INTERNATIONAL MONETARY AND FINANCIAL ECONOMICS

THE PEARSON SERIES IN ECONOMICS

Abel/Bernanke/Croushore
Macroeconomics*

Bade/Parkin
Foundations of Economics*

Berck/Helfand
The Economics of the Environment

Bierman/Fernandez
Game Theory with Economic Applications

Blanchard
Macroeconomics*

Blau/Ferber/Winkler
The Economics of Women, Men and Work

Boardman/Greenberg/Vining/Weimer
Cost-Benefit Analysis

Boyer
Principles of Transportation Economics

Branson
Macroeconomic Theory and Policy

Brock/Adams
The Structure of American Industry

Bruce
Public Finance and the American Economy

Carlton/Perloff
Modern Industrial Organization

Case/Fair/Oster
Principles of Economics*

Caves/Frankel/Jones
World Trade and Payments: An Introduction

Chapman
Environmental Economics: Theory, Application, and Policy

Cooter/Ulen
Law & Economics

Downs
An Economic Theory of Democracy

Ehrenberg/Smith
Modern Labor Economics

Farnham
Economics for Managers

Folland/Goodman/Stano
The Economics of Health and Health Care

Fort
Sports Economics

Froyen
Macroeconomics

Fusfeld
The Age of the Economist

Gerber
International Economics*

González-Rivera
Forecasting for Economics and Business

Gordon
Macroeconomics*

Greene
Econometric Analysis

Gregory
Essentials of Economics

Gregory/Stuart
Russian and Soviet Economic Performance and Structure

Hartwick/Olewiler
The Economics of Natural Resource Use

Heilbroner/Milberg
The Making of the Economic Society

Heyne/Boettke/Prychitko
The Economic Way of Thinking

Hoffman/Averett
Women and the Economy: Family, Work, and Pay

Holt
Markets, Games and Strategic Behavior

Hubbard/O'Brien
Economics*

Money, Banking, and the Financial System*

Hubbard/O'Brien/Rafferty
Macroeconomics*

Hughes/Cain
American Economic History

Husted/Melvin
International Economics

Jehle/Reny
Advanced Microeconomic Theory

Johnson-Lans
A Health Economics Primer

Keat/Young
Managerial Economics

Klein
Mathematical Methods for Economics

Krugman/Obstfeld/Melitz
International Economics: Theory & Policy*

Laidler
The Demand for Money

Leeds/von Allmen
The Economics of Sports

Leeds/von Allmen/Schiming
Economics*

Lipsey/Ragan/Storer
Economics*

Lynn
Economic Development: Theory and Practice for a Divided World

Miller
Economics Today*

Understanding Modern Economics

Miller/Benjamin
The Economics of Macro Issues

Miller/Benjamin/North
The Economics of Public Issues

Mills/Hamilton
Urban Economics

Mishkin
The Economics of Money, Banking, and Financial Markets*

The Economics of Money, Banking, and Financial Markets, Business School Edition*

Macroeconomics: Policy and Practice*

Murray
Econometrics: A Modern Introduction

Nafziger
The Economics of Developing Countries

O'Sullivan/Sheffrin/Perez
Economics: Principles, Applications and Tools*

Parkin
Economics*

Perloff
Microeconomics*

Microeconomics: Theory and Applications with Calculus*

Phelps
Health Economics

Pindyck/Rubinfeld
Microeconomics*

Riddell/Shackelford/Stamos/Schneider
Economics: A Tool for Critically Understanding Society

Ritter/Silber/Udell
Principles of Money, Banking & Financial Markets*

Roberts
The Choice: A Fable of Free Trade and Protection

Rohlf
Introduction to Economic Reasoning

Ruffin/Gregory
Principles of Economics

Sargent
Rational Expectations and Inflation

Sawyer/Sprinkle
International Economics

Scherer
Industry Structure, Strategy, and Public Policy

Schiller
The Economics of Poverty and Discrimination

Sherman
Market Regulation

Silberberg
Principles of Microeconomics

Stock/Watson
Introduction to Econometrics

Studenmund
Using Econometrics: A Practical Guide

Tietenberg/Lewis
Environmental and Natural Resource Economics

Environmental Economics and Policy

Todaro/Smith
Economic Development

Waldman
Microeconomics

Waldman/Jensen
Industrial Organization: Theory and Practice

Walters/Walters/Appel/Callahan/Centanni/Maex/O'Neill
Econversations: Today's Students Discuss Today's Issues

Weil
Economic Growth

Williamson
Macroeconomics

* denotes MyEconLab titles

Visit www.myeconlab.com to learn more.

INTERNATIONAL MONETARY AND FINANCIAL ECONOMICS

Joseph P. Daniels
Marquette University

David D. Van Hoose
Baylor University

PEARSON

Boston   Columbus   Indianapolis   New York   San Francisco   Upper Saddle River
Amsterdam   Cape Town   Dubai   London   Madrid   Milan   Munich   Paris   Montréal   Toronto
Delhi   Mexico City   São Paulo   Sydney   Hong Kong   Seoul   Singapore   Taipei   Tokyo

To Lora,
J.P.D.

To Michael,
D.D.V.

Editor in Chief: Donna Battista
Senior Acquisitions Editor: Noel Seibert
Senior Editorial Project Manager: Carolyn Terbush
Editorial Assistant: Emily Brodeur
Director of Marketing: Maggie Moylan
Executive Marketing Manager: Lori DeShazo
Marketing Assistant: Kim Lovato
Managing Editor: Jeffrey Holcomb
Senior Production Project Manager: Kathryn Dinovo
Senior Manufacturing Buyer: Carol Melville

Creative Director: Jayne Conte
Cover Designer: Suzanne Behnke
Cover Image: Shutterstock-Alexey U
Media Producer: Lisa Rinaldi
Supplements Editor: Kathryn Dinovo
Full-Service Project Management: S4Carlisle
    Publishing Services
Printer/Binder: Edwards Brothers Malloy
Cover Printer: Lehigh-Phoenix Color/Hagerstwon
Text Font: Times LT Std

Credits and acknowledgments borrowed from other sources and reproduced, with permission, in this textbook appear on the appropriate page within text.

Library of Congress Cataloging-in-Publication Data
Daniels, Joseph P.
    International monetary and financial economics / Joseph P. Daniels, David D. VanHoose.—1st Pearson ed.
        p. cm.
    ISBN-13: 978-0-13-246186-3
    ISBN-10: 0-13-246186-2
    1. International finance. I. VanHoose, David D. II. Title.
    HG3881.D3264 2014
    332'.042—dc23

                                                                                2012030878

10 9 8 7 6 5 4 3 2 1

ISBN 10:   0-13-246186-2
ISBN 13:   978-0-13-246186-3

Brief CONTENTS

Chapter 1 Keeping Up with a Changing World—Trade Flows, Capital Flows, and the Balance of Payments   2

Chapter 2 The Market for Foreign Exchange   28

Chapter 3 Exchange-Rate Systems, Past to Present   58

Chapter 4 The Forward Currency Market and International Financial Arbitrage   86

Chapter 5 Interest Yields, Interest-Rate Risk, and Derivative Securities   112

Chapter 6 International Banking, Central Banks, and Supranational Financial Policymaking Institutions   151

Chapter 7 The International Financial Architecture and Emerging Economies   187

Chapter 8 Traditional Approaches to Balance-of-Payments and Exchange-Rate Determination   220

Chapter 9 Monetary and Portfolio Approaches to Balance-of-Payments and Exchange-Rate Determination   243

Chapter 10 An Open Economy Framework   274

Chapter 11 Economic Policy with Fixed Exchange Rates   314

Chapter 12 Economic Policy with Floating Exchange Rates   348

Chapter 13 The Price Level, Real Output, and Economic Policymaking   376

Chapter 14 Domestic Economic Policymaking in a Global Economy   418

Chapter 15 Policy Coordination, Monetary Union, and Target Zones   448

CONTENTS

PREFACE   xliv

PART 1   INTERNATIONAL PAYMENTS AND EXCHANGE   1

CHAPTER 1   **Keeping Up with a Changing World—Trade Flows, Capital Flows, and the Balance of Payments   2**

Why It Is Important to Understand International Money and Finance   3

International Economic Integration: The Importance of Global Trade and Financial Markets   3

    The Real and Financial Sectors of an Economy   4

    World Trade in Goods and Services   4

FUNDAMENTAL ISSUES
How Important Is the Global Market for Goods and Services?   5

    International Transactions in Financial Assets   6

    The Most Globalized Nations   7

ON THE WEB   7
The Most Globalized Firms   8

FUNDAMENTAL ISSUES
How Important Are the International Monetary and Financial Markets?   10

The Balance of Payments   10

ON THE WEB   10
Balance of Payments as a Double-Entry Bookkeeping System   10

Balance-of-Payments Accounts   12

The Current Account   12

🌐 **POLICY NOTEBOOK**
The Combined Current Account Deficit of Developed Nations Translates into a Combined Current Account Surplus for Emerging Countries   13

The Capital Account   14

🖱 **ON THE WEB   15**
The Official Settlements Balance   15

Deficits and Surpluses in the Balance of Payments   16

Other Deficit and Surplus Measures   17

📈 **MANAGEMENT NOTEBOOK**
Trade Deficits: Faulty Indicators of Business Activity   17

Examples of International Transactions and How They Affect the Balance of Payments   18

Example 1: Import of an Automobile   18

Example 2: A College Student Travels Abroad   19

Example 3: A Foreign Resident Purchases a Domestic Treasury Bill   19

Example 4: The United States Pays Interest on a Foreign-Held Asset   20

Example 5: A Charitable Organization in the United States Provides Humanitarian Aid Abroad   20

Examples Combined   20

💱 **FUNDAMENTAL ISSUES**
What Is a Country's Balance of Payments, and What Does This Measure?   20

The Capital Account and the International Flow of Assets   21

Example: A College Student   21

A Capital Account Surplus   21

The United States as a Net Debtor   22

FUNDAMENTAL ISSUES
What Does It Mean for a Country to Be a Net Debtor or Net Creditor? 23

Relating the Current Account Balance and Capital Flows   23

FUNDAMENTAL ISSUES
What Is the Relationship between a Nation's Current Account Balance and Its Capital Flows? 24

Chapter Summary   24
Questions and Problems   25
Online Applications   26
Selected References and Further Readings   27

CHAPTER 2   The Market for Foreign Exchange   28

Exchange Rates and the Market for Foreign Exchange   29

The Role of the Foreign Exchange Market   29

ONLINE NOTEBOOK   31
On the Internet, Currency Trading Spreads to the "Little Guy"   31

ON THE WEB   31

FUNDAMENTAL ISSUES
What Is the Foreign Exchange Market?   32

Exchange Rates as Relative Prices   32

Currency Appreciation and Depreciation   32

FUNDAMENTAL ISSUES
What Does It Mean When a Currency Has Appreciated or Depreciated?   33

Cross Rates   33

Bid–Ask Spreads and Trading Margins   34
The Bid–Ask Spread   34
The Bid–Ask Margin   34

ON THE WEB   35
Real Exchange Rates   35
The Effect of Price Changes   35

Measuring the Overall Strength or Weakness of a Currency:
Effective Exchange Rates   36

Constructing an Effective Exchange Rate   36

A Two-Country Example of an Effective Exchange Rate   37

Constructing Bilateral Weights   37

Determining Relative Exchange Rates   38

What an Effective Exchange Rate Tells Us   38

Real Effective Exchange Rates   39

ON THE WEB   40

FUNDAMENTAL ISSUES
How Is the General Value of a Currency Measured?   40

Composite Currencies   40

Special Drawing Right (SDR)   40

Calculation of the SDR   41

Foreign Exchange Arbitrage   42

FUNDAMENTAL ISSUES
What Is Foreign Exchange Arbitrage?   43

The Demand for and Supply of Currencies   43

The Demand for a Currency   43

*Illustrating the Demand Relationship: The Demand
Curve   43*

MANAGEMENT NOTEBOOK
*Variations in the Dollar's Value Induce Colleges to Adjust
Enrollments in Study-Abroad Programs   44*

A Change in Demand   45

The Supply of a Currency   45

Illustrating the Supply Relationship: The Supply Curve   45

A Change in Supply   46

The Equilibrium Exchange Rate   47

Illustrating the Market Equilibrium   47

Example: A Change in Demand   47

Foreign Exchange Market Intervention   48

FUNDAMENTAL ISSUES
What Determines the Value of a Currency? **49**

Absolute Purchasing Power Parity   49

Purchasing Power Parity   49

Arbitrage and PPP   *50*

Absolute PPP   *50*

*Practical Problems and Shortcomings
of Absolute PPP*   *51*

 MANAGEMENT NOTEBOOK
*Significant Gains from Arbitrage Turn Out to Be Mainly
Theoretical in Canada*   **52**

Relative Purchasing Power Parity   52

ON THE WEB   **52**

FUNDAMENTAL ISSUES
*What Is Purchasing Power Parity, and Is It Useful as a Guide to
Movements in Exchange Rates?*   **54**

Chapter Summary   *54*

Questions and Problems   *55*

Online Applications   *56*

Selected References and Further Readings   *57*

CHAPTER 3   Exchange-Rate Systems, Past to Present   58

Exchange-Rate Systems   59

ONLINE NOTEBOOK
*Foreign Exchange Rates for Virtual Money
Become a Reality*   **59**

FUNDAMENTAL ISSUES
What Is an Exchange-Rate System?   **60**

The Gold Standard   60

The Gold Standard as an Exchange-Rate
System   60

FUNDAMENTAL ISSUES
How Does a Gold Standard Constitute an Exchange-Rate System? 61

Performance of the Gold Standard 62

Positive and Negative Aspects of a Gold Standard 62

The Economic Environment of the Gold Standard Era 62

The Collapse of the Gold Standard 63

The Bretton Woods System 63

ON THE WEB 64
The Bretton Woods Agreement 64

FUNDAMENTAL ISSUES
What Was the Bretton Woods System of "Pegged" Exchange Rates? 66

Performance of the Bretton Woods System 66

The Gold Pool 66

President Nixon Closes the Gold Window 68

The Smithsonian Agreement and the Snake in the Tunnel 68

The Flexible-Exchange-Rate System 69

The Economic Summits and a New Order 69

Performance of the Floating-Rate System 69

ON THE WEB 70
The Plaza Agreement and the Louvre Accord 70

The Euro 72

FUNDAMENTAL ISSUES
What Post–Bretton Woods System of "Flexible" Exchange Rates Prevails Today? 73

Other Forms of Exchange-Rate Arrangements Today 73

Dollarization 74

POLICY NOTEBOOK
U.S. Inflation Creates Economic Pain in El Salvador 74

Independent Currency Authorities 75

FUNDAMENTAL ISSUES
What Is Dollarization, and What Is a Currency Board? 76
Conventional Peg and Pegged with Bands 76
Currency Baskets 76
Selecting a Currency Basket 77

MANAGEMENT NOTEBOOK
*A New Currency Basket Offers Weights
That Vary over Time 78*
Managing the Currency Basket 78
Crawling Pegs 78
Nicaragua's Crawling-Peg Arrangement 79

FUNDAMENTAL ISSUES
*What Types of Pegged-Exchange-Rate Arrangements
Are Used Today? 79*

Fixed or Floating Exchange Rates? 80

FUNDAMENTAL ISSUES
*Which Is Best, a Fixed- or Flexible-Exchange-Rate
Arrangement? 80*

Chapter Summary 80
Questions and Problems 82
Online Applications 83
Selected References and Further Readings 83

PART 2 INTERNATIONAL FINANCIAL INSTRUMENTS, MARKETS, AND INSTITUTIONS 85

**CHAPTER 4   The Forward Currency Market and International
Financial Arbitrage 86**

Foreign Exchange Risk 87
Types of Foreign Exchange Risk Exposure 87
Hedging Foreign Exchange Risk 88

MANAGEMENT NOTEBOOK
Japanese Automakers Ramp Up U.S. Production to Hedge against a Depreciating Dollar **88**

FUNDAMENTAL ISSUES
What Is Foreign Exchange Risk? **89**

The Forward Exchange Market **89**

Covering a Transaction with a Forward Contract **89**

Determination of Forward Exchange Rates **90**

The Forward Exchange Rate as a Predictor of the Future Spot Rate **90**

FUNDAMENTAL ISSUES
What Is the Forward Currency Market, and How Are Forward Exchange Rates Determined? **92**

International Financial Arbitrage **92**

The International Flow of Funds and Interest Rate Determination **93**

Supply **93**

Demand **93**

Determination of the Market Interest Rate **94**

Interest Parity **94**

Exchange Uncertainty and Covered Interest Parity **95**

Covered Interest Arbitrage **96**

Covered-Interest-Parity Grid **96**

Covered Interest Arbitrage and Savings Flows **97**

Adjustment to an Equilibrium **97**

FUNDAMENTAL ISSUES
What Is Covered Interest Parity? **99**

Uncovered Interest Parity **99**

Uncovered Interest Arbitrage **99**

MANAGEMENT NOTEBOOK
Many Hungarians Literally Bet Their Houses on Exchange Rates **100**

Risk and Uncovered Interest Parity   101

Risks Other Than Foreign Exchange Risk   101

Tests of Uncovered Interest Parity   102

📈 MANAGEMENT NOTEBOOK
The Carry-Trade Strategy for International Investment 102

💱 FUNDAMENTAL ISSUES
What Is Uncovered Interest Parity?   103

Foreign Exchange Market Efficiency   103

Market Efficiency   104

Evidence on Foreign Exchange Market Efficiency   104

💱 FUNDAMENTAL ISSUES
What Is Foreign Exchange Market Efficiency?   104

International Financial Markets   104

International Capital Markets   105

International Money Markets   105

Eurobonds, Euronotes, and Eurocommercial Paper   105

Eurocurrencies   106

Origins of the Eurocurrency Market   106

Relationship to the Forward Market   107

💱 FUNDAMENTAL ISSUES
What Are the International Financial Markets?   108

Chapter Summary   108

Questions and Problems   109

Online Applications   110

Selected References and Further Readings   111

CHAPTER 5 Interest Yields, Interest Rate Risk, and Derivative Securities   112

Interest Rates   113

Interest Yields and Financial Instrument Prices   113

Interest Rates and Discounted Present Value   113

Discounted Present Value and the Market Price of Bonds   114

⟋ ON THE WEB   115

⟋ ON THE WEB   116

Perpetuities and the Relationship between Interest Yields and Bond Prices   116

📈 MANAGEMENT NOTEBOOK
Recalculating Libor   117

Term to Maturity and Interest Rate Risk   118

💱 FUNDAMENTAL ISSUES
How Are Interest Yields, Financial Instrument Prices, and Interest Rate Risk Interrelated?   119

The Term Structure of Interest Rates   119

Yield Curves   119

Segmented Markets Theory   120

The Expectations Theory   120

The Preferred Habitat Theory   122

The Risk Structure of Interest Rates   122

Default Risk   123

Liquidity   123

Tax Differences   124

💱 FUNDAMENTAL ISSUES
Why Do Market Interest Yields Vary with Differences in Financial Instruments' Terms to Maturity?   124

Interest Rate Differentials—Excess Returns and Failure of Uncovered Interest Parity   124

Breakdowns of Uncovered Interest Parity and Excess Returns   125

Excess Returns   125

Evidence on Excess Returns   125

Accounting for Differences in Excess Returns to Help Explain International Interest Rate Differences   125

📈 MANAGEMENT NOTEBOOK
Do Excess Returns Vary at Different Bond Maturities? 126

🌐 FUNDAMENTAL ISSUES
*What Factors Explain Why International Interest Rate
Differentials Are Often Inconsistent with the Uncovered-
Interest-Parity Condition? 127*

Real Interest Rates and Real Interest Parity 127

 Real Interest Rates: The Fisher Equation 128

 Real Interest Parity 128

  *Combining Relative Purchasing Power Parity and Uncovered
  Interest Parity 128*

  *Deviations from Real Interest Parity as a Measure of
  International Market Arbitrage 129*

📈 MANAGEMENT NOTEBOOK
*How Long Does It Take for Real Interest Rates to
Converge? 129*

🌐 FUNDAMENTAL ISSUES
*What Are Real Interest Rates, and How Can Real-Interest-
Rate Differentials Serve as Indicators of the Extent to Which
International Markets Are Open to Arbitrage? 130*

Hedging, Speculation, and Derivative Securities 130

 Possible Responses to Interest Rate Risk 130

  Some Strategies for Limiting Interest Rate Risk 131

  Hedging 131

 Derivative Securities 131

  Hedging with Forward Contracts 132

  Speculation with Derivatives 132

  Speculative Gains and Losses 133

🌐 FUNDAMENTAL ISSUES
What Are Derivative Securities? 134

Common Derivative Securities and Their Risks 135

 Forward Contracts 135

 Futures 135

☑ ON THE WEB   136
Interest Rate Futures   136
Stock-Index Futures   136
Currency Futures   136

☑ ON THE WEB   137
Hedging with Currency Futures   137
Daily Futures Settlement   138

Options   139
Stock Options and Futures Options   139
Currency Options   139
Netting   142

Swaps   143
Currency Swaps   143
Types of Swaps   144

Derivatives Risks and Regulation   145
Measuring Derivatives Risks   145
Types of Derivatives Risks   145

💲 FUNDAMENTAL ISSUES
What Are the Most Commonly Traded Derivative Securities?   146

Chapter Summary   146
Questions and Problems   147
Online Applications   149
Selected References and Further Readings   150

CHAPTER 6   International Banking, Central Banks, and Supranational Financial Policymaking Institutions   151

International Dimensions of Financial Intermediation   152
Financial Intermediation   152
Asymmetric Information   153
Adverse Selection   153
Moral Hazard   153
Economies of Scale   154

Financial Intermediation across National Boundaries   154

   International Financial Intermediation   155

   Economies of Scale and Global Banking   155

FUNDAMENTAL ISSUES
*What Accounts for International Financial Intermediation, and
How Do National Banking Systems Differ?   156*

Global Payments and Financial System Risks   156

  Global Payment Systems   157

   Nonelectronic Payment Systems   157

   Electronic Payment Systems   158

ON THE WEB   158
Payment-System Risks   158

   Liquidity Risk   159

   Credit Risk   159

   Systemic Risk   160

   Herstatt Risk   160

FUNDAMENTAL ISSUES
*What Are the World's Major Bank Payment Systems, and How
Do the Risks That Arise in National Financial and Banking
Systems Contribute to the Potential for Financial Instability
and Crises?   161*

Financial Instability and International Financial Crises   161

   *Economic Imbalances and International Financial
Crises   161*

   Self-Fulfilling Expectations and Contagion Effects   162

   Structural Moral Hazard Problems   162

MANAGEMENT NOTEBOOK
From Fish to Finance—and Back to Fish Again?   163

Bank Regulation and Capital Requirements   163

ON THE WEB   164
The Goals of Bank Regulation   164

   Limiting the Scope for Bank Insolvencies and Failures   164

   Maintaining Bank Liquidity   164

   Promoting an Efficient Banking System   164

POLICY NOTEBOOK
Engaging in War Games Pays Off for Bank Regulators   165

ON THE WEB   165
Bank Capital Requirements   166
The Three Pillars of the Basel Regulatory System   167

POLICY NOTEBOOK
Will More Risk-Based Capital Regulation Make Banking More Procyclical?   167
Market-Based Regulation?   168

FUNDAMENTAL ISSUES
What Objectives Do National Banking Regulators Seek to Achieve, and How Do They Implement Their Regulations?   169

Central Banks   169

ON THE WEB   169
Central Bank Assets   170
Central Bank Liabilities and Net Worth   171

FUNDAMENTAL ISSUES
What Are the Main Assets and Liabilities of Central Banks?   172

What Do Central Banks Do?   172
Central Banks as Government Banks   172
Central Banks as Government Depositories   172
Central Banks as Fiscal Agents   172
Central Banks as Bankers' Banks   173
Do Banks "Need" a Central Bank?   173
Lenders of Last Resort   173
Central Banks as Monetary Policymakers   174
Interest Rates on Central Bank Advances   174
Open-Market Operations   176
Reserve Requirements   177
Interest Rate Regulations and Direct Credit Controls   177

FUNDAMENTAL ISSUES
What Are the Primary Functions of Central Banks? *178*

Supranational Financial Policymaking Institutions 178
  The International Monetary Fund 178
  The World Bank 181

FUNDAMENTAL ISSUES
What Are the Two Most Important Supranational Financial Policymaking Institutions, and What Are Their Functions in the International Financial System? *182*

  Chapter Summary *182*
  Questions and Problems *183*
  Online Applications *184*
  Selected References and Further Readings *185*

CHAPTER 7   The International Financial Architecture and Emerging Economies 187

International Capital Flows 188
  Explaining the Direction of Capital Flows 188
    Foreign Direct Investment and Developed Nations *188*

ON THE WEB **188**
    Cross-Border Mergers and Acquisitions *189*

ON THE WEB **190**
    The Emerging Economies *190*

FUNDAMENTAL ISSUES
What Are the Most Important Developments in the Recent Evolution of Global Capital Markets? *191*

  Capital Allocations and Economic Growth 191
    How Capital Inflows Can Smooth the Domestic Economy *192*
    How Capital Inflows Can Contribute to Long-Term Development *192*
  Capital Misallocations and Their Consequences 193
    Market Imperfections *193*

Policy-Created Distortions   193

Financial Instability and Financial Crises   194

Maximizing Benefits and Minimizing Risks   194

Where Do Financial Intermediaries Fit In?   195

FUNDAMENTAL ISSUES
What Is the Relationship between Capital Allocations and Economic Growth, and What Is the Role of Financial Intermediaries in This Relationship?   195

Capital Market Liberalization and International Financial Crises   196

Are All Capital Flows Equal?   196

Portfolio Capital Flows   196

Foreign Direct Investment   196

MANAGEMENT NOTEBOOK
Private Capital Flows: Source of Instability or Engine of Economic Development?   197

The Role of Capital Flows in Recent Crisis Episodes   198

ON THE WEB   198

Foreign Direct Investment as a Stabilizing Element   198

Is There a Role for Capital Controls?   199

FUNDAMENTAL ISSUES
What Is the Difference between Portfolio Capital Flows and Foreign Direct Investment, and What Role Did These Types of Capital Flows Play in Recent Financial Crises?   200

Exchange-Rate Regimes and Financial Crises   200

Schools of Thought on Exchange-Rate Regimes   200

The Corners Hypothesis   201

Dollarization   201

The Benefits of Dollarization   201

The Costs of Dollarization   202

Dollarized Economies   202

Peg, Take the Middle Road, or Float?   202

The "Trilemma"   203

POLICY NOTEBOOK
Differences in Cross-Country Patterns in Addressing the Trilemma Issue   204

FUNDAMENTAL ISSUES
What Type of Exchange-Rate Regime Is Most Appropriate for Emerging Economies?   205

Evaluating the Status Quo   205

Ex Ante *versus* Ex Post *Conditionality at the IMF   205*

ONLINE NOTEBOOK
Data Dissemination via the Internet   206

Searching for a Mission at the World Bank   206

POLICY NOTEBOOK
Should National Policymakers Promote Microlending?   207

ON THE WEB   208
Debt Relief for the Heavily Indebted Poor Countries   209

FUNDAMENTAL ISSUES
What Aspects of IMF and World Bank Policymaking Have Proved Controversial in Recent Years?   210

Does the International Financial Architecture Need a Redesign?   210

Crisis Prediction and Early-Warning Systems   210

Rethinking Economic Institutions and Policies   211

Rethinking Long-Term Development Lending   211
Alternative Institutional Structures for Limiting Financial Crises   212

FUNDAMENTAL ISSUES
What Changes in the International Financial Architecture Have Economists Proposed in Recent Years?   214

Chapter Summary   214
Questions and Problems   215
Online Applications   216
Selected References and Further Readings   217

PART 3 EXCHANGE-RATE AND BALANCE-OF-PAYMENTS DETERMINATION 219

CHAPTER 8 Traditional Approaches to Balance-of-Payments and Exchange-Rate Determination 220

Common Characteristics of the Traditional Approaches 221

Exports, Imports, and the Demand for and Supply of Foreign Exchange 221

Derivation of the Demand for Foreign Exchange 221

Elasticity and the Demand for Foreign Exchange 222

Derivation of the Supply of Foreign Exchange 223

Elasticity and the Supply of Foreign Exchange 224

FUNDAMENTAL ISSUES
How Do the Supply of Exports and Demand for Imports Determine the Supply of and Demand for Foreign Exchange? 226

The Elasticities Approach 226

The Exchange Rate and the Balance of Payments 226

The Role of Elasticity 227

ON THE WEB 228
The Marshall–Lerner Condition 228

FUNDAMENTAL ISSUES
What Is the Elasticities Approach to Balance-of-Payments and Exchange-Rate Determination? 229

Short- and Long-Run Elasticity Measures and the J-Curve 229

Short-Run versus Long-Run Time Horizons 229

The J-Curve Effect 230

MANAGEMENT NOTEBOOK
Industry-Level Evidence of J-Curve Effects for Bilateral Trade between Canada and the United States 231

FUNDAMENTAL ISSUES
What Is the J-Curve Effect? *231*

Pass-Through Effects 232

ON THE WEB 232

MANAGEMENT NOTEBOOK
Market Power and Variations in U.S. Exchange-Rate Pass-Through Effects *232*

FUNDAMENTAL ISSUES
What Are Pass-Through Effects? *233*

The Absorption Approach 233

  Modeling the Absorption Approach 233

    Absorption *234*

    Real Income *234*

    The Current Account *234*

  Determination of the Current Account Balance 234

  Economic Expansion and Contraction 235

    An Economic Expansion *235*

    An Economic Contraction *235*

ON THE WEB 236

FUNDAMENTAL ISSUES
What Is the Absorption Approach to Balance-of-Payments and Exchange-Rate Determination? *236*

  Policy Instruments 236

FUNDAMENTAL ISSUES
How Do Changes in Real Income and Absorption Affect a Nation's Current Account Balance and the Foreign Exchange Value of Its Currency? *237*

Chapter Summary *238*

Questions and Problems *239*

Online Applications *240*

Selected References and Further Readings *241*

CHAPTER 9   Monetary and Portfolio Approaches to Balance-of-Payments and Exchange-Rate Determination   243

Central Bank Balance Sheets   244

A Nation's Monetary Base   244

⊕ POLICY NOTEBOOK
So Many Foreign Exchange Reserves, So Many New Options for Allocating Them   245

A Nation's Money Stock   246

An Open-Market Transaction   246

The Money Multiplier   246

The Relationship between the Monetary Base and the Money Stock   247

✿ FUNDAMENTAL ISSUES
What Are the Main Assets and Liabilities of Central Banks?   248

Managed Exchange Rates: Foreign Exchange Interventions   248

Mechanics of Foreign Exchange Interventions   248

Intervention Transactions   248

Leaning with or against the Wind   249

Financing Interventions   249

✎ ON THE WEB   250

Foreign Exchange Interventions and the Money Stock   250

An Example of a Foreign Exchange Transaction   251

The Effect on the U.S. Money Stock   252

Sterilization of Interventions   252

⊕ POLICY NOTEBOOK
Emerging Nations Weigh the Benefits and Costs of Sterilization   254

✿ FUNDAMENTAL ISSUES
How Do a Central Bank's Foreign Exchange Market Interventions Alter the Monetary Base and the Money Stock?   255

The Monetary Approach to Balance-of-Payments and Exchange-Rate Determination 255

The Cambridge Approach to Money Demand 255

Money, the Balance of Payments, and the Exchange Rate 256

The Relationship between the Money Stock and the Balance of Payments 256

The Relationship between Domestic Prices, Foreign Prices, and the Spot Exchange Rate 256

The Monetary Equilibrium Condition 256

The Monetary Approach and a Fixed-Exchange-Rate Arrangement 257

A Change in Domestic Credit 257

A Change in the Quantity of Money Demanded 258

POLICY NOTEBOOK
The Oil-Rich Middle East Begins to Desert the Sinking Dollar 258

The Monetary Approach and a Flexible-Exchange-Rate Arrangement 259

A Change in Domestic Credit 259

A Change in the Quantity of Money Demanded 260

FUNDAMENTAL ISSUES
What Is the Monetary Approach to Balance-of-Payments and Exchange-Rate Determination? 260

Applying the Monetary Approach: A Two-Country Setting 260

A Two-Country Monetary Model 260

An Example of Exchange-Rate Determination for Two Nations 261

ON THE WEB 262

FUNDAMENTAL ISSUES
How Is the Monetary Approach a Theory of Exchange-Rate Determination in a Two-Country Setting? 263

The Portfolio Approach to Exchange-Rate Determination   263

Households' Allocation of Wealth   263

A Change in the Domestic Money Stock   264

A Change in the Foreign Interest Rate   264

FUNDAMENTAL ISSUES
What Is the Portfolio Approach to Exchange-Rate Determination?   265

To Sterilize or Not to Sterilize?   265

Sterilized Foreign Exchange Interventions and the Monetary Approach   265

Sterilized Foreign Exchange Interventions and the Portfolio Approach   266

Do Interventions Accomplish Anything?   266

FUNDAMENTAL ISSUES
Should Central Banks Sterilize Foreign Exchange Interventions?   268

Chapter Summary   268

Questions and Problems   269

Online Applications   270

Selected References and Further Readings   271

PART 4   OPEN ECONOMY MACROECONOMICS AND POLICY ANALYSIS   273

CHAPTER 10   An Open Economy Framework   274

Measuring an Economy's Performance: Gross Domestic Product and Price Indexes   275

Gross Domestic Product   275

Nominal GDP, Real GDP, and the GDP Price Deflator   276

Real versus Nominal GDP   276

The GDP Price Deflator   277

ON THE WEB   277
Denoting a Base Year   277

POLICY NOTEBOOK
Global Real GDP Calculations Reveal the Rapid Pace of World Economic Growth   279

ON THE WEB   279
Fixed- and Flexible-Weight Price Measures   279
> *The GDP Price Deflator: A Flexible-Weight Price Index*   280
> *Fixed-Weight Price Indexes*   280
> *The Consumer and Producer Price Indexes*   280

MANAGEMENT NOTEBOOK
The Tenuous Link from Chinese Wages to U.S. Consumer Prices   280

ON THE WEB   281
Real Income and Expenditures: The *IS* Schedule   282
> *The Income Identity*   282
> *The Product Identity*   283

FUNDAMENTAL ISSUES
How Do Economists Measure a Nation's Flow of Income and Expenditure and Its Overall Level of Prices of Goods and Services?   284

Private and Public Expenditures   284
> *Saving, Import Spending, and Domestic Consumption Spending*   284

MANAGEMENT NOTEBOOK
The Declining Impact of Interest Rate Variations on U.S. Real Consumption Expenditures   288
> *Desired Investment Spending*   288
> *Government Spending and Net Taxes*   290
> *Export Spending*   291

Equilibrium Income and Expenditures   291
> *Aggregate Desired Expenditures*   292

Equilibrium National Income   292

The Income–Expenditure Equilibrium   293

FUNDAMENTAL ISSUES
How Is Equilibrium Real Income Determined in an Open Economy?   293

The *IS* Schedule   293

The Derivation of the IS *Schedule*   294

Determining the Position of the IS *Schedule*   295

The Multiplier Effect   295

Explaining the Multiplier Effect   297

FUNDAMENTAL ISSUES
What Is the IS *Schedule, and What Factors Determine Its Position?*   297

The Market for Real Money Balances: The *LM* Schedule   298

The Demand for Money   298

The Transactions and Precautionary Motives for Holding Money   298

ONLINE NOTEBOOK
Using the Web to Convert Dollars into African Vouchers   299

The Portfolio Motive for Holding Money   300

The Demand for Real Money Balances   301

The *LM* Schedule   302

Money Market Equilibrium and the LM *Schedule*   303

Determining the Position of the LM *Schedule*   304

FUNDAMENTAL ISSUES
What Is the LM *Schedule, and What Factors Determine Its Position?*   305

The Balance of Payments: The *BP* Schedule and the *IS–LM–BP* Model   305

Maintaining a Balance-of-Payments Equilibrium: The *BP* Schedule   305

Real Income and the Balance of Payments   305

*The Nominal Interest Rate and the Balance of
Payments* 306

The *IS–LM–BP* Model 307

IS–LM *Equilibrium* 307

🎛 FUNDAMENTAL ISSUES
What Is an IS–LM *Equilibrium?* **307**

*Determining a Nation's Balance-of-Payments
Position* 307

🎛 FUNDAMENTAL ISSUES
What Is the BP *Schedule, and How Can We Use the* IS–LM–
BP *Model to Determine a Nation's Balance-of-Payments
Status?* 309

Chapter Summary 309

Questions and Problems 310

Online Applications 311

Selected References and Further Readings 312

CHAPTER 11   Economic Policy with Fixed Exchange Rates   314

The Objectives of Policy 315

Internal Balance Objectives 315

Real-Income Goals 315

🖊 ON THE WEB 316

Employment Goals 317

Inflation Goals 318

External Balance Objectives 319

International Objectives and Domestic Goals 319

External Balance for Its Own Sake 319

🎛 FUNDAMENTAL ISSUES
What Are the Economic Goals of National Policymakers? **320**

The Role of Capital Mobility 320

Capital Mobility and the *BP* Schedule 321

The Case of Low Capital Mobility 321

The Case of High Capital Mobility 322

Perfect Capital Mobility   322

Perfect Capital Mobility and the BP *Schedule   322*

▶ ONLINE NOTEBOOK
A Web Route to Avoiding Lines for Currency Exchange   323

*The Domestic Interest Rate and Balance of Payments with
Perfect Capital Mobility   323*

FUNDAMENTAL ISSUES
*How Does the Degree of Capital Mobility Influence
the Slope of the* BP *Schedule?   324*

Fixed Exchange Rates and Imperfect Capital Mobility   324

Monetary Policy under Fixed Exchange Rates
and Imperfect Capital Mobility   325

POLICY NOTEBOOK
*To Make Its Official Exchange Rate Credible, Venezuela's
Government Has Sometimes Effectively Given Away Caribbean
Vacations   325*

ON THE WEB   325

*Monetary Policy, the Nominal Interest Rate, and Real
Income   325*

*Monetary Policy and the Balance of Payments with
Imperfect Capital Mobility   327*

Sterilized Monetary Policy   327

Nonsterilized Monetary Policy   328

The Monetary Approach Revisited   329

POLICY NOTEBOOK
*What Determines the Choice of a Peg for a Nation's Fixed-
Exchange-Rate System?   329*

FUNDAMENTAL ISSUES
*To What Extent Can Monetary Policy Actions Influence the
Real Income Level of a Small Open Economy with Imperfect
Capital Mobility and a Fixed Exchange Rate?   330*

Fiscal Policy under Fixed Exchange Rates   330

*Fiscal Policy, the Nominal Interest Rate, and Real
Income   330*

Fiscal Policy and the Balance of Payments with Imperfect Capital Mobility 331

The Effects of Fiscal Policy Actions with and without Monetary Sterilization 332

💲 **FUNDAMENTAL ISSUES**
To What Extent Can Fiscal Policy Actions Influence the Real Income Level of a Small Open Economy with Imperfect Capital Mobility and a Fixed Exchange Rate? **334**

Fixed Exchange Rates and Perfect Capital Mobility 335

🌐 **POLICY NOTEBOOK**
Brazilian Policymakers Try to Have It Both Ways **335**

📩 **ON THE WEB** **335**
Economic Policies with Perfect Capital Mobility and a Fixed Exchange Rate: The Small Open Economy 336

Monetary Policy with Perfect Capital Mobility and a Fixed Exchange Rate 336

Fiscal Policy with Perfect Capital Mobility and a Fixed Exchange Rate 337

💲 **FUNDAMENTAL ISSUES**
In What Ways Does Perfect Capital Mobility Alter the Relative Effectiveness of Monetary and Fiscal Policy Actions in a Small Open Economy That Adopts a Fixed Exchange Rate? **337**

Economic Policies with Perfect Capital Mobility and a Fixed Exchange Rate: A Two-Country Example 338

A Two-Country Model with Perfect Capital Mobility and a Fixed Exchange Rate 338

The Effects of a Foreign Monetary Expansion 339

The Effects of a Foreign Fiscal Expansion 340

The Effects of a Domestic Monetary Expansion 342

The Effects of a Domestic Fiscal Expansion 343

⚙ FUNDAMENTAL ISSUES

In a Two-Country Setting in Which One Nation's Central Bank Fixes the Exchange Rate, to What Extent Can Policy Actions in One Nation Influence Economic Activity in the Other Nation?   344

Chapter Summary   344

Questions and Problems   345

Online Applications   346

Selected References and Further Readings   347

CHAPTER 12   Economic Policy with Floating Exchange Rates   348

Floating Exchange Rates and Imperfect Capital Mobility   349

The Effects of Exchange-Rate Variations in the *IS–LM–BP* Model   349

Exchange-Rate Variations and the IS *Schedule   349*

Exchange-Rate Variations and the BP *Schedule   350*

Monetary Policy under Floating Exchange Rates   350

🌐 POLICY NOTEBOOK

Current Account Balances and Exchange-Rate Adjustments   351

Fiscal Policy under Floating Exchange Rates   353

The Case of Low Capital Mobility   353

The Case of High Capital Mobility   354

▶ ONLINE NOTEBOOK

Betting That Higher Capital Mobility and Greater Spending Will Fuel an Iraqi Dinar Appreciation   354

⚙ FUNDAMENTAL ISSUES

How Do Monetary and Fiscal Policy Actions Affect a Nation's Real Income Under a Floating Exchange Rate?   355

Floating Exchange Rates and Perfect Capital Mobility   355

Economic Policies with Perfect Capital Mobility and a Floating Exchange Rate: The Small Open Economy   355

Monetary Policy with Perfect Capital Mobility and a Floating Exchange Rate 355

Fiscal Policy with Perfect Capital Mobility and a Floating Exchange Rate 356

Perfect Capital Mobility and Fixed versus Floating Exchange Rates 357

FUNDAMENTAL ISSUES
How Does Perfect Capital Mobility Influence the Relative Effectiveness of Monetary and Fiscal Policy Actions in a Small Open Economy That Permits Its Exchange Rate to Float? 358

Economic Policies with Perfect Capital Mobility and a Floating Exchange Rate: A Two-Country Example 358

The Effects of a Domestic Monetary Expansion 358

MANAGEMENT NOTEBOOK
A Beggar-Thy-Neighbor Effect Hits Auto Markets of U.S. Trading Partners 360

The Effects of a Foreign Monetary Expansion 360

The Effects of a Domestic Fiscal Expansion 361

The Effects of a Foreign Fiscal Expansion 362

FUNDAMENTAL ISSUES
In a Two-Country Setting with a Floating Exchange Rate, to What Extent Can Policy Actions in One Nation Influence Economic Activity in the Other Nation? 362

Fixed versus Floating Exchange Rates 363

Efficiency Arguments for Fixed versus Floating Exchange Rates 363

Social Costs Stemming from Foreign Exchange Risks 363

Efficiency via a Fixed Exchange Rate? 364

The Pain of Realigning 364

ON THE WEB 365

FUNDAMENTAL ISSUES
What Is the Basic Economic Efficiency Trade-off Faced in Choosing between Fixed and Floating Exchange Rates? 366

Stability Arguments for Fixed versus Floating Exchange
Rates   366

   *Autonomous Expenditure Volatility and Fixed versus Floating
   Exchange Rates   366*

   *Financial Volatility and Fixed versus Floating Exchange
   Rates   368*

   The Stability Trade-Off   370

Monetary Policy Autonomy and Fixed versus Floating
Exchange Rates   371

FUNDAMENTAL ISSUES
*How Does the Choice between Fixed and Floating Exchange
Rates Depend in Part on the Implications for Economic Stability
and Monetary Policy Autonomy?   372*

Chapter Summary   372

Questions and Problems   373

Online Applications   374

Selected References and Further Readings   374

**CHAPTER 13   The Price Level, Real Output, and Economic
Policymaking   376**

Aggregate Demand   377

   The Aggregate Demand Schedule   377

FUNDAMENTAL ISSUES
What Is the Aggregate Demand Schedule?   378

Factors That Determine the Position of the Aggregate
Demand Schedule in an Open Economy   379

   Monetary Policy and Aggregate Demand   379

   *Monetary Policy and Aggregate Demand in an Open
   Economy with a Fixed Exchange Rate   380*

   *Monetary Policy and Aggregate Demand in an Open
   Economy with a Floating Exchange Rate   382*

   *Exchange-Rate Policy and Aggregate Demand in
   an Open Economy   384*

FUNDAMENTAL ISSUES
What Factors Determine the Extent to Which Changes in the Quantity of Money Can Influence Aggregate Demand in an Open Economy?   384

Fiscal Policy and Aggregate Demand   384

Fiscal Policy and Aggregate Demand in an Open Economy with a Fixed Exchange Rate   385

Fiscal Policy and Aggregate Demand in an Open Economy with a Floating Exchange Rate   387

FUNDAMENTAL ISSUES
What Factors Determine the Extent to Which Fiscal Policy Actions Can Influence Aggregate Demand in an Open Economy?   389

Aggregate Supply   389

Output and Employment Determination   389

The Production Function   389

The Marginal Product of Labor   390

The Demand for Labor   391

Wage Flexibility, Aggregate Supply, and the Price Level   392

The Determination of Nominal Wages   392

MANAGEMENT NOTEBOOK
In a Globalized Economy, Higher Corporate Income Taxes Translate into Lower Wages for Workers   393

Employment and Aggregate Supply with Fixed versus Flexible Nominal Wages   394

The Aggregate Supply Schedule with Partial Wage Adjustment   396

FUNDAMENTAL ISSUES
What Is the Aggregate Supply Schedule?   397

Real Output, the Price Level, and Economic Policymaking   397

The Equilibrium Price Level and the Equilibrium Real Output Level   398

The Output and Price-Level Effects of Economic Policies with Floating versus Fixed Exchange Rates   399

Aggregate Demand, Output, and Inflation   *399*

Economic Policies, Output, and Inflation with Floating versus Fixed Exchange Rates   *400*

POLICY NOTEBOOK
Are Nations' Business Cycles More Nearly Synchronized Than in Years Past?   *400*

FUNDAMENTAL ISSUES
How Are a Nation's Price Level and Volume of Real Output Determined, and How Might Economic Policymakers Influence Inflation and Real Output?   *402*

Rules versus Discretion in Economic Policymaking   402

Expectations and the Flexibility of Nominal Wages   402

The Rational Expectations Hypothesis   *402*

Wages, Employment, and Output When Policy Actions Are Anticipated   *402*

Wages, Employment, and Output When Policy Actions Are Unanticipated   *404*

Discretion, Credibility, and Inflation   404

The Inflation Bias of Discretionary Economic Policymaking   *404*

The Incentive to Inflate   *406*

Workers' Response   *406*

The Problem of Policy Credibility   *407*

POLICY NOTEBOOK
When Measured Inflation Expectations Creep Upward, So Does the Apparent Inflation Bias of Discretionary Policymaking   *408*

Making Economic Policies Credible   *408*

ON THE WEB   409
ON THE WEB   410

Support for Central Bank Independence   *410*

FUNDAMENTAL ISSUES
Why Does the Rational Expectations Hypothesis Indicate That Economic Policies May Have Limited Real Output Effects and That the Credibility of Policymakers Is Important?   *411*

Chapter Summary   412

Questions and Problems   413

Online Applications   414

Selected References and Further Readings   415

PART 5   DOMESTIC AND MULTINATIONAL POLICYMAKING IN A GLOBAL ECONOMY   417

CHAPTER 14   Domestic Economic Policymaking in a Global Economy   418

The Policy Assignment Problem   419

Finding the Best Policy Mix for Internal and External Balance   419

Achieving External Balance   420

Achieving Internal Balance   421

Assigning Internal and External Objectives   421

An Incorrect Assignment   422

Difficulties in Solving the Assignment Problem   423

FUNDAMENTAL ISSUES
What Is the Policy Assignment Problem?   423

Exchange-Rate Responses to Policy Actions with Sticky Wages and Prices—Exchange-Rate Overshooting   423

The Long-Run Adjustment of the Exchange Rate to a Monetary Expansion   424

Long-Run Equilibrium   424

Exchange-Rate Adjustment in the Long Run   424

Exchange-Rate Overshooting   425

Moving from the Short Run to the Long Run   425

Tracing the Adjustment of the Exchange Rate   425

Implications of Exchange-Rate Overshooting   427

FUNDAMENTAL ISSUES
What Is Exchange-Rate Overshooting, and Why Might It Occur?   427

Openness and the Output–Inflation Relationship—How
Globalization Alters the Effects of Policies   427

How Increased Openness Can Make Output Less Responsive
to Inflation   428

🌐 POLICY NOTEBOOK
Measuring Openness   429

   Partially Indexed Wage Contracts   430

   Greater Openness and Imported Inputs   430

How Greater Openness Can Increase the Sensitivity of Output
to Inflation   430

   *Openness and Competition in Domestic Product
Markets   430*

📈 MANAGEMENT NOTEBOOK
*Which Nations' Industries Face the Most Extensive
Regulations?   431*

   *Openness, Wage Stickiness, and Central Bank
Independence   432*

Evidence on Openness and the Output–Inflation
Relationship   433

   *Responsiveness of Output to Inflation: International
Evidence   433*

   *Central Bank Independence, Openness, and the Output–
Inflation Relationship   434*

   *Additional Evidence Regarding the Interaction between
Openness and the Output–Inflation Relationship   435*

💱 FUNDAMENTAL ISSUES
*Why Does Increased Openness of a Nation's Economy Have
an Uncertain Net Effect on the Responsiveness of Output to
Changes in the Price Level?   435*

Openness and Inflation   436

The Global Openness–Inflation Relationship   436

🌐 POLICY NOTEBOOK
*Is a More Open Economy More or Less Prone to "Sudden
Stops"?   437*

Just How Strong Is the Openness–Inflation
Relationship?   437

     *Differences in How Openness and Inflation Relate in
Developed versus Less Developed Nations*   437

     *Accounting for Cross-Country Differences in the Impacts of
Globalization*   439

🌐 FUNDAMENTAL ISSUES
*Is There an Inverse Relationship between Openness and
Inflation?*   *439*

New Open Economy Macroeconomics and Its Policy
Implications   439

     Features of the New Open Economy Macroeconomics   440

     Sources of Price Stickiness   440

📈 MANAGEMENT NOTEBOOK
Are Product Prices Really Sticky?   *440*

     Imperfect Competition   *441*

     Dynamic Analysis   *442*

Policy Implications of the New Open Economy
Macroeconomics   442

     Welfare Evaluations   *442*

     Still a Long Way to Go   *443*

🌐 FUNDAMENTAL ISSUES
What Is the New Open Economy Macroeconomics?   *443*

Chapter Summary   *444*

Questions and Problems   *445*

Online Applications   *446*

Selected References and Further Readings   *447*

CHAPTER 15   **Policy Coordination, Monetary Union, and Target Zones**   **448**

International Interdependence   449

     Structural Interdependence and International Policy
Externalities   449

Structural Interdependence and Its Consequences *449*

International Policy Externalities *449*

Accounting for Interdependence: International Policy Cooperation and Coordination 450

International Policy Cooperation *450*

International Policy Coordination *450*

FUNDAMENTAL ISSUES
What Is Structural Interdependence, and How Can It Lead Nations to Cooperate or to Coordinate Their Policies? *451*

Perfect Capital Mobility Revisited: Can International Policy Coordination Pay? 451

The Aggregate Demand Effects of National Monetary Policies 451

Conflicting Monetary Policies and the Potential Role of Policy Coordination 453

A Potential Gain from Policy Coordination 454

The Pros and Cons of International Policy Coordination 455

Potential Benefits of International Policy Coordination 456

Internalizing International Policy Externalities *456*

Getting the Most Out of Limited Sets of Policy Instruments *456*

Gaining Support from Abroad *456*

FUNDAMENTAL ISSUES
What Are the Potential Benefits of International Policy Coordination? *457*

Some Potential Drawbacks of International Policy Coordination 457

How Much Autonomy Should a Nation Sacrifice? *457*

Can Other Countries Be Trusted? *457*

Putting Faith in Other Nations' Policymakers *458*

Could "Successful" Coordination Actually Be Counterproductive? *459*

FUNDAMENTAL ISSUES
What Are the Potential Drawbacks of International Policy Coordination? *462*

The Economics of Monetary Unions   462

Optimal Currency Areas   462

How Separate Currencies and a Floating Exchange Rate Can Be Beneficial   463

   A Shift in Relative Demands   *463*

   A Flexible Exchange Rate   *464*

   When Could Using a Single Currency Pay Off?   *464*

POLICY NOTEBOOK
Will North Americans Eventually Use the "Amero" as a Medium of Exchange? *465*

Rationales for Separate Currencies   465

   Removal of Currency Competition   *465*

   Lack of Fiscal Integration   *466*

Trials and Tribulations of the European Monetary Union   467

ON THE WEB   467

   Does the Eurozone Constitute an Optimal Currency Area?   *467*

POLICY NOTEBOOK
Pros and Cons of an East Asian Monetary Union   *468*

   Fiscal Crisis and the Euro   *468*

POLICY NOTEBOOK
When Have Past Currency Unions Collapsed?   *470*

FUNDAMENTAL ISSUES
Could Nations Gain from Adopting a Common Currency?   *470*

Vehicle Currencies   470

POLICY NOTEBOOK
Determination of Invoicing Currencies in International Trade   *471*

The Dollar's Predominance   471

Evidence Regarding Today's Vehicle Currencies   471

FUNDAMENTAL ISSUES
What Are Vehicle Currencies?   473

Splitting the Difference: Exchange-Rate Target Zones   473

Target Zones   473

Establishing a Target Zone   473

The Behavior of the Exchange Rate Inside the Target Zone   474

Does the Target Zone Model Fit the Facts?   476

Real-World Evidence   476

Salvaging the Target Zone Theory   476

FUNDAMENTAL ISSUES
What Is an Exchange-Rate Target Zone?   477

Chapter Summary   477

Questions and Problems   479

Online Applications   480

Selected References and Further Readings   480

GLOSSARY   483

INDEX   493

PREFACE

Our guiding principle for *International Monetary and Financial Economics* has been to write a textbook accessible to instructors and students seeking to cover the full range of topics appropriate for a complete course in international money and finance. There are a number of texts that focus exclusively on international finance, and there are several good books on open economy macroeconomics. We have aimed to write a book that encompasses both areas, thereby simplifying the instructor's efforts to cover all relevant topics. Furthermore, we have sought to write a more broad-based and accessible text than others that are available—a book that acquaints students with all of the concepts that they must learn to be able to understand and analyze global monetary and financial events at an appropriate level.

HALLMARKS AND APPROACH

The overriding objective of this text is to motivate student learning. Toward this end, we have integrated into the text's contents—discussed in detail in the following sections—more than fifty examples drawn from recent experiences of nations throughout the world. Among these are the following.

Management Notebooks

Businesspeople cannot ignore international developments, which continually present them with both opportunities and challenges. To acquaint students with the variety of international financial issues faced by managers, we have included *Management Notebook* features on topics such as the following:

- Trade Deficits: Faulty Indicators of Business Activity
- Significant Gains from Arbitrage Turn Out to Be Mainly Theoretical in Canada
- Many Hungarians Literally Bet Their Houses on Exchange Rates
- From Fish to Finance—and Back to Fish Again?
- Industry-Level Evidence of J-Curve Effects for Bilateral Trade between Canada and the United States
- The Tenuous Link from Chinese Wages to U.S. Consumer Prices

Policy Notebooks

International monetary and financial policy issues dominate the news. Hence, features covering a wide range of recent policy issues appear at appropriate locations. Topics covered include:

- The Combined Current Account Deficit of Developed Nations Translates into a Combined Current Account Surplus for Emerging Countries
- Emerging Nations Weigh the Benefits and Costs of Sterilization
- Will More Risk-Based Capital Regulation Make Banking More Procyclical?
- Is a More Open Economy More or Less Prone to "Sudden Stops"?
- Will North Americans Eventually Use the "Amero" as a Medium of Exchange?
- Pros and Cons of an East Asian Monetary Union

Online Notebooks

The Internet now plays a central role in international financial markets and the global economy. In features such as the following, students can learn more about the role of worldwide electronic commerce:

- On the Internet, Currency Trading Spreads to the "Little Guy"
- Foreign Exchange Rates for Virtual Money Become a Reality
- Data Dissemination via the Internet
- Using the Web to Convert Dollars into African Vouchers
- A Web Route to Avoiding Lines for Currency Exchange
- Betting That Higher Capital Mobility and Greater Spending Will Fuel an Iraqi Dinar Appreciation

CONTENT STRUCTURE

The fifteen chapters of *International Monetary and Financial Economics* provide the foundation materials for a full one-term course.

Part 1's first three chapters offer a complete introduction to the field. Chapter 1 carefully guides the student through the balance-of-payments accounts, and Chapter 2 gradually introduces all of the fundamental concepts relating to spot exchange markets. Chapter 3 then offers an overview of the history of exchange-rate regimes and alternative exchange-rate arrangements in practice today.

Building on this foundation, Part 2 addresses key issues in international finance. Chapter 4 begins by providing a full discussion of forward exchange markets, international financial arbitrage, and interest parity conditions. Chapter 5 covers determinants of interest yields and risks and explains the key foreign exchange market derivative instruments and their uses in hedging against foreign exchange risks. Chapter 6 gives the student a solid grounding in the international dimensions of private and central banking, and Chapter 7 furnishes an evaluation of financial-integration problems confronted by the world's diverse nations.

Part 3 focuses on alternative approaches to the determination of exchange rates and the balance of payments. Chapter 8 conveys an understanding of the elasticities approach, the Marshall–Lerner condition, and the J-curve and lays out the building blocks of the absorption approach. Chapter 9 provides a painstaking coverage of the monetary approach for both a small open economy and for two countries, as well as a thorough treatment of the portfolio approach.

Part 4's emphasis is on economic policymaking in open economies. Chapter 10 meticulously develops an integrated framework for analyzing the joint determination of simultaneous equilibrium of income and expenditures, the market for real money balances, and the balance of payments. Chapter 11 applies this framework to help the student develop a full comprehension of economic policymaking under fixed exchange rates. Chapter 12 accomplishes the same objective in the case of floating exchange rates and explains conditions under which fixed- versus flexible-exchange-rate arrangements are desirable. Chapter 13 explains the determination of the price level and inflation rate in open economies and assesses the fundamental role of central bank credibility.

Part 5 concludes by imparting to the student a complete understanding of traditional and modern policy issues faced in open economies. Chapter 14 considers the policy assignment problem and exchange-rate overshooting, evaluates how greater international openness influences inflation and the relationship between inflation and real output, and discusses the developments in the area of new open economy macroeconomics. Chapter 15 provides a capstone to the text by pulling together a variety of concepts to evaluate the benefits and drawbacks of international policy coordination, the pros and cons of common currencies (with particular attention to the recent distresses faced by the European Monetary Union), vehicle currencies, and exchange-rate target zones.

Thus, the instructor who utilizes this text will be well positioned to cover every substantive issue in the field today.

PEDAGOGY

In writing *International Monetary and Financial Economics*, we have taken into account that student learning is an active process. In addition to the hallmark notebooks described earlier in the preface, we have developed and included a number of pedagogical features that we hope enhance the active experience of learning for students.

Fundamental Issues and Answers within the Text of Each Chapter

Each chapter begins with five to seven fundamental issues, posed in the form of questions for the student to contemplate while reading the chapter. At appropriate locations within the chapter, these fundamental questions are repeated, and appropriate answers are provided, thereby breaking each chapter into more manageable units for the student seeking to develop an organized understanding of the whole. Students thereby see immediately the relationship between the text materials and the fundamental issues as they read the chapter.

Chapter Summaries

A summary concludes each chapter. The chapter summary's format is a numbered, point-by-point discussion of each of the chapter-opening fundamental issues. Inducing the student to contemplate the key issues covered in each chapter deepens their understanding and thereby further reinforces the circular nature of the learning process.

Emphasis on Vocabulary

Vocabulary can be a hurdle for economics students—and particularly for students in courses in international economics. Consequently, we have included margin definitions of all key vocabulary terms, which are highlighted the first time they appear in the text. Vocabulary terms are further defined in the glossary at the end of the book.

Questions and Problems

Several questions, which seek to elicit qualitative, verbal responses, and problems, which enable students to apply concepts to numerical data, appear at the end of each chapter. They are designed to provide students with additional opportunities to think through key concepts carefully and assure themselves of mastery of chapter material. Suggested answers are provided in the Instructor's Resource Manual.

On the Web and Online Application Features

Each chapter includes On the Web margin references to Web sites relevant to text topics. At these sites, students can see how the chapter's coverage relates to real-world concepts. In addition, each chapter concludes with an Online Application. Every Online Application directs students to a Web site and provides questions aimed at assisting students in applying the site's content in a way that helps to reinforce their understanding of chapter concepts. Each Online Application concludes with follow-up questions to be answered in group or in-class settings.

Selected References and Further Reading

This section of each chapter provides appropriate references for instructors to consult and possibly assign to students as additional readings. These references are current, directly related to the content of the chapter, and often at a level accessible to all students.

SUPPLEMENTS

For this edition, we offer the following supplements for instructors to use in their courses. All resources are available for download through the Instructor's Resource Center. To register, please visit www.pearsonhighered.com/irc.

The Test Bank, written by Heather Kohls of Marquette University and accuracy reviewed by Francis Ahking of the University of Connecticut, includes twenty-five multiple-choice questions and five short essay questions per chapter.

The Instructor's Manual, written by John Mathis of Thunderbird School of Global Management and accuracy reviewed by Joseph Friedman of Temple University, includes a chapter outline, teaching tips, and suggested answers to the end-of-chapter questions for each chapter.

The PowerPoint Presentation, written by Scott Hegerty of Northeastern Illinois University and accuracy reviewed by I-Ming Chiu of Rutgers University, includes lecture notes covering the key topics of each chapter as well as the figures and tables for each chapter.

ACKNOWLEDGMENTS

We would like to thank Noel Seibert, Senior Acquisitions Editor; Carolyn Terbush, Senior Editorial Project Manager; and Kathryn Dinovo, Senior Production Project Manager at Pearson, for all their help throughout the editorial and production process, as well as Diane Kohnen, Project Manager at S4Carlisle. We would also like to thank Joseph Pelzman of George Washington University, who accuracy reviewed the page proofs for the book.

We received helpful feedback from the following professors who reviewed the manuscript:

Jeannette C. Mitchell, *Rochester Institute of Technology*
Heather Kohls, *Marquette University*
Joseph Friedman, *Temple University*
Gil Kim, *California State University, Fresno*
Francis Ahking, *University of Connecticut–Storrs*
Scott W. Hegerty, *Northeastern Illinois University*
Joseph Pelzman, *George Washington University*
Marc Muendler, *University of California, San Diego*
David Beckworth, *Texas State University*
Farida C. Khan, *University of Wisconsin–Parkside*
John Mathis, *Thunderbird School of Global Management*
Robert Murphy, *Boston College*
Sandeep Mazumder, *Wake Forest University*
Yoonbai Kim, *University of Kentucky*

We would like to thank these professors for thoughtful contributions to this edition.

PART 1

■

INTERNATIONAL PAYMENTS AND EXCHANGE

1 Keeping Up with a Changing World—Trade Flows, Capital Flows, and the Balance of Payments

2 The Market for Foreign Exchange

3 Exchange-Rate Systems, Past to Present

1

Keeping Up with a Changing World—Trade Flows, Capital Flows, and the Balance of Payments

Fundamental ISSUES

1. How important is the global market for goods and services?
2. How important are the international monetary and financial markets?
3. What is a country's balance of payments, and what does this measure?
4. What does it mean for a country to be a net debtor or net creditor?
5. What is the relationship between a nation's current account balance and its capital flows?

Between 2006 and 2012, the dollar price of oil increased by more than 100 percent. The average volume of oil imports decreased only slightly during this period. As a consequence, during this interval the dollar value of U.S. oil imports more than doubled. In spite of this upswing in dollars expended on U.S. oil imports, however, the overall annual U.S. trade deficit—the dollar value of total imports of tangible goods in excess of total exports of tangible goods—remained nearly level. Indeed, there were decreases in the annual trade deficit during various intervals between 2006 and 2012. Thus, the annual volume of U.S. exports of tangible goods in excess of tangible imports remained sufficiently large between 2006 and 2011 to compensate for the significant increase in the dollar value of U.S. oil imports. The net result was a drop-off in the annual U.S. trade deficit.

Nevertheless, throughout the 2000s and into the 2010s, the ratio of the average annual U.S. trade deficit to the average U.S. national income level was larger than the nation had experienced in six decades. Furthermore, most economic forecasters predict that larger rather than smaller trade deficits are likely to arise throughout the remainder of the present decade.

How do economists measure international transactions? How are these measures used to gauge the progress of globalization, and what roles do international monetary and financial markets play in the process? What are the institutions that govern and promote integration of international monetary and financial markets? How are these markets linked, and how closely are they linked? To understand why there has been so much attention given to measuring market integration, we must answer these questions.

In this chapter, you will embark upon your study of international monetary and financial economics. You will begin by considering why it is important to understand international money and finance. You will examine some of the most important elements of international money and finance: international trade, international capital flows, and international debt.

WHY IT IS IMPORTANT TO UNDERSTAND INTERNATIONAL MONEY AND FINANCE

During the past two decades, numerous fascinating events have helped shape international monetary and financial markets. The currency values of large developing and emerging economies such as Brazil, Argentina, and South Korea have been volatile; Europe has adopted a common currency; and foreign direct investment in the United States has grown to unprecedented levels. In addition, the countries of Central and Eastern Europe have developed financial and monetary systems; Southeast Asian nations and Russia have experienced significant but highly unsteady growth, punctuated by sharp financial and economic downturns; and the world's poorest economies have become mired in debt crises and economic stagnation. Meanwhile, China has emerged as a major player in global economics and politics. And, a financial crisis that originated in the United States spread across the globe, illustrating the increasing interconnectedness of national economies.

Firms and individuals have expanded their business and investment activities internationally, making these events increasingly important to all of us. As a result, student interest in international economics has grown considerably. In particular, international financial and monetary economics is a topic of increasing interest because of its focus on how the world monetary and financial system works. This knowledge, in turn, aids in understanding the significant global economic events of our age.

Before you begin your examination of international monetary and financial economics, you must understand how to measure the economic activity of a nation. This chapter examines the key measures that economists and statisticians have developed to track a nation's international transactions.

INTERNATIONAL ECONOMIC INTEGRATION: THE IMPORTANCE OF GLOBAL TRADE AND FINANCIAL MARKETS

Perhaps the most interesting economic development of the past thirty-five years is the increasing interconnectedness of national economies. This development has affected policymaking, corporate governance, and the day-to-day lives of many citizens of the world. Because of its importance, economists, political scientists, management and marketing strategists, and other professionals are working within and across disciplines to understand the challenges and prospects presented by the new opportunities and new sources of competition accompanying increased international integration.

Globalization and *integration* are the words most often used in reference to the process of the increasing interconnectedness among national economies. Globalization refers to the broadest scope of the process. It is intended to include increasing market integration, the expansion of world governance and global society, and increased mobility of people and information. International economic integration, by contrast, is narrower in focus and refers to the strengthening of existing international linkages of commerce and the addition of new international linkages. This and several of the following chapters concentrate on the economic integration of the international monetary and financial markets.

Today, many people enjoy greater access to foreign goods and services, global travel, and worldwide communications. They might be surprised, however, to know that the current level of international economic integration is not a new phenomenon. Prior to the outbreak of World War I, the leading economies of the world experienced open trade in goods, services, and financial assets at levels close to those observed today. Unfortunately, unhindered global trade collapsed with the outbreak of the first world war. Despite the nearly universal acceptance among economists of the benefits of free trade, efforts to liberalize global trade in goods, services, and financial assets struggled along until an acceleration began in the 1970s.

Measuring the extent of international economic integration is an important task. It helps policymakers and business managers understand current market trends, so that they may be able to take advantage of opportunities, anticipate potential consequences, and minimize detrimental aspects of global competition. Measuring international economic integration is a daunting task, however. This is especially true in light of two factors: (1) increased trade in services, or *invisibles*, and (2) advances in electronic commerce and communications that greatly complicate efforts to track cross-border trade.

The Real and Financial Sectors of an Economy

In order to measure different types of economic activity, economists typically separate the production and sale of goods and services from exchanges of financial assets. The *real sector* of an economy refers to the production and sale of goods and services, whether these activities are domestic or global. The *financial sector* of an economy refers to transactions in financial assets, whether these transactions are domestic or global. The broadest measures of economic integration focus on the volume of trade in goods and services—a measure of real-sector integration—and the volume of transactions in various types of financial assets—a measure of financial-sector integration. It is important to keep in mind that although we measure these two sectors separately, they are connected:

real sector
A designation for the sector of the economy engaged in the production and sale of goods and services.

financial sector
A designation for the sector of the economy where people trade in financial assets.

> **International economic integration refers to the extent and strength of real-sector and financial-sector linkages among national economies. Real-sector linkages occur through the international transactions in goods and services, whereas the financial-sector linkages occur through international transactions in financial assets.**

World Trade in Goods and Services

Because of reductions in trade barriers, lower transportation costs, and advances in telecommunications, world trade has steadily expanded during the past several decades. As illustrated in Figure 1–1 on the facing page, the volume of world trade in goods and services has exhibited positive growth rates for all but three years during the last three decades. The average rate of growth of total world trade during the last thirty years has been impressive, at approximately 6 percent a year.

Figure 1–2 on the facing page shows the importance of international trade for ten individual nations. This figure plots the sum of each nation's exports and

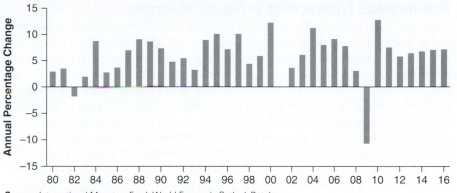

Figure 1–1

Growth in World Trade of Goods and Services

World trade in goods and services has increased at an annual rate of nearly 6 percent since 1980. The cumulative effect of this growth is a more than fivefold increase in the volume of world trade.

Source: International Monetary Fund, World Economic Outlook Database.

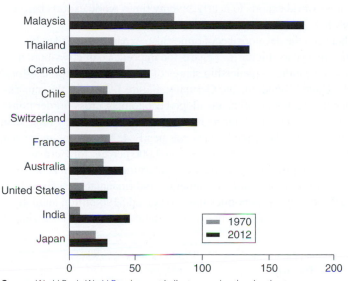

Figure 1–2

Selected Nations' Trade in Goods and Services

The global market for goods and services has become more important for most individual nations. The figure plots the sum of each nation's exports and imports as a percentage of the nation's volume of economic output for the years 1970 and 2012. Hence, the percentage reflects each nation's trade as a share of its overall real-sector activity.

Source: World Bank, World Development Indicators, and authors' estimates.

imports as a percentage of its overall output. Hence, it reflects the importance of international trade as a share of overall transactions in each nation's real sector.

Figure 1–2 shows that, among the nations depicted, global trade in goods and services increased significantly. Generally, larger nations such as the United States and Japan tend to depend less on the global markets for goods and services and more on their domestic markets, relative to the smaller economies of nations such as Thailand and Malaysia.

 Fundamental ISSUES

#1 How important is the global market for goods and services?

Over the last thirty-five years, the volume of world trade in goods and services has grown by almost 6 percent annually. The cumulative effect of this growth is more than a fivefold increase in world trade. As measured by the share of overall real-sector activity, world trade in goods and services has become increasingly more important to developed and developing economies alike.

International Transactions in Financial Assets

Although recent increases in global trade flows are remarkable, they pale in comparison to developments in the international monetary and financial markets. Table 1–1 provides estimates of the annual turnover in the *foreign exchange market*—that is, the market for national currencies and related instruments relative to the volume of world exports of goods. The second column of the table shows that the volume of world trade in goods has increased by more than 900 percent since 1979. Data in the first column, however, indicate that annual foreign exchange turnover, which is the dollar value of total transactions, increased more than 5,000 percent, or more than five times the change in the volume of world exports. The final column of Table 1–1 shows the ratio of foreign exchange turnover to world exports of goods, which is a measure of the amount of international transactions in goods relative to foreign exchange transactions. As the table indicates, within thirty years foreign exchange turnover has grown from about twelve times world exports to nearly seventy times world exports before dropping back somewhat.

Capital flows between the developed economies also expanded considerably during the last twenty-five years. Figure 1–3 charts the importance of cross-border transactions in bonds and equities—ownership shares of the issuing enterprise—for the United States, the United Kingdom, and Germany. Figure 1–3 shows the remarkable increase for each nation. For all of the developed economies, cross-border transactions in bonds and equities increased during the last twenty-two years by more than 1,700 percent. The increase for the United States was nearly 4,000 percent, more than 1,900 percent for the United Kingdom, and more than 4,000 percent for Germany.

The sizable increase in private capital flows to emerging economies is one of the most prominent features of international monetary and financial markets today. Net capital flows to the emerging economies have averaged $190 billion annually since 1990. Although there was a decline in private capital flows to the emerging

Table 1–1

Foreign Exchange Turnover and World Exports

World exports have grown at an impressive rate since 1979. The turnover of foreign exchange, however, has increased from twelve times the volume of world exports of goods to more than sixty times.

	Foreign Exchange Turnover ($ Trillion, annual)	World Exports of Goods ($ Trillion, annual)	Ratio
1979	$17.5	$1.5	12:1
1986	75.0	2.0	38:1
1989	190.0	3.1	61:1
1992	252.0	4.7	54:1
1995	297.5	5.0	60:1
1998	372.5	5.4	69:1
2001	300.0	6.6	45:1
2004	475.0	9.1	52:1
2007	797.8	13.9	57:1
2010	968.0	15.1	62:1

Sources: Held, David, Anthony McGrew, David Goldblatt, and Jonathan Perraton, *Global Transformations*, p. 209; Bank for International Settlements, *Triennial Central Bank Survey*, various issues; International Monetary Fund, *International Financial Statistics*.

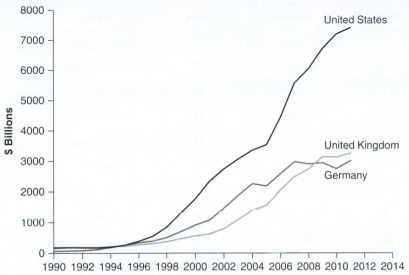

Source: Bank for International Settlements, *BIS Statistics.*

Figure 1–3

Cross-Border Transactions in Bonds and Equities for the United States, Germany, and the United Kingdom

During the past two decades, the developed economies have become more dependent on foreign capital flows. In Germany, the United States, and the United Kingdom, international transactions in bonds and equities have grown by more than 4,000 percent, 3,800 percent, and 1,900 percent, respectively.

economies following the financial crises in East Asia and Russia, worldwide net direct investment continued at a remarkable pace.

The data presented so far show how important global trade in goods, services, and financial assets has become. The data also show, however, that dependence on global markets varies from country to country.

The Most Globalized Nations

In an attempt to rank individual nations according to their degree of globalization, the KOF Swiss Economic Institute combined a number of measures, such as the number of international phone calls; the number of international travelers; the volume of trade in goods, services, and capital; the number of Internet servers per person; and the number of McDonald's restaurants and Ikea stores per person.

On the WEB

To learn more about the KOF Globalization Index, visit the home page of the *KOF Economic Institute* at *http://www.kof.ethz.ch/en/*

Table 1–2 on the following page shows the ranking of the top twenty nations that KOP surveyed. As the table indicates, France is the only one of the largest industrialized nations—the United States, Canada, France, the United Kingdom, Germany, Japan, and Italy—that ranks in the top ten of the most globalized nations. Otherwise, it is the smaller advanced economies with relatively unrestricted financial markets that occupy these positions.

Economists also attempt to determine if globalization is associated with civil liberties, political rights, levels of perceived corruption, and income patterns. There appears to be a clear direct relationship among greater civil liberties, more political rights, lower levels of corruption, and the level of globalization, but there is no clear pattern between the inequality of income patterns and globalization.

Table 1–2

The Top Twenty Globalized Nations

Using several measures of global integration, authors for the KOF Swiss Economic Institute ranked 208 nations, with the top twenty shown here. The smaller advanced economies tend to be the most globalized countries.

Rank	Nation	Rank	Nation
1	Belgium	11	Finland
2	Austria	12	Czech Republic
3	Netherlands	13	Canada
4	Sweden	14	Luxembourg
5	Switzerland	15	Slovak Republic
6	Denmark	16	Germany
7	France	17	Spain
8	Hungary	18	Singapore
9	Portugal	19	Norway
10	Ireland	20	Cyprus

Source: KOF Swiss Economic Institute, *2011 Index of Globalization*; Dreher, Axel, "Does Globalization Affect Growth? Evidence from a New Index of Globalization," *Applied Economics* 38 (10), (2006): 1091–1110; Updated in Dreher, Axel, Noel Gaston, and Pim Martens, *Measuring Globalisation—Gauging Its Consequences*, New York: Springer, 2008.

The Most Globalized Firms

Multinational enterprises (MNEs), which are business organizations based in one nation but conducting their activities in two or more nations, are the engines of increased economic interdependence. According to Professor Alan Rugman of the University of Reading, the five hundred largest MNEs account for about half of the world's trade in goods and services and more than 90 percent of the world's foreign direct investment.

Table 1–3 lists the world's ten largest MNEs based on the value of their foreign assets–assets held in countries other than their home country.

But are these the most globalized firms? In other words, are the activities of these firms really spread out globally? To answer this question, the United Nations Committee on Trade and Development developed a transnationality index. This index measures how "internationalized" a company is using information on its assets, sales, and employees. Specifically, the index is calculated using the average of the company's proportion of foreign assets to total assets, foreign sales to total sales, and employees located abroad to total employees. Table 1–4 ranks the top ten companies based on the value of their transnationality index.

Table 1–4 clearly provides a very different ranking than Table 1–3. Professor Rugman argues that firms with the largest transnationality indexes are from smaller home-market countries, such as Switzerland and Canada, because they must rely on foreign market sales to obtain the benefits from globalizing their operations.

As you can now see, increasing globalization and integration of the world's markets for goods, services, and financial assets is an important issue. We now turn our attention to more detailed measures of an individual nation's transactions in goods, services, and financial assets. In an accounting system, these are used in the balance of payments.

Ranking	Company	Home Country	Industry
1	General Electric	United States	Electrical and Electronic Equipment
2	Royal Dutch/ Shell Group	United Kingdom/ Netherlands	Petroleum
3	Vodafone Group PLC	United Kingdom	Telecommunications
4	British Petroleum Company PLC	United Kingdom	Petroleum
5	Toyota Motor Corporation	Japan	Motor Vehicles
6	ExxonMobil	United States	Petroleum
7	Total	France	Petroleum
8	E.On	Germany	Electricity, Gas, and Water
9	Eléctricité de France	France	Electricity, Gas, and Water
10	ArcelorMittal	Luxembourg	Metal and Metal Products

Table 1–3

The Ten Largest MNEs, Ranked by Foreign Assets

Source: United Nations Conference on Trade and Development, *World Investment Report.*

Ranking	Company	Home Country	Industry
1	Xstrata PLC	United Kingdom	Mining and Quarrying
2	ABB Ltd.	Switzerland	Engineering Services
3	Nokia	Finland	Electrical and Electronic Equipment
4	Pernod Ricard SA	France	Food, Beverage, and Tobacco
5	WPP Group PLC	United Kingdom	Business Services
6	Vodafone Group PLC	United Kingdom	Telecommunications
7	Linde AG	Germany	Chemicals
8	Anheuser-Busch InBev SA	Netherlands	Food, Beverage, and Tobacco
9	Anglo American	United Kingdom	Mining and Quarrying
10	ArcelorMittal	Luxembourg	Metal and Metal Products

Table 1–4

The Top Ten MNEs Ranked by Transnationality

Source: United Nations Conference on Trade and Development, *World Investment Report.*

#2 How important are the international monetary and financial markets?

The international monetary and financial markets have become increasingly important to both developed and emerging economies. Foreign exchange turnover has grown to more than fifty times the volume of world trade in goods. For the developed economies, international transactions in bonds and equities have grown by more than 1,700 percent during the past 20 years, while private capital flows to emerging economies have continued despite several financial crises in the 1990s through the early 2010s.

THE BALANCE OF PAYMENTS

balance-of-payments system

A system of accounts that measures transactions of goods, services, income, and financial assets between domestic residents, businesses, and governments and the rest of the world during specific time period.

The *balance-of-payments system* is a complete tabulation of the total market value of goods, services, and financial assets that domestic residents, firms, and governments exchange with residents of other nations during a given period. Like gross domestic product, a nation's *balance of payments* is a system that accounts for flows of income and expenditures. Unlike gross domestic product, however, the balance of payments includes the flow of financial assets. Table 1–5 provides a summary statement of the U.S. balance-of-payments system that we shall refer to throughout the next several sections of this chapter. The statement is provided every quarter by the Bureau of Economic Analysis.

Get current data on U.S. international transactions at the Bureau of Economic Analysis at *http://www.bea.gov.*

Balance of Payments as a Double-Entry Bookkeeping System

debit entry

A negative entry in the balance of payments that records a transaction resulting in a payment abroad by a domestic resident.

credit entry

A positive entry in the balance of payments that records a transaction resulting in a payment from abroad to a domestic resident.

A *double-entry bookkeeping system* records both sides of any two-party transaction with two separate and offsetting entries: a debit entry and a credit entry. The result is that the sum of all the debit entries, in absolute value, is equal to the sum of all the credit entries. The balance-of-payments system is like a typical double-entry accounting system in that every transaction results in two entries being made in the balance-of-payments accounts. A *debit entry* records a transaction that results in a domestic resident making a payment abroad. A debit entry has a negative value in the balance-of-payments account. A *credit entry* records a transaction that results in a domestic resident receiving a payment from abroad. A credit entry has a positive value in the balance-of-payments account.

In the balance-of-payments accounts, an international transaction that results in a credit entry would also generate an offsetting debit entry, and an international transaction that results in a debit entry would also generate an offsetting credit entry. In the balance-of-payments accounts, therefore, the sum of all the credit entries is equal to, in absolute value, the sum of all the debit entries.

Current Account (millions $)			Capital and Financial Account		
1	**Exports of goods and services and income receipts**	2,500,817	13	**U.S.-owned assets abroad, net [increase/financial outflow (−)]**	−991,447
2	Goods	1,288,699	14	U.S. official reserve assets, net	−1,834
3	Services	548,878	15	U.S. government assets, other than official reserve assets	7,540
4	Income receipts	663,240	16	U.S. private assets abroad, net	−997,153
5	**Imports of goods and services and income payments**	−2,835,620	17	**Foreign-owned assets in the United States, net [increase/financial inflow (+)]**	1,245,736
6	Goods, balance of payments basis	−1,934,555	18	Foreign official assets in the United States, net	349,754
7	Services	−403,048	19	Other foreign assets in the United States, net	895,982
8	Income payments	−498,017	20	**Capital account transactions, net**	−152
9	**Unilateral current transfers, net**	−136,095	21	**Statistical discrepancy (sum of the above items with the sign reversed)**	216,761
10	**Balance on Merchandise Trade (lines 2 and 6)**	−645,856	22	**Balance on Private Capital and Financial Account (lines 16, 19, and 20)**	−101,323
11	**Balance on Goods, Services, and Income (lines 1 and 5)**	−334,803	23	**Balance on Capital and Financial Account (lines 13, 17, and 20)**	254,137
12	**Balance on Current Account (lines 1, 5, and 9)**	−470,898	24	**Overall Balance of Payments (Sum of 12, 21, and 23)**	0

Table 1–5

Summary Statement of the U.S. Balance of Payments

Source: Bureau of Economic Analysis, International Economic Accounts Data, 2010.

To illustrate the double-entry nature of the balance-of-payments system, consider the following example. Suppose a U.S. manufacturer exports a computer to a Canadian firm in exchange for a payment of $2,000. Table 1–6 on the next page shows the transaction's effects on the U.S. balance of payments. The export of the computer is a $2,000 credit, because it results in a $2,000 payment being made to the U.S. firm from the Canadian firm. Because of the double-entry nature of the

Table 1–6

Recording a U.S. Firm's Export in the Balance-of-Payments Accounts

Transaction	Offsetting Entries	Credit	Debit
Computer export	$2,000 computer exported by the U.S.	$2,000	
	$2,000 payment received by the U.S.		–$2,000

system, there is an offsetting $2,000 debit entry made. Note that the sum of the debits in absolute value, $2,000, is equal to the sum of the credits, $2,000.

Balance-of-Payments Accounts

Countries exchange a vast array of goods, services, and financial assets. Economists group these transactions by type. There are different categories for each type of transaction, with various categories combined to form accounts. Therefore, the balance-of-payments system consists of a number of different accounts. Most nations have many accounts. We can understand the balance-of-payments system, however, by focusing on just three accounts: the current account, the private capital account, and the official settlements balance.

current account

Measures the flow of goods, services, income, and transfers or gifts between domestic residents, businesses, and governments and the rest of the world.

The Current Account The *current account* measures the flow of goods, services, and income across national borders. It also includes transfers or gifts from the domestic government and residents to foreign residents and governments, as well as foreign transfers to the domestic country. The four basic categories within the current account are goods, services, income, and unilateral transfers. Table 1–5 shows the exports and imports of goods, services, and income for the United States on lines 1 through 8. Line 9 is for the unilateral transfers category. Let's examine each of these four categories of the current account.

Goods The goods category measures the imports and exports of tangible goods. This category includes trade in foods, industrial materials, capital goods (such as machinery), autos, and consumer goods. An export of any of these items is a credit in the goods category, because this would result in a payment from abroad. An import of any of these items is a debit in the goods category, as this would result in a payment made abroad.

Most economists consider the goods category to be the most accurately measured balance-of-payments category, because this category measures the trade of tangible items that, in many countries, must be registered with customs authorities.

Services The services category measures the imports and exports of services, tourism and travel, and military transactions. Payments, royalties, or fees received from abroad for providing consulting, insurance, banking, or accounting services, for example, are recorded as credits in the service category. Likewise, payments, royalties, or fees sent abroad for the import of these services are debits in the services category. The services category also includes the import and export of military equipment, services, and aid.

To understand how travel and tourism services appear in the balance of payments, consider a domestic college student who traveled abroad during a semester break. Expenditures by this student on items such as a rail pass and hotel accommodations are imports, or debits, in the services category because these services are, in a sense, imported by the student.

The imports and exports of services are much more difficult to measure than exports and imports of goods. Because a nontangible item is not registered at a customs point, it can be very difficult to estimate the amount of services provided internationally. Hence, economists refer to services as *invisibles.*

Income The income category tabulates interest and dividend payments to foreign residents and governments who hold domestic financial assets. It also includes payments received by domestic residents and governments who hold financial assets abroad.

To illustrate how investment income appears in the balance of payments, suppose a U.K. resident receives an interest payment on a German treasury bill. The interest payment is an export, or credit, in the income category of the U.K. balance of payments. The interest payment is a credit, because the U.K. resident received a payment from abroad. Therefore, income payments received by domestic residents who hold financial assets abroad are credits, or exports, whereas income payments made to foreign residents who hold domestic financial assets are debits, or imports.

It is important to note that economists do not record the purchase of a financial asset in the income category. Only the income earned on the financial asset is included in the current account, because income earned on assets can be used for current consumption.

Unilateral transfers The unilateral transfers category measures international transfers, or gifts, among individuals or governments. This category, therefore, records the offsetting entries of exports or imports for which nothing except *goodwill* is expected in return. To illustrate how a gift appears in the unilateral transfers category, suppose the U.S. government sends $500,000 worth of rice as humanitarian aid to a country that had just experienced a flood. The export of the rice appears in the goods category as a credit. However, the U.S. government expects no payment for this export. A debit entry appears in the unilateral transfers category; the United States effectively has imported a $500,000 payment of goodwill from the foreign country. (To consider how the combined current account surpluses or deficits of groups of nations can provide useful information, see *Policy Notebook: The Combined Current Account Deficit of Developed Nations Translates into a Combined Current Account Surplus for Emerging Countries.*)

 **POLICY** Notebook

The Combined Current Account Deficit of Developed Nations Translates into a Combined Current Account Surplus for Emerging Countries

In recent years, the United States and other highly developed nations have been experiencing a combined current account deficit of more than $150 billion per year, as shown in Figure 1–4 on the next page. Until 1997, developed nations were operating with a combined current account surplus, but then they fell into a deficit position that has widened in recent years. Also displayed in Figure 1–4 is the combined current account balance of so-called *emerging countries*—countries with previously less developed economies, such as China and India, in which economic growth is on an upswing. It is no accident that emerging countries' combined current account surpluses have been nearly the mirror image of the deficits of developed nations. Funds to finance the developed nations' current account deficits have come mainly from emerging countries, so net inflows of goods, services, incomes, and transfers from the rest of the world by developed nations must correspond to net outflows of goods, services, incomes, and transfers on the part of the rest of the world—which means primarily emerging countries. Consequently, since 1997 emerging countries have operated with steadily increasing current account surpluses.

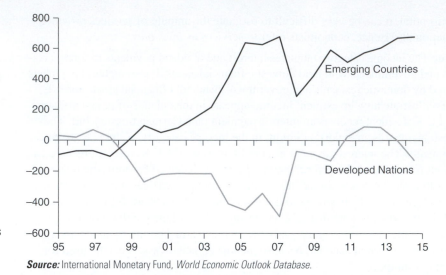

Figure 1–4

Combined Current Account
Balances of Developed Nations
and of Emerging Countries

Source: International Monetary Fund, *World Economic Outlook Database.*

Since 1997, developed nations have experienced higher combined current account deficits, which have been closely mirrored by combined current account surpluses of emerging nations.

For Critical Analysis

If the current account balances of the world's least developed countries—those outside the sets of developed nations and emerging countries—were added to the combined current account surplus of emerging countries, would the result exactly mirror the current account deficit of the world's developed nations? Explain.

capital account

A tabulation of the flows of financial assets among domestic private residents, foreign private residents, and domestic and foreign governments; sometimes referred to as the *financial account.*

private capital account

A tabulation of the flows of financial assets between domestic private residents and foreign private residents.

The Capital Account The *capital account* tabulates cross-border transactions of financial assets among private residents, foreign residents, and domestic and foreign governments. The *private capital account* (sometimes referred to as the *financial account*) measures the outflow of domestic assets abroad and the inflow of foreign assets into the domestic country that result from transactions involving private (nongovernmental) individuals and companies. The private capital account includes transactions of private domestic financial assets and foreign financial assets. It does not include financial assets of the domestic government. These financial assets include physical assets and financial assets such as bonds, bills, stocks, deposits, and currencies.

The private capital account tabulates two types of asset *flows:* investment flows and changes in banks' and brokers' cash deposits that arise from foreign transactions. Investment flows include the following:

- Purchases of foreign securities by domestic residents and purchases of domestic securities by foreign residents
- Lending to foreign residents by domestic residents and borrowing by domestic residents from foreign residents
- Investment by domestic firms in their foreign affiliates and investment by foreign firms in their domestic affiliates

To better understand the potential impact of capital inflows from abroad, economists distinguish between portfolio investment and foreign direct investment.

Portfolio investment refers to an individual's or business's purchase of stocks, bonds, or other financial assets, and deposits. *Foreign direct investment* is the purchase of assets to establish financial control of a foreign entity.

It may be difficult to determine whether the purchase of a foreign asset was intended to earn income or establish financial control. To help distinguish between portfolio and direct foreign investment, economists consider the foreign acquisition of less than 10 percent of the entity's outstanding stock as portfolio investment, and the acquisition of 10 percent or more of the entity's outstanding stock as foreign direct investment.

A debit entry in the capital account, for example, records the purchase of a foreign financial asset by a domestic private resident, because this transaction results in a payment made abroad. Likewise, a credit entry records the purchase of a domestic financial asset by a foreign private resident, as this transaction generates a payment from abroad.

portfolio investment

The acquisition of foreign financial assets that results in less than a 10 percent ownership share in the entity.

foreign direct investment

The acquisition of foreign financial assets that results in an ownership share in the foreign entity of 10 percent or greater.

Access empirical studies on international trade and finance at the *Centre d'Etudes Prospectives et d'Informations Internationales* at *http://www.cepii.fr.*

Table 1–7 shows, using the data from Table 1–5 on page 11, the categories of the capital account for 2010. These three categories tabulate transactions of domestic government assets, domestic private assets, and foreign assets. Changes in private U.S. assets abroad reflect an increase or decrease in private ownership of foreign assets. A net capital outflow means that the net purchases of foreign assets by domestic residents exceeds the net purchases of domestic assets by foreign residents. Changes in foreign assets in the United States reflect an increase or decrease in foreign ownership of domestic assets. A net capital inflow means that the net purchases of domestic assets by foreign residents exceed the net purchases of foreign assets by domestic residents.

The Official Settlements Balance The third and final account, the *official settlements balance,* measures the transactions of financial assets and deposits by official government agencies. Typically, the central banks and finance ministries or treasuries of national governments conduct these types of official transactions.

It is common for foreign central banks and government agencies to keep deposit accounts with other central banks. If, for example, the U.S. Treasury or

official settlements balance

A balance-of-payments account that tabulates transactions of reserve assets by official government agencies.

Category	2010
Private U.S. assets abroad	−997,153
Other U.S. government assets	7,540
Other foreign assets in the United States	895,982
Other capital account transactions	−152
Official settlements balance	347,920

Note: $ millions

Table 1–7

Categories of the Balance-of-Payments Summary Statement That Are Included in the Capital and Financial Account

Federal Reserve were to make a deposit with the Bank of England, the deposit appears as a capital outflow, or *debit*, in the U.S. balance of payments. If, on the other hand, the Bank of England were to make a deposit with the Federal Reserve, the deposit is a capital inflow, or *credit*, in the U.S. balance of payments. In Table 1–5 on page 11, line 14 shows the U.S. official assets that include gold and foreign currencies. U.S. official assets also include assets such as Special Drawing Rights at the International Monetary Fund. These assets will be explained in Chapter 2. Foreign official assets in the United States are shown on line 18 of Table 1–5. The official settlements balance is the sum of lines 14 and 18.

Deficits and Surpluses in the Balance of Payments

If we sum all of the debits and credits that appear in the current account, private capital account, and official settlements balance, the total should be zero. However, this seldom happens in practice. Numerous transactions are missed in the accounting process or hidden from the process intentionally. For example, illegal transactions are hidden from government agencies, and some legal transactions may be hidden from government agencies, such as customs officials, to avoid taxes. Furthermore, government statisticians make errors in their tabulation of credits and debits.

If the sum of the credits and debits in the current account, private capital account, and official settlements is not zero, then an offsetting entry appears in the balance of payments. Economists call this offsetting entry the *statistical discrepancy*. The statistical discrepancy can be very large. Line 21 of Table 1–5 shows that the statistical discrepancy for the United States in 2010 was $216.7 billion!

The *overall balance of payments* is the sum of the credits and debits in the current account, capital account, official settlements, and the statistical discrepancy. Because debit entries offset each and every credit entry, and the statistical discrepancy offsets any errors, the overall balance of payments necessarily is equal to zero.

It is common, and somewhat confusing, when economists and the media refer to balance-of-payments deficits or surpluses. As just explained, ignoring the statistical discrepancy, the overall balance of payments must sum to zero. Therefore, what economists and the media refer to is something other than the *overall* balance of payments.

A balance-of-payments deficit refers to a situation in which the official settlements balance is positive. Ignoring a statistical discrepancy, if the sum of the credits and debits in the current account and the private capital account is negative, private payments made to foreigners exceed private payments received from foreigners. In this case, the official settlements balance must be positive. This is called a *balance-of-payments deficit.* A situation where the sum of the debits and credits in the current and private capital account is positive means that private payments received from foreigners exceed private payments made to foreigners. In this case, the official settlements balance is negative, and there is a *balance-of-payments surplus.* A *balance-of-payments equilibrium* refers to a situation where the sum of the debits and credits in the current account and the private capital account is zero, and thus the official settlements balance is zero. Therefore, we can conclude that:

> **A balance-of-payments equilibrium, ignoring a statistical discrepancy, arises when the sum of the debits and credits in the current account and the private capital account equal zero, so that the official settlements balance is zero. A balance-of-payments deficit corresponds to a positive official settlements balance, and a balance-of-payments surplus corresponds to a negative official settlements balance.**

Other Deficit and Surplus Measures

Economists use other deficit and surplus measures that are part of the balance-of-payments system. The *balance on merchandise trade* is the sum of the debit and credit entries in the merchandise or goods category. If the sum of the debit entries in this category exceeds the sum of the credit entries, then the balance on merchandise trade is negative, and there is a deficit in merchandise trade. If the sum of the debit entries is less than the sum of the credit entries, then the balance on merchandise trade is positive, and there is a merchandise trade surplus. Table 1–5 on page 11 lists goods credits on line 2 and debits on line 6. The sum of the two amounts is the balance on merchandise trade, and this balance appears on line 10 of Table 1–5. Because the debits, or merchandise imports, exceed the credits, or merchandise exports, the total is a negative amount representing a merchandise deficit. (Even though the balance on the goods category of the current account simply summarizes a nation's net flow of imports and exports of tangible goods, some observers view it as an important business indicator. To see why this perspective may be misguided, see *Management Notebook: Trade Deficits: Faulty Indicators of Business Activity.*)

 # MANAGEMENT Notebook

Trade Deficits: Faulty Indicators of Business Activity

The media commonly refer to a negative balance on the goods category of the current account as the *trade deficit*. Stories often interpret an increase in the absolute size of the U.S. trade deficit as good news for U.S. businesses. As Figure 1–5 indicates, however, this interpretation may be misplaced. During years when the U.S. trade deficit was rising, U.S. national income—a key measure of business output—increased at an average annual rate of more than 3.5 percent. During years when the U.S. trade deficit was shrinking, U.S national income rose at an average rate of less than 2 percent per year. Thus, a growing trade deficit is not necessarily an indicator of a weakening national business climate.

For Critical Analysis

Why is a negative balance on the goods category of the current account not necessarily either "good" or "bad" for the economy?

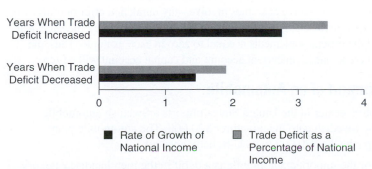

Sources: U.S. Department of Commerce; authors' estimates.

Figure 1–5

Increasing versus Decreasing Trade Deficits and Economic Growth

In contrast to the popular perception that growing U.S. trade deficits are an indicator of a weakening U.S. business climate, the rate of growth of U.S. national income has been significantly higher in years when the trade deficit was growing than in years in which the trade deficit was declining.

The balance on goods, services, and income is the sum of the debit and credit entries that appear in the merchandise, service, and income categories. If the total of the debit entries, or imports, exceeds the sum of the credit entries, or exports, then there is a deficit in goods, services, and income. If the total of the debit entries, or imports, is less than the sum of the credit entries, or exports, then there is a surplus in goods, services, and income. Table 1–5 provides the balance on goods, services, and income on line 11. This amount is negative, indicating that the United States experienced a negative balance, or *deficit,* on goods, services, and income in 2010.

As explained earlier, the current account includes the categories of goods, services, income, and unilateral transfers. Thus, the balance on the current account is the sum of all the debit and credit entries in these categories. The current account balance is the most reported balance-of-payments measure. If the sum of the debit entries exceeds the sum of the credit entries, then there is a current account deficit. If the sum of the debit entries is less than the sum of the credit entries, then there is a current account surplus. Table 1–5 provides the balance on the current account on line 12. This balance is also negative, indicating that the United States experienced a negative balance, or deficit, on the current account in 2010.

The balance on the private capital account reflects the net flow of financial assets purchased by private individuals. As explained earlier, purchases of foreign financial assets by private domestic residents represent a capital outflow, and appear as a debit. Purchases of domestic financial assets by private foreign residents represent a capital inflow and appear as a credit. The balance on the private capital account reflects the net inflow or outflow of capital. If the debit entries exceed the credit entries, there is a net capital outflow. If the debit entries are less than the credit entries, there is a net capital inflow. This balance appears on line 22 of Table 1–5. This negative balance indicates that the United States experienced a deficit on the private capital account, or net outflow of private capital, in 2010.

EXAMPLES OF INTERNATIONAL TRANSACTIONS AND HOW THEY AFFECT THE BALANCE OF PAYMENTS

Now that we have overviewed each category of the balance of payments, let's consider how typical international transactions result in both credit and debit entries and how they affect the various deficit and surplus measures. We shall look at five examples, summarized in Table 1–8.

Each of the examples presents a transaction as it affects the balance of payments for the United States. None of the examples involves any tabulation error or transaction of financial assets by an official government agency. As a result, there is no statistical discrepancy, and the official settlements is equal to zero in each example. Thus, the sum of debit and credit entries in current account and capital account will be zero.

Example 1: Import of an Automobile

An automobile dealer in the United States imports a Swedish automobile and pays the Swedish auto manufacturer $20,000. The automobile manufacturer deposits the $20,000 in its U.S. bank account.

The value of the imported automobile is a debit in the merchandise category because the transaction results in the outflow of currency. The payment is a credit,

	Example 1	Example 2	Example 3	Example 4	Example 5
Merchandise	−$20,000				$200,000
Services		−$1,000			
Income				−$500	
Unilateral transfers					−$200,000
Home assets abroad			−$10,000		
Foreign assets in the home country	$20,000	$1,000	$10,000	$500	
Balance on merchandise					$180,000
Balance on goods, services, and income					$178,500
Balance on current account					−$21,500
Balance on capital account					$21,500

Table 1–8

Balance-of-Payments Examples

or capital inflow, in the foreign assets in the United States category, because the Swedish auto manufacturer now owns a U.S. financial asset, the deposit. The fact that the funds were deposited in a bank in the United States is irrelevant. As long as the payment is made and the foreign entity receives the funds, it is a credit from the standpoint of U.S. balance-of-payments accounting.

Example 2: A College Student Travels Abroad

A college student travels abroad during a break from school, spending $1,000 on hotels and food.

The value of services consumed as a tourist—food, lodging, and transportation—is a debit in the services category, as the consumption of these services results in a payment abroad. The amount of funds the student spends abroad is a credit, or capital inflow, in the foreign assets in the United States category.

Example 3: A Foreign Resident Purchases a Domestic Treasury Bill

A foreign resident purchases a $10,000 U.S. treasury bill from a U.S. brokerage firm.

The payment for the treasury bill is a credit, or a capital inflow, in the foreign assets in the United States category, because the foreign resident now owns a U.S.

financial asset. The payment received by the brokerage firm is a debit, or capital outflow, in the U.S. assets abroad category, because the brokerage firm acquires a foreign deposit.

Example 4: The United States Pays Interest on a Foreign-Held Asset

The U.S. Treasury makes a $500 interest payment to a foreign resident that holds a previously purchased U.S. treasury bill.

The $500 payment made to the foreign resident is a debit in the income category. The payment also is a credit, or capital inflow, in the foreign assets in the U.S. category, because the foreign resident receives $500 of the domestic currency, which also is a domestic financial asset.

Example 5: A Charitable Organization in the United States Provides Humanitarian Aid Abroad

A U.S. charitable organization, as a humanitarian gesture, donates $200,000 of wheat to a country that recently experienced a flood.

The value of the wheat is a credit in the merchandise category because it is an export of a tangible good. The wheat is a donation, with only goodwill expected in return, so the offsetting entry is a debit in the unilateral transfers category. In theory, there is an import of $200,000 of goodwill from the foreign country.

Examples Combined

If these transactions represent all the international transactions of the United States for the period, then we can determine the balance on merchandise trade; balance on goods, services, and income; the current account balance; and the capital account balance in Table 1–8 on page 19. Summing across the row for the merchandise category, we see that the sum of debit and credit entries is $180,000, yielding a surplus on merchandise trade of $180,000. Combining debit and credit entries in the rows for merchandise, services, and income yields the balance on goods, services, and income, which is a surplus of $178,500. Adding the debit and credit entries in the row for unilateral transfers to the entries for merchandise, services, and income yields the current account balance, which is a deficit of $21,500. Combining the entries in the rows for U.S. assets abroad and foreign assets in the United States provides the balance on the capital account. This yields a surplus, or positive balance, of $21,500.

 Fundamental ISSUES

#3 What is a country's balance of payments, and what does this measure?

The balance of payments is an accounting system used to tabulate a nation's international transactions. The balance-of-payments system measures transactions goods, services, income, unilateral transfers, private transactions of financial assets, and official reserves.

THE CAPITAL ACCOUNT AND THE INTERNATIONAL FLOW OF ASSETS

The capital account measures the flow of financial assets, and the current account measures the flow of goods, services, income, and unilateral transfers. Therefore, a starting point for thinking about capital account transactions is to view these transactions as necessary to finance current account transactions.

Consider the following example. If a country runs a current account deficit, the country consumes more goods and services than it produces, and it must import this excess from abroad. Because the country spends more than it earns, it must borrow from abroad to finance purchases of the goods and services. This means that, on net, capital must flow into the economy, thereby yielding a capital account surplus. Viewed from this perspective, a current account deficit is undesirable because a deficit country must borrow from abroad to finance its current consumption. This is a very narrow perspective, however.

A broader way to view a capital account surplus is to recognize that capital may flow into a nation because foreign residents may consider the nation an attractive and promising location for investment. In other words, foreign residents may consider the nation healthy and poised for economic growth that yields sufficiently high returns on their investment. Foreign investment, in turn, expands the capital stock of the nation. An increase in the capital stock can yield a higher future standard of living for the nation's residents. Viewed from this perspective, the capital account surplus, which by definition implies a current account deficit, can be good for a nation.

Example: A College Student

Let's put this discussion in the context of college students. While in college, the students typically spend more than they earn. They pay rent; purchase food, books, and entertainment; and pay tuition. Their earnings usually arise from a part-time job. Often, they borrow from parents, a bank, the university, or from the state or federal government.

Suppose that a student arranges a guaranteed student loan from the federal government. This loan must be paid back, with interest, over a maximum of ten years beginning upon graduation. What is the student's motivation for borrowing? It is likely that the student is making an investment in acquiring *human capital*, which is the knowledge and abilities an individual possesses. If the increase in human capital yields greater increased future earnings that exceed the cost of paying the loan back, then the investment is wise. If the student instead spends all the borrowed funds on current consumption, fails to finish college, and forgoes the higher earnings stream that an education would have provided, then the cost of repaying the loan actually reduces the student's future standard of living.

Clearly what is important is not that the student borrowed, but how the student used the borrowed funds. The key question is this: Did the student invest the funds in education so as to increase future earnings, or were the funds spent on current consumption?

A Capital Account Surplus

A capital account surplus should be viewed in much of the same way: If funds borrowed from abroad add to the capital stock of the nation, and if the resulting increase in future potential output exceeds the cost of borrowing, then the residents of the nation may enjoy an increased ability to consume goods and services in the future. If the borrowed funds finance current period consumption, however, then the burden of repaying the borrowed funds may reduce the nation's future prosperity.

net creditor

A nation whose total claims on foreigners exceed the total claims of foreigners on the nation.

net debtor

A nation whose total claims on foreigners are less than the total claims of foreigners on the nation.

The capital *flows* are the lending and borrowing of a nation's residents over a specific period. These capital flows, on net, add to or reduce the stock of foreign assets held by domestic residents and the *stock* of domestic financial assets held by foreign residents. Economists call a nation that has a stock of foreign financial assets that exceeds the stock of foreign-owned domestic financial assets a ***net creditor***. In contrast, a ***net debtor*** is a nation that has a stock of foreign financial assets that is less than its stock of foreign-owned domestic financial assets. As we have noted, it is not necessarily "good" or "bad" for a nation to be a net debtor or net creditor.

The United States as a Net Debtor

Consider the case of the United States. In the course of its history, it has experienced periods when it was a net creditor and periods when it was a net debtor. The original colonies of the United States began as a net debtor, borrowing from France and the Netherlands to finance Revolutionary War expenditures. The late 1800s was a period of significant net indebtedness. This was also a period of high investment for the United States. The growth potential of the United States attracted considerable foreign capital inflows, resulting in a net debtor position. This investment financed increases in railroads and other physical capital and led to an increase in manufacturing output of approximately 10 percent per year in the latter part of the nineteenth century.

As Figure 1–6 shows, since the 1980s, the United States began experiencing sizable capital inflows and current account deficits. As a result of these inflows, the United States became a net debtor. The popular press has characterized the United States as being the world's largest debtor nation and has claimed that foreigners are "buying up" U.S. businesses and properties. This situation is not necessarily good or bad for the United States. What is important is whether the inflow of capital into the United States is financing current consumption or productive investment.

Figure 1–6

U.S. Net International Investment Position

The United States has been a net debtor nation at various times in its history. In the 1980s, the United States began experiencing sizable net capital inflows and became a net debtor.

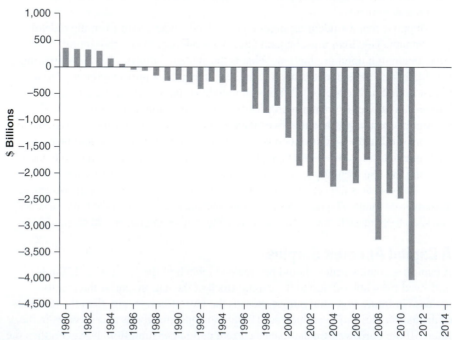

Source: Bureau of Economic Analysis.

Fundamental ISSUES

#4 What does it mean for a country to be a net debtor or net creditor?

A net debtor nation is one whose stock of foreign financial assets held by domestic residents is less than the stock of domestic financial assets held by foreign residents. A net creditor nation is one whose stock of foreign financial assets held by domestic residents is greater than the stock of domestic financial assets held by foreign residents. Being a net debtor or net creditor is not necessarily "good" or "bad." Capital inflows may add to a nation's capital stock and increase an average resident's ability to purchase goods and services in the future.

RELATING THE CURRENT ACCOUNT BALANCE AND CAPITAL FLOWS

It is very important to understand the relationship that exists between a nation's current account and its capital flows. This relationship is derived from accounting identities, not from any specific theory. The basic balance-of-payments identities indicate that a current account deficit occurs when a nation is a net recipient of foreign capital from abroad. Policymakers often debate the potential job losses stemming from a current account deficit, how to reduce the deficit, and the desirability of net capital inflows from abroad. The essence of the debate, however, is whether the benefits of foreign capital investment outweigh the consequences of a trade imbalance and why domestic saving is less than domestic investment.

To illustrate this point, we begin with a nation's domestic saving and domestic investment. Domestic saving includes private saving and public or government saving and is the difference between total domestic income and expenditures. For an open economy, domestic saving can be either positive or negative.

Domestic investment includes expenditures on capital goods and inventories, as well as household and business investment in residential and business construction. If, on one hand, a nation's domestic investment exceeds its domestic saving, its total expenditures exceed the value of its output, and the nation is importing more goods and services than it is exporting. If, on the other hand, domestic saving exceeds its domestic investment, the nation's total expenditures are less than the value of its output, and it is a net exporter of goods and services. The current account balance, therefore, is equal to the difference between domestic saving and domestic investment:

Domestic Saving − Domestic Investment ≡ Current Account Balance

The difference between domestic saving and domestic investment relates to a nation's capital inflows from abroad as well. A nation can finance its domestic investment through either domestic saving or capital inflows from abroad. If a nation's domestic investment exceeds its domestic saving, then it is, on net, importing foreign capital; it is a net borrower from abroad. If, however, domestic saving exceeds domestic investment, then the nation is a net capital exporter or a net lender abroad. Hence, net capital flows, which includes official reserves and other government assets, equal the difference between domestic saving and domestic investment:

Domestic Saving − Domestic Investment ≡ Net Capital Flows

Because both the current account balance and net capital flows must identically equal the difference between domestic saving and domestic investment, they must identically equal each other:

$$\text{Current Account Balance} = \text{Net Capital Flows}$$

This final equation shows that if a nation is experiencing net capital inflows from abroad, it must also be running a current account deficit. If a nation is experiencing net capital outflows, then it must be running a current account surplus.

Based on this relationship between the current account balance and net capital flows, Matthew Higgins and Thomas Klitgaard of the Federal Reserve Bank of New York argue that a high U.S. current account deficit may not necessarily mean that the United States is losing jobs to foreign imports. Rather, large U.S. current account deficits result from sizable capital inflows that finance the gap between U.S. saving and investment spending, including job-creating private investment expenditures. These capital inflows explain, in part, how the United States experienced substantial current account deficits and low unemployment from the 1990s and mid-2000s. During this period, the United States experienced remarkable capital stock growth rates. The increase of capital stock, much of it in high-technology sectors, outpaced the increase in the U.S. labor force growth rate. As a result, U.S. labor productivity rates rose, and increases in overall economic activity created new job opportunities.

Considering the current account and capital account together shows that we should not necessarily view current account deficits as "bad" for an economy. A nation with a current account deficit also experiences capital inflows that are likely financing job-creating investment activity.

 Fundamental ISSUES

#5 What is the relationship between a nation's current account balance and its capital flows?

Basic balance-of-payments identities show that a nation's current account balance must equal its net capital flows from abroad. A nation that is experiencing net capital inflows from abroad—including changes in official reserves and other government assets—is necessarily running a current account deficit. A nation that is experiencing net capital outflows abroad is necessarily running a current account surplus.

Chapter SUMMARY

1. **The Global Market for Goods and Services:** During the past thirty years, reductions in trade barriers, reduced transportation costs, and advances in electronic communication and commerce have spurred dramatic increases in the volume of world trade in goods and services. Since the 1980s, global trade in goods and services has grown, on average, by nearly 6 percent annually. International trade in goods and services, therefore, represents a greater share of real-sector activity for both developed and emerging nations.

2. **The International Monetary and Financial Markets:** During the past thirty years, growth of the international monetary and financial markets has eclipsed growth of global markets for goods and services. Foreign exchange market turnover has grown to sixty times the volume of world trade. In the developed economies, international transactions in bonds and equities have grown by more than 1,700 percent during the past twenty years.

3. **What the Balance-of-Payments System Measures:** The balance of payments is a system of accounts used to record the international transactions of a nation. This system measures trade in goods, services, income, unilateral transfers, private transactions of financial assets, and official reserves. The current account comprises the goods, services, income, and unilateral transfers categories.

4. **Net Debtor and Net Creditor Nations:** A net debtor nation is one whose total claims abroad are less than the total foreign claims on the nation. A net creditor nation is one whose stock of foreign financial assets is greater than the stock of foreign-held domestic financial assets. Being a net debtor is not necessarily "good" or "bad" for an economy. Foreign investment that adds to a nation's capital stock may improve its prospects for prosperity.

5. **The Relationship between a Nation's Current Account Balance and Its Capital Flows:** A nation's current account balance and its capital flows both equal the gap between total domestic saving and domestic investment. Hence, capital flows—including changes in official reserves and other government assets—necessarily equal the current account balance. Hence, a nation that is an importer of capital from abroad is running a current account deficit, whereas a nation that is an exporter of capital abroad is running a current account surplus.

QUESTIONS and PROBLEMS

1. Show the debit and credit entries in each balance-of-payments account—goods, services, income, unilateral transfers—and the current account for the following transactions.
   a. A local college student travels abroad for the holidays and spends $1,000 on food and lodging.
   b. A local auto dealership imports a $20,000 automobile.
   c. The home government gives a drought-stricken nation $1 million as a humanitarian gesture.
   d. You receive a $100 interest payment on a foreign government bond you own.

2. Based on your answers to Question 1, what is the home nation's:
   a. Balance on goods and services?
   b. Current account balance?
   c. Capital account balance?

3. Using the following data (billions of dollars) for a given year, calculate the balance on merchandise trade; balance on goods, services, and income; and the current account balance. Indicate whether these balances are deficits or surpluses.

Exports of goods	719	Imports of goods	1,145
Exports of services	279	Imports of services	210
Net unilateral transfers	−49	Income receipts	284
Income payments	269	Statistical discrepancy	11

4. Using the data in Question 3, calculate the capital account balance. Is the capital account balance a surplus or deficit?

5. What is a balance-of-payments equilibrium? Considering your answers to Questions 3 and 4, is this country experiencing a balance-of-payments deficit or surplus?

6. Using the data in Table 1–5, is there a balance-of-payments surplus or deficit for the United States in 2010?

7. Write out a positive and negative aspect of a nation being a net debtor. Do the same thing for a nation that is a net creditor.

8. Explain why a nation might desire to receive both portfolio investment and direct investment from abroad.

9. Write out a single equation showing the relationship between the current account and net capital inflows, including changes in official reserves and other government assets, as they relate to investment spending and domestic saving.

10. Suppose a nation spends 10 percent of its income on investment and the private sector saves 5 percent. Further, suppose the national government runs a deficit of 1 percent. Using the equation you derived for Question 9 and these data, explain what these conditions mean for the nation's capital account and current account. How might the imbalance be corrected?

11. World Films Inc. has total assets of $1,233 million, foreign assets of $533 million, total sales of $615 million, foreign sales of $227 million, 1,256 total employees, and 322 foreign employees. Music Publishers Worldwide, in contrast, has total assets of $2,456 million, foreign assets of $455 million, total sales of $809 million, foreign sales of $246 million, 2,467 total employees, and 900 foreign employees. Using these values, calculate a transnationality index for each company. Which is the more "global" firm?

12. View each individual component (percent of sales, employees, and foreign assets) of the transnationality index you calculated in Question 11 and compare these across the two companies. How might the global strategies of these two firms differ in terms of exporting abroad or establishing a presence abroad?

13. Consider the data in Table 1–4. Explain why multinational firms of smaller advanced economies tend to be more "global" than multinational firms of the largest developed economies.

14. Consider the data in Tables 1–3 and 1–4 on global assets and the transnationality index. Which set of data is most consistent with the data on the most globalized nations in Table 1–2? Which do you feel is the best measure of a "globalized" firm?

Online APPLICATIONS

This chapter described the remarkable growth in the market for foreign exchange instruments. The following application examines recent survey data on the foreign exchange market.

Internet URL: *http://www.bis.org*

Title: Survey of Foreign Exchange Market Activity

Navigation: Begin at the home page of the Bank for International Settlements (*http://www.bis.org*). On the menu at the top of the page, select *Statistics*. Next select *Foreign Exchange*. Choose the most recent *Triennial Central Bank Survey of Foreign Exchange and Derivatives Market Activity*.

Application: Read the press release and answer the following questions.

1. What was the average daily turnover in the traditional foreign exchange (fx) markets in the most recent survey? Does this represent an increase or decrease in turnover since the previous survey, and what was the increase or decrease?

2. Based on the most recent survey, what was the average daily turnover in the spot market by itself? What percentage of the overall market does this represent?

3. What was the most traded currency pair?

4. What were the market shares of the euro, yen, and the dollar?

SELECTED REFERENCES and FURTHER READINGS

Bhagwati, Jagdish. *In Defense of Globalization*. New York: Oxford University Press, 2004.

Bordo, Michael D., Barry Eichengreen, and Douglas A. Irwin. "Is Globalization Really Different Than Globalization a Hundred Years Ago?" National Bureau of Economic Research, Working Paper No. 7195 (June 1999).

Cavallo, Michele. "Oil Prices and the U.S. Trade Deficit." Federal Reserve Bank of San Francisco, Economic Letter, No. 2006-24 (September 22, 2006).

Frankel, Jeffrey. "Globalization of the Economy," NBER Working Paper Series, No. 7858 (August 2000).

Garner, C. Alan. "Should the Decline in the Personal Saving Rate Be a Cause for Concern?" Federal Reserve Bank of Kansas City, *Economic Review* (Second Quarter 2006): 5–28.

Held, David, Anthony McGrew, David Goldblatt, and Jonathan Perraton. *Global Transformations*. Stanford: Stanford University Press, 1999.

Hellerstein, Rebecca, and Cédric Tille. "The Changing Nature of the U.S. Balance of Payments." Federal Reserve Bank of New York, *Current Issues in Economics and Finance 14*(4) (June 2008).

Higgins, Matthew, and Thomas Klitgaard. "Financial Globalization and the U.S. Current Account Deficit." Federal Reserve Bank of New York, *Current Issues in Economics and Finance 13*(11), December 2007.

Higgins, Matthew, and Thomas Klitgaard. "Viewing the Current Account Deficit as a Capital Inflow." Federal Reserve Bank of New York, *Current Issues in Economics and Finance* (December 1998).

Keidel, Albert. "China's Economic Rise-Fact and Fiction." Policy Brief, 61, Carnegie Endowment for International Peace, (July 2008).

Micklethwait, John, and Adrian Wooldridge. "Globalization Can Be Popular Again." *Wall Street Journal* (April 17, 2000): A34.

Obstfeld, Maurice. "The Global Capital Market: Benefactor or Menace?" *Journal of Economic Perspectives 12*(4) (1998): 9–30.

Pakko, Michael R. "Capital Deepening." Federal Reserve Bank of St. Louis, *National Economic Trends* (May 2000): 1.

Rodrick, Dani. "How Far Will International Economic Integration Go?" *Journal of Economic Perspectives 14*(1) (Winter 2000): 177–186.

Rugman, Alan, M. "From Globalization to Regionalism: The Foreign Direct Investment Dimension of International Finance." In Karl Kraiser, John J. Kirton, and Joseph P. Daniels, eds., *Shaping a New International Financial System: Challenges of Governance in a Globalizing World*. Aldershot, UK: Ashgate Publishing, 2000.

Rugman, Alan M. "Regional Multinationals and Regional Trade Policy: The End of Multilateralism." In Michele Fratianni, Paolo Savona, and John J. Kirton, eds., *Corporate, Public and Global Governance: The G8 Contribution*. Burlington VT: Ashgate Publishing, 2007: 77–86.

Steger, Manfred B. ed. *Rethinking Globalism*. New York: Rowman and Littlefield Publishers Inc., 2004.

United Nations Conference on Trade and Development. *World Investment Report*, 2000. New York: United Nations, 2000.

Valderrama, Diego. "The U.S. Productivity Acceleration and the Current Account Deficit." Federal Reserve Bank of San Francisco, Economic Letter, No. 2007-08 (March 30, 2007).

2

The Market for Foreign Exchange

Fundamental ISSUES

1. What is the foreign exchange market?
2. What does it mean when a currency has appreciated or depreciated?
3. How is the general value of a currency measured?
4. What is foreign exchange arbitrage?
5. What determines the value of a currency?
6. What is purchasing power parity, and is it useful as a guide to movements in exchange rates?

It is 2009. The coordinator of the Palm Springs, California, Coachella Valley Music & Arts Festival is feeling decidedly downbeat about his attempts to line up band performances. Today, a band based in the United Kingdom that he had lined up months ago has dropped out of the festival because it did not like the prevailing rate of exchange of dollars for pounds. In years past, he laments, "when you offered a band $100,000, it used to be that was €75,000, and now it's like €45,000." He marks a line through the band's name on his preliminary schedule, which also contains the marked-out names of three other European bands that have withdrawn in response to the dollar's value in foreign exchange markets. Only one band from Europe, the festival coordinator notes, has not canceled its performance. If the band does drop out, this could be the first time in many years that the festival will fail to offer a performance by a European band. The coordinator wonders if perhaps the dollar's exchange value will recover somewhat in the coming months, so that performing in the festival may be more attractive to European bands next year.

Now fast forward to 2012. Over the preceding six months, the euro has lost more than 3 percent of its value in relation to the dollar. Now the director of the Coachella Valley Music & Arts Festival has a new problem: There are so many good European bands interested in performing at the festival that he realizes that he will have to turn several away. He worries about alienating a few of the bands that he will have to refuse to book. At least this year, he thinks, some of the best bands will be pleased to earn more euros with the dollars that he will be offering.

In this chapter you begin your study of the foreign exchange market. You will learn about foreign exchange and various types of exchange rates. You will explore the forces that determine the value of a currency and investigate how arbitrage generates profits. You will also consider one of the most popular theories of exchange-rate determination.

EXCHANGE RATES AND THE MARKET FOR FOREIGN EXCHANGE

Often, economists speak of foreign trade and capital flows as if the goods, services, and assets are like water flowing from one country to another. Pushing this analogy a little further, we might say that the *foreign exchange market* is the international plumbing. The foreign exchange market is a system of private banks, foreign exchange dealers and brokers, and central banks through which households, firms, and governments buy and sell *foreign exchange,* or another nation's currency. By providing an arrangement for valuing transactions and delivering payments, the foreign exchange system promotes the flows of goods, services, and assets from one nation to another. *Exchange rates,* which are the market prices of foreign exchange, are a critical element of this system.

As an example of the role of exchange rates, suppose you decide to purchase a new audio system. After shopping the local appliance store, you select a receiver and speakers made by a Japanese company that have a dollar price of $300. Your decision to purchase this particular audio system partially depends on the price. Conveniently, the price is denominated in your own currency, the currency you have in your wallet or handbag and in your bank account. Your payment to the appliance store for the Japanese audio system is therefore a simple, straightforward transaction. After receiving your $300 payment, the appliance store can purchase new audio systems from the Japanese company.

The Japanese residents who own the Japanese electronics company, however, must pay the company's workers and suppliers in Japanese yen. They do not want to receive dollars in Japan. Therefore, they deposit the payment with their bank and have the proceeds converted into yen. They can now make their payments from a yen-denominated bank account. How many yen is each dollar worth? In other words, what is the value of the dollar relative to the yen? This is what an exchange rate tells us. An exchange rate expresses the value of one currency relative to another, and therefore converts the value of this transaction into the local currency terms of each party involved.

The Role of the Foreign Exchange Market

What function does the foreign exchange market perform in the previous example? The notion of a foreign exchange market may invoke the image of frantic traders in shirt sleeves and visors hustling money on a cluttered trading floor, with their actions determining the quotations for currencies we see in daily newspapers such as the *Wall Street Journal* and the *Financial Times.* In our example, however, a foreign exchange market was not prominent. The Japanese company used the services of its bank, not the foreign exchange market. Further, the currencies involved, the dollar and the yen, never crossed international borders. Only the audio system did.

Indeed, the actual flow of currencies from one nation to another is an insignificant element of the foreign exchange market. Such flows usually arise only as a result of such activities as tourism or illegal transactions. The financial assets that people typically trade in foreign exchange markets are foreign-currency-denominated financial instruments, such as bonds, stocks, and especially bank deposits.

There are many different foreign exchange instruments and markets. The market in our example is the spot market for foreign exchange. A ***spot market*** is a market for immediate purchase and delivery of an asset, usually within two or three days. The media publish spot rates pertaining to the trading of foreign-currency-denominated deposits among major banks for $1 million or more.

Spot exchange rates are the market prices of foreign exchange in the spot market. Table 2–1 displays spot exchange rates that can be found on the Web sites of daily papers of major business news publishers such as the *Wall Street Journal* or the *Financial Times*. The spot exchange rates in Table 2–1 are for foreign exchange transactions undertaken in the London market and represent the rate that a currency

spot market

A market for contracts requiring the immediate sale or purchase of an asset.

Table 2–1   Foreign Exchange Spot Market Trading

Values below are derived from data for the London closing rates and pertain to transactions among banks in the amount of $1 million or more.

	Currency	U.S. Dollar Per Currency[1]	Previous Close	Currency Per U.S. Dollar	Previous Close	J.P. Morgan Index[2]
Argentina	Peso	0.2275	0.2277	4.3963	4.3915	
Australia	Australian Dollar	1.0382	1.0398	0.9632	0.9617	112.8
Canada	Canadian Dollar	1.0113	1.0126	0.9888	0.9876	141.9
China	Yuan	0.1586	0.1587	6.3040	6.3006	
Czech Republic	Koruna	0.0528	0.0531	18.9229	18.8475	
India	Indian Rupee	0.0193	0.0193	51.8600	51.8600	
Japan	Yen	0.0123	0.0124	81.3100	80.7700	113.5
Malaysia	Ringgit	0.2708	0.2690	3.6925	3.7175	
Mexico	Mexican Peso	0.0762	0.0757	13.1230	13.2153	66.5
New Zealand	NZ Dollar	0.8187	0.8216	1.2214	1.2172	138.2
Phillipines	Peso	0.0234	0.0235	42.6550	42.6050	
Russia	Rouble	0.0339	0.0339	29.4850	29.4943	
Switzerland	Franc	1.0916	1.0935	0.9161	0.9145	141.6
United Kingdom	Pound	1.3842	1.3758	0.7224	0.7268	74.6
Euro	Euro	1.2752	1.2636	0.7842	0.7914	133.3
SDR	SDR	1.5019	1.4973	0.6658	0.6679	
United States	U.S. Dollar					95.1

[1] Closing Midpoint Value
[2] J.P Morgan nominal effective exchange rate index based on a basket of sixteen currencies (2000=100).
Source: *Financial Times*, www.ft.com

sold for at the time the markets closed. Notice in the text at the top of Table 2–1 that the rates "apply to trading among banks in amounts of $1 million and more." This means that the spot exchange rates quoted here pertain to very large transactions. Smaller spot transactions, or "retail" transactions, such as those of individuals and small- to medium-sized businesses, would receive less favorable selling and buying rates. Table 2–1 displays two versions of the spot exchange rate, *U.S. dollar per currency* and *currency per U.S. dollar*. In the next section we shall explain these two versions of the spot exchange rate. We will refer to Table 2–1 often for the examples that appear in this chapter. (To learn about how individuals are getting involved in foreign exchange market trading traditionally dominated by large companies, see *Online Notebook: On the Internet, Currency Trading Spreads to the "Little Guy."*)

ONLINE Notebook

On the Internet, Currency Trading Spreads to the "Little Guy"

When most people think about foreign exchange trading in foreign exchange markets, they envision orders to buy or sell foreign currencies placed by banks, large corporations, and governments. Now online-trading firms, such as FX Solutions and Interbank FX, offer individuals an array of Web-based currency-trading accounts. One of the largest online companies, Gain Capital, claims to have individual clients residing in 140 countries and trading a total of more than $3 billion worth of foreign currencies every day.

To help individuals learn how to trade currencies, most online-trading firms provide free accounts for people to engage in mock trades to gain practice before they put real dollars (and other currencies) at risk. Several, such as FX Solutions, offer online training courses. At Interbank FX, an individual can even open a "Mini Account" for use in making practice trades as small as 50 cents. There is good reason for people to engage in considerable practice before launching into online currency trading. In contrast to online stock brokers, who require individual traders to put up $1 for every $2 of stock trading, online currency firms often permit traders to put up only $1 for every *$400* of currency trading. Thus, it is all too easy for an individual to experience thousands of dollars worth of losses in a short span of time. Of course, rapid gains of the thousands of dollars are also possible, which is what attracts many people to online currency trading.

For Critical Analysis

In principle, how can an individual trader hope to profit from buying yen in advance of an anticipated fall in the value of the U.S. dollar in relation to the Japanese yen?

On the WEB

To open a practice foreign exchange trading account and learn more about the spot market for foreign exchange, go to the Web site of Oanda.com at *http://www.oanda.com*.

#1 What is the foreign exchange market?

The foreign exchange "market" is the system through which people exchange one nation's currency for the currency of another nation. A large portion of the transactions in this market consists of exchanges of foreign-currency-denominated deposits of $1 million or more among large commercial banks. The actual movement of a currency from one country to another is a relatively insignificant feature of activity in the foreign exchange market.

Exchange Rates as Relative Prices

As we indicated in the previous section, the role of the exchange rate is to measure the value of one currency relative to another. An exchange rate, therefore, is a *relative price* that indicates the price of one currency in terms of another currency. Because an exchange rate relates two currencies, economists commonly call an exchange rate a *bilateral exchange rate,* because *bilateral* means "two sides." In Table 2–1 on page 30, there are two columns for the current day's spot exchange rates. The first is the *U.S. dollar per currency,* or how many U.S. dollars it takes to purchase one unit of a foreign currency. For example, in Table 2–1, the exchange rate for the U.S. dollar relative to the euro (€) is 1.2752 $/€, meaning that one must give 1.2752 U.S. dollars in exchange for 1.0 euro.

The exchange rate also expresses how many foreign currency units it takes to purchase one dollar, or *currency per U.S. dollar.* This is simply the reciprocal of the U.S. dollar-per-currency rate. Hence, the rate of exchange of the euro for the U.S. dollar is 1/(1.2752 $/€), or 0.7842 €/$. This means that one must give 0.7842 euros in exchange for 1.0 U.S. dollar. Because there are two different ways to express an exchange rate, it is very important that you determine whether an exchange rate is a U.S.-dollar-per-currency rate or a currency-per-U.S.-dollar rate.

Currency Appreciation and Depreciation Looking at the U.S.-dollar-per-currency rate for the British pound in Table 2–1 on page 30, we see that the rate changed from 1.3758 $/£ to 1.3842 $/£ since the previous day's close. This means that the dollar *depreciated* against the pound because the number of dollars required to purchase one pound increased. In other words, the dollar price of the pound rose. At the same time, the pound *appreciated* relative to the dollar. The currency-per-U.S.-dollar rate changed from 0.7268 £/$ to 0.7224 £/$, indicating that the number of pounds required to purchase one dollar decreased, or the pound price of the dollar fell.

We can determine the rate of appreciation or depreciation by calculating the percentage change in the exchange rate. We calculate the percentage change of an exchange rate by subtracting the old value of the exchange rate from the new value, dividing this difference by the old value, and multiplying by 100. Using the U.S.-dollar-per-currency rates from Table 2–1, the percentage change is

$$[(1.3842 - 1.3758/1.3758)] \times 100 \cong 0.61\%.$$

In words, the pound appreciated relative to the dollar by 0.61 percent.

Fundamental ISSUES

#2 What does it mean when a currency has appreciated or depreciated?

When an exchange rate changes, one currency either gains or loses value relative to another currency. When a currency appreciates, it gains value relative to another currency. When a currency depreciates, it loses value relative to another currency. The percentage change in the exchange rate measures the amount of the currency's appreciation or depreciation.

Cross Rates Table 2–1 on page 30 indicates that, for this particular day, the U.S.-dollar-per-currency and currency-per-U.S.-dollar exchange rates for the euro were equal to 1.2752 \$/€ and 0.7842 €/\$, respectively. Suppose, however, that our interest is in the exchange rate between the British pound and the euro, not the dollar and the euro. To determine this rate, we can compute a ***cross rate,*** which is a third exchange rate that we calculate from two bilateral exchange rates.

In Table 2–1, the U.S.-dollar-per-currency rate for the British pound is 1.3842 \$/£, and the U.S.-dollar-per-currency rate for the euro is 1.2752 \$/€. From these two bilateral rates, it is straightforward to calculate either the British-pound-per-euro rate or the euro-per-British-pound rate.

To calculate the British-pound-per-euro cross rate, we divide the dollar rate for the euro by the dollar rate for the British pound. Thus, we can calculate the pound–euro cross rate in the following manner:

$$\frac{1.2752 \text{ \$/€}}{1.3842 \text{ \$/£}}.$$

Division by a fraction is the same as multiplying by the reciprocal of the fraction. Therefore, we can express the problem as

$$\frac{1.2752}{1.3842} \times \frac{\$}{€} \times \frac{£}{\$}.$$

Notice that in this calculation, the dollar cancels out because it appears in the numerator of one fraction and the denominator of another. This yields the British-pound-per-currency rate for the euro, which equals 0.9213 £/€.

If we wish to determine the euro-per-British-pound rate, we invert the British-pound-equivalent rate, which yields

$$\frac{1}{0.9213 \text{ £/€}} = 1.0855 \text{ €/£}.$$

By using the U.S.-dollar-per-currency rate for the British pound and the euro, we have calculated a cross rate of exchange between the British pound and the euro.

The foreign exchange sections of major newspapers provide cross rates for many high-volume currencies in a cross-rate table. Table 2–2 is an example of a cross-rate table. The table lists the currencies across the top row and the left-hand column. The rates in Table 2–2 are the exchange rates between the currencies of the countries listed on the corresponding row and column. When the same country appears on both the row and the column, the entry is either blank or 1. The first column provides the U.S.-dollar-per-currency rate for each currency listed on the corresponding row. Therefore, the second row provides the foreign-currency-per-U.S.-dollar exchange rates.

cross rate
A bilateral exchange rate calculated from two other bilateral exchange rates.

Table 2–2

Cross-Rate Table
Based on Rates in Table 2–1

	United States	Canada	Euro	United Kingdom
United States	—	0.9888	0.7842	0.7224
Canada	1.0113	—	0.7931	0.7306
Euro	1.2752	1.2610	—	0.9213
United Kingdom	1.3842	1.3687	1.0855	—

Bid–Ask Spreads and Trading Margins

If you live in a large metropolitan area, your bank is likely to have a foreign exchange service. Try calling your bank for a quote on a currency. The person you speak with likely will either quote two rates or will ask whether you are buying or selling. The rate at which the bank is willing to buy the currency from you is the *bid price*. The rate at which the bank is willing to sell the currency to you is the *ask price*, or *offer*.

The Bid–Ask Spread As an example, suppose you are going to London, England, to study economics for a semester. Prior to your trip, you want to exchange dollars for British pounds. From Table 2–1 on page 30, we see that the U.S.-dollar-per-British-pound rate is 1.3842 $/£. Suppose that when you call your local bank and ask for a quote on the British pound, the reply is "840 and 844." Because bankers want to economize on everything, including words, the banker is quoting only the last three decimal points of the spot rate. What was meant, then, is 1.3840 $/£ and 1.3844 $/£. The lower rate, the *bid price* or *buying price,* is the number of U.S. dollars the bank is willing to give you in exchange for one British pound. The higher rate, the *ask price* or *selling price,* is the number of U.S. dollars you would have to give the bank in exchange for one British pound. The spot exchange rates found in tables such as Table 2–1 are the midpoint values between the bid and the ask rates. The difference between the bid price and the ask price is the **bid–ask spread** or bid–offer spread.

The Bid–Ask Margin Typically, banks do not charge fees for foreign exchange transactions. The **bid–ask margin,** or *trading margin*, expresses the bid–ask spread as a percentage, and represents the cost and risk associated with the foreign exchange transaction. We calculate the bid–ask margin as the difference between the ask price and the bid price, divided by the ask price, and multiplied by 100:

$$\text{bid–ask margin} = \frac{\text{ask price } - \text{ bid price}}{\text{ask price}} \times 100.$$

In this example, the bid–ask margin is

$$\frac{1.3844 - 1.3840}{1.3844} \times 100 = 0.0289\%.$$

This bid–ask margin is very small at 0.0289 percent. Currencies with a high trading volume and low exchange variability typically have lower bid–ask margins, indicating the relatively low cost and risk associated with a foreign exchange.

bid–ask spread

The difference between the bid price, or price offered for the purchase of a currency, and the ask price, or price at which the currency is offered for sale.

bid–ask margin

The difference between the ask price, or price at which a currency is offered for sale, and the bid price, or price offered for the purchase of the currency, expressed as a percent of the ask price.

Obtain spot rates and bid price–ask price spreads from the Financial Times at
http://www.ft.com.

Real Exchange Rates

So far, we have discussed ***nominal exchange rates.*** These are exchange rates that
do not reflect changes in price levels in the two nations. The nominal exchange
rate tells us the purchasing power of our own currency in exchange for a foreign
currency. What if we are interested in the amount of foreign *goods and services*
that our currency will buy, however? In other words, what if we really care about
the *purchasing power* of our currency in terms of foreign goods and services? The
real exchange rate adjusts the nominal exchange rate for changes in nations' price
levels and thereby measures the purchasing power of domestic goods and services
in exchange for foreign goods and services. Hence, if we want to know how much
of another country's goods and services that a unit of our own nation's goods and
services can buy, we need to know the value of the real exchange rate.

nominal exchange rate
A bilateral exchange rate that
is unadjusted for changes in
the two nations' price levels.

real exchange rate
A bilateral exchange rate that
has been adjusted for price
changes that occurred in the
two nations.

As an example, consider the case of Mexico from early 2009 through early
2012. This period provides an excellent example because of the relatively large
change in the value of the Mexican peso during that time.

The spot rate for the Mexican peso (Mp) per U.S. dollar was 15.29 Mp/$ in
March 2009 and 13.12 Mp/$ in March 2012. The U.S. dollar, therefore, depreciated
relative to the Mexican peso by 14.2 percent:

$$(13.12 - 15.29)/15.29 \times 100 = 14.2\%.$$

We could also say that the Mexican peso appreciated relative to the U.S. dollar, as
15.29 Mexican pesos were required to purchase one U.S. dollar in March 2009, whereas
the purchase of one U.S. dollar required only 13.12 Mexican pesos in March 2012.

The Effect of Price Changes

Now consider the effect that price changes had on the purchasing power available
to a "typical" U.S. consumer of Mexican goods and services. To determine this
effect, we need to use a price index. Let's use the consumer price index (CPI), because this measurement calculates the change in the prices of a basket of goods and
services consumed by a hypothetical typical consumer.

The CPI for the United States was equal to 108.9 in March 2009 and was equal
to 117.5 in March 2012. In Mexico, the CPI was equal to 118.5 in March 2009 and
was equal to 139.2 in March 2012. Economists often use the percentage change
in the CPI over a given interval as a measure of consumer price inflation during
the period. Therefore, for the United States, inflation from March 2009 through
March 2012 was 7.9 percent. That means that the domestic purchasing power of
each U.S. dollar decreased over this period as the domestic price level rose. For
Mexico, inflation over this period was 17.5 percent. Thus, during the same period
each Mexican peso lost more domestic purchasing power. One can see that the
U.S. dollar depreciated relative to the Mexican peso and, at the same time, each
Mexican peso could buy fewer Mexican goods and services.

For U.S. consumers, that means that the price inflation in Mexico added to the
currency loss brought about by the depreciation of the U.S. dollar relative to the
Mexican peso. To see why this is so, we calculate the real exchange rate by dividing

the nominal Mexican-peso-per-U.S.-dollar exchange rate by the ratio of Mexican prices to U.S. prices. This adjusts the nominal value of the Mexican peso relative to the U.S. dollar by price changes in Mexico relative to price changes in the United States.

Let S_t denote the nominal Mexican-peso-per-U.S.-dollar exchange rate, Mp/\$, at time period t. We shall also let P_t^{US} denote the U.S. CPI at time period t and P_t^M denote the Mexican CPI at time period t. Using this notation, the real Mexican-peso-per-U.S.-dollar exchange rate at time period t, denoted as s_t, is

$$s_t = S_t/(P_t^M/P_t^{US}).$$

Once again, we have a ratio in the denominator of an expression. We can therefore rewrite the expression by multiplying the reciprocal of the ratio in the denominator. The expression then becomes

$$s_t = S_t \times (P_t^{US}/P_t^M).$$

From this expression, we see that the Mexican-peso-per-U.S.-dollar real exchange rate is the Mexican-peso-per-U.S.-dollar nominal exchange rate multiplied by the ratio of U.S. prices to Mexican prices. Using this expression, the Mexican-peso-per-U.S.-dollar real exchange rate for March 2009, s_{2009} is

$$s_{2009} = 15.29 \times (108.9/118.5) = 14.05.$$

Similarly, the Mexican-peso-per-U.S.-dollar real exchange rate for March 2012, s_{2012}, is

$$s_{2012} = 13.12 \times (117.5/139.2) = 11.08.$$

Thus, between March 2009 and March 2012, the real exchange rate decreased in value. This indicates that there was a real depreciation of the U.S. dollar relative to the Mexican peso. The real depreciation, however, was larger than the nominal depreciation. The percentage change in the real exchange rate was 21 percent, whereas the percentage change in the nominal exchange rate was 14 percent. Because the Mexican CPI rose at a rate of 9 percentage points more than that of the U.S. CPI, the inflation differential added to the nominal depreciation.

MEASURING THE OVERALL STRENGTH OR WEAKNESS OF A CURRENCY: EFFECTIVE EXCHANGE RATES

As explained earlier in this chapter, the exchange rates we have discussed so far are bilateral exchange rates, which measure the value of one currency relative to *one* other currency. On any given day, a currency will strengthen, or appreciate, against some currencies and weaken, or depreciate, against others. On a given day, the dollar's value may have fallen against the British pound, Japanese yen, and Canadian dollar. Its value may have risen, however, in relation to the euro, Swiss franc, and Mexican peso. So, some bilateral rates would have fallen and some would have risen. But overall, or in general, is the dollar "stronger" or "weaker"? To answer this question, economists use an *effective exchange rate,* which is a measure of the weighted-average value of a currency relative to two or more other currencies.

effective exchange rate
A measure of the weighted-average value of a currency relative to a selected group of currencies.

Constructing an Effective Exchange Rate
To construct an effective exchange rate, economists must make a number of choices. The first is the basket of currencies in which to measure the effective

exchange rate. It is not practical to measure the value of a currency against every other currency in the world. Thus, economists include only the currencies that they judge to be most important. What constitutes "important" currencies depends on the particular application. If a businessperson wanted to know how changes in the value of the dollar affect U.S. imports and exports, then the individual would want to include the bilateral exchange rates of the largest trading partners of the United States. If a portfolio manager wanted to know how changes in the value of the dollar would affect the return on a portfolio of international assets, then that individual would want to include the bilateral exchange rates of the currencies that represent the largest shares of the portfolio. The currencies that one eventually selects compose what economists call the currency basket.

Next one must select a *base year*. A base year serves as a reference point in time. The base year value is equal to 100. Economists then measure changes from this base year. For example, if 2010 were the base year, then the value of the effective exchange rate for 2010 would be 100. If the effective exchange rate were 125 for 2012, then we know there was a 25 percent increase in the effective exchange rate.

Finally, because an effective exchange rate is a weighted average of bilateral exchange rates, economists must select *weights*. The weights are a means of placing greater emphasis on the more important currencies in the currency basket and less emphasis on the least important currencies in the currency basket. Typically, economists construct weights on either a bilateral or multilateral basis. Bilateral weights reflect the trade flow of an individual country with the United States relative to the total trade of the United States with all of the countries included in the index. Multilateral weights reflect the trade flow of the *individual* country with all countries included in the index relative to the *total* trade volume among all of the countries included in the index. If we consider the value of a single currency (say, the U.S. dollar), a bilateral weighting scheme typically is fine. If we want to compare the performance of the U.S. dollar with the currencies of other countries over the same period, we should use a multilateral weighting scheme.

A Two-Country Example of an Effective Exchange Rate

To illustrate these points, let's use 2008 as the base year and construct a simple effective exchange rate for the United States between 2008 and 2010. For illustrative purposes, we shall use only two of the main trading partners of the United States, Canada and Mexico.

Constructing Bilateral Weights Because we will consider an effective exchange rate for only one country, we shall use bilateral weights. Let X represent exports and M represent imports. Further, let W^b denote the bilateral weight. We calculate the weight placed on the Canadian dollar as the exports of the United States to Canada, X_{Cn}, plus the imports of the United States from Canada, M_{Cn}. This sum of X_{Cn} and M_{Cn} is the total trade of United States with Canada. Likewise, the sum of X_{Mx} and M_{Mx} is the total trade of the United States with Mexico.

To calculate the weight assigned to the Canadian dollar, we divide the total trade of the United States with Canada, $X_{Cn} + M_{Cn}$, by the total trade of the United States with Canada and Mexico, $(X_{Cn} + M_{Cn}) + (X_{Mx} + M_{Mx})$. We can write the formula for the weight of the Canadian dollar as

$$W^b_{Cn} = (X_{Cn} + M_{Cn})/[(X_{Cn} + M_{Cn}) + (X_{Mx} + M_{Mx})].$$

This weight represents the trade of the United States with Canada as a fraction of the total trade of the United States with Mexico and Canada.

During the base year, 2010, U.S. exports to Canada were $248.8 billion and U.S. imports from Canada were $276.5 billion. U.S. exports to Mexico were $163.3 billion, and U.S. imports from Mexico were $229.7 billion. We calculate W_{Cn}^b as

$$W_{Cn}^b = (\$248.8 + \$276.5)/[(\$248.8 + \$276.5) + (\$163.3 + \$229.7)] = 0.57.$$

This weight indicates that of the total trade of the United States with Canada and Mexico, 57 percent was with Canada. Likewise, the weight to be placed on the Mexican peso, W_{Mx}^b, is equal to

$$W_{Mx}^b = (\$163.3 + \$229.7)/[(248.8 + \$276.5) + (\$163.3 + \$229.7)] = 0.43.$$

This weight indicates that of the total trade of the United States with Canada and Mexico, 43 percent was with Mexico. Note that the weights W_{Cn}^b and W_{Mx}^b sum to one. The fact that the weights sum to one is always true regardless of the number of currencies in the basket.

Determining Relative Exchange Rates The next step in constructing the effective exchange rate is to calculate each of the bilateral exchange rates relative to the base-year exchange value. For the example here, the Canadian-dollar-per-U.S.-dollar exchange rate for 2010 was 1.001 C$/$ and for 2012, 0.989 C$/$. Furthermore, the Mexican-peso-per-U.S.-dollar exchange rate for 2010 was 12.195 Mp/$, and for 2012, 13.123 Mp/$. Because 2010 is our base year in this example, we divide the Canadian dollar exchange rate by the 2010 Canadian dollar exchange rate, yielding 1 for 2010 and 0.988 for 2012.

The intuition of this step is as follows. Dividing the current rate by the base-year value yields the value of the currency relative to its value during the base year. Therefore, the fact that the value is equal to 1 in 2010 means that the 2010 value is 100 percent of the 2010 value. The fact that the value is 0.988 in 2012 means that the 2012 exchange value is 98.8 percent of the 2010 exchange value. Completing the same calculations for the Mexican peso yields values of 1 for 2010 and 1.076 for 2012, meaning that the 2010 value is 100 percent of the 2010 value and that the 2012 value is 107.6 percent of the 2010 value. We then multiply these relative exchange values by the appropriate weight. Then we sum the weighted relative exchange values for a given year and multiply by 100. This process yields the effective exchange rate for that year:

$$EER_{2010} = [(0.57)(1) + (0.43)(1)] \times 100 = 100.$$

This effective exchange rate measures the weighted average exchange value of the U.S. dollar against to the Canadian dollar and the Mexican peso relative to the base-year weighted average exchange value of the U.S. dollar against the Canadian dollar and the Mexican peso. In our example, 2010 is the base year, so the value of the effective exchange rate for 2010 is 100. The effective exchange rate for 2012 is

$$EER_{2012} = [(0.57)(0.988) + (0.43)(1.076)] \times 100 = 102.58.$$

This value indicates that the weighted average value of the U.S. dollar against the Canadian dollar and the Mexican peso for 2012 was 102.58 percent of the value for 2010.

What an Effective Exchange Rate Tells Us Now that we have calculated an effective exchange rate, what does it tell us? In the example here, note that the U.S. dollar depreciated relative to the Canadian dollar and appreciated relative to the Mexican peso from 2010 to 2012. So relative to both currencies, did the dollar appreciate or depreciate and by how much? In our example, the value of the effective exchange rate was 100 in 2010 (the base year), and 102.58 in 2012. Because the value of the effective exchange rate rose, the dollar *appreciated,* on average, relative to both currencies during this period. Using the percentage-change formula, the amount of appreciation was [(102.46 − 100)/100] × 100 = 2.58%.

A number of effective exchange rates are available in leading exchange rate sources. As shown in Table 2–1, there are nominal effective exchange rates for a number of currencies. The International Monetary Fund publishes multilateral-weighted nominal and real effective exchange rates in its monthly bulletin, *International Financial Statistics.* The Federal Reserve board publishes a nominal multilateral-weighted effective exchange rate for the U.S. dollar in the *Federal Reserve Bulletin.* The *Financial Times* reports the J.P. Morgan nominal index and the *Wall Street Journal* very recently created its own effective exchange rate index. Figure 2–1 displays the multilateral-weighted nominal effective exchange rates for the U.S. dollar, the euro, and the Japanese yen, since 1980.

Figure 2–1 shows that there was a dramatic increase in the average value of the dollar from 1980 through 1985 and a dramatic decline from 1985 through 1988. Following 1988, there was a steady, general decline in the average value of the dollar until 1995, when the dollar began to gain in value through 2002. In general, the U.S. dollar declined in value following 2002. Following its introduction, the euro declined in value through 2005. Since 2003, the euro has increased in weighted-average value. For the Japanese yen, the figure shows a general increase in value from 1980 through 2000. The yen began at 61 and ended at 154 in 2000, constituting a 152 percent appreciation over the period. From 2000 through 2008, the yen lost value on a weighted-average basis, but began rising in value again in 2009.

Real Effective Exchange Rates Earlier in this chapter, we explained that it is the real exchange rate that indicates changes in international purchasing power. Therefore, it may be desirable to construct a *real effective exchange rate,* which is an effective exchange rate based on real exchange rates as opposed to nominal

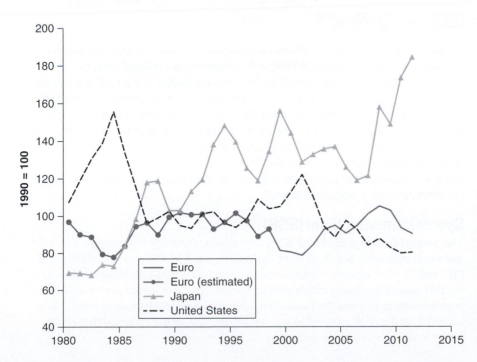

Figure 2–1

Effective Exchange Rates since 1980 from the Bank of England

Between 1985 and 1995, the average value of the U.S. dollar declined, and the average value of the Japanese yen increased. In general, the average value of the dollar declined since the early 2000s, whereas the average value of the yen initially declined but has risen since 2009 . After its introduction, the average value of the euro initially decreased, but the euro's value has risen since 2002.

exchange rates. A real effective exchange rate is calculated in much the same way as a nominal effective exchange rate. In contrast to calculating effective nominal exchange rates, however, we use real exchange rates in computing the real effective exchange rate. Thus, to construct a real exchange rate, we require, in addition to the information already given, CPI data for all countries in the index, as well as for the United States. Then, we would have to convert each nominal exchange rate to a real rate. We then would complete the remaining calculations as described earlier. Question 6 at the end of the chapter gives you the opportunity to construct a real effective exchange rate.

For effective exchange rates for a number of currencies, visit the Web site of the Bank of England at *http://www.bankofengland.co.uk.*

#3 How is the general value of a currency measured?

An effective exchange rate tracks the movement of a currency against a number of currencies. Because an effective exchange rate is a weighted average of a set of bilateral exchange rates, effective exchange rates are very useful as general guides to changes in a currency's value. A real effective exchange rate is based on real bilateral exchange rates, whereas a nominal effective exchange rate is based on nominal bilateral exchange rates.

COMPOSITE CURRENCIES

composite currency
A currency unit in which the value is expressed as a weighted average of a selected basket of currencies.

Sometimes it is useful to denominate transactions and value single currencies relative to composite currencies. A *composite currency,* or *artificial currency unit,* is a currency unit formed from a standardized currency basket composed of a weighted average of several currencies. The most common composite currency is the *Special Drawing Right (SDR),* established and maintained by the International Monetary Fund. Economists typically express the values of this currency relative to the dollar and/or pound. You can find the daily values of the SDR listed in the currency tables of the *Wall Street Journal, Financial Times,* or other leading financial media. Now that you understand the construction of effective exchange rates, understanding a composite currency is straightforward.

Special Drawing Right (SDR)
A composite currency of the International Monetary Fund in which the value is based on a weighted-average value of the currencies of five member nations.

Special Drawing Right (SDR)
The *Special Drawing Right (SDR)* is a composite currency first proposed in 1968 and eventually allocated in 1970 by the International Monetary Fund (IMF). The IMF and sponsoring industrialized nations developed the SDR. Policymakers at the IMF and in the sponsoring nations believed that there would not be sufficient gold reserves to provide the liquidity needed for international transactions. They intended for the SDR to serve as a *reserve currency,* or the currency that central banks would use to settle transactions.

The expected liquidity crises did not occur, so the SDR did not become the primary reserve currency. Nonetheless, the SDR does fulfill some limited functions. It is a means for some countries to finance short-term liquidity shortages, and for some nations it has served as a currency basket for pegging national currencies. (We shall discuss fixed- or pegged-exchange-rate systems and the use of a currency basket in this regard in Chapter 3.)

The IMF defines the SDR in a manner analogous to an effective exchange rate, basing it on a basket of selected currencies. The countries whose currencies constitute the basket are the four individual countries or monetary union of the International Monetary Fund that experienced the greatest exports of goods and services during a recent period of five years. Currently the SDR is based on the U.S. dollar, euro, British pound, and Japanese yen. Multilateral weights, which reflect relative export volumes of the four countries, as well as the relative balances of these four currencies held by all member countries of the IMF, are used in the construction of the SDR.

Calculation of the SDR

On January 1, 1999, the euro replaced the French franc and the German mark in the basket of currencies. The weights of these two currencies, however, were retained and now apply to the euro. To derive the daily SDR value, we begin with the basket as of its last revision. The basket of currencies consists of 0.660 U.S. dollar, 12.100 Japanese yen, 0.111 British pound, and 0.423 euro (in place of the French franc and German mark). We then convert these currency amounts to their U.S. dollar equivalents using daily spot exchange rates. Then we sum the U.S. dollar equivalent amounts for the SDR.

We can use the information in Table 2–1 on page 30 to construct an SDR calculation. Table 2–3 provides SDR currency amounts and the current U.S.-dollar-per-currency rates for the four currencies. We multiply the currency amount, in the second column, by the U.S.-dollar-per-currency rate in the third column, to yield the U.S.-dollar-per-currency amount of each currency in the SDR, given in the fourth column. Then we add the U.S.-dollar-per-currency amounts in the fourth column together to give the U.S.-dollar-per-currency exchange rate of the SDR, 1.5019 $/SDR, which is the value in Table 2–1.

We can calculate the SDR rate of any currency other than the dollar as a cross rate using the U.S.-dollar-per-currency exchange rate of the SDR and the individual currency's U.S.-dollar-per-currency exchange rate. For example, in Table 2–1, the U.S.-dollar-per-currency rate of the Russian ruble is 0.0339 $/Rr and the

Table 2–3

Calculation of the SDR

Currency Amount	Currency Amount in SDR	U.S.-Dollar-per-Currency Rate	U.S. Dollar Equivalent
Euro	0.423	1.2752	0.5394
Japanese yen	12.100	0.0123	0.1488
British pound	0.111	1.3842	0.1536
U.S. dollar	0.660	1.0000	0.6600
SDR1 = $1.5019			1.5019
$1 = SDR0.6658			0.6658

U.S.-dollar-per-currency rate of the SDR is 1.5019. Dividing the second rate, $/SDR, by the first rate, $/Rr, yields the Russian ruble-SDR cross rate, 44.3038 Rr/SDR.

FOREIGN EXCHANGE ARBITRAGE

Many people envision foreign exchange dealers buying and selling currencies at a furious pace and generating magnificent profits. Indeed, some traders have reputations for earning enormous profits in the foreign exchange market. We must understand, however, that an activity known as *arbitrage* leads to these profits. Arbitrage, in its simplest terms, means "buy low–sell high," and is an activity through which individuals seek immediate profits based on price differentials. Individuals can also profit on currencies across time, through currency speculation or hedging. We shall discuss these latter types of activity in Chapters 4 and 5.

spatial arbitrage
The act of profiting from exchange-rate differences that prevail in different markets.

Spatial arbitrage refers to arbitrage transactions conducted across space, such as across two different geographical markets. For spatial arbitrage opportunities to exist, a currency's exchange rate in one market must be different from the exchange rate in another market.

Suppose that you happen to have $1 million line of credit. (Recall that the spot market for foreign exchange is for transactions of $1 million or more.) You notice that the Danish krone (Dkr)-per-U.S.-dollar rate in New York is 5.8426 Dkr/$, and the currency-per-U.S.-dollar rate in London is 5.8134 Dkr/$. Suppose both markets are open and there are no restrictions against buying and selling currencies in either market. Ignoring any brokerage fees, the difference in rates indicates that there is an arbitrage opportunity. In New York, the $1 million would purchase Dkr 5,842,600, while in London it would purchase Dkr 5,813,400. Therefore, you could buy Dkr 5,842,600 for $1 million in New York, and then sell the Dkr 5,842,600 for $1,005,023 in London. Thus, if you bought the krone in New York with dollars and sold it in London for dollars you would make a profit of $5,023. Note that this arbitrage activity would take place across space (in two different markets), hence the term *spatial arbitrage.*

If an arbitrage opportunity exists, foreign exchange traders engage in transactions that reduce or eliminate the arbitrage opportunity. Consider the spatial arbitrage example just given. If foreign exchange traders were to buy the krone in New York and sell it in London, the New York krone-per-U.S.-dollar rate would fall and the London krone-per-U.S.-dollar rate would rise, eliminating the difference in rates. Thus, the opportunity is "arbitraged away."

triangular arbitrage
Three transactions undertaken in three different markets and/or in three different currencies in order to profit from differences in prices.

Triangular arbitrage (or three-way arbitrage), is slightly more complex and involves three or more currencies and/or markets. Again, for triangular arbitrage opportunities to exist, a currency's exchange value must differ across markets. In the previous example, the currency-per-U.S.-dollar exchange rate in one market had to be different from the currency-per-U.S.-dollar exchange rate in another market. For a triangular arbitrage opportunity to exist, one of three exchange rates must not be equal spatially.

Suppose the Danish krone-per-U.S.-dollar rate in New York is 5.8426 Dkr/$, and the British pound-per-U.S.-dollar rate is 0.7224 £/$, while in London the Danish krone-per-pound rate is 7.8452. The two rates in the New York market imply a cross rate between the krone and the pound of 8.0878 Dkr/£ (5.8426 Dkr/$ ÷ 0.7224 £/$ = 8.0878 Dkr/$). Note that the implied cross rate in New York is different from that in the London market. Therefore, an arbitrage opportunity exists. (Again we are ignoring transaction costs.)

Because the krone-per-British-pound rate in London is less than that in New York, as savvy traders we would wish to purchase the pound in London, using the krone. Using the $1 million line of credit, we purchase Dkr5,842,600 ($1 million × 5.8426 Dkr/$ = Dkr5,842,600) in New York.

We then use the Dkr5,842,600 to purchase £744,736 (Dkr5,842,600 ÷ 7.8452 Dkr/£ = £744,736) in London. Then we use £744,736 to purchase $1,030,919 (£744,736 ÷ 0.7224 £/$ = $1,030,919) in New York. This arbitrage activity netted a profit of $30,919. Note that we would have traded *three* currencies in this example, the dollar, pound, and krone, hence the term *triangular arbitrage*.

 **Fundamental ISSUES**

#4 What is foreign exchange arbitrage?

Foreign exchange arbitrage is the act of buying a currency at one price and immediately selling it at a different price. Spatial arbitrage refers to arbitrage activities that span separate markets. Triangular arbitrage refers to arbitrage activities in which the foreign exchange transaction involves more than two currencies.

THE DEMAND FOR AND SUPPLY OF CURRENCIES

So far our discussion has focused on descriptions and calculations. Now let's consider an *analytical model* of the foreign exchange market. We shall use this simple supply and demand model in several of the following chapters. In this framework, we shall assume that there are no obstructions or controls on foreign exchange transactions. In addition, we shall assume that governments do not buy or sell currencies in order to manipulate their values. Under these assumptions, market forces of supply and demand determine the value of a currency.

The Demand for a Currency

The primary function of a currency is to facilitate transactions. Thus, the demand for a currency is a *derived demand.* That is, we derive the demand for a currency from the demand for the goods, services, and assets that people use the currency to purchase. Consider two countries, Germany and the United States. The demand for the euro stems from the U.S. residents' demand for German goods, services, and euro-denominated assets. If U.S. consumers' demand for German goods were to increase, then, indirectly, there would be a rise in the demand for the euro to purchase the German goods. The price the U.S. consumer would have to pay for the euro would be the prevailing U.S.-dollar-per-euro exchange rate.

Illustrating the Demand Relationship: The Demand Curve Figure 2–2 on the next page illustrates this demand relationship. A depreciation of the dollar relative to the euro is an increase in the U.S.-dollar-per-euro exchange rate, as it takes more dollars to purchase each euro. The intuition of the downward-sloping demand curve is that as the dollar depreciates relative to the euro, German goods become relatively more expensive to U.S. consumers. As a result, U.S. consumers desire to purchase fewer German goods and require fewer euros to facilitate the reduced number of transactions. There is, therefore, a negative relationship between the

Figure 2–2

The Demand for Euros

The demand curve illustrates the relationship between quantity demanded and the exchange rate. An increase in the exchange rate from *SA* to *SB* indicates that the U.S. dollar has depreciated relative to the euro. This would make German goods and services relatively more expensive to U.S. consumers. As a result, U.S. consumers would decrease their quantity of euros demanded in buying fewer German goods and services.

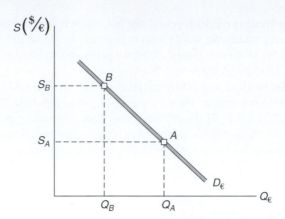

price of the currency and the quantity demanded. We may conclude that a change in the exchange rate results in a movement up and along the demand curve for the euro, as depicted by the movement on the demand curve from point A to point B. This is a *change in the quantity of euros demanded.* (To contemplate how changes in the value of the dollar affects academic institutions' incentives in offerings of study-abroad programs, see *Management Notebook: Variations in the Dollar's Value Induce Colleges to Adjust Enrollments in Study-Abroad Programs.*)

 MANAGEMENT Notebook

Variations in the Dollar's Value Induce Colleges to Adjust Enrollments in Study-Abroad Programs

During the early 2000s, colleges and universities across the United States expanded their menus of study-abroad programs, through which they offered students the opportunity—typically at regular tuition rates—to earn academic credit studying in other nations. Academic administrators based most of these programs in European nations, which have long been popular destinations for U.S. students.

Then, beginning in early 2006, the U.S. dollar's value began to depreciate. Within just two years, the dollar had lost more than 20 percent of its value in relation to the euro, the pound, and other European currencies. Correspondingly, academic institutions experienced increases in the dollar costs of operating study-abroad programs in Europe. As the dollar continued to depreciate into the late 2000s, many colleges and universities began reducing the numbers of students accepted into European-based study-abroad programs.

In the early 2010s, the dollar's value began to rise relative to the euro. Costs of operating in Europe began to decline. U.S. colleges' costs of operating study abroad programs in European nations began to drop back to earlier levels, and colleges responded by raising enrollments toward prior levels.

For Critical Analysis

When more U.S. students respond to a continuing dollar depreciation by opting to participate in study-abroad programs in Argentina, while fewer simultaneously choose programs based in European Monetary Union nations, what are the effects on the quantities demanded of pesos and euros?

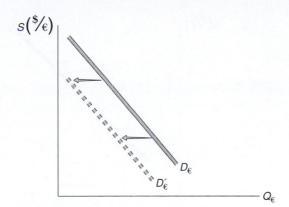

Figure 2–3

A Decrease in the Demand for Euros

A decrease in U.S. consumers' demand for German goods, services, and euro-denominated assets would lead to a decrease in the demand for euros. The decrease in demand is illustrated by a leftward shift of the demand curve from $D€$ to $D'€$.

A Change in Demand Let's suppose that, at a given exchange rate, U.S. consumers' demand for German goods, services, or euro-denominated assets decrease at every exchange rate. Then, as just described, there is a decrease in the quantity of euros demanded at the given exchange rate. This is a *change in the demand* for euros. Figure 2–3 illustrates the change in demand as a *shift* of the demand curve. A rightward shift of the demand curve illustrates an increase in the demand for euros, and a leftward shift illustrates a decrease in the demand for euros.

Because the demand for a currency is a derived demand, the various factors that cause a change in the demand for a currency are all of the factors that cause a change in the foreign demand for that country's goods, services, and assets. We shall discuss these factors in more detail in Chapters 8 and 9.

The Supply of a Currency

To understand the supply of a currency, consider a German consumer's demand for the U.S. dollar, which we may derive from the German consumer's demand for U.S. goods, services, and assets. When the German consumer purchases U.S. dollars in order to buy more U.S. goods, the German consumer exchanges euros for dollars. As a result, there is an increase in the supply of the euro in the foreign exchange market. Thus the German demand for dollars also represents the supply of euros.

Illustrating the Supply Relationship: The Supply Curve Figure 2–4 on the following page depicts the relationship between the German demand for dollars and the supply of euros. The main difference between panel (a) and panel (b) is the labeling of the axes. The vertical axis in panel (b) inverts the euro-per-U.S.-dollar exchange rate, yielding the U.S.-dollar-per-euro exchange rate. On the horizontal axis, the quantity of euros replaces the quantity of U.S. dollars in panel (b).

Viewing panel (a), when the euro appreciates (a decrease in the €/$ exchange rate), U.S. goods are relatively cheaper to German consumers. As a result, German consumers wish to buy more U.S. goods. To do so, they must purchase more U.S. dollars. In other words, there is an increase in the quantity of U.S. dollars demanded, shown by the movement from point A to point B.

Panel (b) shows an equivalent way to express this relationship. When the euro appreciates, the $/€ exchange rate rises. As German consumers purchase more U.S. dollars, they exchange their euros for the dollar, so there is an increase in the quantity of euros supplied. Thus, there is a positive relationship between the $/€ exchange rate and the supply of the euro, illustrated by the upward-sloping supply

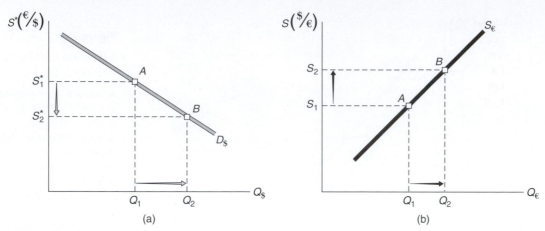

Figure 2–4 The Supply of Euros

Panel (a) depicts the demand for U.S. dollars. The exchange rate in this diagram is the euro-U.S.-dollar rate. A decrease in the euro-per-U.S.-dollar rate leads to an increase in the quantity of U.S. dollars demanded. As more U.S. dollars are purchased with euros, the quantity of euros supplied in the foreign exchange market increases. Panel (b) illustrates the relationship between the exchange rate and the quantity of euros supplied. This exchange rate in panel (b) is the U.S.-dollar-equivalent rate. As this rate rises, which is equivalent a decline in the euro-per-U.S.-dollar rate, the quantity of euros supplied increases. The supply curve, S_ϵ, illustrates the positive relationship between the exchange rate and the quantity supplied.

curve in panel (b). A movement along the supply curve represents a *change in the quantity of euros supplied.* This relationship depends in the elasticity of supply, which is covered in Chapter 8.

A Change in Supply If, at a given exchange rate, there is an increase in the demand for U.S. goods by German consumers, there is an increased demand for dollars. As German consumers purchase dollars to facilitate the additional transactions, they exchange euros for dollars, increasing the quantity supplied of euros in the foreign exchange market at the given rate. This is a *change in the supply of euros,* shown by a rightward shift of the supply curve in Figure 2–5. As shown, we depict an increase in the supply by a rightward shift of the supply schedule. The various factors that cause a change in the supply of a currency are the factors that cause a change in a country's demand for a foreign country's goods, services, and assets, which we shall examine in detail in Chapters 8 and 9.

Figure 2–5

A Shift in the Supply of Euros

An increase in the demand for U.S. dollars by German consumers leads to an increase in the supply of euros. The increase in the supply of euros is illustrated by a rightward shift of the supply curve.

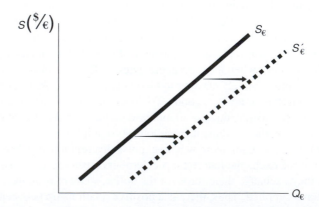

The Equilibrium Exchange Rate

The forces of demand and supply determine the equilibrium, or *market clearing,* exchange rate for a currency. The equilibrium exchange rate is the rate at which the quantity of a currency demanded is equal to the quantity supplied. At the equilibrium exchange rate, the market *clears,* meaning that the quantity demanded is exactly equal to the quantity supplied.

Illustrating the Market Equilibrium Figure 2–6 combines the demand and supply schedules in the same diagram and depicts the point of equilibrium for the foreign exchange market as point *E,* at which the equilibrium exchange rate is S_e, and the equilibrium quantity is Q_e. At exchange rate S_b, there is an excess quantity of euros supplied in the market. The quantity supplied at this rate, Q_2, exceeds the quantity demanded, Q_1. Because there is an excess quantity of the currency supplied, S_b is a *disequilibrium exchange rate.* Hence, the euro will depreciate to the point at which there is no excess quantity supplied. This occurs at point *E.*

Similarly, but in the opposite situation, at exchange rate S_c there is an excess quantity of euros demanded, as the quantity demanded at this rate, Q_2, exceeds the quantity supplied, Q_1. As a result, the euro will appreciate until there is no excess quantity demanded. Again, this takes place at point *E.* This adjustment process continues until the market clears, meaning that the quantity supplied equals the quantity demanded, which is a point of equilibrium. The market remains at this point until something causes one or both of the schedules to shift.

Example: A Change in Demand Figure 2–7 on the next page again shows the market equilibrium at point *E,* with the equilibrium exchange rate labeled S_e and the equilibrium quantity denoted as Q_e. Now consider what happens if there is an increase in the demand for German goods by U.S. consumers. As explained earlier, there is a corresponding increase in the demand for euros by U.S. consumers. This causes the rightward shift of the demand schedule in Figure 2–7. At the initial equilibrium exchange rate, S_e, there is an excess amount of euros demanded, because the quantity demanded at this rate is Q_d' and the quantity supplied is still Q_e. This puts upward pressure on the dollar price of the euro, $/€. The appreciation of the euro relative to the dollar makes U.S. goods relatively cheaper to German consumers. Consequently, German consumers increase their purchases of U.S. goods, exchanging euros for dollars. This increases the quantity of euros supplied, which induces a movement up and along the supply curve, from point *E* to point *E'*.

Figure 2–6

Market Equilibrium

At exchange rate S_b, the quantity of euros supplied is greater than the quantity demanded, and there is downward pressure on the exchange rate. At exchange rate S_c, the quantity of euros demanded is greater than the quantity supplied, and there is pressure for the exchange rate to rise. At exchange rate S_e, the market for the euro is in equilibrium: the quantity demanded is equal to the quantity supplied.

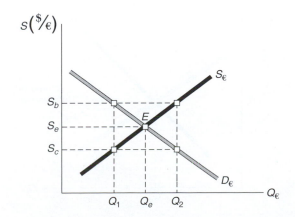

Figure 2–7

A Change in the Demand for Euros

Initially the market for euros is in equilibrium at point E. An increase in U.S. consumers' demand for German goods increases the demand for euros. The increase in the demand for euros is illustrated by a rightward shift of the demand curve. At the initial equilibrium exchange rate S_e, the new quantity demanded exceeds the quantity supplied, as shown by the distance between Q_d' and Q_e. The euro appreciates to S', where the market clears.

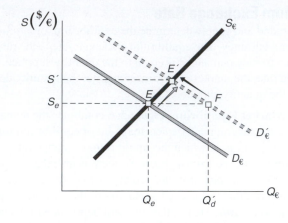

The depreciation of the dollar relative to the euro also makes German goods relatively more expensive to U.S. consumers. U.S. consumers reduce their purchases of German goods due to this change in the exchange rate. As a result, the quantity of euros demanded declines, as shown by the movement up and along the demand curve from point F to point E'. (Note carefully the difference between a change in the demand for the euro, which is a *shift of the demand schedule,* and a change in quantity of euros demanded, which is a *movement along the demand schedule.*) This market adjustment process continues until the quantity demanded equals the quantity supplied, so that the market clears. A new equilibrium occurs at E' and spot exchange rate S', indicating that the euro has appreciated relative to the dollar.

Foreign Exchange Market Intervention

To this point, we have assumed that the value of a nation's currency is determined solely by the forces of supply and demand. That is, the exchange rate has been regarded as *flexible.* Policymakers in some nations prefer to anchor the value of their currency relative to another currency. Consequently, they choose a *fixed-exchange-rate arrangement.* In Chapter 3 you will consider a wide variety of exchange rate arrangements in greater detail. Before we proceed, however, it is helpful to use the supply and demand framework to understand how a policymaker might fix the value of the nation's currency.

Consider the euro appreciation depicted in Figure 2–8. Suppose that European policymakers prefer the value of the euro relative to the dollar to remain steady at

Figure 2–8

Foreign Exchange Market Intervention

An increase in the demand for euros puts pressure on the euro to appreciate relative to the dollar. To maintain the exchange value of the euro, European policymakers purchase dollar-denominated financial instruments. They pay for these purchases with euros, thereby increasing the quantity of euros supplied in the foreign exchange market. The volume of intervention, in terms of euros, is given by the distance between points F and E.

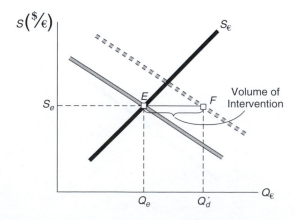

S_e and not to rise to S'. Given the rise in demand from D_ϵ to D'_ϵ, at exchange rate S_e the quantity of euros demanded, Q'_d exceeds the quantity of euros supplied, Q_e. It is this difference between quantity demanded and quantity supplied, depicted as the distance between point F and point E in the figure, which causes the euro to appreciate in value relative to the dollar.

To maintain the value of the euro at S_e, European policymakers would have to increase the quantity of euros supplied to match the quantity demanded. They would accomplish this by purchasing dollar-denominated financial instruments in the foreign exchange market. They would pay for these purchases with euros, thereby increasing the quantity of euros supplied in the foreign exchange market. The volume of their purchases, in euros, is given by the distance between points F and E.

Fundamental ISSUES

#5 What determines the value of a currency?

The interaction between the demand for a currency and the supply of the currency determines the currency's market value. If the exchange rate is free to change, then a currency's value adjusts to its market equilibrium through a market-clearing process. The equilibrium market exchange rate is the value that eliminates any excess quantity of the currency that is demanded or supplied in the market.

PURCHASING POWER PARITY

We often hear that a currency is "undervalued" or "overvalued." What does this mean? A currency will be viewed as over- or undervalued if the current market-determined rate is not consistent with a rate implied by a formal or informal economic model. Therefore, economists would predict that some adjustment is likely to occur in the market. An ***overvalued currency*** is one in which the current market value is stronger than that predicted by a theory or model. This currency is likely to experience a market adjustment that brings about a depreciation in the value of the currency. An ***undervalued currency*** is one in which the current market value is weaker than the value predicted by a theory or model. This currency is likely to experience a market adjustment that brings about an appreciation in the value of the currency.

The first, and oldest, exchange-rate theory used to determine if a currency might be over- or undervalued is known as *purchasing power parity*. Sixteenth-century Spanish scholars first formalized this simple and straightforward theory. Because of its simplicity, economists have given considerable attention to purchasing power parity and its application to a variety of policy and practical issues.

Absolute Purchasing Power Parity
Purchasing power parity (PPP) states that, ignoring transportation costs, tax differentials, and trade restrictions, traded homogeneous goods and services should have the same price in two countries after converting their prices into a common currency. Thus, purchasing power parity is often called the *law of one price*.

To illustrate this, suppose that the market price of a trench coat is $420 in New York. The market price of the same trench coat in London, however, is £300.

overvalued currency
A currency in which the current market-determined value is higher than the value predicted by an economic theory or model.

undervalued currency
A currency in which the current market-determined value is lower than that predicted by an economic theory or model.

purchasing power parity (PPP)
A condition that states that if international arbitrage is unhindered, the price of a good or service in one nation should be the same as the exchange-rate-adjusted price of the same good or service in another nation.

This is because PPP would imply that the dollar equivalent exchange rate of the pound should be 1.4 $/£. Using this rate, we can convert the pound price of the trench coat in London to a dollar price of $420 (£300 × 1.4 $/£ = $420). In other words, under purchasing power parity, the trench coat has the same price in London as it does in New York after adjusting for the exchange rate.

Arbitrage and PPP If, in this example, the market exchange rate is not 1.4 $/£, then an arbitrage opportunity exists. Suppose the exchange rate is equal to 1.5 $/£. Then the dollar price of the trench coat in London is 1.5 $/£ × £300 = $450. The astute arbitrager would be able to buy a trench coat in New York for $420, take it to London and sell it for £300, exchange the £300 for $450 on the foreign exchange market, and earn a profit of $30, ignoring transaction and transportation costs.

The arbitrage activity just described would cause a flow of trench coats from New York to London. The exchange of British pounds for U.S. dollars on the foreign exchange market would generate an increase in the demand for dollars relative to pounds. The three markets (New York trench coat market, London trench coat market, and foreign exchange market) would experience adjustments. The increased demand for trench coats in New York would cause an increase in the price of trench coats in New York. The increased supply of trench coats in London would cause a decrease in price of trench coats in London.

If numerous goods and services were being traded, then there would be an increase in the demand for the dollar relative to the British pound. The increased demand for the dollar relative to the pound would cause the dollar to appreciate relative to the pound. All of these adjustments, which result from the arbitrage activity, would tend to equalize the (same currency) prices of traded goods and services, and thus eliminate the arbitrage opportunity.

At this point we can see that price differences between the two economies can lead to changes in the demand for a currency. In our example, the lower price of trench coats in New York would lead to an eventual increase in the demand for the dollar relative to the pound. Therefore, we would expect an outward shift in the demand curve for the dollar. We may conclude that price differences could be considered a factor of currency demand because relatively lower prices in a nation cause the demand for that nation's currency to increase.

Absolute PPP The above theory of the relationship between prices and exchange rates is absolute purchasing power parity, because it deals with absolute price levels. We can formalize and express absolute PPP as follows. Let S denote the U.S.-dollar-per-currency exchange rate of the pound, $/£. Let P denote the price level in the United States, and let P^* denote the price level in the United Kingdom. Then we can express absolute PPP as

$$P = S \times P^*.$$

In words, the domestic price level should be equal to the multiplication of the foreign price level times the spot exchange rate. Note that the spot rate converts the foreign price level so that it is expressed in terms of the domestic currency. We could say, therefore, that the domestic price level expressed in the domestic currency should equal the foreign price level expressed in the domestic currency. This is the law of one price.

The absolute PPP theory applies to all internationally traded and identical goods and services of the two economies. Consequently, P represents the price level of this *range* of goods, not a single good, as in our previous example. This would imply that arbitrage activity would ensure equality of the same-currency price level of these goods and services across the two economies.

Practical Problems and Shortcomings of Absolute PPP If *all* goods and services are fully and freely tradable across U.S. and British borders, then absolute PPP will hold for all goods. In this instance, we can interpret P as the overall price level of U.S. goods and services and P^* as the overall price level of British goods and services. Note that in this instance, we can rearrange the absolute PPP relationship to solve for the spot exchange rate:

$$S = P/P^*.$$

That is, when absolute purchasing power parity holds for all goods and services, the spot exchange rate equals the U.S. price level divided by the British price level.

Thus, absolute PPP is a theory of exchange rates: If absolute PPP holds, then the bilateral spot exchange rate should equal the ratio of the price levels of the two nations. Hence, the demand and supply schedules in foreign exchange markets should move to positions yielding this bilateral exchange rate. Until they do, one could say that, based on absolute purchasing power parity, one nation's currency is overvalued or undervalued relative to the currency of the other nation.

Even if goods and services are freely tradable and transportation costs are insignificant, we still would anticipate problems in applying absolute PPP to all goods and services of two nations.

One reason is that people in two nations may consume different sets of goods and services. The price levels for the two nations would be based on the prices of different goods, meaning that the arbitrage argument that lies behind the absolute PPP condition could not apply. Arbitrage could not really relate the prices of both sets of goods, so we would be mistaken to infer an exchange rate from the absolute PPP relationship.

Another way to see why absolute PPP is unlikely to hold in the real world is to recall how we calculate a real exchange rate. As you learned earlier, we multiply the spot exchange rate by the ratio of the price levels for two countries. That is, we multiply the exchange rate S by the price-level ratio P/P^*, which tells us that we can write the real exchange rate as $S \times (P^*/P)$.

If absolute PPP holds, then $S = P/P^*$, so that the real exchange rate is equal to

$$S \times (P^*/P) = (P/P^*) \times (P^*/P) = 1.$$

When the real exchange rate is equal to 1, one unit of goods and services in a country, such as the United States, always exchanges one-for-one with a unit of goods and services in another country, such as the United Kingdom. Thus, absolute PPP implies that the real exchange rate is always equal to 1. If people in different countries consume goods and services in different proportions, however, it is highly unlikely that this will be so.

For these reasons, absolute PPP typically fails to hold. Short-run deviations from PPP are significant. As a result, economists discount this form of PPP as a short-run guide. As a long-run theory, it performs only slightly better, with deviations from PPP being eliminated very slowly over time. (To consider real-world factors that hinder full attainment of gains from cross-country arbitrage in trading goods and services, see on the next page *Management Notebook: Significant Gains from Arbitrage Turn Out to Be Mainly Theoretical in Canada.*)

MANAGEMENT Notebook

Significant Gains from Arbitrage Turn Out to Be Mainly Theoretical in Canada

On September 21, 2007, the Canadian dollar—nicknamed the "loonie" after the water fowl depicted on the reverse side of the Canadian dollar coin—reached and then surpassed parity with the U.S. dollar for the first time since 1976. Soon, talk of hundreds of thousands of Canadians streaming across the U.S. border in search of bargains captured the headlines. And, indeed, when the loonie began trading above parity with the U.S. dollar during the months that followed, growing numbers of Canadians began embarking on shopping treks to the United States.

Nevertheless, many Canadians learned that engaging in arbitrage via cross-border shopping is easier in theory than in practice. The government of Canada and provincial governments have stringent limits on quantities of U.S. goods and services that shoppers can transport across the border without paying sales taxes and other duties. In addition, the Canadian government requires residents to pay for expensive alterations to certain U.S.-made durable goods, such as installations of new headlights and bumpers on U.S.-manufactured automobiles, to satisfy Canadian safety codes. Thus, a significant portion of Canadians learned that gains from cross-border arbitrage were much lower than anticipated.

For Critical Analysis

How do limits on cross-border transactions and requirements to pay for alterations to foreign-made products interfere with attainment of the law of one price?

Relative Purchasing Power Parity

The version of PPP discussed in the previous section is *absolute* PPP, because it deals with absolute price levels. *Relative* purchasing power parity is a weaker version of purchasing power parity, as it addresses price changes as opposed to absolute price levels. Relative PPP, as an exchange rate theory, relates exchange rate changes to the differences in price changes across countries.

On the WEB

For weekly articles on the global economy, visit *The Economist* magazine at *http://economist.com*.

We can use the earlier expression for absolute PPP to derive the relative version of PPP. Let's denote the percentage change of a variable by placing the characters "%Δ" in front of the variable. Then, for example, $\%\Delta P$ would represent the change in the price level over a given period. By calculating the change of each variable in the expression for absolute PPP, we can express relative PPP as

$$\%\Delta S = \%\Delta P - \%\Delta P^*.$$

As a guide to exchange-rate changes, relative PPP implies that the change in an exchange rate is equal to the difference in price changes between the two economies. As we discussed in Chapter 1, economists use the percentage change in a price index as a measure of inflation. Let π denote the rate of inflation. In keeping with our earlier example, let π^* be the inflation rate in Britain as measured by the percentage change in the CPI. Let π denote the inflation rate in the United States as measured by the percentage change in the CPI, and let $\%\Delta S$ denote the rate of appreciation or depreciation of the U.S. dollar relative to the British pound as measured by the percentage change in the U.S.-dollar-per-currency exchange rate. Then we can rewrite relative PPP as

$$\%\Delta S = \pi - \pi^*.$$

In words, the appreciation or depreciation of a currency is given by the difference between the two nations' inflation rates.

To show how this version of relative PPP is used as a guide for exchange-rate determination, consider the following example. In 2009, the CPI for the United States was 110.2, and it was 115.2 in 2012. For the United Kingdom, the CPI was 110.8 in 2009, and it was 121.7 in 2012. The U.S.-dollar-per-currency pound exchange rate was 1.4032 in 2009, and it was 1.6031 in 2012. Using these numbers, we can calculate the rates of inflation and currency appreciation or depreciation.

Using the percentage-change formula, the rate of inflation in the United States between 2009 and 2012 was 4.54 percent [(115.2 − 110.2)/110.2 × 100 = 4.54%]. For the United Kingdom, the rate of inflation over this period was 9.84 percent [(121.7 − 110.8)/110.8 × 100 = 9.84%]. The rate of appreciation of the pound, was 14.25 percent [(1.6031 − 1.4032)/1.4032 × 100 = 14.25%]. Substituting the percentages for inflation into the equation for relative PPP yields the implied rate of depreciation (if negative) or appreciation (if positive) of the pound,

$$\%\Delta S = 4.54\% - 9.84\% = -5.30\%.$$

Thus, relative PPP suggests that the percentage change in the U.S.-dollar-per-currency exchange rate of the pound should have been −5.30 percent, or a depreciation of the pound relative to the dollar of 5.30 percent. It was already shown, however, that over this period the pound appreciated relative to the dollar by more than 14 percent. Because the pound actually appreciated relative to the dollar, whereas relative PPP suggest that the pound should have depreciated relative to the dollar, relative PPP suggests that in 2012 the pound is overvalued relative to the dollar. Provided the pound was neither overvalued nor undervalued relative to the dollar in 2009, the market-determined U.S.-dollar-per-currency exchange value of the pound should have decreased, rather than increase, or the U.K. rate of inflation should have been less than that of the United States.

How does relative PPP perform under empirical examination? The evidence shows that relative PPP performs better than absolute PPP. Nonetheless, it is still a poor short-run guide to exchange-rate changes in the major economies and is only slightly better as a long-run guide. Relative PPP does perform well during periods of very high inflation, because during these periods price changes are the dominant influence on the value of a currency.

In conclusion, absolute PPP and relative PPP are common, but perhaps ill-advised, guides to exchange-rate movements. One of their principal shortcomings is that they provide theories based only on the international exchange of goods and services and do not consider financial flows and money stocks.

Fundamental ISSUES

#6 What is purchasing power parity, and is it useful as a guide to movements in exchange rates?

Purchasing power parity is a theory of the relationship between the prices of traded goods and services and the exchange rate. There are two versions of PPP. Absolute PPP relates price levels and the exchange-rate level. Relative PPP relates price changes and changes in the exchange rate. Although both versions are commonly used guides to exchange rates and their movements, generally neither are very useful, particularly in the short run.

Chapter SUMMARY

1. **The Foreign Exchange Market:** The foreign exchange market is a system of private banks, foreign exchange dealers, and central banks through which individuals, businesses, and governments trade foreign exchange, or other nations' currencies. The foreign exchange rate is the rate at which one currency exchanges for another in the foreign exchange market.

2. **Currency Appreciation or Depreciation:** When the domestic currency appreciates relative to a foreign currency, it gains in value relative to the foreign currency. This means people can trade fewer domestic currency units in exchange for each foreign currency unit. When the domestic currency depreciates relative to a foreign currency, it has lost value against the foreign currency. This means people must give more domestic currency units in exchange for each foreign currency unit. When the exchange rate rises, the domestic currency may have appreciated or depreciated, depending on how we express the exchange rate.

3. **How Economists Measure the Overall Value of a Currency:** In the course of a typical trading day, a currency may appreciate against some currencies and depreciate against others. An effective exchange rate is an index that measures the weighted-average value of a currency relative to a basket of currencies. An effective exchange rate, therefore, is a useful measure of general changes in a currency's value.

4. **Foreign Exchange Market Arbitrage:** Foreign exchange arbitrage is the act of profiting from differences between the exchange rates of foreign exchange. Spatial arbitrage refers to an arbitrage transaction that is conducted in two different markets, or separated by space. Triangular arbitrage involves more than two currencies and/or markets.

5. **Determining the Value of a Currency:** The interaction of the forces of supply and demand in the foreign exchange market determines the value of a currency. A currency is over- or undervalued if the market-determined exchange rate is inconsistent with the value predicted by a formal or informal model. Policymakers in some nations fix the exchange value of their currency through foreign exchange market intervention, which is the buying or selling of foreign-currency-denominated financial instruments in foreign exchange markets.

6. **Purchasing Power Parity and Its Usefulness for Predicting Exchange Rates:** Purchasing power parity is a theory of the relationship between the prices of traded goods and services and the exchange rate. There are two versions of purchasing power parity. Absolute PPP relates the price levels of two countries and the level of the exchange rate. Relative PPP relates two nations' inflation rates and the rate of change in the exchange rate. Although both versions are commonly used guides to exchange-rate movements, neither is particularly useful as a short-run guide to exchange-rate movements.

QUESTIONS and PROBLEMS

1. Suppose the U.S.-dollar-per-currency exchange rate of the euro was 1.2201 on Thursday and 1.2168 on Friday. Did the euro appreciate or depreciate relative to the U.S. dollar? How much was the appreciation/depreciation (in percentage-change terms)?

2. Complete the following cross-rate table. The data in the far right-hand column represent the U.S.-dollar-per-currency price of the currencies in the far left-hand column.

	A$	£	€	Sfr	$
Australia					1.0380
United Kingdom					1.3840
Euro					1.2750
Switzerland					1.0916
United States					—

3. Suppose that in New York the euro and British pound trade at the following exchange rates: 1.275 $/€, and $/£ = 1.412. In London, the euro equivalent rate of the pound is 1.198 €/£. Is there an arbitrage opportunity? Why or why not? Calculate the profit to be made on $1,000,000.

4. Suppose we observe the following information for the euro area, Canada, and the United States. The exchange rates given in the table are the currency-per-U.S.-dollar rates.

	S(2011)	S(2012)	CPI(2011)	CPI(2012)	2011 U.S Exports	2011 U.S. Imports
Euro Area	0.672	0.719	118.0	120.4	$261,380	$335,555
Canada	1.00	0.981	117.2	118.8	$274,510	$367,927
United States			122.6	122.3		

Using this information, calculate the 2011 and 2012 effective exchange values for the U.S. dollar using 2011 as the base year. Do the values you calculated indicate an appreciation or depreciation of the U.S. dollar? What is the rate of appreciation or depreciation?

5. Using the data in Question 5, calculate the *real* effective exchange values of the dollar. Do the values you calculated indicate an appreciation or depreciation of the U.S. dollar? What is the rate of appreciation or depreciation?

6. In 2011, the spot rate of exchange between the Turkish lira (TI) and the euro was 2.016 TI/€. In 2012, the rate was 2.348 TI/€. Based on this information, did the euro appreciate or depreciate relative to the Turkish lira? What was the amount, in percentage-change terms, of the appreciation/depreciation?

7. Based on your answer to Question 6, what was the impact of the exchange-rate change on European consumers' purchasing power over Turkish goods and services relative to their purchasing power over European goods and services?

8. In 2011, the CPI for Turkey was 398.2 and the euro-area CPI was 114.4. In 2012, the CPI for Turkey was 456.5 and the euro-area CPI was 120.4. Based on this information, what was the rate of inflation for Turkey and the rate of inflation for the euro area?

9. Based on your answer to Question 8, what was the impact of the different inflation rates on European consumers' purchasing power over Turkish goods and services relative to their purchasing power over European goods and services?

10. Using the information in Questions 6 and 8, calculate the real rate of exchange between the Turkish lira and the euro for 2011 and 2012. In real terms, did the euro appreciate or depreciate relative to the Turkish lira? What was the amount, in percentage-change terms, of the appreciation/depreciation?

11. Using the information in Questions 6 and 8, and according to *absolute* purchasing power parity (PPP), was the euro overvalued or undervalued relative to the Turkish lira in 2012? By what percent?

12. Using the information in Questions 6 and 8, and according to *relative* purchasing power parity (PPP), what is the predicted value of the euro for 2012? Based on your answer, was the euro overvalued or undervalued relative to the Turkish lira in 2012? By what percent?

Online**APPLICATIONS**

This chapter discussed the concept of purchasing power parity. The following application takes you to the publishers of *The Economist* magazine to see if their own subscription prices follow PPP.

Internet URL: *http://economist.com*

Title: Subscription prices of *The Economist* magazine

Navigation: Begin at the home page of *The Economist* (*http://economist.com*). Scroll down to the very bottom of the page and click on "Subscribe."

Application: Select France as the country, and write down the subscription price of a thirteen-week subscription. Next, select Switzerland and write down the subscription price.

1. Write out the expression for purchasing power parity. Rearrange the expression, solving for the spot rate.

2. Substitute in the subscription data you obtained for *The Economist* Web site, and solve for the implied spot rate.

3. Return to the home page. At the top of the page, move the cursor over "Economics" and then scroll down and click on *Markets and Data*. Under "Economic and Financial Indicators," select "Trade, exchange rates, budget balances and interest rates." Obtain the exchange rate between the Swiss franc and the euro. (If exchange rates are given relative to the U.S. dollar, then calculate the cross-rate of exchange between the Swiss franc and the euro.) Compare this exchange rate with that implied by PPP in Question 2. Does PPP hold? If not, is the euro over- or undervalued according to PPP?

SELECTED REFERENCES and FURTHER READINGS

Bird, Graham, and Dane Rowlands. "The Political Economy of the SDR: The Rise and Fall of an International Reserve Asset." In Graham Bird and Dane Rowlands, eds., *The International Monetary Fund and the World Economy, Volume 2.* Cheltenham U.K.: Edgar Elgar, 2007: 481–505.

Bissoondeeal, Rakesh. "Post-Bretton Woods Evidence on PPP under Different Exchange Rate Regimes." *Applied Financial Economics 18*(16–18) (September–October 2008): 1481–1488.

Catão, Luis. "Why Real Exchange Rates?" International Monetary Fund, *Finance and Development 44*(3) (September 2007): 46–47.

Cumby, Robert. "Forecasting Exchange Rates and Relative Prices with the Hamburger Standard: Is What You Want What You Get with McParity?" NBER Working Paper, 5675 (July 1996).

Ding, Liang." Bid–Ask Spread and Order Size in the Foreign Exchange Market: An Empirical Investigation." *International Journal of Finance and Economics 14*(1) (January 2009): 98–105.

Ekpenyong, David B. "Can the Special Drawing Right (S.D.R.) Become an Acceptable Reserve Currency of the International Monetary Fund (I.M.F.) in the Midst of Strong Resistance by Developed Countries Captained by the U.S.A.? A Critical Appraisal. *Journal of Financial Management and Analysis 20*(1) (January–June 2007): 1–15.

Frankel, Jeffrey, and Andrew Rose. "A Panel Project on Purchasing Power Parity: Mean Reversion within and between Countries." *Journal of International Economics 40* (May 2, 1996): 209–224.

Frydman, Roman, Michael Goldberg, Soren Johansen, and Katarina Juselius. "A Resolution of the Purchasing Power Parity Puzzle: Imperfect Knowledge and Long Swings." University of Copenhagen, Department of Economics, Discussion Papers: 08-31 (2008).

Kraus, James. "Forex Trading Sites May Erode Bank Revenue," *American Banker* (May 4, 2000).

Lothian, James, and Mark Taylor. "Real Exchange Rate Behavior: The Recent Float from the Perspective of the Past Two Centuries." *Journal of Political Economy 104* (June 3, 1996): 488–509.

MacDonald, Ronald, and Mark Taylor. "Exchange Rate Economics: A Survey." *IMF Staff Papers 39* (March 1996): 1–47.

O'Connell, Paul. "The Overvaluation of Purchasing Power Parity." *Journal of International Economics 44* (February 1, 1998): 1–19.

Parsley, David, and Shang-Jin Wei. "A Prism into the PPP Puzzles: The Micro-foundations of Big Mac Real Exchange Rates." *Economic Journal 117*(523) (October 2007): 1336–1356.

Rogoff, Kenneth, Kenneth A. Froot, and Michael Kim. "The Law of One Price over 700 Years." IMF Working Paper, WP/01/174 (November 2001).

Taylor, Alan, and Mark Taylor. "The Purchasing Power Parity Debate." University of California at Davis, Department of Economics, Working Papers (2004).

Taylor, Mark. "The Economics of Exchange Rates." *Journal of Economic Literature 33* (March 1995): 13–47.

Walmsley, Julian. *The Foreign Exchange and Money Market Guide.* New York: John Wiley and Sons, Inc. 2000.

3

Exchange-Rate Systems, Past to Present

$⊛¥£€ Fundamental ISSUES

1. What is an exchange-rate system?
2. How does a gold standard constitute an exchange-rate system?
3. What was the Bretton Woods system of "pegged" exchange rates?
4. What post—Bretton Woods system of "flexible" exchange rates prevails today?
5. What is a dollarization, and what is a currency board?
6. What types of pegged-exchange-rate arrangements are used today?
7. Which is best, a fixed- or flexible-exchange-rate arrangement?

In 2005, the Federal Reserve Bank of San Francisco hosted a symposium entitled "Revived Bretton Woods System: A New Paradigm for Asian Development?" A theme of the symposium was the idea that as of the mid-2000s, the international exchange-rate system was operating much like the Bretton Woods system of fixed exchange rates that prevailed from the end of World War II until the early 1970s. Presenters at the symposium argued that although there were no guarantees of fixed parities in terms of gold or the U.S. dollar, many Asian and Middle Eastern countries limited exchange-rate fluctuations relative to the dollar in a manner similar to that under the Bretton Woods system. Some symposium participants even suggested that as long as the U.S. dollar's value held steady against world currencies this perceived new "Bretton-Woods-like" exchange-rate system might continue indefinitely.

How quickly times change. Between 2005 and 2012, the U.S. dollar's value relative to the world's other currencies exhibited considerable volatility and ultimately dropped by a net amount of more than 15 percent. During this period, many Asian and Middle Eastern nations engaged in policies aimed at slowing the dollar's drop in value relative to their own currencies. Nevertheless, by the end of a decade in which the dollar's total loss in world value was roughly one-third, the governments of most of these countries were giving serious consideration to making a clean break from their dollar-centered policy strategies.

Management of a nation's currency is a very important issue. Combined with the way in which a nation conducts its macroeconomic policies, exchange-rate management may result in a stable economic environment that promotes trade and investment, or an unstable environment that puts its industries at a competitive disadvantage. History shows us that, although entered into with the best intentions, few exchange-rate arrangements can avoid speculative and political pressures forever.

EXCHANGE-RATE SYSTEMS

Before you can begin to understand the institutional framework that governs the value of a nation's currency, you must first understand a nation's monetary order. A ***monetary order*** is a set of laws and regulations that establishes the framework within which individuals conduct and settle transactions.

One decision a nation must make is whether its national money will be a commodity money, a commodity-backed money, or fiat money. *Commodity money* is a tangible good that individuals use as means of payment, or a medium of exchange, such as gold or silver coins. *Commodity-backed money* is a monetary unit whose value relates to a specific commodity or commodities, such as silver or gold, and that national authorities will accept in exchange for the commodity. *Fiat money,* which is our money today, is a monetary unit not backed by any commodity. Its value is determined solely by the worth that people attach to it as a medium of exchange.

A nation's monetary order also sets forth the rules that form the nation's exchange-rate system, and, either formally or informally, the nation's participation in an exchange-rate system. An ***exchange-rate system*** is the set of rules governing the value of an individual nation's currency relative to other foreign currencies. (To learn about how an electronic medium of exchange issued by a Hong Kong videogame company for use in a virtual world has gained widespread acceptance as a form of money in the real world, see *Online Notebook: Foreign Exchange Rates for Virtual Money become a Reality.*)

monetary order
A set of laws and regulations that establishes the framework within which individuals conduct and settle transactions.

exchange-rate system
A set of rules that determines the international value of a currency.

ONLINE Notebook

Foreign Exchange Rates for Virtual Money Become a Reality

In China, more than 300 million people regularly conduct exchanges with electronic "Q coins" issued by Tencent Holdings, Limited, a Hong Kong–based company that sells online videogames. In the beginning, the Q coin, which sells for one Chinese yuan (about 13 cents), was a company marketing ploy. Tencent issued the virtual coins to customers for use in buying cellphone ringtones, electronic greeting cards, and virtual equipment such as magical swords used in Web-based videogames. In recent years, however, Q coins have become more readily acceptable in exchange for real-world merchandise, such as antivirus software, movie DVDs, and cosmetics. In addition, growing numbers of gamblers place bets using Q coins. Furthermore, many businesses now operate services that exchange the virtual Q coins for Chinese yuan. A few Web sites even quote rates of exchange of Q coins for foreign currencies. Thus, there is now a developing foreign exchange market for a virtual currency.

For Critical Analysis

Is there any particular reason that currencies that people find acceptable in exchange must be issued by a government?

To better understand the relationships among a monetary order and an exchange-rate arrangement or exchange-rate system, we will examine the history of three important exchange-rate systems: the gold standard, the Bretton Woods system, and the post–Bretton Woods floating-rate system.

Fundamental ISSUES

#1 What is an exchange-rate system?

An exchange-rate system is the set of rules established by a nation to govern the value of its currency relative to foreign currencies. The exchange-rate system evolves from the nation's monetary order, which is the set of laws and rules that establishes the monetary framework within which transactions are conducted.

THE GOLD STANDARD

By the mid-1870s, the major economies of the world had adopted a commodity-backed monetary order for their national currencies. Gold served as the underlying commodity, and the period until 1914 became known as the *gold standard era.* Under this framework, a nation would fix an official price of gold in terms of the national currency, known as the *mint parity,* and establish convertibility at that rate. ***Convertibility*** is the ability to freely exchange a currency for a commodity or another currency at a given rate of exchange. For example, between 1837 to 1933 (except for the suspension of convertibility during the Civil War), the U.S. mint parity of one fine ounce of gold was $20.646, with the dollar convertible at that rate. To maintain the mint parity, or the exchange value between gold and the national currency, a nation must condition its money stock on the level of its gold reserves.

convertibility

The ability to freely exchange a currency for a reserve commodity or reserve currency.

The Gold Standard as an Exchange-Rate System

Other industrialized nations had adopted a commodity-backed order before or shortly after the same time that the United States reinstated convertibility following the Civil War, which ended in 1865. These decisions, though adopted unilaterally, also established each nation's exchange-rate system and informally led to an exchange-rate system among the nations. The gold standard established an exchange-rate system because it meant that people could exchange the dollar both domestically and internationally, at the mint parity rate. Thus, the exchange value between gold and the dollar determined the international value of the dollar.

This also established an exchange-rate system among the countries that had adopted a gold standard. Because each country valued its currency relative to gold, this indirectly established an exchange value between the domestic currency and the currencies of all other countries on a gold standard.

As an example, under the gold standard, Britain's gold parity rate was, as shown in Figure 3–1, £4.252 per fine ounce. Using the gold parity rates of the U.S. dollar and the British pound, we can determine the rate of exchange that existed between the two currencies. The mint parity rate of the United States was $20.646 and the mint parity rate of the British pound was £4.252. As shown in Figure 3–1,

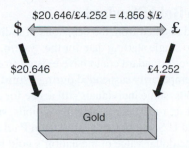

Figure 3–1

The Gold Standard as an
Exchange-Rate System

Countries adopting a gold
standard valued their currencies
relative to gold. The gold parity
rate for the British pound was
£4.252 per troy ounce of gold and
for the U.S. dollar $20.646 per
troy ounce. The gold parity rates
determined the exchange rate
between the two currencies.

the U.S.-dollar-per-currency rate of the British pound, $/£, was therefore
$20.646/£4.252, or 4.856 $/£.

If the exchange rate deviated from this amount, ignoring transportation
costs of gold, then an arbitrage opportunity would have existed. For example,
suppose that, at the mint parity rates just given, the exchange rate between
the U.S. dollar and the British pound was 5 $/£. One would have been able
to take $20.646 and exchange it for one ounce of gold. The gold could then
have been exported to Britain and exchanged for £4.252. The £4.252 would
have exchanged on the foreign exchange market for £4.252 × 5 $/£, or $21.26,
earning a profit of $0.614. If we consider the transportation costs of gold, the
exchange rate between two currencies would remain in a range or band centered
on the ratio of the mint parity values. These transportation and transaction costs
of gold determine the width of the range, because they affect the profitability of
exporting or importing gold.

Under the gold standard, all of the currencies of the nations adopting a gold
standard were linked together, with their exchange values determined in the manner
just described. Just as the mint parities established the exchange rate between the
dollar and the pound, they also established the exchange values among the dollar,
the French franc, and the deutsche mark.

For example, under the gold standard the mint parity of the French franc
was Ffr107.008 and the deutsche mark mint parity was DM86.672. The exchange rate between the dollar and the French franc, therefore, was 5.183 Ffr/$
(Ffr107.008/$20.646). The exchange rate between the dollar and the deutsche mark
was 4.198 DM/$ (DM86.672/$20.646). The link to gold determined all of the cross
rates between the various currencies, as well. It is in this manner that the adoption
of a commodity-backed monetary order by individual nations established the basis
of an exchange-rate system.

Fundamental ISSUES

#2 How does a gold standard constitute an exchange-rate system?

A gold standard constitutes an exchange-rate system for an adopting nation because it
establishes a domestic and international rate of exchange between the domestic currency and gold. A gold standard also links the exchange-rate systems between all of
the nations adopting a gold standard. The exchange value between gold and a nation's
currency indirectly establishes rates of exchange among all of the currencies.

Performance of the Gold Standard

Because the gold standard resulted from the decisions of individual nations made at different times, there is no single starting date for the system. Generally, however, economists consider the gold standard era to have existed from the 1870s onward. Though the system was temporarily suspended during World War I, and eventually collapsed in the early 1930s, some individuals still argue for a return to a gold standard. Some economists at free-market-oriented institutions, such as the Cato Institute (*http://www.cato.org*), and U.S. politicians such as Ron Paul argue that U.S. policymakers should stabilize the dollar value of the nation's gold reserves as a critical first step toward restoring "sound money" to the United States. What is the record of the gold standard, and why do some economists and politicians long for its return?

Positive and Negative Aspects of a Gold Standard As indicated earlier, an important element of a commodity-backed monetary order is that a nation's quantity of money, or its *money stock,* depends directly on the amount of commodity reserves the nation's monetary authority has. A given amount of commodity reserves may support a multiple number of units of money. As an example, between 1879 and 1913 the U.S. money stock was 8.5 times the amount of the monetary gold stock. Thus, *changes* in a nation's money stock depend only on *changes* in the mining and production of monetary gold.

If the supply of gold is rather constant, this particular aspect of a gold standard, therefore, promotes long-run stability of the nation's money stock and long-run stability of real output, prices, and the exchange rate. Another important aspect of a commodity-backed monetary order is that it does not require a central bank. An official authority can maintain the ratio of money stock to gold reserves. Canada and the United States, for example, did not have a central bank during the late 1800s and early 1900s.

A commodity-backed monetary order has some negative aspects, as well. For example, a gold standard has very significant resource costs, such as minting and transportation costs. It can be quite costly for a nation to maintain and exchange a tangible commodity such as gold.

The Economic Environment of the Gold Standard Era Now that you understand these important aspects of a gold standard, let us consider both the conditions that existed and were specific to the 1870–1913 period and the contributions of the gold standard to the world economic environment. First, this period represents a very peaceful period, with no major wars among the participating nations. Second, there was virtually free capital mobility among nations. Finally, London was the center of the world's money and capital markets.

These latter two characteristics enabled the efficient and smooth functioning of the gold standard. Further, the Bank of England, at the center of the world's financial markets, maintained its gold parity values and established the credibility of the system. The apparent concentration of influence in the London market was so significant that economist J. M. Keynes stated that the Bank of England could almost have claimed to be the "conductor of the international orchestra." We can conclude, therefore, that the early gold standard period had some unique characteristics, at least two of which are not prevalent today.

During this period, most nations did indeed experience stable long-run real economic output, prices, and exchange rates. It is this long-run stability that proponents of a return to a gold standard praise. Because there were short-run random changes in the demand and supply of gold, however, there were also short-run random changes in the money stock and in the prices of goods and services. The short-run volatility of the money stock, in part, led to periodic financial and banking instability. Further, the short-run volatility of prices was greater under the gold standard than under the exchange-rate systems that followed.

The Collapse of the Gold Standard

In 1914, after the beginning of World War I, many European nations suspended convertibility of their currencies into gold. For all practical purposes, the gold standard was no longer in effect, and exchange values between currencies did fluctuate. Many nations, therefore, restricted the types and amounts of international payments that their residents could make in hopes of maintaining the prewar values of their currencies.

Since the beginning of the twentieth century, the leading nations recognized the need for an international organization to facilitate payments among nations. Following World War I, the *Bank for International Settlements (BIS)* was founded as part of an effort to facilitate German reparations. Located in Basel, Switzerland, this organization assists central banks in the management of their external reserves, conducts economic research, and is a forum for international monetary policy cooperation.

World War I formally ended with the signing of the Versailles treaty in 1919. There was a general desire among the leading nations to return to a gold standard at the prewar parities. In 1925, the United Kingdom returned to a gold standard at the prewar parity, but other countries, such as France, returned at much lower values. As a result, many believed that the prewar parity rate would result in an overvalued pound. To maintain the parity value, the United Kingdom had to endure high interest rates and high unemployment. The political costs of maintaining the value of the pound became too great, and the United Kingdom abandoned the gold standard in 1931 by suspending the convertibility of the pound to gold. The United States followed suit in 1933. By 1936, most of the industrialized nations had left the gold standard.

What brought about the demise of the gold standard was a return to parity values that led to overvalued currencies, such as the case with the United Kingdom, or undervalued currencies, such as the case with the French franc. In addition, nations facing a worldwide depression decided to pursue objectives such as higher employment levels and real growth rates, rather than to maintain the exchange value of their currencies.

The collapse of the gold standard, combined with the passage of protectionist trade policies such as the Smoot–Hawley Act in the United States, wreaked havoc on international trade flows. As a result, the volume of international trade in 1933 was less than one-third of its 1929 amount. This, in addition to other prevailing economic factors, contributed to the Great Depression, which began with an industrial depression in the United Kingdom in 1926 and the crash of the stock market in the United States in 1929. The Great Depression continued until the outbreak of World War II.

Bank for International Settlements (BIS)
An institution based in Basel, Switzerland, that serves as an agent for central banks and a center of economic cooperation among the largest industrialized nations.

THE BRETTON WOODS SYSTEM

During World War II, the leaders of the United Kingdom and the United States recognized the importance of having a sound monetary order in place when the war ended. The economies of Europe and Japan would be in great need of rebuilding, and therefore would need imports from nations with intact industrial bases, such as the United States. The nations' leaders pressed for negotiations on an exchange-rate system that would facilitate international trade and payments.

Learn more about the existing Bretton Woods organizations at the International Monetary Fund Web site, *http://www.imf.org*, and the World Bank Group Web site, *http://www.worldbank.org.*

Although forty-four nations participated in the conference that led to the postwar exchange-rate system, the primary architects of the system were Harry White of the U.S. Treasury and the renowned British economist John Maynard Keynes. Negotiations concluded with the ratification of a new system in 1944 at a small resort in Bretton Woods, New Hampshire. The conference, although officially called the International Monetary and Financial Conference of the United and Associated Nations, became known as the Bretton Woods Conference; hence, the agreement reached there became known as the Bretton Woods Agreement.

The Bretton Woods Agreement

International Monetary Fund (IMF)

A multinational organization with more than 180 member nations that seeks to encourage global economic growth by promoting international monetary cooperation and effective exchange arrangements and by providing temporary and longer-term financial assistance to nations experiencing balance-of-payments difficulties.

One significant outcome of the Bretton Woods Agreement was the creation of the *International Monetary Fund,* or *IMF*. The IMF's principal function was to lend to member nations experiencing a shortage of foreign exchange reserves. Nations could become members of the IMF by subscribing, or paying a quota or fee. The size and economic resources of a nation determined the initial quota, with 25 percent of the quota paid in gold and 75 percent in the nation's currency. Two other important institutions that arose at the end of the war were the International Bank for Reconstruction and Development (IBRD), known as the *World Bank,* and the *General Agreement on Tariffs and Trade, (GATT)*. The World Bank financed postwar reconstruction and GATT promoted the reduction of trade barriers and settled trade disputes.

pegged-exchange-rate system

An exchange-rate system in which a country pegs the international value of the domestic currency to the currency of another nation.

The exchange-rate system that emerged from the agreement was one of pegged, but adjustable, exchange rates. Under a *pegged-exchange-rate system,* nations fix the value of their currencies to something other than a commodity, such as another nation's currency. As under a gold standard, each nation pegged its exchange rate. In contrast to a gold standard, the U.S. dollar was the anchor of the system. The Bretton Woods system, therefore, was a *dollar-standard exchange-rate system,* which is a system in which nations peg the value of their currencies to the dollar and freely convert their currencies for the dollar at the pegged value.

dollar-standard exchange-rate system

An exchange-rate system in which a country pegs its currency to the U.S. dollar and freely exchanges the domestic currency for the dollar at the pegged rate.

Under the Bretton Woods Agreement, each country could choose to state the par value of its currency in terms of gold, or establish a par value for its currency relative to the U.S. dollar. All but the United States chose the dollar, making the dollar the common unit of value in the system. Each country would then stand ready to buy and sell U.S. dollars in the foreign exchange market to maintain the exchange value of its currency within 1 percent, on either side, of the par value, commonly referred to as the *parity band.*

The United States, by way of contrast, fixed the value of the U.S. dollar to gold at a mint parity of $35 per troy ounce. The United States agreed to buy

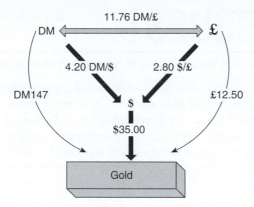

Figure 3–2

The Bretton Woods Exchange-Rate System

In practice, the Bretton Woods system linked all currencies, other than the U.S. dollar, to gold and to each other, through the U.S. dollar. The United States pegged the dollar to gold at a parity rate of $35 per troy ounce. Other nations, such as the United Kingdom and West Germany, pegged their currencies to the dollar. This indirectly established exchange values among the British pound and the deutsche mark, and among the pound and the deutsche mark and gold.

and sell gold with other official monetary agencies in settlement of transactions. Because each country pegged its currency to the U.S. dollar, and the U.S. maintained the value of the dollar relative to gold, this indirectly linked each nondollar currency to gold.

Figure 3–2 illustrates the system and the relationships among gold, the U.S. dollar, the British pound, and the German deutsche mark. The figure shows the dollar with a mint parity value of $35 per troy ounce of gold. The British pound was pegged to the dollar at an exchange rate of 2.80 $/£ and the deutsche mark was pegged to the dollar at an exchange rate of 4.20 DM/$. This system established the link among the British pound and gold, the British pound and the deutsche mark, and the deutsche mark and gold.

Although each country pegged its currency, under the Bretton Woods Agreement it could change the par value with the approval of the IMF. A nation *devalues* its currency when it raises the mint parity value or par value, meaning that a person must offer more units of the currency to purchase a unit of the commodity or foreign currency. A nation *revalues* its currency when it lowers the mint parity value or par value, meaning that one may offer fewer units of the currency to purchase a unit of the commodity or foreign currency. Thus, the Bretton Woods system was an adjustable peg system, rather than a system of fixed exchange rates.

Under the Bretton Woods system, nations used the U.S. dollar to settle international transactions. This made the dollar the primary *reserve currency* of the system, or the currency accepted as a means of settling international debts. Typically, only the United States settled international debts with gold under this system.

One problem encountered during the late 1940s and 1950s was that participating nations did not have sufficient U.S. dollar reserves. The Marshall Plan and the European Payments Union alleviated this dollar-shortage problem. The purpose of the *Marshall Plan,* officially titled the European Recovery Program, was to help rebuild the European economies by supplying financial capital. The inflow of capital funds yielded dollars that the nations could use to conduct current account transactions.

The *European Payments Union* was an arrangement among European nations to help settle deficits and surpluses with each other. Under this arrangement, member nations would track their net monthly deficit or surplus balances with one another. At the end of the month, the nations would settle, in U.S. dollars, only the net balance they had with each other.

devalue

A situation in which a nation with a pegged-exchange-rate arrangement changes the pegged, or parity, value of its currency so that it takes a greater number of domestic currency units to purchase one unit of the foreign currency to which the nation's currency value is pegged.

revalue

A situation in which a nation with a pegged-exchange-rate arrangement changes the pegged, or parity, value of its currency so that it takes a smaller number of domestic currency units to purchase one unit of the foreign currency to which the nation's currency value is pegged.

reserve currency

The currency commonly used to settle international debts and to express the exchange value of other nations' currencies.

#3 What was the Bretton Woods system of "pegged" exchange rates?

The Bretton Woods system was a system of adjustable pegged exchange rates whose parity values could be changed when warranted. Each country established and maintained a parity value of its currency, or peg, relative to gold or the U.S. dollar. All chose the U.S. dollar, making the system a dollar-standard system. Nations could change their parity values, either revaluing or devaluing, with approval of the IMF.

Performance of the Bretton Woods System

Because the United States stated the par value of the dollar in terms of gold while all other participating countries stated their par values in terms of the U.S. dollar, the system had two sets of rules: one for the United States and one for all other countries. Accordingly, the United States had to follow an independent and anti-inflationary monetary policy while standing ready to exchange the dollar for gold at the par value. All other nations had to buy or sell U.S. dollar reserves to keep their domestic currency exchange values against the dollar within the 1 percent parity band.

For most of the period 1945 to 1968, the world economy experienced growth in output and a rapid increase in world trade. Nations did not experience the type of liquidity crises that were prevalent during the gold standard. Consequently, short-run prices were more stable as well. The Bretton Woods system was not without its shortcomings, however.

Because the United States was the only country committed to converting its domestic currency for gold, the system had an inadvertent weakness. Even if the United States followed an anti-inflationary monetary policy, the possibility of a *run on the dollar,* in which traders and official foreign agencies seek to convert the dollar for gold *en masse,* existed. Because there was a limit to the U.S. gold stock, the dollar would not increase in value relative to gold, but it could always decrease in value. This situation made the dollar the target of foreign exchange speculators, as well as nationalistic politicians who opposed the dollar as the standard of the world's exchange-rate system.

The Gold Pool In 1960, the United States and many of the European economies collectively began to intervene in the gold market. The purpose of these interventions was to maintain the dollar price of gold and to ensure the stability of the exchange-rate system. This coordinated arrangement became known as the *gold pool.*

Beginning in 1964, the U.S. government increased federal spending under heightened military involvement in Vietnam and the social programs termed the *Great Society.* The United States experienced a considerable economic expansion accompanied by rising inflation. The United States ran sizable balance-of-payments deficits with Germany and Japan in particular, and as a result, there was a considerable increase in the amount of dollars abroad. What had once been a dollar shortage on the world market was now a dollar glut.

The increase in the volume of dollars on the world market led many traders to believe that the United States would devalue the dollar relative to gold. That is, they anticipated that the dollar's parity value would increase, meaning that they would have to offer more dollars in exchange for a troy ounce of gold. If the parity value of the dollar increased, any individual or government holding dollar reserves would experience a capital loss on those dollar holdings.

In 1967, a devaluation of the British pound, which caused individuals and monetary agencies holding the pound to experience a 14.3 percent capital loss, increased speculation that the United States would devalue the dollar. Because of the speculation that a dollar devaluation was imminent, the demand for gold increased in the London commodities market. To meet the increase in demand and maintain the dollar parity value, the United States had to increase the supply of gold to the market. At one point, U.S. gold sales were so great that the weight of an emergency air shipment from Fort Knox to London collapsed the weighing room floor of the Bank of England.

The participating nations eventually abandoned the gold pool in 1968. Following the end of the gold pool, there was considerable pressure on the central banks of France and Germany to maintain their par values. Eventually, the crisis forced France to devalue the franc relative to the dollar by more than 11 percent. The day after the German elections of September 28, 1969, the German central bank, the *Bundesbank,* sought to maintain the parity value by purchasing $245 million in dollar reserves in the first hour and a half that the market was open. Eventually the deutsche mark was revalued by more than 9 percent. Although these two nations did change their parity values, other European nations did not, so pressure on the system continued.

In early 1971, the U.S. balance on goods and services, illustrated in Figure 3–3, swung from a small surplus to a surprisingly large deficit, further confirming speculation of an overvalued dollar. In May 1971, as the U.S. trade deficit continued to expand, pressure to maintain the parity values between the European currencies, particularly the German mark, and the U.S. dollar climaxed. On May 4, 1971, in order to prevent an appreciation of the deutsche mark relative to the dollar, the Bundesbank bought $1 billion on the exchange market. During the first hour of trading on the following day, the Bundesbank bought more than $1 billion. The Bundesbank then announced that it was abandoning official exchange operations

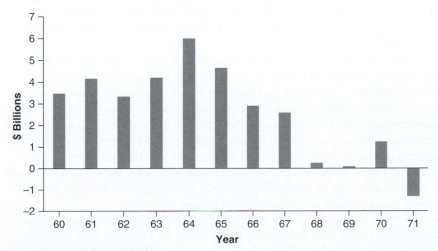

Source: U.S. Bureau of Economic Analysis.

Figure 3–3

The U.S. Balance on Goods, Services, and Income: 1960 through 1971

The U.S. balance on goods and services changed from a small surplus in 1970 to a surprisingly large deficit in 1971. The deficits that emerged early in 1971 reinforced speculations that the dollar was overvalued relative to the other major currencies.

to maintain the parity value. Austria, Belgium, the Netherlands, and Switzerland followed suit.

President Nixon Closes the Gold Window On August 8, 1971, newspapers reported that the French were about to present $191 million of reserves to the United States in exchange for gold so that the French government could make a loan repayment to the IMF. This amount was far short of being a major concern to the United States. In this regard, economist Peter Kenen said, "No one country was large enough to blackmail Washington by demanding gold for dollars, but each was large enough to fear its actions could undermine the monetary system." Nonetheless, speculation against the dollar further increased, and the media reported gold outflows on a daily basis. Eventually, on August 15, 1971, during a televised address, U.S. President Richard Nixon announced that the United States would temporarily suspend the convertibility of the dollar into gold or other reserve assets.

By abandoning the convertibility of the U.S. dollar into gold to foreign central banks, the United States eliminated the anchor of the Bretton Woods system. The incompatibility of U.S. and European macroeconomic policies and the unwillingness of the U.S. government to devalue the dollar or of European governments to revalue their currencies brought about the end of the system. Once again, the world's exchange system was in disarray. Consequently, international trade between nations also fell into a more chaotic state.

The Smithsonian Agreement and the Snake in the Tunnel

In an effort to restore order to the exchange-rate system, the ten nations with the largest share of reserves of the IMF met on December 16 and 17, 1971, at the Smithsonian Institution in Washington, DC. These ten nations—Belgium, Canada, France, Italy, Japan, the Netherlands, Sweden, the United Kingdom, the United States, and West Germany (now Germany)—which together compose the *Group of Ten (G10),* negotiated the Smithsonian Agreement. This established a new exchange-rate system that was similar in many respects to the Bretton Woods system. The agreement established new par values, most representing a revaluation of European currencies relative to the dollar, but with a wider band of 2.25 percent on either side of the parity value. The U.S. dollar, although devalued relative to gold, would not be convertible into gold. Following the conference, President Nixon characterized the agreement to the media as "the most significant monetary agreement in the history of the world."

Shortly after the Smithsonian Agreement, on March 7, 1972, the six member nations of the European Economic Community (EEC; Belgium, France, Italy, Luxembourg, the Netherlands, and West Germany), announced a plan to move toward greater monetary union. The member countries intended to maintain the exchange values of their currencies relative to each other within 2.25 percent. This arrangement became known as the *snake in the tunnel.* Participating nations would maintain exchange values by selling or buying each other's currencies. Collectively, the EEC currencies represented the snake. Whenever the snake would move to the allowable edge of the Smithsonian exchange value—the tunnel—the EEC nations would buy and sell U.S. dollars as needed.

By the middle of 1972, the exchange markets were in turmoil once again. Britain took action first, abandoning the snake in the tunnel in June, only two months after joining. Early in 1973, failure of the Smithsonian Agreement was

Group of Ten (G10)
Belgium, Canada, France, Germany, Italy, Japan, the Netherlands, Sweden, the United Kingdom, and the United States.

on the horizon. Despite enormous diplomatic efforts and a 10 percent devaluation of the dollar against gold by the U.S. Treasury, the European nations participating in the snake announced that they would no longer maintain their parity values relative to outside nations, such as the United States. Thus ended the "most significant monetary agreement in the history of the world," just fifteen months after it began.

THE FLEXIBLE-EXCHANGE-RATE SYSTEM

Although there were attempts to return to some form of an adjustable-pegged system, a *de facto* system of flexible exchange rates emerged. A floating, or *flexible-exchange-rate system,* as described in Chapter 2, is one in which the forces of supply and demand determine a currency's exchange value in the private market. Leading U.S. economists, such as Milton Friedman, had argued in favor of a flexible-exchange-rate arrangement since the early 1950s.

flexible-exchange-rate system
An exchange-rate system whereby a nation allows market forces to determine the international value of its currency.

The Economic Summits and a New Order

Although the world was operating under a floating-rate system, it was not an official system, because the constitution of the IMF forbade floating rates. In 1975, French President Valery Giscard d'Estaing decided to host an informal gathering of the leaders of the major industrialized nations, France, Germany, Italy, Japan, the United Kingdom, and the United States.

Discussions on the exchange-rate system continued between the representatives of the United States and France. On the eve of the summit, the two agreed to a system of flexible exchange rates with coordinated interventions in the foreign exchange market whenever they felt such interventions were required to ensure stability of exchange rates. President Giscard announced the breakthrough at the summit and received immediate endorsement for it from the other participating leaders.

With the leaders of the major industrialized countries endorsing the system envisioned in the French–United States negotiations, the members of the IMF rapidly went about completing the details and revising the constitution of the IMF. Member nations completed the negotiations, known as the *Jamaica Accords,* in Jamaica in 1976.

Within six months of the first economic summit, U.S. president Gerald Ford decided to host an economic summit of his own. President Ford, to the disapproval of President Giscard, also invited Canada to participate. With this action, President Ford institutionalized the summits, now held during the summer of each year and known as the Economic Summit. In 1997, summit host U.S. President William Clinton invited Russian President Boris Yeltsin to attend the summit from beginning to end, although he was excused from the economic meetings. At the 1998 Birmingham summit, British Prime Minister Tony Blair invited President Yeltsin to participate in all the summit meetings, formally expanding the participating nations to eight.

Jamaica Accords
A meeting of the member nations of the IMF, occurring in January 1976, amending the constitution of the IMF to allow, among other things, each member nation to determine its own exchange-rate arrangement.

Performance of the Floating-Rate System

The flexibility of the current exchange-rate system has allowed the major economies to endure some tumultuous economic conditions. Since 1973, which economists recognize as the beginning of the floating-exchange-rate period, the major economies have experienced divergent macroeconomic policies, major internal and external economic shocks, and unprecedented fiscal and current account deficits. By allowing its currency's exchange value to be determined by market forces, a floating-rate country is able to focus monetary policies on domestic objectives. Most nations, however, have experienced periods of dramatic increases and decreases in the exchange values of their currencies.

Learn more about the annual economic summits from the University of Toronto G8 Research Group at *http://www.g8.utoronto.ca.*

Arguably, the greatest challenges to the leading industrialized economies and the exchange-rate system occurred between 1973 and 1974 and in 1979. The outbreak of the Middle East War and an oil embargo imposed in October 1973 resulted in a significant appreciation of the dollar relative to many European currencies and the Japanese yen. In 1979, the Organization of Oil and Petroleum Exporting Countries (OPEC) undertook a series of actions that eventually tripled the price of crude oil on the world market. Already struggling with inflation, oil-importing countries were hard hit by the increase in oil prices. At the end of the 1970s and early 1980s, Canada, France, Italy, the United Kingdom, and the United States were experiencing double-digit or near double-digit rates of inflation.

Also in 1979, U.S. President Jimmy Carter appointed Paul Volcker as chair of the Federal Reserve. Paul Volcker made it publicly known that the Federal Reserve would pursue a single objective of reducing inflation. The Fed's policy actions resulted in a U.S. recession in 1981 and 1982. More important to our discussion, they resulted in very high interest rates and put upward pressure on the value of the dollar relative to other major currencies. (Later chapters examine the effect of monetary policy on interest rates, output, and exchanges rates.) As a result, the dollar began an appreciation that continued until early 1985.

Figure 3–4 illustrates the Federal Reserve's nominal effective exchange value of the dollar relative to several major currencies. The rise of the dollar's value from 1981 through 1985 is one prominent feature of the diagram. The other is the dramatic decline in the dollar's value from 1985 through 1987. We have explained why the dollar appreciated from 1981 through 1985, but why did it peak in 1985 and reverse direction until 1987?

The Plaza Agreement and the Louvre Accord

For some time, the central bankers and finance ministers of a subset of the G10 nations had been meeting to discuss economic conditions and policies. This subgroup included France, Germany, Japan, the United Kingdom, and the United States, and was known as the *Group of Five,* or *G5.* The content, conclusions, and policy outcomes of these meetings had always been secret. In September 1985, the G5 met at the Plaza Hotel in New York to discuss, primarily, the status of the dollar. In an unprecedented move, the participants issued a statement to the media following the meeting. In what is now known as the *Plaza Agreement,* the G5

Group of Five (G5)
The nations of France, Germany, Japan, the United Kingdom, and the United States.

Plaza Agreement
A meeting of the central bankers and finance ministers of the G5 nations that took place at the Plaza Hotel in New York in September 1985. The participants announced that the exchange value of the dollar was too strong and that the nations would coordinate their intervention actions in order to drive down the value of the dollar.

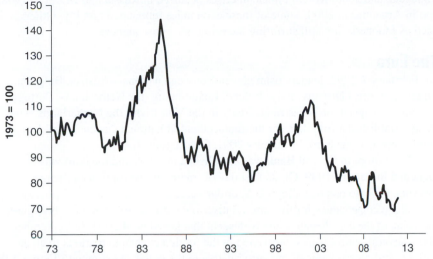

Source: U.S. Federal Reserve Board, http://www.federalreserve.gov.

Figure 3–4

The U.S. Nominal Effective Exchange Rate since 1973 (Nominal Major Currency Index)

Between 1981 and 1985 the U.S. dollar experienced a considerable appreciation in average value relative to several major currencies. Within two years, the appreciation had been reversed. More recently, the U.S. dollar has tended to trade at values below its 1973 level.

announced that it was their belief that the dollar was at a level inconsistent with underlying economic conditions. The G5 said that they would intervene *collectively* to drive down the value of the dollar.

The purpose of the press statement was to convince currency traders that the G5 meant business. The statement and periodic surprise interventions by the G5 appeared to have done just that. As shown in Figure 3–4, the dollar reversed its prior four-year appreciation within the subsequent two years.

Over the next two years, the G5 increased in ranks to include Canada and Italy (becoming consistent with the membership of the annual economic summits at that time). This expanded group is the ***Group of Seven (G7)***. In February 1987, the G7 met at the Louvre in France. Once again the dollar was the focus of discussion. Following the meeting, known as the ***Louvre Accord***, the finance ministers and central bankers announced that the dollar had reached a level now consistent with underlying economic conditions. The G7, therefore, would only intervene in the foreign exchange market as needed to ensure stability.

This meeting defined the exchange-rate management approach of the G7 and G10 economies since 1987. These nations intervene, usually on a collective and unannounced basis, only when a currency or currencies have reached a critical threshold. What is the critical threshold? This is unknown to traders, who are always trying to predict the actions of the finance ministers and central bankers.

Under the Louvre Accord, nations would intervene on behalf of their currencies from time to time. Consequently, the system is not a true flexible exchange-rate system. This type of exchange-rate system is a ***managed float (or dirty float)***, which is a system of flexible exchange rates but with periodic intervention by official agencies.

For the international monetary and financial markets, the 1990s proved no less interesting than the previous two decades. In December 1994, a devaluation of the Mexican peso sparked a financial crisis that caused a collapse in the value of the peso and rattled the economies of Latin America. In 1997, a financial crisis triggered in Thailand affected several economies in East Asia, including Indonesia,

Group of Seven (G7)
The G5 plus Canada and Italy.

Louvre Accord
A meeting of the central bankers and finance ministers of the G7 nations, less Italy, that took place in February 1987. The participants announced that the exchange value of the dollar had fallen to a level consistent with "economic fundamentals" and that central banks would intervene in the foreign exchange market only to ensure the stability of exchange rates.

managed or dirty float
An exchange-rate arrangement in which a nation allows the international value of its currency to be primarily determined by market forces, but intervenes from time to time to stabilize its currency.

Malaysia, and South Korea. Financial crises occurred in Russia and Brazil in 1998, and in Argentina in 2000. Some of these economies rebounded quickly. Others, such as Indonesia, are still suffering the economic consequences.

The Euro

On February 7, 1992, leaders from eleven European nations—Austria, Belgium, Finland, France, Germany, Italy, Ireland, Luxembourg, the Netherlands, Portugal, and Spain—signed the Maastricht Treaty in the Maastricht, the Netherlands. The treaty established a firm date for the replacement of national currencies with a single currency, the euro. In January 2001, Greece joined.

The European Central Bank was established in 1998, and the euro was launched in January 1999. On its first day of trading in the foreign exchange markets, the euro reached a high U.S. dollar value of $1.19. Figure 3–5 provides monthly average values for the euro relative to the dollar. As shown in the figure, the value of the euro began a steady descent that lasted until 2002. In September 2000, several central banks intervened in the foreign exchange markets in an attempt to bolster the value of the euro relative to the dollar. As shown in Figure 3–5, their efforts had only temporary results.

In 2002, euro notes and coins were introduced and central banks began to withdraw national notes and coins from circulation. Finally, in 2002, the euro appreciated relative to the dollar by more than 20 percent without any interventions by central banks.

In the mid-2000s, the euro began a steady appreciation relative to the dollar. This appreciation continued until mid-2008 when the financial crisis spread across many countries. For the next several months, individuals reduced their currency holdings in emerging and developing economies and moved funds to the U.S. dollar as opposed to the euro. The dollar-euro exchange rate stabilized somewhat a few months into 2009, although spillover effects of the crisis into Southern European nations such as Greece caused the euro's value to decline relative to the dollar.

The financial crisis of the late 1990s, the launch of the euro, and the financial crises under way since late in the first decade of this century are very important

Figure 3–5

The Value of the Euro,
1999 to Present

For nearly two years following its introduction, the euro depreciated relative to the dollar. In late 2000, several central banks intervened to support the value of the euro to no avail. Eventually the euro stabilized in the private markets, and began to appreciate relative to the dollar beginning in 2002. This trend continued until the financial crisis of 2008, during which the euro weakened. The euro strengthened once again until 2010, when a debt crisis struck several member countries.

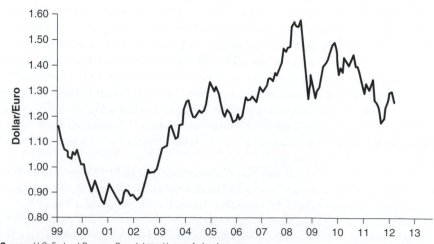

Source: U.S. Federal Reserve Board, http://www.federalreserve.gov.

events that affected and continue to affect financial and monetary markets and policymaking. We shall revisit these events several times throughout the remainder of the text.

Fundamental ISSUES

#4 What post–Bretton Woods system of "flexible" exchange rates prevails today?

Economists typically characterize the post–Bretton Woods exchange-rate system as one of floating exchange rates. Individual nations, however, have adopted a wide variety of exchange-rate arrangements, ranging from pegged to fully flexible exchange rates. Further, the leading industrialized nations periodically intervene in the foreign exchange markets to stabilize their currencies, making the system a managed float as opposed to a truly flexible exchange-rate system.

OTHER FORMS OF EXCHANGE-RATE ARRANGEMENTS TODAY

Since the break-up of the Bretton Woods system, nations have adopted a wide variety of exchange-rate arrangements. Figure 3–6 shows the exchange-rate arrangements that IMF member nations have adopted. The figure shows the percent of those nations that use the currency of another nation or entity as their legal tender, adopt conventional and nonconventional pegs, use limited-flexibility systems, and officially utilize floating systems. The figure shows that nearly 45 percent of member nations claim to have a managed-float or independent-float system.

As Figure 3–6 illustrates, nations have adopted a wide variety of exchange-rate arrangements. The figure, however, does not provide details on the

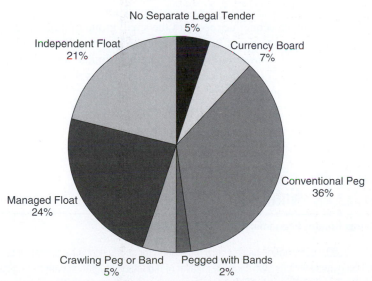

Figure 3–6

Current Foreign Exchange-Rate Arrangements

Currently, more than 44 percent of the member nations of the IMF report to have an independent or managed-float-exchange-rate system. For those countries that peg their currency in some fashion, the U.S. dollar is the most common currency to which they peg their currency values. A currency basket is the second most common currency-peg arrangement.

Source: International Monetary Fund, *Annual Report on Exchange Arrangements and Exchange Restrictions.*

operation of these arrangements. As the 1997 Southeast Asian currency crises painfully showed, the operation of a nation's currency arrangement is of vital importance. Hence, we shall now consider three specific types of arrangements: a crawling peg, a currency-basket peg, and a currency board (or independent currency authority).

Dollarization

Some nations take an even more dramatic approach to exchange-rate management by allowing the currency of another nation to serve as legal tender. As shown in Figure 3–6 on page 73, 21.5 percent of the member nations of the IMF use the currency of another nation. Additional nations also are considering abandoning their domestic currency altogether. This practice is referred to as *dollarization*, but it actually means the use of any other nation's currency, not just the dollar, as legal tender.

Recently Ecuador and El Salvador dollarized their economies. Other Latin American economies already are partially dollarized, and various North, Central, and South American nations, such as Nicaragua and Guatemala, have contemplated dollarization since the late 1990s.

During the early 2000s, dollarization was arguably the leading issue in the field of exchange-rate management. Some economists argue that all developing nations should dollarize. These proponents of dollarization argue that policymakers of small nations bordering large economies with strong currencies should dollarize their economies so as to achieve economic stability. If policymakers give up the national currency and adopt the currency of another nation, the argument goes, they will no longer be able to mismanage their currency. In turn, interest rates and inflation rates should mirror those of the countries whose currency these nations adopted.

Other economists counter that these benefits of dollarization do not outweigh the costs. The costs of dollarization include the loss of discretionary monetary policy and the profits that a central bank generates from producing money. Furthermore, once policymakers choose dollarization, there is no reversing course. Hence, dollarization is typically seen as a last-resort policy action.

After examining the economic record of the small group of dollarized nations, Sebastian Edwards of the National Bureau of Economic Research concluded that dollarized economies have lower rates of inflation than similar nondollarized economies. A cost of this lower inflation rate appears to be a slower rate of economic growth, however. (Having a dollarized economy has created inflation problems for El Salvador in recent years; see *Policy Notebook: U.S. Inflation Creates Economic Pain in El Salvador*.)

POLICY Notebook

U.S. Inflation Creates Economic Pain in El Salvador

Until the late 2000s, dollarization helped lay a foundation for strong economic growth in El Salvador. Doing away with its own currency in favor of monetary integration with its largest trading partner, the United States, enabled El Salvador's government to assure both the nation's citizens and international investors that no unexpected currency devaluations could occur. In addition, adopting the dollar as the nation's currency eliminated all costs of converting currencies for purposes of U.S. trade.

By dollarizing, however, El Salvador effectively outsourced monetary policy to the U.S. central bank, the Federal Reserve. When the annual U.S. inflation rate more than doubled during the 2000s, to above 5 percent at times, so did inflation in El Salvador. Dollar prices of food and crude oil, which El Salvador almost exclusively imports, rose at double-digit annual rates. Thus, the effects of dollar inflation are felt more intensely in El Salvador than in the United States.

For Critical Analysis

Why is El Salvador's government unable to do anything to directly influence the rate of money growth and hence the inflation rate in that nation?

A regional *monetary union,* such as that pioneered by the European Union and discussed earlier in this chapter, is one alternative option to dollarization. This form of regional multilateral policy cooperation is discussed in detail in Chapter 15.

Independent Currency Authorities

Earlier in this chapter, we explained that a gold standard does not require a central bank. Changes in a nation's official gold reserves govern changes in the nation's money stock. A gold standard only requires an official monetary agency that will increase or decrease the money in circulation as required. Some nations today do not have a central bank. Instead, they have an independent monetary authority or currency board.

A ***currency board****, or independent currency authority,* is an independent monetary agency that links the growth of the money stock to the foreign exchange holdings of the currency board. It does this by issuing domestic money in exchange for foreign currency at a fixed exchange rate.

Currency boards were an invention of the British Empire, first established in Mauritius in 1849. The currency-board system peaked in the 1940s and virtually disappeared during the 1960s. The currency board was a means of providing a British colony with a stable and convertible currency. The colony issued its monetary instruments—at a fixed rate of exchange—against the pound sterling assets that the currency board held in London. The colony's money, therefore, was convertible at a fixed rate and was as stable as the pound sterling. The colonies saved considerable resources because they did not need to hold and handle sterling coins and notes.

As practiced today, a currency board pegs its nation's currency to the currency of another nation and buys or sells foreign-currency reserves as appropriate to maintain the parity value. When the monetary authority buys or sells foreign reserves, it changes the amount of domestic money in circulation. This, and this alone, governs changes in the nation's money stock.

The currency board has very limited responsibilities. The currency board does not hold notes or bills issued by the domestic government, does not set reserves requirements on the nation's banks, and does not serve as a lender of last resort to the nation's banks, as a central bank typically does.

currency board or independent currency authority
An independent monetary agency that substitutes for a central bank. The currency board pegs the value of the domestic currency, and changes in the foreign reserve holdings of the currency board determine the level of the domestic money stock.

Because of these limited responsibilities, a currency board cannot engage in discretionary monetary policy, and therefore is shielded from political influence. For this reason, the last few years have seen an increased interest in currency boards. Some economists see currency boards as the best means for some nations to establish a credible approach to price stability.

There are a few independent monetary authorities or currency boards today. Some have been established very recently. Estonia, Lithuania, Hong Kong, and Bulgaria have each established a currency-board arrangement. Some currency boards have been successful, whereas others have failed.

Fundamental ISSUES

#5 What is dollarization, and what is a currency board?

Dollarization is the adoption of another nation's currency as the sole legal tender. Recently, policymakers in Ecuador and El Salvador have dollarized their economies. Policymakers in other nations, such as Nicaragua and Argentina, continue to consider the benefits and costs of dollarization. A currency board (or independent currency authority) supplants a central bank. The responsibilities of a currency board are much more limited than those of a typical central bank. A currency board pegs the value of the domestic currency and buys and sells foreign reserves in order to maintain the pegged value. Changes in the stock of foreign reserves solely determine the domestic money stock. Currency boards, therefore, better isolate monetary policy from domestic political pressures.

Conventional Peg and Pegged with Bands

Currently, the International Monetary Fund considers a pegged-exchange-rate system as one in which policymakers peg the value of the domestic currency at a fixed rate of exchange to a foreign currency. The fixed rate of exchange is called the parity rate. The ***exchange-rate parity bands*** refer to the maximum amounts that the actual exchange rate is allowed to deviate above or below the parity rate. When the parity band allows for a maximum deviation from the parity rate of plus or minus 1 percent, the exchange-rate arrangement is considered a *conventional pegged arrangement*. When the allowed deviation implied by the parity bands is greater than 1 percent, the exchange-rate arrangement is considered a *pegged-exchange rate within horizontal bands*.

Denmark is an example of a system involving a pegged-exchange rate with horizontal bands. Under a framework called ERMII, Denmark pegs the value of the Danish kroner to the euro at a parity rate of 7.46038 (DKr/€). As illustrated in Figure 3–7 on the next page, the spot exchange rate of the krone is allowed to fluctuate within a parity band of plus and minus 2.25 percent (7.62824 and 7.29252, respectively). Denmark has maintained this arrangement since January 1987.

Currency Baskets

The previous section described a pegged-exchange-rate arrangement with bands, which allow for greater flexibility than a currency board or a conventional peg

exchange-rate parity bands

A range of exchange values, with an upper and lower limit within which the exchange value of the domestic currency can fluctuate.

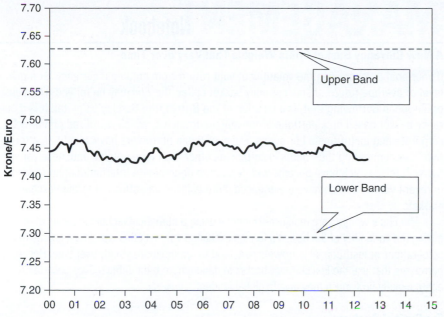

Figure 3–7

Denmark's Peg with Bands

Denmark has maintained a pegged-exchange-rate-with-bands regime to manage the value of its currency relative to the European Currency Unit and, since 1999, relative to the euro. The Danish kroner is allowed to fluctuate within a band of plus and minus 2.25 of the parity rate.

Source: International Monetary Fund, *International Financial Statistics,* http://www.imf.org.

arrangement. For this same reason, policymakers might choose to peg their nation's currency to a weighted average of a number of foreign currencies, known as a *currency-basket peg.* The additional motivation for pegging to a currency basket is that the weighted average of a basket of currencies is likely to be less variable than the exchange rate of a single currency.

To better understand what a currency basket is, imagine that you have six different coins in your hand, each from a different country. Next imagine that you place all of the coins in a basket. Let's allow the sum of the coins in the basket to equal one unit of your own fictitious currency. The value of the coins in the basket is the value at which you would try to maintain your own currency under a currency-basket arrangement.

Selecting a Currency Basket Typically, a nation that adopts a currency-basket peg will have a small number of currencies in the basket. The reason for this is that as the number of currencies to which the nation pegs increases, managing the basket peg becomes more difficult. Most nations using a currency-basket arrangement peg to six or fewer currencies.

The choice of currencies to be included in the basket is similar to the choice made in constructing an effective exchange rate, as discussed in Chapter 2. A basket typically includes selected currencies most prominent in the nation's international trade, capital flows, or international debt settlement. The basket assigns a weight to each currency, similar to the construction of an effective exchange rate. The weights sum to unity as well. The choice of weights reflects the relative importance of each currency in the nation's international transactions. (To consider why private borrowers might choose to use a currency basket to denominate their debts, see on the next page the *Management Notebook: A New Currency Basket Offers Weights That Vary over Time.)*

currency-basket peg

An exchange-rate arrangement in which a country pegs its currency to the weighted average value of a basket, or selected number, of currencies.

MANAGEMENT Notebook

Managing the Currency Basket Under a pegged-exchange-rate arrangement, the nation's monetary authority maintains the exchange rate between the domestic currency and the currency that the nation is pegging to. A currency-basket arrangement introduces an interesting wrinkle. The authority must concentrate on the exchange rate between the domestic currency and the currencies included in the currency basket *and* the cross rates between the currencies in the basket. If these cross rates change, the monetary authority must take action, either depreciating or appreciating the nation's currency so as to maintain the currency-basket value. The weights determine the amount of appreciation or depreciation.

Crawling Pegs

Even after the collapse of the Bretton Woods system, some nations have decided to peg their currencies to the currencies of other nations. There are a number of reasons why a nation may choose to do this. The most common argument for pegged exchange rates is that reducing exchange-rate volatility and uncertainty may yield gains in economic efficiency. Thus, nations that have a large volume of trade with another nation, but a less stable currency, may choose to peg their currency. Pegging to another nation's currency and reducing exchange-rate volatility therefore may promote greater trade and capital flows between the two nations.

The economic conditions of the two nations, however, may be quite different. In later chapters, particularly Chapters 10 through 13, you will see that when the economic conditions of two nations differ, the paths of their exchange rates will likely differ. This situation would make it difficult, if not impossible, to maintain a pegged exchange rate. In this situation, nations that peg the value of their currencies to the currencies of other nations may allow the parity value to continuously change. This type of exchange-rate arrangement is a ***crawling peg.***

crawling peg
An exchange-rate arrangement in which a country pegs its currency to the currency of another nation, but allows the parity value to change at regular time intervals.

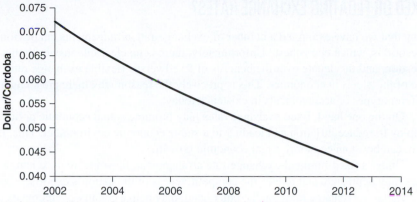

Figure 3–8

Nicaragua's Crawling Peg

Nicaragua's crawling-peg exchange-rate arrangement allows for a steady monthly rate of crawl, or depreciation, of the córdoba relative to the U.S. dollar.

Source: International Monetary Fund, International Financial Statistics, http://www.imf.org.

Nicaragua's Crawling-Peg Arrangement Nicaragua's exchange arrangement of the early 2000s is a very good example of a crawling peg. To promote exchange-rate stability and facilitate exports, Nicaragua pegged the value of its domestic currency, the córdoba, to the U.S. dollar. U.S. and Nicaraguan macroeconomic conditions were quite different, as U.S. inflation remained well below inflation in Nicaragua. Because of this inflation difference, Nicaraguan officials realized that, according to the theory of purchasing power parity, there would be a general tendency for the córdoba to depreciate against the U.S. dollar. Hence, Nicaragua adopted a crawling peg. Figure 3–8 shows, over the entire period, a depreciation of the córdoba relative to the U.S. dollar. As you can see, the córdoba has depreciated at a fairly steady rate.

Some countries, such as Columbia and Chile, have combined features of a crawling peg with the additional flexibility allowed by an exchange-rate band. This type of arrangement is a *crawling band*. Like an exchange-rate band, a crawling band features an upper and lower parity limit. The central parity, however, is adjusted on a regular basis. The upper and lower parity limits, therefore, change on a regular basis, usually allowing for a steady rate of depreciation.

Fundamental ISSUES

#6 What types of pegged-exchange-rate arrangements are used today?

A pegged-exchange-rate arrangement is when policymakers peg the value of the domestic currency at a given parity rate of exchange to a foreign currency. A conventional pegged arrangement allows for a maximum deviation of plus or minus 1 percent from the parity rate, whereas a pegged-with-bands arrangement allows for a deviation of greater than plus and minus 1 percent. Basket-peg and crawling-peg exchange-rate arrangements are other types of pegged-exchange-rate arrangements. Under a basket-peg arrangement, officials peg the domestic currency to a weighted-average value of a small number of currencies. Under a crawling peg, the parity value and the exchange-rate bands are allowed to change at regular intervals. Pegged-with-bands, currency-basket-pegs, and crawling-peg arrangements provide more flexibility than a conventional pegged-exchange-rate arrangement.

FIXED OR FLOATING EXCHANGE RATES?

Now that we have examined a number of exchange-rate arrangements, an obvious question is, which one is best? Unfortunately, there is no clear-cut answer to this question, and the debate over the benefits of fixed versus flexible exchange rates is one of the oldest in economics. This is precisely the reason why there are so many different types of arrangements in existence today.

On the one hand, fixed exchange rates may promote sound economic policy, helping to reduce inflation and leading to a stable economic environment. This, in turn, can boost an economy's real economic growth.

Under a fixed-nominal-exchange-rate arrangement, however, real exchange rates may appreciate and reduce the competitiveness of the nation's exports.

Flexible exchange rates, on the other hand, may help a country overcome external shocks, such as an unusual inflow of capital from abroad or a sudden increase in the price of an imported resource. Flexible exchange rates introduce an additional element of uncertainty and additional volatility, which is the common criticism of flexible rates. In the industrialized nations, however, there is no clear evidence showing that volatility of nominal exchange rates dampens foreign trade or investment.

What is more important than the type of exchange-rate arrangement is that a nation's policymakers conduct sound economic policy. This is perhaps the most overlooked reality in the debate over fixed versus flexible exchange rates. Further, the debate often contrasts the current and imperfect regime with a utopian version of another regime in which governments always conduct policymaking such that it is consistent with the exchange-rate regime. As was shown throughout this chapter, that is not always the case. We shall return to these issues in more detail in Chapters 12 through 15.

 **Fundamental ISSUES**

#7 Which is best, a fixed- or flexible-exchange-rate arrangement?

Whether it is better to peg the value of the domestic currency or allow it to be flexible and market determined is one of the longest-running debates in economics. There is no clear-cut answer, as each arrangement has it own advantages and disadvantages. Sound economic policymaking is more important in creating a stable economic environment than the choice of an exchange-rate arrangement.

Chapter SUMMARY

1. **Exchange-Rate Arrangements or Exchange-Rate Systems:** An exchange-rate arrangement or exchange-rate system is a nation's set of rules that determines the international exchange value of the domestic currency and links a nation's currency value to the currencies of other nations.

2. **A Gold Standard as an Exchange-Rate Arrangement or Exchange-Rate System:** A gold standard constitutes an exchange-rate arrangement for a nation. With a rule of pegging the value of its currency to gold, a nation establishes the international value of its currency in terms of gold. A gold standard also constitutes an exchange-rate system

among those nations adopting a gold standard. With the value of each currency established relative to gold, the exchange value among currencies is also established.

3. **The Bretton Woods System of "Pegged" Exchange Rates:** Under the Bretton Woods system, nations pegged the value of their currencies to the U.S. dollar, which was linked to gold. The parity values that nations pegged their currencies at could be changed, and thus the currency devalued or revalued, with the permission of the IMF. The Bretton Woods system was, therefore, a system of adjustable pegged exchange rates.

4. **The Post–Bretton Woods System of "Flexible" Exchange Rates:** In today's world economy, numerous exchange-rate arrangements are in place, ranging from flexible-exchange-rate arrangements to fixed- or pegged-exchange-rate arrangements. The leading industrialized nations intervene from time to time in the foreign exchange markets. The overall system, therefore, is primarily one of managed floating exchange rates.

5. **Dollarization and a Currency Board or Independent Currency Authority:** Dollarization is the adoption of another nation's currency as the sole legal tender. Recently the nations of Ecuador and El Salvador dollarized by adopting the U.S. dollar as their sole legal currency. A principal argument for dollarization is that it will reduce inflation and interest rates to mirror those of the nation whose currency is adopted. Although comparative empirical evidence on the economic performance of dollarized economies is limited, this evidence indicates that dollarized economies have lower rates of inflation and economic growth than similar nondollarized economies. A currency board substitutes for a central bank but the responsibilities of a currency board are much more limited. The currency board pegs the value of the nation's currency to another nation's currency. It is responsible for maintaining the pegged value of the domestic currency by conditioning the nation's outstanding stock of money on the amount of foreign currency reserves held by the currency board.

6. **Pegged-Exchange-Rate Arrangements:** Policymakers in some nations seek to stabilize the exchange-rate value of their domestic currency through a pegged-exchange-rate arrangement in which the value of the domestic currency is fixed at a given parity rate of exchange to a foreign currency. A conventional pegged arrangement allows for a maximum deviation of plus or minus 1 percent from the parity rate, whereas a pegged-with-bands arrangement allows for a deviation of greater than plus and minus 1 percent. Other policymakers desire the stability of a fixed exchange rate but find it difficult to maintain a rigid parity value. As a result, some nations have adopted either a basket-peg or a crawling-peg exchange-rate arrangement. Under a basket-peg exchange-rate arrangement, a nation pegs the value of its currency to the value of a basket of selected currencies. Under a crawling-peg exchange-rate arrangement, a nation pegs the value of its currency, but the parity rate is adjusted at given time intervals.

7. **Fixed- versus Flexible-Exchange-Rate Arrangements:** There is no clear-cut answer as to whether it is better to peg the value of a nation's currency or to allow the value of the currency to be determined in the market for foreign exchange. Each type of exchange-rate arrangement has its benefits and its costs. Sound economic policymaking is actually more important in creating a sound and stable economic environment than is the choice of exchange-rate arrangement.

QUESTIONS and PROBLEMS

1. Following each statement, write in the name of the exchange-rate regime you think best describes the regime.
   a. The value of the currency is anchored to a given value of another currency and can only deviate by as little as 0.5 percent above or 0.5 percent below that value.
   b. The value of the currency is anchored to a given value of another currency and can only deviate by as little as 1 percent above or 1 percent below that value. That value, however, is increased every trading period.
   c. Only the forces of supply and demand determine the value of the currency.
   d. The value of the currency is anchored to the weighted-average value of a selected group of currencies.
   e. The currency authority anchors the value of the domestic currency one-to-one to the euro. The authority will issue domestic currency notes only when its reserves of the euro rise.
   f. The domestic currency has been replaced with the euro and the euro is the sole legal tender, but the domestic country is not part of the European Monetary Union.
   g. Monetary authorities pretty much let the currency value be determined by market forces, but they will intervene from time to time to move the value in the "right" direction.

2. Describe two primary functions of the International Monetary Fund.

3. Suppose the value of the U.S. dollar is pegged to gold at a rate of $50 per ounce. Next suppose that the value of the British pound is pegged to the U.S. dollar at a rate of $1.50 per pound, and the value of the Canadian dollar is pegged to the U.S. dollar at a rate of $1.38 Canadian dollars per U.S. dollars. Calculate the value of the Canadian dollar and the British pound relative to gold.

4. Using the information in Problem 3, calculate the exchange rate between the Canadian dollar and the British pound.

5. Suppose Argentina decides to peg the value of its currency, the peso, to a basket consisting of 0.50 U.S. dollars and 0.50 euros. Further suppose the exchange rate between the U.S. dollar and the euro is 1.10 $/€. If the basket constitutes one peso, what is the appropriate exchange value between the peso and the dollar, and between the peso and the euro?

6. Based on the information in Problem 5, what is the weight assigned to the U.S. dollar in the currency basket? What is the weight assigned to the euro?

7. Explain the main difference between the exchange-rate systems of the Smithsonian Agreement and the Bretton Woods system. Based on this difference, why do you think the Smithsonian Agreement was so short lived?

8. What is the principal responsibility of a currency board? What three main restrictions on a currency board make it different from a typical central bank?

9. Explain how the Louvre Accord represented a type of exchange-rate system.

10. What factors do you think should be considered when determining the rate of crawl for a crawling-peg exchange-rate system?

11. What, in your opinion, is the chief difference between dollarization and a currency-board system?

Online APPLICATIONS

Along with the IMF and the World Bank, the Bank for International Settlements (BIS) is an important international financial institution. The BIS, however, is perhaps the least known and understood of the three institutions.

Internet URL: *http://www.bis.org*

Title: The Bank for International Settlements

Navigation: Begin at the home page for the BIS located at the Internet URL provided above. Click on the "About BIS" link. Next click on "The BIS in Profile" in the *Related Information* window.

Application: After reading the document titled "The BIS in Profile" and all its parts, answer the following questions.

1. When was the BIS founded, and what is unique about the BIS as an international financial organization?

2. What are the primary services of the BIS?

3. Approximately how many central banks and financial institutions have deposits with the BIS? What is the approximate staff size of the BIS, and from how many nations does the staff come?

4. Approximately what percentage of the world's foreign exchange reserves is held by the BIS?

SELECTED REFERENCES and FURTHER READINGS

Altig, David E. "Dollarization: What's in It for US?" *Federal Reserve Bank of Cleveland, Economic Commentary* (October 15, 2002).

Berg, Andrew, and Eduardo Borensztein. "Full Dollarization: The Pros and Cons." International Monetary Fund, *Economic Issues 24* (December 20, 2000).

Bryant, Ralph C. *Turbulent Waters: Cross-Border Finance and International Governance.* Washington, DC: Brookings Institution Press, 2003.

Calvo, Guillermo A., and Carmen M. Reinhart. "Fear of Floating." NBER Working Paper Number W7993 (November 2000).

Corden, W. Max. *Too Sensational: On the Choice of Exchange Rate Regimes.* Cambridge, MA: MIT Press, 2002.

Craig, Ben, and Christopher Waller. "Dual-Currency Economies as Multiple-Payments Systems." *Federal Reserve Bank of Cleveland Economic Review 36*(1) (Quarter 1, 2000): 2–13.

Daniels, Joseph, Peter Toumanoff, and Marc von der Ruhr. "Optimal Basket-Peg Arrangements for Developing Nations." *Journal of Economic Integration* (March 2001).

Edwards, Sebastian. "Dollarization and Economic Performance: An Empirical Investigation." NBER Working Paper Number W8274 (May 2001).

Edwards, Sebastian, and Igal Magendzo. "A Currency of One's Own? An Empirical Investigation on Dollarization and Independent Currency Unions." National Bureau of Economic Research, Working Paper 9515 (February 2003).

Eichengreen, Barry. *Exorbitant Privilege*. Oxford: Oxford University Press, 2011.

Eichengreen, Barry. *Global Imbalances and the Lessons of Bretton Woods*. Cambridge, MA: MIT Press, 2007.

Garnham, Peter. "Currency Swings Span the Ebu." *Financial Times* (September 23, 2007).

Ghosh, Atish, R., Anne-Marie Gulde, and Holger C. Wolf. *Exchange Rate Regimes*. Cambridge, MA: MIT Press, 2002.

Ho, Corrinne. "A Survey of the Institutional and Operational Aspects of Modern-Day Currency Boards." Bank for International Settlements, Working Paper No. 100 (March 2002).

Salvatore, Dominick, James W. Dean, and Thomas Willett, eds. *The Dollarization Debate*. New York: Oxford University Press, 2003.

Tavlas, George S., and Michael K. Ulan. *Exchange Rate Regimes and Capital Flows*. Thousand Oaks, CA: Sage Publications, 2002.

von Furstenberg, George M. "Can Small Countries Keep Their Own Money and Floating Exchange Rates?" In K. Kaiser, J. Kirton, and J. Daniels, eds., *Shaping a New International Financial System: Challenges of Governance in a Globalizing World*. Aldershot: Ashgate Publishing, 2000: 187–202.

Yeyati, Eduardo Levy, and Federico Sturzenegger. *Dollarization: Debates and Policy Alternatives*. Cambridge, MA: MIT Press, 2003.

PART 2

■

INTERNATIONAL FINANCIAL INSTRUMENTS, MARKETS, AND INSTITUTIONS

4 The Forward Currency Market and International Financial Arbitrage

5 Interest Yields, Interest-Rate Risk, and Derivative Securities

6 International Banking, Central Banks, and Supranational Financial Policymaking Institutions

7 The International Financial Architecture and Emerging Economies

4

The Forward Currency Market and International Financial Arbitrage

Fundamental ISSUES

1. What is foreign exchange risk?
2. What is the forward currency market, and how are forward exchange rates determined?
3. What is covered interest parity?
4. What is uncovered interest parity?
5. What is foreign exchange market efficiency?
6. What are the international financial markets?

For many financial firms on Wall Street and elsewhere around the globe, volatility in asset prices resulting from fluctuations in interest rates made the late 2000s and early 2010s a difficult business climate. Nevertheless, increased exchange-rate variability accompanied the increased volatility in interest rates and asset prices. This rise of exchange-rate instability generated an increase in demand for financial firms' services in reducing clients' exposures to various foreign exchange risks— risks that values of future receipts or obligations will change due to variations in exchange rates. As a consequence, these institutions recorded all-time highs in fee income earned from providing foreign-exchange-risk-reducing services. Indeed, at a number of financial firms, higher fee earnings did much to help offset losses they experienced resulting from declining asset prices. Thus, greater volatility of both exchange rates and interest rates had mixed effects on the profits of a number of financial firms.

What is the relationship between exchange rates and interest rates? How does exchange-rate instability result in greater volatility of interest rates? How do political and fiscal uncertainty affect interest rates? Are foreign exchange markets efficient? In this chapter we examine these questions, particularly the relationship between interest and exchange rates.

FOREIGN EXCHANGE RISK

In Chapter 2 we examined the role of exchange rates in the international market-place. In Chapter 3 you learned that the exchange values of many currencies float and are determined in the foreign exchange market. Consequently, exchange rates vary over time. These exchange rate changes expose households, firms, and others who engage in international transactions to potential risk.

Let's construct an example to show how an international transaction may involve risk from exchange rate changes. Suppose you work for an international property developer based in the United States, and your firm has an interest in commercial real estate in the United Kingdom. The property agents will consider "substantial offers" on the property for a period of three months, at which time they will arrange sale of the property to the party submitting the highest offer. It will take approximately three more months for your employer to close on the transaction and assume possession of the property.

Based on an estimate of the income potential of the property, your managers instruct you to submit a bid of £10 million. Further, suppose that the exchange rate is currently 1.500 dollars per pound ($/£). From your firm's perspective, the price of the bid that you are submitting is $15 million, which is the dollar price of the offer (£10 million × 1.500 $/£ = $15 million). What your managers have communicated to you is that they value the property in the neighborhood of $15 million.

If the sellers of the property accept your offer, you will pay the owner of the property £10 million upon closing, six months from now. Upon acceptance of the offer, your firm has a foreign-currency-denominated obligation that spans time and, therefore, creates a *foreign exchange risk exposure*. **Foreign exchange risk** is the prospect that the value of a foreign-currency-denominated liability or asset will change because of a change in the exchange rate.

Suppose that over the course of the next six months the dollar were to depreciate against the British pound by 5 percent, to 1.575 dollars per pound. In our example, the British pound price of the commercial real estate would still be £10 million. The dollar price, however, would change because of the change in the spot rate. The dollar price of the property would then be $15.75 million (£10 million × 1.575 $/£ = $15.75 million). Because of the change in the exchange rate, the dollar price of the property would rise 5 percent, or $750,000. By agreeing to the future of foreign-currency-denominated transaction, your firm would have incurred an additional 5 percent cost from foreign exchange risk exposure.

Types of Foreign Exchange Risk Exposure

An individual or firm may be exposed to foreign exchange risk in any of three different ways. The first type of foreign exchange exposure, as in our example, is transaction exposure. *Transaction exposure* is the risk that the cost of a transaction, or the proceeds from a transaction, in terms of the domestic currency, may change. A transaction exposure is created when a firm agrees to complete a foreign-currency-denominated transaction some time in the future.

The second type of foreign exchange risk is *translation exposure,* which arises when translating the values of foreign-currency-denominated assets and liabilities into a single currency value. It is easier to understand translation exposure by considering the balance sheet of a multinational corporation. The assets and liabilities, say, of a Swiss multinational corporation, may be denominated in many different currencies. At the end of the year, the accountants at the Swiss corporation tabulate

foreign exchange risk
The risk that the value of a future receipt or obligation will change due to a change in foreign exchange rates.

transaction exposure
The risk that the cost of a transaction, or the proceeds from a transaction, in terms of the domestic currency, may change due to changes in exchange rates.

translation exposure
Foreign exchange risk that results from the conversion of the value of a firm's foreign-currency-denominated assets and liabilities into a common currency value.

the corporation's balance sheet and value all its assets and liabilities in a common currency, the Swiss franc. As the exchange value of the Swiss franc changes, so does the value of assets and liabilities denominated in a foreign currency. The net worth of the company, as reported in the balance sheet, also changes.

economic exposure
The risk that changes in exchange values might alter a firm's present value of the future income streams.

The final type of foreign exchange risk is *economic exposure,* which is the effect that exchange-rate changes have on a firm's present value of future income streams. Economic exposure affects the ability of a firm to compete in a particular market over an extended period. Some economists believe that at least a portion of foreign direct investment results from firms trying to avoid economic exposure. By owning a plant or office in a foreign location of operation, the firm may avoid some of the foreign exchange risk that it would have incurred if all its plants and offices were in domestic locations only.

Hedging Foreign Exchange Risk

hedging
The act of offsetting or eliminating risk exposure.

covered exposure
A foreign exchange risk that has been completely eliminated with a hedging instrument.

When considering foreign exchange risk, it is important to understand that a change in the exchange rate may be positive or negative from the perspective of an individual or firm. Nonetheless, the possibility that the exchange rate may change introduces uncertainty that can make successful planning difficult. An individual or firm decreases or mitigates this uncertainty by reducing or eliminating the foreign exchange risk. *Hedging* is the act of offsetting exposure to risk. An exposure is a *covered exposure* if the hedging activity eliminates *all* of the exposure to risk.

Numerous financial instruments are available to offset foreign exchange risk. In this chapter we examine both covered and uncovered transactions. Chapter 5 examines a variety of hedging instruments, which may or may not fully cover an exposure to foreign exchange risk. (Multinational companies do not always rely solely on financial instruments to hedge against foreign exchange risks; see *Management Notebook: Japanese Automakers Ramp Up U.S. Production to Hedge against a Depreciating Dollar.*)

MANAGEMENT Notebook

Japanese Automakers Ramp Up U.S. Production to Hedge against a Depreciating Dollar

As the U.S. dollar continued to depreciate against the yen during the early 2010s, profits of Japanese automakers Toyota and Honda were reduced. The significant drop in the dollar's value generated large increases in the dollar prices of vehicles exported from Japan to the United States, and the resulting fall in export sales resulted in plummeting export revenues.

In an effort to offset the profit decline and to hedge against future profit falloffs, Japanese automakers began ramping up production of automobiles in the United States. Producing more vehicles in the United States resulted in both production costs and revenues from U.S. sales being denominated in dollars. Hence, this shift in the location of vehicle production provided a natural hedge for Japanese automakers looking to insulate themselves from some of the foreign exchange risks they faced.

Of course, Japanese automakers still faced the fact that the dollar's depreciation meant that dollar-denominated profits earned in the United States translated into fewer profits denominated in yen. To address this source of foreign exchange risks, the automakers had to turn to financial instruments.

For Critical Analysis

How might exposure to foreign exchange risks help to explain why most of the world's large-scale manufacturers operate production facilities in several nations?

Fundamental ISSUES

#1 What is foreign exchange risk?

Foreign exchange risk is the effect that uncertain future values of the exchange rate may have on the value of a foreign-currency-denominated obligation, receipt, asset, or liability. There are three types of exposure to foreign exchange risk: transaction exposure, translation exposure, and economic exposure. In principle, an individual or firm can offset, or hedge, some or all of the exposure to foreign exchange risk. The individual or firm covers the exposure by completely eliminating the risk.

THE FORWARD EXCHANGE MARKET

Chapter 2 examined the spot market for foreign exchange, which is the market for immediate delivery of a foreign currency. Let's assume again that you work for the U.S. property developer with an offer on a U.K. property. It is highly unlikely that your firm would want to purchase the British pound at the time of notification of acceptance of your company's offer. By immediately purchasing the pound, the firm would have $15 million of working capital tied up in a foreign currency for six months. Your firm, therefore, would desire the future delivery of the British pound.

The *forward exchange market* is a market for contracts ensuring the future delivery of a currency at a specified exchange rate. Most forward exchange trades are in the amount of $1 million or more and occur between large commercial banks.

forward exchange market
A market for contracts that ensure the future delivery of a foreign currency at a specified exchange rate.

Covering a Transaction with a Forward Contract

Because a forward contract guarantees a rate of exchange at a future date, it can eliminate foreign exchange risk, or *cover* an exposure. In our example, following acceptance of your firm's offer on the commercial property, the firm has a *short position* in the pound, because it has a future obligation denominated in a foreign currency, the pound. As explained earlier, the firm now has a foreign exchange risk exposure. You could suggest to your superiors that the firm purchase a six-month forward contract on the pound, which would cover the transaction.

Suppose that at the time the property agents accept your firm's offer, the six-month forward rate on the pound is 1.520 $/£. A six-month forward contract for £10 million guarantees that your firm can purchase the £10 million six months from now at an exchange rate of 1.520 $/£. The forward contract guarantees that the final price of the commercial property will be $15,200,000 (£10 million × 1.520 $/£ = $15,200,000). There is no uncertainty about the price of the property, so the transaction is covered.

Firms also can experience transaction exposures that result from foreign-currency-denominated payments that they will receive in the future. In these situations, firms have *long positions,* because they will receive amounts denominated in foreign currencies in the future. In this case, the firms could purchase forward contracts enabling them to sell foreign currencies at guaranteed exchange rates. The forward sell contracts would eliminate all of their foreign exchange risks and would thus cover their receipts.

In both of these examples, firms eliminated positions that had foreign exchange risks by purchasing forward contracts with opposite positions. Firms with short positions in foreign currencies can assume long positions in the forward market by purchasing forward contracts guaranteeing payments denominated in foreign currencies. Firms with long positions in foreign currencies can assume short positions in the forward market by selling currencies in the forward exchange market. By assuming equal and offsetting positions in the forward market, firms can eliminate the uncertainty inherent in their transactions.

Determination of Forward Exchange Rates

For most currencies the forward exchange rates differ from the spot rate, and the forward rates for contracts with different maturity periods typically differ. What determines forward exchange rates?

If there are no currency restrictions or government interventions, the market forces of supply and demand determine forward exchange rates. Figure 4–1 illustrates the downward-sloping demand and upward-sloping supply schedules of the forward exchange market for the British pound. Suppose that a large number of firms and individuals increase their demands for British pounds to be delivered six months from now, perhaps because they have short positions in the pound, as in our previous example.

The Forward Exchange Rate as a Predictor of the Future Spot Rate

The forward exchange rate reflects the supply and demand for a currency for future delivery. It is possible, therefore, that the forward rate provides information on the future spot exchange rate.

Figure 4–1

The Forward Market for the Pound

Initially, the forward market for the pound is in equilibrium at the forward rate of 1.520 $/£. or F_1. With an increase in the demand for the pound forward, the demand schedule shifts to the right from $D_£$ to $D'_£$. For a given supply, the increase in the demand causes the forward rate to rise to F_2, which is an increase in the dollar price of the pound forward.

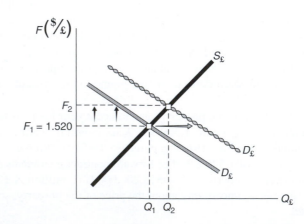

Suppose again that the six-month forward rate for the British pound is 1.520 \$/£ and that the spot rate is 1.500 dollars per pound. Because the dollar-per-pound forward exchange rate is greater than the dollar-per-pound spot exchange rate, the pound is said to trade at a ***forward premium***. In contrast, if the forward exchange rate of a currency is less than the spot exchange rate, the currency is said to trade at a ***forward discount.*** Economists usually state the forward premium or discount in a standardized manner by calculating the *standard forward premium* or *discount* as a percentage and expressing it in annual terms.

forward premium or discount
The difference between the forward exchange rate and the spot exchange rate, expressed as a percentage of the spot exchange rate.

To do this they use the following formula:

$$\text{Standard forward premium/discount} = (F_N - S)/S \times 12/N \times 100,$$

where F_N is the forward rate, S is the spot rate, and N is the number of months of the forward contract. This formula has three parts. The first part is the forward premium, which is the difference between the forward exchange rate and the spot exchange rate relative to the spot rate, expressed as $(F_N - S)/S$. The second part annualizes the forward premium by dividing by the number of months of the contract, expressing the forward premium on a monthly basis, and then multiplying by 12 to express the forward premium on an annual basis. The last part multiplies the annual forward premium by 100 to express it as a percentage. In our example the standard forward premium is

$$(F_N - S)/S \times 12/N \times 100 = (1.520 - 1.500)/1.500 \times 12/6 \times 100$$
$$= 2.667 \text{ percent.}$$

Now let's suppose that a foreign currency trader believes that the pound will appreciate against the dollar by 5 percent over the next six months. The trader's expectation of future appreciation of the pound is different from the forward premium of the pound. Hence, the trader may attempt to profit through a forward currency transaction.

Suppose the trader purchases £1 million forward at a forward rate of 1.520 \$/£. Next let's suppose that the trader's expectation is correct and the pound appreciates by 5 percent, from a rate of 1.500 \$/£ to 1.575 \$/£. In the assumed absence of transaction and opportunity costs, the trader will pay \$1,520,000 to purchase the £1 million forward (£1 million × 1.5200 \$/£ = \$1,520,000). The £1 million that the trader purchased forward will exchange on the spot market at a rate of 1.575 \$/£ to obtain \$1,575,000 (£1 million × 1.575 \$/£ = \$1,575,000), netting a profit of \$55,000.

If other traders share the same expectation, then there is an increase in the total demand for the pound on the forward market. As shown in Figure 4–1, an increase in the demand for the pound on the forward market places upward pressure on the value of pound in the forward market, thereby increasing the amount of the forward premium and eliminating the difference between the forward premium and the expected appreciation. Hence, the following equilibrium condition would hold:

$$(F_N - S)/S = (S_N^e - S)/S,$$

where S_N^e is the spot exchange rate expected to prevail N months from now. In words, this condition states that the forward premium must equal the expected appreciation of the currency, and the forward discount must equal the expected depreciation of the currency.

Based on this equilibrium condition, we might expect a close relationship between the forward exchange rate and the realized future spot exchange rate. This is the reason that we might also expect the forward exchange rate to have some predictive power for movements in the spot rate. Many empirical studies indicate that there is some co-movement between the forward premium or discount and the actual future spot rate. The co-movement is not one-to-one, however. The forward exchange rate sometimes overestimates the future spot exchange rate and sometimes underestimates the future spot exchange rate. We must conclude, therefore, that the forward premium has limited ability in forecasting the future spot exchange rate.

In Chapter 2, you learned about relative purchasing power parity, a condition that relates inflation differentials to exchange-rate changes. Forward exchange-rate premiums and expected changes in spot exchange rates are affected by interest rate differentials. In the following sections, you will explore how economics models the forces of supply and demand that determine interest rates. You will also learn about conditions that relate interest rates to forward exchange-rate premiums and expected spot exchange rates.

 Fundamental ISSUES

#2 What is the forward currency market, and how are forward exchange rates determined?

The forward currency market is the market for contracts that oblige the future delivery of a foreign currency at a specified exchange rate. If there are no exchange controls or government intervention, the forces of supply and demand determine the forward exchange rate in the forward currency market. Some consider the forward exchange rate to be a predictor of the expected future spot rate. In practice, however, the forward exchange rate has limited ability in forecasting the future spot exchange rate.

INTERNATIONAL FINANCIAL ARBITRAGE

Chapter 2 presented the theories of absolute and relative purchasing power parity. As was explained, these are theories of international arbitrage in goods and services. Individuals can also seek profits in the financial markets by shifting funds into interest-bearing assets of other nations.

For example, suppose the interest rate on a U.S. financial instrument is 3.5 percent while the interest rate on a British financial instrument with all the same characteristics, such as risk and length to maturity, is 1.5 percent. Would a saver want to move funds from Britain to the United States? The answer depends on whether the actual return *realized* upon maturity is greater for the U.S. financial instrument as compared with the British financial instrument. The realized return, in turn, depends on the net change in the exchange rate of the British pound relative to the dollar over the life of the asset.

The International Flow of Funds and Interest Rate Determination

If the expected exchange-rate-adjusted return on a similar instrument were greater in one nation as compared with another, and if there were no restrictions on capital flows, then we would see savers move funds from one nation to another. This flow of funds could potentially affect interest rates in both nations, as well as the exchange rate between their currencies. In a competitive market, the supply of and demand for funds available for lending, or *loanable funds,* determine interest rates.

Supply Individuals who save supply loanable funds. There is a positive relationship between the quantity of funds that individuals are willing to save and the rate of return on those funds, or the interest rate. As the interest rate rises, the opportunity cost of accumulating wealth in a non-interest-bearing form increases. This induces individuals to increase their saving by holding more interest-bearing assets.

Various combinations of total saving at different rates of interest compose the market supply schedule for loanable funds. Because there is a positive relationship between the quantity supplied of loanable funds and the rate of interest, the market supply schedule for loanable funds is an upward-sloping curve, as shown in Figure 4–2.

Several factors, including foreign factors, may cause a change in position of the market supply of loanable funds. For instance, if the realized rate of return in another nation rises above that in the domestic nation, households move their savings, or loanable funds, from the domestic country to the foreign country. The market supply of loanable funds in the domestic country would decline, so the supply schedule would shift to the left.

Demand Those who borrow, such as firms that desire to finance investment projects, demand loanable funds. Consistent with the law of demand, as the interest rate on loans increases, the quantity of loanable funds demanded decreases. The market demand schedule for loanable funds is the various combinations of interest rates and quantities of loanable funds demanded.

Because there is a negative relationship between the quantity demanded and the rate of interest, the market demand schedule slopes downward, as illustrated in Figure 4–2. Factors that cause a change in the market demand for loanable funds induce a shift of the demand schedule.

Figure 4–2

The Market for Loanable Funds

In a competitive market setting, the supply and demand of loanable funds determine interest rates. The market-determined equilibrium interest rate is where the quantity demanded of loanable funds is equal to the quantity supplied, shown by point A, with an interest rate R_1. If the interest rate were equal to R_2, the quantity demanded would exceed the quantity supplied, $Q_2^D > Q_2^S$. The excess quantity demanded would cause the interest rate to rise. At point A and interest rate R_1 there would no longer be an excess quantity demanded.

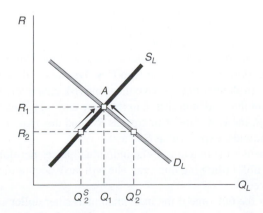

Figure 4–3

A Shift in the Supply of Loanable Funds

Initially the market for loanable funds is in equilibrium at point A with interest rate R_A. The shift of the supply schedule from S_A to S_B illustrates a decrease in the supply of loanable funds. At interest rate R_A, the quantity demanded exceeds the quantity supplied. The interest rate will increase until there is no longer an excess quantity demanded, which occurs at interest rate R_B.

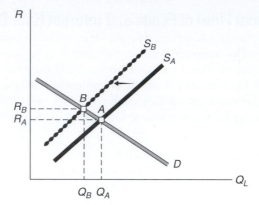

Determination of the Market Interest Rate Point A in Figure 4–2 illustrates a point of market equilibrium, at which the quantity of loanable funds demanded is equal to the quantity of loanable funds supplied. The market interest rate adjusts to satisfy this condition. For example, if in Figure 4–2 the interest rate were equal to R_2, the quantity of loanable funds demanded, Q_2^D, would exceed the quantity of loanable funds supplied, Q_2^S. This excess quantity demanded of loanable funds would put upward pressure on the interest rate, which would rise to R_1 at point A.

Figure 4–3 illustrates how a shift in the market for loanable funds supply schedule affects the market rate of interest. Initially the market for loanable funds is in equilibrium at point A. As in our earlier example, suppose the expected rate of return on foreign instruments became greater than the expected rate of return on similar instruments in the domestic nation. Savers would move funds from the domestic nation to the foreign nation, so the supply of loanable funds in the domestic nation would decline from S_A to S_B. At the interest rate R_2 there would now be an excess quantity of loanable funds demanded, which would cause the interest rate to rise to R_1.

Interest Parity

If expected returns on two similar instruments are different, savers will move funds from one instrument to another. In equilibrium, these rates would be equal. That is, we would have *interest parity,* in which interest rate equalization across nations would ensure that no such flow of funds would occur.

To understand interest parity, consider a resident of the United States who is willing to place her dollar savings in either a U.S. Treasury bill or a United Kingdom Treasury bill. Both instruments have the same risk characteristics. Each is a one-year instrument that is denominated in its home currency. Let's denote the U.S. rate of interest as R, the U.K. rate of interest as R^*, and the spot exchange rate of dollars-per-U.K. pounds, expressed as $/£, as S.

First let's consider the outcome if the individual places her dollar savings in the U.S. Treasury bill. Following one year, she will have accumulated $1+R$ dollars for each dollar saved.

Next consider the outcome if the individual places her dollar savings in the U.K. Treasury bill. First she must exchange each dollar for British pounds at the spot exchange rate of S dollars per pound, to obtain $1/S$ pounds with each dollar. The U.S. resident could then use the $1/S$ British pounds to buy a one-year British treasury bill. After one year, the individual would have accumulated $(1/S)(1+R^*)$ *British pounds.* As a U.S. resident, the saver will likely wish to convert her pound proceeds into dollars. If S_{+1} is the spot exchange rate at the time of maturity, then the *realized return* on the U.K. Treasury bill will turn out to be $(1/S)(1+R^*)S_{+1}$ dollars.

At the time the individual is deciding on which instrument to purchase, however, the U.S. saver does not know what the spot rate will be when the instrument matures. The individual must base her decision on her expectation of what the spot rate will be at the time of maturity. If we denote this expectation as S_{+1}^e, then the *expected return* on the U.K. Treasury bill can be found using the following formula:

$$\text{Expected return} = (1/S)(1+R^*)\,S_{+1}^e.$$

In other words, the saver anticipates that the accumulated $(1/S)(1+R^*)$ British pounds will exchange at the expected future spot exchange rate, S_{+1}^e, for an accumulated savings in dollars of $(1/S)(1+R^*)\,S_{+1}^e$.

Exchange Uncertainty and Covered Interest Parity

If the U.S. saver in our example were to purchase the U.K. Treasury bill, she would have a long position in the pound and would be exposed to foreign exchange risk. She incurs a foreign exchange risk exposure because the actual spot rate that prevails at maturity may turn out to be different from her expectation.

The individual could cover this risk by assuming a short position on the U.K. pound in the forward market, selling the pound forward for the dollar. By purchasing a forward contract, the individual guarantees a rate of exchange at the time of maturity, thereby eliminating all foreign exchange uncertainty.

To cover the foreign exchange risk incurred with the purchase of the British financial instrument, the individual makes two separate foreign exchange transactions. She buys the pound on the spot market, for the purpose of purchasing the U.K. Treasury bill, and sells the pound on the forward market. The amount of savings accumulated with the British treasury bill then depends on the forward exchange rate, as opposed to the future spot exchange rate. If the individual covers her foreign exchange risk, then after one year she would have accumulated $(1/S)(1+R^*)F$ *dollars,* where F is the forward exchange rate.

The U.S. resident who covers the foreign exchange risk with a forward contract, therefore, will be willing to hold both U.S. and U.K. financial instruments if the return on each dollar held in the U.S. financial instrument is equal to the return on each dollar held in the British financial instrument:

$$1+R = (F/S)(1+R^*).$$

Now we can use the fact that

$$F/S = (S/S) + (F-S)/S = 1 + (F-S)/S$$

to rewrite the condition as

$$1+R = [1 + (F-S)/S](1+R^*).$$

Now we can cross-multiply the right-hand side to get

$$1+R = 1 + (F-S)/S + R^* + R^*(F-S)/S.$$

Because R^* and $(F - S)/S$ are both typically small fractions, their product is approximately equal to zero. Making this approximation and subtracting 1 and R^* from both sides of the equation yields

$$R - R^* \cong \frac{F - S}{S}.$$

covered interest parity

A condition relating interest differentials to the forward premium or discount.

This equation is called the covered interest parity condition. ***Covered interest parity*** is a condition that says that the difference between the interest rate on a domestic financial asset and the interest rate on a foreign financial asset should approximately equal the forward premium or discount.

Covered Interest Arbitrage If the covered-interest-parity condition is not satisfied, then a covered-interest-arbitrage opportunity exists. Let's continue with our example and show how an individual conducts covered interest arbitrage. Suppose the dollar-per-U.K.-pound spot rate is 1.500 $/£ and the one-year forward rate is 1.520 $/£.

The U.S. saver in our example will incur a gain if she buys the pound on the spot market and sells the pound in the forward market. For each dollar she exchanges at the spot exchange rate of 1.500 she will receive approximately 0.667 pounds (1/1.500 = 0.667). In twelve months, the forward exchange contract ensures that the pounds she received in exchange for each dollar will trade for 1.520 dollars. The gain on the spot exchange– and forward exchange transactions is approximately 1.33 percent [($1.520 – $1.500)/$1.500] × 100 = 1.33 percent].

Returning to our original question, which instrument should the saver choose? Given that the 3.5 percent return on the dollar-denominated instrument exceeds the 1.5 percent return on the pound-denominated instrument, she will lose 2.0 percent on the pound-denominated instrument. The U.S. saver, however, would gain 1.33 percent on the spot and forward transaction required to cover her purchase of the pound-denominated asset. Nonetheless, in the presumed absence of any transaction costs, the gains on the foreign exchange transactions on the pound fall short of the higher rate of return on the dollar-denominated asset. Hence, the saver should purchase the U.S. Treasury bill.

Covered-Interest-Parity Grid A *covered-interest-parity grid* is a figure that illustrates various combinations of interest rate differentials and forward premiums or discounts. It is a convenient way to illustrate the covered-interest-parity condition.

Figure 4–4 is a covered-interest-parity grid, plotting the interest differential on the horizontal axis and the forward premium or discount on the vertical axis. When the covered-interest-parity condition is satisfied, the interest differential and the forward premium are approximately equal. These combinations of interest rate differentials and forward premiums or discounts lie on, or very close to, a 45-degree ray through the origin. A narrow band around the 45-degree ray reflects the fact that the covered-interest-parity condition is an approximation and that brokerage and sales fees on the various financial instruments cause actual returns to be less than the interest rate. As a result, interest rate differentials and forward premiums or discounts need not be exactly equal. Point A in Figure 4–4 is an example of a combination that satisfies the covered-interest-parity condition.

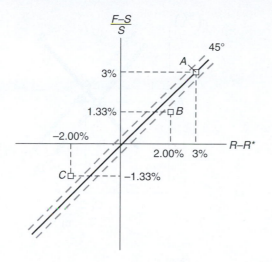

Figure 4–4

The Covered-Interest-Parity Grid

The covered-interest-parity grid illustrates all of the interest differentials and forward premium or discount combinations that satisfy the covered-interest-parity condition. These combinations lie on, or near, the 45-degree ray that intersects the origin. The narrow band reflects transaction and opportunity costs.

Covered Interest Arbitrage and Savings Flows If the covered-interest-parity condition is not satisfied, savers will move funds from one nation to the other as they seek the highest return.

In the previous example, the forward premium on the pound, 1.33 percent, is less than the interest differential, 2.0 percent. This situation, illustrated by point B in Figure 4–4, lies below the 45-degree ray. In this case, and for all situations where the combination of interest differential and forward premium or discount lie below the 45-degree ray, the interest differential between the domestic and foreign financial instruments exceeds the forward premium and individuals should purchase the domestic financial instrument. As a result, savings will flow from abroad into the domestic economy.

Point C in Figure 4–4 illustrates a situation where the combination of interest differential, –2.0 percent, and forward discount –1.33 percent, lies above the 45-degree ray. In this case, individuals should purchase the foreign financial instrument, so that savings will flow from the domestic economy into the foreign economy.

Adjustment to an Equilibrium In our previous example we determined that savings will flow from the United Kingdom to the United States. As a result, there will be pressure on the spot exchange rate, forward exchange rate, and the U.S. and British interest rates to adjust.

To illustrate how the interest rates in the two nations might adjust, we consider the loanable funds markets. To illustrate how exchange rates adjust, we consider the spot and forward markets for foreign exchange. Figure 4–5 on the following page displays each of these market frameworks at an initial equilibrium indicated by point A. Panel (a) shows the spot market for the British pound, panel (b) displays the forward market for the British pound, panel (c) illustrates the loanable funds (L) market in the United Kingdom, and panel (d) displays the market for loanable funds in the United States.

To move savings into the United States, individuals must exchange the British pound for the dollar, so there is an increase in the demand for the dollar. As explained in Chapter 2, the increased demand for the dollar corresponds

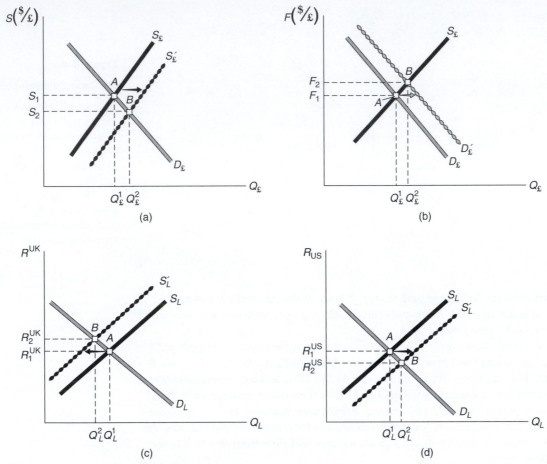

Figure 4–5 Covered-Interest-Parity Example

Panel (a) illustrates the spot market for the British pound. Panel (b) displays the forward market for the British pound. Panel (c) displays the loanable funds *(L)* market in the United Kingdom. Panel (d) illustrates the loanable funds market in the United States. As individuals move funds from pound-denominated to dollar-denominated financial instruments, there is an increase in the demand for the dollar, which is equivalent to an increase in the supply of the pound on the spot market. At the same time, there is an increase in the demand for the pound on the forward market. The flow of funds out of the United Kingdom decreases the supply of loanable funds in the United Kingdom. The flow of funds into the United States increases the supply of loanable funds in that country.

to an increase in the supply of the British pound, shown by a shift of the supply curve in panel *a* from $S_£$ to $S'_£$. As shown in panel (a), the increase in the supply of the British pound in the spot market causes a decline in the spot rate, or a depreciation of the pound relative to the dollar, shown by the movement from S_1 to S_2.

British individuals who purchase the U.S. Treasury instrument will likely desire to receive their principal and interest in British pounds upon maturity. If these individuals cover their exposure to foreign exchange risk, they will purchase the pound forward. This is illustrated by a increases in the demand for the pound in the forward market, shown by a shift from $D_£$ to $D'_£$ in panel (b). The increase in the demand for the pound on the forward market will cause the pound to appreciate relative to the dollar on the forward market, as shown by an increase in the forward rate from F_1 to F_2.

The flow of savings out of the United Kingdom causes a decrease in the supply of loanable funds, shown by the shift of the supply curve from S_L to S_L' in panel (c). A decrease in the supply of loanable funds in the United Kingdom causes an increase in the British interest rate from R_1^{UK} to R_2^{UK}. The flow of savings into the United States causes an increases in the supply of loanable funds from S_L to S_L' in panel (d), which causes the U.S. interest rate to decline from R_1^{US} to R_2^{US}.

There is considerable evidence that covered interest parity normally holds true in developed nations with borders that are open to international bond exchanges and to flows of funds in spot and forward exchange markets.

Fundamental ISSUES

#3 What is covered interest parity?

Covered interest parity is a condition relating the interest rate differential on similar financial assets in two nations to the spot and forward exchange rates. In equilibrium, the interest differential on the two assets is equal to the forward premium or discount. If covered interest parity does not hold, financial arbitrage is possible, and individuals will move savings from one nation to another.

UNCOVERED INTEREST PARITY

In the previous section, we considered financial arbitrage by an individual who hedged all of the foreign exchange risk by making use of a forward exchange contract. Now we consider a situation in which the individual does not use a forward exchange contract.

There are a number of reasons why someone might choose not to use a forward exchange contract to hedge risk. For example, it might be that the transaction is not large enough to warrant a forward contract, which typically has a denomination of at least $1 million. In this situation, the individual might choose not to hedge the transaction at all, or might decide to use some other hedging instrument. Chapter 5 examines alternative hedging instruments. Here, we consider an uncovered transaction, in which the individual does not hedge the exposure to foreign exchange risk at all.

Uncovered Interest Arbitrage

Earlier, we considered a U.S. saver with a choice between a U.S. Treasury instrument and a U.K. Treasury instrument. At the time of the investment decision, the anticipated return on the U.K. financial instrument was $(1/S)\,(1+R^*)\,S_{+1}^e$, where S_{+1}^e is the individual's expectation of next period's actual spot exchange rate. If the U.S. saver does not purchase a forward exchange contract or hedge the foreign exchange risk in any other manner, then the transaction is uncovered and depends, in part, on the saver's expectation of the future spot rate. Following the same basic steps as in our discussion of covered interest parity, we can derive the equilibrium condition representing uncovered interest parity.

uncovered interest parity

A condition relating interest differentials to an expected change in the spot exchange rate of the domestic currency.

Uncovered interest parity is a condition relating the interest differential of similar financial instruments of two nations to the expected change in the spot exchange rate between the two nations. The condition representing uncovered interest parity is

$$R - R^* = \frac{S_{+1}^e - S}{S}.$$

In words, in equilibrium the interest differential between two similar financial instruments should be approximately equal to the expected depreciation or appreciation of the foreign currency. (Nearly 50 percent of all Hungarian home mortgage borrowers engage in uncovered international financial transactions; see *Management Notebook: Many Hungarians Literally Bet Their Houses on Exchange Rates*.)

 # MANAGEMENT Notebook

Many Hungarians Literally Bet Their Houses on Exchange Rates

About half of all mortgage borrowers in Hungary have loans denominated in currencies other than Hungarian forint. For instance, a borrower's mortgage may be valued in Swiss francs, but she makes her mortgage payments in Hungarian forint. Although the interest rate on Swiss-franc-denominated mortgage loans stays constant over the terms of the loans, the value of the interest payment in forint varies with the franc-forint exchange rate. Every time the forint depreciates in relation the Swiss franc, the borrower has to pay more forint.

When asked why they have chosen to finance purchases of their homes by borrowing Swiss francs instead of Hungarian forint, borrowers typically provide the same answer: Market interest rates on loans denominated in Hungarian forint are more than twice as high as rates on Swiss franc loans. In fact, a key reason that Hungarian rates are so much higher than Swiss rates is that most participants in world financial markets anticipate that the Hungarian currency will depreciate considerably in relation to the Swiss franc. Lenders therefore require a higher-interest return on Hungarian financial assets—such as mortgage loans—to induce them to hold Hungarian assets alongside Swiss assets. Thus, the uncovered-interest-parity condition suggests that Hungarian mortgage borrowers can anticipate paying as many forint over the lifetime of a low-interest franc-denominated loan as they would on a high-interest forint-denominated loan.

For Critical Analysis

Why do you suppose that some Hungarian mortgage borrowers who already have Swiss-franc-denominated loans have banded together to lobby for the government of Hungary to adopt a system of fixed exchange rates?

Let's use the information from the covered-interest-arbitrage example, but now suppose the U.S. saver decides not to cover her foreign exchange risk and bases her savings decision on her expectation of the future spot exchange rate. Let's further assume that the U.S. saver expects the future spot exchange rate to be 1.520 dollars per pound.

As in the covered interest arbitrage example, the interest differential between the U.S. Treasury bill and the U.K. Treasury bill is 2.0 percent. If this U.S. saver expects the spot exchange rate to be 1.520 $/£ upon maturity of the British treasury bill, then she expects the U.S. dollar to depreciate relative to the British pound by 1.33 percent [(1.520 − 1.500)/1.500 × 100 = 1.33 percent]. If the individual had her savings in the U.K. Treasury instrument for the year, the number of dollars she would receive in exchange for each British pound would increase by 1.33 percent.

We can state this problem in another manner. The known return on the U.S. financial instrument, paid in dollars, is 3.5 percent. The expected return on the U.K. financial instrument is the sum of the 1.5 percent interest paid on the instrument, in pounds, and the gain in value of the U.K. pound of 1.33 percent, for a total *expected* return on the U.K. Treasury bill, in dollars, of 2.83 percent. The individual would take advantage of this financial arbitrage opportunity by purchasing the U.S. Treasury bill.

If many people undertook the same transaction, the effect on the spot and loanable funds markets would be the same as in the covered-interest-parity example. Because the transaction is uncovered, there is no effect on the forward market. The effect on next period's spot exchange rate, however, would be the same as on the forward market in the covered-interest-parity example.

Risk and Uncovered Interest Parity

Because the purchase of the foreign financial instrument is unhedged in this example, the U.S. saver has a foreign exchange risk exposure. It is very possible that the individual's expectation about the value of the future sport rate will turn out to be incorrect. If this is the case, the realized return on the foreign financial instrument would differ from the expected return.

If a nation's currency value is highly variable, the ability to predict its future value becomes more difficult. If this is the case, individuals will become less confident in their ability to accurately predict the spot rate. This makes the purchase of a foreign financial instrument a much riskier proposition. To induce savers to purchase a risky financial instrument, borrowers may have to offer a higher rate of return on the debt instruments they issue. The inclusion of a risk premium in the uncovered interest parity condition captures this aspect. A *risk premium* is an increase in the return offered on a higher-risk financial instrument to compensate individuals for the additional risk they undertake. The risk premium, ρ, augments the uncovered-interest-parity condition:

$$R - R^* = \frac{S^e_{+1} - S}{S} + \rho.$$

risk premium
An increase in the return offered on a higher-risk financial instrument to compensate individuals for the additional risk they undertake.

Hence, if the domestic financial instrument is the higher-risk instrument, then the positive interest differential should equal the expected depreciation of the domestic currency *plus* an additional amount to compensate individuals for the additional risk they assume with the purchase of the domestic financial instrument.

Risks Other Than Foreign Exchange Risk

The risk premium may reflect risks other than foreign exchange risk. The individual financial instruments may have characteristics that affect their degree of risk. We discuss these instrument-specific risks in Chapter 5.

country risk
The possibility of losses on holdings of financial instruments issued in another nation because of political uncertainty within that nation.

In addition to foreign exchange and instrument-specific risks, there may be *country risk,* which is the risk due to the political and fiscal environment of the nation itself. A government with a considerable amount of external debt may eventually default on that debt, so holding its bonds is a risky proposition. Savers would risk losing the return on their funds, and perhaps their principal as well. Changes in government leadership may lead to increased taxes on foreign investment or restricted outflows of foreign funds. Hence, risk premium may reflect both foreign exchange risk and country risk.

Tests of Uncovered Interest Parity

Uncovered interest parity states that the interest differential for financial instruments of two nations that are similar in all characteristics such as risk and time to maturity should be equal to the expected change in the spot exchange rate between the two nations' currencies.

One problem with testing uncovered interest parity is determining how to measure individuals' expectations of the future spot exchange rate. Economists typically use either survey data on currency traders' expectations or the actual spot rate that prevails at the time the financial instruments mature.

Economists Kenneth Froot and Jeffrey Frankel were two of the first researchers to employ extensive survey data of exchange market traders in a test of uncovered interest parity. The use of survey data is important, because it allows the separation of errors from traders' forecasts of exchange-rate movements from the risk premiums. Their results were similar to those of other researchers: They found that uncovered interest parity does not hold to the extent that covered interest parity does. Froot and Frankel concluded that deviations from uncovered interest parity were due to currency traders' chronic forecast errors and a risk premium. (A commonly used strategy of international investment provides some evidence that the uncovered-interest-parity condition does not always necessarily hold true; see *Management Notebook: The Carry-Trade Strategy for International Investment.*)

 **MANAGEMENT** Notebook

The Carry-Trade Strategy for International Investment

For years, many international investors have utilized a general trading strategy known as the *carry trade.* In the most common version of carry trade, an investor borrows an amount of the currency of a country in which low interest rates prevail—known as the "funding currency." The investor then converts the funds into the currency of a nation in which interest rates are higher—called the "target currency"—and lends that sum at the higher interest rate.

Some investors implement another version of carry trade that they claim focuses on the forward premium. Specifically, they buy currencies that are at a forward discount and sell currencies that are at a forward premium. In fact, however, this version of international carry trade turns out to be equivalent to the first version. As implied by the covered-interest-parity condition, currencies of nations with high interest rates are typically at a forward discount, and currencies of countries with low interest rates are normally at a forward premium. Consequently, buying currencies that are at a forward discount and selling currencies that are at a forward premium is actually equivalent to borrowing currencies of nations with low interest rates and lending currencies of countries with high interest rates.

In any event, if the uncovered-interest-parity condition holds, on average the international carry trade should not be profitable. The concerted actions of those engaging in the carry trade—as well as those of other financial market participants—should narrow interest differentials and cause the currencies of countries with the initially low interest rates to depreciate somewhat, which eventually should yield uncovered interest parity. Nevertheless, there is evidence that investors who successfully implement carry-trade strategies can earn average returns close to those earned by investing in a diversified portfolio of stocks. Furthermore, on average the return from the carry trade is less volatile than the return on a stock portfolio. There is a catch, however. When interest rates do eventually narrow and exchange rates do ultimately adjust toward values consistent with uncovered interest parity, such changes sometimes occur abruptly. Thus, people using carry-trade strategies expose themselves to sudden risks of experiencing significant losses.

For Critical Analysis

What does the evidence regarding profitability of the carry trade imply about the likelihood that uncovered interest parity holds at any given point in time?

 # Fundamental ISSUES

#4 What is uncovered interest parity?

Uncovered interest parity is a condition relating the nominal interest rate differential on two similar financial instruments to the expected change in the spot exchange rate. If there is a sizable amount of foreign exchange risk or country risk, the interest rate differential may also reflect a risk premium, which compensates individuals for the additional risk they assume. Tests of uncovered interest parity show that it does not hold to the extent that covered interest parity does.

FOREIGN EXCHANGE MARKET EFFICIENCY

In this chapter we found that covered interest parity is a condition relating interest differentials to the forward and spot exchange rates. We also learned that uncovered interest parity is a condition relating interest differentials to the spot exchange rate and the expected future spot exchange rate. What is the relationship between these two conditions?

The two conditions are linked through interest rate differentials. Let's suppose that both conditions are satisfied. We can then relate the two conditions through the interest differential as

$$\frac{F - S}{S} = R - R^* = \frac{S^e_{+1} - S}{S},$$

that is, the forward premium is equal to the expected change in the spot rate. We can simplify this relationship by adding S/S to each side, yielding

$$F = S^e_{+1}.$$

In words, the uncovered and covered interest parity conditions imply that the forward exchange rate should equal the spot exchange rate expected to prevail at the time of the settlement of the forward contract.

Market Efficiency

foreign exchange market efficiency

A situation in which the equilibrium spot and forward exchange rates adjust to reflect all available information, in which case the forward premium is, on average, equal to the expected rate of currency depreciation plus any risk premium. This, in turn, implies that the forward exchange rate predicts, on average, the expected future spot exchange rate.

If this last equality is not satisfied, so that the forward exchange rate differs from the expected future spot exchange rate, then financial market traders perceive an arbitrage opportunity. An *efficient market* is one in which market prices adjust quickly to new and relevant information. Hence, market expectations and prices should adjust speedily to eliminate the potential for arbitrage profits. Thus, *foreign exchange market efficiency* exists when the forward exchange rate is a good predictor—often called an *unbiased predictor*—of the future spot exchange rate, meaning that, on average, the forward exchange rate turns out to equal the future spot exchange rate. When the foreign exchange market is efficient, therefore, forward exchange rates should adjust to the point at which the forward premium is equal to the expected rate of currency depreciation.

Evidence on Foreign Exchange Market Efficiency

As indicated earlier, there is considerable evidence that covered interest parity generally holds in the markets for currencies of developed economies. The evidence on uncovered interest parity and, consequently, of foreign exchange market efficiency, is more mixed. To test foreign exchange market efficiency, economists must disentangle the relative contributions of the risk premium from traders' expectation errors. Most studies indicate that risk premiums are important but are divided on whether foreign exchange markets are truly efficient.

 Fundamental**ISSUES**

#5 What is foreign exchange market efficiency?

Market efficiency means that market rates adjust quickly to new and relevant information so that systematic profit opportunities do not exist. Hence, foreign exchange market efficiency means that, in absence of any risk premium, the forward exchange rate should, on average, equal the expected future spot exchange rate.

INTERNATIONAL FINANCIAL MARKETS

In this chapter we have considered various conditions that relate exchange rates and the rates of return on financial instruments of different nations. Chapter 1 discussed the remarkable growth of international financial markets that has taken place over the last few decades. This growth occurred as businesses expanded their operations to foreign markets, and as individuals and fund managers considered new opportunities in foreign markets. New markets developed over time to meet these expanded opportunities.

Generally there is a distinction made between *capital markets* and *money markets*. **International capital markets** are the markets for cross-border exchange of financial instruments that have a maturity of a year or more. International capital market traders also exchange instruments with no distinct maturity. In contrast, **international money markets** are the markets for cross-border exchange of financial instruments with maturities of less than one year.

International Capital Markets

Figure 1–3 on page 7 showed the remarkable increase in cross-border transaction in bonds and equities for the United States, the United Kingdom, and Germany. **Bonds**, which we will discuss in greater detail in Chapter 5, are long-term promissory notes. **Equities,** like bonds, are financing instruments. Equities, however, are ownership shares that might or might not pay the holder a dividend. Equity values rise and fall with savers' perceptions of the value of an enterprise.

International Money Markets

International money markets are markets for cross-border exchange of financial instruments with maturities of less than one year. Although traders exchange a number of different types of instruments in international money markets, foreign exchange instruments are most actively traded. Recall from Chapter 2 that the foreign exchange market consists of spot and forward exchanges of foreign currencies and that the majority of the foreign exchange markets is the trading of foreign-currency-denominated deposits among major banks in amounts of $1 million or more.

As noted earlier, the international capital markets have experienced considerable growth since the early 1970s. The international money markets, however, have experienced astounding growth. Economics periodically estimate the volume of transactions in the foreign exchange markets based on surveys of the largest banks and foreign exchange trading firms. On average, the daily volume of the foreign exchange market approximates two months of activity in the New York Stock Exchange.

The international money markets comprise a number of financial instruments other than spot and forward exchange contracts. These instruments include short-term international bank, government, and corporate notes, and international commercial paper.

Eurobonds, Euronotes, and Eurocommercial Paper

Eurobonds, Euronotes, and *Eurocommerical paper* are financial instruments traded in the international capital and international money markets. The Euromarkets, however, are *nontraditional* markets, because traditional financing activity takes place within the domestic economy and is denominated in the domestic currency.

The Euromarkets, in contrast, allow a corporation to raise funds in other nations or to denominate debt in another currency. For example, a U.K. firm may issue a debt instrument denominated in deutsche marks in the United States. Note that this instruments is a *Euro-instrument,* being a financial instrument denominated in a currency other than that of the country in which the instrument is issued. Hence, these nontraditional markets give businesses the opportunity to borrow from individuals or firms that were previously inaccessible.

Eurobonds are long-term debt instruments issued in a currency other than that of the country in which the instruments is issued. For example, a Canadian business may issue Canadian-dollar-denominated ten-year debt instruments in London. This

international capital markets
Markets for cross-border exchange of financial instruments that have maturities of one year or more.

international money markets
Markets for cross-border exchange of financial instruments with maturities of less than one year.

bonds
Long-term promissory notes.

equities
Ownership shares that might or might not pay the holder a dividend; their values rise and fall with savers' perceived value of the issuing enterprise.

Eurobonds
Long-term debt instruments denominated in a currency other than that of the country in which instrument is issued.

Eurocommercial paper

Unsecured short-term debt instrument issued in a currency other than that of the country in which the instrument is issued.

Euronotes

Short- and medium-term debt instruments issued in a currency other than that of the country in which the instrument is issued.

Eurocurrency

A bank deposit denominated in a currency other than that of the nation in which the bank deposit is located.

Eurocurrency market

A market for the borrowing and lending of Eurocurrency deposits.

is a Eurobond, because it is denominated in a currency, the Canadian dollar, other than that of the country in which it is issued, the United Kingdom.

Eurocommercial paper is an unsecured short-term debt instrument issued in a currency other than that of the country in which the instrument is issued. *Euronotes* are short- to medium-term debt instruments issued in a currency other than that of the country in which the instrument is issued. These instruments, with typical maturities of a few months to one year, have a longer term than Eurocurrencies and a shorter term than Eurobonds.

Eurocurrencies

As businesses expand their operations to foreign markets, and as individuals and funds managers consider new opportunities in foreign markets, international borrowing and lending activities continue to increase. New markets have developed over time to meet these expanded lending and borrowing preferences. One market in particular, the *Eurocurrency market,* which began in the mid-1950s, has grown considerably to facilitate these activities.

Origins of the Eurocurrency Market A *Eurocurrency* is a bank deposit denominated in a currency other than that of the nation in which the bank deposit is located. For example, a Eurodollar deposit is a bank deposit denominated in U.S. dollars, but located in a bank outside of the United States. The *Eurocurrency market* is a market for the borrowing and lending of Eurocurrency deposits. There are at least two competing views on how the Eurocurrency market originated.

The first account of how eurocurrencies began gives credit to Soviet financiers. From the end of World War II to the collapse of the Soviet Union, the Soviet Union conducted many of its international transactions using barter, but it conducted monetary transactions in U.S. dollars, because the dollar was the predominant reserve currency. This required the Soviet Union to maintain dollar-denominated deposits in U.S. banks to conduct these transactions.

As tension between the United States and the Soviet Union increased during the Cold War, the Soviet Union became fearful that U.S. officials might freeze these funds. Soviet financial officials sought to move their funds outside of the United States and outside of the U.S. banking system. Soviet financial officials therefore moved the funds to banks located in Paris and London. These deposits were Eurodollar deposits, or dollar-denominated deposits, located in Europe.

A second and more likely theory of the origins of the Eurocurrency market begins in the mid-1950s. In 1956 the Egyptian government seized control of the Suez Canal, operated by a firm with French and British ties. Over objections of the United States, the United Kingdom and France retook control of the Suez Canal. In retaliation, the U.S. government soon began selling British pounds in the foreign exchange market.

As an attempt to support the pound by restricting its supply in the foreign exchange market, the British government restricted the foreign lending activities of British banks. These lending activities were a very profitable and sizable portion of the British banks' business. British banks soon began advertising that they would accept dollar-denominated deposits. As an inducement, they offered attractive rates on the deposits. When dollar deposits flowed into the British banks, the banks, in turn, deposited the funds in U.S. banks. This allowed the British banks to resume their international lending activities, which they conducted in U.S. dollars instead of British pounds. The media eventually dubbed the dollar-denominated deposits held in the British banks Eurodollars.

Leading financial papers, such as the *Financial Times,* publish Eurocurrency borrowing and lending rates. Table 4–1 shows recent Eurocurrency interest rates for six currencies and their maturity periods, from one year to overnight. The table presents all of the rates on an annual basis. Each column shows two rates. The first is the rate at which major banks would be willing to lend a Eurocurrency deposit. The second displays the rate they would be willing to pay to borrow a Eurocurrency deposit.

Relationship to the Forward Market The maturities of Eurocurrency deposits are similar to those of the forward exchange market. The Eurocurrency market and the forward market are highly integrated because they fulfill some similar roles. These markets allow a bank, firm, or individual to structure a financial arbitrage denominated in the domestic currency. Because of this, Eurocurrency interest rate differentials and the forward premium or discount tend to be in equilibrium, meaning that covered interest arbitrage in the Eurocurrency market is typically not profitable.

Using the equations of our previous examples, let's consider using the Eurocurrency market to conduct financial arbitrage. Suppose you decide to borrow U.S. dollars in the Eurocurrency market, which you then plan to convert into Swiss francs (SFr) to lend in the Eurocurrency market.

Using Table 4–1, let's consider borrowing $1 million for three months. Further, on the same day, the spot rate on the Swiss franc is 0.9130 SFr/$, and the three-month forward rate is 0.9112 SFr/$. The borrowing rate in Table 4–1 is 0.73 percent. First let's calculate how much we will have to pay back, the principal and interest, on the $1 million. Remember that the interest rate is stated on an annual basis, so we will do a simple conversion to put it on a three-month basis, by dividing the interest rate by 12 and multiplying it by 3 (or simply dividing by 4). The principal and interest due on the three-month $1 million loan is

$$\$1,000,000 \times [1 + (0.0073/4)] = \$1,001,825.$$

Using the $1 million we borrowed, we can exchange it for SFr9130,000 ($1 million × 0.9130SFr/$ = SFr913,000). Next we use the SFr913,000 to purchase a Eurocurrency deposit with a return of 0.03 percent. At the end of three months the principal and interest on the Swiss franc Eurocurrency deposit is

$$SFr913,000[1 + (0.0003/4)] = SFr913,068.$$

Table 4–1

Eurocurrency Interest Rates

	Overnight	Three Months	Six Months	One Year
Euro	0.40–0.30	1.17–0.97	1.59–1.39	1.95–1.75
British Pound	0.68–0.48	1.19–0.99	1.57–1.37	2.08–1.88
Swiss Franc	0.24–0.01	0.25–0.03	0.32–0.02	0.54–0.24
Canadian Dollar	1.15–0.80	1.40–1.10	2.07–1.92	1.90–1.60
U.S. Dollar	0.32–0.02	0.73–0.53	1.03–0.83	1.45–1.25
Japanese Yen	0.17–0.07	0.35–0.10	0.55–0.30	0.75–0.50

Source: *Financial Times,* http://www.ft.com.

We will have to repay the Eurodollar loan in dollars in three months, so we will sell the Swiss franc forward at a rate of 0.9112 Swiss francs per dollar. The SFr913,068 million will net $1,002,050 on the forward transaction (SFr913,068/ 0.9112 SFr/$). After we repay the Eurodollar loan, we have $1,002,050 − $1,001,825 = $225. It is most likely that the $225 would not even pay our transaction costs!

Fundamental ISSUES

#6 What are the international financial markets?

The international financial markets are the markets for cross-border exchange of financial instruments. International capital markets are markets for cross-border exchange of financial instruments that have maturities of one year or more, whereas the international money markets exchange financial instruments with maturities of less than one year. The Euromarkets allow corporations to raise funds in other nations or to denominate debt in another currency.

Chapter SUMMARY

1. **Foreign Exchange Risk:** Foreign exchange risk is the possibility that the value of a foreign receipt or payment to be made in the future may vary due to a change in the exchange rate. There are three types of exposure to foreign exchange risk: transaction risk, translation risk, and economic risk. Some financial instruments can partially or completely offset foreign exchange risks. The exposure is *covered* when it is completely offset. The exposure is *uncovered* if it is not offset at all.

2. **The Forward Currency Market and the Determination of Forward Exchange Rates:** The forward currency market is a standardized market for the future delivery of a currency at a guaranteed exchange rate. When there is no government intervention in the market or exchange-rate restrictions, the forces of supply and demand determine forward exchange rates.

3. **Covered Interest Parity:** Covered interest parity is a condition relating interest differentials to the forward premium or discount. In equilibrium, the interest differential is equal to the forward premium or discount. If equilibrium does not hold, the covered-interest-parity condition postulates that savings will flow from one nation to another in search of higher, exchange-rate-adjusted returns. A parity grid illustrates the covered-interest-parity condition.

4. **Uncovered Interest Parity:** Uncovered interest parity is a condition relating the nominal interest rate differential on two similar financial instruments to the expected change in the spot exchange rate. Under uncovered interest parity, transactions are not covered and are subject to foreign exchange risk.

5. **Foreign Exchange Market Efficiency:** The foreign exchange market is efficient if market rates adjust quickly to new and relevant information, eliminating systematic profit opportunities. In absence of any risk premium, the forward rate should, on average, equal the expected future spot rate.

6. **International Financial Markets:** The international financial markets are markets for the cross-border exchange of financial instruments. Typically, there is a distinction made

between international capital markets and international money markets. International capital markets are the markets for cross-border exchange of financial instruments with maturities of one year or more, whereas international money markets are markets for exchange of financial instruments with maturities of less than one year.

QUESTIONSandPROBLEMS

1. Suppose the following information on U.S. dollar and euro rates prevails in the international money market.

Spot rate	1.072 $/€
One-month forward rate	1.089 $/€
Interest rate(€)	3.25% per year
Interest rate ($)	1.75% per year

   a. Illustrate the covered-interest-parity grid and plot the information in a diagram.
   b. Suppose transaction costs are approximately 1 percent. Incorporate this information into the parity grid.
   c. Based on the diagram you constructed, would you move funds to the euro instrument, move them to the U.S. dollar instrument, or maintain your current portfolio?

2. Ignoring transaction costs, use the covered-interest-parity condition to explain your answer in Problem 1.

3. Construct diagrams representing the spot exchange market for the euro relative to the U.S. dollar, the forward exchange market for the euro relative to the U.S. dollar, the loanable funds market in Germany, and the loanable funds market in the United States. Based on your answer to Problem 1, show the potential effects within each of these markets as individuals reallocate their portfolios.

4. Suppose the following situation prevails in the foreign exchange and Eurocurrency markets for the euro (€) and the British pound (£).

One-year Eurocurrency rates:	
Euro	3.125%
British pound	4.250%
Exchange rates:	
Spot	1.5245 €/£
One-year forward	1.4575 €/£

   Explain how an individual would profit from financial arbitrage in this situation. Calculate the percentage return the individual would earn from undertaking arbitrage activity. Keep all of your calculations to four decimal points for accuracy.

5. Suppose the spot exchange rate between the U.S. dollar and the British pound is 1.5492 $/£, the interest rate on a three-month U.S. financial instrument is 1.24 percent, and the interest rate on a similar U.K. financial instrument is 3.66 percent.
   a. Rewrite the uncovered-interest-parity equation to show how it is a guide for the future spot rate.
   b. Based on the given information, calculate the implied expectation of the spot rate between the U.S. dollar and the British pound.

6. Suppose the spot exchange rate between the dollar and the euro is 1.08 \$/€. The dollar can be borrowed for one year at 1.75 percent and the euro can be lent for one year 3.25 percent. What should be the forward premium or discount? What should be the one-year forward rate?

7. Use the information in Problem 6. Assume, however, that the maturity period is six months as opposed to one year. What should be the forward premium or discount be now? What should the forward rate be now?

8. On a particular day, the spot rate between the Czech koruna and the U.S. dollar was 30.35 (CKR/USD), and the representative interest rate on a one-year financial instrument in the Czech Republic was 7.5 percent and 3.5 percent in the United States.
   a. Using uncovered interest parity (UIP), determine the spot rate you would expect to prevail in one year.
   b. Suppose the Czech koruna instrument has a risk premium of 2 percent. What is the expected spot rate now?

9. In recent years, Turkey's current account deficit has exceeded 9 percent of gross domestic product, which has caused some observers to question whether the nation can finance such a large deficit. Draw a diagram of Turkey's loanable funds market and of the spot market for the Turkish Lira. Suppose that a general concern emerges about the nation's large current account deficit that causes people to reallocate their savings away from Turkey. Use your diagrams to illustrate and explain the likely impacts of such a reallocation of savings on Turkey's interest rates and on the exchange value of the Lira

10. A Japanese student is planning on studying for a year at a German university. She desires to save sufficient Japanese yen today to cover the year's tuition costs of €35,000. Suppose that the student has two choices: (a) saving yen in a Japanese account that pays an annual interest rate of 1.18 percent and buying euros forward one year at the current forward exchange rate of 96.846 ¥/€, or (b) buying euros today at the current spot exchange rate of 94.583 ¥/€ and saving the proceeds in a German account that pays an annual interest rate of 3.26 percent. Calculate how many yen each option would require, and determine which of the two options the student should choose.

11. In the late 2000s and early 2010s, recessions struck a number of nations, which shook global confidence levels. During much of this period, many savers viewed the U.S. economy as a "safe haven." Draw diagrams of the U.S. loanable funds market and the spot market for the U.S. dollar. Use your diagrams to explain the likely impacts of the resulting funds flow on the U.S. interest rate and on the exchange value of the U.S. dollar.

Online**APPLICATIONS**

This chapter presented the concepts of foreign exchange risk and country risk. Quantifying country risk is an important yet subjective task. A variety of methods exist and numerous investment agencies provide such estimates. Because the World Bank (IBRD) lends to many nations, country risk is an important consideration.

Internet URL: *http://www.worldbank.org*

Title: The World Bank

Navigation: Begin with the home page of the World Bank. At the top of the home page, click on *About*. Next, under "Resources," click on *Annual Report*. Click on the link for the most recent annual report. Click on the link for *Financial Statements,* and then on *Management's Discussion and Analysis.* Find the page number for *Credit Risk,* under the heading of *Financial Risk Management.*

Application: Go to the page for *Credit Risk* and answer the following questions.

1. Explain how the World Bank evaluates the credit risk of a country, or country risk.

2. In addition to country risk, the World Bank faces "market risk" on its loans. List and describe the primary types of market risk.

3. How, in general, does the World Bank manage exchange-rate risk?

SELECTED REFERENCES and FURTHER READINGS

Al-Loughani, Nabeel E., and Imad A. Moosa. "Covered Interest Parity and the Relative Effectiveness of Forward and Money Market Hedging." *Applied Economics Letters* 7(10) (October 2000): 673–675.

Chakraborty, Avik, and George W. Evans. "Can Perpetual Learning Explain the Forward Premium Puzzle?" *Journal of Monetary Economics 85* (April 2008): 477–490.

Diamandis Panayiotis F., Dimitris A. Georgoutsos, and Georgios P. Kouretas. "Testing the Forward Rate Unbiasedness during the 1920s." *Journal of Financial Markets, Institutions, and Money, 18* (October 2008): 358–373.

Dominguez, Emilio, and Alfonso Novales. "Testing the Expectations Hypothesis in Eurodeposits." *International Money and Finance 19*(5) (October 2000): 713–736.

Flood, Robert P., and Andrew K. Rose. "Uncovered Interest Parity in Crisis: The Interest Rate Defence in the 1990s." Centre for Economic Policy Research, Discussion Paper No. 2943 (September 2001), http://www.cepr.org.

Ichiue, Hibiki, and Kentaro Koyama. "Regime Switches in Exchange Rate Volatility and Uncovered Interest Parity." *Journal of International Money and Finance, 30* (2011): 1436–1450.

Lothian, James, and Mark Taylor. "Real Exchange Rate Behavior: The Recent Float from the Perspective of the Past Two Centuries." *Journal of Political Economy 104* (June 3, 1996): 488–509.

Madsen, Erik Strojer. "Inefficiency of Foreign Exchange Markets and Expectations." *Applied Economics 28*(4) (April 1996): 397–403.

Matacz, Andrew, and Jean-Philippe Bouchaud. "An Empirical Investigation of the Forward Interest Rate Term Structure." *International Journal of Theoretical and Applied Finance 3*(4) (October 2000): 703–729.

Walmsley, Julian. *The Foreign Exchange and Money Markets Guide: Second Edition.* New York: John Wiley and Sons, Inc., 2000.

Wolff, Christian C. P. "Forward Foreign Exchange Rates and Expected Future Spot Rates." *Applied Financial Economics 10*(4) (August 2000): 371–377.

5

Interest Yields, Interest Rate Risk, and Derivative Securities

Fundamental ISSUES

1. How are interest yields, financial instrument prices, and interest rate risk interrelated?

2. Why do market interest yields vary with differences in financial instruments' terms to maturity and risks?

3. What factors explain why international interest rate differentials are often inconsistent with the uncovered-interest-parity condition?

4. What are real interest rates, and how can real-interest-rate differentials serve as indicators of the extent to which international markets are open to arbitrage?

5. What are derivative securities?

6. What are the most commonly traded derivative securities?

For a low-level trader at one of the world's largest banks, Société Générale of France, it all began with a desire to do something more exciting than his assigned task, which was engaging in relatively small transactions involving derivative securities—also known simply as "derivatives." In order to fulfill his dream of trading much larger sums, the trader found a way to hack into the bank's computer and execute trades without approval of senior managers and without their knowledge. Each day for several months, he spent part of his day at the bank engaging in these unauthorized trades. Eventually, the trader failed to hide a single unapproved transaction from a supervisor, who then figured out how to track all of the trader's transactions.

Within a couple of days, the staggering extent of the trader's unauthorized activities was clear to Société Générale: All the derivatives that the trader had purchased summed to about $73 billion—or nearly three times the value of the bank to its shareholders! The bank's senior officers immediately put its staff of traders to work trying to sell off most of the securities, with an aim to keep the $73-billion-dollar exposure to risk secret while acting to minimize the bank's losses. Eventually, the bank was able to sell off many of the securities. Nevertheless, *ultimately the bank experienced a loss equivalent to nearly $7.2 billion—roughly 25 percent of the bank's total market value to its shareholders—as a consequence of this single trader's unauthorized activities.*

What are derivative securities? Are all transactions in derivatives necessarily risky, or can firms sometimes use them to help protect against certain risks, including foreign exchange risks and other types of risks encountered in international financial markets? In this chapter, you will learn the answers to these questions.

INTEREST RATES

Naturally, anyone who chooses to hold a financial instrument must contend with the risks associated with the instrument. For one thing, there is always the possibility that the issuer of the instrument may default. But even financial instruments with extremely low risk of default, such as bonds issued by governments of the United States, the European Union, and Japan, can pose significant risks of loss owing to the potential for the market values of these instruments to vary as interest rates change. To understand how individuals and businesses can seek either to minimize risks owing to interest rate variations or to profit from them, it is necessary first to understand how interest rates and the prices of financial instruments are related.

Interest Yields and Financial Instrument Prices

Holding financial instruments, such as loans or securities, issued by individuals, companies, or governments entails an extension of credit. The amount of credit extended via the purchase of a financial instrument is the ***principal*** amount of the loan or the security. Payments from the issuers that compensate the purchasers for the use of their funds constitute *interest*. The amount of interest as a percentage of the principal of a financial instrument is the *interest rate*. For example, the annual interest rate on a simple-interest, one-year loan is equal to the amount of interest divided by the loan principal, expressed as a percentage.

principal
The amount of credit extended when one makes a loan or purchases a bond.

Interest Rates and Discounted Present Value The issuer of a bond often sells the bond at a *discount*, meaning that the bond's selling price is less than its face value. Therefore, the holder of the bond automatically earns a ***capital gain***. This is an increase in the bond's market value, relative to its market value at the time of purchase, if he or she holds the bond until maturity.

To illustrate the relationship between interest rates and the market values of bonds, consider a specific bond whose maturity is three years. The bond's face value is $10,000. Its annual coupon return is $600. Hence, its nominal yield per year is $600 / $10,000 = 0.06, or 6 percent. The bond's owner receives three payments: $600 at the end of the first year, $600 at the end of the second year, and $10,600 (the principal plus the third year's interest) at the end of the third year. Consequently, the amount that an individual is willing to pay for this bond must equal the value of these payments from the purchaser's perspective at the time that the purchase occurs.

The value today of payments to be received at future dates is the ***discounted present value*** of those payments. The discounted present value of any future amount is how much that amount is currently worth to us, *given* current market

capital gain
A rise in the value of a financial instrument at the time it is sold, as compared with its market value at the time it was purchased.

discounted present value
The value today of a payment to be received at a future date.

Table 5–1

Present Values of a
Future Dollar

This table shows how much a
dollar received a given number of
years in the future would be worth
today at different rates of interest.
For instance, at an interest rate of
8 percent, a dollar to be received
25 years from now would have a
value of less than 15 cents, and a
dollar to be received 50 years from
now is worth about 2 cents.

Year	Compounded Annual Interest Rate				
	3%	5%	8%	10%	20%
1	.971	.952	.926	.909	.833
2	.943	.907	.857	.826	.694
3	.915	.864	.794	.751	.578
4	.889	.823	.735	.683	.482
5	.863	.784	.681	.620	.402
6	.838	.746	.630	.564	.335
7	.813	.711	.583	.513	.279
8	.789	.677	.540	.466	.233
9	.766	.645	.500	.424	.194
10	.744	.614	.463	.385	.162
15	.642	.481	.315	.239	.0649
20	.554	.377	.215	.148	.0261
25	.478	.295	.146	.0923	.0105
30	.412	.231	.0994	.0573	.00421
40	.307	.142	.0460	.0221	.000680
50	.228	.087	.0213	.00852	.000109

interest rates. Table 5–1 displays the discounted present value of a dollar received
at various future dates. As you can see, the future value of a dollar declines faster
at higher interest rates. This implies that the discounted present value of future payments that a holder of a bond receives falls as interest rates increase. As interest
rates rise, therefore, the amount that a buyer is willing to pay for the bond declines.
Hence, computing bond prices requires knowing how to calculate the discounted
present value of a future sum.

Discounted Present Value and the Market Price of Bonds For our example of
a bond with a face value of $10,000 and three annual payments of $600 each, let's
suppose that the prevailing market interest rate is $R = 0.07$, or 7 percent. Let's
also begin by considering the bond's first year's return of $600. Furthermore, let's
note that saving $560.75 for one year at an interest rate of 7 percent would yield an
amount of $560.75 (the initial amount saved) plus 0.07 times $560.75 (the interest
earned). This is equivalent to $560.75 times the factor 1.07, which works out to be
equal to $600.

Hence, from today's perspective, a $600 payment to be received one year from
now at a market interest rate of 7 percent is worth $560.75. It follows that $560.75
is the *discounted present value* of $600 a year from now at the interest rate of
7 percent. This amount is equal to the future payment of $600 divided by $1 + 0.07$,

or $600 / (1.07) = \$560.75$. We can conclude that the formula for calculating the discounted present value of a payment to be received a year from now is

$$\text{Discounted present value} = \frac{\text{Payment one year from now}}{1 + R}.$$

The three-year bond in our example also pays $600 two years following the date of issue. Note that at a market rate of interest of 7 percent, holding $524.06 for two years would yield $600. This is so because if you were to save $524.06 for one year at this interest rate, the accumulated saving after the year would be equal to $524.06 times 1.07, or $560.75. Then if you were to save $560.75 for another year, you would end up with $560.75 times 1.07, or $600 at the end of the second year. This leads us to the conclusion that the discounted present value of $600 to be received two years from now is equal to $600 / [(1.07)(1.07)] = \$600 / (1.07)^2 = \$524.06$.

For a glossary of finance and investment terms, go to *http://www.finance-glossary.com*.

Based on the logic of this calculation, we can determine that a general formula for computing the discounted present value of a payment to be received *n* years in the future is

$$\text{Discounted present value} = \frac{\text{Payment } n \text{ year from now}}{(1 + R)^n}.$$

In our two-year example, $n = 2$, $R = 0.07$, and the payment two years from now is $600.

At the conclusion of the third year, the holder of the three-year bond stands to receive the principal amount of $10,000 and a concluding $600 interest payment. We can calculate the discounted present value of this amount using the earlier formula:

$$\begin{array}{l}\text{Disscounted} \\ \text{value of \$10,600} \\ \text{three years hence}\end{array} = \frac{\$10,600}{(1.07)^3} = \$8,652.76.$$

Thus, today's value of the $10,600 that the bondholder will receive at the time when the three-year bond matures is $8,652.76.

In the absence of transactions costs and risks, the *price* of this three-year bond should be the amount that a buyer perceives the bond to be worth at the purchase date, given a market interest rate of 7 percent. This is the sum of the discounted present values of the payments received in each of the three years. From our previous computations, this sum is

$$\begin{array}{rl}\text{Price of} \\ \text{3-year} \\ \text{bond}\end{array} = \frac{\$600}{(1.07)} + \frac{\$600}{(1.07)^2} + \frac{\$10,600}{(1.07)^3}$$

$$= \$560.75 + \$524.06 + \$8,652.76$$

$$= \$9,737.57.$$

Thus, $9,737.57 is the market value of the three-year bond with a face value of $10,000 and coupon return of $600 when the market interest rate is 7 percent.

On the WEB

Track U.S. interest rates via the Federal Reserve at *http://www.federalreserve.gov/releases/ h15/data.htm/update/*

Perpetuities and the Relationship between Interest Yields and Bond Prices

There are many types of bonds. One particularly useful bond to think about, however, is a **perpetuity**, or a bond that never matures. For instance, the British government has issued perpetuities called *British consols*. The British Parliament called these perpetuities *2.5% Consolidated Stock of 1921*, because they first were introduced in that year and at that nominal interest rate. British consols have no fixed maturity date, although Parliament could redeem these bonds at their par values and in any amounts that it may choose.

Perpetuities such as consols pay a fixed coupon return forever. Let's again denote this annual coupon return as an amount C. If the nominal interest rate is R, then anyone contemplating buying a perpetuity must determine how much to pay for this infinite-life bond. An individual who purchases a perpetuity earns C dollars next year, the year after that, and every year following.

This implies that the discounted present value of the perpetuity is the sum of the discounted present values of C dollars every year into the future. This is an *infinite sum* equal to

$$C/(1 + R) + C/(1 + R)^2 + C/(1 + R)^3 + C/(1 + R)^4 + \dots$$

If we assume that this individual does not have to worry about risks or transactions costs, then this is the amount that the person is willing to pay for this bond. This is so because this amount is today's value of the coupon returns the bond will yield. If everyone else uses the same reasoning, then the actual market price of the perpetual bond, P_B, will equal this sum of discounted present values of coupon returns:

$$P_B = C/(1 + R) + C/(1 + R)^2 + C/(1 + R)^3 + C/(1 + R)^4 + \dots$$

In Problem 1 at the end of the chapter, we give you the opportunity to show that this expression reduces to the simple form,

$$P_B = C/R.$$

This expression tells us that the price of a perpetual, nonmaturing bond is its annual coupon payment divided by the market interest rate. This tells us that if the

perpetuity

A bond with an infinite term to maturity.

perpetuity pays $C = \$100$ per year forever, and if the market interest rate is 5 percent, then the price of the bond is equal to

$$P_B = C/R = \$100/(0.05) = \$20,000.00.$$

Suppose that the market interest rate R increase to 6 percent. Then the ratio C/R falls, and the price of the bond declines. In our earlier numerical example, if the market interest rate increases to 6 percent, then the price of the perpetuity with a $100 annual coupon return declines to

$$P_B = C/R = \$100/(0.06) = \$1,666.67.$$

We can reach the following important conclusion from this pricing formula for a perpetuity:

Holding the coupon payment and all other factors unchanged, the price of an existing bond varies inversely with the nominal interest rate.

This means that if the market nominal interest rate falls, then bond prices rise, and those who hold bonds earn a nominal capital gain. In contrast, if the market nominal interest rate rises, then bond prices decline, and people who hold bonds incur a nominal capital loss.

This inverse relationship between the market interest rate and the market price holds for all types of bonds. For instance, if you take a look back at the market price calculation in our earlier example of a three-year bond on page 115, you will note that if the interest rate had been higher, we would have computed a lower market price for the three-year bond. As you can see, the formula for the price of a perpetuity clearly illustrates this inverse relationship that exists for all financial instruments. (Interest rates charged on many loans in the United States and other nations are based on *Libor*, or the *London interbank offered rate*, which recently has come under considerable scrutiny; see *Management Notebook: Recalculating Libor*.)

MANAGEMENT Notebook

Recalculating Libor

For many years, the London interbank offered rate, or Libor, has been calculated as an average of interest rates that sixteen large international banking institutions report they are paying to borrow funds from other banks. The British Bankers Association (BBA) computes Libor each day and releases its value at 11 A.M. London time. The BBA reports Libor in terms of ten different currencies and at fifteen maturities, or periods of time over which loans mature before final repayment. Because Libor is designed to measure the worldwide cost of funds to banks, increasingly many banks have tied interest rates on a number of corporate and mortgage loan contracts to Libor. Thus, when Libor rises, interest rates rise on various loans in such far-flung locales as St. Petersburg, Russia; São Paulo, Brazil; and Muncie, Indiana. All told, Libor forms the basis for payments on approximately $400 trillion in loans and other financial instruments.

In the late 2000s in the midst of the U.S. financial meltdown and again during the early 2010s as a consequence of the European debt crisis, Libor rose well above the U.S. interbank loan rate, the federal funds rate. In both instances, this occurred because of an unusual increase in the demand for dollar loans among European banks that were suffering an acute lack of dollar-denominated liquidity. Nevertheless, many Libor experts openly questioned whether Libor had risen as much as it should have. When the financial media ran reports on these concerns, Libor suddenly increased. This led many of the experts to suspect that international banks had, in an effort to avoid appearing desperate for cash, reported borrowing at lower interbank rates than they actually paid. When subjected to greater scrutiny, the experts suggested, some of banks had become more honest, at least temporarily, in their reports to the BBA.

In 2012, British government investigations yielded admissions by Libor-participating banks that they had colluded to keep the Libor rate artificially low during the financial meltdown. These actions contributed to artificially low interest rates that were tied to Libor, which benefited borrowers but harmed lenders. As a consequence, many financial institutions around the globe are now searching for a replacement for Libor as an international market interest rate to which they might eventually tie interest rates on other financial contracts. Many new loan contracts are linking lending rates to averages of actual interest rates on internationally traded Eurocurrency instruments.

For Critical Analysis

*Why do you suppose that many financial institutions are considering candidate replacements for Libor that involve averages of **actual** interest rates instead of averages of interest rates reported by other banks?*

Term to Maturity and Interest Rate Risk

Perpetuities are useful bonds to study because the formula for their market price is so simple. Most bonds, however, have a fixed *term to maturity*, or a finite period between the initial purchase of the instrument and the eventual receipt of principal and promised interest payments. It turns out that the term to maturity is a key factor influencing the degree of **interest rate risk** associated with a financial instrument. This is the risk of variations in the market value of the financial instrument due to interest rate variations. Interest rate risk may arise from length of maturity and frequency of payments.

interest rate risk
The possibility that the market value of a financial instrument will change as interest rates vary.

To see why time to maturity plays a key role in determining a financial instrument's interest rate risk, consider an example of two simple instruments. One is a British bond that pays 10,000 pounds sterling after a single year, and the other is a bond that pays £10,000 after the two years have passed. Bonds that pay lump-sum amounts when they mature are called *zero-coupon bonds*.

zero-coupon bonds
Bonds that pay lump-sum amounts at maturity.

In Table 5–2 we calculate the prices of these two bonds for market interest rates of 6 percent and 7 percent. As the table indicates, an interest rate increase from 6 percent to 7 percent induces a fall in the price of each bond. As a result, those holding the bonds would incur **capital losses**, meaning that the market values of the bonds as components of their financial wealth would fall.

capital loss
A decline in the market value of a financial instrument at the time it is sold, as compared with its market value at the time it was purchased.

The calculations in Table 5–2 indicate that the percentage of capital loss on the two-year bond is 1.9 percent, which is more than double the 0.9 percent capital loss on the one-year bond. This is so because the increase in the market interest rate from 6 percent to 7 percent would be applied to both years during which the two-year bond matures. By way of contrast, the same interest rate increase influences the price of the one-year bond only during the one-year lifetime of the bond.

This illustrates that financial instruments' terms to maturity are key determinants of the proportionate capital losses that their owners experience if market

	One-Year £10,000 Zero-Coupon Bond	Two-Year £10,000 Zero-Coupon Bond
Bond Price at 7% Rate	£10,000 / (1.07) = £9,345.79	£10,000 / (1.07)^2 = £8,734.39
Bond Price at 6% Rate	£10,000 / (1.06) = £9,433.96	£10,000 / (1.06)^2 = £8,899.96
Pound Price Change	−£88.17	−£165.57
Percentage Price Change	(−£88.17 / £9,433.96) × (100) = −0.9%	(−£165.57 / £8,899.96) × (100) = −1.9%

Table 5–2

Capital Losses on Bonds with Differing Maturities

This example illustrates that the prices of bonds with longer maturities fall in greater proportion following an expected rise in the market interest rate. Consequently, bonds with longer lifetimes have greater exposure to interest rate risk.

interest rates increase. Instruments with longer terms to maturity expose their owners to greater risk of capital loss. Consequently, holding bonds with longer maturities increases one's exposure to interest rate risk.

Fundamental ISSUES

#1 How are interest yields, financial instrument prices, and interest rate risk interrelated?

Interest yields are rates of return derived from holding financial instruments. The current price of any financial instrument should reflect traders' assessments of the value of the instruments from today's perspective. It follows that a financial instrument's price should depend directly on the discounted present value of current and future returns, which, in turn, depends negatively on the interest rate. Hence, upward movements in interest rates can cause capital losses by unexpectedly depressing market prices, thereby exposing the holder to interest rate risk.

The Term Structure of Interest Rates

What factors determine the actual values of market interest rates? As we shall discuss in Chapters 10 to 15, the overall level of interest rates depends on a number of economic factors. Once the general level of interest rates is determined, the interrelationships among interest rates on various financial instruments depend largely on two key factors. One of these is the instruments' terms to maturity. The other is the underlying risks associated with the financial instruments.

The relationship among interest yields on financial instruments that possess the *same risk, liquidity (ease of convertibility into cash), and tax characteristics* but differing terms to maturity is called the ***term structure of interest rates***. Bond yields normally differ even if bonds with different maturities are identical in every other respect.

Yield Curves We can plot the differences among interest yields for various terms to maturity on a ***yield curve,*** or a chart showing yields on similar bonds with different terms to maturity. Figure 5–1 on the following page displays yield curves for selected nations and the countries of the euro area.

term structure of interest rates
The relationship among yields on financial instruments with identical risk, liquidity, and tax characteristics but differing terms to maturity.

yield curve
A chart giving the relationship among yields on bonds that differ only in their terms to maturity.

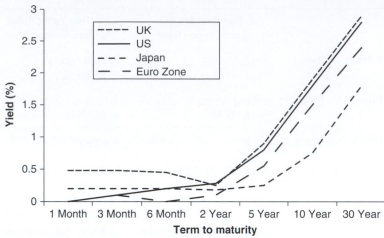

Figure 5–1

Yield Curves for Selected Nations

Typically, yield curves slope upward: interest yields rise at longer terms to maturity.

Source: Authors created based on data from *the Financial Times*, September 24, 2012, www.ft.com.

As you can see, the yield curves in Figure 5–1 slope upward. Most of the time, this is the typical shape of a yield curve, indicating that interest yields normally rise with an increase in the term to maturity of a financial instrument. Nevertheless, at various times nations can experience downward-sloping yield curves. If this circumstance arises, then a country's yield curve is said to be an *inverted* yield curve, because interest yields fall as the term to maturity increases.

Why is it that yield curves typically slope upward? Economists have advanced three fundamental explanations in an effort to answer this question. These are known as the segmented markets theory, the expectations theory, and the preferred habitat theory.

segmented markets theory

A theory of the term structure of interest rates that views bonds with differing maturities as nonsubstitutable, so that their yields differ because they are determined in separate markets.

Segmented Markets Theory The key idea behind the *segmented markets theory* of the term structure of interest rates is that financial instruments with differing terms to maturity are not perfect substitutes. Consequently, they essentially are traded in separate financial markets, even though they may be nearly identical instruments in all respects other than their terms to maturity. Then the interactions between supply and demand conditions within each individual market determine each instrument's yield. Thus, interest yields of financial assets with differing terms to maturity should reflect these natural differences in desired holdings of financial assets based on their terms to maturity.

The segmented markets theory explains why yields may differ across various terms to maturity, but it suffers from two fundamental problems. One is that the theory assumes that financial instruments with different maturities are not perfect substitutes, even though there is considerable evidence that the interest yields on bonds with similar characteristics move together over time. Hence, bonds that differ only on the basis of terms to maturity must be somewhat substitutable. The second difficulty with the segmented markets theory is that it fails to explain why an upward-sloping yield curve should be a "normal" outcome, as it so typically is.

expectations theory

A theory of the term structure of interest rates that views bonds with differing maturities as perfect substitutes, causing their yields to differ solely because traders anticipated that short-term interest rates will rise or fall.

The Expectations Theory A theory that can shed light on both of these issues is called the *expectations theory* of the term structure of interest rates. We can illustrate the basic features of the expectations theory by examining a setting in which an individual plans to save funds over a two-year period. The individual confronts two possibilities. One option is to hold a two-year bond for the two years to maturity. We suppose that this bond has an annual interest yield denoted I. The individual's other option is to hold one-year bonds each year over the two-year interval. If the individual makes this choice, he would place his funds in a one-year bond for the first year at an interest rate of R_1. At the end of the first year, the bondholder would place the principal plus the interest accumulated during the first year in holdings of an additional one-year bond that would mature at the conclusion of the second year. We assume that at the beginning of the two-period planning horizon when the individual must choose which savings strategy to pursue, he anticipates that the one-year bond's interest yield during the second year will be R_2^e.

Naturally, the individual would be willing to hold *either* one-year or two-year bonds only if the return over the two years is expected to be the same under either option. This would be the case if

$$I = (R_1 + R_2^e)/2.$$

Hence, the individual would be indifferent between the alternative savings strategies if the annual interest rate on the two-year bond, I, were equal to the expected *average* annual interest rate from holding one-year bonds, $(R_1 + R_2^e)/2$. If the two-year bond rate were to rise above this expected average of one-year rates, then the individual would hold only two-year bonds. If the two-year bond rate were to fall below this expected average of one-year rates, however, then the individual would hold only one-year bonds each year. As this individual and others participating in financial markets seek to arbitrage between these two choices, the two sides of the equation would, in fact, be driven to an equality in the marketplace.

To see the implications of the expectations theory for the yield curve, suppose that the one-year bond were to pay $R_1 = 0.05$ during the first year and that people expect the one-year bond yield for the next year to be $R_2^e = 0.07$. In equilibrium, therefore, the two-year bond rate I should, under the expectations theory, turn out to be equal to the average of 0.05 and 0.07, which is $(0.05 + 0.07)/2 = 0.06$. In this situation, the current one-year bond rate would be 7 percent, whereas the rate on a two-year bond would be 6 percent. Hence, the yield curve for bonds of one- and two-year maturities would slope upward.

Now consider what would happen if people were to expect a sharp decline in the future one-year bond rate, to $R_2^e = 0.03$. As a result, the two-year bond rate would have to decline to

$$I = (R_1 + R_2^e)/2 = (0.05 + 0.03)/2 = 0.04.$$

Thus, the two-year bond now would yield 4 percent per year. Because the one-year bond yield would be higher, at 5 percent, the yield curve now would be downward sloping, or inverted.

As you can see, unlike the segmented markets theory, the expectations theory of the term structure offers an explanation for why yield curves may slope upward or downward: An upward-sloping yield curve indicates a general expectation that short-term interest rates will rise, whereas a downward-sloping yield curve indicates a general expectation that short-term interest rates will fall. A glaring problem with this conclusion is that yield curves normally slope upward. If interest yields are as likely over long intervals to fall as they are to rise, then the expectations theory cannot provide an explanation for why yield curves generally slope upward.

preferred habitat theory
A theory of the term structure of interest rates that views bonds as imperfectly substitutable, so that yields on longer-term bonds must be greater than those on shorter-term bonds even if short-term interest rates are not expected to rise or fall.

The Preferred Habitat Theory To resolve this problem with the expectations theory, the *preferred habitat theory* of the term structure of interest rates puts together key features of the segmented markets theory and the expectations theory. According to the preferred habitat theory, financial instruments are *imperfectly substitutable* if they have differing maturities but are identical in other respects. The preferred habitat theory proposes that the expectations theory otherwise constitutes an acceptable theory of the term structure.

The key assumption of the preferred habitat theory is that, holding all other factors constant, people usually prefer to hold financial instruments with shorter maturities. The reason is that short-maturity instruments typically are more liquid instruments, making them somewhat more desirable to hold as compared with longer-term instruments. Thus, people have a natural "preference for the habitat" of trading in shorter-term instruments, and so a *term premium* on longer-term bonds would be necessary to induce them to hold these instruments alongside short-term instruments, if all other factors were the same.

term premium
An amount by which the yield on a long-term bond must exceed the yield on a short-term bond to make individuals willing to hold either bond if they expect short-term bond yields to remain unchanged.

In relating the interest yields on short- and long-term bonds, the preferred habitat theory modifies the expectations theory by adding a term premium. In the case of one- and two-year bonds, for instance, the interest yield on the two-year bond thereby would equal

$$I = TP + [(R_1 + R_2^e)/2],$$

where TP is the term premium for the two-year bond. Suppose that $R_1 = R_2^e = 0.05$, so that people expect that the one-year bond rate will remain at 5 percent for both years. In addition, suppose also that people have a decided preference to hold one-year bonds. This leads to a sizable term premium of $TP = 0.01$, or 1 percent, to induce holdings of two-year bonds alongside one-year bonds. As a result, the two-year bond rate is equal to

$$\begin{aligned} I &= TP + [(R_1 + R_2^e)/2] \\ &= 0.01 + [(0.05 + 0.05)/2] \\ &= 0.01 + 0.05 = 0.06. \end{aligned}$$

Hence, the two-year bond rate would equal 6 percent even though people anticipate that the one-year bond rate will stay unchanged at 5 percent. The resulting yield curve relating the yields on one- and two-year bonds slopes upward. This implies that over a long period in which interest rates are equally likely to rise or fall, the yield curve normally would have a positive slope. The preferred habitat theory appears to fit the facts: It indicates that yield curves typically should slope upward. It further predicts that yield curves should steepen if people generally expect short-term interest rates to rise and that they should flatten out, or in extreme cases even become inverted, if people expect sharp declines in short-term interest rates.

risk structure of interest rates
The relationship among yields on financial instruments that have the same maturity but differ because of variations in default risk, liquidity, and tax rates.

The Risk Structure of Interest Rates

Differences in terms to maturity provide one reason that interest rates differ across financial instruments. The *risk structure of interest rates* constitutes the other key reason. This refers to the relationship among yields on financial instruments that have the *same maturity* but differ as a result of default risk, liquidity, and tax considerations.

Default Risk A fundamental reason that financial instruments offer different yields is that savers must take into account *default risk*. This is the possibility that the issuer of a financial instrument may be unable to honor obligations to pay off the principal or interest. The bonds issued by many national governments, and particularly those of the United States and other developed countries, have relatively low default risk. The reason is that as long as governments can enforce their power to tax and to create new money, they can raise taxes to make interest and principal payments on bonds that they issue.

In contrast, financial market traders typically regard bonds issued by governments of a number of less-developed nations as much riskier. The reason is that political instability in these nations makes traders wary of holding these bonds. For instance, a twenty-year bond issued by a nation that has had fifteen changes of government during the past seven years, including perhaps a military coup that led to a renunciation of some past government debt obligations, possesses considerable default risk. Thus, even if the government bond issued by the developing country were to have the same term to maturity, traders would require a higher exchange-rate-adjusted yield to induce them to hold both bonds in their portfolios.

The amount by which this developing country's government bond rate exceeds the Treasury bond rate because of greater risk of debt default risk is the *risk premium*. In this situation, in which the main source of risk stems from political uncertainty, the risk premium arises from perceived *country risk* differences. As we discussed in Chapter 4, country risk can account for risk premiums on bonds issued by various nations for reasons other than political uncertainty. For example, if reports were to emerge that the oil reserves of an otherwise politically stable, oil-producing nation were being depleted, then traders likely would consider bonds issued by that nation as possessing greater country risk as well. We shall discuss issues involving country risk in greater detail in Chapter 7.

Private risks also can account for interest rate risk premiums. For example, consider a twenty-year Italian corporate bond. Even if the Italian company issuing the bond were to have a very good current credit rating, the possibility nonetheless exists that its profitability could decline at any future date within the next twenty years. In contrast to the Italian government, this company could not assess taxes or print money to pay its debt obligations if its fortunes turned sour during that span. Thus, the perceived default risk for the Italian corporate bond would be greater than for a twenty-year Italian government bond. The interest rate on the Italian corporate bond typically would equal the rate on the government bond plus a risk premium.

Liquidity An additional rationale for why bonds of most developing nations typically have yields exceeding exchange-rate-adjusted yields on developed-country bonds with the same terms to maturity is that bonds of developing nations most often are less-liquid financial instruments. This is true because financial markets of a number of developing nations have low trading volumes. Thus, the holder of bonds issued by, say, the British, German, or Japanese government knows that these bonds will be easier to sell in a time of a need for cash, as compared with bonds issued by the governments of Rwanda, Bangladesh, or Vietnam. Hence, yields on the latter bonds will be higher.

Default risk, therefore, is not the only factor that can cause differences between yields on bonds with the same terms to maturity. Another portion of the

default risk
The possibility that an individual or business that issues a financial instrument may be unable to meet its obligations to repay the principal or to make interest payments.

difference between yields on bonds with the same maturity is a *liquidity premium*. Nevertheless, it is very difficult for economists to distinguish between risk and liquidity premiums. For instance, bonds issued by the Russian government are less liquid than U.S. Treasury bonds of the same maturity. A key reason for this liquidity difference is that fewer traders are willing to take on the additional country risk associated with holding Russian bonds.

For this reason, economists apply the term *risk premium* to refer to interest rate differences resulting both from diverging degrees of default risk *and* from distinctive levels of liquidity. When traders or the financial media refer to a risk premium on one bond relative to another, such as the nearly 2-percentage-point differential that often exists between interest yields on U.S. corporate bonds and yields on U.S. Treasury bonds of the same maturity, they generally have in mind a yield difference arising because a bond has greater default risk *and* lower liquidity.

Tax Differences One more reason that bonds with identical maturities may have different interest yields is that nations' tax laws sometimes treat some bonds different than others. For example, in the United States bondholders generally have not been required to pay either federal or state taxes on their interest earnings from holdings of municipal bonds, which are bonds issued by state and local governments. Hence, the pretax and after-tax yields on U.S. municipal bonds are the same, but after-tax yields on U.S. Treasury bonds are typically 0.5 to 1 percentage point lower than their pretax yields. To compensate investors for the greater tax bite on Treasury bonds, market yields on these bonds are higher than market yields on municipal bonds.

 Fundamental ISSUES

#2 Why do market interest yields vary with differences in financial instruments' terms to maturity?

Yields on financial instruments with differing maturities will not be equal for two reasons. One is that differences in short-term and long-term rates may arise from differing expectations about whether future short-term interest rates are likely to rise or fall relative to current interest rates on longer-term instruments. Another is that short-term financial instruments generally are more liquid and less risky than longer-term instruments, so that a term premium is needed to induce individuals to be indifferent between holding either long-term or short-term instruments. Differences in degrees of default risk and liquidity also cause risk premiums to be imbedded in the yields on financial instruments. Because risk premiums differ across instruments, their market yields typically differ even if they have the same terms to maturity. National and state governments also tax some instruments at different rates, which causes their market rates to diverge.

INTEREST RATE DIFFERENTIALS—EXCESS RETURNS AND FAILURE OF UNCOVERED INTEREST PARITY

Chapter 4 discussed why international relationships may exist among interest rates and exchange rates. One such relationship is the uncovered-interest-parity condition. If this condition is satisfied, the interest rate on a U.S. bond, *R*, should equal the interest rate on a foreign bond, R^*, plus the rate at which the domestic currency is anticipated to depreciate during the period that the two bonds mature, $(S_{+1}^e - S)/S$. As also noted in Chapter 4, however, there is little evidence that the uncovered-interest-parity condition is satisfied.

Breakdowns of Uncovered Interest Parity and Excess Returns

What happens if the uncovered-interest-parity condition fails to hold? For instance, what if the expected rate of domestic currency depreciation is greater than the differential between the market interest rates on domestic and foreign bonds, so that $(S_{+1}^e - S)/S$ exceeds the difference between R and R^*? The answer is that in this situation a saver can anticipate earning *excess returns* on foreign bonds.

Excess Returns If the expected rate of currency depreciation exceeds the differential between the interest rate on a domestic bond and the interest rate on a foreign bond, then a domestic resident can anticipate earning a higher return than simply holding the domestic bond and earning the rate R. She can do so by engaging in the following transactions. She can convert dollars to the foreign currency and hold foreign bonds, thereby earning the rate R^*. Then she can obtain more dollars per unit of foreign currency after the foreign bond matures and the domestic currency depreciates. In this way, the U.S. resident can expect to earn an excess return equal to $(S_{+1}^e - S)/S - (R - R^*)$. For instance, if the expected annual rate of depreciation of the dollar relative to the euro is 2 percent, the annual return on a U.S. bond is 6 percent, and the annual return on a German bond is 5 percent, then the excess return equals 2 percent − (6 percent − 5 percent) = 1 percent.

Evidence on Excess Returns Traditionally, economists have argued that the ability of U.S. residents to earn excess returns should be lessened when considering bonds of nations that have the most developed and open financial markets. For this reason, we might expect that measured excess returns should be relatively smaller in more developed nations, as compared with less-developed, emerging nations.

Consider Figure 5–2 on the next page, which displays estimates of excess returns since 1980. As you can see by comparing the plots in the figure, larger excess returns are not always available on bonds issued in various developing economies than in certain advanced nations. Even though it is sometimes possible to earn significant excess returns by holding bonds of other nations, excess returns in most countries are not very large. Thus, although Figure 5–2 indicates that the uncovered-interest-parity condition is rarely satisfied at any given point in time, over longer-run periods there is a propensity for excess returns to noticeably decline. This appears to be true in developing nations as well as in highly advanced countries.

Accounting for Differences in Excess Returns to Help Explain International Interest Rate Differences

Research by various economists suggests several factors that contribute to the somewhat larger and more persistent excess returns observed in emerging economies. Not surprisingly, one factor is the somewhat less-developed and less-open financial markets in these nations, which lessens the scope for uncovered arbitrage to push interest rates and the spot exchange rate to levels consistent with the uncovered-interest-parity condition.

For emerging economies with fixed exchange rates, another set of factors that may contribute to persistent excess returns in less-developed nations is that these countries typically have higher and more volatile interest rates and inflation rates,

Figure 5–2

Estimates of Excess Returns on International Bond Trading

This figure displays average annualized excess returns for sixteen advanced national and for sixteen developing countries. The excess returns are estimated expected percentage changes in the exchange rate minus interest rate differentials.

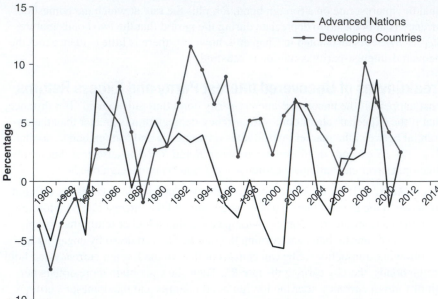

Source: International Monetary Fund, International Financial Statistics, http://www.imf.org.

peso problem

An upward bias in depreciation expectations resulting from a perceived small probability of a large currency realignment.

more variable exchange rates, and less-stable levels of economic activity. These factors can contribute to a ***peso problem***, so-called because first application of the idea was to Mexico. A peso problem is the possibility that traders perceive that there is at least a small probability of a very sizable devaluation of a less-developed nation's currency in response to misalignments of a fixed exchange rate with the exchange rate consistent with underlying economic forces. (We shall have more to say about this issue in Chapter 7.) As a result, there is an upward bias in the expected rate of depreciation of the developing nation's currency, even in times when its value is otherwise relatively stable. A consequence is persistent excess returns in that nation.

Indeed, relatively high levels of economic volatility observed in many emerging nations can contribute to a *risk premium*, which you learned in Chapter 4 can also help explain the failure of uncovered interest parity. Most economic research indicates that risk premiums exist in international financial markets. As yet, however, there is no consensus among economists about the relative contributions of risk premiums, barriers to international arbitrage, or peso problems as factors explaining why excess returns are somewhat more prevalent and persistent in developing nations. (If it holds true, the uncovered-interest-parity condition applies only to bonds with the same maturities, so a natural question is whether excess returns differ across pairings of international financial instruments that vary by maturity; see *Management Notebook: Do Excess Returns Vary at Different Bond Maturities?*)

MANAGEMENT Notebook

Do Excess Returns Vary at Different Bond Maturities?

Uncovered interest parity is one of the most widely studied concepts in international financial economics. To date, however, the only consensus across studies on the concept is that the condition of uncovered interest parity does not appear to hold true for interest rates on bonds with any given term to maturity.

Geert Bekaert of Columbia University, Min Wei of the Federal Reserve, and Yuhang Xing of Rice University have studied uncovered interest parity at different bond maturities. They note that the expectations theory of the term structure of interest rates predicts that uncovered interest parity should hold for any pairing of international financial instruments with the same risk characteristics and the same term to maturity. The expectations theory of the term structure does not usually exactly explain differences in bond interest rates across different maturities, however. Thus, it is conceivable that failure of the expectations theory of the term structure could help account for excess returns on longer-term bonds.

Bekaert, Wei, and Xing, therefore, examined excess returns for twenty years of data for all possible pairings of US, U.K., and German bonds with three-, twelve-, thirty-six- and sixty-month maturities. They sought to determine whether excess returns at longer bond maturities arise due to a breakdown of uncovered interest parity or due to deviations from the expectations theory of the term structure of interest rates. They found that although there are deviations from the predictions of the expectations theory of the term structure at all longer bond maturities, these deviations play at most a minor role in explaining why uncovered interest parity fails to hold for longer-term international financial instruments. Thus, the authors conclude that excess returns at longer maturities arise from a breakdown in uncovered interest parity and not from a failure of the expectations hypothesis of the term structure of interest rates.

For Critical Analysis

Why would we not expect uncovered interest parity to hold for two international financial instruments with differing terms to maturity?

Fundamental ISSUES

#3 What factors explain why international interest rate differentials are often inconsistent with the uncovered-interest-parity condition?

Most evidence indicates that deviations from uncovered interest parity diminish in the long run. Nevertheless, domestic savers can potentially earn excess returns—amounts by which rates of anticipated currency depreciation exceed differentials between the home and foreign interest rates—in international financial markets. These excess returns tend to be slightly larger and more persistent for financial instruments of emerging economies. Obstacles to uncovered arbitrage, peso problems, and risk premiums are all factors that contribute to the existence of excess returns and the failure of uncovered interest parity to hold for these and others of the world's nations.

REAL INTEREST RATES AND REAL INTEREST PARITY

The uncovered-interest-parity condition relates *nominal* interest rate differentials to spot and expected spot exchange rates. This condition is appropriate for evaluating the extent to which arbitrage takes place across international markets if we consider only short- or medium-term financial instruments. Over longer time horizons, however, changes in price levels may affect saving decisions. For example, if the rate of inflation is fairly low, the purchasing power of one dollar of principal changes very little over a three-month time horizon. In the same inflation environment, however, the purchasing power of one dollar of principal can change significantly over a ten-year time horizon. Hence, holders of long-term financial instruments are likely to be motivated by *real* yields as opposed to *nominal* yields.

Real Interest Rates: The Fisher Equation

real interest rate

The nominal interest rate less the rate of price inflation expected to prevail over the maturity period of the financial instrument.

Fisher equation

A condition that defines the real interest rate as the nominal interest rate less the expected rate of inflation.

Economist Irving Fisher defined a financial instrument's ***real interest rate*** as the nominal interest rate less the rate of price inflation expected to prevail during the life of the financial instrument. In what is now known as the ***Fisher equation***, Fisher expressed this definition of the real interest rate as

$$r = R - \pi^e,$$

where r denotes the real interest rate, R denotes the nominal interest rate, and π^e denotes the expected rate of inflation. In other words, the Fisher equation is a condition that defines the real interest rate as the nominal interest rate less the expected rate of inflation.

Typically the Fisher equation is rewritten as

$$R = r + \pi^e.$$

That is, the nominal interest rate is equal to the sum of the real interest rate and the expected rate of inflation. For example, suppose that the nominal rate of interest on a newly issued one-year note is 5 percent. In addition, suppose you expect the rate of inflation to be 3 percent over the next year. Then, according to the Fisher equation, the real interest rate is 2 percent (5 percent minus 3 percent).

Real Interest Parity

The Fisher equation provides an approximation of the real interest rate. By combining uncovered interest parity and relative purchasing power parity, we can use the Fisher equation to establish a condition relating the real rate of interest on financial instruments of two nations that share all of the same characteristics, such as time to maturity and risk.

Combining Relative Purchasing Power Parity and Uncovered Interest Parity
Chapter 2 examined relative purchasing power parity, which is a theory relating changes in the price levels of two nations to changes in the spot exchange rate. For expected price changes, we can express *(ex ante)* purchasing power parity as:

$$\pi^e - \pi^{*e} = (S^e_{+1} - S)/S,$$

where π^e denotes the expected rate of inflation in the domestic nation, π^{*e} denotes the expected rate of inflation in the foreign nation, S^e_{+1} denotes the spot exchange rate that is expected to prevail over the time period considered, and S is the current spot exchange rate. (Recall that in this equation, the spot exchange rate, S, is defined as the number of domestic currency units required to purchase one foreign currency unit.) In other words, the difference in expected rates of inflation is equal to the expected rate of depreciation or appreciation of the domestic currency relative to the foreign currency.

Note that the same term, $(S^e_{+1} - S)/S$, appears on the right-hand side of the equations representing relative purchasing power parity and uncovered interest parity. Hence, we can set these two conditions equal to each other:

$$\pi^e - \pi^{*e} = (S^e_{+1} - S)/S = R - R^*,$$

or

$$\pi^e - \pi^{*e} = R - R^*.$$

We can rearrange this expression to obtain:

$$R - \pi^e = R^* - \pi^{*e}.$$

Note that, according to the Fisher equation, the left-hand side of the equation is equivalent to the domestic real interest rate, r, and the right-hand side of the equation is equivalent to the foreign real interest rate, r^*. Hence, we can also express the equation as

$$r = r^*.$$

This final equation is the ***real-interest-parity*** condition. It indicates that in equilibrium the real interest rates of financial instruments of two nations that share all of the same characteristics, such as time to maturity and risk, are equal. In addition to defining the real rate of interest, Irving Fisher also postulated that the real rate of interest is stable in the long run. Hence, real interest parity is implied by relative purchasing power parity and uncovered interest parity.

real interest parity
A condition that postulates that in equilibrium the real rates of interest on similar financial instruments of two nations are equal.

Deviations from Real Interest Parity as a Measure of International Market Arbitrage Real interest parity holds if international markets are sufficiently open to permit differences in real interest rates to be arbitraged away. Hence, if unhindered international arbitrage occurs, real-interest-rate differentials should not persist over extended time periods. Thus, the existence of persistent real interest differentials would cast doubt on the assumption that international markets are open to arbitrage. Larger deviations from real interest parity naturally indicate less capability to engage in arbitrage across national borders. Smaller deviations from real interest parity indicate that international markets are more open to arbitrage.

Economist Richard Marston of the University of Pennsylvania has shown that real-interest-rate differentials among the industrialized nations are, on average, small. Marston measured how deviations from real interest parity can be decomposed into deviations from relative purchasing power parity and uncovered interest parity. He has shown that because deviations from relative purchasing power parity and uncovered interest parity are small, on average, it is no surprise that deviations from real interest parity are also small. Nonetheless, these deviations may still lead one to conclude that real interest parity does not hold, even for the most developed nations of the world. (Although real interest parity does not appear to hold over near-term time horizons, there is some evidence that deviations from real interest parity are reversed within not much more than two years; see *Management Notebook: How Long Does It Take for Real Interest Rates to Converge?*)

MANAGEMENT Notebook

How Long Does It Take for Real Interest Rates to Converge?

The real-interest-parity condition is derived from the assumption that both the purchasing-power-parity condition and the uncovered-interest-parity condition are satisfied simultaneously. In light of the considerable evidence (discussed in Chapter 2) that purchasing power parity does not hold in the near term, it is unsurprising that the real-world evidence consistently rejects real interest parity over short time horizons.

Nevertheless, we might expect that, given sufficient time for adjustment, both the purchasing-power-parity condition and uncovered-interest-parity condition will more nearly hold, at least on average. To explore this possibility, Citigroup economist Sofiane Sekioua examined data on exchange rates, interest rates on long-term government bonds, and consumer price inflation rates over the period 1923 to 2000 for the United States, the United Kingdom, France, and Japan. Although Sekioua found that real interest parity rarely held at any given point in time during this long interval, deviations from the real-interest-parity condition—caused by terms-of-trade shocks or other factors causing variations in real interest rates—typically tended to reverse within two years' time. Thus, whenever a disturbance in the world economy caused real interest rates to move farther apart, within two years the differential between real interest rates converged back to its previous value. This conclusion provides evidence of a tendency for nations' real interest rates to move toward parity in the long run, even if real interest parity rarely holds true in the short run.

For Critical Analysis

Why is the real-interest-parity condition more likely to hold true over a long time period than over a short time period?

 **Fundamental ISSUES**

#4 What are real interest rates, and how can real-interest-rate differentials serve as indicators of the extent to which international markets are open to arbitrage?

The real interest rate is the nominal interest rate minus expected inflation. If individuals anticipate that purchasing power parity will hold and if the uncovered-interest-parity condition is also satisfied, then real interest parity exists, meaning that real interest rates are equalized across nations. Deviations from real interest parity naturally arise from deviations from purchasing power parity and uncovered interest parity. Thus, the size of deviations from real interest parity provides an indication of the extent to which arbitrage freely takes place across international markets.

HEDGING, SPECULATION, AND DERIVATIVE SECURITIES

Movements in market interest rates cause those who trade in international financial markets to face risks arising from variations in asset returns. They also experience foreign exchange risks that arise from exchange-rate volatility. Let's consider how traders confront these sources of risk.

Possible Responses to Interest Rate Risk

Interest rate risk poses both rewards and challenges to an individual or firm. The rewards arise if an individual or a company finds ways to profit from increases in financial instruments' market values following reductions in market interest rates. The challenges, on the other hand, entail balancing the potential for such capital gains against the possibility of capital losses, or losses incurred if market interest rates decline, thereby reducing the market values of financial instruments.

Some Strategies for Limiting Interest Rate Risk There are various ways that one might seek to limit exposure to interest rate risks. One approach might be to hold bonds with shorter durations, to avoid zero-coupon bonds, and to strive to make certain that all bond holdings yield frequent coupon returns. Another strategy might be to hold mostly short-term financial instruments. Financial instruments with short-term maturities, as we noted earlier, have lower risk of capital losses when interest rates rise as compared with instruments of longer maturity.

There are three problems with this second strategy, however. One is that if the yield curve slopes upward, it is more likely that long-duration instruments will provide greater returns. This is so because if all other factors are unchanged, duration increases with the term to maturity. The higher is the term to maturity, the higher is the interest yield when the yield curve exhibits its normal shape. Consequently, holding only short-duration instruments constitutes a low-return strategy.

Second, continually selling and repurchasing—*rolling over*—short-term instruments can be costly. There are opportunity costs of time that must be devoted to this activity, and traders also incur direct costs in the form of expended effort. Furthermore, rolling over instruments with short terms to maturity entails potentially significant exposure to *reinvestment risk*. This is the possibility that market yields decline by the time the short-term instrument matures, so that a trader could have earned a higher net yield by holding longer-term instruments instead.

Furthermore, holding only short-maturity instruments sacrifices potential benefits that financial market traders could gain from *portfolio diversification*, or spreading risks across holdings of financial instruments with different characteristics. For instance, short-term yields may fall at the same time that long-term yields are rising. Thus, placing funds in a portfolio consisting only of short-term instruments could lead to a lower return than one could otherwise earn by holding a broader mix of instruments. If traders allocate their funds to a portfolio including longer-term instruments, then the rise in yields on these instruments helps offset the effect on the total portfolio return from declines in short-term yields.

Hedging Allocating most funds to holdings of short-term instruments is a potentially costly strategy for addressing interest rate risk. An alternative strategy is to *hedge* interest rate risk using other financial instruments in ways that reduce portfolio risks. A *perfect hedge* constitutes a strategy that fully eliminates such risks.

Market interest rate and exchange-rate conditions can vary from one hour to the next. Consequently, holders of financial instruments must meet two key requirements to hedge against portfolio risks, including interest rate risks and foreign exchange risks. One is sufficient *flexibility* to adapt to various situations. Another is the capability to conduct necessary transactions *rapidly*. The desire to find hedging strategies that combine both flexibility and speed has led to the development of sophisticated financial instruments called *derivative securities*, or *derivatives*.

Derivative Securities

A *forward contract*, such as a forward currency contract that calls for delivery of a financial instrument at a predetermined price on a specific date, represents one type of *derivative security*. In general, a derivative security is any financial instrument with a return that is linked to, or derived from, the returns of other financial instruments. Forward currency contracts fit this definition, because their payoffs to traders depend on spot exchange rates.

reinvestment risk
The possibility that available yields on short-term financial instruments may decline, so that holdings of longer-term instruments might be preferable.

portfolio diversification
Holding financial instruments with different characteristics so as to spread risks across the entire set of instruments.

derivative security
A financial instrument in which the return depends on the returns of other financial instruments.

interest rate forward contract

Contracts committing the issuer to sell a financial instrument at a given interest rate as of a specific date.

Hedging with Forward Contracts As you learned in Chapter 4, foreign exchange market participants use forward currency contracts to protect themselves from foreign exchange risks, or the potential for losses owing to unanticipated variations in spot exchange rates. In a like manner, financial market traders hedge against variability in interest rates by using *interest rate forward contracts*, which are contracts guaranteeing the future sale of a financial instrument at a specified interest rate as of a specific date.

To see how an interest rate forward contract can be a *perfect* hedge for two parties to such a contract, consider an example. Suppose that a London bank feels certain that next year it will receive £10 million in future interest and principal payments from creditworthy customers who have borrowed from the bank. As part of a new management strategy, the bank's managers have decided to reduce the bank's lending next year and to place half of that amount, or £5 million, in default-risk-free five-year notes issued by the British government. The bank's managers wish to guarantee that at the same time the following year, the bank will still find itself earning the current market interest yield on the British government notes, which we shall suppose is equal to 7 percent. At the same time, a German bank's securities portfolio contains several million pounds worth of five-year British government notes that will mature in three years. The German bank's managers think that market interest rates may rise above 7 percent during the next three years, which would imply a fall in the prices of the notes, causing the bank to incur a capital loss on its British note holdings.

To try to hedge against the risks that they face, the London and German banks negotiate an interest rate forward contract. The London bank agrees to purchase five-year British notes valued at 5 million pounds *one year from now* at a price that would yield the 7 percent interest yield currently in effect for those notes. The London bank thereby guarantees that it will earn today's 7 percent market rate a year from now. The German bank also relieves itself of the risk of capital loss within the next year on a significant portion of its portfolio of five-year British notes. This is because the contract guarantees the German bank that the price of the notes will be consistent with a 7 percent yield in the following year.

Speculation with Derivatives As this example and those in Chapter 4 concerning forward currency contracts indicate, traders use derivative securities as hedging instruments for the purpose of protecting a portfolio from risks of loss. This does not mean, however, that traders do not use derivative securities for purposes of risky speculation in the pursuit of profits.

To understand how derivatives transactions may *increase* overall risk, let's slightly change the conditions of the previous example involving the London and German banks. Suppose now that the London bank's managers currently think that the interest cost of their bank's funds, which now averages 6 percent, is likely to be lower by this time next year. Their belief, however, is not consistent with the widespread views of other financial market participants, who generally expect a significant increase in average funding costs that London banks will face during the next year. Nevertheless, the London bank managers are so sure that their expectation will turn out to be correct that they are willing to enter into the interest rate forward contract with the German bank that we already discussed.

Recall that this contract commits the London bank to buy the British government notes at a price consistent with the *current* market yield of 7 percent. This means that if the widespread expectation that banks' average interest funding costs will rise significantly by the following year are correct, then the net interest profit that the London bank would earn on the British government notes would be much lower next year than the London bank's managers currently *speculate* that it will be. For example, if banks' average funding costs were to rise to as high as 7 percent or more, then the London bank would earn a net profit on its British notes of zero or less. Thus, to the extent that the consensus forecast of higher bank funding costs indicates a strong likelihood that this actually will occur, the London bank would have negotiated a speculative contract and added to its overall risk.

This example indicates that while financial market participants can use derivative securities to hedge against risks, they also can use them to engage in speculative activities. Worldwide derivatives trading has increased dramatically since the early 1980s as financial managers found ways to use derivative securities in hedging strategies. At the same time, however, many traders determined that they could earn significant short-run profits by speculating with derivative securities.

Speculative Gains and Losses Some traders learned that such derivatives speculations can turn out to be wrong. The results were sizable speculative losses, the most notable of which we tabulate in Table 5–3 on the following page. Particularly dramatic among these were the 1994 loss of more than $1.5 billion by Orange County, California; the 1995 loss of about $1.4 billion by Britain's Barings Bank; and the 1998 loss of more than $2 billion by a hedge fund called Long-Term Capital Management (LTCM); and the 2008 loss in excess of $7 billion by the French bank Société Générale. The broader consequences of these losses were layoffs for Orange County employees, the collapse of Barings Bank, and a bank bailout of hedge-fund investors mediated by the Federal Reserve, and an emergency campaign by Société Générale to solicit funds from stockholders.

Where did all the "lost" funds tabulated in Table 5–3 end up? The answer is that the funds did not evaporate. Instead, they fell into the possession of individuals, businesses, financial institutions, and government agencies that made the right choices in their own speculative strategies. For instance, in our example involving the London and German banks, if the London bank's managers turn out to be incorrect in their anticipation of a fall in average bank funding costs, then the London bank experiences losses from the interest rate forward contract. The "lost" funds flow to the German bank, which is able to remove the British notes from its portfolio at a 7 percent yield, and hence at an above-market price, in the following year.

This leads us to the following conclusion about losses in derivatives transactions:

> **For each "loser" in derivatives speculation, there also must be a "winner" on the other side of the transaction.**

From society's perspective, gains and losses from derivatives speculation must, in a purely accounting sense, *cancel out*. As we shall discuss, however, this does not mean that governments have not become concerned about the potential for broader fallout from large derivatives losses.

Table 5–3

Major Derivatives Losses since 1990

Many companies and municipalities have experienced huge losses from derivatives.

Estimate of Loss	Company/Municipality	Primary Derivatives
$50 million	First Boston	Options
$260 million	Volkswagen	Currency futures
$100 million	Cargill Fund	Mortgage derivatives
$157 million	Procter & Gamble	Currency futures
$100 million	Florida State Treasury	Mortgage derivatives
$20 million	Gibson Greeting Cards	Swaps
$35 million	Dell Computer	Swaps and options
$20 million	Paramount Communications	Swaps
$150 million	Glaxo, Inc.	Mortgage derivatives
$1,500 million	Orange County, California	Mortgage derivatives
$50 million	Capital Corp. Credit Union	Mortgage derivatives
$195 million	Wisconsin Investment Funds	Swaps
$25 million	Escambia County, Florida	Mortgage derivatives
$1,400 million	Barings Bank, UK	Stock index futures
$65 million	PacifiCorp	Currency options
$83 million	Bank of Tokyo-Mitsubishi	Swaps and options
$3,500 million	Long-Term Capital Management	Swaps
$689 million	United Bank of Switzerland	Stock index futures
$720 million	Deutsche Bank	Swaps and options
$149 million	NatWest Bank	Swaps and options
$691 million	Allied Irish Bank	Currency options
$7,150 million	Société Générale	Stock index futures

 Fundamental ISSUES

#5 What are derivative securities?

Derivative securities are financial instruments that have returns based on the returns of other financial instruments. Traders may use derivative securities to hedge against interest rate and foreign exchange risks. They also may use derivatives to try to earn profits based on speculations about future movements in interest rates and exchange rates.

COMMON DERIVATIVE SECURITIES AND THEIR RISKS

There are several categories of derivative securities. The characteristic that they all share is that their returns stem from returns on other financial instruments. In addition, traders may use them as hedging instruments. Traders also may use these instruments in speculative strategies.

Forward Contracts

In the example of an interest rate forward contract between London and German banks, the London bank agreed to purchase British government notes in the following year at a price consistent with the current market yield. In the terminology of forward contracts, the London bank took a ***long position***, meaning that the London bank is obliged to *purchase* the British government's notes next year at a fixed yield. By way of contrast, the German bank selling the notes took a ***short position***, meaning that the German bank must *sell* the British government notes the following year at the contracted price. By entering into the forward contract, however, the German bank's managers were able to remove the British government notes from their portfolios more quickly, thus avoiding the possibility of incurring a capital loss if market yields were to rise.

Two factors that may limit the market for forward contracts are setting terms of the contract and default risk. Participants in forward contracts must agree to specific contract terms. Sometimes it is difficult for two parties to reach agreement. In our example, we simply assumed that the London and German banks could reach mutually satisfying terms. In reality, reaching an agreement on the terms of forward contracts can be a complex undertaking.

Default risk also somewhat deters the use of forward contracts. In our banking example, the London bank might be better off defaulting on the contract if its funding costs were to rise sharply within a year's time. This could make the German bank less likely to agree to the terms of the contract. Such potential incentives for default make interest rate forward contracts more risky and less liquid, thereby restraining trading volumes somewhat.

long position
An obligation to purchase a financial instrument at a given price and at a specific time.

short position
An obligation to sell a financial instrument at a given price and at a specific time.

Futures

A *futures contract* is an agreement by one party to deliver to another a quantity of a commodity or financial instrument at a specific future date. In contrast to forward contracts, futures contracts specify *standardized* quantities and terms of exchange. Futures contracts specify in advance the amounts to be traded and the guidelines for transactions. Because futures contracts are standardized, parties do not have to spend time working out contract terms.

Holders of futures experience profits or losses on the contracts at anytime before the contract expires. This is because futures contracts require daily cash-flow settlements. By way of contract, profits or losses occur only at the expiration date of a forward contract, which requires settlements only at maturity.

The futures exchange is an organized market that simplifies the task of selling of a futures contract to another party. This makes futures contracts highly liquid. Consequently, futures trading has grown much more rapidly than transactions in forward contracts. This does not mean that derivatives trading outside public futures exchanges is "small potatoes"; the estimated value of worldwide forward contracts and other derivatives transactions amounts to more than $80 trillion, or more than seven times the amount of *annual* U.S. nominal national income.

futures contract
An agreement to deliver to another a given amount of a standardized commodity or financial instrument at a designated future date.

Visit the Futures Industry Association at *http://www2.fiafii.org.*

interest rate futures
Contracts to buy or sell a standardized denomination of a specific financial instrument at a given price at a certain date in the future.

stock-index futures
Promises of future delivery of a portfolio of stocks represented by a stock price index.

currency future
An agreement to deliver to another a standardized quantity of a specific nation's currency at a designated future date.

Interest Rate Futures Contracts requiring delivery of standard quantities of a financial instrument at a specified price and rate of return and on a certain date are *interest rate futures*. Traders undertake transactions in these contracts at the Chicago Board of Trade (CBOT) futures exchange and other exchanges around the world. Each exchange establishes requirements that parties to such a transaction must meet. The financial instruments of futures contracts usually are U.S. Treasury bonds and other government bonds. For example, a trader may enter into a five-year U.S. Treasury note futures contract, which constitutes an agreement to purchase or sell U.S. Treasury notes in standard denominations of $100,000.

Stock-Index Futures Standardized agreements to deliver, on a specified date, a portfolio of stocks represented by a stock price index are *stock-index futures*. For example, in the case of Standard & Poor's (S&P) 500 futures traded at the Chicago Mercantile Exchange, the stock portfolio is representative of market value of the 500 companies listed in the S&P index. Likewise, Nikkei-225 Stock Average futures are based on a portfolio of 225 stocks traded in the Tokyo Stock Exchange. It was a series of bad bets about Nikkei-225 futures traded in the Singapore International Monetary Exchange (Simex) that led to the downfall of Barings Bank in 1995.

To see how to calculate the value of a futures contract, let's consider an example involving an S&P 500 index futures contract. Computing the dollar value of such a contract requires multiplying the current market price of the futures contract by $500. For instance, if the S&P 500 futures price is 400, then the value of the contract is equal to $200,000. If an individual were to take a *short position* with an S&P 500 futures contract, then she would agree to deliver a cash amount of $500 times whatever the futures price turns out to be at the date in the contract. A party on the other end of the transactions, in contrast, would take a *long position* and agree to pay 400 times $500 for this contract today. Thus, if the market price of the futures contract when the date arrives were to equal to 500, then the contract would have a dollar value of $250,000. The individual in the short position would lose $50,000. The buyer in the long position, in turn, would gain $50,000. The buyer in the long position would have paid $200,000 for the $250,000 cash payment that the seller in the short position is obligated to make.

Currency Futures Futures contracts entailing the future delivery of national currencies are *currency futures*. The world's largest currency futures market is the International Monetary Market of the Chicago Mercantile Exchange (CME), in which traders conduct futures transactions in numerous currencies, including those of Australia, Canada, Germany, Japan, Mexico, Switzerland, and the United Kingdom. Figure 5–3 shows how the CME executes trades of currency futures and other derivatives contracts.

Currency futures contracts, like other futures, entail daily cash-flow settlements, whereas currency forward contracts entail a single settlement only at the date of maturity. As a result, the market prices of forward and futures contracts usually differ. In addition, futures contracts typically involve smaller currency

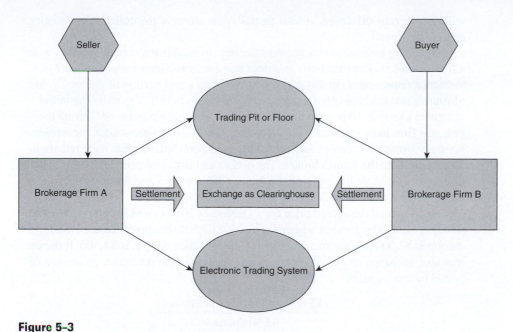

Figure 5–3

How an Exchange. Executes Derivatives Transactions

Buyers and sellers engage in transactions with brokerage firms that are members of an exchange, such as the Chicago Mercantile Exchange. Brokers process these orders in the trading pits or via an electronic trading system, and a clearinghouse linking member firms executes the transactions.

denominations, as compared with forward contracts. Large banking institutions and corporations that transmit large volumes of foreign currencies in their normal business operations are the primary users of forward contracts. Individuals and smaller firms that wish to undertake hedging or speculative strategies typically trade currency futures instead.

 On the WEB

Learn about the Chicago Mercantile Exchange at *http://www.cmegroup.com.*

Hedging with Currency Futures How might one act on a current currency futures quote? Suppose that a British firm has a franchise operation in the United States. The firm's managers anticipate that the current year's profits from this operation will be $3 million, which they plan to convert to British pounds. If the dollar were to depreciate relative to the pound during the year, then the pound-denominated value of the $3 million would be lower at the end of the year. That is, the British firm's exposure to translation risk would cause it to lose a portion of its dollar-denominated profits from its U.S. operation. To hedge against this risk, the firm's managers could take a long position via a pound future that expires in December. As the dollar-denominated profit earnings of the firm decline in value relative to the British pound, the pound-denominated value of the firm's December future will rise, thereby offsetting, at least partially, the effect of the dollar's depreciation against the pound.

Reducing translation risk requires the firm to establish a *margin account* with a futures broker. The firm posts an *initial margin* (sometimes called the *bond performance requirement*) in this account by paying a small portion of the total value of futures that the broker will purchase on the firm's behalf. Typically the initial margin is less than 10 percent of the total value of futures purchased. During the year, the firm must maintain a *maintenance margin* (sometimes called the *minimum bond performance requirement*), which is a minimum balance that must remain in its account with the futures broker. The broker and firm also establish a *marked-to-market* procedure for applying the future contract gains and losses to the firm's account at the close of each trading day.

Suppose that the agreed price for a December 2014 pound future is 1.5486 per pound. The standard size of a pound future is £62,500. Suppose that the initial margin is $2,000 per contract and that the maintenance margin is $1,500. If the current spot exchange rate is 1.5274 per pound, then the firm purchases an amount of pound futures equal to

$$\frac{[\$3 \text{ million}/\$1.5274 \text{ per pound}]}{62,500 \text{ pound}}$$

which is approximately equal to 32. Therefore, purchasing thirty-two standard pound futures contracts provides the best possible futures hedge for the British firm. Note that the firm's initial margin is $32 \times \$2,000 = \$64,000$. Thus, for a $3 million futures account with its broker, the firm must post only $64,000 in its margin account with its broker.

Daily Futures Settlement To illustrate the daily settlement process of a typical futures contract, let's extend our example by supposing that on the first trading day the market closes at a futures price of $1.5294 per pound, so that the firm's thirty-two pound futures appreciate. To keep things simple, let's also assume that the firm pays no brokerage fees. On the first day, the firm earns a dollar profit equal to ($1.5294 per pound − $1.5274 per pound) × 62,500 pounds × 32 = $4,000. The firm's margin account thereby rises from $64,000 (the initial margin) to $64,000 + $4,000 = $68,000.

If the closing futures price on the second trading day drops to $1.5264 per pound, then the firm experiences a dollar loss on the pound futures equal to

($1.5264 per pound − $1.5294 per pound) × 62,500 pounds × 32 = −$6,000.

The firm's margin account thereby falls from $68,000 to $68,000 − $6,000 = $62,000.

Now suppose that the futures price rises to $1.5332 per pound on the third trading day. Then the firm earns a dollar profit equal to

($1.5304 per pound − $1.5264 per pound) × 62,500 pounds × 32 = $8,000,

and the firm's margin account thereby rises from $62,000 to $62,000 + $8,000 = $70,000.

Note how the set of thirty-two futures contracts serves as a hedging instrument for the British firm. If during the course of the year the pound appreciates against the dollar, then the firm's realized pound-denominated value of profits from its U.S. franchise operation declines, so that each dollar of profits from those operations has a smaller pound-equivalent value at the end of the year. As the pound appreciates against the dollar, however, the British company's futures margin position improves, thereby offsetting some or all of the firm's translation risk exposure.

Options

Another type of derivative instrument is an *option*, which is a financial contract providing the holder the right to purchase or sell an underlying financial instrument at a given price. This right does not require the holder to buy or sell. It gives the buyer the *option* to do so. The given price at which the holder of an option can exercise the right to purchase or sell a financial instrument is the option's *exercise price*, which traders also call the *strike price*.

   Call options are options that allow the holder to *purchase* a financial instrument at the exercise price. *Put options* are options that allow the buyer to sell a financial instrument at the exercise price. Traders call an option granting the holder the right to exercise the right of purchase or sale at any time before or including the date at which the contract expires an *American option*. They call an option that allows the holder to exercise the right of purchase or sale *only* on the date that the contract expires a *European option*.

Stock Options and Futures Options Many individuals and firms use options to hedge against risks owing to variations in interest rates or stock prices. To do this, they trade *futures options*, which are options to buy or sell stock-index futures or interest rate futures, and *stock options*, which are options to buy or sell shares in corporations.

   Trading volumes in the stock-index futures market have risen considerably since the 1980s. Paralleling this growth has been broadened trading in the futures options market. In fact, today more options on stock-index futures—essentially derivatives of derivatives—are traded than options based on actual stocks.

Currency Options Contracts that give the owner the right to buy or sell a fixed amount of a given currency at a specified exchange rate at a certain time are *currency options*. Currency *put* options grant the holder the right to sell an amount of currency, whereas currency *call* options grant the holder the right to purchase an amount of the currency. Multinational corporations can purchase currency options directly from banks via *over-the-counter* contracts, but they can also purchase them in organized exchanges.

Limited losses and potential profits from using currency call options Let's consider how a U.S. importer buying €2 million of finished goods for a June payment might hedge against foreign exchange risk using a currency call option. If the current spot rate is $1.3000 per euro, then the €2 million equal $2,600,000. To hedge against an unanticipated change in the exchange rate between now and June, the importer purchases June euro call options. At an exercise exchange rate of $1.3150, as shown in Figure 5–4, the upper limit on the dollar cost of the imported goods is $2,630,000. A June call option with this exercise price has a *premium* of $0.0238 per euro, which is the effective cost of purchasing the contract. Consequently, one contract for the standard amount of €62,500 requires an expenditure of $1,487.50. Covering the €2 million in standard allotments of €62,500 requires exactly thirty-two contracts, for a total expenditure, or *total premium*, of 32 × $1,487.50 = $47,600.

   Once the importer purchases the thirty-two option contracts for $47,600, if the dollar depreciates above $1.3150 per euro, and if we ignore exercise fees that the contract might specify, then the importer would choose to exercise the option.

option
A financial contract giving the owner the right to buy or sell an underlying financial instrument at a certain price within a specific period of time.

exercise price
The price at which the holder of an option has the right to buy or sell a financial instrument; also known as the strike price.

call option
An option contract giving the owner the right to purchase a financial instrument at a specific price.

put option
An option contract giving the owner the right to sell a financial instrument at a specific price.

American option
An option in which the holder may buy or sell a security any time before or including the date at which the contract expires.

European option
An option in which the holder may buy or sell a financial instrument only on the day that the contract expires.

futures options
Options to buy or sell futures contracts.

stock options
Options to buy or sell firm equity shares.

currency option
A contract granting the right to buy or sell a given amount of a nation's currency at a certain price within a specific period of time.

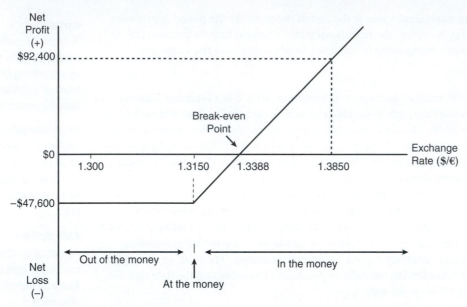

Figure 5–4   Potential Profit and Limited Loss of a Call Option

At a per-contract premium of $0.0238 per euro, each €62,500 contract entails a premium expenditure of $1,487.50, so that the total premiums that the holder of the options pays would be 32 × $1,487.50 = $47,600. The maximum loss that the holder can incur on the option is limited to this amount. At or above the exercise exchange rate of $1.3150 per euro, the holder of the options can exercise the options and recoup at least a portion of the premiums paid for the options. At the spot exchange rate of $1.3388 per euro, the holder's earnings from exercising the options just cover the total premiums paid for the options. At a higher spot exchange rate, the holder of the options earns a net profit. For example, at the spot exchange rate of $1.3850 per euro, the holder earns a net profit of $92,400.

For example, if the dollar depreciates to an exchange rate of $1.3850 per euro, then it costs the importer $2,770,000 to obtain €2 million in the spot market. The exchange-rate change increases the importer's costs by $2,770,000 − $2,600,000 = $170,000. Exercising the option and obtaining the €2 million at the exercise price of $1.3150 per euro, or at a total dollar expenditure of $2,630,000, thereby saves $140,000. Considering the premium that the importer paid for the options, the importer comes out ahead by an amount equal to $140,000 − $47,600 = $92,400.

Note that the firm did not completely hedge against losses if the spot exchange rate turns out to be $1.3850 per euro, because the firm pays a total of $2,630,000 + $47,600 = $2,677,600 using its option contracts. This is $77,600 more than the $2,600,000 that the firm would have to pay if the exchange rate had remained at its initial value of $1.3000 per euro. Hence, the firm still incurs a net loss of $77,600 as a result of a rise in the exchange rate from $1.3000 per euro to $1.3850 per euro. This is better than the $170,000 loss it otherwise would have incurred without the currency options.

A spot exchange rate of $1.3850 per euro is just one possible outcome, however. Figure 5–5 illustrates the limited loss and potential profit resulting from the importer's call options for a range of possible values of the spot exchange rate. The maximum loss that the importer can experience is the total premium of $47,600 for the thirty-two option contracts. Below the strike exchange rate of $1.3150 per euro, the importer is "out of the money," meaning that the firm cannot exercise the options. If the spot exchange rate rises to $1.3150 per euro, however, then the

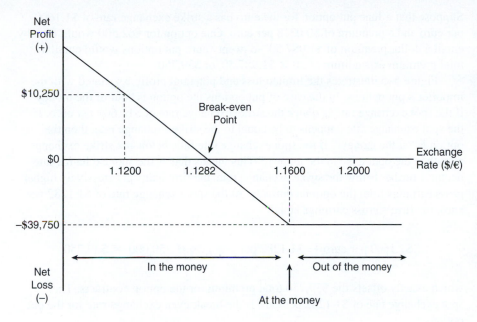

Figure 5–5

Potential Profit and Limited Loss of a Put Option

Given a premium payment of $1,987.50 for each €62,500 contract, the total premiums that the holder of twenty put option contracts pays would be 20 × $1,987.50 = $39,750, and the holder's maximum loss is limited to this amount. At or below the strike exchange rate of $1.1600 per euro, the holder of the options can exercise the options and recover at least part of the premiums paid for the options. At the spot exchange rate of $1.1282 per euro, the earnings that the holder receives just cover the total premium payment. At a lower spot exchange rate, the holder earns a net profit.

importer has the option to exercise the options. At this strike exchange rate, the importer is "at the money." Above the strike exchange rate, the firm is "in the money," meaning that it earns gross receipts that begin to offset the total premium it pays for its options.

If the spot exchange rate rises to $1.3388 per euro, then the gross earnings from exercising the option increases to $47,600, which exactly recoups the total premium of $47,600. Hence, the spot exchange rate of $1.3388 per euro is the *break-even point* for the importer's option contracts. If the spot exchange rate rises above $1.3388 per euro, then the importer earns net profits from its options; that is, its gross earnings exceed the total premium paid for the option contracts. Note that if the spot exchange rate turns out to be $1.3850 per euro in Figure 5–5, then the importer's net gain from the option contracts is equal to

$$(1.3850 \text{ per euro} - \$1.3388 \text{ per euro}) \times €2,000,000 = \$92,400,$$

which is the amount we calculated previously.

Limited losses and potential profits from using currency put options Suppose that the U.S. firm previously discussed also sells export goods through its German distributor and that its receipt for a June shipment will amount to €1,250,000. If the current spot exchange rate is $1.2000 per euro, then the €1,250,000 are equivalent to $1,500,000. To hedge against the possible loss of dollar receipts from this sale of goods, the firm purchases twenty euro put options.

If the euro declines in value against the dollar, say to $1.1200 per euro, then the €1,250,000 would yield only $1,400,000 in June. The firm would lose $100,000 in dollar-denominated receipts that month. Using put options would allow the firm to sell the euros it received from this transaction at a guaranteed price if the euro were to depreciate to, or below, the strike exchange rate for the put options.

Suppose that a June put option for the euro has a strike exchange rate of $1.1600 per euro and a premium of $0.0318 per euro. One option for €62,500 would thereby entail a dollar premium of $1,987.50, so twenty euro put options would entail a total premium expenditure of 20 × $1,987.50, or $39,750.

Figure 5–5 illustrates the limited loss and potential profit associated with the importer's put options. In the case of put options the option is "out of the money" if the spot exchange rate is *above* the strike exchange rate of $1.1600 per euro. If the spot exchange rate happens to be equal to the strike exchange rate, then the option is "at the money." If the spot exchange rate falls *below* the strike exchange rate, then the option is "in the money." This means that as the spot exchange rate declines further below the strike exchange rate, the firm gains progressively higher gross earnings from the option contracts. At the spot exchange rate of $1.1282 per euro, the firm's gross earnings equal

$$(\$1.1600 \text{ per euro} - \$1.1282 \text{ per year}) \times €1,250,000 = \$39,750,$$

which exactly offsets the $39,750 total premium for the option contracts. The spot exchange rate of $1.1282 per euro is the break-even exchange rate for the put options.

Suppose that the euro settles at a dollar value of $1.1200 in the foreign exchange market. The U.S. firm will lose $100,000 in receipts from the euro payment. In this instance, the firm can profit from the option contracts by exercising its options and selling euros at the strike exchange rate of $1.1600 per euro. If the firm purchases €1,250,000 at the prevailing spot exchange rate of $1.1200 per euro, then its payment for the euros in the spot market is $1,400,000. Then it can sell the €1,250,000 to the issuer of the option contracts at an exchange rate of $1.1600 per euro. The firm's gross option profit thereby is equal to

$$(\$1.1600 \text{ per euro} - \$1.1200 \text{ per year}) \times €1,250,000 = \$50,000.$$

Again, the firm will not be perfectly hedged if the spot exchange rate turns out to fall from its initial value of $1.2000 per euro to a level of $1.1200 per euro. But the net option profit of $10,250 (the gross option profit of $50,000 less the $39,750 premium) reduces the $100,000 loss to a net amount of $89,750.

Netting Many multinational firms have both expenditures and receipts that are denominated in foreign currencies, much like the importer in our earlier call option and put option examples. The foreign currency expenditures and receipts may cancel out, on net, much of the risk exposure to exchange rate variations. To see how this works, let's combine the two examples.

If the euro appreciates from, say, $1.2200 per euro to $1.2000 per euro, then the importer's €2 million expenditure rises by

$$(\$1.2300 \text{ per euro} - \$1.2000 \text{ per year}) \times €2,000,000 = \$60,000.$$

Simultaneously, the firm's euro receipts rise by

$$(\$1.2300 \text{ per euro} - \$1.2000 \text{ per year}) \times €1,250,000 = \$37,500.$$

Hence, the firm's *net* loss due to the change in the spot exchange rate is $22,500.

Because the firm's two translation-risk exposures tend to offset each other in this way, the firm may choose to *consolidate* these exposures into a single *net* risk exposure. The process of combining currency risk exposures of payments and receipts into a net risk exposure is called **netting**. For the firm in our example, consolidating its payments and receipts yields a net exposure of €2,000,000 in expenditures minus €1,250,000 in receipts, or €750,000 in net expenditures. Hence, the firm could try to hedge against this *net* risk exposure to a euro appreciation solely through call options. The firm uses call options because the €750,000 net risk exposure requires the *delivery* of the currency in the future. Specifically, the firm hedges the net risk by purchasing twelve euro call options contracts (€750,000 / €62,500 = 12) at a total premium of

$$(\$0.0238 \text{ per euro}) \times (12 \times €62,500) = \$17,850.$$

Netting saves the firm from having to use both call and put options to hedge against exposures relating to both expenditures and receipts. If the firm had not used a netting arrangement, then using both thirty-two call options and twenty put options (as in the separate call and put option examples), the total premiums the firm would have had to pay would have been $47,600 + $39,750 = $87,350. Netting reduces the firm's total premium to $17,850 and thereby reduces its premium expense by $69,500.

Swaps

Swaps are financial contracts in which parties to the transactions exchange flows of payments. An **interest rate swap** is one important type of swap on international financial markets. This is a contract under which one party commits itself to exchange a set of interest payments that it is scheduled to receive for a different set of interest payments owed to another party.

Currency Swaps Another key swap contract is a **currency swap**, which is an exchange of payment flows denominated in different currencies. Figure 5–6 on the next page illustrates a sample currency swap, in which we suppose that International Business Machines (IBM) Corporation earns a flow of yen-denominated revenues from computer sales in Japan, while Toshiba Corporation earns dollar revenues from selling computers in the United States. IBM pays dollar dividends and interest to its owners and bondholders, and Toshiba pays yen-denominated dividends and interest to its owners and bondholders. Therefore, IBM and Toshiba could, in principle, use a currency swap as a mechanism for trading their yen and dollar earnings for the purpose of paying income streams to their stockholders and bondholders.

In addition, firms often use swaps to lock in the domestic currency value of a debt payment or a future receipt. Sometimes swap partners are easier to find than counterparties to forward contracts, because swaps directly match traders that require flows denominated in currencies held by one another.

Using swaps also may allow borrowers to arrange better loan terms. For example, suppose that a U.S. company wishes to obtain a loan denominated in euros to fund a project within the European Monetary Union. The firm has a regional presence inside the United States but is relatively unknown in Europe. Consequently, it might have to pay a risk premium on euro-denominated debt issued in Europe. To avoid paying this risk premium, the firm could issue dollar-denominated debt in

netting
The process of combining separate risk exposures that a firm faces in its foreign-currency-denominated payments and receipts into a single net risk exposure.

swap
A contract entailing an exchange of payment flows between two parties.

interest rate swap
A contractual exchange of one set of interest payments for another.

currency swap
An exchange of payment flows denominated in different currencies.

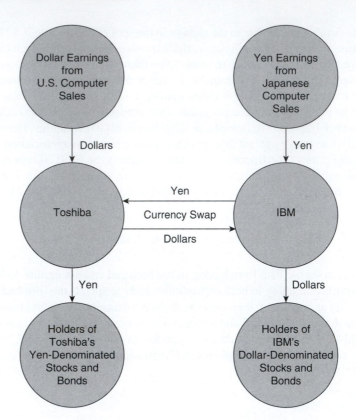

Figure 5–6

A Sample Currency Swap

IBM receives yen earnings from selling computers in Japan, and Toshiba receives dollar earnings from selling computers in the United States. The two companies could use a currency swap contract to trade their yen and dollar earnings to make payments to holders of their stocks and bonds.

the United States. Then it could arrange for an internationally known U.S. bank to transact a dollar-euro swap on relatively favorable terms. This indirect means of obtaining euros by issuing domestic debt and engaging in a currency swap enables the U.S. firm to cover the funding for its euro project while making dollar-denominated interest payments to its U.S. bondholders.

Note that if the euro weakens, the firm can gain on the swap arrangement, but the firm can lose if the euro strengthens. As a result, there is an element of foreign exchange risk that is similar to the risk that the firm could have experienced by taking a long position using a forward contract.

Types of Swaps This has engendered the development of various types of interest rate and currency swaps. The most common swap is the *plain vanilla swap* (sometimes called a *bullet swap*), in which two parties to the swap arrangement agree simply to trade the streams of payments to which each is entitled. There are other, more sophisticated swap contracts, however. For instance, a *cross-currency swap* involves *both* a currency exchange *and* the exchange of a floating interest rate for a fixed interest rate. A *forward swap* delays the actual swap transaction for a period ranging from a few days to a few years. A *swap option* (sometimes called a *swaption*) grants the owner the right to enter into a swap when the swap's market price reaches an exercise or strike price.

Determining the effective returns on these and other derivatives of swap scan be fairly complicated. This has led to the development of a group of financial economists who call themselves *financial engineers* and who seek to develop methods for computing the appropriate market prices of these derivative securities.

Derivatives Risks and Regulation

Financial engineers also seek to determine the risks that traders incur by speculating via derivative securities. This is a conceptually challenging task, partly because simply determining the dollar amounts of derivatives trading can be difficult.

Measuring Derivatives Risks A widely used measure of aggregate derivatives volume, which some use as a rough measure of exposure to derivatives risk, is the *notional value* of derivatives, or the amount of principal that serves as a basis for computing streams of payments. The notional value of foreign exchange derivatives holdings by U.S. banks grew from $1.4 trillion in 1986 to more than $65 trillion in 2013. The estimated notional value of all derivative contracts worldwide in 2013 exceeded $650 trillion, up from just over $43.2 trillion in 1996.

Replacement-cost credit exposure is another popular measure of derivatives-related risk. This is the cost that a party to a derivatives contract faces at current market prices if the other party in the derivative contract defaults before contract settlement. Between 1992 and 1994, the total derivatives replacement-cost credit exposure of U.S. commercial banks amounted to about 5 percent of their assets; today this figure exceeds 10 percent.

Types of Derivatives Risks By holding derivatives, firms expose themselves to three basic types of risk. One type is *derivative credit risk*. This is the risk associated with potential default by a contract party or of an unexpected change in credit exposure resulting from changes in market prices of underlying instruments on which derivative yields depend. The replacement-cost credit exposure measure focuses on this form of derivatives risk.

Another type of risk is *derivative market risk*, which is the risk of potential losses stemming from unexpected payments-system glitches or unusual price changes at the time of settlement. Such events can cause derivative traders' liquidity levels to drop and can slow their normal efforts to adjust their derivatives holdings, thereby exposing them to risks of loss. For instance, if a multinational firm decides to execute a currency option before an anticipated unfavorable price movement, it may try to do so but find that a critical computer link temporarily is "down," thereby causing it to experience a loss when the price changes. In like manner, the price of an underlying asset in a derivatives transaction might fluctuate unexpectedly at the last moment before settlement, also causing the holder to incur a loss.

Finally, derivatives traders must confront *derivative operating risks*, which are risks of loss due to unwise management. Many of the notable derivatives losses summarized in Table 5–3 on page 134 resulted from situations in which firm managers incorrectly valued derivatives and discovered their errors only at settlement. Institutions such as Bankers Trust, which settled several large lawsuits concerning derivatives trading that it performed on behalf of client firms, experienced problems due to inadequate internal controls that resulted in poorly supervised trading by mid-level managers.

As individuals, banks, and companies have become more adept at sorting out the ways in which they can use various derivatives for both hedging and speculation, the markets for these instruments have continued to grow around the world. These markets also have, like those for other financial instruments, become increasingly interconnected. We turn our attention to this development in the next chapter.

derivative credit risks
Risks stemming from the potential default by a party in a derivative contract or from unexpected changes in credit exposure because of changes in the market yields of instruments on which derivative yields depend.

derivative market risks
Risks arising from unanticipated changes in derivatives market liquidity or payments-system failures.

derivative operating risks
Risks owing to a lack of adequate management controls or from managerial inexperience with derivative securities.

Fundamental ISSUES

#6 What are the most commonly traded derivative securities?

The most commonly held and traded derivatives are forward contracts, futures, options, and swaps. Forward contracts include interest rate forward contracts as well as forward currency contracts. Interest rate futures, stock-index futures, and currency futures are the most common types of futures contracts, which differ from forward contracts because traders exchange them in standardized quantities in organized markets in which flows of profits or losses take place daily, rather than only at maturity. The most common options, which are contracts giving the holder the right to buy or sell a financial instrument, are stock options, futures options, and currency options. Interest rate and currency swaps are contracts committing parties to exchanging flows of interest income or payments denominated in different currencies.

Chapter SUMMARY

1. **Interest Yields, Financial Instrument Prices, and Interest Rate Risk:** Interest yields are rates of return derived on financial instruments. The prices of financial instruments should incorporate traders' assessments of the current perceived values of such instruments. Thus, any financial instrument's price should depend directly on the discounted present value of the current and future returns that it yields, which is inversely related to the interest rate. Unanticipated increases in market interest rates can thereby cause capital losses by reducing market prices, exposing the holder of financial instruments to interest rate risk.

2. **Why Market Interest Yields Vary with Differences in Financial Instruments' Terms to Maturity and Risks:** One factor accounting for differences between short-term and long-term interest yields is expectations about whether future short-term interest rates are likely to rise or fall relative to current longer-term interest rates. Another factor is the generally greater liquidity and lower perceived risk of short-term instruments as compared with longer-term instruments, which leads traders to require a term premium to make them indifferent between holding either long-term or short-term instruments. The extent of default risk and liquidity varies across financial instruments, so risk premiums also differ across instruments. Traders require market yields to reflect risk premiums, so financial instruments normally differ even if the instruments have the same terms to maturity. In addition, governments often tax some instruments, which ultimately causes their market yields to diverge.

3. **Factors Explaining Why International Interest Rate Differentials Are Often Inconsistent with the Uncovered-Interest-Parity Condition:** Although departures from uncovered interest parity narrow in the long run, there is evidence that savers in international financial markets can earn excess returns, or amounts by which rates of anticipated domestic currency depreciation exceed differentials between the home and foreign interest rates. Excess returns are generally somewhat higher and longer-lasting on bonds and other financial instruments issued by residents of emerging economies. Factors that contribute to such excess returns and the implied failure of the uncovered-interest-parity condition in these and other countries are barriers to uncovered arbitrage, peso problems, and risk premiums.

4. **Real Interest Rates and How Real Interest Rate Differentials Can Indicate the Extent to Which International Markets Are Open to Arbitrage:** The real interest rate is equal to the nominal rate of interest minus the expected rate of inflation. If the purchasing-power-parity condition is expected to be satisfied and if the uncovered-interest-parity condition also holds, then real interest rates are equalized across nations, and real interest parity exists. Deviations from purchasing power parity and uncovered interest parity result in deviations from real interest parity, so that the size of deviations from real interest parity indicates the degree to which arbitrage can occur across international markets.

5. **Derivative Securities:** These are financial instruments whose returns depend on the returns of other financial instruments. As a result, traders can use these securities to hedge against or speculate on interest rate risks or foreign exchange risks.

6. **The Most Commonly Traded Derivative Securities:** The derivative securities that are most widely held and traded include forward contracts, futures, options, and swaps. Traders commonly use both interest rate forward contracts and forward currency contracts. The most widely traded futures contracts include interest rate futures, stock-index futures, and currency futures. In contrast to forward contracts, futures contracts call for exchange of a standardized amount of financial instruments in highly organized markets, and flows of profits or losses stemming from futures contracts occur daily. The most commonly traded options, or contracts giving the holder the right to buy or sell a financial instrument, are stock options, futures options, and currency options. Swaps are agreements to exchange flows of payments, so interest rate swaps entail exchanges of flows of interest payments, whereas currency swaps are exchanges of payments denominated in different currencies.

QUESTIONSandPROBLEMS

1. The formula for the price of a perpetual, nonmaturing bond with an annual coupon return of C is C/R. Note that the discounted present value of C dollars received each year forever is equal to the infinite sum,

$$P_B = C/(1 + R) + C/(1 + R)^2 + C/(1 + R)^3 + C/(1 + R)^4 + \cdots$$

The amount P_B should be the price that the bearer of the consol would be willing to pay to hold this instrument. And so P_B should equal C/R. Prove that this is true. [*Hint:* Try multiplying the equation above by the factor $1/(1 + R)$. Then subtract the resulting equation from the equation above. Then solve for P_B.]

2. Consider the following data on three Russian bonds, denoted as bond A, bond B, and bond C:

Bond	Term of Maturity	Current Annual Yield
A	5 years	20 percent
B	10 years	17 percent
C	20 years	15 percent

If these bonds are equally risky, then what factor might most likely explain the pattern of yields exhibited by these bonds?

3. Suppose that traders currently anticipate that during the next year the dollar will depreciate by 3.5 percent relative to the euro. At present, the market interest rate on a U.S. Treasury security is 5 percent, and the market interest rate on a German government bond with the same risk characteristics and the same maturity is 3 percent. Is there an excess return available from holding the German government bond? If so, what is the amount of the excess return?

4. Suppose that the annual interest rate on a domestic bond is 5 percent and that the expected rate of inflation is 2 percent per year. Further, suppose that the foreign annual interest rate on a similar bond is 6 percent, while the expected rate of inflation is 4 percent per year.
   a. Applying the concept of uncovered interest arbitrage to the nominal interest rates, what would you expect to happen to the exchange value of the domestic currency during the year?
   b. Applying the concept of relative purchasing power parity to the inflation rates, what would you expect to happen to the exchange value of the domestic currency during the year?

5. Based on the information in Problem 4, what are the domestic and foreign real interest rates? Does real interest parity hold? What flows of funds and real-interest-rate adjustments might you expect to take place between these nations?

6. In what ways does a currency futures contract differ from a forward currency contract?

7. Why is a currency futures option a "derivative of a derivative"? Explain briefly.

8. Suppose your company owes a 500,000 Swiss franc (SFr) payment due in June. If the franc were to appreciate against the dollar, the dollar value of this future payment will increase and your company will experience a loss. Because of this foreign exchange risk exposure, you decide to use a futures contract as a hedge. The initial margin on a franc future is $1,688 and the CME maintenance margin is $1,250.
   a. Explain how you would use franc futures—number of contracts, long or short—and how the futures account would act as a hedge.
   b. Suppose you undertake this transaction with June Sfr futures on the first of the month at the moment the market opens. Show how your initial margin changes daily (for the first through fourth). Indicate if any cash flows are generated or if a margin call occurs.

		Open	High	Low	Settle	Change	Interest
		SWISS FRANC (CME) –125,000 francs; $ per franc					
1st	June	.6251	.6267	.6213	.6252	–.0046	807
2nd	June	.6216	.6216	.6110	.6127	–.0125	980
3rd	June	.6108	.6120	.6029	.6115	–.0012	1,237
4th	June	.6085	.6112	.6058	.6086	–.0029	1,363

   c. How would you close out your position at the end of the fourth day?

9. Using the following table, consider an American-style call option on the euro. The current euro spot exchange rate is $0.9657, and each option contract is for €62,500.

		Calls		Puts	
		Vol.	Last	Vol.	Last
960	Jun	...	...	5	0.0161
980	Jun	14	0.0188	...	...
1000	Jun	1	0.0117	...	...
1020	Jun	1	0.0600	...	0.0100

   a. Is the 980 call option currently in the money, at the money, or out of the money?
   b. Suppose that your corporate economist believes the euro may appreciate against the dollar to an exchange value as high as $1.02 or depreciate to an exchange value as low as $0.96. She therefore purchases eight call contracts to partially hedge an underlying short exposure of $750,000. Draw a diagram illustrating the potential loss or gain on eight call contracts.
   c. Indicate the amount of loss or profit at $0.96, $1.02, and the current spot rate. (Keep all calculations to two decimal places.)
   d. Indicate the break-even rate.
   e. Add to your diagram a line indicating the gain and loss on the underlying exposure as the spot deviates from the current level. Indicate the gain or loss at $0.96 and $1.02.

10. Contrast the pros and cons of using swaps versus forward contracts to cover a long position in a currency, and explain circumstances that are likely to favor using one derivative instead of the other.

Online APPLICATIONS

Internet URL: *http://www.cmegroup.com*

Title: The Chicago Mercantile Exchange (CME)

Navigation: Begin with the CME home page (http://www.cmegroup.com). Click on *About Us*, and then click on *Corporate Overview*. Under "Related Links," click on *Corporate Capabilities*.

Application: Read the document, and then answer the following questions.

1. Based on this document, how many foreign exchange futures contracts trade on the CME? How many foreign exchange options?

2. What are the three main categories of FX Products offered by the CME Group? Give a brief description of each group.

3. What are the two main categories of "Alternative Investment Products" offered by the CME Group? Provide a brief description of each category.

SELECTED REFERENCES and FURTHER READINGS

Bekaert, Gaert, Min Wei, and Yuhang Xing. "Uncovered Interest Rate Parity and the Term Structure." *Journal of International Money and Finance 26* (2007): 1038–1069.

Bartolini, Leonardo. "Foreign Exchange Swaps." Federal Reserve Bank of Boston. *New England Economic Review* (Second Quarter 2002): 11–12.

Chaboud, Alain, and Jonathan Wright. "Uncovered Interest Parity: It Works, But Not for Long." *Journal of International Economics 66* (2005): 349–362.

Ferreira, Alex Luiz, and Miguel León-Ledesma. "Does the Real Interest Parity Hypothesis Hold? Evidence for Developing and Emerging Markets." *Journal of International Money and Finance 26* (2007): 364–382.

Flood, Robert, and Andrew Rose. "Uncovered Interest Parity in Crisis: The Interest Rate Defense of the 1990s." *IMF Staff Papers 49* (2002): 252–266.

Francis, Bill, Iftekhar Hasan, and Delroy Hunter. "Emerging Market Liberalization and the Impact on Uncovered Interest Parity." *IMF Staff Papers 49* (2002): 252–266.

Goswami, Gautam, and Milind Shrikhande. "Economic Exposure and Currency Swaps." *Journal of Applied Finance 17* (Fall–Winter 2007): 62–71.

Gunther, Jeffry, and Thomas Siems, "Debunking Derivatives Delirium." Federal Reserve Bank of Dallas. *Southwest Economy* (March/April 2003): 1–9.

Hoque, Ariful, Felix Chan, and Meher Manzur. "Efficiency of the Foreign Currency Options Market." *Global Finance Journal 19* (2008): 157–170.

Kawaller, Ira. "Hedging Currency Exposures by Multinationals: Things to Consider." *Journal of Applied Finance 18* (Spring–Summer 2008): 92–98.

King, Robert, and André Kurmann. "Expectations and the Term Structure of Interest Rates: Evidence and Implications." Federal Reserve Bank of Richmond. *Economic Quarterly* (Fall 2002): 49–95.

Nardi, Sailcat, and Daniel Waggoner. "Issues in Hedging Options Positions." Federal Reserve Bank of Atlanta. *Economic Review* (First Quarter 2000): 24–39.

Sekiuoa, Sofiane. "Real Interest Parity over the 20th Century: New Evidence Based on Confidence Intervals for the Largest Root and Half-Life." *Journal of International Money and Finance 27* (2008): 76–101.

Wang, Tao, Jian Yang, and Marc Simpson. "U.S. Monetary Policy Surprises and Currency Futures Markets: A New Look." *Financial Review 43* (2008): 509–541.

6

International Banking, Central Banks, and Supranational Financial Policymaking Institutions

Fundamental ISSUES

1. What accounts for international financial intermediation, and how do national banking systems differ?

2. What are the world's major bank payment systems, and how do the risks that arise in national financial and banking systems contribute to the potential for financial instability and crises?

3. What objectives do national banking regulators seek to achieve, and how do they implement their regulations?

4. What are the main assets and liabilities of central banks?

5. What are the primary functions of central banks?

6. What are the two most important supranational financial policymaking institutions, and what are their functions in the international financial system?

On October 24, 2007, a headline on page one of the Wall Street Journal *read, "World's Central Bankers Struggle with Good Times." The article's focus was on complications arising from expansions of foreign exchange reserves, or financial assets denominated in foreign currencies such as the U.S. dollar, flowing to national governments and central banks—government-sponsored financial institutions that provide banking services to governments and privately owned banks and that usually serve as regulators of countries' banking systems. Specifically mentioned in the article were the central banks of emerging nations such as China, Colombia, India, Russia, and Thailand. Yet even in developed nations such as Western European countries, Japan, and the United States, central banks were struggling in 2007 to adjust to "good times." Private banks regulated by central banks in these nations appeared to be performing so well that officials were having difficulty justifying maintaining large and expensive central bank staffs of supervisors and auditors.*

How quickly times can change. By the summer of 2008, central banks of emerging economies were struggling to adjust to a dramatically worsened international financial climate. In Western Europe, Japan, and the United States, the substantial increase in numbers of "troubled" or failing banks induced central banks to increase hiring of accountants and economists to their bank regulatory staffs into the 2010s.

What are the roles of a central bank in an individual nation's financial system and in its economy? What functions do central banks perform in the international financial system and foreign exchange markets? This chapter provides a foundation for answering these questions, which will require the next several chapters to accomplish fully.

INTERNATIONAL DIMENSIONS OF FINANCIAL INTERMEDIATION

What do private banks and central banks do, and what is their role in international financial markets? To answer this question, let's begin by thinking about the role that banks perform in channeling savings to investment projects.

When savers allocate some of their wealth to the purchase of a bond issued by a company, they effectively make a direct loan to that business. In this way, they assist in the *direct finance* of domestic capital investment projects that the company chooses to undertake.

The financing of capital investment projects is not always so direct. It is also possible that a saver may obtain a long-term time deposit at a banking firm chartered by its nation's government. This bank allocates these funds, together with those of other deposit holders, to holdings of bonds issued by the same company as before. In this instance, the saver *indirectly finances* domestic capital investment. The bank, in turn, *intermediates* the financing of the domestic investment.

Financial Intermediation

Figure 6–1 illustrates the distinction between direct and indirect finance. With direct finance, a financial intermediary such as a bank is not involved. A saver lends directly to individuals or firms who undertake capital investment. With indirect

Figure 6–1

Indirect Finance through Financial Intermediaries

Those savers who exchange funds for the financial instruments of companies in financial markets undertake direct finance of the capital investments of those companies. Financial intermediaries make indirect finance possible by issuing their own financial instruments and using the funds that they obtain from savers to finance capital investments of businesses.

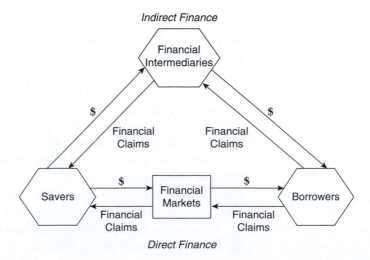

finance, however, another institution channels the funds of savers to those parties who desire to undertake capital investments.

The process of indirect finance, or *financial intermediation,* is the most common way in which funds are channeled from savings to investment. *Financial intermediaries* are the institutions that serve as the "go-betweens" in this process. These intermediaries exist solely to take the funds of savers and allocate those funds to ultimate borrowers. Commercial banks that issue deposits and that allocate funds to making loans or to holding other types of financial instruments are an example of a financial intermediary.

Asymmetric Information Why would any savers desire to direct their funds through some other institution instead of lending them directly to another party? One important reason is *asymmetric information,* or the fact that one party in a financial transaction, such as a borrower, often possesses information not available to another party, such as a lender.

Suppose, for instance, that a Mexican citizen has the opportunity to buy a high-yield bond issued by a public utility located 600 miles from where he resides. The firm plans to use the funds to build an experimental power plant designed to increase electrical-generation efficiency while significantly reducing atmospheric pollution. Unless this Mexican saver happens to be well versed on electrical power generation, it is very difficult for him to assess the true riskiness of this bond. This makes it difficult for him to compare the yield on this bond with yields on alternative financial instruments.

In contrast, the public utility that issues the bond surely has much more information about the prospects for its proposed power plant. It may be that the chances of success in both improved fuel efficiency and better low-pollution performance are very good. Or it could be that the public utility's managers propose the project because of political pressures to increase expenditures in the locale in which the proposed plant would be built, in an effort to increase employment in a high-vote region. In either case, the public utility that issues the bond has information about its riskiness that the saver does not possess.

Adverse Selection Suppose that, in fact, the public utility's managers know at the outset that the long-term prospects for financial success are poor, yet they have chosen to invest in the construction of the power plant in hopes of future support from the Mexican government. In this instance, the public utility's managers know that their bond may have *adverse,* or *bad,* consequences for those who buy the public utility's bonds. This is an example of an asymmetric-information situation known as *adverse selection.* This is the potential for those who desire funds for unworthy projects to be among the most likely to want to borrow or to issue debt instruments. A consequence of adverse selection is that savers are less willing to lend to those seeking to finance high-quality projects: the presence of poor-quality debt instruments (such as the bonds in our public utility example) makes lenders skeptical.

Moral Hazard In contrast, suppose that the managers of the public utility issuing the bond have an honest intention to achieve the specified goals for the power plant and to earn the highest return possible from operating the plant. Nonetheless, after the public utility sells bonds to finance the project, a management change occurs. The new managers, in an effort to cut costs, use inferior materials and techniques in constructing the plant, which ultimately are both inefficient and unprofitable. The result is an increased probability that savers will fail to receive promised interest yields on the public utility's bonds. Such a possibility that a borrower might engage

financial intermediation
Indirect finance through the services of financial institutions that channel funds from savers to those who ultimately make capital investments.

asymmetric information
Possession of information by one party in a financial transaction that is not available to the other party.

adverse selection
The potential for those who borrow funds to undertake unworthy, high-risk investment projects.

moral hazard
The possibility that a borrower might engage in more risky behavior after receiving the funds from a lender.

in behavior that increases risk after financial instrument has been purchased is *moral hazard.* This term refers to the potential "immoral" behavior, from the lender's perspective, that the borrower would have exhibited.

Certainly, one way that the Mexican saver might deal with either problem posed by asymmetric information is to make a number of 600-mile trips to initially evaluate and then continue to monitor the public utility's progress on its capital investment project. By acquiring as much direct information as possible, the saver reduces the asymmetry of information about the bond's risks. Doing this, however, may be very costly to the saver, who incurs direct costs to make the trips, as well as the opportunity costs of lost time.

One reason that financial intermediaries exist is to save potential holders of financial instruments from incurring such costs. Although these institutions cannot eliminate adverse selection and moral hazard problems, they collect information about the underlying riskiness of financial instruments and monitor the continuing performance of those who issue such instruments. For example, intermediaries may specialize in assessing the prospects of bonds that public utilities issue to finance major capital investments, thereby reducing the extent of potential adverse selection problems in the market for these bonds. These intermediaries also keep track of the performances of public utilities in implementing their investments. Public utilities that fail to do a good job of managing their investment projects might have a harder task issuing new bonds in the future, which reduces the potential for moral hazard problems.

Economies of Scale

economies of scale
Cost savings from pooling funds for centralized management.

Another important reason that financial intermediaries exist is *economies of scale.* Some financial intermediaries make it possible for many people to pool their funds together, thereby increasing the size, or *scale,* of the total amount of savings managed by a central authority. This centralization of management reduces the average fund management costs below the levels savers would incur if they all were to manage their savings alone.

If financial intermediaries manage funds for many people at an average cost that is lower than the cost each faces individually, then financial economies of scale exist. *Pension fund companies,* which are institutions that specialize in managing individuals' retirement funds, largely owe their existence to their abilities to provide such cost savings to individual savers. Likewise, *investment companies*— institutions that manage portfolios of financial instruments called *mutual funds* on behalf of shareholders—also exist largely because of economies of scale.

Financial Intermediation across National Boundaries

international financial diversification
Holding financial instruments issued in various countries to spread portfolio risks.

In our example, the Mexican saver contemplates purchasing a bond issued by a Mexican public utility. Another possibility is for the Mexican resident to purchase a bond issued by a public utility located across the border in the United States. There are a number of reasons that the Mexican saver might wish to hold bonds issued by a U.S. company. One reason might be to earn an anticipated higher return. Another reason might be to avoid country risk specific to Mexico by placing at least a portion of his savings in U.S. public utility bonds. More broadly, the saver's goal might be to achieve overall risk reductions via *international financial diversification,* or holding bonds issued in various nations and thereby spreading portfolio risks across both Mexican-issued *and* foreign-issued financial instruments.

A really sophisticated Mexican saver does not just hold financial instruments issued in Mexico and the United States. The saver would place a portion of the wealth with an investment company that offers a ***world index fund,*** which is a carefully designed grouping of globally issued financial instruments that yield returns that historically have tended to move in offsetting directions. By holding a world index fund, the saver consequently earns the average yield on securities of a number of nations while keeping overall risk to a minimum.

world index fund
A portfolio of globally issued financial instruments with yields that historically have moved in offsetting directions.

International Financial Intermediation Holding shares in a world index fund makes the Mexican saver a part of the process of *international financial intermediation.* This refers to the indirect finance of capital investment across national borders by financial intermediaries such as banks, pension fund companies, and investment companies.

The rationales for international financial intermediation are the same as the justifications for the existence of domestic intermediation. For the Mexican saver, for instance, asymmetric information problems are likely to be at least as severe, as compared with evaluating the riskiness of Mexican bonds, when attempting to assess the risk characteristics of U.S. bonds. By placing some wealth in a world index fund managed by an investment company, the saver transfers the task of evaluating and monitoring the prospects and performances of bond issuers across the globe. In exchange for this service, the saver pays the investment company management fees.

Economies of Scale and Global Banking Banks located in various countries take part in the process of international financial intermediation by using some of the funds of deposit holders around the globe to finance loans to individuals and companies based in other nations. Consequently, very few nations' capital investment projects are purely domestically financed. Even bank-financed investment in the United States increasingly stems from loans by non-U.S. banks. The largest U.S. corporations on average use the services of more foreign banks than domestic institutions.

As Table 6–1 indicates, none of the world's ten largest banks are based in the United States. Today most of the largest banking institutions, sometimes called

Table 6–1

The World's Largest Banks

Bank	Country	Assets ($ Billions)
Deutsche Bank, AG	Germany	2,804
BNP Paribus, SA	France	2,547
Industrial & Commerce Bank of China Limited	China	2,459
Barclays Bank	United Kingdom	2,427
Japan Post Bank	Japan	2,320
Crédit Agricole, SA	France	2,233
Royal Bank of Scotland	United Kingdom	2,224
China Construction Bank Corporation	China	1,951
Bank of China	China	1,879
Agricultural Bank	China	1,855

Source: Banker's Almanac, 2012.

megabanks, are located in Europe and Japan. These megabanks typically take in deposits and lend throughout the world. Although they report their profits and pay taxes in their home nations, these megabanks are otherwise fully international banking institutions.

What accounts for the existence of megabanks whose operations span the globe? One possible answer is economies of scale. By increasing their asset port-folios through regional or worldwide expansion, megabanks may be able to reduce average operating costs, thereby gaining efficiency. Research by Yener Altunbas and Philip Molyneux of the University College of North Wales in the United Kingdom found that French, German, and Spanish banks have experienced con-siderable cost reductions as European banking has extended more broadly across national borders. The evidence for economies of scale in banking is more mixed for U.S. banks, although U.S. bank managers themselves commonly offer economies of scale as a key rationale for large-scale mergers in the United States.

Some economists believe that a particular form of economies of scale may explain the existence of megabanks: *economies of scale in information process-ing.* According to this view, the expanding size of these banks reflects the fact that many businesses now have operations that stretch across and among the world's continents. To be able to evaluate and monitor the creditworthiness of these multinational enterprises, banks must also have offices around the globe. This, goes the argument, allows banks to overcome asymmetric information problems more efficiently than they could if they were purely domestic intermediaries. Hence, a key explanation for megabanks hinges on the existence of *both* asymmetric infor-mation *and* economies of scale in international banking operations.

 Fundamental **ISSUES**

#1 What accounts for international financial intermediation, and how do national banking systems differ?

A key reason that financial intermediaries exist is to address problems arising from asym-metric information. One such problem is adverse selection, or the potential for the least creditworthy borrowers to be the most likely to wish to borrow funds. Another is moral hazard, or the possibility that an initially creditworthy borrower may undertake actions that reduce its creditworthiness after receiving funds from a lender. Another reason for the existence of financial intermediaries is the existence of economies of scale, or the ability to spread costs of managing funds across large numbers of savers. A potential justification for international financial intermediation by global banking enterprises is that they may experience economies of scale in information processing by spreading their credit evaluation and monitoring operations around the world.

GLOBAL PAYMENTS AND FINANCIAL SYSTEM RISKS

International financial trading and interbank payments increasingly take place elec-tronically. In the United States, although nonelectronic payments media such as cash and checks account for about 90 percent of all payments, these media account for less than 15 percent of the *dollar value* of these transactions. This implies that the bulk of large-dollar payments, such as interbank payments, is accomplished via electronic transactions.

This revolution in trading and payments technology has reshaped the technical landscape of international finance. The word *bank* derives from the Italian merchant's bench, or *banco,* across which money changed hands in medieval Europe. In today's electronic trading environment, however, this word is becoming a relic of bygone days.

Global Payment Systems

Bank payment transfers take place on ***payment systems,*** which are institutional structures through which individuals, businesses, governments, and financial institutions process payments of funds for goods, services, or financial assets. Table 6–2 lists the world's largest payment systems and gives data on transactions and flows of funds on these systems. There are several types of payment systems, falling into two broad categories: nonelectronic and electronic.

payment system
A term that broadly refers to the set of mechanisms by which consumers, businesses, governments, and financial institutions make payments.

Nonelectronic Payment Systems In most nations, people continue to use coins and currency for the bulk of exchanges. For instance, U.S. residents use coin and currency for more than three-fourths of the total *number* of exchange transactions they make. When an individual makes a purchase using coins and currency, the transaction is final at the moment that the exchange occurs. In contrast, check and debit card transactions are final only after banks transfer funds from the account of the purchaser to the seller. Using checks and debit cards, therefore, requires parties to a transaction to rely upon banks as *payment intermediaries,* or go-betweens in clearing payments that arise from exchanges of goods, services, or financial assets.

In many nations, checks and debit cards are the other main noncash form of nonelectronic payment. Other forms of noncash nonelectronic payments include credit card, money order, and paper-based *giro* transactions. Like check-based

Country/Payment System	Transactions (Millions)	Value ($ Trillions)
European Monetary Union		
TARGET	88.6	760.6
Euro-I	240.5	358.8
Japan		
Zengin	5.2	60.2
BOJ-NET	108.9	943.1
United Kingdom		
CHAPS	32.2	97.4
United States		
Fedwire	144.9	928.4
CHIPS	90.9	365.1

Table 6–2

Transactions and Payment Flows in Major National Payment Systems

Source: Payment systems' statistical publications, various issues; authors' estimates, 2011.

systems, giro systems, which entail transfer of payment orders between banks and other financial institutions, involve payment intermediaries. Giro systems are common in both Europe and Asia and link a number of payment intermediaries besides banks, such as post offices.

large-value wire transfer systems

Payments systems such as Fedwire and CHIPS that permit the electronic transmission of large volumes of funds.

Electronic Payment Systems About 85 percent of the *dollar value* of U.S. electronic payments takes place via *large-value wire transfer systems.* These U.S. wire transfer systems handle fewer than 1 percent of the total *number* of payment transactions. Thus, they clearly specialize in transferring large sums. Such large-value wire transfer systems also are commonplace in other developed nations and handle the bulk of the values of electronic payment transfers. Among these are the TARGET system of the European Monetary Union (EMU), the Bank of Japan NET (BOJNET) system, and the British CHAPS system.

Fedwire

A large-value wire transfer system operated by the Federal Reserve that is open to all banking institutions that legally must maintain required cash reserves with the Fed.

In the United States, there are two key large-value wire transfer systems. One is *Fedwire,* which is owned and operated by the Federal Reserve System on behalf of all financial institutions that must hold reserves at Federal Reserve banks. These institutions pay fees to use Fedwire in transferring funds for two key types of transactions. One is *book-entry security transactions,* which are electronic payments for U.S. Treasury securities. The other main type of Fedwire transaction is interbank payments among bank deposit accounts at Federal Reserve banks that involve credit extensions among banks in an interbank market called the *federal funds market.* The average Fedwire payment exceeds $6 million. The average daily payment volume on the Fedwire system is about $3.5 trillion.

Clearing House Interbank Payments System (CHIPS)

A privately owned and operated large-value wire transfer system linking about 50 U.S. banks, which allows them to transmit large payments relating primarily to foreign exchange and Eurocurrency transactions.

The other major U.S. large-value wire transfer system is the *Clearing House Interbank Payments System (CHIPS).* This is a privately owned system managed by the New York Clearing House Association, which has about 50 member banks. These banks primarily use CHIPS to transfer funds for foreign exchange and Eurocurrency transactions. The average value of a CHIPS transaction is about $4 million, and the average daily payment flow on the CHIPS system exceeds $1.5 trillion.

The BOJNET system performs similar functions as those performed by Fedwire and CHIPS. The same is true of the British CHAPS system, the EMU TARGET system, and other wire transfer systems around the world.

Visit CHIPS at *http://www.chips.org.*

Payment-System Risks

Payment systems face both private and public risks that are *inherent* in financial transactions. Risk increases as the size and scope of the payment system increases. For instance, when any retail outlet accepts currency or coins from a customer, there is a remote possibility that the customer's payment might be counterfeit. Nonetheless, a retailer typically accepts currency and coin payments, because the risk of loss is limited to each individual customer and normally involves a relatively small payment value. In contrast, the risks incurred in multimillion-dollar transactions on large-value wire transfer systems generally are much greater. For this reason, as we discuss in more detail shortly, central banks have become heavily involved in monitoring and supervising the functioning of large-value payment systems.

Three types of risk naturally arise in any payments system: *liquidity risk, credit risk,* and *systemic risk.* Payment intermediaries such as banks take on such risks on behalf of their fee-paying customers. In the realm of international payments, a particular form of payment-system risk known as *Herstatt risk* arises. This is discussed later in this section.

Liquidity Risk You may have noticed that many people are not always punctual in keeping scheduled appointments. Some almost seem to plan on being late to meetings and other engagements. Likewise, many individuals do not always make payments at times that they had promised. This behavior means that those who are to receive promised payments face a risk of loss, perhaps in the form of an opportunity cost, given that late funds could be used for other purposes. In addition, explicit costs could arise from late receipt of a payment. For example, failure to receive a payment at a time it was due could complicate the payment recipient's ability to honor another financial commitment made under the assumption that the payment would arrive on time.

Liquidity risk is the risk that such losses may arise from late receipt of payments. The development of large-value wire transfer systems and other forms of electronic payment systems largely stems from a desire by banks and other payment intermediaries to reduce the amount of liquidity risk by speeding up payment processing. Prior to the advent of modern computer technology that made electronic mechanisms possible, payment intermediaries had to depend on courier or postal services to hand-deliver paper orders for payment. Unanticipated delays in these services exposed payment intermediaries to significant implicit or explicit costs. In contrast, payment intermediaries can initiate wire transfers within minutes, and the actual transfers take place nearly instantaneously.

liquidity risk
The risk of loss that may occur if a payment is not received when due.

Credit Risk A common occurrence in an exchange is for one party to transfer funds before the other party reciprocates with transfer of a good, service, or financial asset. As a result, the party who transfers the funds essentially extends credit to the other party in the transaction, thereby taking on *credit risk.* This is the possibility that the other party in the exchange ultimately might not honor the complete terms of the exchange.

credit risk
The risk of loss that could take place if one party to an exchange were to fail to abide by terms under which both parties originally had agreed to make the exchange.

Payment intermediaries that participate in large-value wire transfer systems have developed intricate systems of rules intended to reduce the exposures to credit risks. These rules detail the responsibilities of both parties to a wire transfer, and they clearly spell out the role of the systems' administrators in mediating disagreements that may arise if parties fail to settle transactions on a timely basis.

In an international context, problems may arise because of different rules and legalities that apply to payments that span national payment systems. For instance, a U.S. payment intermediary may use the CHIPS system to transmit a payment to a Japanese bank that is part of the British CHAPS system. These two large-value wire transfer systems may have slightly different rules about settling payments. Furthermore, the U.S. and British legal systems may have different interpretations of the duties and responsibilities of parties to an exchange. To deal with the potential for such problems in international transactions, central banks of the Group of Ten (G10) nations have developed a common set of rules called *Lamfalussy standards.* These clarify the basic legal payment responsibilities of any payment intermediary that participates in a large-value wire transfer system operated within a G10 nation.

Systemic Risk Liquidity and credit risks are payment-system risks that payment intermediaries assume on an individual basis. Because the payment intermediaries that participate in large-value wire transfer systems are all interconnected, however, the payment intermediaries share some payment-system risks. As a result, payment flows among these intermediaries are interdependent. Consider, for instance, a Los Angeles–based bank expecting a wire transfer from a Philadelphia bank at 1:30 P.M. eastern standard time (EST). Based on this anticipation, the Los Angeles bank commits to wire funds to a bank in St. Louis at 1:45 EST. The St. Louis bank, in turn, agrees to wire funds to a Seattle bank at 2:00 EST, using the funds that it anticipates receiving from the Los Angeles bank. Consequently, if the Philadelphia bank fails to deliver the funds promised at 1:30 EST to the Los Angeles bank, the Los Angeles bank might wire legal title to funds to the St. Louis bank at 1:45 EST that are not really in its possession. In addition, if the Philadelphia bank discovers that some event has occurred that will keep it from sending the funds at all that afternoon, then a full chain of payments may take place, even though there are insufficient funds to cover the payments.

In this example, the risk of an inability by the Philadelphia bank to settle its transaction with the Los Angeles bank is a liquidity or credit risk for the latter bank. For the St. Louis and Seattle banks, however, this situation constitutes *systemic risk.* This is a risk that some payment intermediaries, such as the St. Louis and Seattle banks in our example, may not be able to honor financial commitments because of payment settlement breakdowns in otherwise unrelated transactions

For these payment intermediaries, systemic risk is a negative *externality,* or an adverse spillover effect stemming from transactions in which they were not participants. Another example of a negative externality is air pollution, which can cause those who do not consume the products of manufacturers that pollute the air to incur costs of the polluters' actions, nonetheless. Governments often point to the existence of negative externalities such as air pollution as a justification for government regulation of the activities of polluters. In like manner, central banks typically cite systemic risk arising from the interdependence of payment intermediaries on large-value wire transfer systems as a justification for their supervision and regulation of these systems.

Herstatt Risk Systemic risk spans national borders. On June 26, 1974, a German bank called Bankhaus I. D. Herstatt collapsed. When Herstatt failed, German regulators closed the bank at 3:30 P.M. Frankfurt time. That was after the bank had received foreign currency payments from banks based elsewhere in Europe but before the bank had made dollar payments that it owed to banks in the United States. After all the accounting had been unraveled following Herstatt's collapse, U.S. banks determined that they had lost as much as $200 million. The Herstatt episode unsettled U.S. financial markets and payment systems, and several other payment systems in other countries temporarily shut down.

Since this event, bankers have broadly referred to international payment-system risks as *Herstatt risk.* This form of risk actually encompasses two types of risk that arise primarily from payments processing relating to foreign currency transactions between payment intermediaries based in different countries. First, Herstatt risk refers in part to the direct liquidity and credit risks that payment intermediaries face if they enter into agreements to receive payments from institutions

---

systemic risk
The risk that some payment intermediaries may not be able to meet the terms of payment agreements because of failures by other institutions to settle transactions that otherwise are not related.

externality
A spillover from the actions of one set of individuals to others who otherwise are not involved in the transactions among that group.

Herstatt risk
Liquidity, credit, and systemic risks across international borders.

based in other nations in different time zones. For the U.S. banks that had to wait for millions of dollars of payments or that lost $200 million outright when Herstatt collapsed in 1974, these direct risks turned out to be significant.

Second, and more broadly, however, Herstatt risk also refers to the systemic risks owing to global linkages among national payment systems. Because of time differences separating large payment intermediaries around the globe, these intermediaries face the potential for events that occur in one time zone, such as the German Herstatt failure, to have broader effects on the functioning of payment systems in another time zone. In this sense, Herstatt risk constitutes an *international externality* that arguably requires the cooperative supervisory and regulatory efforts of many central banks.

Fundamental ISSUES

#2 What are the world's major bank payment systems, and how do the risks that arise in national financial and banking systems contribute to the potential for financial instability and crises?

The bulk of the aggregate value of payments takes place on electronic payment systems via payment intermediaries such as banks. Payment-system risks that payment intermediaries face on an individual basis include liquidity risk, or the possibility of incurring losses as a result of delayed receipt of payments, and credit risk, or the possibility that another party may fail to honor fully the terms of a transaction. Systemic risk is the possibility that payment settlement failures among some payment intermediaries may cause further failures in payment settlement among others, potentially resulting in the breakdown of the payment system as a whole. Herstatt risk refers broadly to liquidity, credit, and systemic risks that arise specifically from the international transmission of payments. These various financial risks, together with the potential for currency values to become inconsistent with exchange rates coherent with economic fundamentals, can give rise to financial instability. Such an environment can engender speculative attacks on official exchange rates, trigger self-fulfilling anticipations and contagions, or worsen moral hazard problems, thereby generating international financial crises.

Financial Instability and International Financial Crises

Payment-system risks are one possible source of *financial instability,* a situation in which a nation's financial markets and banking system are unable to allocate funds to the most productive projects. Other sources include major fluctuations in currency values in foreign exchange markets or unexpected difficulties that a country's businesses or government might experience in repaying domestic and foreign debts.

Severe financial instability can potentially trigger a *financial crisis,* or major breakdown in the functioning of a nation's financial markets and its banking system. To be able to limit, or even prevent, international financial crises, policymakers must have a good idea about their underlying causes. In fact, however, there are differing perspectives concerning the main causes of financial crises.

Economic Imbalances and International Financial Crises The traditional view of financial crises focuses on *economic fundamentals,* which are underlying factors such as the nation's current and likely future economic prospects and

financial instability
When a nation's financial sector is no longer able to allocate funds to the most productive projects.

financial crisis
A situation that arises when financial instability becomes so severe that the nation's financial system is unable to function. A financial crisis typically involves a banking crisis, a currency crisis, and a foreign debt crisis.

economic fundamentals
Basic factors determining a nation's current exchange rate, such as the country's present and likely future economic policies and performance.

economic policies pursued by the nation's government or central bank. According to this view, an inconsistency between the value of the exchange rate corresponding to a nation's economic fundamentals and an officially targeted exchange-rate value can engender a financial crisis. If foreign exchange traders perceive that the official value of a nation's currency is higher than its true value in private foreign exchange markets based on economic fundamentals, then there naturally will be a tendency for traders to sell their holdings of assets denominated in that currency to avoid losses. By unloading these assets, risk-averse traders will reduce their losses if it should happen that the government or central bank run out of the foreign currency reserves used to purchase the currency and maintain the official exchange rate.

Furthermore, speculators may seek to profit from their anticipations of an imminent exhaustion of official foreign exchange reserves by selling assets denominated in the nation's currency in an effort to push the government or central bank into giving up on supporting the exchange rate at its officially targeted level. At the same time they can bet on a collapse of the official exchange rate via the long positions they take in markets for futures, options, and swaps. This type of behavior is called a ***speculative attack*** on a nation's official exchange rate.

If a speculative attack is successful, then speculators potentially can earn significant profits from taking these positions. They can do this by effectively selling foreign-currency-denominated assets at the high official prices via arrangements to buy them in derivatives markets at lower prices more nearly consistent with underlying economic fundamentals. Of course, speculators can, and sometimes do, lose these kinds of bets, so speculative attacks do not necessarily succeed. Nevertheless, if the official exchange rate is sufficiently misaligned with the exchange rate that would be consistent with economic fundamentals, the probability that a speculative attack will succeed increases.

Self-Fulfilling Expectations and Contagion Effects A second perspective focuses on the potential role of *self-fulfilling anticipations* and contagion effects that can bring about an international financial crisis even when underlying economic fundamentals are consistent with an officially pegged exchange rate or when governments and central banks otherwise have sufficient foreign exchange reserves, given a slight misalignment of the government's exchange-rate target. According to this view, all that is needed to induce a speculative attack is a relatively widespread perception by traders that a nation's policymakers face relatively high internal costs (perhaps because of resulting political difficulties) from maintaining the official exchange rate.

Suppose, for instance, that currency speculators perceive a lack of resolve on the part of policymakers. They may then attempt to profit from their anticipation that policymakers will give in and devalue a currency rather than accept higher interest rates or other changes that may have negative economic spillovers. If sufficient numbers of speculators develop anticipations that government authorities in a nation lack the will to accept such spillovers, then large sales of assets denominated in the nation's currency can occur. This can induce other risk-averse traders to sell their foreign-currency-denominated assets as well in an effort to avoid losses. Essentially, according to this alternative view a speculative attack takes place simply because of expectations that it will be successful, but not necessarily because of underlying problems with economic fundamentals.

Structural Moral Hazard Problems Finally, a third perspective focuses on flaws within the structure of a nation's financial system as the major factors that lay the groundwork for a crisis situation. From this view, crisis conditions exist when

speculative attack
A concerted effort by financial market speculators to induce abandonment of an exchange-rate target that will yield them profits in derivative markets.

governmental policies create a situation of rampant *moral hazard problems.* For instance, a nation's government might require its banks to make loans to specific firms or industries, and because these firms and industries know that they will receive credit no matter how they use the funds, they commit them to risky undertakings. Many observers of the financial crises in Malaysia and Indonesia during the late 1990s, Argentina in the early 2000s, and the United States and a number of European nations in the late 2000s have argued that such moral hazard problems existed in those nations. Ultimately the risks taken on by those who receive government-directed credit generate actual losses and failures, these observers conclude, which sets off a crisis situation. (Recently, banks in Iceland confronted the country's largest-ever financial crisis; see *Management Notebook: From Fish to Finance—and Back to Fish Again?*)

MANAGEMENT Notebook

From Fish to Finance—and Back to Fish Again?

Iceland's population of about 300,000 people is equivalent to about one-tenth of 1 percent of the population of the United States—that is, about the size of the population of Toledo, Ohio. The nation's annual national income amounts to roughly $20 billion, or just over one-tenth of 1 percent of U.S. national income. By most measures, Iceland is simply a very tiny place compared with the United States. Traditionally, it has stood out in a relative sense in only one area. Its location amid a region surrounded by waters heavily populated with fish gave the nation a comparative advantage over the United States and most other areas in fishing. Indeed, the fishing industry was the lifeblood of the Icelandic economy for centuries.

Between 2000 and 2008, however, Iceland developed a comparative advantage in another industry: banking. In the United States, the assets and liabilities of all commercial banks typically amount to about 85 percent of annual U.S. income. In contrast, by 2008 the total assets and liabilities of Iceland's banking industry—comprised of three banks—amounted to nearly *ten times* the nation's annual income.

The bulk of the funds that the Icelandic banks derived from deposits and other debts had been issued to non-Icelandic residents, and the banks allocated the bulk of these funds as loans to individuals and businesses outside Iceland. This posed a big problem when Iceland's currency rapidly depreciated between the spring and autumn of 2008. By October, when euro-, pound-, and dollar-denominated payments on several of the banks' debts were due, the banks could not come up with sufficient amounts of euros, pounds, and dollars to transmit their promised payments. Ultimately, all three of the nation's banks failed, resulting in the world's largest known banking-system failure in relation to a nation's size.

For Critical Analysis

Which of the explanations for financial instability and crises appears to best explain Iceland's banking meltdown?

BANK REGULATION AND CAPITAL REQUIREMENTS

The common rationale for governmental supervision and regulation of banking institutions is that leaving these institutions to their own devices might result in socially undesirable outcomes, such as banking panics, losses of people's savings, and business collapses that can bring about full-fledged financial crises. Actual national experiences with such events have led to today's broad systems of national banking regulations.

See Federal Reserve regulations at *http://www.newyorkfed.org/banking/regulations.html*.

The Goals of Bank Regulation

Bank regulation and supervision is a fundamental part of the strategies of most nations for reducing the potential for financial instability and, hence, the likelihood of a financial crisis. For most countries, bank regulation aims to achieve three objectives: limiting bank failures, maintaining bank liquidity, and promoting an efficient financial system.

Limiting the Scope for Bank Insolvencies and Failures A key objective of bank regulation is to reduce the potential for widespread failures of banking institutions. A bank reaches a point of *insolvency* if the value of its assets falls below the value of its liabilities, so that its equity, or net worth, is negative. In the absence of governmental action to keep an insolvent bank operating, the bank must declare bankruptcy and halt its operations.

A common feature of bank regulation worldwide is the periodic *examination* of banks' accounting records to verify that the institutions are solvent. Another typical feature of bank regulation is the *supervision* of these institutions via the establishment and enforcement of rules and standards that banks must follow and meet.

Maintaining Bank Liquidity In most countries, banks issue liabilities, such as checking and savings accounts, that function as means of payment or from which customers can withdraw funds on very short notice. An individual bank that has insufficient funds available to meet the cash requirements of its depositors is *illiquid*. If a significant portion of a nation's banking system were illiquid, then there could be adverse effects on the country's flow of payments for goods and services. In the short term, this could depress the nation's level of economic activity.

Consequently, a further objective of bank regulation is to reduce the potential for episodes of widespread bank illiquidity. Governmental regulators thereby conduct bank examination and supervision with this additional goal in mind. Distinguishing illiquidity and insolvency is not always an easy task, however. A bank can experience short-term liquidity problems while remaining solvent, just as someone as wealthy as Donald Trump might lack sufficient ready cash to pull off a big business deal without the aid of other investors. Nevertheless, a bank on the verge of insolvency typically experiences illiquidity. Thus, efforts by government regulators to keep banks liquid sometimes end up perpetuating the lives of insolvent banks that actually should close. This is a key rationale that national regulators often give for conducting periodic examination of banks' accounting ledgers.

Promoting an Efficient Banking System The final goal of bank regulation is to promote low-cost provision of banking services and the banks' attainment of *normal profits*. These are levels of profit just sufficient to compensate bank owners for holding equity shares of banks instead of other businesses.

A basic problem that national bank regulators must confront is the potential for their three regulatory objectives to conflict. On the one hand, one way to improve

insolvency
A situation in which the value of a bank's assets falls below the value of its liabilities.

normal profit
A profit level just sufficient to compensate bank owners for holding equity shares in banks rather than other enterprises.

the likelihood of high bank liquidity and solvency is through a regulatory system that protects existing banks from additional rivalry for customers, thereby allowing banks to earn above-normal profits. On the other hand, a regulatory environment that promotes considerable competition would give banks an incentive to operate efficiently, yet their profit margins might be so low that unexpected declines in economic activity could bring about bouts of bank illiquidity or insolvency. Hence, a nagging issue for any country's banking regulators is deciding to what extent one objective may need to be sacrificed if another is to be attained. (In recent years, bank regulators increasingly have engaged in mock "war games"; see *Policy Notebook: Engaging in War Games Pays Off for Bank Regulators*.)

POLICY Notebook

Engaging in War Games Pays Off for Bank Regulators

According to a sixth-century Chinese general named Sun Tzu, "To know your enemy, you must become your enemy." Government and central-bank banking regulators have been taking Sun Tzu's dictum to heart. To do so, they periodically have their regulatory staffs participate in computer-simulated war games in which the "enemies" are private banks facing collapse. A few years ago, the European Commission's banking authorities ran an exercise in which they pretended that a major corporate insolvency was threatening to bring down two large banks at the same time. British banking authorities also performed drills in which they examined impacts on payment-clearing institutions of unexpected failures of banking subsidiaries. In the United States, the Federal Deposit Insurance Corporation (FDIC) has regularly conducted simulations of events that place stress on the banking system and, as a consequence, the FDIC's deposit insurance fund.

These and other bank-regulation war games entail conducting computer-guided simulations of various stages of a crisis situation. During each stage, teams of staff members seek to coordinate their responses to simulated events, and when each stage concludes they learn the combined effects of all teams' strategies on outcomes for the institutions they regulate. Each team adapts in subsequent stages in an effort to improve its performance. A key objective in conducting regulatory war games has been to encourage teams of bank supervisors to think more carefully about how their own actions potentially can influence real-world outcomes. Another goal has been to help supervisors view themselves from the perspective of managers of the financial institutions that they regulate, so that they can better foresee and react to the actions of those managers. Both objectives of engaging in mock war games were realized when banks encountered turbulence in 2008 and 2009.

For Critical Analysis

Why do you suppose that some national regulatory officials have conducted joint war games involving adverse banking events that have negative financial repercussions that overlap their countries' borders? (Hint: *Recall the concepts of systemic risk and Herstatt risk.*)

On the WEB

See the British Financial Services Authority's objectives of supervision at *http://www.fsa.gov.uk.*

Bank Capital Requirements

Since the late 1980s, a major focus of bank regulation has been on bank capital positions, or the extent to which the financial stakes of bank shareholders provide a cushion against losses. In 1989 the regulators of banks in most advanced market-based economies gathered at the Bank for International Settlements in Basel, Switzerland, to announce a system of *capital requirements.* This international program for bank capital standards intends to account for varying asset risk characteristics into the calculation of required bank capital. Under the Basel capital standards, banks compute ratios of capital in relation to their *risk-adjusted assets.* This is a weighted average of all the bank's assets, in which the weights reflect regulators' perception of distinctive asset risks—100 percent for most loans; 20 percent for interbank deposits and bonds issued by cities, states, and regions; and 10 percent for *off-balance-sheet banking,* such as derivatives trading, that does not affect the reported assets and liabilities of banks but that exposes banks to risk of loss. After computing these various weighted figures, regulators sum them together to obtain an individual bank's total risk-adjusted assets. This weighted sum constitutes the denominator of capital ratios that banks must satisfy.

Under the Basel capital standards, banks have been required to compute ratios relating various measures of capital to risk-adjusted assets. The most basic capital measure is common shareholders' equity (shares of stock held by voting stockholders). There are also two other broader capital measures, called capital *tiers.* The first of these, "Tier 1 capital," or *core capital,* is equal to the sum of shareholders' equity and retained earnings (income not paid out to shareholders). A bank's *total capital* is equal to core capital plus "Tier 2 capital," or *supplementary capital.* This latter measure includes some types of preferred stock (stock shares held by nonvoting stockholders) and most types of subordinated debt.

The current Basel capital requirements apply to both banks and their parent companies. Under the current version of the Basel capital standards, known as *Basel III* and scheduled to be phased in by 2018, banks must satisfy several minimum capital ratio requirements:

1. the base ratio of common shareholders' equity to risk-adjusted assets must always exceed 4.5 percent;
2. an additional "capital conservation buffer" required ratio of common shareholders' equity to risk-adjusted assets must equal to 2.5 percent, which can be violated only if bank managers' bonuses and other compensation are reduced;
3. the ratio of core capital to risk-adjusted assets must always exceed 6 percent;
4. the ratio of total capital to risk-adjusted assets must always exceed 8 percent;
5. at the discretion of bank regulators, an additional "countercyclical" capital requirement ratio of common shareholders' equity to risk-adjusted assets can be assessed up to 2.5 percent.

Thus, banks must always maintain a ratio of core capital to risk-adjusted assets in excess of 6 percent. Inclusive of the capital conservation buffer, the overall required ratio of common shareholders' equity to risk-adjusted assets should always exceed 7 percent. In addition, the ratio of total capital to risk-adjusted assets must always exceed 8 percent. Overall, when the capital conservation buffer is included, a bank's ratio of total capital to risk-adjusted assets must be greater than 10.5 percent. In times in which regulators might choose to add an additional "countercyclical" buffer requirement, the overall required capital ratio could be as high as 13 percent.

capital requirements

Minimum equity capital standards that national regulatory agencies impose on banks.

risk-adjusted assets

A weighted average of bank assets that regulators compute to account for risk differences across assets.

off-balance-sheet banking

Bank activities that earn income without expanding the assets and liabilities that they report on their balance sheets.

core capital

Defined by the Basel capital standards as shareholders' equity plus retained earnings.

total capital

Under the Basel bank capital standards, this is the sum of core capital and supplementary capital.

supplementary capital

A measure that many national banking regulators use to calculate required capital, which includes certain preferred stock and most subordinated debt.

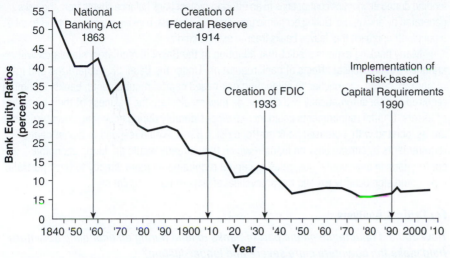

Figure 6–2

Equity as a Percentage of Bank Assets in the United States, 1840–2004

U.S. bank equity ratios fell considerably between the mid-nineteenth and mid-twentieth centuries. Recently they have risen slightly.

Source: Data from Allen N. Berger, et al. "The Role of Capital in Financial Institutions." *Journal of Banking and Finance* (1995): 402; and Federal Deposit Insurance Corporation. http://www.fdic.gov.

How have risk-based capital standards affected actual bank capital ratios? Figure 6–2 shows the induced changes in the core capital ratios of U.S. banks. As the figure indicates, the new standards reversed a long trend toward lower capital ratios.

The Three Pillars of the Basel Regulatory System The national bank regulators that have designed the Basel standards conceptualize them as resting on three levels of support, which they refer to as "pillars." This pillar analogy is appropriate. If any of the three pillars fails to provide support for the overall regulatory scheme, then the framework ultimately is likely to fail to promote long-run safety and soundness of the banking systems of the dozens of nations that have indicated an intention to participate.

Pillar 1 The first pillar of the Basel standards is the set of capital requirements summarized earlier. (A number of observers worry that adoption of Basel III's Pillar 1 capital standards could add to the inherent tendency for the banking industry's fortunes to move with—and add to—variations in broader economic activity; see *Policy Notebook: Will More Risk-Based Capital Regulation Make Banking More Procyclical?*)

POLICY Notebook

Will More Risk-Based Capital Regulation Make Banking More Procyclical?

The public's demand for credit from banks and its supply of deposit funds to banks vary directly with economic activity. That is, when there is an upswing in a nation's economy, its residents desire more loans from banks, and its residents earn higher incomes and hence have more funds available to deposit with banks. Hence, banking tends to be a *procyclical* industry, meaning that upward and downward cycles in activity levels of banks tend to reflect cycles of more general economic activity. Furthermore, bank regulation traditionally has added to these natural procyclical tendencies of banking. By its nature, the bank supervisory process tends to press banks to constrict lending during economics contractions in an effort to protect bank balance sheets from the risks generated by downturns. During economic upswings, in contrast, banking supervisors tend to take a hands-off approach that leaves banks freer to expand credit.

Many banking experts predict that adoption of the Basel III regulatory standards will enhance the procyclical effects of bank regulation. Under the Basel III standardized and internal-risk-based approaches to computing risk-based capital requirements, banks' minimum required capital automatically will change as they recalculate the riskiness of their portfolios of assets. Capital requirements could increase considerably during economic downturns that are associated with increased bank portfolio risks. Banks would respond to higher capital requirements by cutting back on loans—which they already would do during economic contractions in any event. Thus, relating capital requirements more directly to bank portfolio risks could significantly expand the procyclical effects of bank regulation.

For Critical Analysis

How could a reluctance on the part of banks to lend during an economic downturn help make the downturn more severe and longer-lasting?

Pillar 2 The second pillar of the Basel regulatory standards is a set of supervisory-review-process guidelines for national regulators. Several of these guidelines focus on how regulators should enforce the new Basel II capital requirements. Nevertheless, Pillar 3 generally leaves it up to national regulators to determine if banks are well, adequately, or inadequately capitalized relative to ratios specified in the Basel regulatory standards. Thus, there is considerable scope for different levels of enforcement of the Basel standards across countries.

Pillar 3 The third pillar is a set of guiding principles for disclosures of information, which are intended to allow a bank's customers, bondholders, and shareholders to assess key pieces of information about the various risks it faces. Toward this end, the Pillar 3 principles suggest that national regulators should require most banks to release detailed risk information every three to six months.

Market-Based Regulation? The basic idea behind the third, information-disclosure pillar of the Basel regulatory standards is that regulators might be able to rely on "market discipline"—actions by depositors, holders of debt securities issued by banks, and stockholders, such as requiring riskier banks to pay higher rates of return to obtain funds—that might induce banks to maintain tight controls over their exposures to risks. In recent years, critics of the Basel standards have suggested that regulators might be able to rely on market discipline to supervise banks rather than teams of auditors.

market-based regulation
Using information gleaned from financial markets to determine appropriate bank regulatory standards.

These critics have suggested that an alternative way to supervise and regulate banks is ***market-based regulation***, which utilizes measures of risk derived from the markets in which banks participate. One key measure of risk that proponents of market-based regulation have proposed is the market value of banks' subordinated debt instruments, which would act as a fundamental indictor of the riskiness of the institutions' activities. Proponents of market-based regulation argue that much banking supervision and perhaps all capital requirements could be replaced with *regulatory tripwires* based on the depository debt security yields: If the risk premium on a bank's subordinated debt instruments were to rise above a certain threshold, regulators would force the bank to raise additional capital and shed some of its assets to reduce its overall risk.

A fundamental assumption of the marked-based regulatory approach is that private market traders of depository institutions' debt securities have good information about depository institution risks. Another presumption is that the market for depository institution debt instruments is efficient, so that these risks are fully reflected in the market prices of the securities. Thus, financial economists have sought to determine if the yields on depository institution debt securities closely track accounting measures of the issuers' risk characteristics commonly used by bank examiners. A number of studies in the late 1990s and 2000s found considerable evidence that this was the case for large banks' debt securities, thereby lending credence to the idea of linking regulatory enforcement to movements in market yields on depository institution debt instruments. The promise of this approach is that governments could realize significant resource savings if a few regulatory officials and staffs could track market yields, instead of paying large numbers of examiners to do the job.

Fundamental ISSUES

#3 What objectives do national banking regulators seek to achieve, and how do they implement their regulations?

One typical goal of bank regulation is to prevent banks from becoming insolvent, or from having negative net worth. Another regulatory goal is to keep banks from becoming illiquid, or lacking sufficient cash assets to meet the needs of their depositors. A third regulatory goal is for banks to operate at low cost and at normal levels of profit. Bank capital requirements are minimum permitted standards for shareholder ownership stakes relative to measures of bank assets. Since 1990, bank regulators in thirty-five countries have imposed risk-based capital requirements in which banks must maintain minimal allowable ratios of capital relative to total assets and to risk-adjusted assets.

CENTRAL BANKS

The first central bank was the Swedish Sveriges Riksbank (called the Risens Standers Bank until 1867), which began operations as a state-owned institution in 1668. A charge from the Riksdag, the parliament of Sweden, placed day-to-day management of the Riksbank under control of a commission. Initially, the Riksbank did not issue money, but by 1701 the Riksbank had authority to issue "transfer notes" that basically functioned as a form of currency. In 1789, the Riksdag established a National Debt Office that formally issued Swedish government currency, but the Riksbank Act of 1897 made the Riksbank the only legal issuer of currency in Sweden.

On the WEB

Visit the Swedish Riksbank at *http://www.riksbank.se.*

Figure 6–3

The Number of Central Banking Institutions, 1670–Present

The twentieth century witnessed considerable growth in the number of central banks.

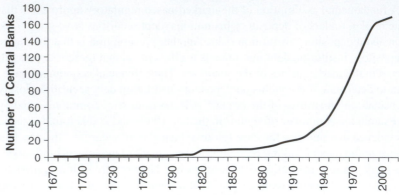

Source: Data from Forrest Capie, et al. *The Development of Central Banking: The Tercentenary Symposium of the Bank of England.* Cambridge, U.K.: Cambridge University Press, 1994, pp. 1–231; and Bank for International Settlements.

In 1694, the British parliament established the Bank of England. It authorized the Bank of England to issue currency notes redeemable in silver. The Bank of England's notes circulated along with other forms of money used at the time, which included notes issued by the government and private finance companies. Until 1800, the Riksbank and Bank of England were the only central banks. The total number of central banks worldwide remained a single digit as late as 1873.

As Figure 6–3 indicates, considerable expansion in the number of central banks occurred beginning in the latter part of the nineteenth century and particularly during the latter part of the twentieth century. Part of this growth stemmed from the establishment of central banks by former colonial states that achieved independence. Although, as we discussed in Chapter 3, some countries have established currency boards, several nations that previously had conducted their monetary and financial dealings without central banks have decided that it is in their best interests to establish these institutions.

Central Bank Assets

The best place to begin any examination of the functions of a central bank is its balance sheet, which is a tabulation of the central bank's assets, liabilities, and net worth. Table 6–3 displays the balance sheet of the Bank of Canada. The table displays Canadian dollar amounts and percentages relative to total assets and to total liabilities and net worth. Because nominal values of central bank assets, liabilities, and net worth change considerably over time while proportionate allocations tend to remain stable, you should concentrate most attention on the percentages in Table 6–3.

Key assets of the central banks include various types of securities and loans. When the Bank of Canada and other central banks lend to private banking institutions, these private banks must pay interest charges to obtain these funds.

Like other central banks, the Bank of Canada maintains holdings of assets denominated in the currencies of other nations. These are foreign-currency-denominated securities and deposits included within the set of securities held by the Bank of Canada. As we have noted in earlier chapters, a key reason that central banks hold such securities and deposits is so that they can trade the assets when they wish to try to change the values of their nations' currencies in foreign exchange markets. This will be discussed in greater detail in the following pages.

Table 6–3   The Balance Sheet of the Bank of Canada

The Bank of Canada (Billions of Canadian Dollars, as of August 24, 2011)

Assets			Liabilities and Capital		
Asset	**Canadian Dollar Amount**	**Percent of Total Assets**	**Liability**	**Canadian Dollar Amount**	**Percent of Total Assets**
Domestic Securities and Bills	68.7	98.9%	Currency Notes	59.5	85.6%
Direct Loans to Private Banks	0.1	0.1%	Bank Reserve Deposits	0.1	0.1%
Other Assets	0.7	1.0%	Government Deposits	7.4	10.7%
Total Assets	69.5	100.0%	Other Liabilities and Capital	2.5	3.6%
			Total Liabilities and Capital	69.5	100.0%

Source: Bank of Canada Banking and Financial Statistics, September 2011.

Central Bank Liabilities and Net Worth

Typically, at least half of a central bank's total liabilities and equity capital is composed of *currency notes*. Accountants designate currency notes as liabilities to indicate that the central banks "owe" holders of the notes something in exchange. For instance, if you had sought to redeem a $1 Federal Reserve note at a Federal Reserve bank before the early 1930s, you could have received gold in exchange. Now, however, you would receive a new $1 Federal Reserve note.

Likewise, if you turned in Canadian-dollar-denominated notes to the Bank of Canada, you also would receive new Canadian dollar notes in exchange. So in what sense are these notes really liabilities? The answer is that if the government of Canada decided to close down the nation's central bank, it would be liable to holders of its notes for the Canadian dollar value of goods and services at the time of the closure.

Another liability of the central banks is bank reserve deposits. In many nations, private banks hold some of these deposits to meet legal requirements established by the central banks (though this is not the case in Canada). In addition, however, banks typically hold a portion of deposits at central banks as *excess* reserves. These reserve holdings help to facilitate check clearing and transactions with the central bank and other private banks, including transfers of funds that they may lend to one another in their nations' **interbank funds markets**. These are markets for very short-term loans among banks. These loans have large denominations and typically have maturities between one day and one week. As we will discuss, the market interest rates on these loans perform important roles in monetary policymaking.

interbank funds markets
Markets for large-denomination interbank loans and one-day to one-week maturities.

Table 6–3 also indicates another deposit liability of the Bank of Canada. The Canadian government's Department of Finance draws on these deposit funds to make payments such as purchases of goods and services or tax refunds.

Like private companies, central banks issue ownership shares. Table 6–3 indicates that the Bank of Canada's equity capital, which is subsumed with the "other liabilities and capital" category, is comparatively low in relation to its assets.

Fundamental ISSUES

#4 What are the main assets and liabilities of central banks?

The primary assets of central banks are government securities, loans to private banking institutions, and foreign-currency-denominated securities and deposits. Key central bank liabilities are currency notes and reserve deposits of private banking institutions.

WHAT DO CENTRAL BANKS DO?

The tasks of central banks fall into three broad categories. First, central banks perform banking functions for their nations' governments. Second, central banks provide financial services for private banks. Third, central banks conduct their nations' monetary policies. Let's consider each of these categories in turn.

Central Banks as Government Banks

Governments often argue that they "need" central banks. For instance, a primary motivation for the founding of the Bank of England in 1694 was the desire for the Bank to raise government funds to finance one of Britain's wars with France. In like manner, a justification that the French government gave for establishing the Banques de France in 1800 was to better manage the nation's public debt that had ballooned as France and Britain continued their military buildups.

Even in countries where providing financial services to governments has not been the key justification for a central bank, central banks typically have become the main governmental banking institution. For example, in the United States, in which there had been long-standing opposition to central banks before the founding of the Federal Reserve System in 1913, the U.S. Treasury quickly began to rely on Federal Reserve banks as providers of depository services.

Central Banks as Government Depositories As we noted earlier, a significant liability of central banks is government deposits. National governments may hold these deposits at a single central bank office or in various regional branch offices of central banks.

For instance, the U.S. Treasury holds deposits at each of the twelve Federal Reserve banks. These regional banks clear checks drawn on those accounts. They also accept deposits of fees and taxes paid by U.S. residents and firms. Furthermore, they make payments at the direction of the U.S. Treasury, just as a private bank makes payments on behalf of a private customer.

Central Banks as Fiscal Agents Central banks typically operate as *fiscal agents* for national governments, meaning that they issue, service, and redeem government debts. Treasury departments or finance ministries issue securities such as bills, notes, and bonds to cover shortfalls between tax receipts and expenditures on goods and services. In nations with highly developed financial markets, treasury departments or finance ministries issue these securities at auctions.

In their role as fiscal agents, central banks often review, tabulate, and summarize bids to purchase the securities, issue securities to successful bidders, and process the purchasers' payments to the government. For example, in the United States the Federal Reserve banks operate *book-entry security systems,* which are systems of computerized accounts of U.S. Treasury sales of bills, notes, and bonds and of

fiscal agent

A term describing a central bank's role as an agent of its government's finance ministry or treasury department, in which the central bank issues, services, and redeems debts on the government's behalf.

book-entry security systems

Computer systems that the Federal Reserve uses to maintain records of sales of U.S. Treasury securities and interest and principal payments.

interest and principal payments on these instruments. When an institution with a book-entry security account desires to sell U.S. Treasury securities, it instructs the Federal Reserve bank that maintains its book-entry security account to transfer the title of ownership from its account to the book-entry security account of the institution that has agreed to purchase the security. The Federal Reserve bank then makes the transfer electronically.

In emerging nations with less-developed financial markets, central banks may play more direct roles. They may effectively act as investment banks for their governments by lining up private individuals or firms willing to purchase new government security issues. In nations with particularly thin secondary securities markets, central banks even purchase the securities directly from government treasury departments or finance ministries. To help broaden the markets for government securities, central banks in some countries, such as South Korea, have even imposed regulations requiring private banks to purchase government bills, notes, and bonds. Economists say that such rules make private banks *captive buyers* of government debt.

Central Banks as Bankers' Banks

Although the immediate rationale for the 1694 founding of the Bank of England was to improve the government's ability to finance wartime expenditures, the British parliament also justified creating the Bank of England to stabilize London financial markets and limit periodic fluctuations in the availability of currency and credit throughout England.

Do Banks "Need" a Central Bank? In later years, governments of other nations offered similar rationales for the establishment of central banks. Many proponents of these institutions, in fact, have contended that private banks *need* a central bank. As already discussed, the key rationale for such a "need" is the idea that financial markets are subject to *externalities,* or situations in which transactions among individuals or firms can spill over to affect others.

According to this view, central banking institutions perform socially useful roles in supervising and regulating the processes and systems through which individuals, firms, and banks exchange payments. Hence, private banks "need" a central bank to keep payment systems operating smoothly on a day-to-day basis and to repair any breakdowns in these systems.

Lenders of Last Resort We noted earlier that the most dramatic sort of financial breakdown is a *systemic* failure, in which large numbers of banking institutions fail. The classic example of this type of systemic failure is a *bank run,* in which large numbers of bank customers lose confidence in the ability of banks to maintain their asset values and, hence, anticipate depletion of the banks' net worth. As a result, customers seek to liquidate their deposits, which actually does push large numbers of banks into insolvency.

In principle, a central bank can keep bank runs from occurring by serving as the financial system's ***lender of last resort*** that stands ready to lend to any temporarily illiquid but otherwise solvent bank. By lending funds when necessary, the central bank might prevent such illiquidity from leading to a general loss of confidence that can lead to a systemwide run on the bank. In the years following its establishment, the Bank of England also came to function as a lender of last resort for banks suffering temporary liquidity problems that posed short-term threats to their individual solvency and to the broader stability of the British financial system.

lender of last resort
A central banking function in which the central bank stands willing to lend to any temporarily illiquid but otherwise solvent banking institution to prevent its illiquid position from leading to a general loss of confidence in that institution.

In response to critics' attacks on the Bank of England's policies, supporters of the Bank offered this as another justification for the Bank's existence.

Central Banks as Monetary Policymakers

Even though most central banks devote the bulk of their resources, including the time and effort of their employees, to the tasks of providing services to their nations' governments and banking institutions, most media attention on central bankers focuses on their monetary policymaking function. As you will learn in Chapters 10 through 15, there is a good reason for this: In a number of economic settings, central banks can considerably affect the price level and, potentially, real economic activity.

policy instruments

A financial variable that central banks can control in an effort to attain their policy objectives.

Central banks, of course, do not set a nation's price level. Nor do they add much to a nation's real output, aside from the services that they provide to governments and private banks. Nevertheless, they have access to a number of ***policy instruments,*** which for central banks are financial variables that they can control, either directly or indirectly. By altering these policy instruments, a central bank can bring about variations in market interest rates, thereby changing the volumes of money and credit in its nation's economy and generating changes in the value of its nation's currency. Such financial market effects can, in turn, induce changes in the level of a country's economic activity.

Interest Rates on Central Bank Advances Traditionally, a key central bank policy instrument has been the interest rate charged on *advances,* or loans, to private banks.

Alternative approaches to Central Bank advances In the European Monetary Union, the European Central Bank (ECB), which is the governing institution within the European System of Central Banks (ESCB), has long set *two* interest rates on central bank advances. One of these rates is a rate slightly below prevailing interbank funds rates. The ECB establishes credit quotas for all private banks within the European Monetary Union, and these banks often borrow up to these limits.

Lombard rate

The specific name given to the interest rate on central bank advances that the European Central Bank and Swiss National Bank set above current market interest rates.

The other interest rate on central bank advances in the ESCB and Switzerland is traditionally known as the ***Lombard rate,*** which is an interest rate that these nations' central banks set *above* current market interest rates. (The ECB refers to this rate as the *marginal interest rate.*) Hence, the Lombard rate is a ***penalty rate,*** meaning that private banks can get Lombard credit from the ECB and Swiss National Bank only by incurring an above-market penalty. Banks can borrow at this penalty rate whenever they unexpectedly find themselves illiquid. Because European Monetary Union and Swiss banks can finance a known amount of daily funds borrowings at the below-market *discount rate* and cover unanticipated credit requirements at the above-market Lombard rate, the market interest rate in European Monetary Union and Swiss interbank funds markets tends to vary between these two central bank rates. Consequently, when they establish values for the discount and Lombard rates, the ECB and Swiss National Bank place lower and upper limits on daily interest rate variations.

penalty rate

The general term for any interest rate on central bank advances that is set above prevailing market interest rates.

The Bank of Japan also advances credit to private banks. In contrast to the ECB and Swiss National Bank, however, the Bank of Japan does not establish fixed credit quotas for banks. Instead, it engages in discretionary rationing of credit on a daily basis. The effective value of the Bank of Japan's lending rate also varies with the term of its loans. To accomplish this, the Bank of Japan calculates the total interest charge on advances to private banks based on the period of the loan *plus* one additional day. As a result, if the Bank of Japan were to restrict advances to a bank to one-day maturities on a Tuesday, whereas on the previous Monday it had permitted two-day advances, its action on Tuesday effectively would raise the interest charge on advances to that bank. Thus, Japanese banks can face several different interest charges by the Bank of Japan from day to day.

The Bank of England and the Bank of Canada each set a single discount rate, but they choose to use their lending rates solely as penalty rates. Since 2003, the U.S. Federal Reserve System has also set its lending rate on advances, which it nonetheless calls its *discount rate*, as a penalty rate above the interbank rate, which in the United States is known as the *federal funds rate*. In 2008, the Federal Reserve began paying interest on required and excess bank reserves at rates generally below the market federal funds rate. If the market federal funds rate were to fall to the rate paid on excess reserves, banks of course would simply hold excess reserves instead of lending in the interbank market. Thus, the Federal Reserve's new policy structure places an upper limit—the lending rate on advances—and a lower limit—the rate of interest paid on excess reserves—on movements in the market federal funds rate.

Central Bank interest rates and other market interest rates Even though every central bank has its own policy regarding the interest rate (or rates) it establishes for advances of credit to private banks, in principle each central bank can influence other short-term interest rates by varying the rate (or rates) that it charges. In the European Monetary Union, for instance, the ECB can induce a rise in the average interbank funds rate by pushing up both the discount rate and the Lombard rate, thereby raising both the lower and upper limits for movements in the interbank rate. Alternatively, it can induce less "dramatic" changes in the level of the interbank funds rate by raising just one of its interest rates, and this is a more common manner in which the ECB tries to bring about gradual interest rate adjustments within the European Monetary Union.

The adjustments in other market interest rates occur as a result of the term structure of interest rates, which we discussed in Chapter 5. For instance, a rise in the one-day interbank funds rate induced by an increase in the ECB's rates on advances will cause bond traders, provided that they do not regard the policy action as transitory, to expect higher one-day rates in the future. Because other market rates are averages of one-day funds rates, they will increase following a long-lived rise in the one-day interbank funds rate.

In Japan, the Bank of Japan can try to generate an increase in the interbank funds rate either by raising its quoted lending rate or by shortening the maturity of its advances, thereby raising the effective discount rate. Either action tends to raise the effective cost to Japanese banks of raising funds through central bank advances, which induces them to offer higher rates to borrow privately in the interbank market. The result is a rise in the average Japanese interbank funds rate and, via the term structure of interest rates, an increase in the general level of interest rates on other Japanese financial instruments.

Finally, an increase in the lending rate on central bank advances often induces increases in other interest rates via an ***announcement effect.*** In connection with rates on central bank advances, this is a change in private market interest rates that results from an *anticipation* of near-term changes in interest rates. A rise in the central bank lending rate signals to private banks that an increase in other rates is likely. Central banks already strenuously ration advances in these countries, so a

announcement effect
A change in private market interest rates or exchange rates that results from an anticipation of near-term changes in market conditions signaled by a central bank policy action.

lending rate increase does not necessarily induce further declines in private bank borrowing from these central banks. Nevertheless, because of the announcement effect, private banks will respond by increasing their current borrowing in the interbank market today, before the interbank funds rate rises. The result is a self-fulfilling prophesy. As private banks raise their demand for loans from other banks, they bid up the general level of the interbank funds rate.

Open-Market Operations A second fundamental type of monetary policy instrument available to many central banks is *open-market operations.* This term refers to central bank purchases or sales of government or private securities. In normal times, central banking institutions that engage in open-market operations—such as the U.S. Federal Reserve—buy or sell only government securities. Some, such as the Federal Reserve, buy securities in secondary markets, rather than purchasing them directly from the government. At the Federal Reserve, voting members of the *Federal Open Market Committee (FOMC)*— the seven Federal Reserve Board governors and five Federal Reserve bank presidents—set the overall strategy of open-market operations at meetings that take place every six to eight weeks. They explain this strategy in the *FOMC Directive,* which outlines the FOMC's policy objectives, establishes short-term federal funds rate goals, and lays out specific target ranges for monetary aggregates. The Federal Reserve Bank of New York's *Trading Desk* then implements the *Directive* from day to day during the weeks between FOMC meetings.

Outright transactions versus repurchase agreements The Trading Desk's open-market operations typically occur within a one-hour interval each business morning. The Trading Desk conducts two types of open-market operations. One is called an *outright transaction.* This is an open-market purchase or sale in which the Trading Desk is not obliged to resell or repurchase securities at a later date. The other kind of operation is a *repurchase agreement transaction,* which commits the seller of a security to repurchase the security at a later date. The Trading Desk often buys securities from dealers under agreements for the dealers to repurchase them at a later date. The Trading Desk also commonly uses *reverse repurchase agreements* when conducting open-market sales, which are agreements for the Trading Desk to repurchase the securities from dealers at a later time.

When a central bank purchases a security, it typically makes payment to the prior owner by crediting the owner's deposit account at a banking institution. When the bank receives the funds, its reserves increase. The Trading Desk often uses outright purchases or sales when it wishes to permanently change the aggregate level of bank reserves. In contrast, it typically uses repurchase agreements when its main goal is to keep the current level of reserves from changing for some external reason. Nevertheless, the Trading Desk can substitute repurchase agreement transactions for outright purchases or sales to change the overall reserve level by continuously mismatching repurchase-agreement transactions as needed.

Alternative procedures for open-market operations Because the ECB is able to use its discount rate–Lombard rate system for advances to constrain market interest rates from day to day, it does not conduct open-market operations each day. Instead, it offers a set of repurchase agreements at a regular weekly auction. This enables the ECB to maintain a desired level of bank reserves from week to week.

The Bank of Canada also conducts open-market operations once per week. However, it usually participates directly in the Canadian Treasury's weekly auction

---

open-market operations
Central bank purchases or sales of government or private securities.

of government bills of indebtedness. Thus, many of the Bank of Canada's open-market operations are outright transactions, with some purchases made directly from the government.

At the Bank of Japan, most open-market operations involve the purchase or sale of *privately issued* financial instruments, including commercial bills and paper and bank certificates of deposit. In the past, this has allowed the Bank of Japan to try to directly influence a variety of market interest rates. Since the late 1980s, however, the Bank of Japan has aimed its open-market operations primarily at influencing the Japanese interbank funds rate. As we shall discuss shortly, this procedure parallels the approach adopted by most central banks in industrialized countries.

Open-market operations are much less common in less-developed and emerging economies. The reason for this is simple: These nations do not have well-developed markets for government securities and other short-term instruments. This makes it difficult for central banks in these countries to find a critical mass of banks and other institutions that regularly trade securities on a daily or weekly basis.

Reserve Requirements As we will discuss in greater detail, a key objective of a central bank's policies typically is to influence the aggregate reserves in its banking system. In years past, therefore, an important instrument of monetary policy has been *reserve requirements.* These are rules specifying portions of transactions (checking) and term (time and savings) deposits that private banks must hold either as vault cash or as funds on deposit at the central bank.

Today, however, reserve requirements are less important instruments of monetary policy. Certainly, central banks rarely change reserve requirements in an effort to exert direct effects on the quantities of money and credit or on the levels of market interest rates. Central banks offer reserve requirements mainly to ensure that private banks are sufficiently liquid to be able to make rapid day-to-day reserve adjustments in response to unexpected events. To assist banks in this endeavor, most central banks assess reserve requirements on an average basis: Banks must meet their reserve requirements, but they need do so only on average over a period of one or two weeks.

Interest Rate Regulations and Direct Credit Controls In a number of nations, and especially in those with less-developed financial markets, central banks traditionally have used more blunt means of influencing the quantities of money and credit. In East Asia, for instance, central banks commonly place restrictions on interest rates that private banks may pay their depositors. They sometimes use these limits as monetary policy instruments. For example, raising the allowable interest rate that banks may pay on deposits potentially can induce individuals and firms to hold more deposits, thereby increasing the amount of deposits, including those that circulate as money.

In nations such as China and Russia, central banks also use *direct credit controls,* which are explicit quantity constraints on how much credit banks and other financial institutions may extend to individuals and firms. If central banks in these nations wish to contract the growth of money and credit, perhaps in an effort to contain inflation, then they tighten credit constraints. If the central banks wish to induce higher growth in money and credit, perhaps to encourage increased near-term economic growth, then they loosen the controls somewhat.

reserve requirements
Central bank regulations requiring private banks to hold specified fractions of transactions and term deposits either as vault cash or as funds on deposit at the central bank.

Fundamental ISSUES

#5 What are the primary functions of central banks?

Central banks are the main depository institutions for national governments, and they serve as fiscal agents operating the systems through which governments issue debt instruments and make interest and principal payments, as well as promote broader markets for government debt instruments. Central banks also provide banking services for private banking institutions and function as lenders of last resort, providing liquidity in the event of systemic failures such as bank runs. Finally, central banks conduct monetary policy by determining values for their policy instruments, which may include interest rates on central bank advances, open-market operations, reserve requirements, and interest rate and credit restrictions. They vary these policy instruments to influence total bank reserve levels and interbank funds rates.

SUPRANATIONAL FINANCIAL POLICYMAKING INSTITUTIONS

Central banks are national institutions that have responsibility for conducting banking and monetary policy functions within the borders of their own nations. Although central banks can choose to coordinate efforts in the face of international financial instability or crises, typically such efforts are worked out on an ad hoc basis, *following* instability or crisis events. In recognition of the possible inability of national central banks to prevent crises and of the potential for crises to spread internationally, many nations have developed multinational institutions intended to limit the likelihood of crisis and to contain crises when they occur.

There are two supranational organizations at the center of current multilateral efforts to prevent and stem international financial crises: the International Monetary Fund and the World Bank.

The International Monetary Fund

The *International Monetary Fund (IMF)* is a multinational organization that promotes international monetary cooperation, exchange arrangements, and economic growth. It provides temporary financial assistance to nations experiencing balance-of-payments difficulties. Figure 6–4 on the next page charts the growth of IMF membership since the founding of the organization in July 1944. Currently, the IMF has 182 member nations.

quota subscription
The funds deposited by IMF member nations that together form the pool of funds that IMF managers can use for loans to member nations experiencing financial difficulties.

When a country joins the IMF, it deposits funds to an account called its *quota subscription.* These funds, which are measured in terms of Special Drawing Rights (SDRs; see Chapter 2 to see how the SDR is calculated), form a pool from which the IMF can draw to lend to members. Figure 6–5 displays current quota subscriptions for selected IMF member nations.

The IMF sets each nation's quota subscription based on its real national income. The quota subscription determines how much a member can borrow from the IMF under the organization's standard credit arrangements. It also determines the member's share of voting power within the IMF. The U.S. quota subscription, for instance, is just over 17 percent of the total funds provided by all member nations, so this is the IMF voting share held by the United States.

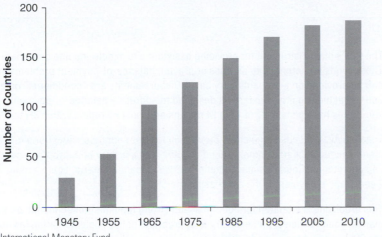

Figure 6–4

Growth in IMF Membership since 1945

The number of member nations in the International Monetary Fund is now about six times larger than it was when the organization was founded.

Source: International Monetary Fund.

When the IMF considers providing financial support to a member country, it normally imposes specific limitations on the actions of that country's government. This IMF policy, called ***conditionality,*** requires countries to cooperate with the IMF in establishing plans for the nation's financial policies. Sometimes the IMF will not extend assistance to a nation unless it takes certain actions before receiving the loan. As part of broader satisfaction of conditionality requirements, the IMF may only request a general commitment to aim policies in a certain direction, known as *low conditionality.* In this case, the IMF is said to have a *policy understanding* with the nation. Alternatively, the IMF may impose *high conditionality.* Then it requires a nation to aim for specific, quantifiable targets, called *performance criteria.* Failure to meet these targets can lead to suspension of IMF loan disbursements.

conditionality

The set of limitations on the range of allowable actions of a government of a country that is a recipient of IMF loans.

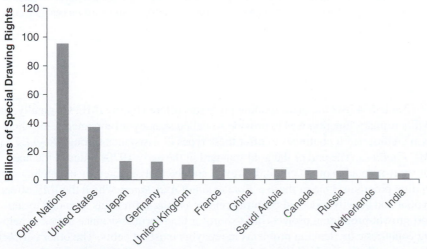

Figure 6–5

IMF Quota Subscriptions

The quota subscription of each member nation in the IMF, which is denominated in SDRs, depends on the nation's real national income. A country's quota subscription determines its share of voting power within the IMF and how much it is eligible to borrow under standard IMF credit arrangements.

Source: International Monetary Fund.

Table 6–4 IMF Financing Facilities

Nonconcessional Facilities	
Stand-by Arrangements (SBAs)	The IMF's main instrument for providing assistance to middle-income countries. These funds are intended to address or prevent balance-of-payment problems and can be provided on a precautionary basis. Disbursements are "conditional" on a country achieving program targets designed to address a balance-of-payments problem. Loans have a maturity of 12 to 24 months and must be repaid within 3½ to 5 years.
Flexible Credit Line (FCL)	This facility is intended as a crisis-prevention tool for countries with strong fundamental economic performance, sound policies, and a history of appropriate policy implementation. Countries must meet preset qualification criteria. Loans are for 1 to 2 years and repayment is the same as for the SBA.
Precautionary Credit Line (PCL)	This credit line is intended for countries with strong fundamental economic performance, sound policies, and a history of appropriate policy implementation (as under the FCL) and that face "moderate" vulnerabilities and do not qualify for large-scale adjustments (as under the SBA). The credit line can be drawn upon if a need arises unexpectedly.
Extended Fund Facility	This facility was established in 1974 to assist countries in addressing long-term balance-of-payments problems. Loans are typically for 3 years and must be repaid with 4½ to 10 years from disbursement.
Concessional Facilities	
Extended Credit Facility (ECF)	The IMF's main instrument for providing medium-term loans to lower-income countries that have "protracted" balance-of-payments problems. These loans have a zero interest rate with a grace period of 5 ½ years and a 10-year maturity.
Standby Credit Facility (SCF)	Provides loans to lower-income countries with short-term balance-of-payments requirements. These loans have a zero interest rate with a grace period of 4 years and an 8-year maturity.
Rapid Credit Facility (RCF)	Provides rapid financing to lower-income countries with "urgent" balance-of-payments requirements. These loans have a zero interest rate with a grace period of 5 ½ years and a 10-year maturity.
Emergency Assistance	Emergency assistance is available for countries that experience a natural disaster or are emerging from a conflict. Loans are subject to interest and must be repaid within 3¼ to 5 years.

Source: International Monetary Fund.

Table 6–4 lists the main funding programs offered by the IMF. Originally, the IMF's primary function was to provide so-called standby arrangements and short-term credits, and it continues to offer these types of assistance through *Regular IMF Facilities.* The end of the gold standard in the early 1970s reduced the need for short-term adjustment credit, however, and the IMF adapted by expanding other lending programs. One of these is *Concessional Assistance,* which the IMF offers to poor and heavily indebted countries, either as long-term loans intended to support growth-promoting projects or as short- or long-term assistance aimed at helping countries experiencing problems in repaying existing debts. The other is *Other Financing Facilities.* Under these funding programs, the IMF seeks to assist any qualifying member experiencing an unusual fluctuation in exports or imports, a loss of confidence in its own financial system, or spillover effects from financial crises originating elsewhere.

The World Bank

The other key supranational institution that provides support to nations experiencing financial problems is the ***World Bank.*** This institution, which also was created during the 1944 Bretton Woods conference, is more narrowly specialized than the IMF. The World Bank makes loans solely to about100 developing nations with an aim toward reducing poverty and improving living standards. It estimates that within its client nations, about 3 billion people live on less than $2 per day, about 40,000 die of preventable diseases each day, and more than 100 million never attend schools of any type.

In contrast to the IMF, the World Bank has always specialized in relatively long-term loans used to fund long-term development and growth. Its initial objective was to provide assistance to countries in the post–World War II rebuilding period. In the 1960s it refocused its mission by broadening its scope to encompass global antipoverty efforts.

Whereas nations' governments commonly used IMF loans to supplement their overall budgetary resources, countries typically seek loans from the World Bank to fund specific projects, such as improved irrigation systems or better hospitals. Nevertheless, in recent years some of the World Bank's programs have overlapped with IMF efforts to finance longer-term structural adjustments and debt-refinancing activities within heavily indebted nations.

The World Bank is composed of five separate institutions, which are listed and described in Table 6–5. These institutions lend to both governments and private firms. They also provide advice and assistance in various aspects of development finance, including resolving disputes that may arise between foreign investors and developing countries. The world's wealthiest countries fund most of its activities, although the World Bank also raises some of its funds in international capital markets.

World Bank
A sister institution to the International Monetary Fund that is more narrowly specialized in making loans to about 100 developing nations in an effort to promote their long-term development and growth.

Table 6–5   World Bank Institutions

International Development Association	On behalf of 165 member countries, specializes in funding loans aimed toward poverty reduction in developing nations.
International Bank for Reconstruction and Development	On behalf of 184 member nations, provides loans and other forms of development assistance to middle-income countries and the more creditworthy developing nations.
International Finance Corporation	On behalf of 176 member nations, promotes private-sector investment in developing countries by committing its own funds, brokering loans from private sources, and offering advice to private firms.
Multinational Investment Guarantee Agency	On behalf of 165 member countries, promotes foreign direct investment in developing nations by offering political risk insurance guarantees to lenders and investors.
International Center for Settlement of Investment Disputes	On behalf of 143 member nations, provides conciliation and arbitration facilities for settling investment disputes arising between foreign investors and developing nations.

Source: World Bank.

In recent years, critics of the World Bank have questioned just how much the institution's activities really assist developing nations. Some economists and policymakers have raised questions as well about the usefulness of the current activities of the International Monetary Fund. We shall address these issues in Chapter 7.

Fundamental ISSUES

#6 What are the two most important supranational financial policymaking institutions, and what are their functions in the international financial system?

The International Monetary Fund and the World Bank are multinational economic organizations consisting of more than 180 member nations. One of the IMF's broad objectives is to encourage economic growth by facilitating international monetary cooperation and effective exchange arrangements. Another fundamental IMF goal is to hinder or combat international crises by providing temporary and longer-term financial assistance to nations experiencing balance-of-payments difficulties. The World Bank also seeks to promote economic growth, but it does so primarily via longer-term loans to support investment projects within the world's less-developed nations.

Chapter SUMMARY

1. **The Process of International Financial Intermediation and How National Banking Systems Differ:** A key reason that financial intermediaries exist is to address problems arising from asymmetric information. One such problem is adverse selection, or the potential for the least creditworthy borrowers to be the most likely to seek to issue financial instruments. Another is moral hazard, or the possibility that an initially creditworthy borrower may undertake actions that reduce its creditworthiness after receiving funds from a lender. In addition, financial intermediaries may take advantage of economies of scale, or the ability to spread costs of managing funds across large numbers of savers. A potential justification for international financial intermediation by global banking enterprises is that they may experience economies of scale in information processing by spreading their credit evaluation and monitoring operations across the world. Finally, different laws concerning secrecy and tax treatment of banking accounts can lead to differences in the functioning of national banking systems.

2. **The World's Major Bank Payment Systems and How the Risks That Arise in National Financial and Banking Systems Contribute to the Potential for Financial Instability and Crises:** The largest-valued payments processed by banks are transmitted through electronic payment systems such as the Fedwire and CHIPS systems that operate in the United States. As payment intermediaries, individual banks face a variety of risks in transmitting payments, including liquidity risks associated with the possibility of delayed receipt of payments and credit risks arising from the potential for other parties to fail to honor payment obligations. As interconnected payment intermediaries, banks also face systemic risks, which arise from the possibility for settlement failures among some institutions to result in payment breakdowns among others. They also face Herstatt risks, which are liquidity, credit, and systemic risks relating to international payments. These financial risks, together with the potential for exchange rates to become misaligned with currency values consistent with economic fundamentals, can contribute

to financial instability. In such a climate, speculative attacks on official exchange rates, self-fulfilling anticipations and contagion effects, or existing moral hazard problems can result in international financial crises.

3. **The Objectives That National Banking Regulators Seek to Achieve and How They Implement Their Regulations:** A key regulatory goal is the prevention of bank in-solvency, or negative net worth. An additional objective is the prevention of widespread bank illiquidity, or the general inability of banks to meet the cash requirements of their depositors. A third regulatory goal is to induce banks to operate at low cost and at normal profit levels. Currently, bank regulators in thirty-five nations require banks based in their countries to meet risk-based capital standards. Under these requirements, banks must maintain minimal allowable ratios of capital relative to total assets and to risk-adjusted assets.

4. **The Main Assets and Liabilities of Central Banks:** Key central bank assets are gov-ernment securities, loans to private banks, and foreign-currency-dominated securities and deposits. The primary liabilities of central banks are currency notes and reserve deposits of private banks.

5. **The Primary Functions of Central Banks:** Central banks are depositories for funds held by national governments and act as fiscal agents by operating the systems through which governments issue debt instruments, making interest and principal payments to those who hold government debt, and developing markets for government debt instru-ments. Central banks perform financial services for private banks and operate as lenders of last resort by providing liquidity to stem bank runs or other systemic banking problems. Furthermore, central banks vary policy instruments, such as interest rates on central bank advances, open-market operations, reserve requirements, and interest rate and credit restrictions, in an effort to affect interbank funds rates and total bank reserves.

6. **The Two Most Important Supranational Financial Policymaking Institutions and Their Functions in the International Financial System:** The IMF and World Bank are multinational economic organizations that are owned and operated by more than 180 nations. The IMF exists to promote global economic growth by encouraging international monetary cooperation and effective exchange arrangements and to limit the scope for international financial crises by providing temporary and longer-term financial assistance to nations experiencing balance-of-payments difficulties. Like the IMF, the World Bank's function is to encourage economic growth, but the World Bank seeks to fulfill this duty mainly by extending relatively long-term loans to fund investment projects by govern-ments or firms located in the least-developed nations of the world.

QUESTIONS and PROBLEMS

1. Why might a U.S. resident choose to hold a deposit in a U.S. bank that allocates a sig-nificant portion of its assets to international loans and securities, instead of making such loans or purchasing such securities personally?

2. Of the list of factors explaining the existence of financial intermediaries, which one do you believe is the most important reason for the existence of commercial banks? Explain your reasoning.

3. The complete failure of one bank to repay the full amount of a loan to a second bank in the same country could leave the second bank unable to transmit promised repayments to a third bank in the same nation and to a fourth bank in another country. What types of payment-system risks exist?

4. What single factor do you conclude plays the most significant role in accounting for the large sizes attained by the banks listed in Table 6–1? Support your answer.

5. Suppose that a Japanese bank has total assets of ¥1,000 million. Of these assets, 80 percent consists of loans to businesses, and the remainder is holdings of cash assets and government securities. The bank engages in derivatives trading that Japanese regulators assign a credit equivalence exposure value of ¥400 million. The bank's equity capital amounts to ¥100 million, and the bank has no subordinated debt. Does this bank meet Basel I capital requirements?

6. What are the key assets and liabilities of central banks?

7. In your view, what is the single most important role of a central bank? Could a central bank perform this role without performing its other roles? Explain your reasoning.

8. Draw a T-account for listing assets (on the left) and liabilities (on the right) of the Federal Reserve System. Place each of the items listed below, which are assumed to be the Fed's only assets and liabilities, in the correct location in the Fed's T-account. Calculate the Fed's total assets and its total liabilities. Show your work, and explain very briefly. Write words and sentences.

U.S. Treasury bills	$250 billion
Funds that private banks hold on deposit with Federal Reserve banks	$160 billion
Federal Reserve loans to private banks	$ 10 billion
Federal Reserve notes in circulation	$490 billion
Dollar value of euro-denominated cash securities the Fed holds on deposit with the European Central Bank	$ 50 billion
U.S. Treasury notes and bonds	$340 billion

9. Suppose that a nation's central bank does not use open-market operations to conduct monetary policy. How could the central bank vary the interest rate(s) that it charges on its advances to prevent the sum of total assets in its balance sheet from changing when it increases its reserves of foreign currencies through purchases in the foreign exchange market?

10. In what ways do the current functions and objectives of the International Monetary Fund and the World Bank overlap? In what ways do they have different functions and pursue different goals?

OnlineAPPLICATIONS

Internet URL: *http://www.bis.org*

Title: Statistics on Payment Systems in the Group of Ten Countries

Navigation: Begin with http://www.bis.org. In the popup menu under *Monetary and Financial Stability*, click on *Committee on Payment and Settlement Systems*. Scan down the *Publications by Category* list and click on *Red Book: CPSS Countries*, and then click on *statistics on payment and settlement systems in the CPSS countries* for the most recent year. Open the PDF file entitled *Comparative Tables*, which contains tables of payment-system data for G10 countries listed in alphabetical order, and answer the following questions.

Application: You can use the data in this report to make a number of cross-country comparisons. Here, let's focus on comparing the relative use of checks and automated teller machine (ATMs and point-of-sale [POS] devices) in Belgium and the United States.

1. Look at Table 1 ("Basic statistical data") for Belgium (the first country in the report) and the United States (the last country in the report). On a separate sheet of paper, write down each nation's population in the latest available year, and write down the average exchange rate for the euro (given in euros per dollar) for that year. Next, scroll to Table 9 ("Use of payment instruments by non-banks: value of transactions per payment instrument") for each country. What was the *dollar value* of total checks (spelled "cheques" in the tables) issued in each nation during this year (use the average euro exchange rate for the year to convert the Belgian value of checks issued into dollars)? What was the average *per-capita dollar value* of checks issued in each nation (divide each nation's dollar value of checks issued by its population)? Based on your per-capita figures, in which of the two nations are checks a relatively more important means of payment for the average resident?

2. Now consider Table P53 ("Payments processed by selected interbank funds transfer systems: value of transactions") for each nation. For the most recent year, what was the total *dollar value* of transactions processed by the largest interbank transfer system in each country? What was the average *per-capita dollar value* of the systems' transactions in each nation? Based on your per-capita figures, in which of the two nations are the largest-value transactions processed?

SELECTED REFERENCES and FURTHER READINGS

Adrian, Tobias, and Hyun Song Shin. "Liquidity, Monetary Policy, and Financial Cycles." *Federal Reserve Bank of New York Current Issues in Economics and Finance 14* (January/February 2008).

Bandt, de, Olivier, and Philip Hartmann. "Systemic Risk: A Survey." European Central Bank Working Paper No. *35* (November 2000).

Bank for International Settlements. *The New Basel Capital Accord: An Explanatory Note* (January 2001).

Barth, James, Gerald Caprio, Jr., and Ross Levine. *Rethinking Bank Regulation: Till Angels Govern.* Cambridge: Cambridge University Press, 2006.

Bech, Morten, Christine Preisig, and Kimmo Soramäki, "Global Trends in Large-Value Payments." *Federal Reserve Bank of New York Economic Policy Review* (2008).

Becher, Christopher, Marco Galiati, and Merxe Tudela. "The Timing and Funding of CHAPS Sterling Payments." *Federal Reserve Bank of New York Economic Policy Review* (2008).

Beck, Thorsten, Asli Demirgue-Kunt, and Maria Soledad Martinez Peria. "Reaching Out: Access to and Use of Banking Services across Countries." *Journal of Financial Economics 85* (2007): 234–266.

Bordo, Michael, "A Brief History of Central Banks." *Federal Reserve Bank of Cleveland Economic Commentary* (2007).

Borio, Claudio. "The Implementation of Monetary Policy in Industrial Countries: A Survey." BIS Economic Papers, No. *47* (July 1997).

Chiuri, Maria Concetta, Giovanni Ferri, and Giovanni Majnoni. "The Macroeconomic Impact of Bank Capital Requirements in Emerging Economies: Past Evidence to Access the Future." *Journal of Banking and Finance 26* (2002): 881–904.

Daniels, Joseph, and David VanHoose. "Currency Substitution, Seigniorage, and Currency Crises in Interdependent Economies." *Journal of Economics and Business 55* (May–June 2003): 221–232.

Demirgüc-Kunt, Asli, and Edward Kane. "Deposit Insurance around the Globe: Where Does It Work?" World Bank and Boston College, 2002.

Duttagupta, Rupa, and Paul Cashin. "The Anatomy of Banking Crises." International Monetary Fund Working Paper No. WP/08/93, April 2008.

Fry, Maxwell. *Money, Interest, and Banking in Economic Development,* 2nd ed. Baltimore: Johns Hopkins University Press, 1995.

Fry, Maxwell, Charles Goodhart, and Alvaro Almeida. *Central Banking in Developing Countries.* London: Routledge, 1996.

Goodhart, Charles. *The Evolution of Central Banks,* Cambridge, MA: MIT Press, 1988.

Humpage, Owen. "A New Role for the Exchange Stabilization Fund." *Federal Reserve Bank of Cleveland Economic Commentary* (August 2008).

Kopecky, Kenneth, and David VanHoose. "Bank Capital Requirements and the Monetary Transmission Mechanism." *Journal of Macroeconomics 26* (2004): 443–464.

Kopecky, Kenneth, and David VanHoose. "A Model of the Monetary Sector with and without Binding Capital Requirements." *Journal of Banking and Finance 28* (2004): 633–646.

Kutar, Ali, and Josef Brada. "The Evolution of Monetary Policy in Transition Economics." *Federal Reserve Bank of St. Louis Review 82* (March/April 2000): 31–40.

Smith, Roy, and Ingo Walter. *Global Banking,* 2nd ed. Oxford: Oxford University Press, 2003.

VanHoose, David. "Bank Capital Regulation, Economic Stability, and Monetary Policy: What Does the Academic Literature Tell Us?" *Atlantic Economic Journal 36* (March 2008): 1–14.

VanHoose, David. "Market Discipline and Supervisory Discretion in Banking: Reinforcing or Conflicting Pillars of Basel II?" *Journal of Applied Finance 17* (Fall/Winter 2007): 105–118.

VanHoose, David. "Theories of Bank Behavior under Capital Regulation." *Journal of Banking and Finance 31* (December 2007): 3680–3697.

7

The International Financial Architecture and Emerging Economies

Fundamental ISSUES

1. What are the most important developments in the recent evolution of global capital markets?

2. What is the relationship between capital allocations and economic growth, and what is the role of financial intermediaries in this relationship?

3. What is the difference between portfolio capital flows and foreign direct investment, and what role did these types of capital flows play in recent financial crises?

4. What type of exchange-rate regime is most appropriate for emerging economies?

5. What aspects of IMF and World Bank policymaking have proved controversial in recent years?

6. What changes in the international financial architecture have economists proposed in recent years?

The mid-2000s were problematic for the International Monetary Fund (IMF). Loans outstanding fell to the lowest level in a quarter of a century, and as a consequence the IMF experienced a significant drop in revenues. In response, top officials pulled out all stops to cut costs and to find other sources of revenues. As part of its effort to cut its costs by $100 million per year, the institution launched a 15 percent staff reduction, from more than 2,600 employees to closer to 2,200. Because far fewer countries were borrowing funds from the IMF, there was less economic analysis for the institution to perform and hence fewer tasks for economists. Many of the job cuts were economist positions. To generate more revenues, the IMF began gradually selling off about 400 metric tons of gold, or more than 12 percent of the total quantity of gold in its possession. The IMF used funds from these gold sales to establish an endowment of international securities that it hoped would yield a rate of return of nearly $400 million per year.

Thus, when the global financial crisis began in the United States in 2008 and shifted to Europe in the early 2010s, the IMF found itself short of the staff required to assist emerging nations in developing and implementing policies aimed at halting banking meltdowns. The IMF also had to scramble for funds to lend to these nations.

What is the International Monetary Fund's responsibility within the international financial system? This is one of several questions that we shall consider in this chapter, which focuses on capital flows to and from the world's emerging nations and the role of supranational institutions such as the IMF.

INTERNATIONAL CAPITAL FLOWS

Financial crises that took place in developing and developed economies alike have induced policymakers and economists around the world to reconsider the *international financial architecture*—that is, the international institutions, national policies and regulatory agencies, and international agreements that govern activity in the international monetary and financial markets. Whether the world's nations should alter the shape of the international financial architecture and, if so, what types of reforms should be adopted are among the most important global policy issues today.

international financial architecture
The international institutions, governmental and nongovernmental organizations, and policies that govern activity in the international monetary and financial markets.

This chapter examines how different types of global capital flows affect the stability and growth of a nation's economy and considers the role of capital flows in recent financial crises. In addition, this chapter discusses efforts by multinational institutions such as the International Monetary Fund and the World Bank to prevent, predict, and respond to such crises. It also examines recent proposals for restructuring or redirecting the activities of these institutions.

Explaining the Direction of Capital Flows

Since the collapse of the Bretton Woods system, the most important feature of the international financial system has been the increased volume of financial flows between nations. As you learned in Chapter 1, in recent years there has been dramatic growth of the volume of transactions in the international capital markets. To understand the nature of this recent upswing, it is important to account for differences between the capital flows experienced by developed countries and emerging economies. It is also crucial to distinguish between foreign direct investment (FDI) and portfolio capital flows.

Foreign Direct Investment and Developed Nations Growth in FDI is one of the most important developments in the evolution of global capital markets. FDI is the acquisition of foreign financial assets that results in an ownership share of 10 percent or more. Hence, an *FDI inflow* is an acquisition of domestic financial assets that results in foreign residents owning 10 percent or more of a domestic entity. An *FDI outflow* is an acquisition of foreign financial assets that results in domestic residents owning 10 percent or more of a foreign entity.

On the WEB

Get annual data on global foreign direct investment flows from the United Nations Conference on Trade and Development (UNCTAD) at *http//www.unctad.org*.

	FDI Inflows (%)	FDI Outflows (%)	World Exports (%)
1971–1975	19.8	17.3	24.0
1976–1980	18.5	17.4	18.1
1981–1985	2.1	2.4	-0.6
1986–1990	31.5	34.6	14.5
1991–1995	20.0	15.7	8.3
1996–2000	33.4	29.1	8.0
2001–2005	−2.4	−0.8	5.7
2006–2010	9.0	15.2	4.5
2011–2015*	16.4	16.7	5.6

Table 7–1

Average Annual Growth of World FDI and World Exports

During the 1970s, world FDI inflows and outflows and world exports all grew at rates exceeding 17 percent. The average annual growth rates of these flows fell dramatically during the global recession of the early 1980s, during the early 2000s, and again in 2008.

Source: UNCTADSTAT, unctadstat.inctad.org, and IMF *World Economic Outlook Database.* *IMF and authors' estimates.

Table 7–1 provides growth rates of world FDI inflows, outflows, and world exports. As shown in the table, both FDI flows and exports grew by 17 percent or more during the 1970s. In the first half of the 1980s, these growth rates declined and world exports actually contracted in the wake of an emerging-economy debt crisis and a global recession. According to data gathered by the United Nations Conference on Trade and Development (UNCTAD), since 1980 the global stock of FDI has increased by more than twentyfold to a level of more than $19 trillion. Nonetheless, because of global economic downturn, a precipitous drop in FDI flows occurred in from 2001 through 2003 and following the global economic crisis beginning in 2008.

FDI flows, indeed much of long-term capital flows, tend to be concentrated among the developed nations. Table 7–2 provides the geographical distribution of FDI inflows given in Table 7–1. The table shows that, on average, 60 percent of FDI inflows goes to the developed nations. In the years immediately following the major emerging-economy financial crises of 1995 and 1998, FDI inflows to the developed economies spiked upward as FDI inflows to the emerging economies declined. During 2002, however, the United States and the United Kingdom accounted for half of the decline in FDI among those nations with reduced FDI inflows. In contrast, during the early 2000s, China became a leading recipient of FDI flows and the only emerging economy ranked among the top-ten recipients.

Cross-Border Mergers and Acquisitions Cross-border mergers and acquisitions (M&As) are the driving force behind the recent surge in FDI within the developed economies. *Cross-border mergers and acquisitions* are the combining of firms in different nations. A merger occurs when a firm absorbs the assets and liabilities of another firm. An acquisition occurs when a firm purchases the assets and liabilities of another firm. Changes in national tax codes, relaxation of business regulations and labor laws, and a changing shareholder culture spurred a dramatic increase in cross-border M&A deals.

cross-border mergers and acquisitions

The combining of firms located in different nations in which one firm absorbs the assets and liabilities of another firm (merger) or purchases the assets and liabilities of another firm (acquisition).

Table 7–2

Geographical Distribution of FDI Inflows, Percent of Total Inflows

FDI inflows are highly concentrated in the developed nations. On average, more than 60 percent of FDI inflows goes to the developed nations.

	1990–1995	1996–2000	2001–2005	2006–2010	2011–2015
Developed Nations	50.5	67.8	57.6	68.9	73.0
Developing Nations	37.1	29.2	37.1	26.1	22.7
Transition Economies	3.3	3.0	5.4	5.0	4.3

Source: UNCTADSTAT, unctadstat.unctad.org.

Consistent with the geographical pattern of FDI, M&A activity is concentrated among developed nations, with more than 80 percent of total flows within the United States, Japan, and the European Union. According to data gathered by the Organization for Economic Cooperation and Development, European companies were the leading purchasers in M&A deals. The United States, on the other hand, consistently attracts more M&A deals than any other nation, capturing more than 20 percent of global M&A purchases. As shown in Figure 7–1, M&A flows increased dramatically after the mid-1990s, to a peak of over $1 trillion annually in 2000. These flows temporarily declined from 2001 through 2003, rising again and then falling during the global financial crisis in 2009.

For data on M&A and capital flows, visit the home page of the Organization for Economic Cooperation and Development at *http://www.oecd.org*.

The Emerging Economies A second important development in the recent evolution of global capital markets is the growth of private capital flows to the emerging economies. Figure 7–2 illustrates the most recent data on these flows. In the figure, capital flows are separated into foreign direct investment and portfolio investment. As shown in the figure, private FDI and portfolio flows to the emerging and developing economies have averaged over $300 billion since 2005. There was a decline

Figure 7–1

Cross-Border Merger-and-Acquisition Inflows

Cross-border mergers and acquisitions are the driving force behind recent increases in FDI. Most of these inflows are to the developed nations.

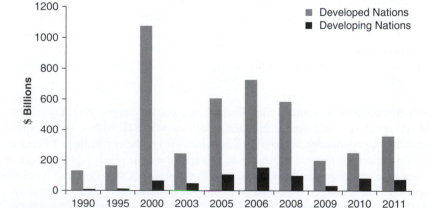

Source: UNCTADSTAT, unctadstat.unctad.org.

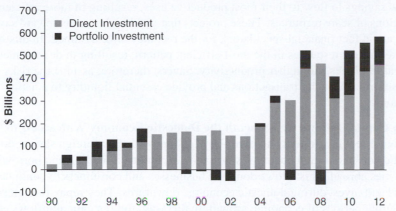

Figure 7–2

Net Private Capital Flows
to Emerging Economies

Private capital flows to the
emerging economies have grown
at a remarkable rate since 1990.
Despite the financial crises in
Mexico in 1994, East Asia in 1997,
Russia in 1998, Brazil in 1999,
and Argentina in 2001, direct
investment continued to flow to
the emerging economies. Private
capital flows declined following the
global recession that began in 2008.

Source: International Monetary Fund, *World Economic Outlook Database.*

in these flows during the early 2000s, when a number of emerging and developing
economies suffered financial crises. Although portfolio capital flows turned negative in 2006 and 2008, FDI flows remained relatively robust in spite of the global
financial crisis.

Private capital flows to emerging and developing economies that experienced financial crises, such as Mexico, Russia, and the economies of Southeast
Asia, exhibited a similar pattern. In general, there was a dramatic increase in
capital flows to these economies prior to the crisis, with a large share of the
capital inflows being short-term portfolio capital inflows. Many economists
believe that the systems of financial intermediaries in these nations were over-
whelmed by such large capital inflows. The crises were typically sparked by
a reversal of portfolio flows. Following most of their crisis episodes, most of
these nations were able to attract a greater proportion of capital flows in the
form of FDI.

Fundamental ISSUES

#1 What are the most important developments in the recent evolution of global capital markets?

Two important developments in the global capital markets are the growth of foreign direct
investment (FDI) among developed nations and surging private capital flows to emerging
economies. Normally, FDI has been concentrated among the United States, Japan, and
the European Union, where the rise of cross-border mergers and acquisitions has recently
contributed to FDI within these regions. Since the early 1990s, capital flows to emerging economies have also increased significantly. Despite a drop in capital flows to both
developed and emerging economies during the early and late 2000s, capital flows to these
nations have averaged more than $440 billion a year since 2005.

Capital Allocations and Economic Growth

Advocates of capital market liberalization—allowing relatively open issuance and
competition in stock and bond markets—argue that unhindered capital movements

allow savings to flow to their most productive uses, resulting in more efficient allocations of scare resources. Those projects that yield high returns reward savers, who are in fact financial speculators, for the risk they have assumed. In this way, markets direct resources in the most efficient pattern, resulting in development of real resources and higher productivity. Savers, therefore, assume the risks in cross-border financial transactions and provide essential liquidity to a nation's economy.

How Capital Inflows Can Smooth the Domestic Economy With access to foreign direct investment and portfolio capital provided by foreign savers, domestic households and businesses then may expand their lending and borrowing activities abroad. This allows domestic businesses and consumers to continue to spend and invest during domestic economic downturns. They repay foreign savers during periods of economic growth. In this way, foreign capital inflows can help to offset domestic business cycles, providing greater stability to the domestic economy.

Hence, domestic savers can diversify internationally and reduce their exposure to domestic economic shocks. These positive aspects of foreign capital inflows allow domestic savers to enjoy higher risk-adjusted rates of return, spurring even higher levels of saving and investment activity. In turn, increased saving and investment induce additional economic growth.

How Capital Inflows Can Contribute to Long-Term Development For developing nations, access to global capital in the form of FDI and portfolio capital inflows considerably reduces the cost of financing investment projects. This permits domestic firms and individuals to undertake more investment projects, which contributes to the development of real resources. In the long run, this translates into higher standards of living and higher rates of economic growth. Additionally, private savings from abroad may substitute for uncertain development aid from foreign governments that often comes with inefficiency costs associated with bureaucratic red tape and constraints.

As you learned in Chapter 6, financial intermediaries typically perform an important role in allocating savings in a nation's economy. For emerging economies, *financial-sector development*—the development and strengthening of financial institutions, payment systems, and regulatory agencies—is necessary to attract global capital and promote domestic saving. Economic theory indicates, however, that financial-sector development may either increase or decrease saving. As just discussed, financial-sector development can improve the allocation of domestic and foreign savings flows. Nevertheless, wider availability of the various hedging instruments described in Chapter 5 potentially can reduce precautionary saving. In addition, improvements in household credit markets may allow agents to borrow more than they might have otherwise to engage in current consumption or to initiate projects that previously might have been deemed unworthy of financial support. Hence, if financial-sector development induces lower total *net* saving—saving less borrowing—economic growth actually could suffer.

In general, economists have two opposing points of view of the contribution of the financial sector to long-run economic development. Some economists argue that the development of real resources, including physical resources such as plant and equipment, and the development of technology and human capital are the crucial determinates of long-run economic performance. According to this view, the financial sector does not play an important role in the long run.

financial-sector development
The strengthening and growth of a nation's financial sector institutions, payments systems, and regulatory agencies.

An alternative view is that the development of the financial sector induces changes in economic fundamentals. The financial sector can, as explained, attract foreign capital and affect private agents' long-run saving and borrowing decisions, and, therefore, long-run investment strategies. In this way, development of the financial sector influences long-run economic performance.

Why financial development evolves differently across nations is still somewhat unclear. Recent research on the casual relationship between financial development and real-sector growth, however, tends to support the second view. This research concludes that financial development does indeed affect economic growth by promoting savings and directing funds to the most productive investment projects.

Capital Misallocations and their Consequences

In spite of the arguments for capital market liberalization, *financial market imperfections* (such as the type discussed in Chapter 6) and *policy-created distortions* may cause a nation's financial system to fall short in contributing to its economic development.

Market Imperfections Many economists argue that one type of market imperfection, *asymmetric information,* is pervasive in financial markets. As discussed in Chapter 6, asymmetric information can bring about an inefficient distribution of capital through resulting problems of *adverse selection, herding behavior,* and *moral hazard.*

Adverse selection is the potential for those who want funds for unworthy projects to be the most likely to want to borrow. Adverse selection can make savers less willing to lend to or hold instruments, including instruments of those seeking to finance high-quality projects. Additionally, poor information may result in herding behavior. Herding behavior occurs when savers who lack full information base their decisions on the behavior of others who they feel are better informed. In a global context, herding behavior can be a catalyst for *contagion,* the spread of financial instability to regional levels. Herding behavior can also lead to a reduction of asset prices or currency values that greatly exceed what would be warranted.

Another potential problem is moral hazard, or the potential for a borrower to engage in much riskier behavior after issuing a debt instrument. For instance, moral hazard may arise when a domestic government implicitly or explicitly guarantees that a firm or bank will not be allowed to fail. Knowing that it will not be allowed to fail, the firm may engage in higher-risk projects in search for higher returns. International organizations, such as the International Monetary Fund, have also been accused of creating moral hazard in much the same way, by standing ready to bail out sovereign nations facing liquidity crises. The argument goes that if the sovereign government knows the IMF is willing to loan it funds when the government runs out of foreign reserves, the government will not conduct its policies in a manner prescribed by its exchange-rate arrangement.

Policy-Created Distortions Capital flows may also respond to policy-created distortions, leading to an inefficient and capricious allocation of capital. A *policy-created distortion* results when a government policy leads a market to produce a level of output that is different from the desired level of output, or economically efficient level of output. Microeconomic policies such as tariffs on imports and subsidies to specific industries, for example, protect producers in those industries

policy-created distortion
When a government policy results in a market producing a level of output that is different from the economically efficient level of output. The policy, therefore, causes a less-than-optimal allocation of an economy's scarce resources.

from foreign competition. This type of protection is typically offered to industries that are not competitive in global markets. Yet, by protecting the industry, these policy measures result in a different level of output and higher economic profits than would be experienced in a competitive environment. In turn, these higher profits attract capital flows into the protected industry and away from other, perhaps more productive industries. Differential national taxation policies, trade restrictions, and macroeconomic policies are but a few policy-created distortions that may lead to a misallocation of capital.

In addition, differing national regulations of financial transactions may generate *regulatory arbitrage.* Domestic institutions may locate abroad or conduct certain types of operations abroad in order to avoid domestic regulation and supervision. Such regulatory-avoidance behavior diminishes the regulatory abilities of governments and exposes domestic intermediaries to the very types of risk regulators seek to minimize.

Though these distortions result from domestic economic policies, they should be viewed in an international context as well. In principle, the absence of international cooperation and coordination can bring about potential "race to the bottom," or a movement toward the regulatory and tax environment of the least stringent nation. The potential role of multinational policy cooperation and coordination in reducing this possibility is discussed later in this chapter.

Financial Instability and Financial Crises When market imperfections and policy-created distortion are severe, they may result in financial instability, a situation in which the financial sector is unable to allocate funds to the most productive projects. Severe financial instability can potentially trigger a financial crisis, or complete breakdown in the functioning of financial markets. Chapter 6 provided some evidence on the costs of financial crises experienced by various nations. A key policy objective of all nations, therefore, is to reduce the potential for the types of problems just described, creating a stable financial environment.

Maximizing Benefits and Minimizing Risks For some emerging economies, capital market liberalization can be a mixed blessing. Capital inflows allow residents of emerging economies to finance trade and investment opportunities that otherwise would be impossible. Nevertheless, a portion of funds from abroad can flow out of a nation just as quickly as funds flow in, putting severe strains on a nation's financial system and affecting the exchange value of the nation's currency.

capital market liberalization

Policy actions designed to allow relatively open issuance and competition in a nation's stock and bond markets.

Is *capital market liberalization,* which is allowing relatively open issuance and competition in stock and bond markets, the right policy for an emerging economy, or should these nations continue to restrict capital flows? John Williamson of the World Bank and Molly Mahar of the Federal Reserve Bank of San Francisco studied the economic performance of thirty-four nations that undertook some degree of financial liberalization. The authors found that only two nations, the United Kingdom and Singapore, were spared systemic economic crises following liberalization. Nonetheless, they concluded that financial liberalization has, in general, led to more efficient allocations of capital and deepening of the nations' financial markets.

Economists continue to try to understand how policymakers in emerging economies might liberalize their capital markets while avoiding financial instability and crises. The proper balance between short-term and long-term capital inflows, the effectiveness of capital controls, the contribution of financial intermediaries in allocating capital inflows, the role of the exchange-rate regime, and the structure and responsibilities of international institutions such as the IMF and World Bank are important issues that we shall discuss in the remainder of this chapter.

Where Do Financial Intermediaries Fit In?

There are several ways in which financial intermediaries can contribute to financial stability and spur greater economic growth. One key function of financial intermediaries is to funnel savings to borrowers with minimum inefficiencies. The process of intermediation can be costly and, therefore, absorbs a fraction of each dollar of savings being channeled to a borrower. An efficient intermediary absorbs a smaller fraction of each dollar and can channel a greater portion of each dollar of savings on to the borrower. As a result, a greater portion of the nation's saving is invested, spurring greater economic growth. Reducing reserve requirements and unnecessary and costly regulations may improve the efficiency of a nation's financial intermediaries.

As described in Chapter 6, another way that financial intermediaries reduce inefficiencies is by making it possible for many people to pool their funds together. This increases the amount of total savings managed by a single authority. This centralization can yield *economies of scale* that reduce average fund-management costs below the levels that savers would incur if they were to manage their savings alone. In this way, intermediaries may increase the amount of savings ultimately invested by reducing unnecessary costs.

An efficient system of financial intermediaries may also reduce the degree of information asymmetries, thereby improving capital allocations and enhancing financial market stability. By specializing in the assessment of the quality of debt instruments and continuously monitoring the performance of firms that issue these instruments, financial intermediaries are able to reduce the extent of information imperfections.

In addition, intermediaries provide a means for savers to pool risks. If savers are unable to pool risks, they will only invest in the most liquid projects. More productive but less liquid projects are not financed, resulting in lower potential economic growth.

Hence, intermediaries perform a multifaceted role. Relying on their informational capabilities, they evaluate investment projects, determine those with the highest potential return, and induce savers to invest in higher-risk but more profitable projects by providing a means of sharing risks at reduced average costs. Because of their important role in allocating capital, their supervision and regulation is a key element of various proposals for the reform of the financial architecture.

Fundamental ISSUES

#2 What is the relationship between capital allocations and economic growth, and what is the role of financial intermediaries in this relationship?

When a nation's financial intermediaries direct funds to the most productive investment projects, they contribute to a higher level of real economic growth. Efficient financial intermediaries reduce the costs of financing investment projects, pool risks, and reduce the impact of financial market imperfections. Consequently, they encourage more saving and finance more investment projects.

CAPITAL MARKET LIBERALIZATION AND INTERNATIONAL FINANCIAL CRISES

Recent research by economists indicates that capital market liberalization—the elimination or removal of restrictions on capital flows—generally leads to improvements in capital allocations and further development of a nation's financial sector. Capital market liberalization, however, also carries risk. How have international capital flows contributed to recent financial crises?

Are All Capital Flows Equal?

Although capital market liberalization and access to global capital may reduce the cost of investment projects and spur economic growth, the resulting collective debt obligations may destabilize the economy. The maturity structure of a nation's public and private foreign debt is one important aspect. Attracting both short-term and long-term debt allows for a diversified portfolio of debt instruments, a manageable repayment structure, and, therefore, a more stable portfolio of debt.

Because governments, firms, and households have different borrowing needs, and because investment projects have different time horizons, it is important that a nation's financial sector attract both short-term portfolio capital flows and long-term direct investment capital. In most nations, economists consider portfolio investment as the purchase of financial instruments that results in less than a 10 percent ownership share. Portfolio capital flows tend to have a shorter term to maturity and lower borrowing costs, and are typically viewed as a means of generating near-term income. On the other hand, foreign direct investment is a long-term investment strategy in which the source of funds establishes financial control. Because portfolio capital and FDI represent different investment strategies, have different maturity structures, and have different borrowing costs, they are not equivalent in terms of their potential short-run and long-run consequences.

Portfolio Capital Flows Portfolio capital deals, which are short-term in nature, are easier to arrange, have lower borrowing costs, and do not require a firm to relinquish financial control to a foreign entity. Over time, portfolio capital inflows may improve capital allocations within a nation and help a nation's financial sector develop. Because portfolio capital is a nonownership and relatively liquid form of investment, however, portfolio capital flows (often referred as *hot-money flows*) can reverse direction quickly. Portfolio capital flight from a developing country can leave its fragile financial sector short of much needed liquidity, generating financial instability. This can trigger a financial crisis that can threaten both the solvency of a nation's financial intermediaries and the viability of its exchange-rate regime.

Foreign Direct Investment By way of contrast, FDI is a relatively illiquid, ownership form of investment that can have a stabilizing effect on a nation's economy. As noted earlier, FDI most often occurs when multinational firms establish foreign affiliates or enter into strategic alliances with foreign firms. In doing so they seek long-term commitments. As multinational firms become entrenched in foreign nations, they establish valuable relationships and networks with customers and suppliers. One would not expect, therefore, that multinational firms engaging in FDI would enter and exit foreign nations with much frequency. The potential for long-lasting commitments and corporate entrenchment is what makes FDI a stabilizing influence on a nation's economy. These long-term arrangements, however, are more difficult to arrange and result in some degree of foreign ownership of domestic firms.

Hence, portfolio capital and direct investment offer different positive and nega-tive features. Because capital flows are not all equal, it is important for a nation's financial sector to create an environment that attracts both long-term and short-term capital. In this way, capital allocations are improved, spurring real-sector and financial-sector development, while minimizing financial instability. (To contemplate why the volatility of capital flows matters, see *Management Notebook: Private Capital Flows: Source of Instability or Engine of Economic Development?*)

MANAGEMENT Notebook

Private Capital Flows: Source of Instability or Engine of Economic Development?

Figure 7–3 displays index measures of worldwide cross-border flows of portfolio stock investment, portfolio bond investment, and foreign direct investment since 1990. Both forms of international portfolio investment dropped during the 1990s. Indeed, the portfolio bond index exhibited *negative* values during the late 1990s and into the early 2000s, indicating net *outflows* of funds held in bonds during this interval. The figure highlights the fact that port-folio investment, especially in bonds, has been considerably more volatile than foreign direct investment, which grew steadily until the early 2000s, leveled off for a few years, and then increased again during the mid-2000s. All forms of global investment dropped in 2009.

There is considerable evidence that greater volatility of private international invest-ment tends to be associated with a slower pace of economic development. For instance, since 1970, the variability of private investment flows—concentrated heavily in portfolio investment—to Argentina, South Africa, and Venezuela has been two to three times greater than the worldwide average, and the economic growth in these nations has aver-aged below 2 percent per year. In contrast, private investment flows to China, Indonesia, and Pakistan—which have been mainly in the form of foreign direct investment—since 1970 have been less than half as volatile as the global average. Annual rates of economic growth in Indonesia and Pakistan have averaged 5 percent, and China's average annual rate of growth has been about 9 percent. Thus, much of the world's foreign direct investment

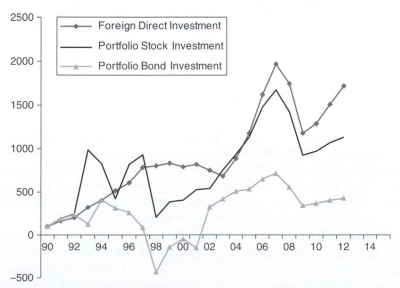

Source: World Bank, www.worldbank.org; authors' estimates.

Figure 7–3

Worldwide Flows of Portfolio Stock Investment, Portfolio Bond Investment, and Foreign Direct Investment since 1990

Prior to recent financial turmoil, portfolio stock investment and, especially, portfolio bond investment have exhibited much greater volatility than foreign direct investment.

flowing to developing nations is making its way to countries in Asia, which continue to experience a faster pace of economic development than South American and African countries.

For Critical Analysis

Why might greater volatility in private international investment inflows hinder economic development and growth?

The Role of Capital Flows in Recent Crisis Episodes

The 1994 to 1995 Mexican financial crisis illustrates well the consequences of relying too heavily on portfolio capital flows. Figure 7–3 on page 197 shows the distribution of private capital flows to the emerging economies of the western hemisphere. During the early and mid-1990s, the region experienced a dramatic increase in private capital inflows. Portfolio capital accounted for a large portion of these inflows, however. The combination of political instability in Mexico and rising interest rates in developing nations sparked a decrease in portfolio capital inflows during late 1994. During 1995, net portfolio capital flows to the region decreased nearly 100 percent. This drop in capital flows put considerable downward pressure on the exchange values of the currencies of most nations in the region and led to the complete collapse of the crawling-peg arrangement in Mexico.

A similar situation unfolded for several emerging economies of Asia, such as Thailand, Malaysia, Indonesia, and Korea, in the late 1990s, and Russia in the 2000s. Although the emerging economies of Asia were able to attract a greater proportion of FDI flows prior to the 1997 financial crisis, portfolio capital and other short-term capital flows still accounted for more than 40 percent of total private capital flows. The value of the Thai baht and the other currencies of the region collapsed in late 1997 and early 1998, along with a significant outflow of capital from the region that paralleled the capital outflows experienced during the Mexican crisis.

For international development data, visit the home page of Harvard University's Center for International Development at *http://www.cid.harvard.edu*.

The lesson learned from these events is that excessive reliance on portfolio capital flows can be destabilizing. It is important to note, however, that outflows of foreign portfolio capital were not the root cause of these financial crises. Foreign capital outflows were a symptom, triggered by a loss of confidence in the nation's macroeconomic and microeconomic policies, its political stability, and the soundness of its financial markets and real productive and manufacturing sectors.

Foreign Direct Investment as a Stabilizing Element Because FDI is a stabilizing element, many nations strive to create an environment that attracts FDI. Table 7–2 on page 190, however, indicates that FDI is concentrated among the developed countries. An important policy issue for emerging economies, therefore, is how to attract FDI and minimize the reliance on portfolio capital flows in financing investment projects.

In considering policy approaches to achieve this goal, some policymakers argue that nations should pay less attention to the nationality of multinational corporations. They argue that a nation's policymakers should consider instead the positive impact that locating production or distribution operations of a foreign firm within a country can have on the country's employment and income. Their claim is that multinational firms invest in foreign markets because they perceive advantages to doing so: skilled workforces, good distribution networks, developed supply chains, access to finance, and so on. A country that invests in education, research, training, and infrastructure, therefore, can expect to continually attract FDI, enabling the country to maintain high levels of employment and income. In this way, a nation could create a spiral of growth and investment, whereby domestic investment and FDI continually reinforce one another.

Following the international financial crises of the 1990s and early 2000s, academics, private agencies, and international policy groups generated a large body of policy recommendations for nations to improve the mix of capital inflows. Improving the information available on businesses, banks, and government finances is a particular point of emphasis in these recommendations. In general, the proposals call for improved and standardized dissemination of information by sovereign governments, rigorous financial disclosure, and the use of internationally recognized and accepted auditing and accounting standards and improved corporate governance standards so that lenders may monitor borrowers' financial decisions. Other recommendations include improving risk-management techniques by banks, restructuring international debt, and placing *capital controls* on short-term capital inflows.

Is There a Role for Capital Controls? Some economists believe that countries cannot limit their efforts to attracting FDI. They contend that emerging nations should take steps to reduce their level of reliance on portfolio capital flows. Economists favoring greater government intervention often advocate **capital controls** on short-term portfolio flows as a way to pace the gradual liberalization of financial markets.

capital controls
Legal restrictions on the ability of a nation's residents to hold and exchange assets denominated in foreign currencies.

Most economists are skeptical of controls on capital flows, however. Sebastian Edwards of the University of California in Los Angeles studied the effect of Chile's capital controls on the composition of that country's capital flows and its macroeconomic stability. He concluded that regardless of the type and extent of legislation imposed, the private sector eventually finds ways of getting around the restrictions. Edwards argues that controls on capital *outflows* should be avoided, as they are particularly ineffective in this regard.

Controls on capital *inflows,* however, may prove to be effective in the short run and slow the pace of short-term inflows and lengthen the maturity of foreign debt. By lengthening the maturity of debt, they give policymakers an opportunity to liberalize capital markets and allow the financial sector to develop. During the 1990s, for example, Chile placed a number of constraints on foreign capital inflows, which included restrictions on borrowing from abroad. These controls resulted in a decline of short-term capital inflows as a share of overall capital inflows, from more than 95 percent to 3 percent, in less than ten years. Though some of the capital controls were removed in the 2000s, short-term capital flows remained below 20 percent of overall flows.

Some economists believe these capital controls contributed to Chile's solid economic and exchange value performance. Others, though, see the capital controls as a hindrance to optimal capital allocation and a contributor to Chile's stagnant stock prices. They instead credit Chile's economic performance to appropriate economic policies.

Edwards concluded that capital controls should be used as a "temporary stop-gap" measure. He argued that capital controls create additional borrowing costs and should eventually be removed. In fact, Chile now faces greater competition from other South American nations for foreign capital than it did in the 1990s. For all practical purposes, policymakers have, therefore, ended Chile's remaining capital controls in hopes of reducing the cost of foreign capital.

Fundamental ISSUES

#3 What is the difference between portfolio capital flows and foreign direct investment, and what role did these types of capital flows play in recent financial crises?

Because portfolio capital inflows constitute a nonownership, income-generating form of investment, they tend to be shorter-term and more liquid than FDI. An excessive reliance on portfolio capital flows for financing investment projects, therefore, can be destabilizing. By way of contrast, FDI represents a long-term financial control strategy and, therefore, may have a stabilizing effect for the economy. An excessive reliance on portfolio capital flows appears to be one of the factors that contributed to the recent financial crises in the emerging economies.

EXCHANGE-RATE REGIMES AND FINANCIAL CRISES

The contribution of exchange-rate policies to the financial crises of the 1990s and early 2000s is of particular interest to international economists. Countries that experienced financial crises—such as Mexico in the mid-1990s; the economies of Southeast Asia, Brazil, and Russia in the late 1990s; and Turkey and Argentina in the early 2000s—all had some type of fixed-exchange-rate regime. Hence, it appears, at least on the surface, that pegged-exchange-rate regimes somehow contributed to the crises.

Schools of Thought on Exchange-Rate Regimes

Two schools of thought on exchange-rate regimes emerged shortly before the financial crises just described. The first school of thought holds that policymakers should not peg currency values to explicit targets or parity values.

According to this school of thought, currency-market participants can closely monitor policymakers' actions by observing differences between the spot exchange rate and the official parity rate. It is possible, therefore, that currency-market participants perceive even small misses from the parity rate, which cause them to determine whether the exchange-rate regime was not credible or trustworthy. If currency-market participants view the exchange-rate peg as noncredible and sell domestic-currency-denominated assets in large volumes, policymakers might not have sufficient foreign exchange reserves to maintain the parity rate, and the exchange-rate regime will collapse. Hence, this school of thought suggests that exchange rates should be fully flexible.

Conversely, the second school of thought indicates that an explicit exchange value target is necessary for policymakers to establish credibility with market participants. By targeting the exchange rate, policymakers make a transparent commitment to their exchange-rate policy. According to this line of thought, an exchange-rate target or parity value constitutes a rule for the conduct of monetary policy. In this way, policymakers are more credible because currency-market participants can closely monitor exchange-rate policy and force policymakers to maintain their commitment to the exchange-rate target. Hence, this school of thought suggests that exchange rates should be fixed or pegged.

The Corners Hypothesis

What followed is that many economists became skeptical of the soundness of *inter-mediate* or *middle-ground* exchange-rate regimes—regimes with limited exchange-rate flexibility, such as adjustable pegs, crawling pegs, and basket pegs. Mass selling of currencies by currency-market participants forced many of the crisis countries—Mexico, Thailand, Korea, Indonesia, Russia, and Brazil, for example—to abandon their intermediate exchange-rate regimes.

Hence, a third view on exchange-rate management, the ***corners hypothesis*** view, emerged. This theory suggests that policymakers should make a firm commit to an exchange-rate regime that lies at one extreme or the other. That is, policymakers should establish a currency board or even dollarize their economies, or allow their currencies to float freely in the foreign exchange market, and avoid intermediate exchange-rate regimes.

The corners hypothesis sparked a great deal of research that compared and contrasted exchange-rate regimes and economic and political conditions specific to each of the crisis countries. In the meantime, international organizations such as the IMF and the G7 urged policymakers in emerging economies to abandon intermediate pegged-exchange-rate regimes in favor of flexible-exchange-rate regimes, or even to dollarize their economies.

Dollarization

Since the collapse of Argentina's currency-board exchange-rate arrangement in the early 2000s, growing numbers of economists have recommended that emerging economies abandon their domestic currencies altogether and fully dollarize their economies. As discussed in Chapter 3, dollarization is the adoption of a foreign currency as sole legal tender.

The Benefits of Dollarization Andrew Berg and Eduardo Borensztein, IMF economists and experts on dollarization, contend that dollarization has both benefits and costs for emerging economies. They argue that the most important benefit of dollarization is that it eliminates currency risk and thereby reduces risk premiums and interest rates in emerging economies. Country risk remains however, so, interest rates will not fully converge to those of the developed economies.

Another proposed benefit of dollarization is that adopting the U.S. dollar or the euro might promote greater economic integration with large economies such as the United States or the European Union than might otherwise be possible when emerging economies maintain their own currencies. Greater integration with these

corners hypothesis
The view that policymakers should choose fully flexible or hard-peg-exchange-rate regimes over intermediate regimes such as adjustable-peg, crawling-peg, or basket-peg arrangements.

large economies might, in turn, promote greater economic growth and stability within the dollarizing economy.

The Costs of Dollarization The loss of seigniorage revenues—a government's profit from issuing its own money (see Chapter 6)—is an important cost of dollarizing an economy. There are two components to this cost. First, the central bank would have to "buy" back all of the domestic currency in circulation with U.S. dollars. Second, the central bank would give up any future seigniorage revenue. Berg and Borensztein estimate that dollarizing Argentina's economy would require an initial $15 billion to buy back pesos and another $1 billion annually in lost seigniorage revenues.

Another important cost of dollarization is the loss of the lender-of-last-resort function. As discussed in Chapter 6, as a lender of last resort, a central bank stands willing to lend to a domestic bank that is temporarily illiquid. Hence, in a dollarized economy, policymakers cannot respond if a bank becomes temporarily illiquid and are thus unable to restore confidence in the domestic banking system.

Dollarized Economies Table 7–3 lists fully dollarized economies. All of the countries in the table have relatively small populations and economies. Three dollarized only recently. East Timor and Ecuador adopted the U.S. dollar in 2000, and El Salvador adopted the U.S. dollar in 2001. The small number of dollarized economies makes it difficult for economists to reliably estimate the benefits and costs of dollarizing an economy. For this reason, economists are closely monitoring the performances of these economies.

Peg, Take the Middle Road, or Float?

So what type of exchange-rate regime should emerging-economy policymakers choose in hopes of avoiding a financial crisis? Recently, growing numbers of

Table 7–3

Dollarized Economies

Since the end of World War II, only five nations dollarized: Cyprus, Montenegro, East Timor, El Salvador, and Ecuador. Cyprus adopted the Turkish lira in 1974, but later joined the European Monetary System. All of the dollarized economies are relatively small nations in terms of their population and overall economic output.

Country	Currency Adopted	Date of Dollarization
East Timor	U.S. dollar	2000
El Salvador	U.S. dollar	2001
Ecuador	U.S. dollar	2000
Kiribati	Australian dollar	1943
Montenegro	German mark/euro	1999
Marshall Islands	U.S. dollar	1944
Micronesia	U.S. dollar	1944
Monaco French	franc/euro	1865
Nauru	Australian dollar	1914
Palau	U.S. dollar	1914
Panama	U.S. dollar	1904
San Marino	Italian lira/euro	1897

Source: IMF, *Exchange Arrangements and Restrictions.*

economists have rejected the corners hypothesis. The main arguments against the corners hypothesis are that it lacks any theoretical basis and lacks empirical support. Hence, even though many of the crisis-stricken economies employed intermediate exchange-rate regimes, that does not necessarily imply that their exchange rate regimes have been to blame for the crisis.

Economists who reject the corners hypothesis claim that there is no single type of exchange-rate regime that is right for all countries, and that for any given country, no single type of regime may be appropriate at all times. Rather, as discussed in Chapter 3, economic and legal institutions and sound economic policymaking are more important than the choice of an exchange-rate regime in that they determine the viability of a given exchange-rate regime. Consequently, all three categories of exchange-rate regimes—hard peg, intermediate peg, and floating—are appropriate for some countries.

The "Trilemma"

The appropriateness of the exchange-rate regime may be better understood in the context of the "impossible trinity dilemma," or *trilemma*. Economists Joshua Aizenman and Reuven Glick claim that it was a three-part policy mix—a combination of pegged exchange rates, discretionary monetary policy, and capital market liberalization—that led to the financial crises discussed in this chapter. Their explanation of the trilemma is that a nation may simultaneously choose any two, but not all three of the following: fixed exchange rates, discretionary monetary policy, and capital market liberalization.

Figure 7–4 illustrates the trilemma. As shown in the figure, the three sides of the triangle represent the three potential goals of fixed exchange rates, discretionary monetary policy, and capital market liberalization. The top of the triangle represents the combination of closed capital markets, fixed exchange rates, and discretionary monetary policy. This is the combination pursued by countries such as Mexico and many Asian economies prior to their financial crises. Prior to a

Trilemma

The idea that policymakers may choose a combination of two, but not all three of the following policy options: fixed exchange rates, discretionary monetary policy, and liberalized capital markets.

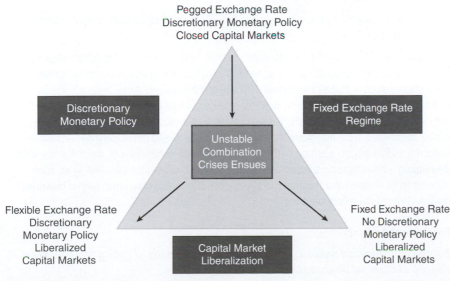

Figure 7–4

The Trilemma

According to the trilemma, as a country moves toward liberalized capital markets, a stable policy configuration requires that policymakers forego either discretionary monetary policy or fixed exchange rates.

Source: Adapted from Joshua Aizenman and Reuven Glick. "Sterilization, Monetary Policy, and Global Financial Integration." NBER Working Paper W13902 (March 2008).

crisis, each of these economies began to liberalize or open up its capital markets, representing a movement toward the base of the triangle.

According to the trilemma, as a country moves toward liberalized capital markets, a stable policy configuration requires that policymakers forego either discretionary monetary policy or fixed exchange rates. This stable combination is represented by a movement down one side of the triangle or the other. An unstable configuration is trying to pursue all three goals, represented by a movement through the middle of the triangle. Countries such as Mexico and South Korea suffered financial crises and subsequently allowed their currencies to float, thereby moving to the combination of exchange-rate flexibility, capital market liberalization, and discretionary monetary policy represented by a movement to the bottom-left corner of the triangle. (To consider how different groups of nations have confronted the issue of the trilemma, see *Policy Notebook: Differences in Cross-Country Patterns in Addressing the Trilemma Issue.*)

POLICY Notebook

Differences in Cross-Country Patterns in Addressing the Trilemma Issue

Are there systematic differences in how distinct groups of nations configure policymaking in relation to the trilemma issue? To explore this question, Joshua Aizenman of the University of California–Santa Cruz, Menzie Chinn of the University of Wisconsin, and Hiro Ito of Portland State University have considered for 170 nations the following measures of the dimensions of the trilemma:

1. Monetary independence: correlation of a given nation's interest rate with a "base country" within a selected group of nations

2. Exchange-rate stability: A measure of the volatility of a given nation's exchange rate vis-à-vis the currency of the "base country"

3. Financial openness: an index measure of the extent to which capital controls constrain financial flows

Aizenman, Chinn, and Ito find evidence of striking differences in the trilemma choices of industrialized countries as compared with those of emerging and developing nations. Their study suggests that since the mid-1970s—and particularly since the early 1990s—industrialized countries have opted strongly in favor of more exchange-rate stability and increased financial openness, which necessitated a considerable drop in monetary independence. In contrast, their measures indicated that emerging and developing nations moved toward a middle-ground position with respect to all three dimensions of the trilemma, with developing nations tending to favor somewhat more exchange-rate stability. Thus, there appears to be distinctive differences in how industrialized and nonindustrialized countries have addressed the trilemma issue.

For Critical Analysis

For the industrialized nations, what are the pros and cons of opting for a substantial degree of financial openness?

$ ¥ Fundamental ISSUES
£

#4 What type of exchange-rate regime is most appropriate for emerging economies?

The most appropriate exchange-rate regime for emerging economies is a hotly contested and contemporary debate. Some economists argue that policymakers should commit to a hard-peg-exchange-rate regime or a fully flexible exchange-rate regime. Others argues that no single regime is appropriate for all emerging economies and that intermediate regimes, such as crawling-peg and basket-peg regimes, may be appropriate for some emerging economies. Dollarization is yet another option that is available to emerging-economy policymakers.

Evaluating the Status Quo

The experiences with crises in the 1990s and 2000s induced a number of economists and policymakers to offer proposals for restructuring the IMF and the World Bank. Before examining these proposals, it is important to consider the current policies of these institutions.

***Ex Ante* versus *Ex Post* Conditionality at the IMF** Like any other lender, the IMF encounters two key problems. One is *adverse selection,* or the possibility that some borrowers most interested in obtaining funds may be the most likely to misuse them. The other is *moral hazard,* or the potential for a borrower to take on greater risks after receiving a loan than the lender desires. The IMF's policy of imposing conditionality terms on borrowers seeks to address the moral hazard problem. Most observers, however, agree that there are two at least two weaknesses in the IMF's approach. First, IMF officials do not publicly announce the terms of the institution's lending agreements with specific nations. This means that it is solely up to the IMF to monitor whether borrower nations are wisely using funds donated by other countries. Often, private investors can discern that a country has failed to abide by its agreement with the IMF only when the IMF undertakes an action such as withholding a scheduled loan installment. Swift adverse market reactions following such IMF moves can place borrower nations in even worse financial straits, making it even more difficult for the borrower to meet the terms of its original agreement with the IMF. Thus, the IMF's policy of keeping loan agreements secret can undermine its efforts to protect members' funds from misuse.

Second, it is common for IMF officials to initially place only very general conditions on the loans extended. They tend to switch to high conditionality only after a borrower nation has already enacted policies that violate the original low-conditionality arrangement. By that point, of course, the IMF has already failed to avoid the moral hazard problem.

Critics argue that IMF secrecy and its tendency to impose high conditionality only when pressed to do so effectively amount to firm conditionality only on an *ex post,* or after-the-fact, basis. They contend that this after-the-fact, discretionary approach to establishing conditions under which the IMF lends, which they call ***ex post conditionality,*** undermines the IMF's credibility both with actual borrowers *and* with prospective borrowers. This lack of credibility, they argue, increases the

***ex post* conditionality**
The imposition of IMF lending conditions after a loan has already been granted.

likelihood for moral hazard problems while also widening the scope of the adverse selection problem by attracting borrower nations that are most likely to try to take advantage of vague conditions of a policy of low conditionality.

ex ante conditionality

The imposition of IMF lending conditions before the IMF grants the loan.

To reduce the extent of both problems, IMF critics have long suggested the use of *ex ante conditionality,* or conditions for IMF loans that are publicly known in advance. They have also pushed for imposing a few straightforward conditions, so that it is easy for everyone to monitor whether borrower nations have complied. (The IMF does recommend that nations make available a standard set of economic data. See *Online Notebook: Data Dissemination via the Internet*.) To date, however, the IMF has maintained its generally secretive and discretionary lending policies.

ONLINE Notebook

Data Dissemination via the Internet

The International Monetary Fund assists member nations in preparing and publishing data. To aid in this task, economists at the IMF maintain two data systems, the General Data Dissemination System (GDDS) and the Special Data Dissemination System (SDDS). The GDDS is available to all IMF members, and IMF provides the SDDS to member countries having or seeking access to international capital markets. According to the IMF, both the GDDS and the SDDS are expected to enhance the availability of timely and comprehensive statistics, promoting sound macroeconomic policies and contributing to the improved functioning of financial markets.

The IMF recommends that countries publish important economic information on a timely basis. It also encourages publication via the Internet. The GDDS section of the IMF Web page provides quick links to agencies of member countries that are responsible for publishing the GDDS data.

For Critical Analysis

What are the benefits of providing economic information over the Internet to those countries seeking foreign capital inflows?

Searching for a Mission at the World Bank The World Bank currently extends more than $15 billion annually in lending assistance to developing nations, with more than $120 billion in outstanding loans. In some nations, particularly in Africa, attracting private investment has proved difficult. Consequently, the World Bank has been a key source of credit for these nations. Nevertheless, as Figure 7–5 on the next page indicates, only about 23 percent of lending by the World Bank has been directed to African countries.

Even though more than $100 billion in private capital flows has recently flowed into developing nations, the World Bank continues to make many of its loans to nations that have little trouble attracting private funds. For instance, in the late 1990s, when foreign investors sought to finance the construction of China's largest thermal power plant, makers of the power plant turned them away because they were able to get a loan from the World Bank at more favorable terms.

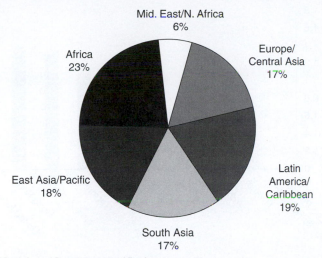

Source: World Bank Annual Report, www.worldbank.org.

Figure 7–5

The Distribution of World Bank Lending

Even though Africa has the world's poorest nations, it has received only 23 percent of recent World Bank loans. Nonetheless, Africa remains the top priority of the World Bank, and this percentage has been increasing, albeit slowly.

Although the World Bank's official mission is to lend to people in developing nations with projects that cannot attract private capital, the development agency increasingly competes with private investors. In such competitions, the institution typically wins out over private lenders by offering loans at below-market rates. Critics of such loans argue that they often distort the market for private capital and encourage the kind of inefficient investment that contributed to East Asia's economic woes in the late 1990s. They also contend that countries such as China are inappropriate recipients of development assistance. After all, China has substantial foreign currency reserves, and it has persistently run an annual current account surplus in the tens of billions of dollars. As a result, China is a net exporter of capital. Nevertheless, because policymakers are offered below-market interest rates, China typically borrows between $1.5 billion and $3 billion from the World Bank each year.

The World Bank faces pressure from nations that are net donors to its lending pool to maintain a significant revenue stream of its own, thereby reducing the donors' risks of loss. Because of this constraint, projects in developing nations that are most likely to maintain stable and reasonably high returns are also the ones that are most likely to attract the interest of private investors. By way of contrast, projects in the poorest and most needy countries are least likely to yield steady payoffs for the World Bank. (Some observers suggest that private lenders issuing small loans to people in the poorest nations could accomplish more than the World Bank does with its large credit packages; see *Policy Notebook: Should National Policymakers Promote* Microlending?)

Should National Policymakers Promote *Microlending*?

Muhammad Yunus of Bangladesh, the 2006 winner of the Nobel Peace Prize, contends that access to private credit, rather than credit from institutions such as the World Bank, is vital for promoting economic growth in poverty-stricken countries. Figure 7–6 displays both the

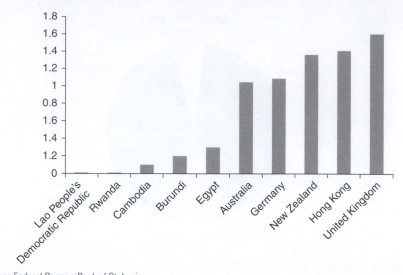

Figure 7–6

The Ratio of Private Credit to GDP in Selected Nations

This figure displays the top-five and bottom-five nations of the world ranked according to ratios of private credit to GDP.

Source: Federal Reserve Bank of St. Louis.

top-five and the bottom-five nations of the world ranked by their ratios of private credit to gross domestic product (GDP). Access to credit in these nations is very limited, so ratios of private credit to GDP are low.

Common features of the bottom-five nations are significant stocks of informally used but officially unowned capital goods and bureaucratic and inefficient governments. These characteristics, Yunus suggests, hinder economic development. Private lenders are more likely to grant loans if borrowers can provide marketable collateral in the form of capital assets that lenders can obtain if a borrower defaults, but loan applicants cannot offer as collateral capital assets that they do not officially own. Furthermore, even if an applicant has legal title to capital assets, a lender is unlikely to accept them as collateral if government rules and inefficiencies inhibit the marketability of those assets in the event that the borrower defaults.

Yunus received the Nobel Peace Prize for his efforts to promote the operations of *microlenders*, banking institutions that specialize in making very small loans, collateralized by personally owned items such as bicycles or water buffalo, to entrepreneurs seeking to lift themselves up from the lowest rungs of poverty. In some of the poorest nations in which microlending activities are beginning to flourish, tens of millions of people are getting access to credit for the first time in their lives. As a consequence, ratios of private credit to GDP in several of these nations are now rising.

For Critical Analysis

How could it be possible for small loans to many individuals to generate greater economic development than a few large loans to a few borrowers?

 On the WEB

To learn more about microlending and microfinancing, visit the Web site of Accion International at *http://www.accion.org*.

Debt Relief for the Heavily Indebted Poor Countries

Debt relief for the poorest and most heavily indebted nations is currently one of the most perplexing and onerous policy problems. Beginning in the 1980s, a number of low-income nations' stocks of international debt became so large that these countries found that they could no longer make all of their debt service payments to creditor nations such as the United States, Japan, France, and Germany and to institutions such as the International Monetary Fund and the World Bank.

Creditor nations and international organizations attempted to provide relief by continuing to lend to debtor nations and rescheduling some of their short-term debts. The rationale for debt relief is twofold: Some of the debt was incurred long ago by corrupt governments that are no longer in power, and servicing the debt has reduced funding for education and welfare programs. Many of the negotiations took place through the Paris Club. The **Paris Club** was formed in the 1950s as a forum for multilateral negotiations between debtor and creditor nations for rescheduling official debt. Though an ad hoc organization, it has a permanent secretariat provided by the French finance ministry. The **London Club** was established in the 1970s to facilitate, in a similar manner, negotiations on private debt owed to commercial banks. In addition to the efforts of these two bodies, the Millennium Fund was recently established to generate private-sector donations to be used for debt relief.

Despite efforts to provide debt relief, the debt problems of the poorest nations became even worse, and their stock of debt doubled in five years. By the turn of the century, the nations were fulfilling less than half of their debt obligations, and more than $60 billion of the debt was in arrears. By the late 1990s, the industrialized nations redoubled their efforts to provide meaningful debt relief. In 1996, the leaders of the leading seven industrialized nations agreed upon the **HIPC Initiative** (heavily indebted poor countries), which was subsequently endorsed by the IMF and the World Bank. The HIPC Initiative was intended to establish a set of conditions required for debt relief and a means to deliver multilateral relief, but it failed to live up to the expectations of both creditor and debtor nations.

In 1999, intensive public pressure led to the **Cologne Debt Initiative** (CDI). The CDI was intended to provide faster, broader, and deeper relief. The CDI expanded the list of HIPC nations from twenty-six to thirty-three and promised to relieve 70 percent of the approximately 197 billion of these nations' debts by the early 2000s. Within a few years, the list of nations considered for debt relief under these initiatives expanded to forty-one. Twenty-three nations reached a phase in the set of conditions that allowed for some limited debt relief, and ten are still being considered.

The expanded HIPC Initiative is not without its problems, though. Funding continues to be a major concern. More than 15 percent of the more than $100 billion in relief promised by the leading industrialized nations is to come from nations that were not party to the initial policy negotiations. Some of these creditor nations are reluctant to be part of a plan that was negotiated without their involvement. Another problem is that because more than 50 percent of the debt is currently not being serviced, forgiving a majority of the *debt stock* will not necessarily relieve the burden of *debt servicing*. Part of the funding for the CDI was to come from the sales of gold stocks. These sales, however, have the potential to depress gold prices, harming a number of the HIPC countries that depend on gold exports. Additionally, another fear is that debt relief may merely displace much-needed development assistance.

Paris Club
A forum that allows debtor nations to initiate negotiations with creditor nations to reschedule payments on official debt.

London Club
A forum for debtor nations to initiate negotiations with private-sector lenders to reschedule payments on commercial bank debt.

HIPC Initiative
A program of debt relief for the heavily indebted poor countries developed by the leaders of the seven major industrialized nations. The initiative established a set of conditions and time table required for debt relief.

Cologne Debt Initiative
A follow-up program to the HIPC Initiative that expanded the list of nations that could potentially qualify for debt relief, expanded the amount of proposed debt relief, and accelerated the time table.

Fundamental ISSUES

#5 What aspects of IMF and World Bank policymaking have proved controversial in recent years?

The IMF has received criticism for failing to publicize the conditions it places on loans to member countries. Critics have also questioned the IMF's tendency to make such conditions very general and hard to measure. Both aspects of IMF policymaking, they argue, increase the potential for moral hazard by making it easier for borrowers to commit IMF funds to riskier projects. Although the World Bank directs a significant portion of its financial assistance to the world's poorest countries, it also makes a large amount of loans in countries that receive significant private capital inflows. In some of these nations, critics argue, the World Bank makes financial markets less efficient by offering loans at below-market interest rates.

DOES THE INTERNATIONAL FINANCIAL ARCHITECTURE NEED A REDESIGN?

Multinational institutions have confronted two types of criticisms in recent years. One set of critics believes that these institutions are correctly designed and structured but contends nevertheless that these institutions could do a much better job of heading off financial crises before they occur. Another group criticizes the operations of, and in some cases even the existence of, multinational financial institutions. According to this latter group, at a minimum the international financial architecture requires some retuning, and it may even require a redesign.

Crisis Prediction and Early-Warning Systems

Before considering what factors aid in predicting financial crises, and how multinational institutions might head off financial crises, it would be helpful if economists agreed about what constitutes a crisis. There are, however, different views on how to determine that a crisis has occurred. Jeffrey Frankel of Harvard University and Andrew Rose of the University of California at Berkeley, for instance, propose that a crisis definitely exists when a nation's currency experiences a nominal depreciation of at least 25 percent within a year that follows a depreciation of at least 10 percent the previous year. Most economists, however, have considered more flexible index measures of speculative pressures that take into account exchange-rate changes and variations in foreign exchange reserves. They consider a crisis to have occurred when such an index exceeds a threshold that depends on the normal, historical pattern of variation that the index has exhibited in prior years.

financial crisis indicator
An economic variable that normally moves in a specific direction and by a certain relative amount in advance of a financial crisis, thereby helping to predict a coming crisis.

In such studies, economists seek to determine whether they can identify any economic variables that serve as *financial crisis indicators,* or factors that typically precede such crises and thereby aid in predicting them. One such study is by Morris Goldstein of the Institute for International Economics, Graciela Kaminsky of George Washington University, and Carmen Reinhart of the University of Maryland. These authors consider ratings of the countries' debts as one indicator. These would include credit ratings by Moody's and other credit rating bureaus, for example, which might reflect moral hazard problems. In addition, however, the authors evaluated a large set of potential *leading indicators* of financial crises that included exchanges rates, interest rates, national income levels, quantities of money and circulation, and the like. Such variables, naturally, reflect economic fundamentals that the traditional view of financial crises predicts should play important roles, and these variables also provide important information that traders use to form expectations.

These authors found that credit ratings do not help predict financial crises. This could be because moral hazard problems are not a key causal factor in crises, but it is also possible that rating agencies such as Moody's do not have sufficient information to accurately assess the scope of moral hazard and its implications for the true creditworthiness of international borrowers. The authors find that several economic fundamentals together tend to do a better job of predicting financial crises than any single indicator.

The objective of studies searching for financial crisis indicators is to develop an *early-warning system,* or a mechanism for monitoring financial and economic data for signals of trouble that might eventually evolve into a crisis. The idea is that if a multinational institution could develop an effective early-warning system, it would receive sufficient warning to intervene speedily and head off a crisis before it occurs.

There is some optimism inside and outside the IMF and World Bank that economists may ultimately develop a reliable early-warning system. Many economists remain skeptical, however. Some doubt that any single view of the causes of international financial crises—shifts in economic fundamentals, speculation driven by self-fulfilling expectations, or moral hazard problems caused by inadequate conditions on domestic or multinational loans—can single-handedly "explain" every crisis. Thus, these skeptics doubt that any early-warning system based on a limited set of indicators is likely to improve the capability of multinational institutions to react quickly enough to prevent them from occurring.

early-warning system
A mechanism that multinational institutions might use to track financial crisis indicators to determine that a crisis is on the horizon, thereby permitting a rapid response to head off the crisis.

Rethinking Economic Institutions and Policies

The strongest critics of multinational institutions contend that there is little evidence that these institutions have developed the capability to head off financial crises before they occur. Indeed, some critics contend that multinational institutions themselves can contribute to the likelihood of international financial crises. Accordingly, these critics argue, the world's nations should consider making fundamental reforms in the structure of these institutions.

Rethinking Long-Term Development Lending Not all lending by supranational institutions is related to crisis situations. As discussed earlier, both the IMF and the World Bank make longer-term loans intended to foster growing standards of living in many of the world's poorer nations.

Since the early 1990s, one of the main themes of development economics has been that markets work better at promoting growth when a developing nation has more effective institutions, such as basic property rights, well-run legal systems, and uncorrupt government agencies. Considerable evidence indicates that countries grow more slowly where property rights are not well enforced, the rule of law is weak, and governments are corrupt, even if the countries otherwise permit markets to function without regulatory hindrances.

This implies that a top priority of supranational organizations dedicated to higher standards of living in developing nations should be finding ways to improve those nations' fundamental institutions. At the most basic level, economists emphasize the paramount importance of laying basic market foundations, such as property and contract rights. This requires constructing credible legal systems to enforce laws and setting up the kinds of institutions that are likely to lead to better national policies, perhaps including establishment of independent central banks and transparent budget processes for fiscal authorities.

Furthermore, creating structural reforms consistent with achieving a higher long-term growth rate requires nations to develop strategies for making reforms last. This requires building a consensus for reform and sometimes may entail compensating those who lose when reform is enacted.

A key issue is what, if anything, a supranational institution such as the World Bank can do to promote pro-growth institutional improvements within developing nations. From one standpoint, there is little that the IMF and World Bank can do. After all, the shapes of national institutions are largely political matters for the people of developing nations to decide.

Nevertheless, numerous economists have suggested that the IMF and World Bank should adopt strict policies against countries that fail to promote individual property rights, law enforcement, and anticorruption efforts. This would, they argue, give countries an incentive to shape up their institutional structures.

Other economists, in contrast, advocate direct financial assistance to governments attempting to implement such institutional reforms. Funds put to such use, they argue, could compensate those who lose power as a result of reform efforts and could help fund infrastructures required to make reforms work. Those proposing this more active role for supranational lenders contend that the result could be much larger long-term returns for borrower nations and donor nations alike, as compared with the piecemeal payoffs from such projects as dams, power plants, and bridges.

Alternative Institutional Structures for Limiting Financial Crises Most proposals for altering the international financial architecture focus on multinational policymaking relating to financial crises. There have been many proposals relating to this issue. A few of these are summarized in Table 7–4. They range from relatively minor changes in existing institutions and procedures to replacement of existing multinational institutions with new institutions.

There are, nonetheless, several features common to a number of the proposals. These include more frequent and in-depth releases of information by both multinational lenders and national borrowers, adoption of improved financial and accounting standards for those receiving funds from multinational lenders, making both high and *ex ante* conditionality the norm for IMF lending, and, in several proposals, increased efforts to induce private lenders to extend credit. Beyond these areas of common ground, however, proposals typically diverge sharply. Some call for more oversight of the IMF, whereas others suggest a wholesale change in the IMF's management structure. Still other proposals would, if adopted, entail dismantling the IMF and replacing it with new forms of multinational institutions.

So far, few proposals for altering the international financial architecture have led to actual change. The IMF has adopted some minor changes in its procedures for collecting and releasing information, and it has stiffened some of the financial and accounting standards that borrowers must follow to obtain credit.

Naturally, the member nations of the IMF would have to agree to the adoption of more dramatic proposals for change. To date there has been little movement in this direction. Nevertheless, debate on the desirability of minor changes in the status quo versus potentially significant departures continues. Undoubtedly, proposals for an altered international financial architecture will continue to generate global debate in the years to come.

National Proposals	
Canada Proposal for Emergency Standstill Clause	Under this proposal, countries would establish rules for restricting capital outflows that threaten international financial stability.
France Proposal for an IMF Council Composed of National Finance Ministers	The proposal would upgrade an "Interim Committee" of national finance composed of national finance ministers to the status of the ultimate governing and decision-making body for the International Monetary Fund.
United Kingdom Proposal for a Standing Committee for Global Financial Regulation	This proposed committee would encompass the IMF, World Bank, and Bank for International Settlements and would establish and implement international standards for financial regulation and economic policymaking.
Private Proposals	
Calomiris-Meltzer Proposals for Strict International Lending Rules	Although these economists' proposals are different in certain respects, they share the idea that current multinational institutions might be replaced with a single institution that makes only short-term loans to illiquid countries.
Garten's Proposals for a Global Central Bank	This proposal envisions a new multinational institution overseen by the G7 and rotating emerging-economy members that would engage in open-market operations using funds raised from members and international taxes.
Soros's Proposal for an International Investor Insurance Agency	Under this proposal, nations would create a public corporation that would insure investors against debt defaults up to a specified ceiling level.
International Proposals	
IMF Proposals for Internal Reforms	This proposal entails, among other things, requiring borrowers to provide more in-depth financial information and to adopt better accounting standards and to release more IMF data and information to the public.
G7 Proposals for a Larger Role for Private-Sector Lenders	This proposal extends the IMF proposals by calling for greater private-sector involvement in providing funds to distressed nations and providing incentives for private lenders to be willing to participate.
G22 Proposals for Greater Accountability, Stronger Financial Systems, and Crisis Container	Under this proposal, the IMF would be required to prepare a "Transparency Report" for each nation receiving an IMF loan, nations requesting loans would have to follow common financial and accounting principles, and international loan renegotiations would be mandatory in the event that crises take place.

Table 7–4

A Sampling of Proposals to Restructure the International Financial Architecture

Source: Barry Eichengreen. *Toward a New International Financial Architecture.* Washington, D.C.: Institute for International Economics, 1999, Appendix A.

#6 What changes in the international financial architecture have economists pro-posed in recent years?

Many critics of the IMF and the World Bank have argued that they should develop early-warning systems to aid in predicting and perhaps even preventing international financial crises. A fundamental problem that these institutions face in such efforts, however, is that there is little agreement about why crises occur and, hence, about what indicators should be used to try to predict crises. A common theme of existing proposals for altering the international financial architecture is to enforce stronger conditions on the long-term and short-term loans that multinational institutions extend to borrowers. Many proposals also entail more publicity of the internal operations and lending policies of the Interna-tional Monetary Fund and the World Bank. Some proposals, however, argue for changing the management structure of IMF and the World Bank, supplementing these institutions with additional multinational institutions, or even replacing them with new multinational institutions that would follow different procedures or pursue different objectives.

ChapterSUMMARY

1. **Important Developments in the Evolution of Global Capital Markets:** The growth of foreign direct investment among the developed economies and the growth of private capital flows to the emerging economies are two of the most important developments taking place in the global capital markets. FDI has been concentrated among the triad countries of the United States, Japan, and the European Union. Over the last decade, pri-vate capital flows to the emerging economies averaged more than $150 billion annually.

2. **The Relationship between Capital Allocation and Economic Growth and the Role of Financial Intermediaries in This Relationship:** When a nation's financial-sector institutions allocate funds to their most productive use, it spurs the development of real resources and higher productivity. Financial intermediaries play an important role in this process by reducing the costs of financing investment projects, pooling risk, and reducing the impact of financial market imperfections.

3. **The Difference between Portfolio Capital Flows and Foreign Direct Investment and the Role of These Capital Flows in Recent Financial Crises:** Portfolio capital flows are a nonownership form of investment and tend to have short-term maturities. FDI represents an ownership strategy and tends to be long term in maturity. Recent financial crises demonstrate that an excessive reliance on portfolio capital flows can destabilize an economy. FDI, on the other hand, may have a stabilizing influence on an economy.

4. **The Appropriate Exchange-Rate Regime for Emerging Economies:** There is con-siderable debate over the exchange-rate regime best suited for the emerging economies. Economists disagree about whether policymakers in emerging economies should adopt a hard-peg arrangement, a fully flexible arrangement, or an intermediate arrangement such as a crawling-peg or basket-peg arrangement. Dollarization of the economy is yet another option that policymakers may consider.

5. **Aspects of IMF and World Bank Policymaking That Have Been Controversial in Recent Years:** Although the IMF can place strong and measurable conditions on its

loans to member countries, it often fails to do so. The IMF also does not release complete information about the conditions it places on loans. It is arguable that these aspects of IMF policymaking make it easier for borrowers to use IMF funds for unworthy projects, thereby increasing the scope of the moral hazard problem in international financial markets. The World Bank provides a significant percentage of the credit available to the world's poorest countries, but it also extends large numbers of loans to governments and private companies located in countries that receive relatively large volumes of private capital inflows. It is possible that by offering loans to these governments and companies at interest rates below private market levels, the World Bank contributes to less-efficient financial markets in those nations.

6. **Changes in the International Financial Architecture Proposed by Economists in Recent Years:** Numerous economists have favored greater IMF and World Bank efforts to head off crises by developing early-warning systems that would permit them to predict and more rapidly respond to international financial crises. Nevertheless, skeptics doubt that such efforts will bear fruit in light of general disagreement among economists about why crises occur and, therefore, about what indicators the IMF or World Bank might use to attempt to predict crises. Proposals for redesigning the international financial architecture include adding and enforcing stricter and more measurable conditions for borrowers to meet before receiving long-term and short-term loans from the IMF and World Bank. Another common feature of many proposals is the release of more public information about the internal operations and lending policies of these institutions. A few proposals suggest more dramatic changes, such as new management structures for the IMF and the World Bank, adding additional multinational institutions to supplement their activities, or replacing existing multinational institutions with new institutions that would operate differently or aim to achieve different objectives.

QUESTIONS and PROBLEMS

1. This chapter discussed the important functions of financial intermediaries. Explain the difference between direct and indirect financing. Next explain why a nation might desire a strong and stable system of financial intermediaries *and* a robust bond market.

2. List three benefits of portfolio capital and three benefits of foreign direct investment. Give one negative aspect of each. Explain why it is undesirable to rely on portfolio capital only. Explain why it is undesirable to rely on FDI only.

3. Suppose a nation has a pegged-exchange-rate system and you are the nation's chief central banker. Construct a supply-and-demand diagram of the spot exchange market for the domestic currency. Explain, using the diagram, how the central bank must react to portfolio capital inflows and outflows so as to maintain the currency peg.

4. Explain how allowing foreign banks to enter and compete in the domestic financial sector might improve capital market allocations. Explain how, in general, competition among financial intermediaries is important to financial stability.

5. Explain how savers and borrowers might benefit from regulation of a nation's financial intermediaries. Does regulation impose costs? How do these costs affect long-run economic development?

6. Suppose you are a policymaker in an emerging economy. Explain what types of capital flow you would try to encourage. What policy actions might you take to encourage these types of flows?

7. You are the finance minister of an emerging economy. You have the responsibility of maintaining an exchange-rate regime in which the value of the domestic currency is pegged to the currency of a large trading partner. Explain what policy actions or operations you would take to maintain the exchange-rate regime under the following circumstances:
   a. There is an increased inflow of short-term (portfolio) capital that you believe is only temporary in nature.
   b. There is an increased inflow of long-term (direct investment) capital that you believe will persist for at least a few years.

8. Some observers have responded to harsh criticisms of World Bank policies by arguing that the World Bank's members have saddled it with conflicting goals. Do you agree that the World Bank confronts conflicting objectives? If not, why not? If so, which of the allegedly conflicting goals do you think should take precedence?

9. Construct a table with three columns that lists each of the views on the causes of international financial crises in the left-hand column. In the second column of the table, list at least one possible financial crisis indicator corresponding to each view that might be tracked in an IMF early-warning system for predicting financial crises. In the third column, propose how to evaluate whether each potential indicator you have proposed actually helps predict a crisis. Does this exercise help explain why economists have a hard time constructing reliable early-warning systems?

10. Table 7–4 on page 213 lists a plan by Jeffrey Garten to establish a global central bank funded by credit lines from national governments and/or revenues from taxes on various international transactions. This central bank would be authorized to conduct open-market purchases and sales of securities issued in the financial markets of member nations. Discuss the strengths and weaknesses that you see in this proposal.

11. Should multinational institutions lend funds at interest rates below, equivalent to, or above private-market interest rates? Take a stand, and support your position.

12. Consider Figure 7–4 on page 203. Suppose a developing country is occupying the middle of the trilemma and suffers a financial crisis. As a response to the crises, policymakers decide to forgo discretionary monetary policy in favor of exchange-rate stability and open capital markets. What exchange-rate regimes do you think are *most* consistent with this policy configuration?

Online APPLICATIONS

Policymakers in emerging economies are completing bilateral investment agreements with policymakers in the advanced economies with the hope of attracting foreign direct investment. The United Nations Conference on Trade and Investment is the organization within the United Nations responsible for matters related to FDI. This application acquaints you with the *World Investment Report,* the main annual report of UNCTAD.

Internet URL: *http://www.unctad.org*

Title: The World Investment Report

Navigation: Begin at *http://www.unctad.org,* the address for the home page of UNCTAD. Click on *Publications* at the top of the page. Click on *Flagship Reports.* Under the *World Investment Report,* click on the link for the download page of the most recent report.

Click on *Downloads.* Click on *Overview.*

Application: Use the *Overview of the World Investment Report* to answer the following questions:

1. Describe the change in FDI inflows and outflows during the last few years.

2. Describe the change in mergers and acquisitions during the last few years.

3. List the top-ten FDI recipients. Are there any developing countries in this list?

4. List the top-ten nonfinancial transnational corporations from developing countries. What industries are represented in this list? How do these industries differ from those in the list of the top-ten nonfinancial transnational corporations from the developed countries?

SELECTED REFERENCES and FURTHER READINGS

Aizenman, Joshua, and Reuven Glick. "Sterilization, Monetary Policy, and Global Financial Integration." NBER Working Paper W13902 (March 2008).

Backé, Peter, and Cezary Wójcik. "Unilateral Euroisation: A Suitable Road towards Joining the Euro Area for Central and Eastern European EU Accession Countries?" In *Alternative Monetary Regimes in Entry to EMU,* Bank of Estonia (2002).

Barry Eichengreen. *Toward a New International Financial Architecture.* Washington, D.C.: Institute for International Economics, 1999, Appendix A.

Berg, Andrew, and Eduardo R. Borensztein. "The Pros and Cons of Full Dollarization." In Salvatore, Dominick, James W. Dean, and Thomas D. Willett, eds., *The Dollarization Debate.* New York: Oxford University Press, 2003.

Bordo, Michael, and Christopher Meissner. "The Role of Foreign Currency Debt in Financial Crises: 1880–1913 vs. 1972–1997." Rutgers University, March 2006.

Calvo, Guillermo A., and Frederic S. Mishkin. "The Mirage of Exchange Rate Regimes for Emerging Market Countries." NBER Working Paper 9808 (June 2003).

Choe, Hyuk, Bong-Chan Kho, and René Stulz. "Do Foreign Investors Destabilize Stock Markets? The Korean Experience in 1997." *Journal of Financial Economics 54* (1999): 227–264.

Edwards, Sebastian, "How Effective Are Capital Controls?" *Journal of Economic Perspectives 13*(4) (Fall 1999): 65–84.

Edwards, Sebastian, and Igal Magendzo. "A Currency of One's Own? An Empirical Investigation on Dollarization and Independent Currency Unions." National Bureau of Economic Research Working Paper 9514 (February 2003).

Frankel, Jeffrey. "Experiences of and Lessons from Exchange Rate Regimes in Emerging Economies." John F. Kennedy School of Government, Harvard University, Faculty Research Working Paper Series RWP03-011 (February 2003).

Fratianni, Michele. "Financial Crises, Safety Nets and Regulation." Working Paper, Indiana University Kelly School of Business (September 2008).

Ghosh, Atish R., Anne-Marie Gulde, and Holger C. Wolf. *Exchange Rate Regimes.* Cambridge, MA: MIT Press, 2002.

Goldstein, Morris, Graciela Kaminsky, and Carmen Reinhart. *Assessing Financial Vulnerability: An Early Warning System for Emerging Markets.* Washington D.C.: Institute for International Economics, 2000.

Kaiser, Karl, John. J. Kirton, and Joseph P. Daniels, eds. *Shaping a New International Financial System: Challenges of Governance in a Globalizing World.* Aldershot, U.K.: Ashgate Publishing Ltd., 2000.

Kose, M. Ayhan, Eswar Prasad, Kenneth Rogoff, and Shang-Jin Wei. "Financial Globalization: A Reappraisal." NBER Working Paper No. 12484 (August 2006).

Kumar, Anil. "Does Foreign Direct Investment Help Emerging Economies?" *Federal Reserve Bank of Dallas Economic Letter* (January 2007).

Lee, Jong-Wha, and Kwanho Shin. "IMF Bailouts and Moral Hazard." *Journal of International Money and Finance 27* (2008): 816–830.

Mourmouras, Alex, and Wolfgang Mayer. "Overcoming Barriers to Reform: On Incentive-Compatible International Assistance." IMF Working Paper WP/07/231 (September 2007).

Reinhart, Carmen M., and Kenneth S. Rogoff. *This Time Is Different: Eight Centuries of Financial Folly.* Princeton, NJ: Princeton University Press, 2009.

Salvatore, Dominick, James W. Dean, and Thomas D. Willett, eds. *The Dollarization Debate.* New York: Oxford University Press, 2003.

Straetmans, Setfan, Roald Versteeg, and Christian Wolff. "Are Capital Controls in the Foreign Exchange Market Effective?" C.E.P.R. Discussion Paper 6727 (2008).

Yeyati, Eduardo Levy, and Federico Sturzenegger. *Dollarization: Debates and Policy Alternatives.* Cambridge, MA: MIT Press, 2003.

PART 3

∎

EXCHANGE-RATE AND BALANCE-OF-PAYMENTS DETERMINATION

8 Traditional Approaches to Balance-of-Payments and Exchange-Rate Determination

9 Monetary and Portfolio Approaches to Balance-of-Payments and Exchange-Rate Determination

8 | Traditional Approaches to Balance-of-Payments and Exchange-Rate Determination

Fundamental ISSUES

1. How do the supply of exports and demand for imports determine the supply of and demand for foreign exchange?
2. What is the elasticities approach to balance-of-payments and exchange-rate determination?
3. What is the J-curve effect?
4. What are pass-through effects?
5. What is the absorption approach to balance-of-payments and exchange-rate determination?
6. How do changes in real income and absorption affect a nation's current account balance and the foreign exchange value of its currency?

During the mid-2000s, the dollar depreciated by more than 5 percent relative to the currencies of major U.S. trading partners and lost more than 10 percent of its value in relation to the euro. As a consequence, U.S. imports became more expensive, and the U.S. trade deficit began to increase. Then, between early 2007 and the onset of the U.S. financial meltdown in 2008, the dollar depreciated an additional 12 percent relative to major trading partners' currencies and dropped an additional 16 percent in relation to the euro. The U.S. trade deficit, however, began to shrink as the annual rate of growth in the dollar value of exports surged above 10 percent.

Why did the U.S. trade deficit apparently rise in response to the dollar depreciation of the mid-2000s but then eventually decline as the dollar continued to depreciate? As you will learn in this chapter, differences between the short- and long-run degrees of responsiveness of the home-currency values of exports and imports help provide an answer to this question. This chapter considers two traditional approaches to balance-of-payments and exchange-rate determination, and Chapter 9 describes two more modern approaches.

COMMON CHARACTERISTICS OF THE TRADITIONAL APPROACHES

Economists developed the two traditional approaches between the early1920s through the 1960s, when the world economy was quite different from that of today. These models, therefore, share some common characteristics. Because the major economies had adjustable-peg-exchange-rate arrangements under both the gold standard and the Bretton Woods system, economists focused their efforts on understanding the effect of a devaluation on a nation's balance of payments. We can, however, use these approaches to examine the effects of a currency depreciation as well, as you will learn in this chapter.

When these approaches were developed, capital flows did not dominate the foreign exchange market as they do today. As a result, both approaches assume that capital flows exist solely to finance international transactions of goods and services. Hence, capital flows are not explicitly considered in the models, which focus only on a nation's trade in goods and services. By distinguishing the effects of trade flows from the effects of capital flows, however, these approaches contribute to our understanding of exchange-rate and balance-of-payments determination.

The two traditional approaches differ in their emphasis on the economic variables that influence a nation's balance of payments and the exchange value of its currency. The first approach, the *elasticities approach*, emphasizes price effects, whereas the second, the *absorption approach*, emphasizes income effects. We begin with the elasticities approach, which centers on the relationship between a nation's imports and exports and the supply of and demand for foreign exchange.

EXPORTS, IMPORTS, AND THE DEMAND FOR AND SUPPLY OF FOREIGN EXCHANGE

The traditional approaches to balance-of-payments and exchange-rate determination assume that capital flows occur only as a means of financing current account transactions. Hence, the quantity of foreign exchange demanded and the quantity of foreign exchange supplied depend only on international transactions of goods and services.

Derivation of the Demand for Foreign Exchange

We explained in Chapter 2 that when a nation's residents import goods and services, they require foreign currencies to pay for these imports. Thus, the quantity of a currency demanded in the foreign exchange market is derived from the nation's demand for imports. In this chapter we provide a more complete derivation of the demand for foreign exchange, involving U.S. residents' demand for euros. In this setting, in which capital flows are ignored, the quantity of euros demanded by residents of the United States is equal to the value of their demand for imported European-produced items.

Suppose that U.S. residents export music CDs to Europe and import champagne from Europe. For simplicity, we shall assume that in euros, the "world" price of a bottle of champagne is €20 and that the "world" price of a music CD is €10. Furthermore, we shall assume that the euro prices of these two goods are given. Panel (a) of Figure 8–1 on the following page illustrates a hypothetical import demand curve for champagne in the United States. Point *A* of panel (a) indicates that at a price of $26 per bottle, the quantity of champagne demanded is 11 million

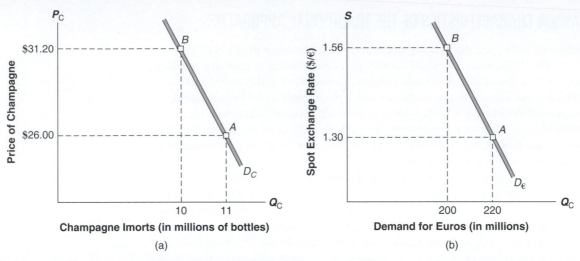

Figure 8–1 The U.S. Import Demand Curve and the Demand for the Euro
Panel (a) illustrates a hypothetical import demand curve as combinations of the quantities of champagne demanded by U.S. residents at various prices, such as those denoted by points *A* and *B*. The value of U.S. imports determines the quantity of foreign exchange demanded. For example, at a spot exchange rate of 1.30 $/€, the U.S. price of a bottle of champagne is $26, at which U.S. residents import 11 million bottles of champagne. At a world price of €20 per bottle, the value of U.S. imports is €220 million. Point *A* in panel (b) shows the combination of €220 million of foreign exchange demanded and the spot exchange rate 1.30 $/€. Panel (b) depicts the demand for foreign exchange as combinations of the quantities of foreign exchange demanded at various exchange rates, such as those denoted by points *A* and *B*.

bottles, and point *B* indicates that at a price of $31.20 the quantity of champagne demanded is 10 million bottles. The hypothetical import demand curve containing points *A* and *B* and denoted D_C illustrates all of the various combinations of import prices and quantities demanded.

This import demand curve determines U.S. residents' demand for foreign exchange, or euros. At a spot exchange rate of 1.30 $/€, the world price of champagne in U.S. dollars is $26 (€20 × 1.30 $/€ = $26). Hence, at a spot exchange rate of 1.30 $/€, the United States imports 11 million bottles of champagne. The euro value of U.S. imports at this spot exchange rate and, therefore, the quantity of euros demanded, is €220 million (€20 ×11 million = €220 million). Point *A* of panel (b) shows this combination of the spot exchange rate and the quantity of euros demanded.

At a spot exchange rate of 1.56 $/€, the U.S. price of a bottle of champagne in dollars is $31.20 (€20 × 1.56 $/€ = $31.20). Point *B* of panel (a) indicates that at this price, the United States imports 10 million bottles of champagne. The euro value of U.S. imports at this spot exchange rate and, therefore, the quantity of euros demanded is €200 million (€20.00 × 10 million = €200 million). Point *B* of panel (b) shows this combination of the spot exchange rate and the quantity of euros demanded. The demand curve formed by connecting points *A* and *B* and denoted $D_€$ in panel (b) illustrates all of the various combinations of spot exchange rates and quantities of euros demanded.

price elasticity of demand
A measure of the proportional change of the quantity demanded to a proportional change in price.

price elasticity of supply
A measure of the proportional change of the quantity supplied to a proportional change in its price.

Elasticity and the Demand for Foreign Exchange
Price elasticity of demand is a measure of the responsiveness of the quantity demanded to a change in price. Likewise, *price elasticity of supply* is a measure of the responsiveness of the quantity supplied to a change in price. Elasticity tells us

the proportionate change in quantity demanded or supplied in response to a given proportionate change in price.

Figure 8–1 shows that if the price of a bottle of champagne increases from $26 to $31.20, the quantity of champagne demanded falls from 11 million bottles to 10 million bottles. Suppose that for the same increase in price, the quantity of champagne demanded falls to 9 million bottles, as denoted by point B' in panel (a) of Figure 8–2. We would say that in this second case, the quantity of champagne demanded is more responsive to the change in price. In this second case, therefore, the demand for champagne is *more* elastic. As shown in panel (a) of Figure 8–2, the new demand curve formed by points A and B' and denoted D'_C is more elastic over the same price range as compared with the previous demand curve D_C.

As explained earlier, at a spot exchange rate of 1.56 $/€ the dollar price of champagne is $31.20. Using the import demand curve D'_C, at a price of $31.20 the United States imports 9 million bottles of champagne. The euro value of U.S. imports at this spot exchange rate, which is the quantity of euros demanded at point B' on the euro demand curve $D_€$, is equal to €180 million (€20 × 9 million = €180 million). The new foreign exchange demand curve formed by points A and B' and denoted D'_C is more elastic over the same range of exchange rates than the previous demand curve $D_€$. Consequently, the elasticity of the import demand curve influences the elasticity of the foreign exchange demand curve. A more elastic import demand curve yields a more elastic demand for foreign exchange. A less elastic import demand curve yields a less elastic demand for foreign exchange.

Derivation of the Supply of Foreign Exchange

In the traditional, trade-based theory of exchange-rate determination, the supply of foreign exchange to a nation results from its exports of goods and services. To

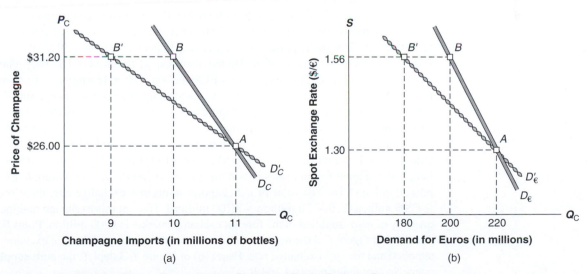

Figure 8–2   The Elasticity of Import Demand and the Elasticity of Foreign Exchange Demand
The elasticity of import demand determines the elasticity of foreign exchange demand. In panel (b), $D_€$ denotes the foreign exchange demand curve derived from the import demand curve D_C, and $D'_€$ denotes the foreign exchange demand curve derived from the import demand curve D'_C. In panel (a), the import demand curve denoted D'_C is more elastic than the demand curve D_C. As a result, the foreign exchange demand curve denoted D'_C is more elastic than the foreign exchange demand curve $D_€$.

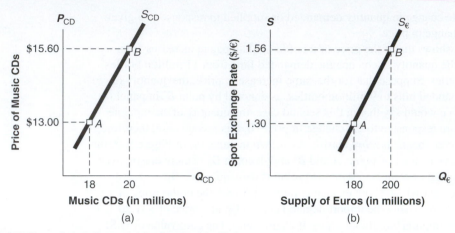

Figure 8–3 The U.S. Export Supply Curve and the Supply of the Euro

Panel (a) illustrates a hypothetical export supply curve for United States as combinations of the quantities of music CDs supplied at various prices, such as those denoted by points A and B. The value of U.S. exports determines the quantity of euros supplied. For example, at a spot exchange rate of 1.30 $/€, the U.S. price of music CDs is $13, at which U.S. businesses export 18 million music CDs. At a world price of €10 per CD, the euro value of U.S. exports is €180 million. Point A in panel (b) shows the combination of €180 million of foreign exchange supplied and the spot exchange rate 1.30 $/€. Panel (b) illustrates the supply of foreign exchange as combinations of the quantities of foreign exchange supplied at various exchange rates, such as those denoted by points A and B.

purchase goods and services from foreign residents, domestic residents provide foreign currency. Hence, the domestic nation's supply of exports implies a supply of foreign exchange.

Panel (a) of Figure 8–3 illustrates a hypothetical export supply curve for the United States. Point A shows that at a price of $13.00, the quantity of music CDs supplied by U.S. producers for export is 18 million CDs, and point B shows that at a price of $15.60 per CD, the quantity of music CDs supplied is 20 million CDs.

Recall that the world price of music CDs is €10 per CD. At an exchange rate of 1.30 $/€, the U.S. dollar price of music CDs is $10 per CD (€10 × 1.30 $ / € = $13.00), at which the residents of the United States export 18 million CDs. The value of the U.S. exports at this exchange rate is €180 million (€10 × 18 million = €180 million). Thus, at an exchange rate of 1.30 $ / €, the quantity of foreign exchange supplied is €180 million. Point A in panel (b) of Figure 8–3 illustrates this combination of the spot exchange rate and the quantity of euros supplied in the foreign exchange market.

If the U.S. dollar depreciates relative to the euro, from 1.30 $ / € to 1.56 $ / €, the U.S. dollar price of music CDs rises to $15.60 per CD (€10 × 1.56 $ / € = $15.60). Panel (a) of Figure 8–3 indicates that at this price U.S. producers are willing to export 20 million CDs. The value of U.S. exports at this new exchange rate, therefore, is €200 million (€10 × 20 million = €200 million). Thus, at this exchange rate the quantity of euros supplied in the foreign exchange market is €200 million. Point B in panel (b) of Figure 8–3 shows this combination of the quantity of foreign exchange supplied and the spot exchange rate. Panel (b) of Figure 8–3 depicts the euro supply curve $S_€$, containing points A and B.

Elasticity and the Supply of Foreign Exchange

Just as the elasticity of import demand determines the elasticity of the demand for foreign exchange demand, the elasticity of export supply also determines the elasticity of the supply of foreign exchange. Along the CD supply curve S_{CD} in panel (a) of Figure 8–3, if the price of music CDs rises from $13 per CD at point A to $15.60 per CD at point B, the quantity of music CDs supplied by U.S. producers increases from 18 million CDs to 20 million CDs. Suppose that, for the same price change, the quantity of music CDs supplied instead increases to 22 million CDs, shown at point B' on the CD supply curve D'_{CD} in panel (a) of Figure 8–4. In this second case, the quantity of music CDs supplied is more responsive to the price increase, so the proportional change in quantity supplied in response to the same proportional change in price is greater for the supply curve S'_{CD} than for the CD supply curve S_{CD}. Hence, over this price range, the supply curve S'_{CD} is more elastic than the supply curve S_{CD}.

Because the supply of exports determines the supply of foreign exchange, the elasticity of the supply of exports determines the elasticity of the supply of foreign exchange. At an exchange rate of 1.56 $/€ and a world price for music CDs of €10, the U.S. dollar price of a music CD is $15.60. If U.S. producers of music CDs export 22 million CDs at this exchange rate, then the value of U.S. exports to Europe, and thus the quantity of euros supplied by European residents, is €220 million (€10 × 22 million = €220 million).

Point B' in panel (b) of Figure 8–4 shows this new combination of the spot exchange rate and the quantity of euros supplied. As the figure shows, the foreign exchange supply curve containing points A and B' and denoted S'_C is more elastic over this range of exchange rates than the original supply curve $S_{€}$. Thus, the elasticity of the export supply curve determines the elasticity of the foreign exchange supply curve. If the supply of exports is more elastic, the supply of foreign exchange is also more elastic. Likewise, if the supply of exports is less elastic, the supply of foreign exchange is also less elastic.

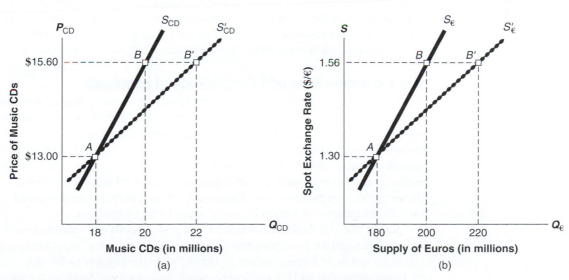

Figure 8–4   The Elasticity of Export Supply and the Elasticity of Foreign Exchange Supply
The elasticity of export supply determines the elasticity of foreign exchange supply. In panel (b), $S_{€}$ denotes the foreign exchange supply curve derived from the export supply curve S_{CD}, and S'_C denotes the foreign exchange supply curve derived from the export supply curve S'_{CD}. In panel (a), the export supply curve S'_{CD} is more elastic than the supply curve S_{CD}. As a result, the foreign exchange supply curve S'_C is more elastic than the foreign exchange supply curve $S_{€}$.

Fundamental ISSUES

#1 How do the supply of exports and demand for imports determine the supply of and demand for foreign exchange?

In an environment where capital flows occur only to finance current account transactions, the supply and demand for foreign exchange are determined by a nation's imports and exports of goods and services. When a nation's residents import goods and services, they must pay for these imports with foreign exchange. Thus, the demand for imports generates a demand for foreign exchange. Likewise, when a nation's residents export goods and services, they require foreign exchange as payment for these exports. Thus, the supply of exports generates a supply of foreign exchange.

THE ELASTICITIES APPROACH

elasticities approach

An approach that emphasizes changes in the prices of goods and services as the main determinant of a nation's balance of payments and the exchange value of its currency.

The *elasticities approach* centers on changes in the prices of goods and services as the determinant of a nation's balance of payments and the exchange value of its currency. As already explained, elasticity is a measure of the responsiveness of quantity to a change in price.

The previous section also showed that a change in the exchange rate affects the domestic currency price of goods and services.

For example, the U.S. dollar price of imported champagne rises when the U.S. dollar depreciates against the euro. As a result, residents of the United States import fewer bottles of champagne. Hence, a change in the exchange rate affects the domestic prices of imported and exported goods and services. In turn, the quantity of imports demanded and the quantity of exports supplied change as the domestic price varies. Elasticity measures thereby help us to determine the amount by which the quantity of imports demanded and the quantity of exports supplied adjust in response to a change in the exchange rate. In principle, this can be a useful tool when considering how to reduce a balance-of-payments deficit.

The Exchange Rate and the Balance of Payments

To understand the effects of a currency devaluation or currency depreciation and the roles of the elasticities of import demand and export supply, let's consider a country that currently experiences a current account deficit. Figure 8–5 illustrates the two foreign exchange demand curves D_{ϵ} and D'_C from Figure 8–2 and the two foreign exchange supply curves S_{ϵ} and S'_C from Figure 8–4. Suppose that the spot exchange rate between the U.S. dollar and the euro is 1.30 \$/€. As Figure 8–5 shows, at this spot exchange rate, the quantity of foreign exchange demanded exceeds the quantity of foreign exchange supplied by €40 million.

Recall that U.S. residents' demand for imported goods and services generates their demand for foreign exchange and that U.S. producers' supply of exports yields the supply of foreign exchange. Hence, when the quantity of foreign exchange demanded by U.S. residents exceeds the quantity of foreign exchange supplied by U.S. producers to Europeans, the United States experiences a current account deficit. The difference, €40 million in this example, or its dollar equivalent amount of \$52 million (€40 million × 1.30 \$ / € = \$52 million), is the amount of the U.S. current account deficit.

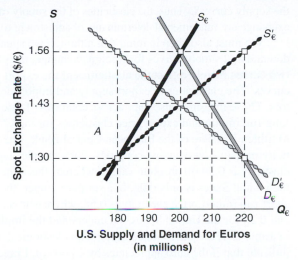

Figure 8–5   The Current Account Deficit

The current account deficit is equivalent to the difference between the quantity of foreign exchange demanded and the quantity of foreign exchange supplied. At a spot exchange rate of 1.30 \$/€, U.S. residents demand €220 million in foreign exchange and European residents supply €180 million in foreign exchange. Thus, at an exchange rate of 1.30 \$/€, the current account deficit is €40 million. The extent to which a currency depreciation will improve the current account deficit depends on the elasticity of foreign exchange demand and supply. When demand and supply are relatively more elastic, a smaller depreciation is required to eliminate the current account deficit.

Let's suppose the U.S. government is willing to allow the value of the U.S. dollar to depreciate relative to the euro. As Figure 8–5 illustrates, when the number of U.S. dollars required to purchase each euro increases, the quantity of foreign exchange demanded decreases, and the quantity of foreign exchange supplied increases. In other words, U.S. producers' exports of goods and services rise, and U.S. residents' imports of goods and services fall.

The Role of Elasticity   How much of a depreciation of the U.S. dollar is required to completely eliminate the current account deficit? As Figure 8–5 also illustrates, the answer to this question depends of which set of supply and demand curves we consider. Take a look at the foreign exchange demand curve denoted D'_ϵ and the foreign exchange supply curve denoted S'_C in Figure 8–5. The difference between the quantity of foreign exchange demanded and the quantity supplied and, therefore, the current account deficit, is eliminated at an exchange rate of 1.43 \$ / €. In other words, a 10 percent depreciation [(1.43 − 1.30) / 1.30 × 100 = 10%] of the U.S. dollar relative to the euro eliminates the current account deficit.

In contrast, if we consider the foreign exchange demand curve D_ϵ, and the foreign exchange supply curve S_ϵ in Figure 8–5, a 10 percent depreciation of the U.S. dollar relative to the euro does not completely eliminate the current account deficit. A deficit of \$28.6 million remains (€20 million × 1.43 \$ / € = \$28.6 million). The spot exchange rate would have to change to 1.56 \$/€ in order to completely eliminate the deficit. Hence, according to Figure 8–5, a 20 percent depreciation is required [(1.56 − 1.30) / 1.30 × 100 = 20%].

Because the demand curve D'_C is more elastic relative to demand curve D_ϵ, a 10 percent depreciation generates a larger change in the quantity of foreign exchange demanded along curve D'_C than it does along the less elastic demand curve D_ϵ. Likewise, a 10 percent depreciation generates a larger change in the quantity of foreign exchange supplied along the relatively more elastic supply curve S'_C than it does along the supply curve S_ϵ. Thus, the elasticities of the supply of and demand for foreign exchange are fundamental determinants of adjustment to a balance-of-payments deficit.

We must also keep in mind that although we speak of the elasticities of the demand and supply curves for foreign exchange, the elasticity measures of these two curves merely reflect the elasticities of the export supply and import demand curves. The elasticities of export supply and import demand depend on many factors. These measures also vary across countries. Table 8–1 provides short-run and long-run import and export price elasticities for the G7 economies, as estimated by Matthieu Bussière of the European Central Bank. The table shows how these elasticity measures vary across countries. For example, Japan's short-run export price elasticity is 0.39 (in absolute value), whereas the same measure for Germany and the United States is only 0.08. In a similar manner, the absolute value of Japan's short-run import price elasticity is 0.58, whereas it is only 0.33 for Germany and 0.23 for the United States. To understand the implications of the elasticities in Table 8–1, consider France's short-run elasticities. The values in Table 8–1 indicate that if the euro appreciates by 1 percent, France's export prices decline by 0.32 percent and its import prices decline by 0.52 percent. Table 8–1 also shows that, in general, long-run elasticities are larger in absolute value than short-run elasticities. In the next section we will explain the economic theory behind this and the implications for a nation's trade balance following a depreciation or appreciation of its currency.

Learn more about research conducted at the European Central Bank at *http://www.ecb.int/*.

The Marshall–Lerner Condition Based on the previous example, it appears that a depreciation will always improve a balance-of-payments deficit to some extent, if not in full. This is not necessarily the case. It is theoretically possible that a depreciation can increase the difference between the quantity of foreign exchange supplied and the quantity of foreign exchange demanded. Likewise, an appreciation may

Table 8–1

Measures of Import and Export Price Elasticities

	Canada	Germany	France	Italy	Japan	U.K.	U.S.
Export Price Elasticity							
Short Run	−0.17	−0.08	−0.32	−0.24	−0.39	−0.23	−0.08
Long Run	−0.19	−0.08	−0.39	−0.28	−0.34	−0.27	−0.16
Import Price Elasticity							
Short Run	−0.45	−0.33	−0.52	−0.56	−0.58	−0.39	−0.23
Long Run	−0.49	−0.36	−0.76	−0.72	−0.63	−0.48	−0.29

Source: Matthieu Bussière. "Exchange Rate Pass-through to Trade Prices: The Role of Non-Linearities and Asymmetries." European Central Bank Working Paper Series, No. 822 (October 2007).

increase the difference between the quantity of foreign exchange demanded and the quantity of foreign exchange supplied. *Exchange-rate instability* is this type of situation where a depreciation causes an excess quantity of foreign exchange supplied to increase, and a currency appreciation causes an excess quantity of foreign exchange demanded to increase.

The *Marshall–Lerner condition* specifies the necessary condition for exchange-rate stability. The condition and its derivation are quite complex and are beyond the scope of our discussion here. However, we can state the condition as it applies to the single-country example we have considered to this point. According to the Marshall–Lerner condition, exchange-rate stability results when the sum of the absolute values of the elasticity of import demand and the elasticity of export supply exceed unity. The Marshall–Lerner condition is met in most situations. It is possible, however, that if we consider a very short time horizon, the Marshall–Lerner condition may not be met.

exchange-rate instability

A situation in which a currency depreciation increases the difference between the quantity of foreign exchange supplied and the quantity of foreign exchange demanded instead of reducing the difference.

Marshall–Lerner condition

A necessary condition for exchange-rate stability, in which the sum of the elasticity of import demand and the elasticity of export supply must exceed unity.

Fundamental ISSUES

#2 What is the elasticities approach to balance-of-payments and exchange-rate determination?

The elasticities approach is a theory of balance-of-payments and exchange-rate determination that emphasizes the effect of price changes. A currency depreciation or appreciation may change the domestic currency price paid for imports and the price received for exports, thus leading to changes in the quantity of imports demanded and the quantity of exports supplied. The amounts by which the quantity of imports demanded and the quantity of exports supplied (and, therefore, the balance of payments) change is determined by the elasticity of export supply and the elasticity of import demand.

Short- and Long-Run Elasticity Measures and the J-Curve

Many factors determine the elasticity of export supply and import demand. The time horizon considered is particularly important, however, when considering the correction of a current account deficit.

Short-Run versus Long-Run Time Horizons The Marshall–Lerner condition implies that the elasticities of export supply and import demand must be sufficiently elastic for a depreciation to reduce the nation's balance-of-payments deficit. Elasticity measures generally differ over the time horizon that is considered. Because a longer time interval provides households and businesses the time needed to adjust to price changes, supply and demand tend to be relatively more price elastic over longer time periods and relatively less elastic over shorter time periods. For example, in the short run, households and businesses may be obligated by contract to complete a purchase of an imported good. Further, households and businesses might not have the opportunity to find domestic suppliers of imported goods and services, and thus might alter their planned expenditures on imports.

Over longer time horizons, however, if the prices of imported goods and services rise, households and business can adjust their planned expenditures. They can seek out alternatives to imported goods and services and reduce their reliance on imports. Hence, over longer time intervals, households and businesses are more responsive to price changes, and over shorter time intervals they are less responsive to price changes. We can conclude, therefore, that import demand and export supply tend to be relatively more elastic over long time intervals and relatively less elastic over short time intervals.

The J-Curve Effect Import demand and export supply are less elastic in the short run. Consequently, a depreciation of the domestic currency is unlikely to immediately improve a nation's balance-of-payments deficit. It is even possible that a depreciation could cause a nation's balance of payments to worsen before it improves, a phenomenon known as the *J-curve effect*.

J-curve effect

A phenomenon in which a depreciation of the domestic currency causes a nation's balance of payments to worsen before it improves.

To understand how the J-curve effect might arise, consider an extreme example in which the quantity of imports demanded and quantity of exports supplied are completely unresponsive to price changes, or completely in elastic, in the short term. Using the original import demand curve D_C in panel (a) of Figure 8–1 on page 222 and the export supply curve S_{CD} in panel (a) of Figure 8–3 on page 224 at an exchange rate of 1.30 \$ / €, the value of U.S. imports is \$286 million (\$26 × 11 million = \$286 million), and the value of U.S. exports is \$234 million (\$13 × 18 million = \$234 million). Hence, the U.S. current account deficit is \$52 million.

Let's think about how a depreciation of the U.S. dollar to a spot exchange rate, from 1.30 \$ / € to 1.56 \$ / €, affects the current account deficit in this situation. Because the quantity of exports supplied and the quantity of imports demanded are unresponsive to price changes, these quantities do not vary with a change in the spot exchange rate. If the spot exchange rate rises to 1.56 \$ / €, the U.S. price of a music CD increases, to \$15.60, and the U.S. price of a bottle of champagne also rises, to \$31.20. Thus, the value of U.S. exports rises, to \$280.8 million (\$15.60 × 18 million = \$280.8 million), while the value of U.S. imports also increases, to \$343.2 million (\$31.20 × 11 million bottles = \$343.2 million).The U.S. current account deficit thereby *widens* by \$10.4 million, to \$52 million.

As time passes, U.S. households and businesses will be able to find alternatives to the relatively more expensive imported goods and services. Thus, the quantity of imported goods and services will begin to decline, as indicated by the import demand curve D_C in panel (a) of Figure 8–1. Likewise, foreign households and businesses will be able to shift their expenditures to the relatively cheaper U.S. exports. Consequently, the quantity of U.S. goods and services exported will begin to rise, as indicated by the supply curve S_{CD} in panel (a) of Figure 8–3. Eventually, as shown in Figure 8–5 on page 227, the current account deficit will be eliminated.

Figure 8–6 illustrates the hypothetical J-curve that results. Initially, at time t_1, the U.S. current account deficit is \$52.0 million. Following the depreciation of the U.S. dollar to a spot exchange rate from 1.30 \$ / € to 1.56 \$ / €, the current account deficit widens to \$62.4 million at time t_2. As time passes, the deficit narrows until it is eventually eliminated at time t_3. The graph shows the initial worsening of the current account deficit before it improves, resulting in a J-shaped curve. (There is evidence that J-curve effects do exist even at the level of commodities produced by specific industries; see *Management Notebook: Industry-Level Evidence of J-Curve Effects for Bilateral Trade between Canada and the United States.*)

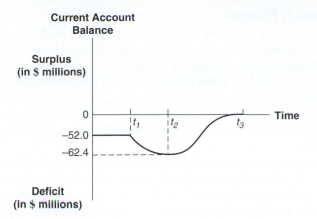

Figure 8–6

The J-Curve

Initially, the United States has a current account deficit of $52 million. At time t_1 the dollar depreciates. In the short run, import demand and export supply may be relatively inelastic. In this situation, the current account actually widens to $62.4 million at time t_2. Eventually, as business and households have time to adjust their planned expenditures on imports and exports, the deficit improves.

MANAGEMENT Notebook

Industry-Level Evidence of J-Curve Effects for Bilateral Trade between Canada and the United States

Most research exploring the J-curve effect examines how a nation's aggregate trade balance responds to changes in its currency's value. In a recent study, Mohsen Bahmani-Oskooee and Marzieh Bolhasani of the University of Wisconsin–Milwaukee instead considered bilateral trade data for Canada and the United States from the early 1960s through the 2000s. In addition, they evaluated export and import data for industries producing more than 152 commodities. They found that a real depreciation of the Canadian dollar exerts short-run effects on the trade balance for two-thirds of these industries. In about half of industries, a Canadian real depreciation translates into favorable J-curve effects on Canadian industry-level trade balances.

For Critical Analysis

Why might there be disparities in short- and long-run responses to currency depreciations of trade balances for different commodities? (Hint: Consider how the extent to which short- and long-run elasticities of demand and supply can vary across different industries.)

Fundamental ISSUES

#3 What is the J-curve effect?

The J-curve effect is a phenomenon where, following a devaluation or depreciation of the domestic currency, a nation's balance-of-payments deficit may actually worsen before it improves, forming a J-shaped curve. The J-curve effect results from the demand for imports and supply of exports being inelastic in the short run. Hence, following a devaluation or depreciation of the domestic currency, the quantity of imports demanded and the quantity of exports supplied do not change much. As a result, the balance-of-payments deficit, as valued in the domestic currency, widens. The J-curve effect is sometimes, but not always, observed following a domestic currency depreciation or devaluation.

Pass-Through Effects

pass-through effect
The effect of a currency depreciation that results in higher domestic prices of imported goods and services.

In our example, a depreciation of the U.S. dollar improved the U.S. current account deficit. Part of the improvement was brought about by a decrease in the quantity of imports demanded. This reduction in the quantity of imports demanded resulted from an increase in the U.S. dollar price of imported goods caused by the currency depreciation. Economists refer to this effect, in which a currency depreciation results in higher domestic prices of imported goods and services, as the ***pass-through effect***. In other words, the currency depreciation is passed through to domestic prices.

If, for some reason, the currency depreciation is not passed through to domestic prices of imported goods and services, the currency depreciation may not improve the current account deficit. Similarly, if a currency appreciation does not reduce the price of imported goods and services, the appreciation may not reduce a current account surplus. Hence, it is important to understand how much of a change in the exchange value of the domestic currency is passed through to domestic prices because of the implications for a nation's balance of payments.

Visit the Brookings Institution at *http://www.brook.edu* for economic, foreign policy, and governmental studies and research.

There have been many studies of pass-through effects indicating that the degree of pass-through varies across nations, across time, and across industries within nations. One reason that exchange value changes might not be passed through is that foreign producers may alter the prices of their products to offset the change in a currency's exchange value and maintain their market share in the domestic nation. (The degree of market power possessed by U.S. firms likely influences the extent of exchange-rate pass-through; see *Management Notebook: Market Power and Variations in U.S. Exchange-Rate Pass-Through Effects*.)

MANAGEMENT Notebook

Market Power and Variations in U.S. Exchange-Rate Pass-Through Effects

One factor affecting the extent of exchange-rate pass-through relates to the degree of market power possessed by foreign firms compared with domestic firms. For instance, consider a possible situation in which foreign producers exporting goods to the United States confront a U.S. industry in which a few domestic firms possess significant ability to influence prices. In the face of depreciation in the dollar's value, the foreign producer may fear losing considerable market share if it passes through the exchange-rate change by raising the prices of its goods. In contrast, if the goods of foreign producers compete with items produced by numerous domestic producers with sales that are small percentages of U.S. market shares, the foreign firms may be more willing to allow more pass-through of the dollar depreciation to their prices.

Federal Reserve Bank of New York economists Rebecca Hellerstein, Deirdre Daly, and Christina Marsh have found evidence supporting this argument. As a rough measure of market power of foreign producers relative to domestic producers in various industries, they use the ratio of imports to domestic production. Consistent with idea that relative market shares of foreign and domestic producers influence the extent of the pass-through effect, these researchers note that the percentage of pass-through to U.S. import prices is positively related to the ratio of imports to domestic production in U.S. markets: As the ratio of imports to domestic production increases across U.S. industries, so does the extent of pass-through of dollar depreciations to prices of imported products.

For Critical Analysis

In light of the relationship between the ratio of imports to domestic production and the extent of pass-through to prices of imported products, what might be signified by the fact that many economists have found evidence that the extent of exchange-rate pass-through effects has declined in the United States during the past twenty-five years?

Fundamental ISSUES

#4 What are pass-through effects?

A pass-through effect occurs when a change in the exchange value of the domestic currency results in a change in the domestic prices of imported goods and services. Hence, when the domestic currency depreciates, a pass-through effect results in higher domestic prices of imported goods. When the domestic currency appreciates, a pass-through effect results in lower domestic prices of imported goods and services. Economists have determined that the degree of pass-through varies across nations, across time, and across industries. The degree of pass-through is very important because it has implications for the effect of the change in the value of the domestic currency on the nation's balance of payments.

THE ABSORPTION APPROACH

The two traditional balance-of-payments and exchange-rate approaches emphasize different variables. The elasticities approach emphasizes prices as a determinant of the balance of payments and exchange rate. The *absorption approach*, however, assumes that prices remain constant and emphasizes changes in real domestic income. Hence, the absorption approach is a real-income theory of balance-of-payments and exchange-rate determination. Because of the assumption of constant prices, economists view the absorption approach as a short-run approach to balance-of-payments and exchange-rate determination.

Modeling the Absorption Approach

The absorption approach separates the market values of a nation's expenditures on final goods and services into four basic categories: consumption expenditures, investment expenditures, government expenditures, and expenditures on imports.

absorption approach
A theory of balance-of-payments and exchange-rate determination that emphasizes the role of a nation's expenditures, or absorption, and income. According to the absorption approach, if a nation's real income exceeds the amount of goods and services that it absorbs, then the nation will run a current account surplus.

Exports are not included, because they represent another nation's expenditures on domestic final goods and services. Because prices are assumed to be constant, the values in each category are real measures.

Absorption Economists refer to the total of these four categories of expenditures as *domestic absorption*. That is, a nation absorbs goods and services for consumption, investment, and public-sector purposes, as well as imports from abroad. Hence, *absorption* is a nation's total expenditures on final goods and services. We shall express the identity representing a nation's absorption as

absorption

A nation's total expenditures on final goods and services net of exports.

$$a \equiv c + i + g + im,$$

where a denotes absorption, c denotes real consumption expenditures, i denotes real investment expenditures, g denotes real government expenditures, and im denotes the nation's real expenditures on imported goods and services.

Real Income A nation's real income, on the other hand, is equivalent to the real expenditures on its output of final goods and services. Hence, real income is equal to real consumption expenditures, real investment expenditures, real government expenditures, and other nations' real expenditures on its output, or its real exports. We shall represent a nation's real income as

$$y \equiv c + i + g + x,$$

where y denotes real income and x denotes real exports.

The Current Account As explained earlier in this chapter, capital flows were not very important at the time the elasticities and absorption approaches were developed. Hence, the current account was the focus of economists' attention. In the absorption approach, the current account balance, ignoring any unilateral transfers, is represented by the difference between foreign real expenditures on exports and domestic real expenditures on imports. This is represented as

$$ca \equiv x - im,$$

where ca denotes the real current account balance. If real exports exceed real imports, the nation is running a current account surplus. If real exports are equal to real imports, the nation's current account is balanced. If real exports are less than real imports, the nation is running a current account deficit.

Determination of the Current Account Balance

According to the absorption approach, a nation's current account balance is determined by the difference between its income and absorption. This can be seen by subtracting the equation representing absorption from the equation for the nation's real income:

$$y - a = (c + i + g + x) - (c + i + g + im),$$

Combining terms on the right-hand side, we obtain

$$y - a = x - im.$$

Finally, we can substitute ca for the value $x - im$, as the difference between the two is the current account balance. In doing so, we obtain the standard equation representing the absorption approach:

$$y - a = ca.$$

Hence, a nation's current account balance is determined by the difference between its real income and its absorption.

For example, suppose the nation's income exceeds its absorption, $y > a$; that is to say, it is producing more output than it absorbs. In this situation, the right-hand side of the equation is positive, which implies that the nation is running a current account surplus ($y > a$: current account surplus). Likewise, when a nation's income is less than its absorption, it runs a current account deficit ($y < a$: current account deficit). Finally, when a nation's income is equal to its absorption, its current account is balanced.

Economic Expansion and Contraction

Though it is a simple theory, the absorption approach is useful in understanding the performance of a nation's current account balance and the exchange value of its currency during periods of economic expansion and during periods of economic contraction, or recessions. It is often presupposed, particularly in popular media reports, that a nation experiencing an economic contraction will spend less on imported goods and services, so that its current account balance will improve and its currency will appreciate. Likewise, observers typically argue, a country undergoing an economic expansion will spend more on imported goods and services so that its current account balance will deteriorate and its currency will depreciate. In the real world things do not always turn out this way. The absorption approach helps explain why this is so.

An Economic Expansion Consider a nation whose current account initially is balanced. Suppose that this nation experiences an economic expansion. As real income rises, so, typically, do real expenditures, or absorption. Returning to the equation for the absorption approach:

$$y - a = ca,$$

when real income, y, rises and absorption, a, rises, it is unclear whether the nation will have a current account deficit or surplus. This depends on which element, real income or absorption, rises *faster*. If real income rises faster than absorption—that is, if domestic output rises faster than domestic expenditures—the nation will experience a current account surplus. If absorption rises faster than real income, the nation will experience a current account deficit. If real income and absorption rise at the same rate, the current account will remain unchanged.

We can examine the impact on the exchange value of the domestic currency in a similar manner. We return to our previous equation that appeared in our derivation of the absorption approach:

$$y - a = x - im.$$

If, during the course of an economic expansion, real income rises faster than absorption, then the nation's exports must rise relative to its imports. As a result, the domestic currency appreciates. If absorption rises faster than real income, the nation's imports must rise relative to its exports. As a result, the domestic currency depreciates.

An Economic Contraction Likewise, during the course of an economic downturn, if real income falls faster than absorption, then exports decline relative to imports, and the domestic currency depreciates. If absorption declines faster than real income, then the nation's exports rise relative to its imports, and the domestic currency appreciates.

In conclusion, the absorption approach shows us why a nation enjoying an economic expansion often experiences a currency appreciation, whereas a nation in a recession often experiences a currency depreciation. What is important is the *relative* change in real income and absorption. The absorption approach, as we shall discuss next, also illustrates the limited effectiveness of policy actions designed to reduce a current account deficit.

On the WEB

To access research conducted by economists at the Federal Reserve Bank of New York, visit the Bank's research page at *http://www.ny.frb.org/research/*.

Fundamental ISSUES

#5 What is the absorption approach to balance-of-payments and exchange-rate determination?

The absorption approach emphasizes a nation's real income and expenditures as determinants of its balance of payments and the exchange value of its currency. According to the absorption approach, if a nation's real income exceeds the amount of goods and services that it absorbs, then the nation will run a current account surplus. If a nation's real income is less than the amount of goods and services it absorbs, then the nation will run a current account deficit. If real income and absorption are equal, the nation's current account will be balanced.

Policy Instruments

We must recall the economic environment during which the absorption model was developed to fully appreciate its policy implications. The absorption approach was developed in the 1950s, with credit typically given to Sidney Alexander, an economist at the International Monetary Fund. As explained in Chapter 3, during this period most nations participated in the Bretton Woods system of adjustable-peg-exchange-rate arrangements.

As we noted in Chapter 6, policymakers have access to a number of *policy instruments*, which are variables that they can determine, either directly or indirectly. We will be discussing monetary and fiscal policy in greater detail in Chapter 11. In the absorption approach, and under adjustable pegged exchange rates, policymakers have two instruments, an *absorption instrument* and an *expenditure-switching instrument*. The **absorption instrument** refers to a government's ability to raise or reduce a nation's absorption by changing its own purchases of domestic output, g, or by influencing consumption and investment expenditures through changes in taxes. A change in government spending results in a change in g, whereas a change in taxes affects households' planned consumption expenditures and businesses investment expenditures, resulting in a change in c and i. It is unclear, however, how a decrease in expenditures might affect real income in the context of the absorption model. Thus, it is also unclear as to whether the use of an absorption instrument will be effective in reducing a current account deficit.

absorption instrument
A government's ability to increase or decrease a nation's absorption by changing its own purchases of domestic output or by influencing consumption and investment expenditures.

Nevertheless, the absorption approach also shows the potential consequences of attempting to stimulate the domestic economy through increased government expenditures. Suppose that policymakers in an economy experiencing a recession increase government spending, *g*, in an attempt to stimulate output. If the increase in government expenditures causes absorption to rise faster than output, then the nation's current account balance will worsen.

The ***expenditure-switching instrument*** is the ability of the government to alter, or "switch," private expenditures among imports and exports by adopting policies that change their relative costs. This can be accomplished in two ways. First, the government can impose trade restrictions. These commercial policies would raise the price of imported goods and services, leading consumers and business to purchase fewer imports and more goods and services produced domestically. Domestic income rises as the domestic production of the imported goods and services rises, while the absorption of imported goods and services declines and the absorption of domestic goods and services rises. These types of policies, however, often lead to retaliation from the nation's trading partners.

Another way to induce expenditure switching is by changing the exchange value of the domestic currency. A devaluation of the domestic currency causes foreign goods and services to become relatively more expensive. Consequently, domestic consumers and businesses may switch from imported to domestically produced goods and services. A revaluation of the domestic currency would have the opposite effect.

Expenditure switching, according to the absorption approach, does not necessarily improve the current account balance. If households and businesses switch directly between imported goods and services and domestically produced goods and services, leaving overall absorption the same, and if the level of real income remains the same, then there is no change in the current account balance. As demonstrated earlier, the current account balance changes only if there is an increase in real income relative to absorption. This is accomplished only if a policy action stimulates greater output of exports relative to expenditures on imports. Hence, a devaluation alone may have limited usefulness in correcting a current account deficit.

expenditure-switching instrument
A government's ability to alter, or switch, expenditures among imports and exports by enacting policies that change their relative prices.

 **Fundamental** ISSUES

#6 How do changes in real income and absorption affect a nation's current account balance and the foreign exchange value of its currency?

According to the absorption approach, if real income rises faster than absorption, then exports rise relative to imports, the nation's balance of payments improves, and the domestic currency appreciates. If absorption rises faster than real income, then imports rise relative to exports, the nation's balance of payments deteriorates, and the domestic currency depreciates. The two types of policy instruments in the absorption model, the absorption instrument and the expenditure-switching instrument, may have negligible effects on a nation's current account imbalance. Hence, it is unclear if these instruments will increase real income relative to absorption.

Chapter SUMMARY

1. **A Nation's Supply of Exports and Demand for Imports Determine Its Demand for and Supply of Foreign Exchange:** If capital flows occur only to finance current account transactions, then the supply and demand for foreign exchange is determined by a nation's imports and exports of goods and services. When a nation's residents import goods and services, they must pay for these imports with foreign exchange. Hence, the nation's residents supply foreign exchange. Likewise, when a nation's residents export goods and services, they require foreign exchange as payment for these exports, which yields their demand for foreign exchange.

2. **The Elasticities Approach to Balance-of-Payments and Exchange-Rate Determination:** The elasticities approach is a theory of balance-of-payments and exchange-rate determination that focuses on the effects of price changes. A currency depreciation or appreciation may change the domestic currency price paid for imports and the price received for exports, thus leading to changes in the quantity of imports demanded and the quantity of exports supplied.

3. **The J-Curve Effect:** The J-curve effect is a phenomenon in which a nation's balance-of-payments deficit may actually worsen before it improves following a currency depreciation or devaluation. What results is a "J-shaped" curve as the balance of payments adjusts over time. The J-curve effect results from low short-run price elasticities of demand for imports and supply of exports. In the long run, however, these elasticities are larger because consumers and businesses have more time to adjust to the price changes. Hence, in the long run, the balance of payments is likely to improve following a depreciation of the domestic currency.

4. **Pass-through Effects:** A pass-through effect arises when a change in the exchange value of the domestic currency results in a change in the domestic prices of imported goods and services. Hence, when the exchange value of the domestic currency changes, it may or may not be passed through and result in a change in the domestic prices of imported goods and services. The degree of pass-through varies across nations, across time, and across industries. The degree of pass-through is very important because it influences the response of a nation's balance of payments to a change in value of the domestic currency.

5. **The Absorption Approach to Balance-of-Payments and Exchange-Rate Determination:** The absorption approach to balance-of-payments and exchange-rate determination emphasizes a nation's real income and expenditures. According to the absorption approach, if a nation's real income exceeds the amount of goods and services that it absorbs, the nation will run a current account surplus. If a nation's real income is less than the amount of goods and services that it absorbs, the nation will run a current account deficit. If real income and absorption are equal, the nation's current account will be balanced.

6. **Changes in Real Income and Absorption and a Nation's Current Account Balance and the Exchange Value of Its Currency:** The absorption approach illustrates that if real income rises faster than absorption, exports rise relative to imports, the nation's balance of payments improves, and the domestic currency appreciates. If absorption rises faster than real income, imports rise relative to exports, the nation's balance of payments deteriorate, and the domestic currency depreciates. A similar argument holds when real income and absorption decline.

QUESTIONS and PROBLEMS

1. Price elasticity is calculated as the percentage change in quantity divided by the percentage change in price. If we let a subscript A denote the old value and a subscript B denote the new value, price elasticity is calculated as

$$\frac{\left[\dfrac{Q_B - Q_A}{1/2\,(Q_A + Q_B)}\right]}{\left[\dfrac{P_B - P_A}{1/2\,(P_A + P_B)}\right]}$$

   If the absolute value of the price elasticity measure is greater than unity, we say it is elastic. If it is less than unity, we say it is inelastic. If it is equal to unity, we say it is unit elastic. Using this formula, calculate the elasticity of foreign exchange demand in panel (b) of Figure 8–1 on page 222 and the elasticity of foreign exchange supply in panel (b) of Figure 8–3 on page 224.

2. Based on the elasticity calculations in Problem 1, what is the change in the quantity of imports demanded and the quantity of exports supplied when the U.S. dollar depreciates relative to the euro by 1 percent? Answer this question both in absolute terms and in percentage change.

3. Refer to Table 8–1 on page 228. Which nation has the most *inelastic* import prices in the short run? Which nation has the most *elastic* import prices in the short run?

4. Refer to Table 8–1 on page 228. Suppose the U.S. dollar depreciates by 1 percent.
   a. What is the resulting short-run change in U.S. import prices?
   b. What is the resulting short-run change in U.S. export prices?
   c. Based on your answers in (a) and (b), what is the likely short-run impact on the U.S. trade balance?

5. Refer to Table 8–1 on page 228.
   a. What value represents the estimate of long-run exchange-rate pass-through for the United States?
   b. Does this value represent full exchange-rate pass-through, partial or incomplete pass-through, or no exchange-rate pass-through?

6. Refer to the values for the U.K. import price elasticity in Table 8–1 on page 228. Give some reason why import prices respond to exchange-rate changes to a lesser degree in the short run than in the long run.

7. Brazil is a major global supplier of coffee beans and Germany is a major importer of coffee beans. Suppose Brazil invoices and sells its coffee beans on the international market in U.S. dollars at the international market price of $1.20 per pound. The exchange rate between the dollar and the euro is 1.40 $ / €, and the exchange rate between the Brazilian Real and the U.S. dollar is 2.4 BR / $. Now suppose the euro depreciates by 5 percent relative to the U.S. dollar, but the exchange value between the Real and the dollar remains constant.
   a. What is the likely impact on the number of units of coffee Brazil exports to Germany?
   b. What is the likely impact on the value of Brazil's exports in terms of the Real?
   c. Suppose Brazil's coffee exporters want to maintain their market share in Germany. How much should they reduce the dollar price of their exported coffee? What is the new value of this export price in terms of the Brazilian Real?

8. Suppose that a nation experiences a recession and falling unemployment during the first half of year.
   a. Write out a single equation representing the absorption approach. Define each variable and explain the meaning of the equation.
   b. Suppose this nation has a fixed exchange rate. Explain, using the equation and according to the absorption approach, if the country's balance of payments will rise or fall.
   c. Suppose this nation has a flexible exchange rate. Explain, using the equation and according to the absorption approach, if the country's currency will be appreciating or depreciating.

9. Suppose that real consumption expenditures in a nation are $10,000, real investment expenditures are $8,000, real government expenditures are $5,000, real expenditures on imports are $1,000, and real exports are $500.
   a. What are the nation's levels of real income and absorption?
   b. What is its trade balance?

10. Suppose that the government of the nation described in Question 9 devalues the domestic currency and, as a result, imports fall by $50, exports rise by $50, and real consumption expenditures rise by $25. What is the trade balance now? Did the devaluation improve the balance of payments?

11. Suppose the Chinese economy expands at a faster pace than that of its trading partners. Using the absorption approach, explain why the Chinese yuan might depreciate relative to the currencies of its trading partners. Explain why the Chinese yuan might appreciate relative to the currencies of its trading partners.

Online APPLICATIONS

This chapter presented the elasticities approach to balance-of-payments and exchange-rate determination and the J-curve effect. A J-curve pattern is sometimes observed for a nation's external balance following a depreciation or devaluation. That is, following a depreciation or devaluation, the external balance may decrease before it increases. This application asks you to consider the opposite scenario: Does the external balance *increase* before it decreases following an *appreciation*?

Internet URL: *http://www.statcan.gc.ca*

Title: *Statistics Canada*

Navigation: Begin at the home page of Statistics Canada. In the center of the page, click on the *Key resource* tab. Under *Data tables* , click on *Summary Tables*. In the left-hand panel, under *Tables By*, click on *Subject*. In the list of subjects, click on *International Trade*. Next click on *Trade Patterns*. In the list of categories, click on *Imports, Exports, and Trade Balance of Goods on a Balance-of-Payments Basis by Country or Country Grouping.*

Application: From January 2008 through January 2012, the real effective exchange index of the Canadian dollar increased from 92.0 to 11.4. Using the data you obtained on Canada's international trade, consider the impact of this change on the trade balance of Canada.

1. Calculate the percentage increase in the real effective exchange rate. As the trade balance data show, in 2008 and 20011, Canada maintained a trade surplus. What do you

think, however, would be the impact of the change in the real effective exchange rate on the surplus? Would you expect it to increase or decrease?

2. What was the actual change in Canada's overall trade balance over this time period? Does the trade balance display a "J-curve" pattern (explain)? Was the change in the balance of trade consistent across all five country groupings or did it differ across groups?

3. What was the percentage change in Canada's imports?

4. Using your answer to Question 3, calculate Canada's exchange-rate elasticity of import demand.

SELECTED REFERENCES and FURTHER READINGS

Alexander, Sidney S. "Effects of a Devaluation: A Simplified Synthesis of Elasticities and Absorption Approaches." In Norman C. Miller, ed., *Open Economy Macroeconomics. Volume 1.* Cheltenham, U.K. and Northampton, MA: Elgar, 2006: 89–102.

Bahmani-Oskooee, Mohsen, and Marzieh Bolhasani. "The J-Curve: Evidence from Commodity Trade between Canada and the U.S." *Journal of Economics and Finance 32*(3) (July 2008): 207–225.

Bussiére, Matthieu. "Exchange Rate Pass-Through to Trade Prices: The Role of Non-Linearities and Asymmetries." European Central Bank, Working Paper Series, No. 822 (October 2007).

Campa, José Manuel, and Linda S. Goldberg. "Exchange Rate Pass-Through into Import Prices." *Review of Economics and Statistics 87*(4) (2005): 679–690.

Dekle, Robert, Jonathan Eaton, and Samuel Kortum. "Global Rebalancing with Gravity: Measuring the Burden of Adjustment." *IMF Staff Papers 55*(3) (2008): 511–540.

Duasa, Jarita. "Determinants of Malaysian Trade Balance: An ARDL Bound Testing Approach." *Global Economic Review 36*(1) (March 2007): 89–102

Erceg, Christopher J., Luca Guerrieri, and Christopher Gust. "Trade Adjustment and the Composition of Trade." *Journal of Economic Dynamics and Control 32*(8) (August 2008): 2622–2650.

Gagnon, Joseph E. "Long-Run Supply Effects and the Elasticities Approach to Trade." Board of Governors of the Federal Reserve System, International Finance Discussion Paper #754, http://www.federalreserve.gov/pubs/ifdp/ (January 2003).

Gagnon, Joseph E., and Jane Ihrig. "Monetary Policy and Exchange Rate Pass-Through." Working Paper, Division of International Finance, Federal Reserve Board of Governors of the Federal Reserve System (March 2002).

Hellerstein, Rebecca, Deirdre Daly, and Christina Marsh. "Have U.S. Import Prices become Less Responsive to Changes in the Dollar?" *Federal Reserve Bank of New York Current Issues in Economics and Finance 12*(6) (September 2006).

Iley, Richard A., and Mervyn K. Lewis. *Untangling the US Deficit: Evaluating Causes, Cures and Global Imbalances.* Cheltenham, U.K. and Northampton, MA: Elgar, 2007.

Kumar Narayan, Paresh, and Seema Narayan. "The J-Curve: Evidence from Fiji." *International Review of Applied Economics 18*(3) (July 2004): 369–380.

Mahmud, Syed F., Aman Ullah, and Eray M. Yucel. "Testing Marshall–Lerner Condition: A Non-Parametric Approach." *Applied Economics Letters 11* (2004): 231–236.

Miller, Norman C. "A General Approach to the Balance of Payments and Exchange Rates." *Journal of International Economic Integration 1*(1) (1986): 85–122.

Papaioannou, Stefan, and Kei-Mu Yi. "The Effects of a Booming Economy on the U.S. Trade Deficit." *Federal Reserve Bank of New York Current Issues in Economics and Finance 7*(7) (February 2001).

Sekine, Toshitaka. "Time-Varying Exchange Rate Pass-Through: Experience of Some Industrial Countries," Bank for International Settlements, Monetary and Economic Department, BIS Working Papers, No. 202 (March 2006).

9 Monetary and Portfolio Approaches to Balance-of-Payments and Exchange-Rate Determination

Fundamental ISSUES

1. What are the main assets and liabilities of central banks?
2. How do a central bank's foreign exchange market interventions alter the monetary base and the money stock?
3. What is the monetary approach to balance-of-payments and exchange-rate determination?
4. How is the monetary approach a theory of exchange-rate determination in a two-country setting?
5. What is the portfolio approach to exchange-rate determination?
6. Should central banks sterilize foreign exchange interventions?

Some of them have names that sound at home in the corporate world, such as China Investment Corporation, Korea Investment Corporation, and Temasek Singapore. The names of others, including Abu Dhabi Investment Authority, Kuwait Investment Authority, and Qatar Investment Authority, come closer to revealing their true connections. And some of names that are quite revealing, such as Government Pension Fund-Global, Government of Singapore Investment Corporation, and Stabilization Fund Russia. All of these entities are known as sovereign funds. Each of these sovereign funds is operated by its nation's government. Nevertheless, each one pursues the same goal that a private company would pursue, namely, profit maximization.

Most of the assets held by sovereign funds are not denominated in the domestic currencies of the countries in which the sovereign funds are based. Instead, their assets are mainly denominated in various foreign currencies and, in particular, the U.S. dollar. Taken together, the assets of all sovereign funds total to well over $5 trillion, or nearly one-third of U.S. annual national income. Yet all these assets of sovereign funds are just a fraction of the total foreign-currency-denominated assets held by nations such as China, Korea, Russia, and Singapore. And foreign-currency-denominated assets continue to accumulate in these and other nations, to the tune of as much as $2 billion per week.

Through what process are governments around the globe accumulating so many assets denominated in foreign currencies such as the dollar? In this chapter, you will learn that the process has a lot to do with the policies of the nations' central banks. More generally, you will learn about financial-markets-oriented approaches to balance-of-payments and exchange-rate determination that help us understand this and other important issues.

CENTRAL BANK BALANCE SHEETS

Chapter 6 detailed the various objectives and functions of a central bank. In that chapter, you learned that in many countries the central bank acts as the government's agent, conducting transactions in the foreign exchange markets at the government's request. We now consider how foreign exchange market interventions alter the nation's *monetary base* and its *money stock*.

A Nation's Monetary Base

monetary base

Central bank holdings of domestic securities and loans plus foreign exchange reserves, or the sum of currency and bank reserves.

domestic credit

Total domestic securities and loans held as assets by a central bank.

A nation's ***monetary base*** is equal to the sum of central bank holdings of domestic securities and loans and foreign exchange reserves. Economists call total domestic securities and loans ***domestic credit,*** so the monetary base by definition is the domestic credit plus the central bank's foreign exchange reserves. The sum of domestic credit and foreign exchange reserves corresponds to between 80 and 90 percent of the assets of major central banks. Consequently, for the purpose of understanding how central banks conduct monetary policy, let's simplify things by considering the stripped-down central bank balance sheet depicted in Figure 9–1. In the figure, we assume that the only assets of a central bank are domestic credit and foreign exchange reserves, which together compose the monetary base.

Note that it is also true that at least two-thirds of central bank liabilities are composed of currency issued by major central banks and reserves that private banks hold on deposit with the central banks. Thus, in Figure 9–1 we list these two central bank liabilities. Because assets must equal liabilities in this simplified balance sheet, we reach an important conclusion:

> **The monetary base constitutes the bulk of central bank assets and liabilities. Viewed from the asset side of a central bank's balance sheet, the monetary base is equal to domestic credit plus foreign exchange reserves. Viewed from the liability side of the central bank's balance sheet, the monetary base is equal to currency plus bank reserves.**

Figure 9–1 illustrates a simplified balance sheet of the central bank. In the figure, domestic credit *(DC),* which is the central bank's holdings of securities and loans, and foreign exchange reserves *(FER),* valued in terms of the domestic currency, constitute the central bank's assets. Currency outstanding *(C)* and the total reserves of banks *(TR)* constitute the central bank's liabilities. Because the assets

Figure 9–1

A Simplified Central Bank Balance Sheet

Assets	Liabilities
Domestic credit	Currency
Foreign exchange reserves	Bank reserves
Monetary base	Monetary base

of the central bank equal its liabilities, we can express the nation's monetary base as either the sum of domestic credit and foreign exchange reserves or the sum of currency outstanding and the total reserves of banks:

$$MB = DC + FER, \text{ or } MB = C + TR.$$

For our discussion in this chapter, it will be convenient to focus on the asset side of the central bank's balance sheet and express the nation's monetary base *(MB)* as the sum of domestic credit and foreign exchange reserves. Hence, allowing Δ to denote the change in a variable, we can express the change in a nation's monetary base as

$$\Delta MB = \Delta DC + \Delta FER.$$

This expression tells us that a nation's monetary base will change because of a change in domestic credit or in foreign exchange reserves, or in both. (Recently, central banks and governments holding most of the world's foreign exchange reserves have been rethinking how to allocate them; see *Policy Notebook: So Many Foreign Exchange Reserves, So Many New Options for Allocating Them.*)

POLICY Notebook

So Many Foreign Exchange Reserves, So Many New Options for Allocating Them

At various times in recent years, official dollar inflows to China have been as high as $20 billion per *month*, which helps to explain how, as shown in Figure 9–2, the People's Bank of China and the Chinese government have stockpiled the world's largest stock of foreign exchange reserves. In past years, Chinese officials have mainly opted to hold only the safest securities, such as U.S. Treasury bonds.

The safest government bonds, however, offer the lowest rates of return. In recent years, Chinese officials have been expanding their list of choices for allocating foreign exchange reserves by investing some of those funds with Blackstone Group and other U.S. private-equity firms. Policymakers in Russia, Singapore, and South Korea have been seeking higher returns by using considerable portions of their reserves to purchase corporate stocks and bonds in the United States and other nations.

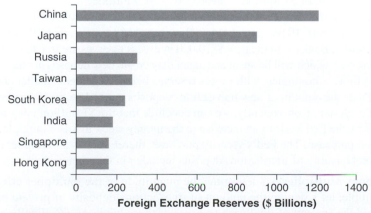

Figure 9–2

Countries with Largest Holdings of Foreign Exchange Reserves

Central banks and governments of Asian nations hold the largest stocks of foreign exchange reserves.

Source: International Monetary Fund, International Financial Statistics; authors' estimates.

For Critical Analysis

In light of evidence that higher-risk financial instruments offer higher rates of return, what is one possible drawback associated with investing foreign exchange reserves in privately issued financial instruments instead of government bonds?

A Nation's Money Stock

There are a variety of measures of a nation's money stock, which we shall denote *M*. The simplest measure, and the one we shall use, is the sum of the amount of currency in circulation and the amount of transactions deposits in the banking system. Most nations have a fractional-reserve banking system. Central banks typically require that private banks maintain a fraction of their customers' transactions deposits as reserves. This fraction determines the maximum increase in the money stock that a change in the total reserves of the banking system can create.

An Open-Market Transaction To see why this is so, consider an example. Suppose the reserve requirement is 10 percent. Next consider an open-market operation, in which the U.S. Federal Reserve System (the "Fed") purchases $1 million of securities from a securities dealer. When the Fed purchases the $1 million in securities, the domestic credit component of the Fed's balance sheet rises by $1 million, so the monetary base rises by $1 million. The securities dealer may have the Fed wire the payment to the dealer's account, say at a bank in Chicago. The Fed completes the transaction by applying a $1 million credit to the Chicago bank's reserve account at the Federal Reserve Bank of Chicago, and the amount of total reserves of the private bank increases by $1 million. The private bank then earmarks these funds for the dealer's transactions deposit account with the bank. The Fed has, therefore, created an additional $1 million in total reserves, and the nation's money stock immediately rises by $1 million.

The effect of the Fed's action does not end here, however. Of the $1 million in total reserves, 10 percent, or $100,000, is required reserves and $900,000 is excess reserves. The bank in Chicago is free to lend out the $900,000 in excess reserves. If the individuals who receive the $900,000 in loans spend these funds, then the recipients of these funds ultimately may redeposit them at other banks, thereby creating $900,000 in new transactions deposits. Because of this lending activity, the amount of domestic credit, and thus the money stock, can rise by an additional $900,000, for a total increase of $1 million + $900,000 = $1.9 million.

Once again the story does not necessarily end here. Of the $900,000 in new transactions deposits, 10 percent, or $90,000 are required reserves and $810,000 are excess reserves. Banks with the new $810,000 in excess reserves are free to lend the excess reserves, which will be spent and again may create new deposits at other banks.

This process continues, with excess reserves being 10 percent smaller at each step and thus the amount of new transactions deposits created being 10 percent larger at each step. Consequently, we can conclude that the $1 million open-market purchase by the Fed leads to an increase in the money stock that is a multiple of the $1 million purchase. The Fed's security purchase, therefore, has a multiplier effect on the total quantity of transactions deposits included in the money stock.

The Money Multiplier To determine the magnitude of the multiplier effect in this example, let's denote the amount of transactions deposits of private banks as *TD* and the amount of total cash reserves of these banks as *TR*. Finally, we denote the reserve requirement ratio as *rr*. If banks were to hold only the amount of reserves required by the Fed, then total reserves in the banking system would be $TR = (rr \times TD)$. Any change in total reserves due to changes in transactions deposits at banks would be

$$\Delta TR = rr \times \Delta TD.$$

Solving this equation for ΔTD by dividing each side of the equation by rr yields

$$\Delta TD = (1/rr) \times \Delta TD.$$

Thus, the *maximum* amount by which transactions deposits may rise is equal to the change in total reserves times a *multiplier* equal to $1/rr$. In our example, the Fed's security purchase causes an initial increase of $1 million in the private bank's reserves, so ΔTR equals $1 million. Further, the reserve requirement ratio is 10 percent, so rr equals 0.10 and $1/rr$ equals 10. As a result, the maximum possible change in total transactions deposits in the banking system, ΔTD, equals 10 times $1 million, or $10 million. Therefore, in our example, the Fed's $1 million securities purchase ultimately can increase the amount of transactions deposits, and thus the money stock, by $10 million. The ratio $1/rr$ is the transactions deposit multiplier. Under an assumption that the monetary base is comprised solely of transactions deposits, the transactions deposit multiplier is also the **money multiplier (m),** which is the number by which a reserve measure is multiplied to obtain the amount of the money stock of an economy.

Realistically, the final multiplier effect of an open-market transaction is less than the amount given by the money multiplier as derived here. One reason is that most people hold some money in the form of currency and do not deposit all of their funds in transactions deposits accounts. Hence, at each step in the process banks have fewer funds to lend than that given in the example. Another reason that the multiplier typically is smaller than $1/rr$ is that many banks hold some excess reserves—or, in other words, they do not lend out all excess reserves at each step of the multiplier process.

money multiplier
The number by which a reserve measure is multiplied to obtain the total money stock of an economy.

The Relationship between the Monetary Base and the Money Stock

This example, in which we assume that the monetary base consists solely of transactions deposits, describes a relationship between the monetary base and the money stock. That is, the money stock is equal to the monetary base times the money multiplier. As we include the amount of currency in circulation as a component of the monetary base, the money multiplier becomes more complex and is no longer equal to $1/rr$. (The derivation of the money multiplier in a situation where the monetary base includes currency in circulation is left as a problem at the end of this chapter.) Regardless of the complexity of the money multiplier, we can express the relationship between the money stock and the monetary base as

$$M = m \times MB = m(C + TR) = m(DC + FER).$$

Further, we can express a change in the nation's money stock as the value of the money multiplier times the change in the nation's monetary base:

$$\Delta M = m \times \Delta MB = m(\Delta C + \Delta TR) = m(\Delta DC + \Delta FER).$$

Using this equation, we can examine the effect of an open-market operation, as depicted in our previous example, on the nation's money stock. First we must recognize that the change in total reserves of the banking system—the initial $1 million increase in the private bank's reserve account at the Chicago Fed—is equivalent to a $1 million change in domestic credit, because the Fed purchased $1 million in securities. The change in cash outstanding and foreign exchange reserves, however, is zero. Assuming that the money multiplier is 10, substituting these values into the previous equation yields

$$\Delta M = 10 \times \$1 \text{ million} = \$10 \text{ million}.$$

Thus, $10 million is the maximum possible change in the nation's money stock.

 Fundamental**ISSUES**

#1 What are the main assets and liabilities of central banks?

The primary assets of central banks are government securities and loans to private banking institutions, referred to as domestic credit, and foreign-currency-denominated securities and deposits. Key central bank liabilities are currency notes and reserve deposits of private banking institutions. The sum of domestic credit and foreign-currency-denominated securities and loans corresponds to 80 to 90 percent of the assets of major central banks. The sum of currency notes and reserve deposits of private banking institutions corresponds to at least two-thirds of the liabilities of major central banks. A nation's monetary base constitutes the bulk of central bank assets and liabilities.

MANAGED EXCHANGE RATES: FOREIGN EXCHANGE INTERVENTIONS

If central banks seek to attain international objectives, then they typically do so in part through foreign exchange interventions, buying or selling financial assets denominated in foreign currencies in an effort to influence exchange rates. Nevertheless, even if central banks focus on domestic policy objectives, leaving finance ministries the task of pursuing international goals, they often still find themselves intimately involved in the mechanics of foreign exchange interventions. The reason is that in their role as government depositories and fiscal agents, they usually conduct foreign exchange interventions on behalf of their governments. Under these circumstances, as we shall discuss, central banks may wish to undertake actions to prevent the interventions from complicating their strategies for attaining their domestic objectives.

Mechanics of Foreign Exchange Interventions

To attain international goals, central banks often attempt to alter the values of their nations' currencies in the foreign exchange markets via foreign exchange interventions. Now that you have learned about the balance-sheet compositions, structures, and functions of central banks, we can consider how they conduct foreign exchange market interventions in an effort to influence exchange rates.

Intervention Transactions Central banks normally conduct foreign exchange interventions via *spot market* transactions. A key reason is that central banks often wish for their interventions to convey clear signals of their policy intentions to foreign exchange market traders. Sizable spot transactions are readily detectable by traders, thereby improving the likelihood that traders will observe central bank interventions and be able to infer the objectives of the central banks.

Most central banks do not use forward market transactions in their interventions. Central banks commonly use swap transactions, however, to adjust the composition of their portfolios of foreign exchange reserves. In this respect, swaps, which we discussed in Chapter 5, are a useful means of adding to a central bank's holdings of a particular currency shortly before a period of spot market intervention with one of those currencies. The U.S. dollar, the Japanese yen, and the euro are the key vehicle currencies of the world, so these are the currencies that central banks commonly stockpile using swap transactions in advance of interventions.

Leaning with or against the Wind A central bank intervenes either on its own account or on behalf of its national government in an effort to influence the value of its nation's currency in the foreign exchange market. If a central bank intervenes to support or speed along the current trend in the value of its nation's currency in the foreign exchange market, then economists say that its interventions are *leaning with the wind.*

In contrast, economists say that a central bank's interventions intended to halt or reverse a recent trend in the value of its nation's currency are *leaning against the wind.* Most often, central banks lean against the wind solely to halt, at least temporarily, sharp swings in market exchange rates. Consequently, a key rationale for many instances of leaning against the wind is simply to reduce volatility in exchange rates. A central bank does not necessarily lean against the wind with an aim to bring about long-term reversals in the trend value of its nation's currency; although in some instances this might be an ultimate goal of a central bank or finance ministry upon whose behalf the central bank conducts a policy of leaning against the wind.

Financing Interventions If central banks intervene in foreign exchange markets on their own behalf, then they do so using their own reserves of assets denominated in foreign currencies. Many central banks have "war chests" of foreign currency reserves in the event that they should desire to conduct interventions on their own account. In like manner, governments often maintain reserves of foreign-currency-denominated assets.

To better understand how central banks and finance ministries fund their interventions, it is helpful to review the mechanics of foreign exchange market interventions in the United States, Europe, and Japan. In the United States, the U.S. Treasury has primary responsibility for undertaking foreign exchange interventions. Consequently, the Treasury usually determines the timing and extent of U.S. interventions, even though the Federal Reserve conducts these interventions on the Treasury's behalf. The U.S. Treasury's position is that it has the legal authority to order the Federal Reserve to use its own foreign exchange reserves as well as those of the Treasury, and in the past the Federal Reserve has conducted Treasury interventions using its own reserves as well as those of the Treasury. Recently, this has become a source of tension within the Federal Reserve System, as some Federal Reserve officials have openly questioned this "subservience" of the Federal Reserve to the Treasury.

Nonetheless, the U.S. government maintains a separate *Exchange Stabilization Fund (ESF)* that it can use to finance its interventions when Federal Reserve foreign exchange reserves are not involved. If ESF officials intervene in support of the dollar's value by selling assets denominated in foreign currencies, they

leaning with the wind
Central bank interventions to support or speed along the current trend in the market exchange value of its nation's currency.

leaning against the wind
Central bank interventions to halt or reverse the current trend in the market exchange value of its nation's currency.

initially deposit the dollars obtained in the transaction in a Treasury deposit at the Federal Reserve. The Treasury Department then issues a nonmarketable security to the ESF, which purchases the Treasury security from its account with the Federal Reserve, which credits the Treasury's deposit account. To ensure that this sequence of transactions has no ultimate effect on the Federal Reserve's balance sheet, and hence on the monetary base, the Treasury then withdraws these funds from its deposit account at the Federal Reserve and redeposits them at private banks.

The Japanese mechanism for official interventions is much like that of the United States. The national budget of Japan includes the Foreign Exchange Fund Special Account, through which the Ministry of Finance can fund interventions, using the Bank of Japan as its agent for actually conducting transactions in foreign exchange markets. The Ministry of Finance uses this account much like the U.S. Treasury uses the Exchange Stabilization Fund, although it does not take any steps to automatically shield the Japanese money stock from the effects of its actions.

Visit the Bank of Japan at *http://www.boj.or.jp/en.*

By law, the European Central Bank's sole responsibility is to maintain price stability. Hence, the strength or weakness of the euro should be a concern to the European Central Bank (ECB) only in how it affects inflation. During the first eighteen months following its issue in January 1999, however, the euro depreciated relative to the dollar by approximately 25 percent, generating much concern on the part of the ECB. By September 2000, the ECB convinced the United States, Japan, Canada and Britain to join it in an effort to bolster the value of the euro. Fifteen years to the day following the Plaza Agreement, a coordinated effort to do so took place, with $3 to $5 billion euros being purchased by the central banks of these nations. This action only temporarily halted the depreciation of the euro. Although previously assuring the markets that the ECB would only intervene with the cooperation of the United States, the ECB intervened on its own four more times in 2000, with little impact on the value of the euro.

From 2000 to 2008, the euro strengthened significantly against other major currencies, including the U.S. dollar and the Japanese yen, to the point where some European leaders questioned if the euro was "too strong." This time, however, the European Central Bank refused to intervene.

Foreign Exchange Interventions and the Money Stock

As explained earlier, foreign exchange interventions are purchases or sales of foreign-currency-denominated assets. To show how central banks conduct their interventions through the private banking system, changing the monetary base and thereby altering the money stock, we consider only the purchase or sale of foreign-currency-denominated bank deposits. These deposits are assets of domestic individuals, firms, brokers, and banks, which they hold on deposit at foreign banks. Hence, foreign exchange transactions of the central bank affect the balance sheets of domestic private banks *and* the balance sheets of foreign private banks.

Indirectly, therefore, foreign exchange interventions influence the domestic money stock *and* potentially the foreign nation's money stock.

An Example of a Foreign Exchange Transaction To illustrate the consequences of a central bank's foreign exchange interventions, we shall focus on a two-country example using the simplified central bank balance sheet presented earlier. For purposes of illustration, let's suppose that the two countries are the United States and Japan. Figure 9–3 presents the simplified balance sheets of the Federal Reserve and the Bank of Japan. As our example unfolds, we use these balance sheets to show the change in the components of the monetary base of each nation.

Let's suppose that the money multiplier of the United States is 2.1 and the money multiplier of Japan is 2.6. Also, let's suppose that the Bank of Japan chooses to lean against the wind, so that it wishes to slow or halt, at least temporarily, an appreciation of the yen relative to the dollar. The Bank of Japan, therefore, purchases a $1 million bank deposit from a Tokyo foreign exchange dealer at a spot exchange rate of 110 ¥/$.

If the dealer instructs the Bank of Japan to wire the payment to its account at a Tokyo bank, the Bank of Japan applies a ¥110 million ($1 million × 110 ¥/$) credit to the Tokyo bank's reserve account at the Bank of Japan. The private bank then earmarks those funds for the transactions deposit account at the dealer's bank. As a result, the transactions deposits of the Japanese banking system rise by ¥110 million and the foreign exchange reserves of the Bank of Japan rise by $1 million (or, if valued in yen terms, by ¥110 million). Figure 9–4 (p. 252) shows the effect of the foreign exchange purchase on the Bank of Japan's balance sheet. There is an increase in the foreign exchange reserves component of ¥110 million, with a resulting increase in the Japanese monetary base of ¥110 million.

As discussed earlier, the initial increase in transactions deposits leads to a multiple increase in the Japanese money stock. The increase in the Japanese money stock is equal to the Japanese money multiplier times the ¥110 million increase in the monetary base. Using the same equations as in our open-market-operation example, we can express the impact on the Japanese money stock as

$$\Delta M_J = m_J \times \Delta MB_J = m_J \times (\Delta DC_J + \Delta FER_J).$$

In this instance, the change in domestic credit is zero, the change in foreign exchange reserves is ¥110 million, and the Japanese money multiplier is 2.6.

Simplified Balance Sheet of the Federal Reserve

Assets	Liabilities
Domestic credit	Currency
Foreign exchange reserves	Bank reserves
Monetary base	Monetary base

Simplified Balance Sheet of the Bank of Japan

Assets	Liabilities
Domestic credit	Currency
Foreign exchange reserves	Bank reserves
Monetary base	Monetary base

Figure 9–3

The Simplified Balance Sheets of the Federal Reserve and the Bank of Japan

The simplified balance sheets of the Federal Reserve and the Bank of Japan express the monetary base as the sum of the central bank's assets, domestic credit, and foreign exchange reserves, and as the sum of its liabilities, currency, and bank reserves.

Figure 9–4

The Effect of a Foreign Exchange Purchase on the Bank of Japan's Balance Sheet

When the Bank of Japan purchases ¥110 million of foreign reserves, the foreign exchange reserves component of the monetary base rises. The Bank of Japan pays the foreign exchange dealer by applying a ¥110 million credit to the reserves of the dealer's bank.

Figure 9–4

Simplified Balance Sheet of the Bank of Japan

Assets	Liabilities
Domestic credit	Currency
Foreign exchange reserves +¥110 million	Bank reserves +¥110 million
Monetary base +¥110 million	Monetary base +¥110 million

Substituting these values into the last equation, the change in the Japanese money stock is

$$\Delta M_J = 2.6 \times (\$0 + ¥110 \text{ million}) = 2.6 \times ¥110 \text{ million} = ¥286 \text{ million}.$$

Hence, the foreign exchange transaction of the Bank of Japan increases the Japanese money stock by ¥286 million.

The Effect on the U.S. Money Stock Following the purchase of a dollar-denominated deposit, the Bank of Japan has a $1 million claim on a U.S. bank. The Bank of Japan presents this claim to the Fed. The Fed "clears" the Bank of Japan's claim on the U.S. bank by assuming the liability itself. This action reduces the reserves of the U.S. bank by $1 million. As shown in Figure 9–5, the domestic credit component of the U.S. monetary base decreases by $1 million. The U.S. money stock declines by a multiple of the change in the monetary base. Using the previous equation, the change in the U.S. money stock is

$$\Delta M_{US} = m_{US} \times \Delta MB_{US} = m_{US} \times (\Delta DC + \Delta FER).$$

sterilization

A central bank policy of altering domestic credit in an equal and opposite direction relative to any variation in foreign exchange reserves so as to prevent the monetary base from changing.

In this example, the U.S. money multiplier is 2.1, the change in domestic credit is a negative $1 million, and the change in foreign reserves is zero. The change in the U.S. money stock, therefore, is

$$\Delta M_{US} = 2.1 \times (-\$1 \text{ million} + \$0) = \$2.1 \times (-\$1 \text{ million}) = -\$2.1 \text{ million}.$$

The foreign exchange market transaction of the Bank of Japan that results in a ¥110 million increase in the Japanese money stock also results in a $2.1 million decrease in the U.S. money stock.

Sterilization of Interventions

A central bank *sterilizes* foreign exchange interventions when it buys or sells domestic assets in sufficient quantities to prevent the interventions from influencing the domestic money stock. As we noted earlier in this chapter, a key money measure is the *monetary base*, which we can view as either the sum of domestic

Figure 9–5

The Effect of a Foreign Exchange Purchase by the Bank of Japan on the Fed's Balance Sheet

When the Bank of Japan purchases $1 million of dollar-denominated bank deposits, it then presents the deposits to the Fed. The Fed assumes the liability and reduces the U.S. bank's reserve account by $1 million. This, in turn, reduces domestic credit and the monetary base by $1 million.

Simplified Balance Sheet of the Fed

Assets	Liabilities
Domestic credit −$1,000,000	Currency
Foreign exchange reserves	Bank reserves −$1,000,000
Monetary base −$1,000,000	Monetary base −$1,000,000

credit plus foreign exchange reserves or as the sum of domestic currency and bank reserves. Thus, sterilization of the sale of foreign exchange reserves requires an equal-sized expansion of domestic credit, perhaps via a central bank open-market purchase, that would maintain an unchanged monetary base.

The mechanics of U.S. foreign exchange interventions entail accounting entries that lead to nearly immediate and complete sterilization. Japan, for example, also follows policies intended to assure at least long-term sterilization of interventions.

Many other countries officially espouse a policy of sterilizing foreign exchange interventions, but in practice some find it difficult to fully offset the effects of the resulting changes in net foreign assets. Thus, many interventions by central banks around the world are at least partly nonsterilized, so that interventions cause changes in relative quantities of national moneys in circulation. It is through this channel that many economists think that interventions actually may influence market exchange rates.

In the preceding example, the Bank of Japan may have intervened in the foreign exchange market in pursuit of an external objective. The consequence is a change in the domestic money stock. Suppose, however, that the change in the Japanese money stock conflicts with the internal objectives of the Bank of Japan. In this case, the Bank of Japan desires to offset, or *sterilize,* the effect of the foreign exchange intervention on the Japanese money stock. The Bank of Japan can sterilize the foreign exchange transaction through an offsetting open-market transaction.

To sterilize the effect of the foreign exchange transaction, the Bank of Japan must offset the increase in foreign exchange reserves with an equivalent decrease in domestic credit. To do this, the Bank of Japan must engage in an open-market sale of securities. When the Bank of Japan sells ¥110 million of Japanese government securities to a domestic dealer, domestic credit falls by ¥110 million. The dealer pays for the securities by wiring funds from a transactions deposit account to the Bank of Japan. The Bank of Japan clears the transaction deposit by reducing the total reserves of the dealer's bank. Thus, transactions deposits fall by ¥110 million.

Figure 9–6 illustrates the combined effect of the foreign exchange transaction and the open-market transaction on the Bank of Japan balance sheet. When both transactions are conducted simultaneously, domestic credit falls by ¥110 million, and foreign exchange reserves rise by ¥110 million. The foreign exchange

Simplified Balance Sheet of the Bank of Japan

Assets	Liabilities
Domestic credit −¥110 million	Currency
Foreign exchange reserves +¥110 million	Bank reserves +¥110 million −¥110 million
Monetary base	Monetary base

Figure 9–6   The Combined Effects of a Foreign Exchange Transaction and Sterilization
When the Bank of Japan purchases ¥110 million of foreign exchange reserves, the foreign exchange reserves component of the monetary base rises. The Bank of Japan pays the foreign exchange dealer by applying a ¥110 million credit to the bank reserves of the dealer's bank. The Bank of Japan sterilizes the foreign exchange transaction through an open-market sale of securities. This reduces the domestic credit component of the monetary base. To complete the open-market transaction the Bank of Japan reduces bank reserves. Thus, the monetary base is unchanged.

transaction results in a ¥110 million increase in private bank reserves, and the open-market transaction results in a ¥110 million decrease in private bank reserves. The net effect on private bank reserves is zero. Furthermore, Figure 9–6 illustrates that the net effect on the Japanese monetary base is zero.

The sterilized foreign exchange transaction leaves the Japanese monetary base, and, therefore, the Japanese money stock unchanged. Combining the foreign exchange transaction and the open-market transaction in the equations representing the relationship between the money stock and the monetary base, we can express the effect on the money stock as

$$\Delta M_J = m_J \times (\Delta DC_J + \Delta FER_J)$$
$$= 2.6 \times (-\text{¥}110 \text{ million} + \text{¥}110 \text{ million}) = 0.$$

Hence, a fully sterilized foreign exchange intervention has no effect on the Japanese money stock.

The Federal Reserve may also desire to sterilize the effect of the Bank of Japan foreign exchange transaction on the U.S. money stock. If so, the Fed can also undertake an offsetting open-market transaction. (In many emerging nations, there has been a trend toward more sterilization of foreign exchange market interventions; see *Policy Notebook: Emerging Nations Weigh the Benefits and Costs of Sterilization*.)

# POLICY Notebook

Emerging Nations Weigh the Benefits and Costs of Sterilization

The key benefit of sterilizing foreign exchange market interventions is that doing so prevents a nation's money supply from expanding or contracting, thereby contributing to inflationary or disinflationary conditions. Sterilization can entail an expense, however, depending on whether rates of return on domestic financial instruments are higher or lower than rates of return on foreign financial instruments. For instance, consider a central bank that is accumulating foreign exchange reserves and is sterilizing its actions by selling domestic securities. If the average rate of return on foreign financial instruments is less than the average rate of return on domestic financial instruments, then sterilization entails incurring a per-unit opportunity cost equal to the differential between the two rates of return.

Joshua Aizenman of the University of California at Santa Cruz and Reuven Glick of the Federal Reserve Bank of San Francisco have utilized techniques for measuring the degree to which foreign exchange interventions are sterilized. Based on these measures, they conclude that the sterilization is more commonplace in recent years than previously, particularly in countries of Asia and Latin America. Apparently more central banks are determining, after weighing the benefits and costs of sterilization, that an increased degree of sterilization is appropriate for their nations.

For Critical Analysis

When a central bank incurs an interest-differential opportunity cost by engaging in sterilization, who ultimately incurs the cost? (Hint: *In most countries, who ultimately owns central banks?*)

Fundamental ISSUES

#2 How do a central bank's foreign exchange market interventions alter the monetary base and the money stock?

Central bank foreign exchange market interventions increase or reduce the foreign exchange reserves component of the monetary base. Thus, purchases (sales) of foreign assets increase (reduce) the monetary base. A nation's money stock is a multiple of the monetary base. Hence, foreign exchange transactions change the nation's money stock by a multiple of the change in the monetary base. Sterilization changes the domestic credit component of the monetary base in an opposite direction, thereby eliminating the effect of the foreign exchange transaction on the monetary base and the money stock.

THE MONETARY APPROACH TO BALANCE-OF-PAYMENTS AND EXCHANGE-RATE DETERMINATION

Chapter 8 presented the two traditional approaches to balance-of-payments and exchange-rate determination, the elasticities and absorption approaches. As explained earlier, these approaches focused on transactions in goods and services and ignored financial markets. After the collapse of the Bretton Woods system, economists sought to develop approaches to understanding balance-of-payments and exchange-rate determination that allowed for floating exchange rates and greater integration of goods and financial markets across economies. Their efforts yielded the *monetary approach,* which quickly became popular among many economists. As you will now learn, the preceding material laid all the groundwork for understanding the role of money in determining a nation's balance of payments and the exchange value of its currency.

The ***monetary approach*** to balance-of-payments and exchange-rate determination postulates that changes in a nation's balance of payments and the exchange value of its currency are a monetary phenomenon. That is, balance-of-payments deficits or surpluses or exchange-rate variations result from differences between the quantity of money supplied and the quantity of money demanded.

Although the monetary approach is a recent development relative to the theories presented in Chapter 8, its roots can be traced back to the philosopher David Hume and his price-specie flow model. This approach begins with a formal model of the demand for, and supply of, money balances.

monetary approach
Relates changes in a nation's balance of payments and the exchange value of its currency to differences between the quantity of money demanded and the quantity of money supplied.

The Cambridge Approach to Money Demand

The monetary approach begins with the ***Cambridge equation,*** which is a theory of the demand for money developed in the late nineteenth century by economists at Cambridge University. The Cambridge equation is

$$M^d = kPy,$$

where M^d denotes the total quantity of nominal money balances that all households desire to hold, k is a fraction between zero and one, P is the aggregate price level in the economy, and y is total real income. Because P is the aggregate price level and y is real income, multiplying the two together yields nominal income. Hence, the Cambridge equation constitutes a hypothesis that people hold a fraction of their nominal income as money.

Cambridge equation
A theory of the demand for money developed by economists at Cambridge University. The Cambridge equation postulates that the quantity of money demanded is a fraction of nominal income.

Money, the Balance of Payments, and the Exchange Rate

As discussed earlier, a nation's quantity of money is equal to a money multiplier times the monetary base:

$$M = m(DC + FER).$$

As before, we have expressed the monetary base as the sum of domestic credit and foreign exchange reserves.

The Relationship between the Money Stock and the Balance of Payments
Chapter 1 examined the identities that make up a nation's balance-of-payments system. Recall that the current account balance plus the capital account balance is equal to the official settlements balance. The official settlements balance consists mainly of changes in the central bank's foreign exchange reserves. To simplify our discussion, we will assume the nation's foreign exchange reserves are equivalent to its official settlements balance.

Using this accounting identity, we can relate a nation's money stock to its balance of payments. Remember also from Chapter 1 that an increase in the official settlements balance (or, in this case, the foreign exchange reserves component of the monetary base) is equivalent to a balance-of-payments surplus. Likewise, a decrease in foreign exchange reserves is equivalent to a balance-of-payments deficit. If foreign exchange reserves are unchanged, then the nation's overall balance of payments continues to be zero. Hence, we can relate changes in the nation's money stock to changes in its balance of payments.

The Relationship between Domestic Prices, Foreign Prices, and the Spot Exchange Rate Economists who use the monetary approach assume that purchasing power parity holds in the long run. As explained in Chapter 2, absolute purchasing power parity postulates that the equilibrium domestic price level of traded goods and services is equal to the foreign price level of traded goods and services times the spot exchange rate between the two nations' currencies. Hence, absolute purchasing power parity is expressed as

$$P = SP^*,$$

where P is the domestic price level, S is the spot exchange rate (expressed in domestic currency units per foreign currency unit), and P^* is the foreign price level.

The Monetary Equilibrium Condition The relationship among the Cambridge equation of money demand, the money stock (and, therefore, the balance of payments), the foreign price level, and the spot exchange rate can be determined through an equilibrium condition in which the quantity of money demanded equals the money stock:

$$M^d = M.$$

First we substitute the equation for the quantity of money and the Cambridge equation into the equilibrium condition $M^d = M$, which yields

$$kPy = m(DC + FER).$$

Next, we use the expression for absolute purchasing power parity to substitute in for the domestic price level to obtain

$$m(DC + FER) = kSP^*y.$$

In words, in equilibrium the actual money stock equals the quantity of money demanded. Proponents of the monetary approach, however, use this relationship to explain how key variables affect the nation's balance of payments and the exchange value of its currency.

The Monetary Approach and a Fixed-Exchange-Rate Arrangement

According to the monetary approach, an event that causes a difference between the quantity of money demanded and the quantity of money supplied generates a change in the nation's balance of payments or in the spot exchange value of its currency. In addition, the monetary approach postulates that the event triggers an automatic adjustment process that eventually brings the economy back to an equilibrium at which the quantity of money demanded equals the quantity of money supplied.

To understand the automatic adjustment process of the monetary approach, we must take into account the type of exchange-rate arrangement the nation has adopted. Hence, we must examine the monetary approach under both fixed- and flexible-exchange-rate arrangements.

A Change in Domestic Credit Consider a nation that is small, so that its economy has no effects on the price levels of foreign nations. In addition, suppose that its central bank pegs the exchange value of its currency. If the nation's central bank increases domestic credit through an open-market purchase of securities, then the open-market purchase causes the nation's money stock to rise through the multiplier process. All other things constant, the open-market operation thereby causes the actual money stock to exceed the quantity of money demanded.

In this situation, households find that the quantity of money that they hold exceeds the quantity they desire to hold. Households reduce their money holdings by increasing their purchases of goods and services. Some of these additional purchases are purchases of foreign goods and services. Depending on the type of exchange-rate arrangement, the increase in the demand for foreign goods and services will have one of two effects. Under a fixed-exchange-rate arrangement, the additional purchases of foreign goods and services will generate a balance-of-payments deficit, with no change in the exchange value of the domestic currency. Under a flexible-exchange-rate arrangement, the additional purchases of foreign goods and services will cause the domestic currency to depreciate, with no change in the balance of payments.

Under a fixed-exchange-rate arrangement the nation's monetary authorities must intervene via a sale of foreign exchange reserves in order to maintain the pegged exchange value of its currency through a sale of foreign exchange reserves. As a result, foreign exchange reserves decline, while the spot exchange rate remains constant.

Let's consider the size of the foreign exchange intervention that the monetary authorities must undertake to maintain the pegged-exchange value of the domestic currency. We shall denote the pegged-exchange value of the domestic currency as S and the new level of domestic credit as DC'. At this new level of domestic credit, the money stock exceeds the quantity of money demanded, expressed as

$$m(DC' + FER) > kSP^*y.$$

To prevent the domestic currency from depreciating, the domestic central bank must reduce the quantity of money supplied so that it equals the quantity of money demanded. To do so, the central bank must sell sufficient foreign reserves to exactly offset the increase in domestic credit, returning the money stock to its original level. At this level, households' desired quantity of money again equals the quantity of money supplied.

As discussed earlier, a decline in foreign exchange reserves is equivalent to a balance-of-payments deficit. The amount of the balance-of-payments deficit, therefore, is equal to the change in the foreign exchange reserves component of the monetary base, which is equal to the change in domestic credit brought about by the central bank's open-market transaction. We can conclude that, under a fixed-exchange-rate arrangement, the monetary approach indicates that an increase in domestic credit generates a balance-of-payments deficit, whereas a decrease in domestic credit results in a balance-of-payments surplus.

A Change in the Quantity of Money Demanded Let's continue our example of a small nation that pegs the exchange value of its currency. Suppose that instead of a change in domestic credit there is an increase in either the foreign price level or real income. According to the Cambridge equation that we modified by including absolute purchasing power parity, an increase in either of these two variables causes an increase in the quantity of money demanded.

In this situation, households find that their desired quantity of money falls short of their current money holdings. Households will increase their money holdings by reducing their expenditures on goods and services. As a result, households' demands for domestic *and* foreign goods and services decline. The decline in demand for foreign goods and services results in either a balance-of-payments surplus or an appreciation of the domestic currency. To maintain the pegged-exchange value of the domestic currency, the central bank must buy foreign reserves.

Let's consider the size of foreign exchange intervention the central bank must undertake to maintain the pegged-exchange value of the domestic currency. Let's also continue to denote the pegged-exchange value of the domestic currency as *S,* and let's denote the higher foreign price level or higher level of real income as $(P*y)'$. The higher foreign price level or higher level of real income causes the quantity of money demanded to exceed the quantity of money supplied, expressed as

$$m(DC + FER) < kS(P*y)'.$$

To prevent the domestic currency from appreciating, the domestic monetary authorities must increase the quantity of money supplied so that it equals the quantity of money demanded. To accomplish this, the central bank buys foreign exchange reserves. The increase in foreign exchange reserves is equivalent to a balance-of-payments surplus, with the size of the surplus equal to the change in foreign exchange reserves. We can conclude that a rise in either the foreign price level or domestic real income results in a balance-of-payments surplus. Likewise, a decline in either the foreign price level or domestic real income results in a balance-of-payments deficit. (Recently, even nations that are certain that they want to peg their currencies are rethinking the currency to which they wish to peg; see *Policy Notebook: The Oil-Rich Middle East Begins to Desert the Sinking Dollar.*)

 **POLICY Notebook**

The Oil-Rich Middle East Begins to Desert the Sinking Dollar

As the U.S. inflation rate approached 6 percent during the late 2000s, oil-producing Middle Eastern nations that had long pegged their currency values to the dollar began to reconsider. By the end of 2007, both Syria and Kuwait had switched to pegging to broader currency baskets. At that time, Qatar's finance minister, Youssef Hussein Kamal, dismissed rumors that his country might be next in line, saying, "Why should I change the peg when 100 percent of my exports and products are in the U.S. dollar?" Nevertheless, when the government of the United Arab Emirates announced in 2008 that it was contemplating an end to its own dollar peg, Qatar's support for its own peg began to waver. Some experts predict that within a few years, all the nations of the oil-rich Middle Eastern region will have switched from dollar pegs to currency-basket pegs.

The reason is that keeping their exchange rates pegged to the value of the dollar in the face of a higher U.S. price level required allowing their own levels of prices to rise. To see why, note that in our simple monetary model, with the exchange rate fixed at a given value $S = \bar{S}$, the purchasing-power-parity condition yields $P = \bar{S} \times P^*$, where for a Middle Eastern nation P is the domestic price level and P^* is the U.S. price level. This implies that in order to keep its exchange rates fixed, a rise in the U.S. price level would require each of these nations to allow its own price level to increase. Maintaining their dollar pegs therefore required these nations essentially to "import" U.S. inflation into their own small open economies—something they were not willing to do.

For Critical Analysis

When oil-producing Middle Eastern countries were pegging to the dollar, how did their reserves of dollars have to adjust to keep their exchange rates fixed as the U.S. price level increased?

The Monetary Approach and a Flexible-Exchange-Rate Arrangement

Suppose now that the small nation we have been considering no longer pegs the exchange value of the domestic currency. Initially, its central bank allows the spot exchange rate to be freely determined in the foreign exchange market. Under a flexible-exchange-rate arrangement such as this, the domestic central bank does not intervene in the foreign exchange market. The foreign exchange reserves component of the monetary base, therefore, remains unchanged, and the nation has neither a balance-of-payments surplus nor a balance-of-payments deficit. The spot exchange rate, as we have seen, is determined by the quantity of money supplied and the quantity of money demanded.

A Change in Domestic Credit Suppose that, as in the earlier example, the domestic central bank increases domestic credit through a purchase of securities. Domestic credit and the domestic money stock rise, and the money stock exceeds the quantity of money demanded.

In this situation, households find that their money holdings exceed the quantity of money they desire. Households reduce their money holdings by increasing their expenditures on goods and services, with some of these expenditures on foreign goods and services. As households increase their expenditures on foreign goods and services, the domestic currency depreciates.

The domestic currency will continue to depreciate until the quantity of money supplied equals the quantity of money demanded. It is in this regard that the spot exchange rate is determined by the quantity of money supplied and the quantity of money demanded. We can conclude, therefore, that under a flexible-exchange-rate arrangement, the monetary approach indicates that an increase in domestic credit results in a depreciation of the domestic currency, whereas a decline in domestic credit results in an appreciation of the domestic currency.

A Change in the Quantity of Money Demanded If the foreign price level or domestic real income increases, then according to the Cambridge equation, the quantity of money demanded increases. As a result, the quantity of money demanded exceeds the quantity of money supplied.

In this situation, households find that their current money holdings fall short of the quantity desired. Households increase their money holdings by reducing their expenditures on domestic and foreign goods and services. The decrease in demand for foreign goods and services causes the domestic currency to appreciate. This appreciation continues until the quantity of money supplied once again equals the quantity of money demanded, so that households find that their actual money holdings match their desired money holdings.

We can conclude, therefore, that under a flexible-exchange-rate arrangement, the monetary approach theorizes that an increase in the foreign price level or domestic real income results in an appreciation of the domestic currency. By way of contrast, a decline in the foreign price level or domestic real income results in a depreciation of the domestic currency.

Fundamental ISSUES

#3 What is the monetary approach to balance-of-payments and exchange-rate determination?

The monetary approach postulates that changes in the balance of payments or exchange rate result from differences between the quantity of money supplied and the quantity of money demanded. Additionally, the monetary approach assumes that when an event causes a difference between the quantity of money supplied and the quantity of money demanded, it triggers an automatic adjustment that eventually eliminates the difference. Under a fixed-exchange-rate arrangement, a difference between the quantity of money supplied and the quantity of money demanded causes a change in the nation's balance of payments. Under a flexible-exchange-rate arrangement, the exchange value of the domestic currency changes.

APPLYING THE MONETARY APPROACH: A TWO-COUNTRY SETTING

We have not yet considered how changes in the quantity of money supplied and demanded *in another nation* might affect the spot exchange rate. Economists have, however, found the monetary approach very illuminating in examining how the balance-of-payments accounts and currency values of *two nations* interact.

A Two-Country Monetary Model

To extend the monetary approach in a two-country setting, we must specify a Cambridge equation of money demand for each nation. We shall denote the individual nations with subscripts *A* and *B*. The Cambridge equations, equilibrium conditions, and absolute-purchasing-power-parity condition for the two nations are as follows:

$$M_A^d = k_A P_A y_A, \qquad M_B^d = k_B P_B y_B$$
$$M_A = M_A^d, \qquad M_B = M_B^d$$
$$P_A = S P_B.$$

where the spot exchange rate S is expressed as the number of units of Country A's currency per unit of Country B's currency.

To derive a single expression for the spot rate, we first substitute the Cambridge equation for each nation into the equilibrium conditions to yield

$$M_A = k_A P_A y_A, \qquad M_B = k_B P_B y_B.$$

Next, we substitute the absolute-purchasing-power-parity condition into the equilibrium condition for Country A, which yields

$$M_A = k_A S P_B y_A, \qquad M_B = k_B P_B y_B.$$

Now we divide Country A's equilibrium condition by Country B's equilibrium condition:

$$\frac{M_A}{M_B} = \frac{k_A S P_B y_A}{k_B P_B y_B},$$

or, more simply:

$$\frac{M_A}{M_B} = S \times \frac{k_A y_A}{k_B y_B}.$$

Finally, we rearrange the expression by dividing each side of the equation by the ratio of each nation's quantity of money demanded, to obtain:

$$S = \frac{M_A}{M_B} \times \frac{k_B y_B}{k_A y_A}.$$

This expression illustrates the monetary approach to exchange-rate determination in a two-country setting. That is, the spot exchange rate is determined by the *relative quantities of money supplied* and the *relative quantities of money demanded*.

With this specification we can see how a change in the relative money stocks or in the relative quantities of money demanded brings about a change in the spot exchange rate. For example, if there is an increase in the money stock of Country A, all other things unchanged, then the spot exchange rate rises. That is, Country A's currency depreciates relative to Country B's currency. If there is an increase in the real income of Country A, then the *relative* quantity of money demanded declines and the spot exchange rate falls, or Country A's currency appreciates relative to Country B's currency.

An Example of Exchange-Rate Determination for Two Nations

Suppose that Australian nominal GDP is A\$1,084,900 million and that Australian real GDP is A\$957,630 million. In addition, New Zealand's nominal GDP is NZ\$175,090 and its real GDP is NZ\$136,990. During the same period, Australia's money stock is A\$225,921 million, and New Zealand's money stock is NZ\$23,537 million. Now we can calculate the fraction of nominal income held as money, *k,* for each nation by dividing the money stock by nominal GDP. These calculations show that the fraction of nominal income held as money balances in Australia is 0.21 and that the fraction of nominal income held as money balances in New Zealand is 0.13.

To learn more about the economies of New Zealand and Australia, visit the Reserve Bank of New Zealand at *http://www.rbnz.govt.nz* and the Reserve Bank of Australia at *http://www.rba.gov.au*.

Using this information, we can employ the two-country monetary approach to calculate the equilibrium spot exchange rate between the Australian dollar and the New Zealand dollar. Using a subscript A to denote Australia and a subscript NZ to denote New Zealand, we can express the two-country monetary approach for this example as

$$S = \frac{M_A}{M_{NZ}} \times \frac{k_{NZ} y_{NZ}}{k_A y_A}.$$

Substituting the values of the money stock and real GDP for each nation into this equation yields

$$S = \frac{A\$225,921}{NZ\$23,537} \times \frac{0.13(NZ\$136,990)}{0.21(A\$957,630)}$$

or

$$S = 0.8500.$$

Thus, the equilibrium spot exchange rate between the Australian dollar and the New Zealand dollar is 0.8500 Australian dollars per New Zealand dollar.

Now let's consider the effect of an increase in the Australian monetary stock. Suppose the Australian money stock rises by 5 percent to A\$237,217, while the New Zealand money stock remains the same. Substituting this new value for the Australian money stock in the previous equation yields a new value for the spot exchange rate of

$$S = \frac{A\$237,217}{NZ\$23,537} \times \frac{0.13(NZ\$136,990)}{0.21(A\$957,630)}$$

or

$$S = 0.8925.$$

Hence, the increase in the Australian money stock causes the equilibrium spot exchange rate to increase from 0.8500 A\$/NZ\$ to 0.8925 A\$/NZ\$. The resulting depreciation of the Australian dollar relative to the New Zealand dollar is 5 percent $[(0.8925 - 0.8500)/0.8500 - 100 = 5\%]$.

Thus, the two-country monetary approach indicates that the spot exchange rate is determined by the relative quantity of money demanded and the relative quantity of money supplied. A nation that increases its money stock causes its currency to depreciate. Similarly, a nation that experiences an increase in the quantity of money demanded, all other things constant, experiences an appreciation of its currency.

Fundamental ISSUES

#4 How is the monetary approach a theory of exchange-rate determination in a two-country setting?

According to the monetary approach in a two-country setting, the spot exchange rate is determined by the relative quantity of money supplied and the relative quantity of money demanded. In general, if all other things are the same, a nation that increases its money stock causes its currency to depreciate. In contrast, a nation whose households demand a larger quantity of money experiences an appreciation of its currency.

THE PORTFOLIO APPROACH TO EXCHANGE-RATE DETERMINATION

The monetary approach to balance-of-payments and exchange-rate determination focuses on the quantity of money demanded and the quantity of money supplied. The portfolio approach expands the monetary approach by recognizing that households may desire to hold other financial instruments, such as domestic and foreign securities. Hence, the ***portfolio approach*** postulates that the exchange value of a nation's currency is determined by the quantities of domestic money and domestic and foreign securities demanded and the quantities of various financial instruments supplied in the markets for these instruments.

Households' Allocation of Wealth

To make our exposition of the portfolio approach simple, we focus on only three types of financial instruments: domestic money, domestic bonds, and foreign bonds. The portfolio approach assumes that individuals earn interest for holding bonds but receive no interest for holding money. It follows that households have no incentive to hold the foreign currency, which they can obtain in the spot exchange market if they wish to conduct a foreign transaction.

As discussed in Chapters 4 and 5, however, the domestic and foreign bonds have elements of risk that money does not. To balance the risk and returns on these instruments, households desire to distribute their wealth over all three types of instruments. A ***wealth identity*** expresses this notion as

$$W \equiv M + B + SB^*,$$

where W denotes household wealth, M denotes the wealth that households desire to hold as money, B denotes the wealth that households desire to hold as domestic bonds, S denotes the spot exchange value of the domestic currency defined as domestic currency units per foreign currency units, and B^* denotes the wealth that households desire to hold as foreign bonds. A wealth identity shows the types of assets that constitute the household's total stock of wealth.

The portfolio approach, therefore, assumes that the exchange value of a nation's currency is determined by the quantities of each of these financial instruments supplied and the quantities demanded. Hence, in contrast to the monetary approach, differences between the quantities of domestic and foreign bonds demanded and supplied are as important as the differences in the quantities of domestic money demanded and supplied.

portfolio approach
Relates changes in a nation's balance of payments and the exchange value of its currency to the quantities demanded and supplied of domestic money, domestic securities, and foreign securities.

A Change in the Domestic Money Stock Let's consider, within the context of the portfolio model, the effect of an open-market operation on the exchange value of the domestic currency. Suppose the central bank wishes to increase the domestic money stock and undertakes an open-market purchase of domestic bonds. As explained earlier, the open-market purchase causes the domestic money supply to rise and the domestic interest rate to decline.

As the domestic interest rate declines, households find they are no longer satisfied with their current allocation of wealth. The decline in the domestic interest rate causes a decline in the quantity of domestic bonds demanded by households. Households have the same stock of wealth to allocate over all three instruments, however. Hence, as the quantity of domestic bonds demanded falls, the quantity of domestic money and foreign bonds demanded increases. Figure 9–7 illustrates the effect on the spot exchange rate of the change in households' quantity demanded of all three instruments. Initially, the spot exchange market is in equilibrium at point $A,$ at which the domestic interest rate is equal to R_1. As households buy more foreign bonds, the demand for the foreign currency rises, shown by the rightward shift of the demand curve from $D_{FC}(R_1)$ to $D_{FC}(R_2)$. As a result of the increase in demand for the foreign currency, the spot exchange rate rises from S_1 to S_2. Thus, the domestic currency depreciates. We can conclude, therefore, that the portfolio approach postulates that a decline in the domestic interest rate results in a depreciation of the domestic currency, and a rise in the domestic interest rate results in an appreciation of the domestic currency.

Consistent with the monetary approach to exchange-rate determination, the portfolio approach predicts that an open-market purchase of securities leads to a domestic currency depreciation. There is a striking difference between the two approaches, however. The monetary approach attributes a currency depreciation to changes in the quantity of *money* demanded and supplied. The portfolio approach attributes a currency depreciation to changes in the quantities demanded and supplied of *all the instruments* that constitute households' stock of wealth.

A Change in the Foreign Interest Rate Consider the effect of a rise in the foreign interest rate on the spot exchange rate. Because of the change in the foreign interest rate, households desire to hold larger quantities of foreign bonds and smaller quantities of domestic money and domestic bonds.

Figure 9–8 on the next page shows the effect of a change in the foreign interest rate on the spot exchange rate. Initially, the spot exchange market is in equilibrium

Figure 9–7

A Decrease in the Domestic Interest Rate

Initially the spot exchange market is in equilibrium at point A with the initial domestic interest rate denoted R_1. When the domestic interest rate declines, households buy more foreign bonds. As a result, their demand for the foreign currency rises, shown by the rightward shift of the demand curve from $D_{FC}(R_1)$ to $D_{FC}(R_2)$. The increase in the demand for the foreign currency causes the domestic currency to depreciate from S_1 to S_2.

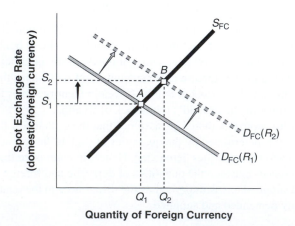

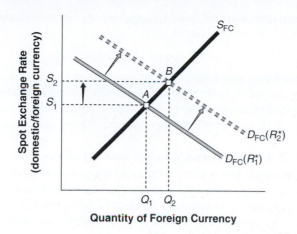

Figure 9–8

An Increase in the Foreign Interest Rate

Initially, the spot exchange market is in equilibrium at point A with the initial foreign interest rate denoted R_1^*. When the foreign interest rate rises to R_2^*, households buy more foreign bonds. Households' demand for the foreign currency rises, shown by the rightward shift of the demand curve from $D_{FC}(R_1^*)$ to $D_{FC}(R_2^*)$. As a result, the domestic currency depreciates from S_1 to S_2.

at a spot exchange rate denoted S_1 at which the foreign interest rate is equal to R_1^*. As households liquidate some of their holdings of domestic money and domestic bonds and begin buying foreign bonds, the demand for the foreign currency rises, shown by the rightward shift of the demand curve from $D_{FC}(R_1^*)$ to $D_{FC}(R_2^*)$. The increase in demand for the foreign currency causes the spot exchange rate to rise from S_1 to S_2. Thus, the domestic currency depreciates. We can conclude that the portfolio approach indicates that an increase in the foreign interest rate causes a depreciation of the domestic currency, and that a decline in the foreign interest rate causes an appreciation of the domestic currency.

$ ¥ £ € Fundamental ISSUES

#5 What is the portfolio approach to exchange-rate determination?

The portfolio approach assumes that households desire to hold domestic and foreign securities along with their holding of money. Hence, the portfolio approach postulates that the value of a nation's currency is determined by the quantity of money and securities demanded and the quantity supplied. An increase in the domestic interest rate causes the domestic currency to appreciate, whereas an increase in the foreign interest rate causes the domestic currency to depreciate.

To Sterilize or Not to Sterilize?

As explained earlier, many nations, such as the United States, fully sterilize their foreign exchange market interventions as a matter of routine. Should nations routinely sterilize their interventions? The answer to this question depends on whether sterilized foreign exchange interventions affect the exchange value of the domestic currency. The monetary and portfolio approaches to exchange-rate determination offer conflicting answers to this question.

Sterilized Foreign Exchange Interventions and the Monetary Approach

According to the monetary approach to exchange-rate determination, differences between the nominal quantity of money supplied and the nominal quantity of money demanded determine the spot exchange rate. Recall the expression for the money stock:

$$M = m(DC + FER),$$

where DC denotes domestic credit, FER denotes foreign exchange reserves, and m is the money multiplier. In the monetary approach, foreign exchange interventions affect the spot exchange value of the domestic currency by increasing or decreasing the domestic monetary base, thereby increasing or decreasing the domestic money stock.

For example, a foreign exchange market intervention that increases foreign exchange reserves leads to a multiple increase in the money stock. Complete sterilization of this intervention entails an open-market sale of securities that reduces domestic credit by an amount equivalent to the increase in foreign exchange reserves. As a result of the open-market transaction, the domestic monetary base remains unchanged, and so does the domestic money stock.

Because sterilized intervention leaves the domestic money stock unchanged, there is no difference between the quantity of money supplied and the quantity of money demanded. Therefore, there is no effect on the exchange value of the domestic currency. Thus, according to the monetary approach, fully sterilized foreign intervention is *ineffective*, because it leaves the exchange value of the domestic currency unchanged.

Sterilized Foreign Exchange Interventions and the Portfolio Approach

According to the portfolio approach, changes in the exchange value of the domestic currency result from differences between the quantities of money and bonds supplied and the quantities demanded. The simple portfolio model assumes that households allocate their wealth across three types of financial instruments—domestic money, domestic bonds, and foreign bonds. Now let's consider the effect of a fully sterilized foreign exchange intervention in this portfolio model.

Foreign exchange reserves typically are foreign-currency-denominated financial instruments, such as treasury bills and bonds. When domestic monetary authorities purchase foreign exchange reserves, the quantity of foreign bonds demanded increases. The increase in the quantity of foreign bonds demanded causes the domestic currency to depreciate.

The purchase of foreign exchange reserves results in an increase in the domestic monetary base and an increase in the domestic money stock. The central bank sterilizes the intervention through an open-market sale of domestic bonds, reducing domestic credit and leaving the domestic monetary base and money stock unchanged. The open-market transaction, however, increases the quantity of domestic bonds available. Hence, sterilized foreign exchange intervention is, in effect, an exchange of domestic bonds for foreign bonds. According to the portfolio approach, the exchange of domestic for foreign bonds results in a depreciation of the domestic currency. Thus, sterilized intervention can be effective.

Do Interventions Accomplish Anything?

If sterilized interventions have no effects, then the implication would be that interventions would be redundant policies. After all, any central bank can vary the amount of money it places in circulation relative to other world currencies through purely domestic policy actions, such as varying interest rates on advances or engaging in open-market operations, which alter the monetary base. Consequently, an important issue for international monetary economists is whether foreign exchange interventions can and do have independent short- and long-term effects on market exchange rates.

Most economists contend that sterilized foreign exchange interventions can, at least in theory, have at most two types of immediate effects on exchange rates. They call one of these the ***portfolio balance effect***: If the exchange rate is viewed as the relative price of imperfectly substitutable assets such as bonds, then changes in government or central bank holdings of bonds and other assets denominated in various currencies can influence exchange rates by affecting the equilibrium prices at which traders are willing to hold these assets. For example, if an intervention reduces the supply of domestic assets relative to foreign assets held by individuals and firms, then the expected return on domestic assets must fall to induce individuals and firms to readjust their portfolios. A reduction in the anticipated rate of return on domestic assets, in turn, requires an appreciation of the domestic currency. Hence, a finance ministry or central bank purchase of domestic currency can, through the portfolio balance effect, cause the value of the domestic currency to rise.

The other possible effect is an intervention *announcement effect* or *signaling effect,* in which foreign exchange interventions may provide traders with previously unknown information that alters their willingness to demand or supply currencies in the foreign exchange markets. The announcement effect can exist, therefore, only if a government or central bank intervention clearly reveals some kind of "inside information" that traders did not have prior to the intervention. For instance, a central bank that plans to conduct a future anti-inflation policy by contracting its money stock may reveal this intention by leaning against the wind in the face of a recent downward trend in the value of its nation's currency. If currency traders believe this message provided by the central bank's intervention, then they will expect a future appreciation and will increase their holdings of the currency. This concerted action by currency traders then causes an actual currency appreciation. Thus, the announcement effect of the intervention, like the portfolio balance effect, induces a rise in the value of the domestic currency.

A major study of foreign exchange market interventions during the 1980s and early 1990s by Kathryn Dominguez of the University of Michigan and Jeffrey Frankel of the University of California at Berkeley found evidence that both effects were at work during that period, especially in the latter part of the 1980s when many of the world's governments conducted sizable interventions. Dominguez and Frankel found that during this interval, in which central banks coordinated several interventions, the *announcements* of the interventions actually had larger effects on exchange rates than the actual magnitudes of the interventions themselves. This, in their view, provides strong evidence of announcement effects in interventions. Particularly in the case of coordinated interventions, traders seem to have viewed interventions as signals of government and central bank commitments to future policy changes and reacted by altering their desired holdings of domestic and foreign assets. The result was changes in market exchange rates, at least in the short run.

More recently, Lucio Sarno and Mark P. Taylor have examined the history of foreign exchange interventions and surveyed the large number of empirical studies conducted since the Plaza Accord. They conclude that coordinated foreign exchange interventions–even those interventions that are sterilized by monetary policymakers–can indeed affect exchange rates. In their opinion, the evidence on foreign exchange interventions supports both the portfolio explanation and the announcement or signaling explanation. They claim, however, that as economies

portfolio balance effect
An exchange-rate adjustment resulting from changes in government or central bank holdings of foreign-currency-denominated financial instruments that influences the equilibrium prices of the instruments.

become more financially integrated and the degree of substitutability of nation's financial assets increases, the portfolio effect is likely to diminish, making the announcement or signaling of foreign exchange interventions even more important for policy effectiveness.

Fundamental ISSUES

#6 Should central banks sterilize foreign exchange interventions?

According to the monetary approach to exchange-rate determination, sterilized foreign exchange interventions are not effective, meaning that these interventions leave the domestic money supply unchanged. According to the portfolio approach, sterilized interventions can be effective, as they alter households' holdings of domestic and foreign bonds. The empirical evidence indicates that sterilized interventions may have some effect on the spot exchange value of a currency through both an announcement effect and a portfolio effect.

Chapter SUMMARY

1. **Central Bank Assets and Liabilities:** The sum of domestic credit—government securities and loans to private banking institutions—and foreign-currency-denominated securities and deposits constitutes the bulk of the assets of major central banks, and the sum of currency notes and reserve deposits of private banking institutions constitutes the bulk of the liabilities of major central banks.

2. **Central Bank Foreign Exchange Market Interventions, the Monetary Base, the Money Stock, and Sterilization:** Central bank foreign exchange interventions alter the nation's monetary base by changing foreign exchange reserves. The change in the monetary base eventually leads to a change in the money stock that is a multiple of the change in the monetary base. Sterilization of a foreign exchange intervention by an open-market transaction can partially or fully offset the effect of the foreign exchange intervention on the monetary base and, therefore, the money stock.

3. **The Monetary Approach to Balance-of-Payments and Exchange-Rate Determination:** The monetary approach to balance-of-payments and exchange-rate determination postulates that changes in a nation's balance of payments or the exchange value of its currency are a monetary phenomenon. That is, these changes are due to a difference between the quantity of money supplied and the quantity of money demanded. In a fixed-exchange-rate arrangement, differences between the quantity of money supplied and the quantity of money demanded determine a nation's balance of payments, whereas in a flexible-exchange-rate arrangement, differences between the quantity of money supplied and the quantity of money demanded determine the spot exchange value of the nation's currency.

4. **The Two-Country Monetary Approach to Exchange-Rate Determination:** Economists often use a two-country monetary approach to exchange-rate determination. According to the two-country monetary approach, the spot exchange rate is determined by the relative quantities of money supplied and the relative quantities of money demanded. A rise in the money stock of one nation causes that nation's currency to depreciate, whereas a rise in one nation's quantity of money demanded causes that nation's currency to appreciate.

5. **The Portfolio Approach to Exchange-Rate Determination:** The portfolio approach assumes that households desire to hold both domestic money and domestic and foreign bonds. Households allocate their wealth across these instruments in order to balance risk and return. As a result, the exchange value of a nation's currency is determined by the quantities of money and domestic and foreign bond demanded and supplied. According to the portfolio approach, an increase in the domestic interest rate results in an appreciation of the domestic currency, whereas an increase in the foreign interest rate results in a depreciation of the domestic currency.

6. **Sterilized versus Nonsterilized Foreign Exchange Interventions:** According to the monetary approach to exchange-rate determination, sterilized foreign exchange interventions are not effective, meaning that they leave the domestic money supply unchanged. According to the portfolio approach, however, sterilized interventions can be effective, because they alter households' holdings of domestic and foreign bonds and, therefore, their relative demands for the foreign currency. Empirical evidence indicates that sterilized interventions may have some effect on the spot exchange value, indicating the possibility of a portfolio effect.

QUESTIONS and PROBLEMS

1. Illustrate a simple balance sheet of the central banks of Japan and Australia. Show in your diagram the effect on the components of the monetary base of each nation of the Bank of Japan selling A$1 million bank deposits. Assume that the spot exchange rate is 58.6 yen-per-Australian dollar (¥/A$).

2. Suppose that the reserve requirement in Australia is 20 percent and that the reserve requirement in Japan is 8 percent. Also suppose that the monetary base consists only of transactions deposits. Using the information in Question 1, what is the maximum possible change in the money stock in each nation?

3. Suppose Japan partially sterilizes the foreign exchange transaction in Question 1 by buying ¥47.5 million of securities. What is the total change in the Japanese money stock that results from both the foreign exchange transaction and the open-market transaction?

4. This chapter presented a simple example of a money multiplier where it was assumed that as the money stock expands, households wish to hold all of their money balances as transactions deposits. Suppose that households wish to hold some fraction of their money balances as currency. Let b denote households' ratio of currency balances to transactions deposits (C/TD). Finally, assume the reserve requirement is 10 percent.
   a. What is the value of the money multiplier if b is zero? (*Hint:* This is the same as the example presented earlier in the text.)
   b. What is the value of the money multiplier if b is 25 percent? (*Hint: b* enters the money multiplier formula in the same way that the reserve requirement does.)

5. Write out an equation representing the monetary approach to balance-of-payments and exchange-rate determination. Suppose that domestic credit equals $1000 million, foreign exchange reserves equal $80 million, the money multiplier is 2, the fraction of nominal income that individuals desire to hold in money balances is 20 percent, the foreign price level is 1.2, and the spot exchange value of the domestic currency is 2. Using this information, what is:
   a. the money stock in the domestic economy?
   b. the level of real income of the domestic economy?

6. Using the information in Question 5, suppose the domestic central bank increases domestic credit by $10 million through an open-market purchase of securities.
   a. Under a fixed-exchange-rate regime, what is the effect of this open-market transaction on the nation's balance of payments?
   b. Under flexible exchange rates, all other things constant, what is the new exchange value of the domestic currency? Is this an appreciation or depreciation?

7. Using the information on the Australian and New Zealand economies on page 261 of this chapter, calculate the effect of a 3 percent increase of New Zealand's monetary base on the following:
   a. the New Zealand money stock.
   b. the equilibrium spot rate under flexible exchange rates.

8. Write out the wealth identity. Using this identity, explain the impact of a central bank open-market sale of bonds on the exchange value of the domestic currency. Now suppose that the exchange rate is pegged. Using the wealth identity, explain the impact of the open-market operation on the domestic nation's balance of payments.

9. Illustrate the spot exchange market for the domestic currency using the supply-and-demand framework. Explain and illustrate the effect of a central bank open-market sale of bonds on the exchange value of the domestic currency.

10. Write out a wealth identity for both the domestic economy and the foreign economy. Using this identity, explain the impact of an open-market sale of bonds by the central bank of the foreign economy on the exchange value between the domestic and foreign currencies.

Online APPLICATIONS

This chapter explained the operation of a currency-basket peg and exchange-rate intervention and its effect on a central bank's reserves. This application examines both concepts in the context of Russia's currency-basket-peg arrangement.

Internet URL: *http://www.cbr.ru/eng/*

Title: Bank of Russia

Navigation: Begin on the home page of the Bank of Russia, the central bank of Russia. On the left-hand side of the page, under the heading *Macroeconomic Indicators*, click on *Russia's International Reserves*. On the left-hand side of the page, enter January 2008. Record the value of Russia's international reserves each January from 2008 through January 2012. Before leaving this page, read the description of Russia's international reserves that is provided in the footnote to the table.

Application: Beginning in 2008, in order to increase the flexibility of the Russian ruble against the U.S. dollar, Russia managed the value of the ruble by pegging it to a basket of currencies that included the euro and the U.S. dollar. During the first six months of 2008, when global oil prices were increasing, there was pressure on the ruble to appreciate. However, oil prices began to decline in the second half of 2008 and through 2009, causing pressure for the ruble to depreciate. In 2010, as a global economic recovery began, oil prices stated to rise again, putting pressure on the ruble to appreciate.

1. Explain the various accounts and assets that comprise Russia's international reserves.

2. Plot the value of Russia's international reserves from January 2008 to January 2012. What was the year-to-year change in the dollar value of international reserves over this

period? What was the year-to-year percentage change in international reserves over this period?

3. Explain how the exchange-rate regime contributed to a decrease in Russia's international reserves from 2008 to 2009

4. Explain how the exchange-rate regime led to an increase in Russia's international reserves from January 2008 through January 2012.

SELECTED REFERENCES and FURTHER READINGS

Aizenman, Joshua, and Jaewoo Lee. "International Reserves: Precautionary vs. Mercantilist Views, Theory and Evidence." International Monetary Fund, IMF Working Paper, WP/05/198 (October 2005).

Aizenman, Joshua, and Reuven Glick. "Sterilization, Monetary Policy, and Global Financial Integration." *Review of International Economics 17*(4) (September 2009): 777–801.

Bordo, Michael D., Owen Humpage, and Anna J. Schwartz. "The Historical Origins of U.S. Exchange Market Intervention Policy." National Bureau of Economic Research, Working Paper 12662 (November 2006).

Brandner, Peter, Harald Grech, and Helmut Stix. "The Effectiveness of Central Bank Intervention in the EMS: The Post 1993 Experience." *Journal of International Money and Finance 25* (2006): 580–597.

Cerra, Valerie, and Sweta Chaman Saxena. "The Monetary Model Strikes Back: Evidence from the World." International Monetary Fund, IMF Working Paper, WP/08/73 (March 2008).

Cushman, David O. "A Portfolio Balance Approach to the Canadian-U.S. Exchange Rate." *Review of Financial Economics 16*(3) (2007): 305–320.

Daniels, Joseph. "Optimal Sterilization Policies in Interdependent Economies." *Journal of Economics and Business 48*(1) (January 1997): 43–60.

de Freitas, Lebre, and Francisco Jose Velga. "Currency Substitution, Portfolio Diversification, and Money Demand." *Canadian Journal of Economics 3* (August 2006): 719–743.

Dominguez, Kathryn M.E. "When Do Central Bank Interventions Influence Intra-Daily and Longer-Term Exchange Rate Movements?" *Journal of International Money and Finance 25* (2006): 1051–1071.

Engel, Charles, and Kenneth D. West. "Exchange Rates and Fundamentals." University of Wisconsin Working Paper, http://www.ssc.wisc.edu/econ/Working Papers/ (April 29, 2003).

European Central Bank. "The Accumulation of Foreign Reserves." Occasional Paper Series, Number 43 (February 2006).

Evans, Martin D. D. "Portfolio Balance, Price Impact, and Secret Intervention." National Bureau of Economic Research, NBER Working Paper 8356 (2001).

Gonçalves, Fernando M. "Accumulating Foreign Reserves under Floating Exchange Rates." International Monetary Fund, IMF Working Paper WP/08/96 (April 2008).

Miller, Victoria. "Getting Out from Between a Rock and a Hard Place: Can China Use Its Foreign Exchange Reserves to Save Its Banks?" *Journal of International Financial Markets, Institutions, and Money 16* (2006): 345–354.

Rapach, David E., Mark E. Wohar. "Testing the Monetary Model of Exchange Rate Determination: Evidence from a Century of Data." *Journal of International Economics 58* (2) (2002): 359–385.

Reitz, Stefan, and Mark P. Taylor. "Japanese and Federal Reserve Intervention in the Yen-US Dollar Market: A Coordination Channel of FX Operations?" Department of Economics, Deutsche Bundesbank, and Department of Economics, University of Warwick, http://ssrn.com/abstract=1157679 (April 2008).

Sarno, Lucio, and Mark P. Taylor. "Official Intervention in the Foreign Exchange Market: Is It Effective and, If So, How Does It Work?" *Journal of Economic Literature 39*(3) (2001): 839–868.

Stella, Peter. "Central Bank Financial Strength, Policy Constraints and Inflation." International Monetary Fund, IMF Working Paper WP/08/49 (February 2008).

Wonchang, Jang. "How to Intervene in FX Market: Market Microstructure Approach." *Journal of Economic Development 32*(1) (June 2007): 105–128.

PART 4

■

OPEN ECONOMY MACROECONOMICS AND POLICY ANALYSIS

10 An Open Economy Framework

11 Economic Policy with Fixed Exchange Rates

12 Economic Policy with Floating Exchange Rates

13 The Price Level, Real Output, and Economic Policymaking

10 An Open Economy Framework

$\$¥$ Fundamental **ISSUES**

1. How do economists measure a nation's flow of income and expenditures and its overall level of prices of goods and services?
2. How is equilibrium real income determined in an open economy?
3. What is the *IS* schedule, and what factors determine its position?
4. What is the *LM* schedule, and what factors determine its position?
5. What is an *IS–LM* equilibrium?
6. What is the *BP* schedule, and how can we use the *IS–LM–BP* model to determine a nation's balance-of-payments status?

In contrast to the United States, in which about 70 percent of annual national income goes to consumption of goods and services by households, in China only about 35 percent of national income goes to household consumption. Furthermore, China's share of national income going to consumption spending has declined by more than 10 percentage points during the past decade. One reason that consumption is a smaller share of national income in China is that Chinese households save nearly 20 percent of China's national income, whereas U.S. households typically save less than 6 percent of U.S. national income. Nevertheless, even as the consumption share of national income has declined in China, so has the share of national income going to savings, which is about 5 percentage points lower than a decade ago.

Clearly, given that households are simultaneously consuming and saving less of China's national income, the share of national income being spent in other sectors of the economy must be rising. In fact, share of national income going to spending by both private firms and the Chinese government has been increasing.

How do we measure the aggregate value of a nation's total production of goods and services and the total flow of income to those who produce it? What factors contribute to determining the equilibrium level of national income in an open economy? These are the questions that we shall begin to discuss in this chapter.

MEASURING AN ECONOMY'S PERFORMANCE: GROSS DOMESTIC PRODUCT AND PRICE INDEXES

To track the overall performances of national economies and the transactions between economies, we require aggregate, or *macroeconomic*, performance measures. These measures include gross domestic product and the national income it generates, price indexes, and the balance of payments. We begin with the most important of these macroeconomic variables, *gross domestic product (GDP)*.

Gross Domestic Product

Economists cannot simply add together the quantities of very different items such as annual oil production, the provision of educational services, and the production of stereo equipment, because their units of measurement are different. We therefore total the *market values* of all final goods and services, measured in terms of prices and expressed in units of a nation's currency. Hence, **gross domestic product (GDP)** is the total of all *final* goods and services produced *domestically* during a given interval (such as a year) and valued at market prices.

> **gross domestic product (GDP)**
> The market value of all final goods and services produced within a nation's borders during a given period.

Economists include only the final goods and services that individuals, businesses, and governments exchange in *markets*. They multiply market prices of goods and services by the quantities of these goods and services produced and sold during a given interval, such as a year. For this reason, GDP excludes non-market transactions such as house-cleaning services, yard work, or fence painting provided by roommates or family members. This activity does not take place in a formal market in which the spouse or roommate receives payment for providing such services. In addition, because GDP measures a nation's production, it includes only the values of *goods and services*. GDP does not include the exchange of stocks, bonds, or other such financial assets, which do not involve the production of new output.

Finally, GDP counts only the production of goods and services in their *final form* during a specific interval. If a computer manufacturer purchases microchips from various suppliers and uses them in the production of laptop computers and sells the assembled computers within the same year, then only the final price of the *computer* counts in tabulating that year's GDP. The market value of the microchips is not separately included in GDP because their market value is reflected in the sale price of the laptop computers.

Nevertheless, if the computer manufacturer stores some microchips or perhaps some partially assembled laptop computers at its assembling facility, then we count the market values of these microchips—as well as all partially assembled and unsold assembled computers—as *inventory investment* for that year. Inventory investment includes all of the production during the year that firms did not sell for final consumption. The tabulation of GDP always includes such inventory investment, which ensures that GDP measures all production during a given year.

GDP also includes the value of *depreciation*, which is the value of *capital goods* such as machines or tools that are repaired or replaced if businesses are to maintain their existing amount of capital. Depreciation expenses reflect the consumption of or wear and tear on physical capital that occurs during the current-year production of goods and services. The term *gross* means that GDP does not adjust for depreciation. Economists subtract depreciation from GDP to obtain *net domestic product*.

Nominal GDP, Real GDP, and the GDP Price Deflator

Figure 10–1 shows that GDP for the United States, Germany, Mexico, and South Korea has risen each year since 1955. There are two reasons for these increases. One is that in most years the nations' production of goods and services has actually increased. During this period, businesses in these countries expanded their resources and developed innovative ways to increase their production.

This does not mean that these nations' actual production increased in every year, however. Aggregate production actually declined in some years, even though GDP for those years increased. The reason that measured GDP still rose in such years is that the prices of goods and services increased in almost every year. Because economists compute GDP using market prices to value the production of firms, general price increases, or inflation, raise the *measured value* of output. Thus, we cannot conclude from Figure 10–1 that total production of goods and services actually increased every year. At least a part of the overall rise in the annual GDP data in the figure occurred because of inflation.

It follows that relying on GDP data that are unadjusted for inflation would, during periods when inflation is prevalent, result in persistent *overstatements* of the true amount of aggregate production. Making reliable comparisons of an economy's year-to-year level of aggregate production thereby requires adjusting GDP figures to account for inflation.

Real versus Nominal GDP Consider a situation in which it is clear why we need to adjust for inflation. Suppose that your employer were to promise you a 10 percent annual wage increase. If the prices of all goods and services remained unchanged, then the purchasing power of your labor income would rise by 10 percent. If the prices of the goods and services you consume were to increase by 10 percent during the coming year, however, then the pay raise would do nothing more than maintain your purchasing power. As a result, your *real* income, or income adjusted for price changes, would be no higher than it was before the wage increase.

Figure 10–1

Growth of Nominal GDP of Selected Nations

Nominal GDP has increased each year in the United States, Germany, Mexico, and South Korea because actual production has risen and because the price level has increased.

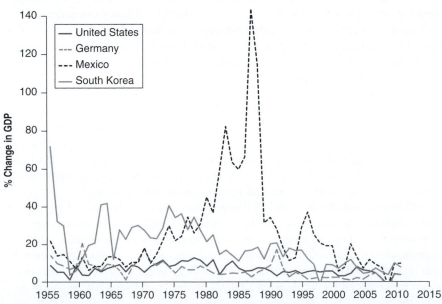

Source: Data from International Monetary Fund, *International Financial Statistics.*

Likewise, if GDP were to rise by 10 percent from one year to the next only because the prices of goods and services rose at that rate, then the aggregate production of goods and services actually would not have changed. The year-to-year change in GDP, then, would be a very poor measure of the *real* annual change in aggregate production.

Economists have addressed this problem by developing an inflation-adjusted measure of GDP, known as **real gross domestic product**, or *real GDP*. This measure of aggregate output takes price changes into account. As a result, real GDP better gauges the economy's true volume of productive activity.

To keep real GDP and the unadjusted GDP measures separate, economists classify the unadjusted GDP measure as **nominal gross domestic product**, or *nominal GDP*. This means that nominal GDP is computed in current dollar terms without any adjustment for inflation.

The GDP Price Deflator Real GDP is intended to gauge a nation's actual production volume. Thus, multiplying real GDP by a measure of the overall price level for all goods and services should render the value of real GDP in terms of current prices, which, by definition, is nominal GDP. Let's denote real GDP as y and the overall price level as P. Then it follows that nominal GDP, which we shall denote as Y, must be

$$Y \equiv y \times P.$$

Hence, nominal GDP is equal to real GDP times the overall price level.

Economists call the factor P the **GDP price deflator**, or simply the *GDP deflator*. We call P a *deflator* because if we rearrange the previous equation to solve for y, we obtain

$$y \equiv \frac{Y}{P}.$$

Thus, real GDP (y) is equal to nominal GDP (Y) adjusted by dividing, or "deflating," by the factor P. For example, suppose that South Korean nominal GDP measured in current prices, Y, is equal to 1351.2 trillion won (KW1351.2 trillion) but the value of the GDP deflator, P, is equal to 1.21. Computing real GDP, then, entails dividing the KW1351.2 trillion nominal GDP by 1.21, to get approximately KW1116.7 trillion for South Korean real GDP.

On the WEB

Learn more about the South Korean economy at Statistics Korea at *http://kostat.go.kr.*

Denoting a Base Year A value of 1.21 for the GDP deflator P gives us little useful information unless we also have a point of reference for judging what this value means. Economists provide such a reference point by defining a **base year** for the GDP deflator. A base year is a year in which nominal GDP is equal to real GDP ($Y = y$), so that the value of the GDP deflator by definition is equal to one ($P = 1$). Therefore, if the base year were, say, 2003, and the value of P in 2013 were equal to 2, then this would indicate that between 2003 and 2013 the overall level of prices would have doubled.

real gross domestic product
A price-adjusted measure of aggregate output, or nominal GDP divided by the GDP price deflator.

nominal gross domestic product
The current market value of all final goods and services produced by a nation during a given period with no adjustment for prices.

GDP price deflator
A measure of the overall price level; equal to nominal gross domestic product divided by real gross domestic product.

base year
A reference year for price-level comparisons, which is a year in which nominal GDP is equal to real GDP, so that the GDP deflator's value is equal to one.

The South Korean government currently uses 2005 as the base year for the GDP deflator. Panel (a) of Figure 10–2 shows the values of the South Korean GDP deflator since 1970. As you can see, the overall level of prices increased by a factor of almost 37, from 0.033 to about 1.21 between 1970 and 2013. This means that an item that required KW1 to purchase in 1970 would have required nearly KW37 to purchase in 2013.

Panel (b) plots South Korea's real and nominal GDP figures since 1970. Note that in 2005, nominal and real GDP are equal because 2005 is the base year in which $P = 1$, so that $Y = y$. Clearly, adjusting for price changes has a significant

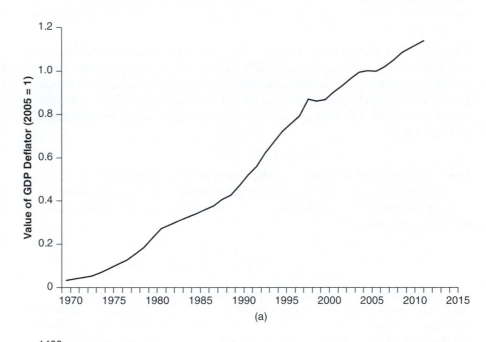

(a)

Figure 10–2

The GDP Deflator and Real and Nominal GDP

Panel (a) shows annual values of the GDP deflator for South Korea. Panel (b) displays South Korean nominal GDP and real GDP. As panel (b) shows, because real GDP accounts for changes in prices, it exhibits less growth each year.

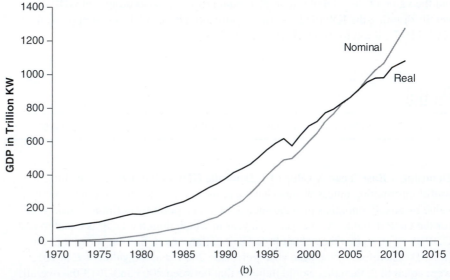

(b)

Source: Bank of Korea, www.bok.or.kr/eng

effect on our interpretation of GDP data. This is why it is so important for us to convert nominal GDP into real GDP using the GDP price deflator. Thus:

> **Only real GDP data can provide useful information about true year-to-year changes in an economy's productive performance.**

(Economists typically measure the pace of a nation's economic growth as the rate of change in real GDP per capita, or real GDP per person; to think about how they measure *world* economic growth, see *Policy Notebook: Global Real GDP Calculations Reveal the Rapid Pace of World Economic Growth*.)

POLICY Notebook

Global Real GDP Calculations Reveal the Rapid Pace of World Economic Growth

To compute world per capita real GDP, economists must account for the fact that prices of goods and services in different countries are measured in terms of the nations' various currencies, such as the dollar, the euro, and the yen. Thus, economists typically begin by converting the value of every country's GDP into U.S. dollars, which is accomplished by multiplying the country's GDP by the exchange rate of the dollar for its currency. Then they engage in purchasing-power-parity adjustments to take into account how nations' price levels vary in relation to the U.S. price level. Next, they develop *worldwide* GDP deflators to adjust the resulting global GDP measure for inflation, thereby computing a measure of world *real* GDP. Dividing world real GDP by the estimated world population yields world per capita real GDP. Finally, by computing annual percentage changes in world per capita real GDP, economists measure global economic growth.

World per capita real GDP increased at an average annual rate of only 1.3 percent per year between 1870 and 1913. The highest average global economic growth rate recorded subsequently was 2.9 percent, which occurred during the period 1950–1973. During the first decade of this century, world per capita real GDP grew at an average annual rate of 3.1 percent, the highest average rate of measured global economic growth in human history.

For Critical Analysis

Based on what you learned about relative purchasing power parity in Chapter 2, why do you suppose that purchasing-power-parity adjustments are part of the procedure for computing world real GDP?

On the WEB

To obtain various GDP measurements on a wide variety of countries, visit the Penn World Tables at *http://pwt.econ.upenn.edu*.

Fixed- and Flexible-Weight Price Measures

The GDP deflator is an example of a *price index*. A price index is a measure of the general price level calculated by tracking the prices of a specific set of goods and services from period to period (usually month to month). As in the case of the GDP deflator, economists must select a base year for any alternative price index. In addition, economists must also determine the types of goods and services and their significance in the index. Weighting the goods in the index usually follows two types of approaches: a flexible-weight basis or a fixed-weight basis.

The GDP Price Deflator: A Flexible-Weight Price Index The GDP price deflator employed in the previous section to convert nominal GDP to real GDP is an example of a flexible-weight price index. A flexible-weight price index is a price index in which weights on various goods and services change automatically as the output of goods and services varies over time.

Fixed-Weight Price Indexes Alternative measures of the overall price level are fixed-weight price indexes. Economists calculate the measures of the economy-wide price level by selecting a fixed set of goods and services and then tracking the prices of these specific goods and services from year to year.

As a simple example of such a fixed-weight price index, let's construct one of our own. Let's call it the "college consumer price index." Suppose that the "typical" college student spends one-fourth of his or her available resources on tuition, one-fourth on housing, one-fourth on food and clothing, and one-fourth on supplies and other expenses. We could then go out and collect information on the average prices of each of these components of the typical college student's expenses. Then we could multiply each one by one-fourth. Summing the results would then yield a numerical value for our college consumer price index.

consumer price index (CPI)

A weighted sum of the prices of goods and services that the government determines a typical consumer purchases each year.

The Consumer and Producer Price Indexes The agencies of national governments compute actual, overall *consumer price indexes (CPIs)* in the same basic manner as in our fictitious example. CPIs, however, are weighted sums of the prices of a full set of goods and services that governments determine typical domestic consumers purchase. Various categories of expenditures that governments incorporate into their weighting scheme for CPIs are a typical consumer's annual purchases of food and beverages, shelter, fuel and other utilities, transportation, and medical care. In the United States, the Bureau of Labor Statistics (BLS) is the government agency that collects the price data to compute the CPI. The BLS samples prices on about 95,000 different items. In addition, the BLS calculates a number of alternative consumer price indexes, such as CPIs for urban consumers, for rural consumers, and so on. (To contemplate whether there is a link between wages earned by Chinese workers and consumer prices paid by U.S. residents, see *Management Notebook: The Tenuous Link from Chinese Wages to U.S. Consumer Prices.*)

MANAGEMENT Notebook

The Tenuous Link from Chinese Wages to U.S. Consumer Prices

Every few months during recent years, media outlets such as the *Wall Street Journal* ran articles with headlines such as, "Change in China Hits U.S. Purse" or "U.S. Shoppers Foot Bill for Soaring Pay in China." Such articles suggest that 10 to 15 percent annual increases in Chinese labor costs and associated 3 to 4 percent hikes in average prices of U.S. imports from China as explanations when there are sudden monthly jumps in the annualized rate of increase of U.S. consumer prices.

To be sure, U.S. residents import a considerable amount of items from China. U.S. imports from China constitute about 16 percent of total U.S imports and account for about 70 percent of the U.S. merchandise trade deficit. Nevertheless, during recent years, U.S. imports from China have made up only about 2.5 percent of the annual U.S. GDP flow. Could higher wages paid to Chinese workers really cause the U.S. CPI inflation to ratchet upward in a given month? According to analysis by Galina Hale and Bart Hobijn of the Federal Reserve Bank of San Francisco, the answer is certainly no. Hale and Hobijn provide evidence that U.S. imports of goods and services from China account for only 2.7 percent of U.S. personal consumption expenditures. Furthermore, they find that of this amount, only 1.2 percent actually represented China-produced content. Thus, during a year in which the average prices of Chinese imports into the United States happen to rise by 4 percent, the annualized U.S. CPI inflation rate would at most rise by less than 0.05 percentage point. For a single month, however, the CPI inflation impact would be about 0.004 percentage point. Thus, Hale and Hobijn conclude, "[I]t is unlikely that recent increases in labor costs and inflation in China will generate broad-based inflationary pressures in the United States."

For Critical Analysis

Given that China recently passed Canada to become the largest national source of U.S. imports, could higher labor costs in any single nation in the world likely have a substantial effect on U.S. consumer price inflation? Explain.

Source: Galina Hale and Bart Hobijn, "The U.S. Content of 'Made in China,'" Federal Reserve Bank of San Francisco, *Economic Letter* 2011-25 (August 8, 2011).

Another fixed-weight price index that many governments calculate is the ***producer price index (PPI)***. This is a weighted average of the prices of goods at which a typical business firm sells its products. Like the CPI, most governments compute several versions of the PPI. The basic categories used in various PPI weighting schemes are finished goods; intermediate materials, supplies, and components; crude materials that require extensive additional processing by a business firm; and food materials.

Economists often prefer to use the GDP deflator as a basic measure of the overall, or economy-wide, price level. Nevertheless, as you know from your own experience, the media most commonly report inflation rates using annual percentage changes in the CPI. Further, the United States and many other countries use the CPI to adjust certain government benefits, such as government pensions and welfare payments, to account for price changes.

We should note, however, that the GDP price deflator and the CPI generally give us the same basic indications about the overall price level. Figure 10–3 on the next page shows annual values of the GDP price deflator and the CPI for the United States since 1959. As you can see, both follow roughly the same path. From a broad perspective, therefore, both price measures provide similar information.

producer price index (PPI)

A weighted average of the prices of goods and services that the government determines a typical business receives from selling its products during a given period.

On the WEB

To obtain monthly consumer price and producer price information, visit the U.S. Bureau of Labor Statistics at *http://www.bls.gov.*

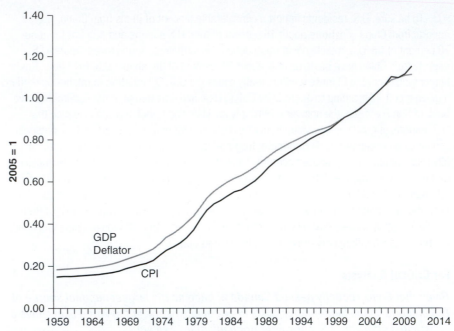

Figure 10–3

U.S. GDP Deflator and Consumer Price Index

Although the U.S. GDP deflator and the U.S. CPI are computed differently, they tend to move closely together over time.

Source: Data from *Economic Report of the President*, various issues.

REAL INCOME AND EXPENDITURES: THE *IS* SCHEDULE

real consumption spending

The real amount of expenditures by households on domestically produced goods and services.

real saving

The amount of income that households save through financial markets.

real net taxes

The amount of real taxes paid to the government by households, net of transfer payments.

transfer payments

Governmentally managed income redistributions.

real import spending

The real flow of expenditures by households for the purchase of goods and services from firms in other countries.

To understand the factors that influence a nation's overall economic performance as measured by its GDP, we must consider the determination of its equilibrium level of real income.

Figure 10–4 shows the flows of income and expenditures in a typical economy. By examining these flows, we can deduce key relationships that must exist among various components of income and expenditures.

The first of these relationships concerns the real value of household income, y, and the real value of firms' output. As you can see in Figure 10–4, once households receive income payments, they can allocate them to several uses. Nevertheless, ultimately all real household income flows back to firms. Consequently, the total real value of firms' output also must equal y:

> The real value of household income is equal to the real value of the output produced by firms.

By definition, therefore, real income and real output are equivalent.

The Income Identity The circular-flow diagram in Figure 10–4 indicates that a nation's households can allocate their real income in four ways. One income allocation is to *real consumption spending*, c, which is the real value of household expenditures on domestically produced goods and services. Additionally, households can allocate part of their real income to *real saving*, s. Households save by purchasing financial claims issued in financial markets. *Real net taxes*, t, are total tax payments, net of *transfer payments*, which are governmentally mandated redistributions of income among various households. A final possible household income allocation is to real expenditures on *foreign-produced goods* and services, which economists call *real import spending*, im. (Throughout, we shall assume that only households import foreign-produced goods and services.)

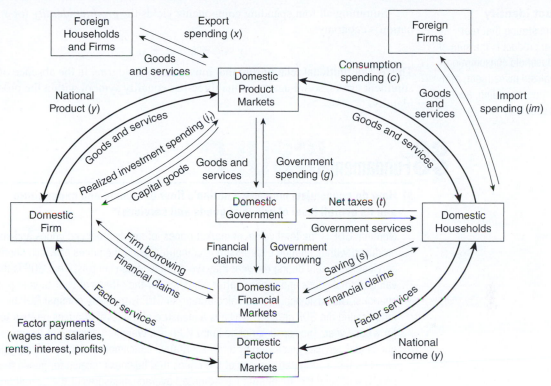

Figure 10–4   The Circular Flow of Income and Expenditures

The earnings that firms derive from producing goods and services and supplying them in product markets ultimately flow to households, which own the firms and the factors of production. Households consume domestic goods and services, import foreign goods and services, save, and pay net taxes. Households, firms, the government, and foreign residents purchase the goods and services that firms produce.

It follows that real income must equal the sum of real consumption, real saving, real net taxes, and real imports:

$$y \equiv c + s + t + im.$$

This is called the **income identity**. The three-bar equality symbol means that the income identity is a definitional relationship that must always hold true.

The Product Identity Figure 10–4 shows that a nation's firms borrow part of real household saving and, in exchange, provide financial claims, such as stocks and bonds. Firms issue these claims in financial markets, and they use the funds that they attract from households to purchase services and goods—such as capital goods, from other firms—and to finance inventories of unsold goods. Together, these real expenditures of firms on goods and services constitute **real realized investment spending**, denoted i_r.

Part of household saving may also be channeled to the nation's government. The government then uses these funds to cover any budget deficit, or the difference between real government spending, g, and real net taxes, t. Like firms, the government borrows by issuing bonds and other financial claims to savers in financial markets.

As Figure 10–4 indicates, household consumption, firm realized investment, and government spending are the three *domestic* components of total spending on domestically produced output. The final component of spending on domestically produced goods and services is expenditures by foreign residents on the output that domestic firms export abroad, or the nation's **real export spending**, denoted x.

income identity
A truism stating that real income is allocated among real household consumption, real household saving, real net taxes, and real imports.

real realized investment spending
Actual real firm expenditures in the product markets.

real export spending
Real value of goods and services produced by domestic firms and exported to other countries.

product identity
A truism stating that real national product is the sum of real household consumption, real realized investment, real government spending, and real export spending.

Summing all four spending components yields the ***product identity*** for a nation's economy:

$$y \equiv c + i_r + g + x.$$

This is a definitional relationship that must always hold true, in the absence of measurement errors, so we again use the three-bar equality symbol within the product identity.

#1 How do economists measure a nation's flow of income and expenditure and its overall level of prices of goods and services?

Nominal GDP is the total value, at market prices, of newly produced goods and services produced within a nation's borders. It is computed using the prices at which goods and services were sold during the year they were produced. In contrast, real GDP is the value of final goods and services after adjusting for the effects of year-to-year price changes. The basic approach to calculating real GDP is to divide nominal GDP by a price index called the GDP deflator, which is a measure of the level of prices relative to prices for a base year. The consumer price index (CPI) is a weighted average of the prices of goods and services purchased by a representative consumer, and the producer price index (PPI) is a weighted average of the prices that business receive for goods that they sell. The CPI and PPI are alternative weighted-average measures of the overall price level, in which the weights of different goods are invariant over time. An examination of a nation's circular flow of real income and expenditures reveals three fundamental relationships. One is that the real value of income must equal the real value of output. A second is the income identity, which says that all real income must be split among real consumption, real saving, real net taxes, and real imports. The third is the product identity, which states that the real value of total output of goods and services must equal the sum of real consumption, real realized investment, real government spending, and real exports.

Private and Public Expenditures

The circular-flow diagram in Figure 10–4 shows how a nation's flows of income and expenditures are related, but it does not tell us the *magnitudes* of those flows. The various identities that these flows satisfy must hold for a nation experiencing a significant expansion of real output and very low labor unemployment, as well as for a nation in the depths of a recession with record unemployment rates.

To understand how the equilibrium levels of a nation's real income and expenditures are determined, we must develop more concrete hypotheses about the factors that influence total expenditures on domestically produced goods and services. We shall then be able to combine these hypotheses to develop a complete theory of real income determination in an open economy.

real disposable income
A household's real after-tax income.

Saving, Import Spending, and Domestic Consumption Spending A key factor influencing household saving and expenditures on domestic- and foreign-manufactured goods and services is ***real disposable income***, which is real income, net of tax payments, or $y_d \equiv y - t$. Because the income identity states that

$y \equiv c + s + t + im$, we can subtract real net taxes t from both sides of the identity to write disposable income as

$$y_d \equiv y - t \equiv c + s + im.$$

Thus, households can use their after-tax income to buy domestically produced goods and services, to save, or to purchase foreign-produced goods and services. If we use the symbol Δ to refer to a change in a variable, then it follows that a change in disposable income can be written as

$$\Delta y_d \equiv \Delta c + \Delta s + \Delta im.$$

In words, households may allocate any additional disposable income to additional domestic consumption, additional saving, and additional import expenditures. Dividing both sides of this identity by Δy_d yields the following expression:

$$\frac{\Delta y_d}{\Delta y_d} = 1 \equiv \frac{\Delta c}{\Delta y_d} + \frac{\Delta s}{\Delta y_d} + \frac{\Delta im}{\Delta y_d}.$$

Thus, the sum of a change in consumption stemming from a change in disposable income ($\Delta c/\Delta y_d$), a change in saving resulting from a change in disposable income ($\Delta s/\Delta y_d$), and a change in real imports stemming from a change in disposable income ($\Delta im/\Delta y_d$) must be equal to 1.

The first ratio on the right-hand side of this identity, $\Delta c/\Delta y_d$, is the *marginal propensity to consume (MPC)*. The MPC is the change in real consumption induced by a change in real disposable income. If $\Delta c/\Delta y_d$ is equal to a value of $0.75, for example, then this numerical value indicates that a one-unit rise in real disposable income induces households to increase their expenditures of domestically produced goods and services by 0.75 units. In the United States, for instance, each one-dollar rise in after-tax income thereby induces a 0.75 increase in consumption of U.S.-produced output.

The second ratio, $\Delta s/\Delta y_d$, is the *marginal propensity to save (MPS)*. The MPS is a change in real saving resulting from a change in real disposable income. If $\Delta s/\Delta y_d$ is equal to 0.15, then a one-unit rise in real disposable income spurs households to raise their real saving by 0.15 units. An MPS value of 0.15 for the United States, therefore, implies that each one-dollar increase in disposable income leads to a $0.15 rise in saving by U.S. households.

The third ratio, $\Delta im/\Delta y_d$, is the *marginal propensity to import (MPIM)*. The MPIM is additional real import expenditures stemming from additional income earnings. If $\Delta im/\Delta y_d$ is equal to 0.10, then each additional unit of real after-tax household income results in a 0.10 unit rise in real import spending. A value of the MPIM equal to 0.10 for the United States indicates that each one-dollar rise in real after-tax household income causes U.S. households to increase real expenditures on imported goods and services by $0.10.

Because $MPC \equiv \Delta c/\Delta y_d$, $MPS \equiv \Delta s/\Delta y_d$, and $MPIM \equiv \Delta im/\Delta y_d$, we can rewrite the previous identity as

$$MPC + MPS + MPIM \equiv 1.$$

Using the hypothetical numerical values discussed earlier for the United States, the $0.75 of each new dollar of U.S. real after-tax income used for consumption of U.S. goods and services, the $0.15 of additional disposable real income allocated to saving, and the $0.10 of disposable real income spent on imported goods and services must sum to each dollar of additional disposable real income.

marginal propensity to consume (MPC)

The additional consumption resulting from an increase in disposable income; a change in consumption spending divided by a corresponding change in disposable income; the slope of the consumption function.

marginal propensity to save (MPS)

The additional saving caused by an increase in disposable income; a change in saving divided by a corresponding change in disposable income; the slope of the saving function.

marginal propensity to import (MPIM)

The additional import expenditures stemming from an increase in disposable income; a change in import spending divided by a corresponding change in disposable income; the slope of the import function.

The saving function A key determinant of household saving is disposable income. Let's consider a functional relationship, called the *saving function*, that captures this idea:

$$s = -s_0 + (MPS \times y_d).$$

According to this relationship, total household saving is equal to a constant amount, $-s_0$, plus an amount that depends on disposable income, $MPS \times \Delta y_d$. A graph of the saving function is shown in panel (a) of Figure 10–5. The function's intercept is s_0, and its slope is equal to the marginal propensity to save *(MPS)*, which indicates the portion of additional real disposable income, y_d, that households allocate to saving. The quantity $MPS \times y_d$ is *induced saving*, or the amount of saving spurred by after-tax income earnings.

We assume that the intercept of the saving function, $-s_0$, is a negative number. This is because if disposable income is equal to zero, then households must reduce their existing wealth to buy goods and services. The quantity $-s_0$ is *autonomous dissaving*, which is the amount by which households draw upon their current wealth to purchase domestically produced goods and services and foreign imports, irrespective of their after-tax income earnings.

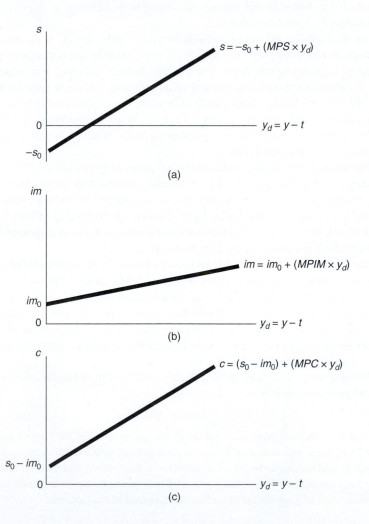

Figure 10–5

The Saving, Import, and Consumption Functions

Panel (a) shows the saving function, in which the intercept $-s_0$ represents autonomous dissaving. The marginal propensity to save, $MPS = \Delta s/\Delta y_d$, is the slope of the saving function. Panel (b) displays the import function. This function's intercept, im_0, is autonomous imports, and marginal propensity to import, $MPIM = \Delta im/\Delta y_d$, is the function's slope. Finally, panel (c) shows that real consumption of domestic goods and services, c, is equal to disposable income less saving and import expenditures, so the intercept of the consumption function is $s_0 - im_0$, which is autonomous consumption. The consumption function's slope is equal to the *MPC*, or $1 - MPS - MPIM$.

The import function The amount of spending on imported goods and services also varies with the amount of real income. Consider the following *import function*:

$$im = im_0 + (MPIM \times y_d).$$

The intercept of this function, which appears in panel (b) of Figure 10–5, is im_0. This is *autonomous import spending*, or household import expenditures that take place irrespective of the amount of total after-tax household income.

As we discussed in Chapter 8, a currency depreciation or devaluation may induce an increase in a nation's imports, and so we might expect that the magnitude of autonomous import spending depends on the exchange rate. As a simplification, however, we shall assume that this is not the case. As you will see, we shall be able to capture the essential features of the effects of a depreciation or devaluation on total national expenditures and income by assuming that exchange-rate changes influence export spending.

The quantity $MPIM \times y_d$ is *induced import spending*. This is the amount of import expenditures that stems directly from the receipt of disposable income.

The consumption function From the disposable income identity, $y_d \equiv c + s + im$, we know that households allocate their disposable income earnings to domestic consumption, saving, and import expenditures. Consequently, a domestic consumption function follows from our hypotheses about the forms of the saving and import functions. If we substitute the saving function, $s = -s_0 + (MPS \times y_d)$, and the import function, $im = im_0 + (MPIM \times y_d)$, into the disposable income identity, the result is

$$y_d = c + s + im$$

or

$$y_d = c - s_0 + (MPS \times y_d) + im_0 + (MPIM \times y_d).$$

We can rearrange the last equation by solving for c. The result is the consumption function:

$$c = (s_0 - im_0) + [(1 - MPS - MPIM) \times y_d].$$

This straight-line function appears in panel (c) of Figure 10–5. The consumption function's intercept is equal to $s_0 - im_0$. This is **autonomous consumption**, or the amount of real expenditures on domestically produced goods and services that would occur regardless of the magnitude of real disposable income. As long as the majority of total disposable income stays within the nation's borders, its autonomous consumption is a positive number. Thus, the intercept $s_0 - im_0$ is greater than zero, as shown in panel (c) of Figure 10–5.

The slope of the consumption function is equal to $1 - MPS - MPIM = \Delta c/\Delta y_d \equiv MPC$. Thus, the slope of the consumption function is the marginal propensity to consume (MPC). It follows that if we sum together the MPC, the MPS, and the $MPIM$, we can make substitutions to obtain

$$MPC + MPS + MPIM = 1.$$

And so, as we noted earlier, the three marginal propensities add up to a value of 1. (Although real disposable income is the primary determinant of consumption in our basic model, another factor that can also influence consumption is the interest rate; see *Management Notebook: The Declining Impact of Interest Rate Variations on U.S. Real Consumption Expenditures*.)

autonomous consumption

The amount of household consumption spending on domestically produced goods and services that is independent of the level of real income.

MANAGEMENT Notebook

The Declining Impact of Interest Rate Variations on U.S. Real Consumption Expenditures

The main determinant of real consumption spending is real disposable income, but there are also other determinants of real consumption expenditures. One of these is the interest rate, because an increase in the interest rate induces an increase in saving at any given level of real income. A higher interest rate also raises borrowing costs for businesses and households, which gives them an incentive to decrease spending.

Figure 10–6 depicts estimated effects, given a constant price level, of a 1-percentage-point increase in the interest rate on real U.S. consumption expenditures over four periods: 1945–1959, 1960–1974, 1979–1989, and post-1989. During the earliest period, a 1-percentage-point interest rate increase led on average to a decline of almost 2 percent in real consumption spending. Since the 1950s, however, the responsiveness of real consumption expenditures to a change in the interest rate has fallen. For the most recent period since 1990, the estimated impact of an interest rate increase on real consumption spending is negligible.

Federal Reserve economists suggest that one explanation for the reduced sensitivity of real consumption to interest rate changes is that more U.S. employers are able to cushion their responses to higher U.S. interest rates by borrowing internationally. As a consequence, employers are less likely than in years past to reduce workers' hours or engage in layoffs when U.S. interest rates increase. Thus, households' disposable incomes are less likely to decline in the face of a higher U.S. interest rate, and households are better able to maintain their consumption levels.

For Critical Analysis

Does an interest rate change cause a movement along or a shift in the consumption function?

Desired Investment Spending Expenditures on capital goods comprise the bulk of firm investment spending. In principle, domestic firms could import capital goods from other nations. To keep things simple, however, we shall assume that firms' investment spending is on domestic goods only.

Although variations in real income can potentially influence real investment, a key factor determining the amount of investment expenditures is the rate of interest. The interest rate that matters for investment is the *real interest rate*, denoted r. As in Chapter 5, we denote the nominal interest rate as R. We denote the expected inflation rate as π^e, where we use the Greek letter π to denote the inflation rate and

Figure 10–6

Estimated Impacts of a 1-Percentage-Point Interest Rate Increase on Real U.S. Consumption Spending since 1945

The estimated effects of a 1-percentage-point increase in the interest rate on real consumption spending have declined over time, indicating that consumption expenditures have become less sensitive to interest rate changes.

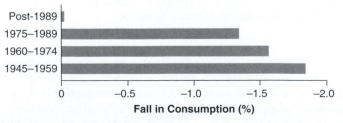

Source: Board of Governors of the Federal Reserve System.

the e superscript to denote the expected inflation rate. Then we can express the real interest rate as

$$r = R - \pi^e.$$

The real interest rate is equal to the nominal interest rate minus the expected inflation rate.

To produce goods and services, firms typically purchase or install capital goods, such as office buildings, computer equipment, factories, and the like. When evaluating the long-term profitability of such investment expenditures, firm owners compare the real return on investment—the real value of the annual flow of production that new capital goods makes possible—with the opportunity cost of incurring the investment expenditure. This opportunity cost is the real rate of interest that firm owners could earn if they were to save the funds instead. Consequently, if the real interest rate, r, increases, then desired real investment, i, declines. This inverse relationship between desired investment spending and the interest rate is shown as the *investment schedule*, labeled i in panels (a), (b), and (c) of Figure 10–7.

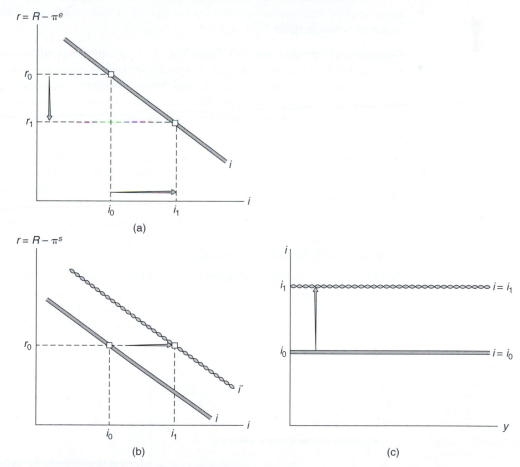

Figure 10–7 Factors Causing Changes in Desired Investment
Panels (a) and (b) show two key factors that can induce an increase in desired real investment expenditures. One, which panel (a) depicts, is a decline in the real interest rate resulting from a fall in the nominal interest rate or a rise in anticipated inflation. This causes a movement along the investment schedule. The other, shown in panel (b), follows from a shift in the investment schedule itself, so that a rise in desired investment takes place at any given real interest rate. As panel (c) indicates, either cause of an increase in desired investment spending generates an upward shift in the investment curve graphed against real income.

As shown in panel (a) of Figure 10–7, a decrease in the real interest rate from r_0 to r_1 causes desired real investment spending to rise from i_0 to i_1. Such a fall in the real interest rate could take place because of a decrease in the nominal interest rate or an increase in the expected inflation rate.

Panel (b) of Figure 10–7, however, displays another way in which desired investment may rise from i_0 to i_1. The desired investment schedule itself may shift to the right, meaning that an increase in desired investment could take place without a change in the real interest rate. Such a shift in the investment schedule may result from an increase in the anticipated real return on investment projects.

Panel (c) of Figure 10–7 shows that, whether induced by a fall in the real interest rate or expectations of higher real returns on investment, an increase in desired investment causes investment to rise at any given level of aggregate income, y. Thus, even though some amount of investment may be income-induced in the real world, to keep things as simple as possible we shall assume that investment is *autonomous*, or unrelated to income. And so, if we measure investment along the vertical axis, as in panel (c), and measure real income along the horizontal axis, an increase in desired investment results in an upward shift in a horizontal desired investment schedule, from $i = i_0$ to $i = i_1$.

Government Spending and Net Taxes The levels of public expenditures and net taxes chosen by a nation's government typically depend on a variety of factors, including the political structure that defines the government's role in the economy. These factors lie outside the scope of this text, as our objective is to understand how a government's spending and taxation decisions affect the economy once they have been adopted.

Government expenditures We shall assume that political and other factors that lead a government to choose any particular level of public expenditures are determined outside of our model. Thus, we shall assume that real government spending is equal to an autonomous amount, $g = g_0$. Panel (a) of Figure 10–8 shows that this implies that the *government spending schedule* is horizontal. If the government raises its spending from $g = g_0$ to $g = g_1$, then the government spending schedule shifts upward by the increase in spending.

Net taxes The governments of countries around the world assess a wide variety of taxes, including income taxes, value-added taxes, sales taxes, excise taxes, property taxes, and the like. The dependence of many governments' tax revenues on the levels of consumption expenditures and incomes indicates that, realistically, net taxes

Figure 10–8

The Government Spending and Net Tax Schedules

A key assumption of the basic open-economy framework is that government spending is autonomous, so that the government spending schedule is horizontal, as shown in panel (a). An increase in government spending thereby causes an upward shift in this schedule. Another assumption is that net taxes are autonomous, so that the net tax schedule in panel (b) also is horizontal. An increase in net taxes results in an upward shift in this schedule.

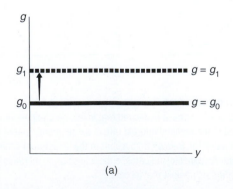

(a)

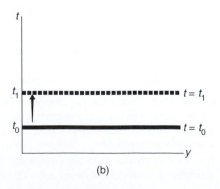

(b)

depend on their nations' real income levels. Nonetheless, we again shall simplify by assuming that net taxes are autonomous and equal to a lump-sum quantity. Panel (b) of Figure 10–8 shows that with this simplification, the *net tax schedule* is, like the government spending schedule, horizontal. Consequently, an increase in net taxes from an amount $t = t_0$ to a larger amount $t = t_1$ shifts the net tax schedule upward by the amount of the tax hike, as depicted in panel (b).

Export Spending Two key factors determine foreign expenditures on a nation's exports. One is the real incomes of foreign residents who buy domestically produced goods. If real income levels rise in other countries, export spending on a nation's domestic output tends to increase.

As discussed in Chapter 8, the other key factor affecting the volume of spending on a nation's exports is the exchange rate. For instance, if the domestic currency appreciates, so that obtaining a unit of domestic currency requires additional units of foreign currency, then domestic exports become more expensive to foreign residents, and they will reduce their spending on domestic exports.

The domestic level of real income, y, has no effect on real exports, however. This implies that foreign expenditures on domestic exports are strictly autonomous with respect to *domestic* income. As a result, the *export schedule* is horizontal, as depicted in Figure 10–9. An increase in foreign real income levels or a depreciation of the domestic currency causes exports to increase from an amount x_0 to a larger amount x_1. Thus, either occurrence results in an upward shift in the export schedule, as shown in Figure 10–9.

Equilibrium Income and Expenditures

We shall define the equilibrium flow of total expenditures and real income as follows:

> **In equilibrium, the aggregate desired expenditures on domestically produced goods and services by households, firms, the government, and foreign residents are equal to total real income.**

Because real income and the real value of domestically produced goods and services are equivalent, the equilibrium flow of real income is that level of all domestically produced and sold output that households, firms, the government, and foreign residents desire to purchase. If any real income remains unspent, then this indicates that firms produced "too much" output, giving them an incentive to cut back on sales and causing real income to change. In equilibrium, however, there is no tendency for the flow of real income and expenditures to change, so the

Figure 10–9

The Export Schedule

Changes in domestic income have no direct effect on export expenditures. Thus, the export schedule is horizontal. If foreign incomes rise or the domestic currency's value depreciates, however, export spending rises, causing an upward shift in the export schedule.

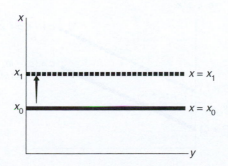

equilibrium level of real income and expenditures must satisfy the condition that all income ultimately is spent.

Aggregate Desired Expenditures The aggregate amount of spending on domestically produced goods and services is the total of household consumption expenditures, desired investment spending, government expenditures, and spending on exports of domestic output by residents of other nations. Hence, aggregate desired expenditures on domestic goods and services are equal to $c + i + g + x$.

Figure 10–10 shows how to sum these components of aggregate desired expenditures. We begin by graphing the upward-sloping household consumption function, $c = (s_0 - im_0) + (MPC \times y_d)$. We now take into account, however, that disposable income, y_d, by definition is equal to total real income, y, minus the current lump-sum amount of real net taxes, $t = t_0$. Substituting $y - t_0$ for y_d allows to rewrite the consumption function as

$$c = (s_0 + im_0) - [MPC \times (y - t_0)].$$

aggregate expenditures schedule

A schedule depicting total desired expenditures on domestic goods and services by households, firms, the government, and foreign residents at each and every level of real national income.

or

$$c = (s_0 + im_0) - (MPC \times t_0) + (MPC \times y).$$

This means that if we measure real income along the horizontal axis, the intercept of the consumption function, $(s_0 - im_0) - (MPC \times t_0)$, accounts for the consumption-reducing effect of taxes. The slope of the consumption function is still equal to the marginal propensity to consume, MPC.

By adding the vertical distance $i_0 + g_0 + x_0$ to the amount of consumption at each possible real income level, we obtain the ***aggregate expenditures schedule***, $c + i + g + x$. The aggregate expenditures schedule displays the total amount of spending on domestically produced goods and services by households, firms, the government, and foreign residents at any given level of domestic real income. The vertical intercept of this schedule is ***aggregate net autonomous expenditures***, or $(s_0 - im_0) - (MPC \times t_0) + i_0 + g_0 + x_0$. This quantity is the net level of spending that is determined independently from the current real income level. The slope of the schedule is the same as the slope of the consumption function, MPC.

aggregate net autonomous expenditures

The total amount of autonomous consumption, autonomous investment, autonomous government spending, and autonomous export spending, which is assumed to be independent of the level of national income.

Equilibrium National Income As noted earlier, the equilibrium flow of real income is that level at which households, firms, the government, and foreign residents desire to purchase all domestically produced goods and services. Hence, a nation's *equilibrium real income* is the real income level at which aggregate

Figure 10–10

Deriving the Aggregate Expenditures Schedule

Summing the combined amount of desired investment spending, government spending, and export expenditures with the level of consumption at each point along the consumption function yields the aggregate expenditures schedule, $c + i + g + x$.

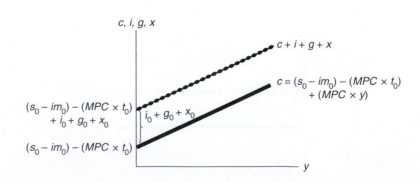

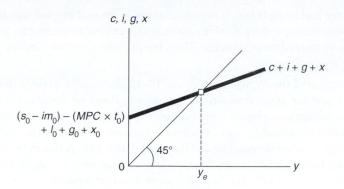

Figure 10–11

The Determination of Equilibrium
Real Income

Equilibrium real income arises at the
point at which aggregate desired
real expenditures, $c + i + g + x$,
equal aggregate real income. This
is true at the single real income
level, y_e, at which the aggregate
expenditures schedule crosses the
45-degree line.

desired expenditures are equal to the real value of domestically produced output.
From the circular-flow diagram in Figure 10–4 on page 283, we know that the
real value of output is equal to real income. Thus, in equilibrium real income is
equal to aggregate desired expenditures on domestic goods and services, or
$y = c + i + g + x$.

The Income–Expenditure Equilibrium Figure 10–11 shows the determination of
a single income–expenditure equilibrium. The aggregate expenditure curve is taken
from Figure 10–10; it displays all combinations of real income and desired expenditures by households, firms, the government, and foreign residents. A ***45-degree line***
cuts in half the 90-degree angle of the coordinate axes on the diagram. At any point
along this 45-degree line, the level of real income is equal to the level of aggregate
desired expenditures, so each point on the 45-degree line potentially can satisfy our
definition of equilibrium. Hence, the *single point* at which the two schedules inter-
sect is the single point that satisfies the equilibrium condition $y = c + i + g + x$.
The equilibrium level of real income at this point is denoted y_e.

45-degree line

A line that cuts in half the
90-degree angle of the coordinate axes on a diagram relating real income to aggregate
desired expenditures and that
provides a potential set of
equilibrium points at which
real income equals aggregate
desired expenditures.

Fundamental ISSUES

#2 How is equilibrium real income determined in an open economy?

In equilibrium, aggregate desired expenditures equal real income. In an open economy,
household consumption of domestically produced goods and services, firm-desired investment spending, government spending, and export spending by foreign residents make
up aggregate desired expenditures. Desired investment, government spending and net
taxes, and export spending are autonomous, whereas consumption spending is positively
related to disposable income, and so the aggregate expenditures schedule has the same
slope as the consumption function. Equilibrium real income is determined by the intersection of this schedule and the 45-degree line.

The *IS* Schedule

Figure 10–11 makes clear that the equilibrium level of real income depends on the
position of the aggregate expenditures schedule. This schedule's position, in turn,
depends on the amount of net autonomous expenditures, including autonomous
investment spending. Because ***autonomous investment spending*** is negatively

**autonomous investment
spending**

Desired investment expenditures that are independent of
the level of real income.

related to the real interest rate, however, changes in the real interest rate alter autonomous investment spending, total net autonomous expenditures, and the position of the aggregate expenditures schedule. Thus, interest rate variations induce variations in equilibrium real income.

The Derivation of the *IS* Schedule Figure 10–12 shows how a rise in the nominal interest rate can affect equilibrium real income. Panel (a) displays the desired investment schedule as graphs, with the *nominal* interest rate measured along the vertical axis. This schedule slopes downward because of the negative relationship between real investment spending and the real interest rate. A rise in the nominal interest rate, from R_1 to R_2, given the expected inflation rate, π^e, causes desired real investment spending to decline from i_1 at point A to i_2 at point B.

Such a decline in desired investment, as shown in panel (b), results in a fall in net autonomous expenditures. Consequently, a rise in the nominal interest rate

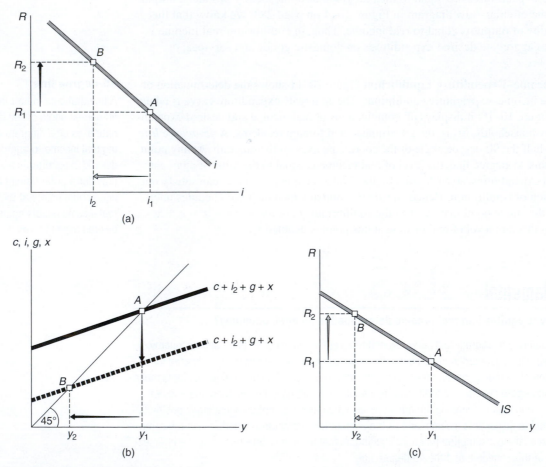

(a)

(b)

(c)

Figure 10–12 The Derivation of the *IS* Schedule

A rise in the nominal interest rate, given the expected inflation rate, raises the real interest rate and induces a reduction in investment spending. Therefore, as indicated in panel (a), an increase in the nominal interest rate induces a movement from point A to point B along the investment schedule and causes a decline in desired investment spending. This, as panel (b) shows, reduces aggregate desired expenditures, resulting in a reduction in equilibrium real income, from y_1 at point A to y_2 at point B. Consequently, the new combination of real income and the nominal interest rate consistent with equilibrium real income and expenditures, which is y_2 and R_2 at point B in panel (c), lies above and to the left of the original combination y_1 and R_1 at point A. It follows that the *IS* schedule, which shows all combinations of real income and the nominal interest rate consistent with equilibrium real income and expenditures, slopes downward.

causes the aggregate desired expenditures schedule to shift downward, resulting in a decline in equilibrium real income, from y_1 to y_2. As a result, as displayed in panel (c), there is a movement from the initial real income–nominal interest rate combination, y_1 and R_1 at point A consistent with equilibrium real income, to a new combination, y_2 and R_2 at point B.

Point A and point B represent real income–nominal interest rate combinations that lie on an **IS schedule**, which is a set of combinations of real income levels and nominal interest rates that maintains equilibrium real income. The IS schedule was first developed in 1937 by Sir John Hicks of Oxford University. Hicks derived the schedule by assuming a simple economy with no government sector or international trade, so that aggregate desired expenditures were equal to $c + i$. From the income identity, with no taxes and no imports, real income therefore would, by definition, equal $y \equiv c + s$. Thus, when Hicks imposed the equilibrium condition $y = c + i$, he could write it as $c + i = c + s$. After subtracting c from both sides, this yielded $i = s$, or investment equals saving, hence the term IS as a label for the resulting relationship that we have derived more generally in Figure 10–12.

Determining the Position of the *IS* Schedule To derive the IS schedule in Figure 10–12, we consider only the effects of a rise in the nominal interest rate on desired investment spending. We assume that all other factors affecting autonomous desired expenditures are unchanged. These factors include autonomous consumption, autonomous saving, government expenditures, autonomous net taxes, autonomous imports, and autonomous export spending. Increases in government expenditures or autonomous export spending, for example, cause a rise in aggregate desired expenditures, as shown in panel (b) of Figure 10–13. Likewise, reductions in autonomous saving, imports, or net taxes also generate such an upward shift in the aggregated desired expenditures schedule by inducing a rise in consumption spending at any given interest rate.

As panel (c) of Figure 10–13 indicates, the result of any one of these possible sources of an increase in autonomous expenditures is a new real income–nominal interest rate combination, y_2 and R_1 at point B, that lies to the right of the original combination, y_1 and R_1 at point A. Therefore, any of the factors just listed that cause an increase in aggregate desired expenditures generate a *rightward shift* in the IS schedule, such as the shift depicted in panel (c).

By way of contrast, any factor that causes a *reduction* in aggregate desired expenditures shifts the IS schedule *leftward*. Such factors include reductions in government spending or autonomous export expenditures or increases in autonomous saving, net taxes, or autonomous import expenditures.

The Multiplier Effect The amount by which the IS schedule shifts in response to a change in net autonomous expenditures depends on the size of the ***multiplier effect***. This term refers to the fact that a given one-unit change in aggregate net autonomous expenditures causes a greater-than-one-unit change in equilibrium real income in the same direction. In panel (b) of Figure 10–13, a one-unit movement in the intercept of the aggregate desired expenditures schedule $c + i + g + x$ induces an increase in equilibrium real income that exceeds one unit.

Some algebra helps to illustrate how to determine the size of the multiplier effect. The income–expenditure equilibrium condition is $y = c + i + g + x$. Let's substitute from our consumption function, $c = (s_0 - im_0) - (MPC \times t_0) + (MPC \times y)$, and, for purposes of illustrating the multiplier effect, assume that net taxes and desired investment, government spending, and export spending are

IS schedule
A set of possible combinations of real income and the nominal interest rate that is necessary to maintain the income–expenditure equilibrium, $y = c + i + g + x$, for a given level of aggregate net autonomous expenditures.

multiplier effect
The ratio of a change in the equilibrium real income to an increase in autonomous net aggregate expenditures. When the aggregate expenditure schedule shifts vertically, the equilibrium level of national income changes by a multiple of the amount of the shift, and the IS schedule shifts by this magnitude.

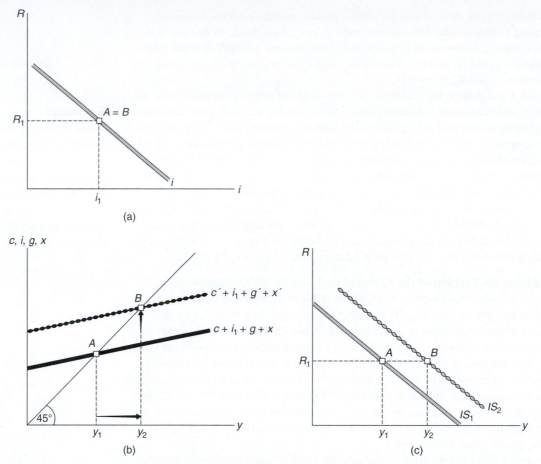

Figure 10–13   A Change in Autonomous Expenditures and the Position of the *IS* Schedule

An increase in aggregate desired expenditures, which might result from a reduction in autonomous saving, autonomous import expenditures, or net taxes or from an increase in autonomous government spending or autonomous export expenditures, causes the aggregate expenditures schedule to shift upward, as shown in panel (b). Hence, at a given interest rate and level of investment expenditures, displayed in panel (a), equilibrium real income increases following the movement from point A to point B in panel (b). This implies that a new real income–interest rate combination maintaining equilibrium real income and expenditures, y_2 and R_1 at point B in panel (c), lies on a new *IS* schedule to the right of the original combination y_1 and R_1 at point A on the initial *IS* schedule. Thus, a rise in autonomous expenditures shifts the *IS* schedule to the right.

all autonomous. This permits us to rewrite the income–expenditure equilibrium condition as

$$y = (s_0 - im_0) - (MPC \times t_0) + (MPC \times y) + i_0 + g_0 + x_0.$$

Subtracting $MPC \times y$ from both sides of this equation, we obtain

$$y - (MPC \times y) = (s_0 - im_0) - (MPC \times t_0) + i_0 + g_0 + x_0.$$

Because the left-hand side is equal to $(1 - MPC) \times y$, we can write this equation as

$$1 - MPC \times y = (s_0 - im_0) - (MPC \times t_0) + i_0 + g_0 + x_0.$$

Finally, let's divide both sides of the equation by $(1 - MPC)$ to obtain a final expression for equilibrium real income:

$$y = [1/(1 - MPC)] \{(s_0 - im_0) - (MPC \times t_0) + i_0 + g_0 + x_0\}.$$

The expression tells us that equilibrium real income is equal to the ratio $1/(1 - MPC)$ times aggregate net autonomous expenditures, $(s_0 - im_0) - (MPC \times t_0) + i_0 + g_0 + x_0$. The ratio $1/(1 - MPC)$ is the ***autonomous expenditures multiplier***, which determines the size of the multiplier effect on equilibrium real income resulting from a variation in net autonomous expenditures. The MPC is a fraction, so the multiplier is greater than 1. For example, if the marginal propensity to save is equal to 0.10 and the marginal propensity to import is equal to 0.15, then the marginal propensity to consume is equal to $MPC = 0.75$. Then the multiplier is equal to $1/(1 - MPC) = 1/(1 - 0.75) = 1/0.25 = 4$. A $1 million increase in aggregate net autonomous expenditures in Figure 10–13 causes a $4 million rise in equilibrium real income.

Explaining the Multiplier Effect Why is there a multiplier effect? To answer this question, let's again suppose that $MPC = 0.75$ and that the nation we are considering is the United States. Then each one-dollar rise in disposable income raises consumption spending by $0.75. If autonomous export expenditures, for example, rise by an amount equal to $1 million, then such a spending increase immediately raises U.S. real income by $1 million. Because we have assumed that taxes are a lump sum, real disposable income rises by $1 million, spurring household consumption spending to increase by 75 percent of $1 million, or $750,000. This raises the disposable income of all firms from which the government or foreign residents purchase domestically produced goods and services by $750,000. At this point, therefore, the $1 million increase in autonomous export spending increases total real income by $1.75 million.

The total process of spending increases is not yet finished, however. Owners and employees at exporting domestic firms that have gained $750,000 in new sales and income earnings are now able to raise their consumption spending by 75 percent of this amount, or by $0.75 \times \$750,000 = \$562,500$. Furthermore, this spending increase causes a rise in disposable income of $562,500 for other domestic firm owners and workers, who then raise their consumption spending by $0.75 \times \$562,500 = \$421,875$.

In the end, the total rise in real income caused by the initial $1 million increase in autonomous export expenditures is equal to the sum of all these increases (\$1 million + \$750,000 + \$562,500 + \$421,875 + . . .) in spending. As we determined earlier, if the MPC is equal to 0.75, then the total rise in real income caused by a $1 million increase in autonomous exports is equal to $1 million $\times 1/(1 - 0.75) = \$1$ million $\times 4 = \$4$ million. This, then, is the amount that the *IS* schedule shifts to the right in panel (c) of Figure 10–13 following an upward shift of the aggregate expenditures schedule equal to $1 million in additional autonomous export spending in panel (b).

autonomous expenditures multiplier

A measure of the size of the multiplier effect on equilibrium real income caused by a change in aggregate autonomous expenditures, which is equal to $1/(MPS + MPIM) = 1/(1 - MPC)$.

Fundamental ISSUES

#3 What is the *IS* schedule, and what factors determine its position?

The *IS* schedule is a downward-sloping set of all combinations of real income and the nominal interest rate for which aggregate desired expenditures equal real income. The *IS* schedule shifts rightward if there is an increase in autonomous desired expenditures arising from a fall in autonomous saving, import spending, or taxes, or from a rise in autonomous government spending, investment, or export spending. In contrast, a rise in autonomous saving, import spending, or taxes or a fall in autonomous government spending, investment, or export spending would shift the *IS* schedule to the left.

THE MARKET FOR REAL MONEY BALANCES: THE *LM* SCHEDULE

In Chapters 6 and 9, you learned that the two key liabilities of central banks—reserves held by private financial institutions and currency held by the nonbank public—together comprise the monetary base. In addition, you learned that there are two important central bank assets corresponding to these liabilities. These are domestic credit and foreign exchange reserves. Consequently, we can consider the quantity of money issued by a central bank from the perspective of either the asset or liability side of the central bank's balance sheet.

How much of the money that a central bank issues do people really want to hold? A friend might mention that a common acquaintance "has lots of money," and the friend might enviously state that one of her goals in life is to "make just as much money." It might seem apparent that we all would like to have as much money as possible. Yet central banks typically must *require* financial institutions to hold minimal amounts of reserves by imposing legal reserve requirements. If they did not do this, many financial institutions would hold nearly zero reserve balances. Inducing the nonbank public to hold the money that central banks issue sometimes can be an even more difficult proposition. For instance, in Russia since the 1990s, many people have preferred to use U.S. dollars, rather than the ruble, for transactions.

We may conclude that people around the world do not necessarily really "want more money" than they already possess. What they really want is more *wealth*. As noted in Chapter 9, although money is a way to hold part of one's wealth, in many circumstances holding money balances issued by a central bank is not in one's best interest. How much of an individual's wealth that a person desires to hold as money balances is the individual's *demand for money*.

The Demand for Money

To see why holding as much money as possible might not be a good idea, think for a moment about how much interest you earn on the central-bank-issued currency you have on hand at the moment. The amount of interest that you earn on such currency holdings is zero. In contrast, if you had sufficient currency to place in a bank deposit or to buy a government bond, then you could convert that currency into an interest-bearing asset that would yield you a return greater than zero.

The Transactions and Precautionary Motives for Holding Money

Viewed from this perspective, why would anyone hold non-interest-bearing forms of money? The answer, of course, is the reason that you probably have some currency on hand yourself at this moment: You desire to hold money to buy things, because money is a widely accepted medium of exchange.

The early-twentieth-century British economist John Maynard Keynes referred to this basic motive for holding money as the *transactions motive*. This is the incentive to hold non-interest-bearing money for use as a medium of

transactions motive
The motive to hold money for use in planned exchanges.

exchange in planned transactions. For example, it is handy to have some cash or coins on hand to use in payment for a snack and soft drink or juice after each round of afternoon classes. Money also can be very useful for purchasing groceries from week to week and for making rent and utility payments from month to month. (To find out how U.S. immigrants can go online to convert their dollars into vouchers that family members back home can use to conduct transactions in their own currencies, see *Online Notebook: Using the Web to Convert Dollars into African Vouchers*.)

ONLINENotebook

Using the Web to Convert Dollars into African Vouchers

Many Kenyan and Ugandan immigrants to the United States have pursued higher-wage jobs that are generating higher incomes for themselves and for their families. Many of these immigrants, however, have at least temporarily left family members behind. If one of these U.S. immigrants wishes to transform hard-earned U.S. dollars into vouchers that these family members can use in transactions for food, health care, and other items back in Kenya or Uganda, the individual can click on Mama Mike's Web site. Mama Mike's is a Nairobi-based company that offers vouchers online in exchange for U.S. dollars. Once an online vender purchase has been completed, an immigrant's family members in Africa receive notification that they can pick up their vouchers in locations scattered throughout Kenya and Uganda. Then they can use the vouchers in transactions for goods and services at participating merchants.

For Critical Analysis

In light of the fact that Mama Mike's receives dollar payments from immigrants but reimburses Kenyan and Ugandan merchants for its vouchers in those nations' currencies, in what type of market must Mama Mike's regularly transact?

Keynes coined the term ***precautionary motive*** to describe a related reason to hold money. This is the desire to hold money in case a need arises to make previously unplanned transactions. For instance, there is always a chance that the hard disk in your personal computer will malfunction and need repair, or that you might be in a clothing retailer and discover a sale on jeans that you "need" but nonetheless did not previously plan to purchase. Most people try to keep additional cash on hand to cover such contingencies.

A key determinant of how much money any of us chooses to hold to satisfy our own transactions and precautionary motives depends largely on our relative incomes. If you happen to be a student whose income is relatively low, so that you spend the bulk of your income on tuition, rental payments, and the like, then you may have to limit the number of times that you purchase a soft drink each week. You also may be less likely to buy an article of clothing that happens to be on sale, because your budget for such contingencies may be limited. By way of contrast, a wealthier student who receives a large monthly allowance may purchase afternoon snacks along with soft drinks, and that student may keep significant sums of cash on hand to purchase sale merchandise on shopping trips.

precautionary motive
The motive to hold money for use in unplanned exchanges.

These commonsensical considerations led Keynes, as well as many of his predecessors, to argue that one key determinant of desired money holdings is one's income. A rise in income leads, via the transactions and precautionary motives for holding money, to an increase in the demand for money balances.

portfolio motive

Modern term for Keynes's essential argument for a speculative motive for holding money, in which people hold both money and bonds and adjust their holdings of both components of financial wealth based on their anticipations concerning interest rate movements.

The Portfolio Motive for Holding Money In addition to the transactions and precautionary motives for holding money, Keynes also proposed the existence of a *speculative motive*. This incentive to hold non-interest-bearing cash, he reasoned, stems from the interaction between changes in the nominal interest rate and the price of an interest-bearing financial asset such as a bond. The modern term for this incentive to hold money is, as discussed in Chapter 9, the *portfolio motive*, which refers to the motive for people to adjust their desired mix of money and bond holdings based on their speculations about interest rate movements and anticipated changes in bond prices. To the extent that this motive influences desired money holdings, changes in the nominal interest rate can thereby affect the quantity of money demanded.

Bonds, money, and financial wealth To understand the essential elements of the reasoning behind the portfolio motive, let's suppose a person allocates her financial wealth only between money holdings, M, and holdings of another financial asset that we shall call a "bond," B. The distinguishing characteristic of money is that the nominal price of money is always equal to 1 unit of money (for instance, $1, €1, ¥1, etc.), whereas the nominal price of a bond can fluctuate. Thus, as discussed in Chapter 5, a person who holds a bond earns a *capital loss* if the nominal price of the bond declines over a given period or a *capital gain* if the nominal price of the bond rises during another interval. A one-dollar bill issued by the Federal Reserve System, a one-euro note issued by the European Central Bank, and a one-yen note issued by the Bank of Japan have the same *nominal* values of $1, €1, or ¥1, respectively, across time. Therefore, an individual cannot incur a nominal capital loss or earn a nominal capital gain if he holds all his financial wealth in the form of currency notes issued by these or other central banks.

To contemplate how an individual chooses shares of her financial wealth to split between money and bonds, let's suppose that at a given time her nominal financial wealth is equal to some amount W. The individual allocates this amount of wealth between holdings of non-interest-bearing holdings of money, M, and holdings of interest-bearing bonds, B. As before, we shall denote the nominal interest return on bonds as R. Hence, at this given point in time, the individual's financial wealth must equal to her money holdings plus her bond holdings (assuming she holds only domestic bonds):

$$W \equiv M + B.$$

If wealth is fixed at a point in time, then it must be true that the sum of changes in money and bond holdings must equal zero, or $\Delta M + \Delta B \equiv 0$. In other words, a change in the individual's bond holdings, ΔB, must be countered by an offsetting change in money holdings in the opposite direction, $-\Delta M$. For instance, if this individual had $12,000 in financial wealth, of which she holds $6,000 as money and $6,000 as bonds, then if she wishes to reduce her bond holdings by $3,000, she must increase her money holdings by $3,000, leaving $9,000 in cash and $3,000 in bonds.

The *wealth constraint* that the individual faces provides the basis for an interaction between interest rate changes and the individual's demand for money. As we discussed in Chapter 5, the fact that bonds earn a nominal interest return means that variations in the nominal interest rate alter the market prices of bonds and, consequently, the individual's desired bond holdings. Altering her bond holdings, however, requires the individual to vary her money holdings. Thus, interest rate changes will induce her to alter her desired money holdings.

The portfolio motive How might an individual alter her money and bond holdings as part of a speculative strategy concerning expected changes in interest rates? The individual will recognize that future capital gains or losses from bond holdings depend directly on whether interest rates rise or fall in the future. Given her *anticipation* of future interest rate movements, she realizes that as interest rates change, she should change her mix of money and bonds.

Suppose that the current market interest rate rises to a level that a given individual believes is rather high. As you learned in Chapter 5, interest yields and bond prices are inversely related. As a result, this individual's anticipation is that if the current interest rate is "high," then the interest rate likely will decline in the future, implying that bond prices likely will rise. This means that she anticipates a future capital gain on bonds that she holds as part of her financial wealth. To further increase her anticipated capital gains from bond holdings, this individual decides to allocate more of her financial wealth to bonds in the present. But her financial wealth is fixed now, so this requires that she reduce her money holdings. Consequently, for this individual a current rise in the market interest rate causes a current reduction in desired money holdings. *Her demand for money depends negatively on the market interest rate*.

The Demand for Real Money Balances Before we think about combining the transactions, precautionary, and speculative motives to consider the total demand for money, we need to consider the appropriate measure of money holdings.

When asked how much cash you have on hand, you might take a look and reply, "Oh, about $25." This would be the nominal, face value of the currency and coins in your possession. But if you think about it for a moment, you will realize that what really matters to you is the purchasing power of the money that you hold.

Real money balances Suppose, for instance, that you decide to carry $25 in cash to cover a day's purchases. You might plan to spend $15 to purchase lunch and $5 to purchase an afternoon snack between classes, which would leave you with $5 in precautionary balances for that day. Now suppose that the price level doubles shortly after you leave for campus. This doubles the price of the lunch you had planned to buy, to $30. In addition, the price of the intended afternoon snack rises to $10. Now the $25 that you had carried from home does not even cover all the lunch items that you had planned to purchase. Furthermore, you have to give up your afternoon snack. Effectively, the purchasing power of the $25 in cash drops to half its previous value. Purchasing the same lunch and snack during the coming day requires twice as much money, or $50. Thus, doubling of prices requires a doubling of your nominal money balances if you wish to maintain the purchasing power necessary to cover the day's expenses.

This example indicates that the real purchasing power of a person's nominal cash balances is the price-adjusted value of one's nominal money holdings, or ***real money balances***, denoted by $m \equiv M/P$. Thus, by definition real money balances are equal to nominal money holdings, M, divided by the GDP price deflator, P.

real money balances
The price-level-adjusted value of the nominal quantity of money, defined as the nominal money stock divided by the price level.

The demand schedule for real money balances What matters for determining the transactions and precautionary demands for real money balances is a person's *real* income. Consequently, a rise in aggregate real income raises the total demand for money across all individuals. A decline in aggregate real income, in contrast, reduces the demand for real money balances. The logic of the portfolio motive for holding money continues to apply to the *nominal* interest rate, however, because real financial wealth still must be split between real holdings of money and bonds. Changes in the nominal interest rate thereby induce changes in the split of real wealth between real money balances and real bond holdings that are equivalent to alterations in the split between nominal holdings of money and bonds.

To take into account these determinants of the demand for real money balances, we can draw a *money demand schedule*, or a graphical depiction of the relationship between the quantity of money demanded and the nominal interest rate. Panel (a) of Figure 10–14 depicts a sample money demand schedule. The negative slope of the money demand schedule reflects the inverse relationship between the quantity of real money balances demanded and the nominal interest rate implied by the portfolio motive for holding money. In addition, we label the schedule $m^d(y_1)$ to indicate that the *position* of the money demand schedule depends on the current level of real income, such as a real income level y_1.

Panel (b) of Figure 10–14 illustrates the effect of an increase in real income, from y_1 to a larger amount y_2. Higher real income increases the volume of planned transactions by all individuals in the economy, thereby increasing their holdings of real money balances for transactions purposes. In addition, the rise in real income raises total precautionary money holdings. Therefore, at any given nominal interest rate, people desire to hold more real money balances, so the money demand schedule shifts rightward, as shown in panel (b) by the shift from $m^d(y_1)$ to $m^d(y_2)$.

The *LM* Schedule

As we noted earlier, a central bank cannot force people to hold the nominal stock of money that it issues. People must be willing to hold it. The price level and the nominal interest rate are the factors that influence people's willingness to hold money balances. In Chapter 13 we shall consider how the price level is determined. For now we shall concentrate on how the nominal interest rate adjusts to make people satisfied with holding a quantity of money, *given* a particular price level.

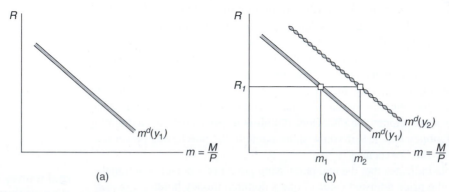

(a) (b)

Figure 10–14 The Money Demand Schedule
The demand for real money balances, $m \equiv M/P$, is the total demand for real purchasing power. As shown in panel (a), the demand for real money balances slopes downward as a result of the portfolio motive for holding real money balances. The demand for real money balances shifts rightward when real income rises, as displayed in panel (b), because of the transactions and precautionary motives for holding real money balances.

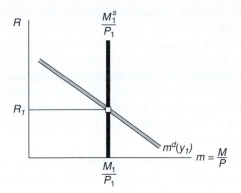

Figure 10–15

Money Market Equilibrium

The equilibrium nominal interest rate is the interest rate at which the quantity of real money balances demanded equals the quantity of real money balances supplied by the central bank. This occurs at the point where the demand schedule for real money balances crosses the real money supply schedule.

Money Market Equilibrium and the *LM* Schedule We shall assume that the central bank sets a given nominal quantity of money supplied, by determining the quantity of domestic credit and foreign exchange reserves. The supply of real money balances then is equal to M_1^s/P_1, where P_1 is the current price level. Figure 10–15 depicts the supply of real money balances, together with the money demand schedule from Figure 10–14. Given the quantity of money supplied $M_1^s = M_1$, the *equilibrium* nominal interest rate is equal to R_1. At this interest rate, people are willing to hold the nominal quantity of money, M_1, issued by the central bank, *given* the current level of prices, P_1. Hence, the market for real money balances is in equilibrium.

Figure 10–16 illustrates the effect of a rise in real income on the equilibrium nominal interest rate. A rise in real income, from y_1 to a higher level y_2, increases the demand for real money balances. As a result, as shown in panel (a) of Figure 10–16, the money demand schedule shifts to the right, from $m^d(y_1)$ to $m^d(y_2)$. At the initial equilibrium interest rate R_1 at point A, there is an excess quantity of real money balances demanded. This implies an excess quantity of bonds supplied, because people desire to hold fewer bonds as they seek to increase their real money balances. As a result, bond prices decline, so the equilibrium nominal interest rate rises, to R_2 at point B. Thus, in panel (b), there is a movement from an initial real income–nominal interest rate combination, y_1 and R_1 at point A, to a new combination, y_2 and R_2 at point B. Both real income–nominal interest rate combinations are

Figure 10–16

The Derivation of the *LM* Schedule

If real income rises from an initial amount y_1 to a higher level y_2, then the demand for real money balances increases, causing the equilibrium nominal interest rate to rise from R_1 at point A in panel (a) to R_2 at point B. Consequently, as shown in panel (b), the real income–interest rate combinations y_1 and R_1 at point A and y_2 and R_2 at point B maintain equilibrium in the market for real money balances, given the current supply of real money balances. Both of these points lie on an *LM* schedule.

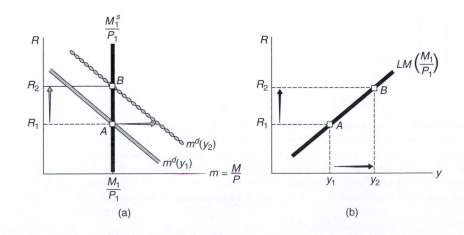

(a)   (b)

representative points of money market equilibrium along the schedule displayed in panel (b), which is labeled *LM*.

LM schedule

A set of combinations of real income and the nominal interest rate that maintains money market equilibrium.

An *LM schedule* is a set of all combinations of real income levels and nominal interest rates that maintain equilibrium in the money market. John Hicks gave the *LM* schedule its name in 1937, when he referred to the demand for money as desired liquidity, *L*. Because money market equilibrium required equality between desired liquidity and the quantity of money balances supplied by a central bank, *M*, Hicks noted that $L = M$ must always hold along the schedule for money market equilibrium, hence the term *LM*.

Determining the Position of the *LM* Schedule It is crucial to recognize that our derivation of the *LM* schedule in Figure 10–16 depended on an unchanging supply of real money balances equal to M_1/P_1. For this reason, we have labeled the *LM* schedule as $LM(M_1/P_1)$ in panel (b) of the figure to indicate that we have derived this set of real income–nominal interest rate combinations *given* the nominal money stock M_1 and the price level P_1. If there had been a different position for the real money supply schedule, then we would have developed a different set of combinations of real income and the nominal interest rate consistent with money market equilibrium. That is, we would have derived a different *LM* schedule.

To see this, suppose that the central bank increases the nominal money stock while real income and the price level remained unchanged. As shown in panel (a) of Figure 10–17, this causes a rise in the real money stock, from M_1/P_1 to M_2/P_1. Real income remains unchanged at y_1, but the equilibrium nominal interest rate declines, from R_1 at point *A* to R_2 at point *B*.

After the increase in the nominal money stock, a new real income–interest rate combination, y_1 and R_2 at point *B* in panel (b) of Figure 10–17, maintains equilibrium in the market for real money balances. This combination is on a new *LM* schedule, $LM(M_2/P_1)$, that lies below and to the right of the initial *LM* schedule,

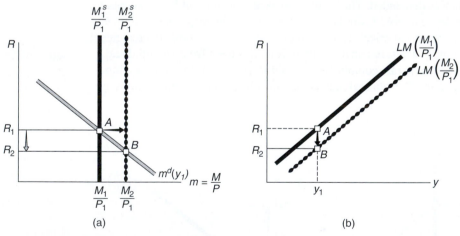

(a)   (b)

Figure 10–17   Changes in the Real Money Supply and in the Position of the *LM* Schedule

Panels (a) and (b) show the effects of a rise in the real money supply owing to an increase in the nominal quantity in circulation by a nation's central bank with an unchanged price level. The result in the market for real money balances, as shown in panel (a), is a rise in the supply of real money balances and a resulting movement from equilibrium point *A* to equilibrium point *B*. Because real income does not change following the decline in the equilibrium interest rate, the new real income–interest rate combination y_1 and R_2 at point *B* in panel (b) lies directly below the original combination y_1 and R_1 at point *A*. Consequently, the *LM* schedule shifts downward and to the right.

$LM(M_1/P_1)$. Holding the price level fixed, therefore, a rise in the nominal money stock raises the supply of real money balances and shifts the *LM* schedule downward and to the right. In contrast, a decline in the money stock with an unvarying price level shifts the *LM* schedule upward and to the left.

A change in the price level also alters the amount of real money balances, causing the *LM* schedule to shift. For the time being, however, and in Chapters 11 and 12 that follow, we shall assume that the price level is fixed. We shall explore the ramifications of changes in the price level in Chapter 13.

 Fundamental ISSUES

#4 What is the *LM* schedule, and what factors determine its position?

The *LM* schedule is an upward-sloping set of all combinations of real income and the nominal interest rate that maintain equilibrium in the market for real money balances. The *LM* schedule shifts downward and to the right if there is an increase in the nominal money stock or a fall in the price level. A decrease in the money stock or a rise in the price level causes the *LM* schedule to shift upward and to the left.

THE BALANCE OF PAYMENTS: THE *BP* SCHEDULE AND THE *IS–LM–BP* MODEL

You have seen so far in this chapter that the *IS* schedule is a downward-sloping set of real income–nominal interest rate combinations that yields equilibrium real income. You also have learned that the *LM* schedule is an upward-sloping set of real income–nominal interest rate combinations that maintains money market equilibrium.

In addition, you have learned that the level of real income also affects a nation's import expenditures. This means that the level of real income must influence a country's trade balance and, consequently, its current account balance. Furthermore, you have seen that the nominal interest rate influences bond holdings within a nation, which implies that the nominal interest rate must affect a country's capital account balance. This reasoning indicates that real income and the nominal interest rate together must determine a nation's balance of payments.

Maintaining a Balance-of-Payments Equilibrium: The *BP* schedule

Recall from Chapter 1 that the *overall* balance of payments is the sum of the current account balance, the private capital account balance, and the official settlements balance. A *balance-of-payments equilibrium,* however, is defined as a situation in which the current account balance and capital account balance sum to zero, so that the official settlements balance also equals zero.

Real Income and the Balance of Payments What real income levels and nominal interest rates would a nation require to maintain a balance-of-payments equilibrium? To consider this question, take a look at Figure 10–18 on the next page. Suppose that the current account and capital account sum to zero at point *A*, at a nominal interest rate equal to R_1 and a real income level equal to y_1. Thus, at point *A* there is a

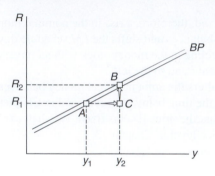

Figure 10–18 The *BP* Schedule

If real income rises from y_1 at point *A*, at which the balance of payments balance is equal to zero, to y_2 at point *C*, then a nation's import expenditures increase, and its trade balance declines. The result is a balance-of-payments deficit at point *C*. Reattaining a balance-of-payments equilibrium requires an increase in the nominal interest rate, which induces foreign residents to hold more of the nation's financial assets, thereby improving its capital account balance. Hence, a point such as point *B*, which is above and to the right of point *A*, represents another real income–interest rate combination consistent with a balance-of-payments equilibrium. The set of all such combinations is the *BP* schedule.

balance-of-payments equilibrium. Now suppose that real income rises, to the level y_2 at point *C*. At this point, higher real income stimulates a rise in import spending. This reduces the trade balance and depresses the current account balance. Consequently, under our assumption that a balance-of-payments equilibrium exists at point *A*, it follows that at point *C* the sum of the current account balance and the private capital account balance is negative. Thus there is a *balance-of-payments deficit* at point *C*.

The Nominal Interest Rate and the Balance of Payments If real income remains at y_2 in Figure 10–18, then what changes are necessary to reattain a balance-of-payments equilibrium? The answer is that the nominal interest rate must rise by an amount sufficient to make domestic financial assets, such as domestic bonds, more attractive to residents of other nations. Because they could earn higher returns on domestic bonds than they could prior to the rise in the domestic interest rate, foreign residents would increase their holdings of domestic financial assets.

Thus, if real income remains equal to y_2 but the nominal interest rate rises, then the result is a real income–nominal interest rate combination such as point *B* in Figure 10–18. If the interest rate increase from R_1 to R_2 is sufficient to reattain a balance-of-payments equilibrium, then point *B*, like point *A*, represents a balance-of-payments equilibrium. In fact, points *A* and *B* lie on a set of real income–nominal interest rate combinations that would maintain a balance-of-payments equilibrium. This set of combinations slopes upward. At higher real income levels, the resulting increases in imports reduce the current account balance, thereby requiring higher nominal interest rates to spur purchases of domestic assets sufficient to raise the capital account balance and reattain balance-of-payments equilibrium.

The set of real income–nominal interest rate combinations maintains a balance-of-payments equilibrium, so that along the **BP schedule** the sum of the current account and capital account is equal to zero. The implication of the *BP* schedule is that at any given time there is a single set of combinations of real income and the nominal interest rate along which a nation can achieve a balance-of-payments equilibrium.

Note that our derivation of the *BP* schedule hinges on an implicit, yet important, assumption—the exchange rate remains unchanged. An important implication is that variations in the exchange rate can alter the position of the *BP* schedule. We shall discuss this point in greater detail in Chapter 12.

BP schedule

A set of real income–nominal interest rate combinations that is consistent with a balance-of-payments equilibrium in which the current account balance and capital account balance sum to zero.

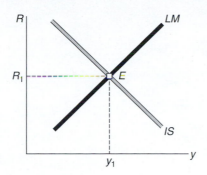

Figure 10–19

IS–LM Equilibrium

At point *E*, where the *IS* and *LM* schedules cross, the market for real money balances is in equilibrium at the same time that real income equals aggregate desired expenditures.

The *IS–LM–BP* Model

We now have three schedules with which to work. The *IS* schedule is a set of real income–nominal interest rate combinations that maintains equilibrium real income; the *LM* schedule consists of real income–nominal interest rate combinations that maintain equilibrium in the market for real money balances; and the *BP* schedule is the set of real income–nominal interest rate combinations for which the current account and the capital account sum to zero at the current exchange rate. Now let's put the schedules together to consider how equilibrium real income, the equilibrium nominal interest rate, and a nation's balance-of-payments status are jointly determined.

IS–LM Equilibrium   Let's begin by considering the simultaneous determination of the equilibrium real income level and the equilibrium nominal interest rate via the *IS* and *LM* schedules alone. Figure 10–19 shows how to combine these two schedules. At point *E*, the two schedules cross. Real income is equal to aggregate desired expenditures at the real income level y_1, because point *E* is on the *IS* schedule. Point *E* also is on the *LM* schedule, and so the money market is in equilibrium at the nominal interest rate R_1.

Point *E* is a point of **IS–LM equilibrium**. It is a point that is shared by both the *IS* schedule and the *LM* schedule. At this point, equilibrium real income is attained simultaneously with the nominal interest rate that maintains equilibrium in the money market.

IS–LM equilibrium

A single point shared in common by the *IS* and *LM* schedules, at which the economy simultaneously attains both an income–expenditure equilibrium and equilibrium in the money market.

$\overset{\$\,¥}{\underset{£\,€}{\circledast\circledast}}$Fundamental ISSUES

#5 What is an *IS–LM* equilibrium?

An *IS–LM* equilibrium is a single point that the *IS* and *LM* schedules share in common. At this point, both real income and the nominal interest rate are consistent with an equilibrium flow of real income and equilibrium in the market for real money balances.

Determining a Nation's Balance-of-Payments Position   Panel (a) of Figure 10–20 shows a situation in which a nation's current account and capital account sum to zero at the current *IS–LM* equilibrium. Because an *IS–LM* equilibrium occurs at point *E* on the *BP* schedule, both the equilibrium nominal interest rate and the equilibrium real income level are consistent with a balance-of-payments equilibrium.

In panel (b), the *IS–LM* equilibrium point *E* lies below and to the right of the *BP* schedule. Consequently, the current equilibrium real income level, y_1, induces

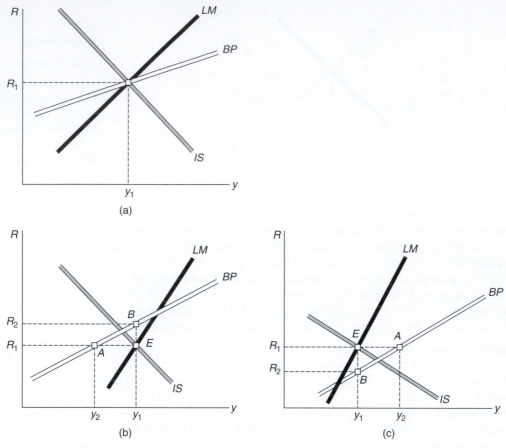

(a)

(b)   (c)

Figure 10–20 *IS–LM* Equilibrium and the *BP* Schedule

At an *IS–LM* equilibrium point *E* that lies along the *BP* schedule in panel (a), the equilibrium nominal interest rate and equilibrium real income level yield import expenditures and capital flows consistent with a balance-of-payments equilibrium. An *IS–LM* equilibrium point *E* that lies to the right of the *BP* schedule, as in panel (b), however, corresponds to a real income–nominal interest rate combination that yields import expenditures and capital outflows sufficiently high to produce a balance-of-payments deficit. Panel (c) shows the final possibility, which is an *IS–LM* equilibrium point *E* that lies to the left of the *BP* schedule. This point corresponds to a real income–nominal interest rate combination that yields import expenditures and capital outflows sufficiently low to yield a balance-of-payments surplus.

import expenditures that are too high, at the current equilibrium interest rate, R_1, to maintain a balance-of-payments equilibrium. At this interest rate, real income would have to fall to y_2 at point *A* to reduce imports pending and, thus, raise the current account balance. Alternatively, the nominal interest rate would have to rise to R_2 to induce sufficient capital inflows at point *B*. From either perspective, it is clear that point *E* in panel (b) is an *IS–LM* equilibrium point at which, given the current exchange rate, there is a *balance-of-payments deficit,* meaning that the sum of the current account balance and the capital account balance is less than zero.

Finally, panel (c) in Figure 10–20 displays a situation in which the *IS–LM* equilibrium point *E* lies above and to the left of the *BP* schedule. In this situation, the current equilibrium real income level, y_1, yields import spending that is too low, at the current equilibrium interest rate, R_1, to produce a balance-of-payments equilibrium. At the interest rate R_1, real income would have to rise to y_1 at point *A* to spur import expenditures and reduce the current account balance. Alternatively, the nominal interest rate would have to decline to R_2 to induce offsetting capital outflows at point *B*. We may conclude that point *E* in panel (c) is an *IS–LM* equilibrium point at which, given the current exchange rate, there is a *balance-of-payments surplus,* so that the sum of the current account balance and the capital account balance is positive.

As you can see, the *IS–LM–BP* model is a useful tool for examining the determination of the equilibrium nominal interest rate, equilibrium real income, and the state of the balance of payments. In the following two chapters, we shall use this open economy framework to help understand how monetary and fiscal policy actions influence these variables in alternative exchange-rate settings.

Fundamental ISSUES

#6 What is the *BP* schedule, and how can we use the *IS–LM–BP* model to determine a nation's balance-of-payments status?

The *BP* schedule is a set of real income–nominal interest rate combinations for which the sum of the current account balance and the capital account balance is equal to zero. Hence, if an *IS–LM* equilibrium occurs at a point on the *BP* schedule, then a balance-of-payments equilibrium results. An *IS–LM* equilibrium above or below the *BP* schedule, however, results in a balance-of-payments surplus or deficit, respectively.

Chapter SUMMARY

1. **Measuring a Nation's Flow of Income and Expenditures and Its Overall Price Level:** Gross domestic product (GDP) is the value of total final production that occurs, during a given time period, within a country regardless of the ownership of resources. GDP can be measured in nominal terms, or not adjusted for price changes, or in real terms, with price changes eliminated by using a deflator or price index. The GDP price deflator is a flexible-weight price index, whose weights on various goods and services change automatically as the output of goods and services varies over time. Another measure of a nation's price level is the consumer price index (CPI). The CPI is a weighted average of the prices of a fixed basket of goods and services purchased by the average or typical consumer. The circular flow of income and expenditures implies three fundamental relationships. One is that the real value of income must equal the real value of output. Another is the income identity, which states that all real income must be allocated to real consumption, real saving, real net taxes, and real imports. The third relationship is the product identity, which states that the real value of total output of goods and services must equal the sum of real consumption, real realized investment, real government spending, and real exports.

2. **The Determination of Equilibrium Real Income in an Open Economy:** The equilibrium level of real income is equal to aggregate desired expenditures at that income level. The components of aggregate desired expenditures in an open economy are household consumption spending on domestically produced goods and services, firm desired investment expenditures, government spending, and export expenditures by residents of other nations. If desired investment, government spending and net taxes, and export spending are autonomous, while consumption spending is positively related to disposable income, then the aggregate expenditures schedule has the same upward slope as the

consumption function, and equilibrium real income is determined by the intersection of this schedule and the 45-degree line.

3. **The *IS* Schedule and the Factors That Determine Its Position:** The *IS* schedule is a downward-sloping set of all combinations of real income and the nominal interest rate for which aggregate desired expenditures equal real income. An increase in autonomous desired expenditures arising from a fall in autonomous saving, import spending, or taxes or from a rise in autonomous government spending, investment, or export spending shifts the *IS* schedule rightward. A rise in autonomous saving, import spending, or taxes or a fall in autonomous government spending, investment, or export spending would, in contrast, shift the *IS* schedule leftward.

4. **The *LM* Schedule and the Factors That Determine Its Position:** The *LM* schedule is an upward-sloping set of all combinations of real income and the nominal interest rate that maintains equilibrium in the money market. An increase in the nominal quantity of money or a reduction in the price level shifts the *LM* schedule downward and to the right. In contrast, a decrease in the money stock or a rise in the price level causes the *LM* schedule to shift upward and to the left.

5. ***IS–LM* Equilibrium:** An *IS–LM* equilibrium is the point at which the *IS* and *LM* schedules cross. At such an equilibrium point, real income and the nominal interest rate simultaneously achieve an equilibrium flow of real income and equilibrium in the market for real money balances.

6. **The *BP* Schedule and How We Can Use the *IS–LM–BP* Model to Determine a Nation's Balance-of-Payments Status:** The *BP* schedule is a set of real income–nominal interest rate combinations for which the sum of the current account balance and the capital account balance is equal to zero. Therefore, attainment of an *IS–LM* equilibrium along the *BP* schedule results in a balance-of-payments equilibrium. An *IS–LM* equilibrium above or below the *BP* schedule, however, implies a balance-of-payments surplus or deficit, respectively.

QUESTIONS and PROBLEMS

1. Consider the following data ($ billions) for a given year, and calculate gross domestic product:

Consumption spending	$4,000
Net interest	600
Rental income	200
Investment spending	1,300
Profits	750
Wages and salaries	5,000
Depreciation	100
Government spending	1,500
Net export spending	−200

2. Refer to the circular-flow diagram in Figure 10–4 (p. 283), and identify flows that constitute *leakages* from the economy's overall spending flow. Now identify the flows that are *reinjections* into the overall flow of expenditures. What is definitionally true of these leakages and reinjections? Explain.

3. Explain the meanings of the intercepts and slopes of the saving, import, and consumption functions. In addition, explain in your own words, without reliance on any algebraic equations, why the marginal propensities to save, import, and consume domestic goods must sum to one.

4. Explain the distinction between a country's level of desired investment and its level of realized investment. Why are these two quantities equal at the equilibrium level of real income?

5. Suppose that in Japan, the value of the *MPS* is 0.20 and the value of the *MPC* is 0.45. What is the marginal propensity to import *(MPIM)?* If disposable income in Japan were to rise from ¥90 trillion to ¥100 trillion, by how much would Japan's consumption rise? By how much would its saving rise? By how much would its imports rise? Is the sum of your answers equal to the change in income?

6. Suppose that the value of a nation's autonomous spending multiplier is equal to 4. The marginal propensity to save is equal to 0.15, and the economy is open to international trade. What is the value of the marginal propensity to import? Show your work.

7. Suppose that the U.S. GDP deflator is equal to one and that the U.S. nominal money stock is equal to $1.8 trillion. If the demand schedule for real money balances is given by the straight-line function (measured in trillions of dollars), $m^d = (0.9 \times y) - (100 \times R)$, then what is the equation for the economy's *LM* schedule? Show your work, and solve for R on the left-hand side of the equation that you derive. Finally, if y is equal to $8 trillion, then what is the equilibrium nominal interest rate?

8. Suppose that desired investment spending is determined by the equation (measured in trillions of dollars), $i = 7.4 - (100 \times R)$. If government spending is equal to $2 trillion, real consumption spending is equal to a *fixed* value of $3 trillion, and export spending is equal to $1 trillion, then what is the straight-line equation for the *IS* schedule? (*Hint:* Set y equal to $c + i + g + x$ and solve the resulting expression with R on the left-hand side of your solution.) Finally, if the nominal interest rate is 5.4 percent (that is, 0.054), what is the equilibrium level of real income?

9. Use your answers to Questions 7 and 8 to calculate the single real income–nominal interest rate combination for an *IS–LM* equilibrium.

10. Suppose that the current account and capital account sum to a number less than zero at the equilibrium real income–nominal interest combination that you calculated in Question 9. Would the *IS–LM* equilibrium point lie above or below the *BP* schedule? Explain your reasoning.

Online APPLICATIONS

In the early part of this chapter, we discussed how real income must equal *aggregate desired* expenditures on domestically produced goods and services at the equilibrium *aggregate* real income level. Large nations, such as the United States, can experience considerable differences in *regional* economic activity, however. A good resource for information about the economic performance of different regions of the United States is the Federal Reserve's *Beige Book*. This publication is compiled by the Federal Reserve's

Board of Governors in Washington, D.C., but it receives considerable input from staff economists at the twelve Federal Reserve banks.

Internet URL: *http://www.federalreserve.gov*

Title: The Beige Book

Navigation: Begin with the Federal Reserve Board's address (http://www.federalreserve .gov). Click on *Monetary Policy*, next click on *Reports*, and then click on *Beige Book*. Select most recent date and read the summary.

Application: Read the *Beige Book Summary* and answer the following questions:

1. What measures of overall business activity does the *Beige Book's* analysis consider? According to these measures, are there regional variations in business activity at present? What is the outlook for overall U.S. business activity?

2. Have recent variations in exchange rates or in trade with other nations affected the U.S. economy? Have these variations induced differential effects across geographical regions of the United States?

For Group Study and Analysis: Assign groups of students to individual Federal Reserve districts (or sets of districts grouped by geographic region). Have each group study the portion of the most recent *Beige Book* relevant to its district or region. Ask each group to summarize the economic performance of its district or region and to identify key factors that appear to have influenced this performance.

SELECTED REFERENCES and FURTHER READINGS

Branson, William. *Macroeconomic Theory and Policy*. New York: Macmillan, 1978.

Clayton, Gary E., and Martin Gerhard Giesbrecht. *A Guide to Everyday Economic Statistics*, 7th ed. New York: McGraw-Hill, 2009.

Council of Economic Advisors. *Economic Report of the President*. Washington, D.C.: U.S. Government Printing Office, various issues.

Davis, George, and Bryce Kanago. "The Cyclical Behavior of Prices and Relative Prices." *Economic Inquiry 46* (October 2008): 576–586.

De Vroey, Michel, and Kevin Hoover. "Introduction: Seven Decades of the IS-LM Model." *History of Political Economy 36* (Supplement 2004): 1–11.

Frumkin, Norman. *Guide to Economic Indicators*, 7th ed. New York: Wiley, 2010.

Hale, Galina, and Bart Hobijn, "The U.S. Content of 'Made in China,'" Federal Reserve Bank of San Francisco, *Economic Letter* 2011-25 (August 8, 2011).

Harris, Laurence. *Monetary Theory*. New York: McGraw-Hill, 1981.

Hicks, John. "Mr. Keynes and the Classics: A Suggested Interpretation." *Econometrica 5* (April 2, 1937): 147–159.

International Monetary Fund. *World Economic Outlook*. Washington, D.C., various issues.

Keynes, John Maynard. *The General Theory of Employment, Interest, and Money*. New York: Harcourt Brace Jovanovich, 1964.

Savov, Stoyadin. "Equilibrium in an Open Economy." *Economic Thought* (2002): 3–20.

Sorensen, Bent, and Oved Yosha. "Producer Prices versus Consumer Prices in the Measurement of Risk." *Applied Economics Quarterly 53* (2007): 3–17.

U.S. Department of Commerce. *Survey of Current Business.* Washington, D.C., various issues.

11

Economic Policy with Fixed Exchange Rates

Fundamental ISSUES

1. What are the economic goals of national policymakers?
2. How does the degree of capital mobility influence the slope of the *BP* schedule?
3. To what extent can monetary policy actions influence the real income level of a small open economy with imperfect capital mobility and a fixed exchange rate?
4. To what extent can fiscal policy actions influence the real income level of a small open economy with imperfect capital mobility and a fixed exchange rate?
5. In what ways does perfect capital mobility alter the relative effectiveness of monetary and fiscal policy actions in a small open economy that adopts a fixed exchange rate?
6. In a two-country setting in which one nation's central bank fixes the exchange rate, to what extent can policy actions in one nation influence economic activity in the other nation?

For many years, the International Monetary Fund (IMF) was unwavering in its support of free flows of capital across countries' borders, and its official "guidance" to national governments advocated open markets for flows of investment funds. The IMF did not levy penalties against countries with policies contrary to this stance, but imposing limits on capital flows stigmatized countries whose governments adopted such restrictions.

Recently, however, the IMF altered its position in favor of a "very pragmatic" view on policies limiting cross-border capital flows. It adopted a new guidance framework, under which it continues to encourage governments to try to deepen their nations' capital markets in order to fully absorb financial inflows. At the same time, the IMF encourages governments to act prudently to prevent surges of capital inflows from creating "damaging distortions" for their nations' economies.

As you learned in Chapter 7, restrictions on cross-border flows of funds such as those now viewed "very pragmatically" by the IMF are known as *capital controls*. In this chapter, you will learn about the implications of capital controls for national monetary and fiscal policymaking in systems of fixed exchange rates.

THE OBJECTIVES OF POLICY

Until the early 1970s, much of the world participated in various types of fixed-exchange-rate systems. Consequently, the appropriate management of monetary and fiscal policies under fixed exchange rates has been an important issue. Even today, about one-third of nations around the globe engage in some form of currency-pegging arrangement. To contemplate how effective policies conducted by national governments and central banks may be, however, we first need to think about what goals they may desire to pursue.

Internal Balance Objectives

In Chapter 10, we introduced the *IS–LM–BP* framework. We use this framework to examine the factors that determine a nation's equilibrium nominal interest rate, its equilibrium real income, and its balance-of-payments position. Changes in the nominal money stock can influence the position of the *LM* schedule, and variations in government spending and taxation policies can affect the position of the *IS* schedule. Consequently, such policy actions could affect a nation's economic performance, and so central banks and governments might contemplate adopting policy strategies with an explicit intention to achieve specific national economic goals.

One aim of central banks and governments could be to achieve *internal balance,* which refers to the attainment of purely domestic policy objectives. Although national policymakers might seek to achieve a number of internal balance objectives, three objectives typically top any policymaker's list of internal balance goals, as discussed next.

Real-Income Goals One internal balance objective of policymakers might be to achieve the highest possible growth in its citizens' livings standards. Measuring how much a country is growing in terms of annual increases in real national income requires adjusting for population growth. Hence, most economists agree that the best available measure of the growth in overall living standards within any nation is the growth rate of ***per capita gross domestic product***, or per capita GDP. This is the total value of final goods and services produced within a nation during a given year divided by the number of the nation's residents. Per capita GDP, therefore, is a measure of material well-being for the average resident of a country, and the growth rate of per capita GDP is a measure of the improvement of an average resident's living standards over time. As Table 11–1 indicates, average annual growth rates of per capita real GDP vary considerably across nations.

Is per capita GDP growth an appropriate policy objective? Some economists question whether central banks and/or governments should try to fine-tune their nations' real growth. One reason is that there are significant problems in measuring and interpreting per capita GDP data. Although per capita income growth may be calculated easily if dependable data are available, the governments of many developing nations do not have the resources to collect accurate real income data, and many do not carefully tabulate their nations' populations.

per capita gross domestic product

The total value of final goods and services produced within a country during a given year divided by the number of people residing in the country.

Table 11–1

Annual Rates of Growth of Per Capita Real GDP in the G7 Nations (%)

	1980–1989	1990–1999	2000–2009	2010–2019*
Canada	1.9	1.3	1.0	1.5
France	1.9	1.4	0.7	1.3
Germany	1.8	1.6	0.9	2.1
Italy	2.4	1.4	0.0	0.5
Japan	3.9	1.2	0.6	1.9
United Kingdom	2.8	2.0	1.2	1.4
United States	2.5	1.9	0.7	1.7

*IMF estimates.
Source: Data from International Monetary Fund, *World Economic Outlook Database.*

There also are some conceptual problems stemming from using the rise in per capita GDP as a measure of economic growth. One is that this measure fails to indicate how a nation's income is *distributed* among the residents of a nation. A country's per capita GDP might grow very rapidly during years in which the incomes of its poorest residents decline even further. In addition, the rate of increase in per capita real GDP is at best an *indicator* of improvements in the average well-being of a nation's residents. This is so because real living standards can improve without per capita income growth, if people, on average, enjoy more leisure time while producing as much as they did before. Furthermore, measured per capita GDP growth does not fully account for *quality* changes that take place over time. Improvements in goods and services that residents of a nation produce and consume are not taken into account in the compilation of GDP statistics. Finally, the well-being of a country's citizens likely depends on more than just the value of the nation's output of goods and services. For instance, if the act of producing those goods and services significantly damages the environment, then overall living standards could decline, on net, even if the country's citizens have higher real incomes and more goods and services available for consumption.

Learn about cross-country per capita income growth and inequality from information from the World Bank at *http://www.worldbank.org.*

Can national policymakers influence real living standards? Despite these problems, economists generally regard growth in per capita GDP as the best available overall measure of a nation's economic growth. For this reason, policymakers might wish to conduct policies intended to maintain high and stable rates of growth in per capita GDP.

This does not necessarily mean, however, that such policies of central banks and governments *can* influence nations' economic growth rates. As we shall discuss in greater detail in Chapter 13, many economists believe that over intervals longer than several years, the monetary policies of central banks have meager effects on real output growth. Furthermore, some economists have concluded that over periods spanning decades, the ability of nations' governments to spur economic growth via their spending and taxation policies is secondary in comparison with broader factors, such as the tastes, preferences, education, and other attributes of those nations' residents.

Nevertheless, it might be possible that trying to attain high and stable per capita GDP growth could help limit fluctuations in aggregate real income relative to *natural real GDP*, or the level of real GDP along the long-run growth path that the economy otherwise would tend to follow in the absence of cyclical fluctuations. Intervals in which such fluctuations take place are known as *business cycles*. Even if policymakers were to agree that they might not have much influence on a nation's natural GDP, they still might feel obligated to try to conduct policies that might reduce the frequency and extent of business-cycle fluctuations.

Employment Goals Labor is a key factor of production, and in most democratic countries workers account for the bulk of the electorate. Even leaders of nondemocratic societies are likely to feel obliged to pay attention to the interests of workers. Thus, governments and central banks usually feel pressure to follow policies intended to reduce the size and volatility of worker unemployment rates.

To track the extent of aggregate unemployment within their nations, governments tabulate *unemployment rates*. A nation's unemployment rate is the percentage of its labor force that is unemployed. Governments define the term *labor force* in various ways, so national unemployment rates are not always strictly comparable across countries. Nevertheless, Table 11–2 shows recent average unemployment

natural real gross domestic product
A level of real GDP that lies on a nation's long-run growth path.

business cycles
Periods of fluctuation in real GDP around its natural level.

unemployment rate
The percentage of a nation's labor force that is unemployed.

Table 11–2

Unemployment Rates in Selected Nations (%)

	2008	2009	2010	2011	2012	2013*	2014*	2015*
Australia	4.3	5.6	5.2	5.1	5.2	5.2	4.8	4.7
Canada	6.2	8.3	8.0	7.5	7.4	7.3	7.1	6.9
France	7.8	9.5	9.8	9.7	9.9	10.0	9.8	9.4
Germany	7.6	7.7	7.1	6.0	5.6	5.5	5.3	5.3
Hong Kong	3.5	5.2	4.3	3.4	3.5	3.5	3.4	3.2
Italy	6.8	7.8	8.4	8.4	9.5	9.7	9.8	9.4
Japan	4.0	5.1	5.1	4.5	4.5	4.4	4.3	4.2
Korea	3.2	3.7	3.7	3.4	3.3	3.3	3.3	3.3
Spain	11.3	18.0	20.1	21.6	24.2	23.9	22.8	21.9
Sweden	6.2	8.3	8.4	7.5	7.5	7.7	7.0	6.5
Taiwan	4.1	5.9	5.2	4.4	4.4	4.3	4.2	4.1
United Kingdom	5.6	7.5	7.9	8.0	8.3	8.2	7.8	7.4
United States	5.8	9.3	9.6	9.0	8.2	7.9	7.5	7.0

*IMF estimates.
Source: International Monetary Fund, *World Economic Outlook Database*.

frictional unemployment

The fraction of a nation's labor force composed of people who are temporarily out of work.

structural unemployment

The fraction of a nation's labor force composed of people who would like to be employed but who do not possess skills and other characteristics required to obtain jobs.

natural rate of unemployment

The sum of the rates of frictional and structural unemployment, or the unemployment rate that would arise if a nation's economy were always on its long-run growth path.

cyclical unemployment

The fraction of a nation's labor force composed of individuals who have lost employment owing to business-cycle fluctuations.

rates for several nations. As you can see, there has been considerable variation in unemployment rates. Many nations have experienced double-digit unemployment rates, whereas in other countries average unemployment rates have been much lower.

There are three components of the unemployed portion of a nation's labor force. One is *frictional unemployment*. This is the portion of the labor force made up of people who are out of work temporarily, perhaps because they recently left one job and will not begin another for a few weeks. Another is *structural unemployment*, or the portion of the labor force composed of people who would like to have jobs but who do not possess skills and other attributes necessary to obtain gainful employment. The sum of the ratios of those who are frictionally and structurally unemployed as a ratio of the labor force is the *natural rate of unemployment*, or the unemployment rate that would arise if the economy could stay on its long-run growth path. At any point along this path, there would naturally be people between jobs or people lacking characteristics necessary to obtain employment. Remaining variations in the overall unemployment rate along an economy's growth path would arise from changes in the third category of unemployment. This is *cyclical unemployment*, or the portion of the labor force composed of individuals who have lost their jobs as a result of business-cycle fluctuations. One possible internal balance objective of national governments is to minimize cyclical unemployment.

Inflation Goals To some extent, all members of society bear inflation costs. Nonetheless, some bear the brunt of these costs to a greater degree than others. Those who are particularly harmed by inflation are business owners who experience forgone profit opportunities and who must incur the costs of changing prices, savers, financial institutions that are creditors, and people who pay the largest portion of taxes. Table 11–3 summarizes these costs.

The inflation costs summarized in Table 11–3 provide a strong rationale for policymakers to try to maintain low inflation and to limit inflation volatility. Most policymakers, therefore, include maintaining low and stable inflation, in addition to attaining high growth in per capita real income and minimizing cyclical unemployment rates, as a part of their definition of internal balance.

Table 11–3

The Costs of Inflation and Inflation Variability

Type of Cost	Cause
Resources expended to economize on money holdings (more trips to banks, etc.)	Rising prices associated with inflation
Costs of changing price lists and printing menus and catalogs	Individual product/service price increases associated with inflation
Redistribution of real income from individuals to the government	Inflation that pushes people into higher, nonindexed nominal tax brackets
Reductions in investment, capital accumulation, and economic growth	Inflation variability that complicates business planning
Slowed pace of introduction of new and better products	Volatile price changes that reduce the efficiency of private markets
Redistribution of resources from creditors to debtors	Unexpected inflation that reduces the real value of debts

External Balance Objectives

In addition to purely domestic, internal balance objectives, a nation's government and central bank may also be concerned about international payment flows. Thus, these policymakers may desire to achieve *external balance*, or the attainment of objectives for international flows of goods, services, income, and assets for the relative values of their national currencies.

Why would a nation's residents desire for policymakers to pursue external balance objectives? One reason is that international factors help determine domestic outcomes in open economies. If residents of a nation engage in significant volumes of trade with other nations, international considerations may affect a nation's ability to achieve its output, employment, and inflation objectives. Consequently, internal and external balance objectives may go hand in hand. Another reason, however, is that a number of a nation's citizens may have immediate interests in the international sectors of their nation's economy. They may perceive that international variables themselves—such as the nation's merchandise trade balance or its current account balance—should be ultimate policy goals.

International Objectives and Domestic Goals As we discussed in Chapter 10, two factors that play a role in determining a country's aggregate desired expenditures are export expenditures on the nation's output of goods and services by residents of other nations and import spending by its own residents on foreign-produced goods and services. An increase in export expenditures increases aggregate desired expenditures, whereas a rise in import spending reduces the fraction of disposable income available for consumption of domestically produced output. Therefore, both of these international factors affect the position of a country's *IS* schedule and thereby influence the equilibrium level of real income.

It follows that a government or central bank must take into consideration the volumes of export and import expenditures when contemplating appropriate policy strategies. At a minimum, a national policymaker must account for the real income effects of trade-related expenditures that are unrelated to purely domestic influences. More broadly, however, a policymaker may reach the conclusion that achieving a nation's internal balance objectives may require careful attention to international factors. For example, a policymaker may seek to achieve balanced merchandise trade as part of a general strategy intended to achieve the nation's domestic output, employment, and inflation objectives.

External Balance for Its Own Sake Policymakers in most countries, however, typically regard external balance objectives as a set of goals that is separable from its internal balance objectives. Workers and business owners in industries that export large portions of their output often push their governments to enact policies that promote exports. At the same time, workers and business owners in industries that rely on domestic sales of their output may pressure government and central bank officials to pursue policies that restrain imports. Persistent efforts by both of these interest groups could induce a nation's policymakers to seek merchandise trade and balance-of-payments *surpluses* as external balance objectives.

History is replete with examples of nations that have sought to achieve persistent surpluses in their balance-of-payments accounts. For example, in the seventeenth and eighteenth centuries, successive generations of British citizens

mercantilism

A view that a primary determinant of a nation's wealth is its inflows of payments resulting from international trade and commerce, so that a nation can gain by enacting policies that spur exports while limiting imports.

advocated a national policy of *mercantilism*. The view of this school of thought is that inflows of payments relating to international commerce and trade are a primary source of a nation's wealth. During this period, therefore, British mercantilists advocated governmental and central bank policy actions designed to promote exports and to hinder imports. A fundamental difficulty with mercantilist thought, of course, is that if all countries simultaneously try to attain trade and payments surpluses through import limitations, international commerce likely would be stymied. Realization of this self-defeating aspect of mercantilism led to its decline in the nineteenth century. Mercantilist thought supports the interests of special interest groups in any open economy, however, so these groups still use mercantilist arguments today in an effort to pressure policymakers to maintain trade and current account balances, if not surpluses.

The interests of exporters and importers also may make exchange-rate objectives part of the mix of external balance goals. If export industries are a predominant political interest group, a country's policymakers also face pressures to reduce the exchange value of its currency. By way of contrast, in a nation in which domestic industries have considerable political clout, policymakers may be lobbied to push up the value of the nation's currency.

Fundamental ISSUES

#1 What are the economic goals of national policymakers?

There are two categories of economic goals that governments and central banks often pursue. One consists of internal balance objectives, which are goals for national real income, employment, and inflation. The other consists of external balance objectives, which are goals for the trade balance and other components of the balance of payments.

THE ROLE OF CAPITAL MOBILITY

The manner in which monetary and fiscal policy actions may influence a nation's economic performance relative to either internal or external balance objectives depends considerably on the extent of *capital mobility*. This term refers to the degree to which funds and financial assets are free to flow across a nation's borders. A nation with *high capital mobility* is one that is open to and experiences considerable cross-border flows of funds and financial assets.

capital mobility

The extent to which financial resources can flow across a nation's borders.

After accounting for differing risks across alternative assets and nations that issue the assets, owners of financial assets around the world seek the highest available returns. Many are willing and able to shift their funds from one nation to another. Typically, therefore, flows of funds across national boundaries are significant if the returns to reallocations are high enough and if barriers to such flows are insignificant. Some nations, however, have imposed legal impediments, called *capital controls*, that restrict the ability of their residents to hold and exchange assets denominated in the currencies of other nations. Capital controls, introduced in Chapter 7, inhibit flows of funds and assets across the borders of a country and can lead to *low capital mobility* for nations that adopt such controls. Furthermore, many less developed nations do not possess well-developed banking systems or financial markets, which often has kept their capital mobility low.

Capital Mobility and the *BP* Schedule

As you learned in Chapter 10, we can infer whether a nation would experience a balance-of-payments surplus or deficit at a given *IS–LM* equilibrium nominal interest rate–real income combination by referring to the *location* of the *BP* schedule. The extent of capital mobility, it turns out, affects the *slope* of the *BP* schedule. As you will see later in this chapter, the degree of capital mobility and the resulting slope of the *BP* schedule determine how monetary and fiscal policy actions ultimately influence a nation's economic performance.

The Case of Low Capital Mobility As you learned in Chapter 10, a balance-of-payments equilibrium, in which the current account balance and capital account balance sum to zero, occurs if an *IS–LM* equilibrium arises at a point along the *BP* schedule. Thus, an *IS–LM* equilibrium point below and to the right of the *BP* schedule implies that a nation is experiencing a balance-of-payments deficit. Below the *BP* schedule, the nominal interest rate is so low at a given level of real income that either capital flows out of the nation, thereby causing a capital account deficit, or capital inflows are too meager to offset the nation's current account deficit. To the right of the *BP* schedule, real income is so high at a given nominal interest rate that the induced level of import spending results in a current account deficit. Either a capital account deficit or a current account deficit contributes to a balance-of-payments deficit, but which is the *predominant* reason for a balance-of-payments deficit? The answer depends on the degree of capital mobility and the slope of the *BP* schedule.

Let's begin by thinking about required adjustments of real income and nominal interest rates necessary to maintain balance-of-payments equilibrium when there is low capital mobility. This situation arises because of capital controls or other impediments to flows of funds and assets. When there is low capital mobility, the *BP* schedule is relatively *steep*. To see why this is so, consider panel (a) of Figure 11–1. Suppose that the real income–nominal interest rate combination y_1 and R_1 at point A

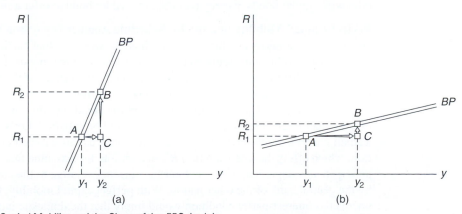

(a)   (b)

Figure 11–1   Capital Mobility and the Slope of the *BP* Schedule

Panel (a) illustrates that the *BP* schedule is relatively steep when there is low capital mobility. If there is a balance-of-payments equilibrium at point *A*, then if real income rises to y_2, imports increase, causing a current account deficit at point *C*. With low capital mobility, a relatively large increase in the nominal interest rate is needed to induce foreign residents to overcome barriers to capital inflows sufficient to achieve a new balance-of-payments equilibrium at point *B*. In contrast, as shown in panel (b), a comparatively smaller increase in the nominal interest rate is required to induce sufficient capital inflows when there are fewer barriers to capital mobility, so that the *BP* schedule is relatively shallow with higher capital mobility.

is consistent with balance-of-payments equilibrium. If real income rises to y_2, then imports increase, generating a current account deficit at point C. Thus, low capital mobility requires a very sizable increase in the nominal interest rate to induce residents of other nations to circumvent capital controls and increase their holdings of domestic financial assets in amounts sufficient to improve the capital account balance to reattain balance-of-payments equilibrium.

It follows that a rise in real income from y_1 to y_2 in panel (a) requires a relatively large increase in the nominal interest rate, say to R_2 at point B, to ensure that the sum of the current account balance and capital account balance would equal zero. Points A and B thereby lie on a relatively steep BP schedule. Stated differently, a relatively steep BP schedule indicates that a nation's degree of capital mobility is relatively low.

The Case of High Capital Mobility In contrast, if capital mobility is relatively high, then the BP schedule is relatively *shallow*, as shown in panel (b) of Figure 11–1. As before, if real income rises from y_1 at point A, at which there is balance-of-payments equilibrium, to y_2 at a point B, then the result is an increase in imports. This causes a current account deficit at the point C.

If capital mobility is high, then a relatively small rise in the nominal interest rate, perhaps from R_1 to R_2 in panel (b), is sufficient to induce other nations' residents to raise their holdings of domestic financial assets in sufficient quantities to improve the capital account balance and reattain balance-of-payments equilibrium. Hence, the BP schedule containing points A and B in panel (b) has a relatively shallow slope. In other words, a relatively shallow BP schedule indicates that the degree of capital mobility is relatively high.

Perfect Capital Mobility

In Chapter 4, you learned about the *uncovered-interest-parity condition*. This condition states that if bonds denominated in two different currencies otherwise are perfect substitutes, then the difference between the interest rates on the bonds should equal the expected rate of depreciation. You also learned that uncovered interest parity does not always hold, because there may be distinctive risk characteristics of these otherwise similar bonds, thereby requiring the riskier bond to offer a risk premium.

Perfect Capital Mobility and the BP Schedule Another key reason that the uncovered-interest-parity condition may not hold, however, is that barriers to capital mobility can inhibit substitution between otherwise identical bonds. Imperfect capital mobility, therefore, is a common explanation for the failure of the uncovered-interest-parity condition to be met in a number of nations.

But this means that for a nation with *perfect* capital mobility, we would expect that the uncovered-interest-parity condition should be satisfied. Let's suppose that a small nation's bonds have the same degree of risk as those issued in a large nation, which offers the interest return R^*. In addition, let's assume that people do not anticipate any depreciation of the domestic currency relative to the currency issued by the central bank of the other nation. With perfect capital mobility, therefore, the uncovered-interest-parity condition would imply that the domestic interest rate, R, should be *equal* to the foreign interest rate, R^*. Thus, as shown in Figure 11–2, under these assumptions the domestic interest rate would not vary from the foreign interest rate R^* as domestic real income varies. As a result, the domestic BP schedule is *horizontal* under perfect capital mobility. (The Internet is helping make foreign currencies so mobile that they can now be delivered to your front door; see *Online Notebook: A Web Route to Avoiding Lines for Currency Exchange*.)

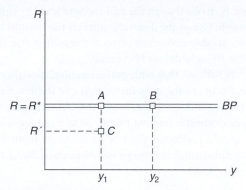

Figure 11–2   The *BP* Schedule with Perfect Capital Mobility

We suppose that the bonds issued in foreign nations, which offer the interest return R^*, have the same risks as domestic bonds. In addition, we assume that domestic and foreign residents do not anticipate any depreciation of the domestic currency relative to the currency issued by the central bank of the other nation. With perfect capital mobility, it follows from the uncovered-interest-parity condition that the domestic interest rate, R, is equal to the foreign interest rate, R^*. This implies that the domestic *BP* schedule is horizontal under perfect capital mobility. Both point *A* and point *B* are consistent with balance-of-payments equilibrium, but if the interest rate declines to R' at point *C*, the domestic interest rate is less than the foreign interest rate so that capital flows out of the domestic country. There is a domestic balance-of-payments deficit at point *C*.

 **ONLINE**Notebook

A Web Route to Avoiding Lines for Currency Exchange

For years, people outside large cities have had a hard time obtaining foreign currencies in advance of a trip abroad. More than half of banks in small communities do not offer currency-exchange services. Many of the remainder actually arrange transactions through larger commercial banks and charge sizable fees to arrange currency exchanges.

Today, anyone with access to the Internet can go to the Web site of Travelex Group, a Canadian firm that ships foreign currencies and foreign-currency-denominated travelers checks in quantities ranging from $200 to $1,500. The company earns revenues from exchange fees that it factors into currency-conversion rates, and it provides free two-day shipping for amounts above $500. If you want foreign currency in a hurry, however, you can pay for next-day shipping.

For Critical Analysis

Why do you suppose that the rates of exchange offered by Travelex and other currency-exchange firms are not as favorable as those at which currencies trade among large financial institutions?

The Domestic Interest Rate and Balance of Payments with Perfect Capital Mobility Any point along the *BP* schedule in Figure 11–2 is a point at which the current account balance and the capital account balance sum to zero. Thus, the real income–nominal interest rate combination y_1 and R at point *A* in Figure 11–2 is a point of balance-of-payments equilibrium, because it lies on the *BP* schedule. So is point *B*. Even though the real income level y_2 is higher at point *B*, the smallest conceivable rise in the domestic interest rate would be sufficient to generate capital inflows sizable enough to offset the resulting rise in imports. Capital is fully mobile, so the *BP* schedule is horizontal.

It follows that with perfect capital mobility, variations in the nominal interest rate are the only factor that can induce balance-of-payments deficits or surpluses. For instance, at point *C* directly below point *A* in Figure 11–2, the lower domestic interest rate *R'* would induce a significant capital outflow. Savers would reallocate their bond holdings from domestic bonds to equally risky, fully substitutable foreign bonds in pursuits of the higher returns available on the foreign bonds.

Fundamental ISSUES

#2 How does the degree of capital mobility influence the slope of the *BP* schedule?

With low capital mobility, a significant rise in a nation's interest rate is required to generate the capital inflows needed to offset the greater imports that result from a rise in the nation's real income level. Because the *BP* schedule is the set of real income–nominal interest rate combinations that maintains balance-of-payments equilibrium, this means that the *BP* schedule is steeply sloped with a low degree of capital mobility. As capital mobility increases, the *BP* schedule becomes more shallow. In the extreme case of perfect capital mobility, the *BP* schedule is horizontal at the level of the foreign interest rate.

FIXED EXCHANGE RATES AND IMPERFECT CAPITAL MOBILITY

As we discussed in Chapter 3, many nations still choose to fix their exchange rates. These nations may consider their residents' costs in hedging against foreign exchange risks to be greater than the benefits of a flexible-exchange-rate system's shock-absorbing features. How does the adoption of a fixed exchange rate influence the transmission of economic policies enacted by governments and central banks?

At this point, we are not in a position to develop complete answers to this question, because the *IS–LM–BP* framework developed in Chapter 10 does not tell us anything about unemployment or inflation. It also is silent concerning the relationship between actual GDP and the natural GDP level. We shall not try to explain how the effects of economic policies relate to these broader internal balance objectives until Chapter 13. Nevertheless, we can still use the *IS–LM–BP* framework to develop some essential answers to this question. To accomplish this, we shall interpret achieving a higher level of real income as a nation's only internal balance objective and maintaining balance-of-payments equilibrium as the overriding external balance objective. Thus, we rule out mercantilist-driven desires for simultaneous current and capital account surpluses. It would be straightforward to account for such goals, but we leave it to you in Problem 1 at the end of the chapter. Under this interpretation of the basic *IS–LM–BP* model, we shall demonstrate that our answers depend on the degree of capital mobility.

Monetary Policy under Fixed Exchange Rates and Imperfect Capital Mobility

As we noted in Chapter 7, a key problem of maintaining a fixed exchange rate through foreign exchange interventions is making a commitment to a particular exchange rate credible. For now, however, let's suppose that a country has established a credible fixed-exchange-rate commitment. We shall revisit the credibility issue in Chapters 13, 14, and 15. (Establishing a credible fixed-exchange-rate arrangement is difficult if the official value of the fixed exchange rate is considerably different from what a free market would have delivered and if black markets are prevalent; see *Policy Notebook: To Make Its Official Exchange Rate Credible, Venezuela's Government Has Sometimes Effectively Given Away Caribbean Vacations*.)

 # POLICY Notebook

To Make Its Official Exchange Rate Credible, Venezuela's Government Has Sometimes Effectively Given Away Caribbean Vacations

Even though the going black-market exchange rate in recent years has been 6 to 7 Venezuelan bolivars per U.S. dollar, the Venezuelan government's official fixed exchange rate has remained at 4.3 bolivars per U.S. dollar. Naturally, the substantial differences between the black-market exchange rate and the official exchange rate have given Venezuelan residents an incentive to buy dollars at the official exchange rate and then sell those dollars at the higher black-market rate.

Nevertheless, in recent years the Venezuelan government has allowed the nation's residents to spend as much as $5,000 on credit cards at the official exchange rate. This has enabled Venezuelan residents to holiday on Caribbean islands, where they have been able to convert their $5,000 quota for dollar purchases into dollars. Then they have returned to Venezuela and converted any unspent dollars back into bolivars—in a few cases not only covering much of the expense of making the trip but also making a profit.

For Critical Analysis

How could the Central Bank of Venezuela adjust its foreign exchange reserves to try to push the black-market bolivar–dollar exchange rate closer to the official fixed exchange rate?

 On the WEB

Visit the Web site of Venezuela's central bank, the Central Bank of Venezuela, at *http://www.bcv.org.ve/EnglishVersion/Index.asp*.

We shall begin by thinking about the effects of monetary policy under fixed exchange rates. First, however, we need to consider how monetary policy actions influence nominal interest rates and real income.

Monetary Policy, the Nominal Interest Rate, and Real Income A country's equilibrium nominal interest rate and the equilibrium level of real income arise in an *IS–LM* equilibrium, such as point *A* in panel (b) of Figure 11–3. As shown in panel (a), the amount of money demanded at the real income level y_1 crosses the

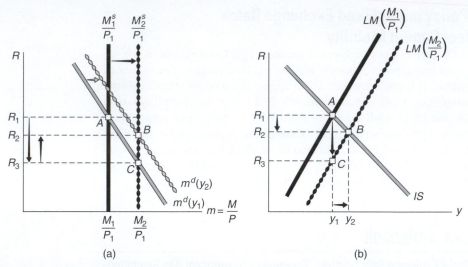

Figure 11–3   The Effects of Expansionary Monetary Policy

A central bank policy action that increases the nominal quantity of money in circulation causes, if the price level is unchanged, an increase in the supply of real money balances. This generates a decline in the money-market equilibrium interest rate from R_1 at point A to R_3 at point C in panel (a), which results in a downward shift in the LM schedule by the distance A–C in panel (b). The decline in the interest rate, however, induces a rise in desired investment and a consequent movement down along the IS schedule to a new IS–LM equilibrium point B at the higher real income level y_2. As real income increases, the demand for real money balances rises in panel (a), causing the equilibrium interest rate to rise to R_2, which corresponds to an upward movement along the new LM schedule in panel (b), from point C to point B. On net, therefore, the rise in the nominal money stock causes a reduction in the equilibrium nominal interest rate and an increase in equilibrium real income.

liquidity effect

A reduction in the equilibrium nominal interest rate stemming from an increase in the nominal quantity of money in circulation.

supply of real money balances at the equilibrium nominal interest rate R_1, so that equilibrium is maintained at point A in the money market.

Now suppose that the central bank undertakes an expansionary monetary policy by increasing the nominal quantity of money, from M_1 to M_2. At a given price level, P_1, this causes a rise in the supply of real money balances, resulting in a decline in the equilibrium nominal interest rate, to R_3 at point C in panel (a). This decline in the nominal interest rate at the income level y_1 is the amount by which the LM schedule shifts downward in panel (b), from point A to point C. The fall in the nominal interest rate generates a rise in desired real investment spending, which in turn causes equilibrium real income to rise toward y_2 at point B in panel (b). Thus, there is a movement along the IS schedule from point A to point B. The result of this increase in real income is an increase in the demand for real money balances in panel (a), from $m^d(y_1)$ to $m^d(y_2)$. This causes the equilibrium nominal interest rate to rise back up toward R_2 at point B in panel (a). In panel (b) this can be visualized as movement back up along the LM schedule from point C to point B. Point B, therefore, is the final equilibrium point, with a net decline in the equilibrium nominal interest rate, from R_1 to R_2, and an increase in equilibrium real income, from y_1 to y_2.

We may conclude that, provided that the price level is unchanged, an expansionary monetary policy action causes a *liquidity effect*—the term for a fall in the equilibrium nominal interest rate induced by an increase in the nominal money stock—that stimulates desired investment and expands equilibrium real income. Hence, the channel through which monetary policy actions are transmitted to the economy is through a liquidity effect that alters desired investment and thereby changes the real income level.

Monetary Policy and the Balance of Payments with Imperfect Capital Mobility
Now let's contemplate the balance-of-payments implications of an expansionary monetary policy action when a nation has low capital mobility. As shown in panel (a) of Figure 11–4, we shall assume that initially the country attains balance-of-payments equilibrium at point A on the relatively steep BP schedule. An increase in the nominal quantity of money, from M_1 to a larger amount M_2, causes the LM schedule to shift downward and to the right, resulting in a new IS–LM equilibrium point below and to the right of the BP schedule. Hence, a monetary expansion generates a balance-of-payments deficit at point B in Figure 11–4.

It is important to recognize that because capital mobility is low, the key reason that a balance-of-payments deficit occurs at point B is a rise in real income. This rise in real income stimulates an increase in imports and thereby causes a trade deficit to occur. The equilibrium interest rate declines, but because capital mobility is low, relatively little capital flows out of the country. Thus, the primary explanation for the existence of a balance-of-payments deficit at point B in panel (a) is the trade deficit stemming from increased import expenditures at the higher income level y_2.

Panel (b) of Figure 11–4 illustrates a situation in which capital mobility is relatively high, though still imperfect, so that the BP schedule is relatively shallow. In contrast to the example in panel (a), a decline in the nation's equilibrium interest rate to R_2 causes a significant outflow of capital, so at point B the nation experiences a sizable capital account deficit, which is a key contributor to the balance-of-payments deficit it experiences at this new equilibrium point.

Sterilized Monetary Policy   At point B in either panel of Figure 11–4, the fact that a nation experiences a balance-of-payments deficit means that there would be market pressures for the nation's exchange rate to change. With low capital mobility, as in panel (a), the increase in equilibrium real income at point B induces the nation's residents to seek to acquire other nations' currencies so that they may purchase more imports. This raises the demand for foreign exchange and places downward pressure on the nation's currency value. By way of contrast, at point B in panel (b), in which there is high capital mobility, the fall in the equilibrium interest rate

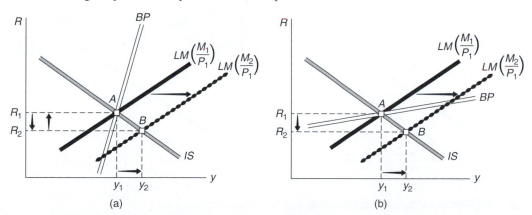

(a)   (b)

Figure 11–4   The Initial Effects of Monetary Policy with a Fixed Exchange Rate
Both panels show how a monetary expansion initially affects the nominal interest rate and real income under a fixed exchange rate. In panel (a) the BP schedule is relatively steep, indicating a situation of low capital mobility. The decline in the equilibrium interest rate that occurs following a movement from point A to point B induces little capital outflow, but the rise in equilibrium real income stimulates greater import spending. The result is a balance-of-payments deficit at point B. In contrast, in panel (b) the BP schedule is much more shallow, implying a situation of high capital mobility. In this case, the decline in the equilibrium interest rate spurs a significant capital outflow that makes a key contribution to the resulting balance-of-payments deficit at point B.

induces residents to acquire more foreign assets. This also entails acquiring greater volumes of foreign currencies, which tends to depress the value of the nation's currency in the foreign exchange markets.

To keep the exchange value of its nation's currency from declining at point *B* in either panel of Figure 11–4, a central bank would have to sell some of its foreign exchange reserves. This would offset the rise in the demand for foreign currencies by its own citizens by raising the supply of foreign currencies in the foreign exchange markets. But if the central bank were to sell some of its foreign currency reserves, its assets would decline. This would require a decline in its liabilities, including some of its money liabilities in circulation. Hence, the domestic money stock would begin to fall. To keep this from happening, the central bank would have to add sufficient *domestic* assets, such as domestic government bonds, to its own portfolio. This action would prevent its total assets from falling. This, as we discussed in Chapter 9, would be a *sterilized* intervention, because this action would prevent changes in foreign exchange reserves from affecting the nation's money stock.

Nonsterilized Monetary Policy Both panels of Figure 11–4 illustrate outcomes if a central bank sterilizes its interventions to maintain a fixed exchange rate. But what would happen if the central bank chose not to sterilize, perhaps because its external balance objective is to maintain balance-of-payments equilibrium? Figure 11–5 provides the answer to this question. As in Figure 11–4, panels (a) and (b) of Figure 11–5 depict the initial effects of a monetary expansion with low capital mobility and high capital mobility, respectively. In each panel, at a new equilibrium point *B* the nation experiences a balance-of-payments deficit. Because this tends to depress the value of the nation's currency in foreign exchange markets, the nation's central bank must sell some of its foreign exchange reserves to keep the exchange rate fixed.

In the absence of sterilization, the central bank's assets would decline, which would require a reduction in the amount of circulating money liabilities that it issues. Consequently, the nation's nominal money stock would begin to decline. As both panels of Figure 11–5 indicate, failure to sterilize ultimately would cause the

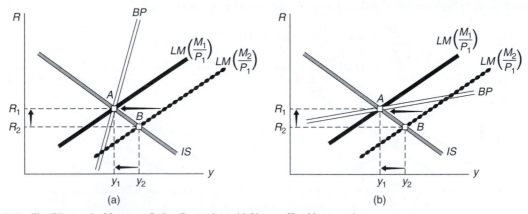

Figure 11–5   The Effects of a Monetary Policy Expansion with Nonsterilized Interventions
Panels (a) and (b) illustrate the final effects of an increase in the nominal quantity of money that, as shown in Figure 11–4, first causes a rightward shift in the *LM* schedule and a movement from point *A* to point *B*. In panel (a) there is relatively low capital mobility, so a balance-of-payments deficit stems mainly from higher import expenditures, whereas in panel (b) there is significant capital mobility, so the balance-of-payments deficit at point *B* results mainly from capital inflows. In either case, the balance-of-payments deficit implies an increased demand for foreign currencies by the nation's residents, which tends to depress the value of the nation's currency in foreign exchange markets. To keep the exchange rate from changing, the nation's central bank must sell foreign exchange reserves. If the central bank does not sterilize this action, this causes a reduction in the quantity of money in circulation and an ultimate movement back to point *A*.

nation's quantity of money to decline from M_2, the level to which the central bank originally had raised the nation's money stock, back to M_1, the initial quantity of money before the monetary expansion. Thus, the central bank's sales of foreign exchange reserves to maintain a fixed exchange rate eventually cause the *LM* schedule to shift back to its original location, and the initial *IS–LM* equilibrium point A ultimately is reattained. A *nonsterilized* monetary expansion with a fixed exchange rate thereby leads to an eventual contraction of the money stock. As long as no other factors change, the economy then would reattain its initial equilibrium real income level and interest rate, leading to reattainment of balance-of-payments equilibrium at point *A*.

The Monetary Approach Revisited Figure 11–5 illustrates the implications of the monetary approach to the balance of payments outlined in Chapter 9. According to the monetary approach, committing to a fixed exchange rate causes a nation's money stock to vary with changes in foreign exchange reserves that are necessary to keep the exchange rate fixed. If monetary policy actions are nonsterilized, then the result is an automatic adjustment toward balance-of-payments equilibrium and toward the preexpansion equilibrium real income level and nominal interest rate. Hence, we may conclude the following:

> **According to the monetary approach to the balance of payments, efforts to affect real income and the balance of payments via nonsterilized monetary expansions or contractions ultimately are ineffective policy actions if exchange rates are fixed.**

Could sterilization prevent this eventual adjustment to balance-of-payments equilibrium? If a central bank attempts to sterilize indefinitely, so as to maintain real income at y_2 at point *B,* then a persistent balance-of-payments deficit places continual downward pressure on the value of the nation's currency. No central bank has sufficient foreign exchange reserves to keep the exchange rate fixed and to conduct sterilized monetary expansions for long. Ultimately, nations that try to push up their real income levels by way of monetary expansions either must eventually permit their money stocks to contract or must devalue their currencies. The latter option applies, naturally, if central banks run short of foreign exchange reserves to sell to support fixed exchange rates. To help prevent speculative attacks on their foreign exchange reserves—efforts by private speculators to profit from bets that central banks will be unable to support a fixed exchange rate—central banks sometimes try to build up large stocks of foreign assets. (Several key factors enter into a nation's policymakers' decision regarding the currency with which they wish to maintain a fixed rate of exchange; see *Policy Notebook: What Determines the Choice of a Peg for a Nation's Fixed-Exchange-Rate System?*)

 **POLICY** Notebook

---

What Determines the Choice of a Peg for a Nation's Fixed-Exchange-Rate System?

A recent study by Christopher Meissner of the University of Cambridge and Nienke Oomes of the International Monetary Fund examined more than one hundred nations that fixed their exchange rates during the 1980s and 1990s. These researchers found that the most important criterion influencing a nation's choice of which currency to peg its exchange rate to is the country's network of trading partners. If most of the countries with which a nation conducts trade fix the rates of exchange of their currencies vis-à-vis the U.S. dollar, for instance, then that nation is more likely to peg its currency's value to the dollar as well.

Meissner and Ooomes found that there are other factors affecting the choice of a currency peg. One factor that appears to matter is whether the volume of economic activity in a currency-pegging nation tends to experience ebbs and flows in conjunction with volume of economic activity in the country to which it chooses to fix its exchange rate. Another key factor is the currency denomination of the nation's debt; if the bulk of its debt is denominated, say, in euros, then a nation is more likely to peg the value of its currency to the euro.

For Critical Analysis

Why do you suppose that Meissner and Oomes suggest that increasing use of the euro as a currency peg plus the euro's growing importance in denominating global debt instruments may result in its further increasing use as a currency peg?

 **Fundamental ISSUES**

#3 To what extent can monetary policy actions influence the real income level of a small open economy with imperfect capital mobility and a fixed exchange rate?

The initial effects of monetary policy actions with a fixed exchange rate depend considerably on the extent to which the central bank of a small open economy sterilizes by preventing variations in its foreign exchange reserves from affecting the nation's nominal money stock. Under the monetary approach to the balance of payments, the immediate effects of unsterilized monetary policy actions on real income ultimately are reversed by offsetting changes in the quantity of money in circulation.

Fiscal Policy under Fixed Exchange Rates

As with monetary policy, the degree of capital mobility has a major bearing on the real income effects of *fiscal policy actions,* which are variations in the government's spending or taxation policies. In addition, the effects of fiscal policy actions depend in part on whether the central bank sterilizes interventions to maintain a fixed exchange rate. Before we discuss these issues, however, let's determine exactly how fiscal policy actions affect the equilibrium nominal interest rate and the equilibrium level of real income.

Fiscal Policy, the Nominal Interest Rate, and Real Income Figure 11–6 displays the effects, within the *IS–LM* framework, of a rise in real government spending, from an amount equal to g_1 to a larger amount equal to g_2. As we discussed in Chapter 10, the increase in government spending causes the *IS* schedule to shift to the right by the amount of the rise in spending times the autonomous expenditures multiplier, $1/(1 - MPC)$. Hence, at the initial equilibrium interest rate, R_1, real income rises from y_1 to y_3, which is equal to the distance between the initial equilibrium point A and point C. This increase in real income, however, raises the demand for real money balances, thereby causing an increase in the equilibrium nominal interest rate, from R_1 to R_2. Thus, there is upward movement along the *LM* schedule from point A to point B. This increase in the equilibrium nominal interest

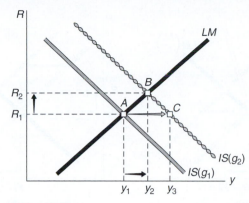

Figure 11–6   The Effects of Expansionary Fiscal Policy

An increase in government spending shifts the *IS* schedule rightward by the amount of the rise in spending times the autonomous expenditures multiplier, shown by the movement from point *A* to point *C*. This causes equilibrium real income to rise, thereby inducing an increase in the demand for real money balances. As a result, the equilibrium nominal interest rate rises, as shown by the movement upward along the *LM* schedule from point *A* to point *B*. Holding inflation expectations unchanged, the real interest rate increases, thereby causing a decline in desired investment expenditures and a movement back along the *IS* schedule from point *C* to point *B*. Thus, a rise in government spending crowds out some amount of private investment expenditures. Nevertheless, on net the increase in government spending generates a rise in the equilibrium nominal interest rate and an increase in equilibrium real income.

rate reduces investment expenditures, thereby causing real income to decline some-what, to y_2, as shown by a movement back along the new *IS* schedule from point *C* to point *B*. The amount of the fall in real income from y_3 back toward y_2 is equal to the decline in investment spending times the autonomous expenditures multiplier, $1/(1 - MPC)$.

The *net* effect of the increase in real government expenditures is an in-crease in the equilibrium real income level. Nevertheless, equilibrium real income no longer rises by the full amount predicted by the basic multiplier analysis discussed in Chapter 10. In fact, a fiscal-policy-induced increase in equilibrium real income typically is smaller, because of the decline in invest-ment stemming from a rise in the interest rate. This fall in investment following a rise in government spending is called the ***crowding-out effect***. By inducing a rise in the nominal interest rate that reduces private investment expenditures, an increase in government spending "crowds out" some amount of private invest-ment, thereby offsetting to some extent the rise in equilibrium real income that otherwise would occur. Note that a tax reduction has the same sort of crowding-out effect.

In contrast, a reduction in government spending or a tax increase, holding other factors constant, generates a decline in the equilibrium interest rate, thereby stimulating private investment. Of course, national governments may reduce their spending or raise their taxes for reasons other than those associated with their purely macroeconomic effects. Nonetheless, the *IS–LM* model indicates that fiscal policy changes may have broad effects on national economic performance, irre-spective of governmental objectives in adopting such changes.

Fiscal Policy and the Balance of Payments with Imperfect Capital Mobility

Both panels in Figure 11–7 on the following page depict the balance-of-payments effects stemming from an increase in government spending. In panel (a), capital mobility is relatively low, so the *BP* schedule is relatively steep. In contrast, in

crowding-out effect
A decline in real private invest-ment spending induced by a rise in the demand for money and the equilibrium nominal interest rate caused by a rise in equilibrium real income that follows an expansionary fiscal policy action.

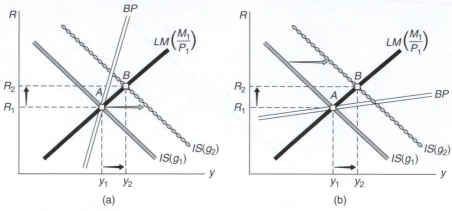

Figure 11–7   The Initial Effects of Expansionary Fiscal Policy with a Fixed Exchange Rate
Both panels show how an increase in real government expenditures initially induces an increase in the equilibrium nominal interest rate and a rise in equilibrium real income. In panel (a) the *BP* schedule is relatively steep, which implies a situation of low capital mobility. The increase in the equilibrium interest rate that occurs following a movement from point *A* to point *B* induces little capital inflow, but the rise in equilibrium real income stimulates greater import spending. The net result is a balance-of-payments deficit at point *B*. In contrast, in panel (b) the *BP* schedule is much more shallow, which indicates a situation of high capital mobility. In this case, the rise in the equilibrium interest rate generates a significant capital inflow that more than offsets the higher imports owing to the increase in equilibrium real income. This results in a balance-of-payments surplus at point *B* in panel (b).

panel (b) there is relatively high capital mobility, and so the *BP* schedule is relatively shallow. The initial equilibrium point in each panel is denoted as point *A*, at which there is an *IS–LM* equilibrium along the *BP* schedule, and so we assume that there is balance-of-payments equilibrium before any fiscal policy action takes place.

In each panel of Figure 11–7, an increase in government spending causes the *IS* schedule to shift to the right, from $IS(g_1)$ to $IS(g_2)$. This yields a new equilibrium point *B* with a higher nominal interest rate R_2 and a higher real income level y_2. In panel (a), the rise in equilibrium real income induces a rise in imports that causes the nation to experience a trade deficit. The rise in the equilibrium interest rate generates an inflow of some financial resources from other nations, but with low capital mobility this inflow is not very significant. Thus, on net there is a balance-of-payments deficit, as point *B* lies below and to the right of the *BP* schedule in panel (a).

Panel (b) in Figure 11–7 illustrates a situation in which capital mobility is much greater. In this case, the rise in the equilibrium interest rate owing to the increase in government spending causes a significant inflow of financial resources from abroad. As a result, there is a sizable capital account surplus that more than offsets the trade deficit stemming from the rise in equilibrium income and the consequent increase in imports. Hence, panel (b) shows that with very high capital mobility, an increase in government spending results in a balance-of-payments surplus, with point *B* above and to the left of the *BP* schedule.

The Effects of Fiscal Policy Actions with and without Monetary Sterilization
At point *B* in panel (a) of Figure 11–7, the existence of a balance-of-payments deficit places downward pressure on the nation's currency value. To keep the exchange rate fixed, the central bank must intervene by selling foreign exchange reserves. If the central bank sterilizes by trading domestic securities to maintain an unchanged quantity of money in circulation, then the nation remains at point *B* in panel (a)

only for as long as the central bank's foreign exchange reserves last. Persistent operations with a balance-of-payments deficit, however, would likely deplete the central bank's foreign exchange reserves. Eventually the central bank would have to devalue or abandon a fixed exchange rate.

In contrast, in panel (b) of Figure 11–7 there is a balance-of-payments surplus at point B, so there is *upward* pressure on the nation's currency value in the foreign exchange market. Maintaining a fixed exchange rate thereby requires the central bank to *purchase* additional foreign exchange reserves. To sterilize the effect that an accumulation of more foreign exchange reserves has on the money stock, the central bank has to sell domestic bonds. This allows the economy to remain at point B in panel (b) of Figure 11–7 for as long as the central bank's holdings of domestic bonds remain undepleted.

Figure 11–8 illustrates the outcomes that result if the central bank is unwilling to sterilize in the face of an increase in government spending. Again, both panels of Figure 11–8 display movements from an initial point A with balance-of-payments equilibrium to point B at which there is an international payments imbalance. In the case of low capital mobility depicted in panel (a), nonsterilization results in a decrease in the nation's money stock. This is because the central bank sells foreign exchange reserves to maintain the nation's fixed exchange rate in the face of a balance-of-payments deficit at point B. The *LM* schedule shifts upward and to the left as the quantity of money in circulation declines from M_1 to M_2. This ultimately leads to a new *IS–LM* equilibrium at point C, with a higher equilibrium interest rate, R_3, and a somewhat lower equilibrium real income level, y_3. The fall in real income generates a decline in import spending, thereby reducing the trade deficit and yielding balance-of-payments equilibrium at point C. This ends

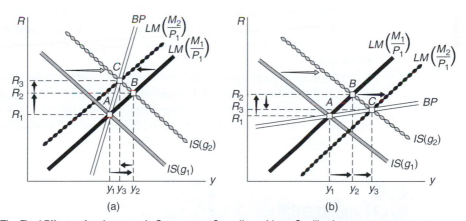

(a)   (b)

Figure 11–8 The Final Effects of an Increase in Government Spending without Sterilization
The panels of this figure illustrate the final effects of an increase in real government expenditures that, as shown in Figure 11–7, first cause a rightward shift in the *IS* schedule and a movement from point A to point B. In panel (a) there is relatively low capital mobility, so a balance-of-payments deficit results from higher import spending that more than offsets meager capital inflows. Hence, the nation's residents raise their demand for foreign currencies, which reduces the value of the nation's currency. To keep the exchange rate fixed, the nation's central bank sells foreign exchange reserves. Without sterilization, these generate a reduction in the quantity of money in circulation, and a movement to point C tends to offset the effect of the rise in government spending on real income. In contrast, in panel (b) there is significant capital mobility. It is so significant that capital outflows more than offset increased imports, resulting in a balance-of-payments surplus at point B. The nation's residents reduce their desired holdings of foreign currencies, which raises the value of the nation's currency in foreign exchange markets. To keep the exchange rate from changing, the nation's central bank purchases foreign exchange reserves. This raises the money stock and induces a movement to point C that *reinforces* the real income effect of the increase in government spending.

pressure on the central bank to sell foreign exchange reserves to defend the fixed exchange rate.

In panel (b) of Figure 11–8, in which capital mobility is relatively high, there is a balance-of-payments surplus at point B following a rise in government spending, because the nation experiences significant capital inflows following the rise in the nominal interest rate from R_1 to R_2. Consequently, the central bank starts to accumulate foreign exchange reserves in its efforts to maintain a fixed exchange rate. If the central bank does not sterilize, then the nation's money stock grows as the central bank's foreign exchange reserves increase, causing the LM schedule to shift down and to the right. As a result, the equilibrium interest rate declines to R_3, reducing the capital inflow and eventually yielding balance-of-payments equilibrium at point C along the BP schedule.

Figures 11–7 and 11–8 illustrate a key implication of the monetary approach to the balance of payments: Under a fixed exchange rate, fiscal policy actions force a central bank to respond to international payments imbalances by reducing or accumulating foreign exchange reserves. As the examples in Figures 11–7 and 11–8 demonstrate, the real income effects of fiscal policy actions hinge on central bank decisions about whether to sterilize and on the degree of capital mobility.

In our examples we have focused on variations in government expenditures, although in most respects the basic analysis also applies to the effects of tax changes. Nevertheless, two factors complicate the ultimate effects that tax variations have on a nation's equilibrium interest rate and real income level. One is the potential for *Ricardian equivalence* to reduce the effect of a tax change on aggregate desired expenditures. Named for David Ricardo, an eighteenth-century British economist, Ricardian equivalence refers to the possibility that a nation's residents may view a tax cut that is deficit-financed as an indication that a future tax increase will be required to repay government borrowings. This induces them to save the proceeds of the current tax cut to permit such future repayments. To the extent that Ricardian equivalence may hold for a given nation, the economic effects of tax changes are dampened.

The second complication is that governments typically collect the bulk of their revenues via taxation of income. Evaluating the full effects of tax changes requires assessing the interaction among tax-rate changes across ranges of household and firm income levels. Tax changes may also affect household work effort, firm production, and, ultimately, aggregate expenditures.

Fundamental ISSUES

#4 To what extent can fiscal policy actions influence the real income level of a small open economy with imperfect capital mobility and a fixed exchange rate?

The immediate effect of an expansionary fiscal policy action is an unambiguous rise in the nation's real income level. Ultimately, however, the effects of fiscal policy actions on real income in a small open economy with a fixed exchange rate depend to some extent on a central bank's decision about sterilization. Sterilization can mute this effect somewhat, but nonsterilized interventions in support of a fixed exchange rate reinforce the rise in real income that a fiscal expansion generates.

FIXED EXCHANGE RATES AND PERFECT CAPITAL MOBILITY

As already discussed, the degree of capital mobility influences the ultimate effects of fiscal policy actions. There is considerable evidence that capital mobility has increased for many nations of the world, and in particular for countries in North America, Western Europe, and East Asia. If nations were to reach a point at which flows of funds and financial assets were as mobile *across* their borders as *within* their borders, then they would experience *perfect capital mobility*, and the uncovered-interest-parity condition would hold. Let's begin by considering how economic policies work in a small open economy with perfect capital mobility. Then we shall consider how policy actions that are undertaken in one economy might spill over to affect another nation when capital is fully mobile. (Brazilian policymakers have recently sought to take advantage of higher mobility of capital across its borders by operating a government-owned sovereign wealth fund, but there seems to be some uncertainty about whether they wish for the exchange rate to be flexible or fixed; see *Policy Notebook: Brazilian Policymakers Try to Have It Both Ways*.)

 **POLICY**Notebook

Brazilian Policymakers Try to Have It Both Ways

According to the Central Bank of Brazil, the value of the nation's currency, the real, is determined solely by market forces, hence the nation has a floating exchange rate. If one asks the nation's finance minister, however, a different answer is forthcoming. The Brazilian finance ministry recently created a sovereign wealth fund, which allocates government-owned reserves of foreign currencies to investments around the globe. Is the primary aim of the sovereign wealth fund, like those established by nations such as Norway and Singapore, to profit from its investments? Not according to Brazil's finance minister. Even though current rules say that intervention in currency markets is the sole prerogative of the Central Bank of Brazil, the finance minister has publicly stated that the sovereign wealth fund's key goal will be to prevent the real from appreciating. This policy conflict is leaving investors guessing about whether Brazil has a floating exchange rate or a pegged exchange rate.

For Critical Analysis

How could the Central Bank of Brazil utilize its own foreign exchange reserves to prevent Brazil's sovereign wealth fund from preventing changes in the real's value in foreign exchange markets?

 **On the WEB**

Visit the Web site of Brazil's central bank, the Central Bank of Brazil, at *http://www.bcb.gov .br/?english.*

Economic Policies with Perfect Capital Mobility and a Fixed Exchange Rate: The Small Open Economy

If an economy is small relative to the rest of the world, then changes in its real income or its nominal interest rate have negligible repercussions for other nations. Thus, for a small open economy, foreign incomes and interest rates are "given."

Monetary Policy with Perfect Capital Mobility and a Fixed Exchange Rate

Figure 11–9 depicts the effects of a monetary expansion in a small open economy that has perfect capital mobility and a fixed exchange rate. With perfect capital mobility, uncovered interest parity holds, so that the home interest rate is equal to the sum of the foreign interest rate, anticipated home currency depreciation, and a risk premium. If we assume that there is no anticipated depreciation of the domestic currency and no risk premium, then the domestic interest rate must equal the foreign interest rate. Hence, the *BP* schedule in the figure is *horizontal* at the foreign interest rate, R^*, because with perfect capital mobility even a very small variation in the nation's nominal interest rate induces very large shifts of financial resources across the nation's borders.

An expansionary monetary policy, such as an increase in the money stock from M_1 to M_2, shifts the *LM* schedule to the right. This results in a movement from an initial *IS–LM* at point *A* on the *BP* schedule to new *IS–LM* equilibrium at point *B* below the *BP* schedule. The equilibrium domestic interest rate declines to R_2, below the foreign interest rate R^*. This induces significant flows of capital out of the small open economy, which results in a balance-of-payments deficit. To prevent a decline in the value of the nation's currency, the central bank sells foreign exchange reserves. If it sterilizes its foreign exchange market interventions, then the central bank can maintain an equilibrium point *B* for at least some period of time. If the central bank's interventions are not sterilized, however, the resulting decline in foreign exchange reserves ultimately causes the nation's money stock to fall back to its original level.

Once again, we conclude that an expansionary monetary policy action ultimately has no effect on real income when the central bank maintains a fixed exchange rate. Because it must intervene in the foreign exchange market to keep the exchange rate from changing, the central bank effectively must "undo" its own policies.

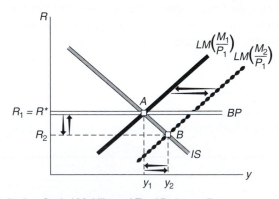

Figure 11–9 Monetary Policy with Perfect Capital Mobility and Fixed Exchange Rates
This figure shows the effects of an unsterilized increase in the quantity of money if there is perfect capital mobility, so that the *BP* schedule is horizontal. The result is a rightward shift of the *LM* schedule along the *IS* schedule, from point *A* to point *B*. The resulting decline in the nominal interest rate induces capital outflows and results in a balance-of-payments deficit. To keep the nation's currency from depreciating, the central bank sells foreign exchange reserves, which causes the nation's money stock to fall back to its initial value, causing the *LM* schedule to shift back to point *A*. Hence, unsterilized monetary policy actions have no long-lived effects on equilibrium real income.

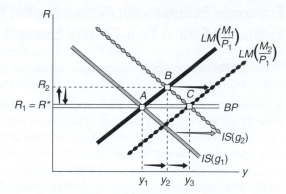

Figure 11–10 Fiscal Policy with Perfect Capital Mobility and Fixed Exchange Rates
An increase in real government expenditures shifts the *IS* schedule rightward along the *LM* schedule, from point *A* to point *B*. The resulting rise in the nominal interest rate induces capital inflows. This results in a balance-of-payments surplus, which tends to place upward pressure on the value of the nation's currency. To prevent such an appreciation, the central bank must purchase foreign exchange reserves, causing the money stock to increase and shifting the *LM* schedule rightward to a final equilibrium at point *C*.

Fiscal Policy with Perfect Capital Mobility and a Fixed Exchange Rate In contrast, the extent to which fiscal policy actions can influence real income under a fixed exchange rate is enlarged if capital is completely mobile. To see this, consider Figure 11–10. An increase in government spending from g_1 to g_2 causes the *IS* schedule to shift rightward, resulting in an equilibrium at point *B* above the *BP* schedule. The small open economy's equilibrium nominal interest rate rises above the foreign interest rate, to R_2, so the nation experiences a balance-of-payments surplus as the higher domestic interest rate induces significant inflows of capital from abroad.

At point *B* in Figure 11–10, the central bank begins to accumulate foreign exchange reserves in its efforts to keep the exchange rate from changing. If the central bank sterilizes indefinitely, then the economy remains at point *B*. In the absence of sterilization, however, the increase in foreign exchange reserves leads to a rise in the quantity of money in circulation, and the *LM* schedule shifts rightward until it again achieves balance-of-payments equilibrium at a new *IS–LM* equilibrium point *C* on the *BP* schedule. Consequently, fiscal policy has its greatest possible effect on equilibrium real income when capital is perfectly mobile.

Fundamental ISSUES

#5 In what ways does perfect capital mobility alter the relative effectiveness of monetary and fiscal policy actions in a small open economy that adopts a fixed exchange rate?

With perfect capital mobility and fixed exchange rates, the real income effects of monetary actions are muted. Under a policy of nonsterilized central bank interventions, in fact, monetary policy actions have no effect on a small open economy's real income level. In contrast, fiscal policy actions have their largest possible short-run effects on the nation's level of real income, particularly with nonsterilized central bank interventions.

Economic Policies with Perfect Capital Mobility and a Fixed Exchange Rate: A Two-Country Example

Some nations, such as the United States, China, Japan, and Germany, clearly do not fit the small-open-economy assumption. Variations in the economic performance of such nations can, in fact, affect economic outcomes in other countries.

A Two-Country Model with Perfect Capital Mobility and a Fixed Exchange Rate To try to understand how policy actions or other economic developments in one country might have spillover effects on other nations, let's imagine a "world" composed of *two* nations that are of roughly equal size and that engage in international trade of goods, services, and financial assets. Clearly, in such a world our small-open-economy assumption is violated, because each nation accounts for about half of the world's output.

Figure 11–11 illustrates the determination of equilibrium real income levels and equilibrium nominal interest rates in the two nations when financial resources flow freely across their borders. In one nation, which we shall call the *domestic economy*, an *IS–LM* equilibrium arises at point A in panel (a), at which equilibrium real income is equal to y_1 and the equilibrium nominal interest rate is equal to R_1. If there is perfect capital mobility, then in the absence of any domestic currency depreciation, uncovered interest parity implies that this equilibrium domestic interest rate must be equal to the equilibrium foreign interest rate, R_1^* in panel (b). This value for the foreign interest rate, in turn, stems from a foreign *IS–LM* equilibrium at point A in panel (b), where the equilibrium level of foreign real income is equal to y_1^*. We continue to assume that prices are unchanged in both the domestic country and the foreign country.

An important implication of Figure 11–11 is that perfect capital mobility imposes a constraint on interest rate movements in the domestic and foreign economies. Although the *IS* and *LM* schedules in both nations shift as a result of economic policy actions, their final locations ultimately must be consistent, absent

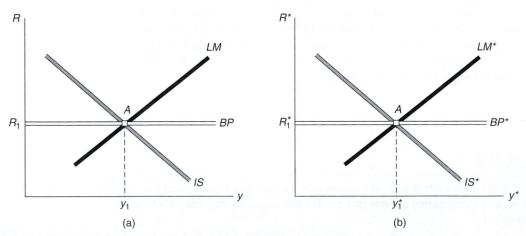

(a)   (b)

Figure 11–11 A Two-Country Framework with Perfect Capital Mobility and a Fixed Exchange Rate
This figure shows how equilibrium real income levels and nominal interest rates arise in two nations whose borders are fully open to flows of financial resources. For the domestic country, an *IS–LM* equilibrium arises at point A in panel (a), at which equilibrium real income is equal to y_1 and the equilibrium nominal interest rate is equal to R_1. In the absence of any domestic currency depreciation, uncovered interest parity implies that the equilibrium domestic interest rate must equal the equilibrium foreign interest rate, R_1^* in panel (b), which is determined by *IS–LM* equilibrium for the foreign nation. This is point A in panel (b), at which the equilibrium level of foreign real income is equal to y_1^*.

any expected currency depreciation, with equality of the domestic and foreign interest rates. In contrast to the small-open-economy framework we considered earlier, nominal interest rates in both nations may change in response to monetary or fiscal policy actions. Nevertheless, the free movement of financial resources between the two nations ultimately must drive the countries' interest rates to the same value.

The Effects of a Foreign Monetary Expansion Consider Figure 11–12, which illustrates the effects of an increase in the quantity of money in circulation in the foreign economy. For purposes of illustration, we assume that the domestic nation's central bank wants to keep the value of the domestic currency fixed relative to that of the foreign currency. Consequently, the domestic central bank must intervene as necessary in the foreign exchange market to maintain its nation's goal of a fixed exchange rate. The foreign central bank, in contrast, pursues its own independent monetary policy by increasing the foreign money stock.

Fixing the exchange rate Note that an alternative way to examine a system of fixed exchange rates in a two-country framework is to suppose that both countries work together to adjust a "world money stock" as necessary to keep the exchange rate linking their two currencies unchanged. In our two-country example, however, we wish to be more realistic. In real-world fixed-exchange-rate systems, such as the Bretton Woods system of the 1950s and 1960s and the Exchange-Rate Mechanism (ERM) of the European Monetary System (EMS) of the 1980s and 1990s, nations typically fixed their exchange rates relative to the currency of a "center country" in the system (the United States in the Bretton Woods system and Germany in the EMS). For instance, you might think of Germany as the *foreign country* that determined its own monetary policy in our two-country framework and of France as the *domestic country* whose central bank sought to maintain a fixed exchange rate.

In this type of fixed-exchange-rate system, a rise in the foreign money stock causes the foreign LM schedule to shift rightward, from $LM^*(M_1^*/P_1^*)$ to $LM^*(M_2^*/P_1^*)$

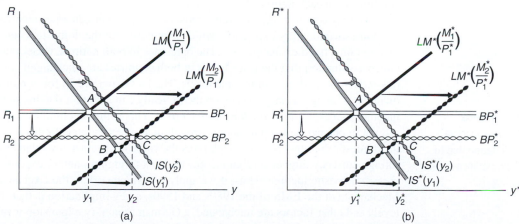

(a)   (b)

Figure 11–12 The Effects of a Foreign Monetary Expansion in the Two-Country Model with a Fixed Exchange Rate
An increase in the foreign money stock causes the foreign LM schedule to shift rightward in panel (b). This causes an initial decline in the equilibrium foreign interest rate, thereby inducing a flow of financial resources from the foreign country to the domestic country. To keep its currency from appreciating relative to the foreign currency, the domestic central bank would have to buy foreign assets, resulting in a rise in the domestic money stock and a rightward shift in the domestic LM schedule in panel (a). Equilibrium nominal interest rates in both nations fall to the same level, which stems the flow of financial resources from the foreign country to the domestic country, thereby pushing the balance of payments back into equilibrium in each nation. On net, equilibrium real income levels in both nations increase, so there is a locomotive effect associated with a foreign monetary expansion.

in panel (b), thereby resulting initially in a decline in the foreign interest rate and a rise in foreign real income indicated by a movement from point A to point B. The fall in the foreign interest rate relative to the domestic interest rate induces a flow of financial resources from the foreign country to the domestic country, causing the foreign nation to experience a balance-of-payments deficit and the domestic nation to experience a balance-of-payment surplus. The resulting decline in the demand for foreign currency and rise in the demand for domestic currency in the foreign exchange markets places upward pressure on the value of the domestic currency relative to the foreign currency.

To keep its currency from appreciating relative to the foreign currency, the domestic central bank buys assets denominated in the foreign currency. If the domestic central bank's interventions are nonsterilized, then this action increases the quantity of domestic currency in circulation, thereby increasing the domestic money stock. Thus, in Figure 11–12 the domestic LM schedule shifts to the right, from $LM(M_1/P_1)$ to $LM(M_2/P_1)$ in panel (a), toward the new IS–LM equilibrium point B. At the same time, however, the rise in foreign real income induces an increase in foreign import spending, which corresponds to an increase in domestic exports. Hence, the domestic IS schedule shifts to the right in panel (a), which yields the final equilibrium point C. On net, there is a reduction in the equilibrium domestic interest rate, from R_1 to R_2, and a rise in equilibrium domestic income, from y_1 to y_2 at point B.

Reattaining equilibrium Finally, the rise in domestic real income causes the foreign IS schedule to shift to the right, from $IS(y_1^*)$ to $IS^*(y_2^*)$ as domestic residents import more foreign goods, which induces an increase in foreign exports. Consequently, the final equilibrium point in panel (b) is point C. Note that in equilibrium, perfect capital mobility requires that the nominal interest rates in both nations fall to the same level. This stems the flow of financial resources from the foreign country to the domestic country, thereby pushing the balance of payments back into equilibrium in each nation.

We may conclude that a foreign monetary expansion generates a corresponding domestic monetary expansion, which is required for the domestic central bank to maintain a fixed exchange rate. The outcomes in both nations, under our maintained assumption that the price levels in both countries are unchanged, are interest rate reductions and rises in income levels. The fact that a rise in foreign income owing to a foreign money expansion theoretically can lead to a rise in *domestic* income is an example of the ***locomotive effect***. This is the potential for income growth in one nation to spur income growth in another country. In this case, when the domestic country's central bank fixes the value of its currency relative to the foreign currency, higher foreign income due to a foreign monetary expansion increases domestic income. Thus, if we apply our framework to the Exchange-Rate Mechanism of the EMS of the 1980s and 1990s, a key implication is that if price levels and other factors are unchanged, a German monetary expansion would have raised equilibrium income levels both in Germany and in France.

The Effects of a Foreign Fiscal Expansion In principle, it is also possible for income in one nation to grow *at the expense* of income growth in another nation. To see why this may occur, consider Figure 11–13, which illustrates the effects of a foreign fiscal expansion. As shown in panel (b), given the initial level of domestic real income, a rise in foreign government spending, from g_1^* to g_2^* shifts the foreign IS schedule rightward, from $IS^*(g_1^*, y_1)$ to $IS^*(g_2^*, y_1)$. This causes a movement up

locomotive effect

A stimulus to real income growth in one nation due to an increase in real income in another country.

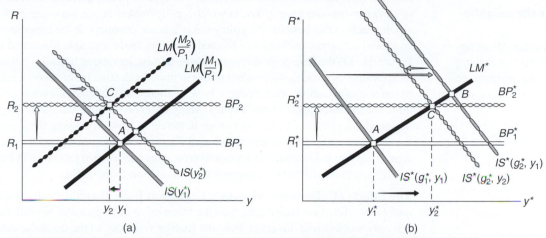

Figure 11–13 The Effects of a Foreign Fiscal Expansion in the Two-Country Model with a Fixed Exchange Rate

An increase in foreign government spending shifts the foreign *IS* schedule rightward in panel (b), causing a rise in the foreign interest rate that induces a flow of financial resources from the domestic country to the foreign country. To keep the value of its currency fixed relative to the foreign currency, the domestic central bank must sell foreign exchange reserves, causing a decline in the domestic money stock and a leftward shift in the domestic *LM* schedule in panel (a). If the rise in domestic exports caused by the rise in foreign real income is insufficient to offset the effect of the decline in domestic investment caused by the rise in the domestic interest rate, then equilibrium domestic real income falls. This is an example of a beggar-thy-neighbor effect.

along the foreign *LM* schedule, to point *B*, which generates an initial increase in foreign real income and the foreign interest rate. The resulting differential between the new equilibrium foreign interest rate and the domestic interest rate induces a flow of financial resources from the domestic country to the foreign country that tends to depress the value of the domestic currency.

To keep the value of its currency fixed relative to the foreign currency, the domestic central bank sells foreign exchange reserves, which depresses the amount of domestic currency in circulation. The resulting decline in the domestic money stock, assuming nonsterilized domestic interventions, causes the domestic *LM* schedule to shift to the left in panel (a), from $LM(M_1/P_1)$ to $LM(M_2/P_1)$, which yields point *B*. At the same time, however, the increase in foreign income stimulates foreign import spending, so domestic exports rise. As a result, the domestic *IS* schedule shifts rightward, which generates the final equilibrium point *C*. Note that the net effect on equilibrium domestic real income could go either way. Panel (a) illustrates a situation in which, on net, equilibrium domestic real income *declines*, from y_1 to y_2, as domestic real investment falls off in response to the higher domestic interest rate by a greater amount than the increase in domestic exports stemming from the rise in foreign real income.

Finally, panel (b) shows that the assumed net decline in domestic real income causes the foreign *IS* schedule to shift back to the left slightly, from $IS^*(g_2^*, y_1)$ to $IS^*(g_2^*, y_2)$. On net, the movement from the initial equilibrium point *A* to the final equilibrium point *C* in panel (b) causes foreign real income to rise from y_1^* to y_2^* and causes the foreign interest rate to rise from R_1^* to R_2^*, which is equal to the domestic interest rate, R_2.

With perfect capital mobility and a domestic policy of maintaining a fixed exchange rate, therefore, a foreign fiscal expansion causes equilibrium foreign income to rise. In principle, however, it can generate a decline in equilibrium domestic

beggar-thy-neighbor effect

A policy action of one nation that benefits that nation's economy but worsens economic performance in another nation.

income. International economists refer to this type of policy effect as an example of a *beggar-thy-neighbor effect*, in which a policymaker in one nation embarks on a policy action that benefits the policymaker's home economy at the expense of worsened economic performance in another nation. In the example illustrated in Figure 11–13, the foreign government is able to raise income at home by raising its spending. A possible by-product of this action is a decline in the income level of the domestic nation, whose central bank maintains a fixed rate of exchange of domestic currency for foreign currency. Many observers argued that such a beggar-thy-neighbor effect took place in Europe in the early 1990s following the significant fiscal expansion during the reunification of Germany. During that period, there was a significant rise in German and French interest rates and a sharp recession in France, as the French central bank maintained its commitment to the ERM.

The Effects of a Domestic Monetary Expansion If the domestic central bank maintains a fixed exchange rate, then the locomotive or beggar-thy-neighbor effects can only work in one direction, from the foreign economy to the domestic economy. Domestic policy actions cannot influence the foreign economy. Figure 11–14 helps to illustrate this point by examining the effects of a *domestic* monetary expansion, under the assumptions that price levels in both nations are unchanging and that the domestic central bank maintains a fixed rate of exchange between the domestic and foreign currencies.

A rise in the domestic quantity of money causes the domestic *LM* schedule to shift rightward, from $LM(M_1/P_1)$ to $LM(M_2/P_1)$, as shown in panel (a) of Figure 11–14. This pushes down the domestic nominal interest rate, from R_1 toward R_2. Consequently, there is a shift of financial resources away from the domestic nation, which begins to experience a capital account deficit and, hence, a balance-of-payments deficit. The resulting reduction in the demand for domestic currency and rise in the demand for foreign currency places downward pressure on the value of the domestic currency.

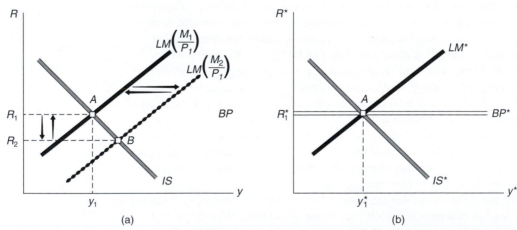

Figure 11–14 The Effects of a Domestic Monetary Expansion in the Two-Country Model with a Fixed Exchange Rate
An increase in the domestic money stock causes the domestic *LM* schedule to shift rightward in panel (a), which pushes down the domestic nominal interest rate and induces a flow of financial resources from the domestic nation to the foreign nation. To keep the exchange rate from changing, the domestic central bank would have to sell foreign exchange reserves. If the domestic central bank's interventions to maintain the fixed exchange rate are nonsterilized, this action would cause the domestic money stock to decline to its initial level. Thus, equilibrium foreign real income is unchanged in panel (b), implying that the domestic central bank's policy of a fixed exchange rate insulates the foreign economy from the effects of domestic policy actions.

To keep the rate of exchange of domestic currency for foreign currency fixed, the domestic central bank sells foreign exchange reserves. As in the small-open-economy example that we considered in Figure 11–10 on page 337, if the domestic central bank sterilizes this action by purchasing domestic bonds, then for some time the domestic economy might remain at the equilibrium nominal interest rate R_2 and the corresponding equilibrium real income level y_2. If the domestic central bank's interventions to maintain the fixed exchange rate are nonsterilized, however, then its sales of foreign exchange reserves cause the domestic money stock to decline to its initial level. Ultimately, therefore, the domestic LM schedule shifts back to its original position, so that the initial domestic monetary expansion has no long-lived effect on the domestic economy. The domestic policy action also has no effect on the foreign economy. Effectively, the domestic central bank's objective of maintaining a fixed exchange rate *insulates* the foreign economy from the effects of domestic policy actions.

An important implication of this example is that the domestic central bank's commitment to the fixed exchange rate entails a sacrifice of its ability to conduct independent monetary policy actions. A real-world implication, therefore, is that under the ERM during the 1980s and 1990s, the Bank of France could not undertake policies to influence French real income.

The Effects of a Domestic Fiscal Expansion What happens if the domestic country's government seeks to influence domestic real income through fiscal policy actions? Figure 11–15 shows the effects of an expansionary domestic fiscal policy action when the domestic central bank maintains a fixed value of the domestic currency relative to the foreign currency. At the initial level of foreign real income, an increase in government spending from g_1 to g_2 causes the domestic IS schedule to shift rightward, from $IS(g_1, y_1^*)$ to $IS(g_2, y_1^*)$ in panel (a). This initial movement to

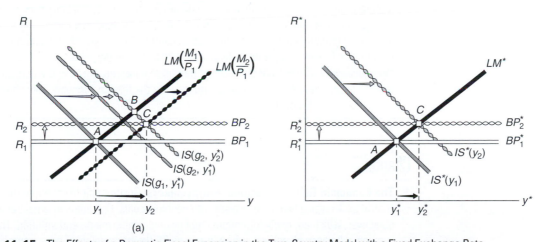

(a)

Figure 11–15 The Effects of a Domestic Fiscal Expansion in the Two-Country Model with a Fixed Exchange Rate
An increase in domestic government expenditures causes the domestic *IS* schedule to shift rightward in panel (a). The initial result is a rise in the domestic nominal interest rate and a flow of financial resources from the foreign country to the domestic country. The increase in foreign exports due to the rise in domestic real income causes the foreign *IS* schedule to shift rightward in panel (b). Thus, there is a locomotive effect on foreign real income, which, in turn, causes domestic exports to rise, causing the domestic *IS* schedule to shift to the right again in panel (a). If the domestic central bank conducts nonsterilized purchases of foreign exchange reserves to keep the exchange rate fixed, then the domestic money stock also increases, causing the domestic *LM* schedule to shift rightward and the domestic nominal interest rate to fall back somewhat. At points *C* in both panels, balance-of-payments equilibrium is reattained at higher domestic and foreign interest rates and real income levels.

point *B* causes domestic real income and the domestic nominal interest rate to rise, and financial resources begin to move from the foreign country to the domestic country. Hence, the domestic nation begins to experience a balance-of-payments surplus.

In panel (b), the increase in domestic real income and the resulting rise in domestic import spending generates an increase in foreign exports, so the foreign *IS* schedule shifts to the right. This causes a rise in equilibrium foreign real income that, in turn, stimulates domestic exports and causes the domestic *IS* schedule to shift further to the right in panel (a), from $IS(g_2, y_1^*)$ to $IS(g_2, y_2^*)$. At the same time, however, with nonsterilized central bank purchases of foreign exchange reserves to keep the exchange rate unchanged, there is a rise in the domestic money stock. Consequently, the domestic *LM* schedule shifts rightward, causing the domestic nominal interest rate to fall back somewhat at the final domestic equilibrium point *C*, at which balance-of-payments equilibrium is reattained. The expansionary fiscal policy action leads to a rise in domestic real income and also generates a rise in foreign real income. Hence, the domestic fiscal expansion has a locomotive effect in this two-country framework. The implication for the ERM in Europe of the 1980s and 1990s was that a French fiscal expansion could, given fixed French and German price levels, raise German real income as well as French real income.

Fundamental ISSUES

#6 In a two-country setting in which one nation's central bank fixes the exchange rate, to what extent can policy actions in one nation influence economic activity in the other nation?

If there is perfect capital mobility and the domestic nation's central bank fixes the exchange rate, then foreign monetary policy expansions can lead to a rise in real income in both the foreign and domestic countries. In contrast, a foreign fiscal expansion tends to stimulate foreign income while leading to a reduction in domestic income. Domestic monetary policy actions cannot influence foreign real income, because the domestic central bank's efforts to fix the exchange rate insulate the foreign economy from changes in domestic monetary policies.

Chapter SUMMARY

1. **The Economic Goals of National Policymakers:** Government fiscal authorities and central banks typically pursue two sets of economic goals. One set is internal balance objectives, which are goals for national real income, employment, and inflation. The other is external balance objectives, which are goals for the trade balance, other components of the balance of payments, and exchange rates.

2. **The Degree of Capital Mobility and the Slope of the *BP* Schedule:** If the degree of capital mobility for a nation is low, then the balance-of-payments deficit stemming from higher imports resulting from a given rise in the nation's real income level could be offset only by capital inflows generated by a sizable increase in the nation's interest rate. The *BP* schedule is the set of real income–nominal interest rate combinations consistent with balance-of-payments equilibrium, and so this reasoning implies that the *BP* schedule is

steeply sloped if capital is relatively immobile. A rise in the degree of capital mobility makes the *BP* schedule more shallow. The *BP* schedule is horizontal in the extreme case of perfect capital mobility.

3. **The Influence of Monetary Policy Actions on the Real Income Level of a Small Open Economy with Imperfect Capital Mobility and a Fixed Exchange Rate:** The immediate effects of monetary policy actions with a fixed exchange rate depend considerably on the extent to which the central bank of a small open economy sterilizes the effects of its foreign exchange operations on the nation's nominal money stock. Unsterilized monetary policy actions, which are consistent with an external balance objective of maintaining balance-of-payments equilibrium, require changes in the quantity of money in circulation that ultimately offset the initial monetary policy actions undertaken by a central bank.

4. **The Influence of Fiscal Policy Actions on the Real Income Level of a Small Open Economy with Imperfect Capital Mobility and a Fixed Exchange Rate:** Expansionary fiscal policy actions have the direct effect of increasing equilibrium real income in a small open economy with a fixed exchange rate. The size of a given fiscal action's effect on real income depends in part on whether the central bank sterilizes interventions in support of a fixed exchange rate. Nonsterilized interventions that are consistent with maintaining a fixed exchange rate tend to reinforce a rise in real income from a fiscal expansion.

5. **Perfect Capital Mobility and the Relative Effectiveness of Monetary and Fiscal Policy Actions in a Small Open Economy That Adopts a Fixed Exchange Rate:** With perfect capital mobility and fixed exchange rates, nonsterilized monetary policy actions have no effect on a small open economy's real income level, but fiscal policy actions have their largest possible short-run effects on the nation's level of real income when central bank interventions in support of a fixed exchange rate are nonsterilized.

6. **The Influence of Policy Actions in a Nation on Economic Activity in Another Nation When One Nation's Central Bank Fixes the Exchange Rate:** If there is perfect capital mobility and the domestic nation's central bank fixes the exchange rate, then foreign monetary policy expansions can induce an increase in both nations' real income levels. By way of contrast, a foreign fiscal expansion tends to stimulate foreign income while depressing domestic income. Because the domestic central bank's efforts to maintain a fixed exchange rate tend to insulate the foreign economy from changes in the domestic interest rate and real income level, domestic monetary policy actions cannot influence foreign real income.

QUESTIONS and PROBLEMS

1. As noted at the beginning of the chapter, mercantilist interests often press for pursuing a balance-of-payments *surplus* as an external balance objective. Suppose that a nation were to adopt the goal of attaining a *specific* balance-of-payments surplus. How could the *BP* schedule be altered to account for this policy goal? Would the nation's central bank be under more or less pressure to sterilize when confronted with this external balance objective? Explain your reasoning.

2. Suppose that a national government adopts, and is able to enforce, a system of capital controls that permits absolutely no flows of financial resources across its borders. What would be the shape of this nation's *BP* schedule? Explain, in your own words, what

effects, if any, an expansionary fiscal policy action would have on equilibrium real income in such an environment.

3. If the central bank of a small open economy maintains a fixed exchange rate but conducts unsterilized monetary policies, how would a contractionary monetary policy action ultimately affect the nation's balance of payments and its real income level, assuming that the price level is unchanged? Support your answer.

4. Explain in your own words why the degree of capital mobility is a crucial determinant of the initial effects on a nation's balance of payments and its equilibrium income level following a reduction in government spending with a fixed exchange rate.

5. If the central bank of a small open economy with very high (though imperfect) capital mobility maintains a fixed exchange rate and conducts unsterilized monetary policies, would a contractionary fiscal policy action induce the nation's money stock to expand or contract as a result? Explain.

6. Is your answer to Question 5 different if capital mobility is very low? Explain.

7. Consider a two-country model in which the domestic central bank fixes the exchange rate using unsterilized foreign exchange market interventions. Begin with an initial equilibrium like the one illustrated in Figure 11–12 on page 339, and work out the effects of a foreign fiscal contraction.

8. Redo Question 7, but this time examine the effects of a domestic fiscal contraction.

9. In our two-country framework with perfect capital mobility, we assumed that the domestic central bank acted alone to maintain a fixed exchange rate. Suppose instead that both the foreign and domestic central banks work together to buy and sell foreign and domestic currencies in sufficient quantities to keep the exchange rate fixed. In such an environment, could a domestic monetary expansion lead to a change in equilibrium real income in the foreign nation? If so, would there be a locomotive effect or a beggar-thy-neighbor effect?

10. Suppose, as in Question 9, that both the foreign and domestic central banks work together in the two-country model to keep the exchange rate fixed. In this setting, could a domestic fiscal expansion lead to a change in equilibrium real income in the foreign nation? If so, would there be a locomotive effect or a beggar-thy-neighbor effect?

Online APPLICATIONS

Internet URL: *https://www.cia.gov/library/publications/the-world-factbook/geos/ly.html*

Title: The CIA World Factbook–Libya

Navigation: Start at the home page for the Central Intelligence (http://www.cia.gov) and click on *World Factbook* in the *Quick Links* window. In the country dropdown menu, select *Libya*. Finally, select *Economy*.

Application: Scan through the description until you reach the *Economy* discussion. Then answer the following questions:

1. Based on the data provided, what was the government deficit in Libya for the latest available year? Where does Libya government deficit rank relative to other nations listed in the *Factbook*? What was its public debt? How might the government try to reduce its deficit and public debt?

2. What was per capita GDP in Libya for the most recent year for which data are available? What factors appear to account for this relatively low figure?

SELECTED REFERENCES and FURTHER READINGS

Aizenman, Joshua, and Reuven Glick. "Pegged Exchange Rate Regimes: A Trap?" *Journal of Money, Credit, and Banking 40* (2008): 817–835.

Aizenman, Joshua, and Nancy Marion. "The High Demand for International Reserves in the Far East. What's Going On?" *Journal of the Japanese and International Economies 22* (2003): 887–893.

Daniels, Joseph, and David VanHoose. "Trade Openness, Capital Mobility, and the Sacrifice Ratio." *Open Economies Review 20* (2009): 473–487.

Daniels, Joseph, and David VanHoose. "Two-Country Models of Monetary and Fiscal Policy: What Have We Learned? What More Can We Learn?" *Open Economies Review 9* (1998): 263–282.

Dooley, Michael P. "A Survey of Literature on Controls over International Transactions." *International Monetary Fund Staff Papers 43* (December 1996): 639–687.

Edwards, Sebastian. "Capital Controls, Capital Flow Contractions, and Macroeconomic Vulnerability." *Journal of International Money and Finance 26* (2007): 814–840.

Frankel, Jeffrey, "Monetary Policy in Emerging Markets: A Survey," National Bureau of Economic Research, Working Paper No. 16125 (June 2010).

Frenkel, Jacob, and Assaf Razin. "The Mundell-Fleming Model a Quarter Century Later." *International Monetary Fund Staff Papers 34* (1987): 567–620.

Magud, Nicolas, and Carmen Reinhart. "Capital Controls: An Evaluation." In *Capital Controls and Capital Flows in Emerging Economies: Policies, Practices, and Consequences*, ed. Sebastian Edwards. Chicago: University of Chicago Press, 2007, pp. 645–674.

Meissner, Christopher, and Nienke Oomes. "Why Do Countries Peg the Way They Peg? The Determinants of Anchor Currency Choice." *Journal of International Money and Finance 28* (2009): 522–547.

Rogoff, Kenneth. "Rethinking Capital Controls. When Should We Keep an Open Mind?" *Finance and Development 39* (December 2002).

12 Economic Policy with Floating Exchange Rates

Fundamental ISSUES

1. How do monetary and fiscal policy actions affect a nation's real income under a floating exchange rate?

2. How does perfect capital mobility influence the relative effectiveness of monetary and fiscal policy actions in a small open economy that permits its exchange rate to float?

3. In a two-country setting with a floating exchange rate, to what extent can policy actions in one nation influence economic activity in the other nation?

4. What is the basic economic efficiency trade-off faced in choosing between fixed and floating exchange rates?

5. How does the choice between fixed and floating exchange rates depend in part on the implications for economic stability and monetary policy autonomy?

At one time or another since 2009, governments or central banks in a number of nations have been actively seeking to reduce the exchange values of their currencies in foreign exchange markets. According to one Wall Street Journal *headline, the difficulty has been that "Rising Currencies Bedevil World Economies." Another has summed up the situation succinctly: "Currency Wars—A Fight to Be Weaker."*

Of course, not every nation's currency can be "weaker" at the same time. As several nations' policymakers have been fretting over how to alleviate steady upward pressure on their currencies' exchange values, it has also been the case that policymakers in other countries have been satisfied with steady currency depreciations. Indeed, for a handful of countries, persistent depreciations were anticipated by-products of expansionary monetary and fiscal policy strategies.

How do expansionary monetary and fiscal policy actions affect a nation's economic activity under a floating exchange rate? What are the advantages and disadvantages of a floating exchange rate for economic policymaking? As experiences associated with the so-called currency war of the early 2010s suggest, these are questions of real-world significance. We shall address them in this chapter.

FLOATING EXCHANGE RATES AND IMPERFECT CAPITAL MOBILITY

When it chooses to maintain a fixed exchange rate, a nation's central bank shoulders two burdens. First, it must stand ready to intervene in the foreign exchange market by purchasing and selling foreign-currency-denominated assets. Thus, the central bank must be willing to accumulate or expend foreign exchange reserves. Second, it must decide whether to sterilize its foreign exchange market interventions. If it fails to sterilize, then the central bank effectively sacrifices control of the quantity of money in circulation.

By permitting the exchange rate to float, a central bank relieves itself from these burdens. You will learn in this chapter that adopting a floating exchange rate also increases the potential for monetary policy actions to exert effects on a nation's economic performance. Fiscal policy, in contrast, may lose at least some of its potency when exchange rates float.

The Effects of Exchange-Rate Variations in the *IS–LM–BP* Model

Before we consider how monetary and fiscal policy actions may influence a nation's economic performance under floating exchange rates, we first need to consider how changes in the exchange rate exert effects in the *IS–LM–BP* framework.

Exchange-Rate Variations and the *IS* Schedule Figure 12–1 shows how a depreciation in the value of a nation's currency influences the *IS* schedule. A fall in the value of a nation's currency makes imports more expensive, inducing the nation's residents to reduce their import spending. Simultaneously, the effective prices of the nation's export goods faced by other nations' residents decline. Consequently, expenditures on the nation's exports increase.

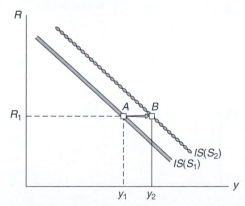

Figure 12–1   The Effects of a Currency Depreciation on the *IS* Schedule

A decline in the value of a nation's currency corresponding to a rise in the exchange rate from S_1 to S_2 makes imports more expensive for a nation's residents, inducing them to cut back on their import expenditures. At the same time, the nation's export goods become less expensive for foreign residents, so foreign expenditures on the nation's exports rise. Together, these effects cause an increase in the nation's aggregate autonomous expenditures at any given nominal interest rate, such as R_1, so the real income level consistent with an income–expenditure equilibrium increases from y_1 at point A to y_2 at point B. Consequently, the *IS* schedule shifts rightward.

Both of these effects generate a rise in the nation's aggregate autonomous expenditures at any given nominal interest rate, such as R_1 in Figure 12–1. As a result, the real income level (y) consistent with an income–expenditure equilibrium increases from y_1 at point A to y_2 at point B. Hence, the IS schedule shifts to the right, from $IS(S_1)$ to $IS(S_2)$, following a rise in the exchange rate, from S_1 to S_2, which entails a depreciation of the home currency.

Exchange-Rate Variations and the BP Schedule The depreciation of a nation's currency also alters the position of the BP schedule. Remember that the BP schedule consists of all real income–interest rate combinations that maintain balance-of-payments equilibrium, holding all other factors unchanged. As already discussed, however, a currency depreciation causes a nation's exports to rise and its imports to fall at any given real income level and at any given nominal interest rate. Therefore, as shown in Figure 12–2, at a given real income–nominal interest rate combination, such as y_1 and R_1 at point A on the BP schedule labeled $BP(S_1)$, a rise in the exchange rate from S_1 to S_2 generates an improvement in the trade balance that results in a balance-of-payments surplus at point A.

This means that for the balance of payments to return to equilibrium, the nation's real income must increase to a level, such as y_2, at which sufficient import spending takes place to return the trade balance to its previous level. As a result, point B lies on a new BP schedule, denoted $BP(S_2)$, following the home currency depreciation. We may conclude that a currency depreciation causes the BP schedule to shift to the right.

Monetary Policy under Floating Exchange Rates

Panels (a) and (b) of Figure 12–3 illustrate the effects of an expansionary monetary policy action under floating exchange rates for a small open economy. Each panel assumes that there is an initial $IS–LM$ equilibrium at point A on the BP schedule labeled $BP(S_1)$, so that at the outset there is a balance-of-payments equilibrium at the prevailing exchange rate, S_1. The BP schedule is very steep in panel (a), which indicates low capital mobility. In panel (b), the BP schedule is much more shallow, implying a much higher degree of capital mobility.

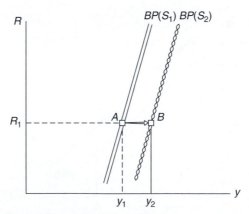

Figure 12–2   The Effects of a Currency Depreciation on the BP Schedule

At a given real income–interest rate combination, such as y_1 and R_1 at point A on the BP schedule labeled $BP(S_1)$, an increase in the exchange rate from S_1 to S_2 results in an improvement in the trade balance. Consequently, a balance-of-payments surplus occurs at point A. Reattainment of balance-of-payments equilibrium requires an increase in the nation's real income to a level such as y_2, which generates a sufficient increase in import expenditures to return the trade balance to its previous level. Hence, point B lies on the scheduled denoted $BP(S_2)$ following the home currency depreciation, which implies that a currency depreciation causes the BP schedule to shift to the right.

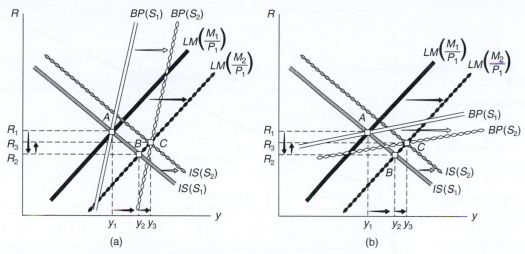

Figure 12–3   The Effects of an Increase in the Money Stock with a Floating Exchange Rate

An increase in the money stock causes the *LM* schedule to shift rightward, so in both panels (a) and (b) there is an initial movement from point *A* to point *B*. Because point *B* lies below and to the right of the *BP*(S_1) schedule, there is a balance-of-payments deficit at point *B* in both panels. The rise in import spending and acquisition of foreign financial assets by the nation's residents and the reduction in export spending and acquisition of domestic financial assets by foreign citizens causes the home currency to depreciate, so the exchange rate rises from S_1 to S_2. As a result, the *IS* and *BP* schedules shift rightward. At the final equilibrium point *C*, balance-of-payments equilibrium is reattained in both panels, so that there is no further upward pressure on the exchange rate.

An increase in the money stock from M_1 to M_2 causes the *LM* schedule to shift rightward. Hence, in both panels of Figure 12–3 there is an initial movement from point *A* to point *B*. Because point *B* lies below and to the right of the *BP*(S_1) schedule, there is a balance-of-payments deficit at point *B*. In panel (a), in which capital mobility is low, the reason for this balance-of payments deficit is the rise in import spending owing to an increase in real income from y_1 to y_2. In panel (b), in which capital mobility is high, the balance-of-payments deficit results from the outflow of capital spurred by the decline in the interest rate from R_1 to R_2.

The rise in import spending and acquisition of foreign financial assets by the nation's residents and the reduction in export spending and acquisition of domestic financial assets by foreign citizens places downward pressure on the value of the nation's currency. Thus, the domestic currency depreciates; the value of the exchange rate would rise from its initial value S_1 to a higher level, S_2. (In a number of countries since the early 2000s, reductions in exports relative to imports that resulted in current account deficits have indeed been associated with currency depreciations; see *Policy Notebook: Current Account Balances and Exchange-Rate Adjustments*.)

POLICYNotebook

Current Account Balances and Exchange-Rate Adjustments

Do nations with current account deficits tend to experience currency depreciations, consistent with the theory of exchange-rate adjustment to policy actions? Do currencies of countries with current account surpluses tend to appreciate? Take a look at Figure 12–4 on the following page, which plots the relationship between percentage changes in effective exchange rates for selected nations since 2002 and the nations' current account balances as percentages of their levels of GDP. As you

Figure 12–4

The Relationship between Percentage Changes in Effective Exchange Rates and Current Account Balances as Percentages of GDP for Selected Nations since 2002

Consistent with the theory of exchange-rate adjustments to policy actions, countries with current account deficits tend to experience currency depreciations, and nations with current account surpluses tend to experience currency appreciations.

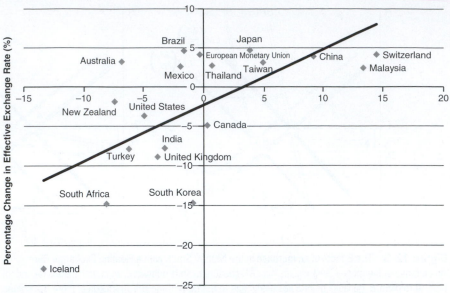

Source: Bank for International Settlements, *www.bis.org.*

can see, the percentage changes in effective exchange rates of countries that experienced current account deficits were generally negative, implying depreciating currencies. In contrast, nations with current account surpluses were predisposed to experience appreciating currencies. Furthermore, the figure indicates that higher ratios of current account deficits or surpluses to GDP were associated with greater proportionate adjustments in exchange rates. Thus, consistent with the theory of policy adjustments under floating exchange rates, currency depreciations do indeed appear to accompany current account deficits, and currency appreciations and current account surpluses also tend to go together.

For Critical Analysis

How is it possible that for a few countries in Figure 12–4, current account deficits were accompanied by appreciating currencies, while for a few others current account surpluses were accompanied by depreciating currencies? (Hint: Why do discussions of theoretical effects of policy actions on exports, imports, and exchange rates always presume that other things are equal?)

The domestic currency depreciation raises the domestic price of foreign goods and reduces the foreign price of domestic goods. Consequently, the rise in the exchange rate from S_1 to S_2 causes export spending to rise and import spending to fall, raising total expenditures on domestic goods. This causes the *IS* schedule to shift to the right, from $IS(S_1)$ to $IS(S_2)$. At the same time, as discussed earlier, the depreciation causes the *BP* schedule to shift to the right, from $BP(S_1)$ to $BP(S_2)$. Following these adjustments in the positions of the *LM, IS,* and *BP* schedules, the point *C* represents the new *IS–LM–BP* equilibrium. At this point, balance-of-payments equilibrium occurs on the new *BP* schedule, and so there is additional pressure on the value of the domestic currency.

Figure 12–3 demonstrates that, with either low or high capital mobility, an increase in the money stock tends to induce a rise in equilibrium real income, holding other factors such as the price level unchanged. Under a floating exchange rate, therefore, an increase in the quantity of money unambiguously constitutes an expansionary policy action that induces at least a near-term increase in a nation's real income level.

Fiscal Policy under Floating Exchange Rates

Fiscal policy actions can also alter the value of a small nation's currency if the nation's exchange rate floats. Whether the nation's currency depreciates or appreciates depends on the degree of capital mobility.

The Case of Low Capital Mobility Panel (a) of Figure 12–5 depicts the effects of an increase in government spending when the extent of capital mobility is relatively low. With the exchange rate initially unchanged at its initial value of S_1, an increase in government spending causes the IS schedule to shift to the right, from $IS_1(g_1, S_1)$ to $IS_1(g_2, S_1)$. This yields a new IS–LM equilibrium at point B, which lies to the right of the initial BP schedule, labeled $BP(S_1)$. Therefore, the immediate effect of the rise in government spending is a balance-of-payments deficit caused by an increase in import spending resulting from a rise in real income from y_1 to y_2.

The nation's currency depreciates in the face of the balance-of-payments deficit. The resulting rise in the exchange rate, from S_1 to a higher level, S_2, induces net export expenditures to increase. This causes the IS schedule to shift rightward once more, to $IS_2(g_2, S_2)$. Furthermore, the currency depreciation causes the BP schedule to shift to the right, from $BP(S_1)$ to $BP(S_2)$. Following these shifts in the IS and BP schedules, the new IS–LM–BP equilibrium is at point C. The exchange rate S_2 constitutes the new equilibrium exchange rate, because there is no tendency for the nation's currency to depreciate further once balance-of-payments equilibrium is reattained at point C. The increase in government spending also induces a higher equilibrium real income level, y_3, at this final equilibrium point.

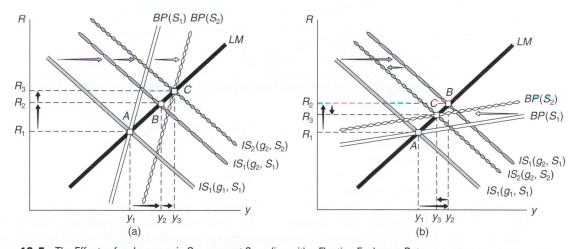

Figure 12–5 The Effects of an Increase in Government Spending with a Floating Exchange Rate
In both panels, an increase in government expenditures causes an initial rightward shift in the IS schedule, thereby inducing a movement from point A to point B, which leads to an increase in the equilibrium nominal interest rate and an increase in equilibrium real income. In panel (a), in which the relatively steep slope of the BP schedule implies low capital mobility, greater import spending more than offsets a small capital inflow in causing a balance-of-payments deficit to arise at point B. This induces a currency depreciation that shifts both the IS and BP schedules to the right, leading to a final equilibrium with a balance-of-payments equilibrium at point C. In panel (b), in which the relatively shallow slope of the BP schedule implies high capital mobility, significant capital inflows more than offset greater import expenditures in causing a balance-of payments surplus to occur at point B. This induces a currency appreciation that shifts both the IS and BP schedules leftward, leading to a final balance-of-payments equilibrium at point C.

The Case of High Capital Mobility When capital is very mobile, as in panel (b) of Figure 12–5 on the previous page, the ultimate effects of an increase in government spending are different from those shown in panel (a). The initial effect of a rise in government spending, however, is the same and is shown by the movement from point A to point B in panel (b), as the IS schedule shifts rightward, from $IS_1(g_1, S_1)$ to $IS_1(g_2, S_1)$.

Nevertheless, with high capital mobility the resulting rise in the interest rate from R_1 to R_2 causes significant capital inflows into this nation. This induces a balance-of-payments surplus at point B, above the initial BP schedule, denoted $BP(S_1)$. As foreign residents acquire more of the nation's currency to purchase domestic financial assets, the nation's currency value appreciates. The domestic price of foreign goods declines as the foreign price of domestic goods rises, which spurs import expenditures and reduces export spending. Hence, the result of the fall in the exchange rate (which implies a home currency appreciation), from S_1 to S_2, is a decline in total expenditures on the nation's goods, and so the IS schedule shifts leftward, from $IS(g_2, S_1)$ to $IS(g_2, S_2)$. The currency appreciation also causes the BP schedule to shift leftward, from $BP(S_1)$ to $BP(S_2)$.

At the final equilibrium point C in panel (b), equilibrium real income on net is higher than before, at y_3 as compared with the beginning level of y_1. Nonetheless, comparing panel (b) with panel (a) indicates that high capital mobility fundamentally changes the nature of the economy's adjustments following a rise in government spending. The result is a reduction in the extent to which equilibrium real income increases following a given increase in government spending. (To learn about why one Web site suggests that investors willing to utilize its services might profit from exchanging U.S. currency for Iraqi currency, see *Online Notebook: Betting That Higher Capital Mobility and Greater Spending Will Fuel an Iraqi Dinar Appreciation*.)

ONLINE Notebook

Betting That Higher Capital Mobility and Greater Spending Will Fuel an Iraqi Dinar Appreciation

In the spring of 2004, a new site called BetOnIraq.com appeared on the Web. At the site, an individual can arrange purchases of dinar, the currency of Iraq, with U.S. dollars. The site suggests that purchasing dinar could prove to be a good investment if the lengthy U.S. military intervention in Iraq succeeded in establishing markets and opening the nation's borders to inflows of capital. If private and government spending in the nation increase considerably over time, the site suggests, the Iraqi currency should appreciate in relation to the dollar.

So far, a dollar-denominated bet on the Iraqi dinar has been a good one. The more than 1,400 dinar that could have been purchased at BetOnIraq.com with each U.S. dollar in the fall of 2006 can now be converted back to about $1.10. Thus, since the autumn of 2006, the dinar has appreciated by approximately 10 percent in relation to the dollar.

For Critical Analysis

If aggregate expenditures in Iraq do indeed rise considerably but the Iraqi government should decide to put stringent capital controls in place, would you anticipate that the Iraqi dinar would continue to appreciate? Why or why not?

#1 How do monetary and fiscal policy actions affect a nation's real income under a floating exchange rate?

An expansionary monetary policy action results in a balance-of-payments deficit that causes a nation's currency to depreciate, thereby spurring export spending while inhibiting import expenditures. Therefore, expansionary monetary policy actions cause a nation's equilibrium real income to increase in the short run. The effects of fiscal policy actions on a nation's balance of payments and the value of its currency hinge on the degree of capital mobility. Under most circumstances, an expansionary fiscal policy action causes at least a slight short-term increase in a nation's real income level. The extent of the rise in real income declines as the degree of capital mobility rises.

FLOATING EXCHANGE RATES AND PERFECT CAPITAL MOBILITY

How would *perfect* capital mobility affect the transmission of monetary and fiscal policy actions to a nation's balance of payments and real income level under *floating* exchange rates? We consider this question first for the case of a small open economy. Then we contemplate this issue in a two-country framework. As in Chapter 11, we assume throughout that there is no anticipated currency depreciation or appreciation, so that the uncovered-interest-parity condition implies that the nominal interest rate for the small open economy is equal to the large-country nominal interest rate, R^*.

Economic Policies with Perfect Capital Mobility and a Floating Exchange Rate: The Small Open Economy

Recall that variations in economic activity within a small open economy do not affect the world economy, so variations in its output, interest rate, or price level cannot influence corresponding values in the rest of the world. Let's think about how monetary and fiscal policies affect a small open economy's real output and interest rate under the assumption that the price level does not vary.

Monetary Policy with Perfect Capital Mobility and a Floating Exchange Rate
Figure 12–6 on the following page depicts the effects of an increase in the money stock in a small open economy with a floating exchange rate and with perfectly mobile capital and, hence, a horizontal *BP* schedule. An increase in the money stock from M_1 to M_2 causes the *LM* schedule to shift rightward, inducing a movement from the initial equilibrium point *A* to a new point of *IS–LM* equilibrium, denoted *B*. At point *B*, the induced decline in the equilibrium interest rate, from R_1 to R_2, generates considerable capital outflows. This causes the country to start to experience a balance-of-payments deficit.

The balance-of-payments deficit, in turn, places downward pressure on the value of the nation's currency, so the exchange rate rises from its initial level, S_1, to a higher value, S_2. Thus, import spending declines, and export spending rises. The resulting increase in net expenditures on the nation's goods causes the *IS* schedule to shift to the right, from $IS(S_1)$ to $IS(S_2)$. At the final equilibrium point *C*, the sum of the nation's current account balance and its capital account balance again is equal to zero, so there is no further pressure on the value of its currency. The exchange

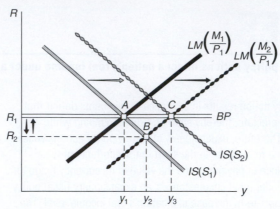

Figure 12–6 The Effects of an Increase in the Money Stock with a Floating Exchange Rate and Perfect Capital Mobility
If there is perfect capital mobility under a floating exchange rate, an increase in the amount of money in circulation causes a rightward shift of the *LM* schedule along the *IS* schedule, from point *A* to point *B*, which induces a decline in the nominal interest rate that leads, in turn, to capital outflows. The resulting balance-of-payments deficit causes the nation's currency to depreciate. This results in higher export spending and lower expenditures, so the *IS* schedule shifts rightward to a final equilibrium at point *C*.

rate S_2 is the new equilibrium exchange rate. Finally, real income increases as fully as possible, from y_1 to y_3, or by the amount of the horizontal distance that the *LM* schedule shifts to the right. Monetary policy has the largest possible immediate effect on real income with a floating exchange rate and perfect capital mobility.

Fiscal Policy with Perfect Capital Mobility and a Floating Exchange Rate
Figure 12–7 illustrates the effects of an increase in government spending, from g_1 to g_2, in a small open economy with a floating exchange rate and perfectly mobile capital. The direct effect of this policy action is a rightward shift in the *IS* schedule at the initial exchange rate, from $IS(g_1, S_1)$ to $IS(g_2, S_1)$, and a movement from point *A* to point *B*. At the new equilibrium point *B*, the initial rise in the interest rate induces significant capital inflows and thereby leads to the onset of a balance-of-payments surplus.

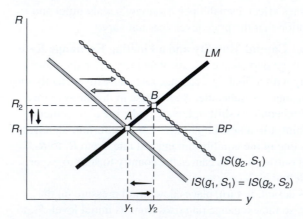

Figure 12–7 The Effects of an Increase in Government Spending with a Floating Exchange Rate and Perfect Capital Mobility
If there is perfect capital mobility under a floating exchange rate, an increase in government expenditures shifts the *IS* schedule rightward along the *LM* schedule, from point *A* to point *B*. The resulting rise in the nominal interest rate induces capital inflows that lead to a balance-of-payments surplus that causes a currency appreciation. Consequently, export spending declines and export expenditures increase, causing the *IS* schedule to return to its original position at point *A*.

The balance-of-payments surplus at point B generates an appreciation of the country's currency, which causes import spending to rise and export expenditures to fall. As a result, total aggregate spending on domestic output declines, and the IS schedule shifts leftward, from $IS(g_2, S_1)$ to $IS(g_2, S_2)$, which is the same as the original position of the IS schedule. Thus, the final equilibrium is point A once again, and real income is unaffected, on net, by the rise in government spending. We may conclude that with perfect capital mobility, fiscal policy actions have *complete crowding-out effects.* Any increase in government spending crowds out an equal amount of net export spending by foreign residents because of the currency appreciation that the fiscal policy action causes. On net, therefore, equilibrium real income is unaffected by the fiscal policy action.

Perfect Capital Mobility and Fixed versus Floating Exchange Rates Let's compare our conclusions about the effects of monetary and fiscal policies under perfect capital mobility and a *floating* exchange rate with those we reached in Chapter 11 when we considered an environment with perfect capital mobility and a *fixed* exchange rate. Recall from Chapter 11 that nonsterilized central bank interventions to maintain a fixed exchange rate cause a nation's money stock to change in the same direction as resulting movements in its foreign exchange reserves. Thus, an initial effort by a central bank to expand the quantity of money in circulation ultimately is offset fully by a reduction in the quantity of money as the central bank sells foreign exchange reserves to relieve resulting downward pressure on the value of its nation's currency. Nonsterilized monetary policy actions thereby cannot affect equilibrium real income with a fixed exchange rate.

In contrast, an expansionary fiscal policy action, such as an increase in government spending, exerts its largest possible effect on equilibrium real income with fixed exchange rates and perfectly mobile capital. This is true, as you learned in Chapter 11, because maintaining a fixed exchange rate in the face of a rise in government expenditures requires purchases of foreign exchange reserves that, if unsterilized, cause an expansion of the quantity of money in circulation. This equiproportionate rise in the nominal money stock reinforces the expansionary effect that the fiscal policy action has on equilibrium real income.

Under a floating exchange rate, however, there is no automatic adjustment of the quantity of money in response to a fiscal policy action. Instead, as illustrated in Figure 12–7, the *exchange rate* adjusts, which leads to a crowding-out effect on net export spending that fully dampens the effect that an increase in government spending otherwise would have on equilibrium real income.

A monetary policy action, by way of contrast, induces both a direct rise in real income and an exchange-rate adjustment that reinforces this real income increase, as shown in Figure 12–7 Thus, an expansionary monetary policy action exerts its largest possible effect on the equilibrium level of real income in a small open economy if the exchange rate floats and capital is perfectly mobile.

Table 12-1 summarizes comparisons of the real income effects of economic policy actions with fixed versus floating exchange rates for a small open economy with perfectly mobile capital. This table yields the following important conclusions about the real-income effects of monetary and fiscal policies under perfect capital mobility:

1. **With perfectly mobile capital, monetary policy actions have minimal effects on equilibrium real income in a small open economy if the exchange rate is fixed. Monetary policy actions have their largest possible real income effects if the exchange rate floats.**

Table 12-1

Real Income Effects of Economic Policies for a Small Open Economy with Perfect Capital Mobility under Fixed versus Floating Exchange Rates

Exchange-Rate Setting	Monetary Policy Effect	Fiscal Policy Effect
Fixed exchange rate	Minimum effect	Maximum effect
Floating exchange rate	Maximum effect	Minimum effect

2. **With perfect capital mobility, fiscal policy actions exert their largest feasible effects on equilibrium real income in a small open economy if the exchange is fixed. Fiscal policy actions have minimal real income effects if the exchange rate floats.**

Fundamental ISSUES

#2 How does perfect capital mobility influence the relative effectiveness of monetary and fiscal policy actions in a small open economy that permits its exchange rate to float?

With perfect capital mobility and a floating exchange rate, the monetary policy actions exert their greatest possible effects on equilibrium real income in a small open economy. In contrast, fiscal policy actions have no short-run real income effects under a floating exchange rate and perfect capital mobility.

Economic Policies with Perfect Capital Mobility and a Floating Exchange Rate: A Two-Country Example

In Chapter 11, we considered the implications of policy actions for the economic performance of two nations that were completely open to cross-border capital flows, under the assumption that one nation's central bank intervened in the foreign exchange market to keep the rate of exchange for the two nations' currencies fixed. Now let's apply that two-country example to a setting with a floating exchange rate, while maintaining our assumption of no anticipated currency appreciations or depreciations.

The Effects of a Domestic Monetary Expansion First, let's think about the effects of an action by the domestic central bank to increase the amount of domestic money in circulation. As shown in panel (a) of Figure 12–8, this shifts the domestic LM schedule to the right. As a result, the domestic interest rate falls from its initial equilibrium value of R_1 at point A toward a lower value of R' at point B, which is below the BP schedule, denoted BP_1, that prevails at the initial equilibrium exchange rate. This decline in the domestic interest rate induces a shift in financial resources from the domestic country to the foreign country, thereby raising the domestic demand for foreign currency and reducing the foreign demand for domestic currency. As a result, the value of the domestic currency depreciates, and the value of the foreign currency appreciates. Thus, the equilibrium exchange rate rises from its initial value of S_1 to a higher level, S_2.

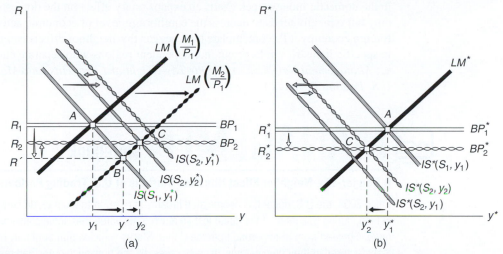

Figure 12–8 The Effects of a Domestic Monetary Expansion in the Two-Country Model with a Floating Exchange Rate
An increase in the domestic money stock shifts the domestic *LM* schedule rightward, causing a movement from point *A* to point *B* in panel (a). The resulting decline in the domestic interest rate causes financial resources to flow from the domestic country to the foreign country, thereby causing the domestic currency to depreciate relative to the foreign currency. The rise in the equilibrium exchange rate from S_1 to S_2 induces a rise in net expenditures on domestic output and a decline in net spending on foreign output, so on net the domestic *IS* schedule shifts rightward in panel (a), whereas the foreign *IS* schedule shifts leftward in panel (b). At the final equilibrium points labeled points *C* in both panels, domestic real income is higher, and foreign real income is lower. Thus, the domestic monetary expansion has a beggar-thy-neighbor effect on the foreign country.

The domestic currency depreciation induces a rise in net expenditures on domestic output, so at the initial level of foreign real income the domestic *IS* schedule shifts rightward in panel (a) of Figure 12–8, from $IS(S_1, y_1^*)$ to $IS(S_2, y_1^*)$. At the same time, the corresponding foreign currency appreciation and induced reduction in net expenditures on foreign output at the initial level of domestic real income causes the foreign *IS* schedule to shift to the left in panel (b), from $IS^*(S_1, y_1)$ to $IS^*(S_2, y_1)$. The resulting lower foreign real income causes domestic exports to decline, which shifts the domestic *IS* schedule to the left, to $IS(S_2, y_2^*)$ in panel (a) and to $IS^*(S_2, y_2)$ in panel (b). Finally, higher domestic real income induces increased foreign exports, which shifts the foreign *IS* schedule to the right. If domestic imports are highly responsive to a rise in domestic income, then the foreign *IS* schedule could shift farther back toward, or even beyond, point *A*, but panel (b) illustrates the more typical case in which foreign real income declines on net.

The equilibrium domestic nominal interest rate converges to an equality with the equilibrium foreign interest rate, with $R_2 = R_2^*$ at points *C* in both panels, as the *BP* schedules for both nations shift downward because of the *simultaneous* decline in nominal interest rates in both nations. In contrast to the small-open-economy case considered earlier in this chapter, both nations are sufficiently large that their policymakers can influence the overall world interest rate.

At point *C* in panel (a), the equilibrium level of domestic real income, y_2, exceeds the initial equilibrium value, y_1. At point *C* in panel (b), however, equilibrium foreign real income, y_2^* lies below its initial level, y_1^*. We may conclude that under a floating exchange rate and perfect capital mobility, a domestic monetary expansion can have a *beggar-thy-neighbor effect* on the foreign country. That is, an increase in the domestic money stock exerts an expansionary effect on the domestic economy but typically tends to depress the equilibrium level of economic activity in the foreign economy. (To contemplate how beggar-thy-neighbor effects can take place in specific industries in large but interdependent regions with separate currencies, see *Management Notebook: A Beggar-Thy-Neighbor Effect Hits Auto Markets of U.S. Trading Partners*.)

MANAGEMENT Notebook

A Beggar-Thy-Neighbor Effect Hits Auto Markets of U.S. Trading Partners

Since 2008, the U.S. dollar has depreciated broadly in relation to most world currencies. Indeed, during this interval the dollar lost so much of its value that some consumers in other regions gained from re-importing from the United States vehicles that originally had been manufactured in their own nations. In many cases, by the time such autos had reached U.S. shores, re-expressing their dollar prices in home currencies resulted in effective prices in local currencies that were as much as 20 percent lower than the prices of other home-manufactured vehicles.

U.S. auto dealers, of course, were only too happy to earn profits from selling foreign-manufactured automobiles to non-U.S. consumers, thereby boosting their export sales. Such transactions, however, reduced the sales of auto dealers in other locales, such as Japan, where imports of vehicles from the United States rose by 40 percent after 2008. Thus, auto dealers in the United States gained from the dollar depreciation at the expense of non-U.S. auto dealers.

For Critical Analysis

Why do you suppose that some foreign households have purchased two or even three vehicles from U.S. auto dealers in recent years?

If you think back to Chapter 11, you will recall that if the domestic monetary authority intervenes in the foreign exchange market to fix the exchange rate, then domestic monetary policy actions have no ultimate effect on either domestic or foreign real income levels or nominal interest rates in a two-country world with perfect capital mobility. Figure 12–8 on the previous page indicates that if the exchange rate floats, domestic monetary policy can affect levels of real income and interest rates in both nations within the same two-country world. Hence, the foreign economy is no longer insulated from domestic monetary policy actions under a floating exchange rate.

The Effects of a Foreign Monetary Expansion Note that we could have just as easily considered the effect of a foreign monetary expansion in Figure 12–8. Such an example produces a mirror image: A rightward shift of the foreign *LM* schedule, a rightward shift of the foreign *IS* schedule as the foreign currency's value depreciates, and a leftward shift of the domestic *IS* schedule as the domestic currency's value appreciates. Thus, with a floating exchange rate and perfect capital mobility, an increase in the foreign money stock generates a decline in equilibrium nominal interest rates in both nations, a rise in equilibrium foreign real income, and a decline in equilibrium domestic real income.

You saw in Chapter 11 that if the domestic central bank maintains a fixed exchange rate, then a foreign monetary expansion induces the domestic central bank to increase the domestic money stock, so there is a *locomotive effect,* as both nations' real income levels would rise in response. Figure 12–8 shows that the *opposite* result occurs in a two-country world with a floating exchange rate. In such a world, a foreign monetary expansion instead typically generates a beggar-thy-neighbor effect.

The Effects of a Domestic Fiscal Expansion In Figure 12–9, we consider the effects of an increase in domestic government spending in the two-country model under a floating exchange rate. The direct effect of a rise in domestic government expenditures, at the initial equilibrium exchange rate, S_1, and the initial foreign real income level, y_1^*, is a rightward shift in the domestic IS schedule in panel (a), from $IS(g_1, S_1, y_1^*)$ to $IS(g_2, S_1, y_1^*)$. As a result, the equilibrium domestic nominal interest rate rises toward R' at point B in panel (a), which causes an inflow of financial resources from the foreign country. To acquire domestic financial assets, foreign residents would increase their demand for domestic currency. The domestic currency appreciates, and the foreign currency depreciates. Consequently, the equilibrium exchange rate declines from S_1 to a smaller value, S_2.

The domestic currency appreciation generates a reduction in net expenditures on domestic goods and services, causing the domestic IS schedule to shift back to the left. At the same time, the foreign currency depreciation leads to an increase in net spending on foreign goods and services, which induces a rightward shift in the foreign IS schedule. As equilibrium real income levels in both nations increase, so do exports, which tend to push both nations' IS schedules to the right. In panel (a), we assume that domestic exports respond more strongly to the domestic currency appreciation than to the rise in foreign real income, so that there is a net leftward

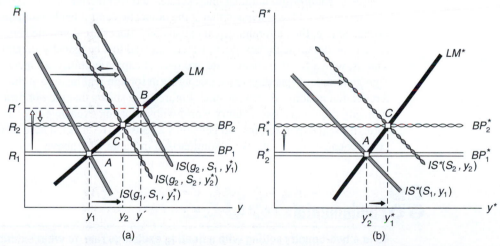

(a)   (b)

Figure 12–9   The Effects of a Domestic Fiscal Expansion in the Two-Country Model with a Floating Exchange Rate
An increase in domestic government expenditures causes the domestic IS schedule to shift rightward in panel (a), causing a movement from point A to point B. The resulting increase in the domestic interest rate induces an inflow of financial resources from the foreign country that causes an appreciation of the domestic currency relative to the foreign currency. The fall in the equilibrium exchange rate from S_1 to S_2 induces a reduction in net expenditures on domestic goods and services, which causes the domestic IS schedule to shift leftward in panel (a), and it causes an increase in net spending on foreign goods and services, which causes the foreign IS schedule to shift rightward in panel (b). At points C in both panels, the equilibrium levels of real income in the two nations are higher than their initial values, so the domestic fiscal expansion has a locomotive effect on the foreign country.

Table 12-2

Cross-Country Effects of Economic Policy Actions in the Two-Country Model with Perfect Capital Mobility under Fixed versus Floating Exchange Rates

Exchange-Rate Setting	Monetary Policy Effect	Fiscal Policy Effect
Fixed exchange rate	Locomotive effect	Beggar-thy-neighbor effect
Floating exchange rate	Beggar-thy-neighbor effect	Locomotive effect

shift of the domestic *IS* schedule, to $IS(g_2, S_2, y_1^*)$, which generates a final equilibrium at point *C*. In panel (b), we show the combined rightward shifts in the foreign *IS* schedule following the foreign currency depreciation and rise in domestic real income by the movement to $IS^*(S_2, y_2)$ at point *C*. The equilibrium foreign nominal interest rate rises toward convergence with the equilibrium domestic interest rate, with $R_2 = R_2^*$ at points *C* in both panels, as the *BP* schedules for both nations shift upward.

At points *C* in both panels of Figure 12–9 on the previous page, the equilibrium levels of real income in the two nations exceed their initial values. Thus, under a floating exchange rate and perfect capital mobility, a domestic fiscal expansion has a *locomotive effect* on the foreign country. An increase in domestic government spending results in expansions of real income levels in both nations.

The Effects of a Foreign Fiscal Expansion The example in Figure 12–9 could have been altered to evaluate the effect of a foreign fiscal expansion. Again, a mirror image of effects takes place: a rightward shift of the domestic *IS* schedule, a leftward shift of the foreign *IS* schedule as the foreign currency's value appreciates, and a rightward shift of the domestic *IS* schedule as the domestic currency's value depreciates. Hence, we may conclude that with a floating exchange rate and perfectly mobile capital, an increase in foreign government spending generates increases in equilibrium nominal interest rates and real income levels in both nations.

In Chapter 11 you learned that if the domestic central bank maintains a fixed exchange rate, then a foreign fiscal expansion induces the domestic central bank to reduce the domestic money stock, which can lead to a beggar-thy-neighbor effect. That is, with a fixed exchange rate and perfect capital mobility, an increase in foreign government spending can cause a rise in foreign real income at the expense of a reduction in domestic real income. Figure 12–9 shows that the *opposite* outcome typically occurs in a two-country world with a floating exchange rate, in which a foreign fiscal expansion instead generates a locomotive effect. These differences in cross-country policy effects are summarized in Table 12-2 above.

Fundamental ISSUES

#3 In a two-country setting with a floating exchange rate, to what extent can policy actions in one nation influence economic activity in the other nation?

With a floating exchange rate and interdependent economies, an expansionary monetary policy action in one nation tends to raise equilibrium real income in that nation while reducing equilibrium real income in the other country. In contrast, an expansionary fiscal policy action in one nation tends to stimulate equilibrium real income levels in both countries.

FIXED VERSUS FLOATING EXCHANGE RATES

Which is preferable: a fixed exchange rate, or a floating exchange rate? If this choice were simple, then the wide variety of exchange-rate arrangements that we surveyed in Chapter 3 would not exist. In addition, individual nations would not have fixed their exchange rates during some periods in their history while permitting them to float during other intervals. If it were an easy matter to decide whether to fix exchange rates or to let exchange rates float, all nations would have made the same choice, and they would have maintained the same exchange-rate systems over the years.

This observation indicates that there must be pros and cons associated with these alternative exchange-rate arrangements. That is, nations must confront *economic trade-offs* when choosing between fixed and floating exchange rates. A choice of one type of exchange-rate system or the other must entail balancing the potential gains from that choice with the potential losses.

The fundamental trade-offs between fixed versus floating exchange rates cut across two dimensions: *economic efficiency* and *economic stability*. As you will learn, the most *efficient* exchange-rate system may or may not be the one that attains greater stability of an economy's overall real income performance. This is what makes the choice of the "best" exchange-rate system potentially very difficult.

Efficiency Arguments for Fixed versus Floating Exchange Rates

Economic efficiency is the attainment of the least-cost allocation of scarce resources. Therefore, *the most efficient exchange-rate system is the set of exchange-rate arrangements that permits residents of a nation to direct resources to their alternative uses at minimum cost.* To evaluate whether a fixed exchange rate or a floating exchange rate may better contribute to economic efficiency, we need to contemplate the costs that a nation's residents face under the alternative systems.

economic efficiency
The allocation of scarce resources at minimum cost.

Social Costs Stemming from Foreign Exchange Risks In Chapters 4 and 5, you learned about how currency exchanges in the forward exchange market and financial transactions involving various derivative securities may be used to hedge against foreign exchange risks. Such hedging activities entail expenditures of resources. For instance, banks must pay salaries to traders who possess the expertise necessary to plan hedging strategies and to conduct derivatives transactions on their behalf.

In addition, holding and trading derivatives exposes banks and other firms to risks. As we discussed in Chapter 5, these include *credit risks* associated with potential default by a contract counterparty, *market risks* arising from potential liquidity crunches or payment-system failures, and operating risks stemming from the potential for poor derivatives management. On the one hand, failure to control these risks can result in sizable losses, as noted in Chapter 5. On the other hand, establishing and maintaining management systems to monitor and contain derivatives risks can entail sizable resource expenses. Losses stemming from derivatives risks and the costs of limiting such losses constitute another set of costs associated with hedging activities.

Furthermore, governmental concerns about the potential for *systemic risks,* such as the systemic payment-system risks discussed in Chapter 6, can lead to the establishment of elaborate systems of regulatory oversight of financial institutions. The costs incurred by governments in examining and supervising financial institutions represent further costs that stem from hedging activities in the face of foreign exchange risks.

Efficiency via a Fixed Exchange Rate? Many observers argue that the efficiency trade-off between fixed and floating exchange rates favors adopting a system of fixed exchange rates. The basis of their argument is simple. If rates of exchange among currencies are fixed, then exchange-rate volatility and the related risks by definition should be significantly muted, if not eliminated. As a result, there is little incentive to undertake foreign exchange hedging activities, and so the associated costs are minimized. A system of fixed exchange rates thereby would be most efficient.

Figure 12–10 shows how a trade-weighted index measure of the dollar's value, or effective exchange rate (see Chapter 2), has behaved since the concluding years of the Bretton Woods system of fixed exchange rates. As you can see, the dollar's overall exchange value has varied considerably during the past five years. Undoubtedly, exchange-rate variability under floating exchange rates has spurred increased hedging activities and raised the related costs.

Does this mean that social costs resulting from foreign exchange risks are always lower under a system of fixed exchange rates? Not necessarily. "Fixed" exchange rates are never permanently fixed. In a system of fixed exchange rates, people face the possibility of exchange-rate *realignments*, or changes in official target values for currency values. Consequently, there can be substantial risks arising from political instability or other factors that may influence governmental authorities who determine the "appropriate" exchange rates to fix.

realignment

A change in an official exchange-rate target.

The Pain of Realigning Indeed, foreign holders of Mexican government bonds and firm stocks learned this lesson the hard way in 1994. Until December of that year, the Mexican government sought to keep the value of the peso within an official "trading band"—or allowable range of exchange-rate variation—relative to the U.S. dollar. Mexico's objective in pursuing this policy was to keep its inflation rate more in line with U.S. inflation and thereby promote a stable environment for

Figure 12–10

Exchange-Rate Volatility under Floating Exchange Rates

Since the end of the Bretton Woods system of fixed exchange rates, the British pound's value has exhibited several periods of variability. This variability was most pronounced during the early 1990s and after the financial crisis that began in 2008.

increased trade with the United States, Canada, and other nations. An indication of the apparent success of the Mexican policy was a November 18, 1994, headline in the *Wall Street Journal,* which read, "Mexico Posts Surprisingly Solid Growth, As Turnaround in Economy Advances." A figure accompanying the article, titled "On the Move," showed recent Mexican GDP growth of nearly 5 percent per year.

Visit the Bank of Mexico at *http://www.banxico.org.mx/indexEn.html.*

Nonetheless, between February and December of 1994, the peso's value declined by more than 10 percent relative to the dollar, to the bottom of the Mexican government's trading band. Then, on December 21, the Mexican government unexpectedly devalued the peso. In that single day, the peso's value relative to the dollar shot down by 12.7 percent. During the week following the devaluation, the peso's value fell by a total of more than 35 percent.

For U.S. residents who held peso-denominated financial assets, this meant that within a single week's time they had lost more than one-third of the dollar value of their holdings. In early 1995 the Federal Reserve intervened in the dollar–peso exchange market to support the peso's value, and the U.S. Treasury made more than $40 billion in loan guarantees to the Mexican government. These actions helped the peso's market value recover considerably. Consequently, for most foreign holders of Mexican bonds and stocks, the devaluation caused short-term "paper losses" that were not actually realized at maturity. Nevertheless, a number of non-Mexican bondholders and stock traders did experience significant losses as a result of the 1994 peso devaluation.

This example shows that a "fixed" exchange-rate system is not necessarily risk-free. Indeed, the potential for unhedged losses arguably may be greater under a fixed exchange rate, as compared with a floating-exchange-rate system. This is because a fixed exchange rate can lull some holders of financial assets into a sense of complacency, leading them to take unhedged trading positions that yield large losses when unexpected devaluations occur.

We may conclude that a system of floating exchange rates increases the potential for day-to-day foreign exchange risks, requiring potentially significant expenditures of resources associated with hedging activities. This is an efficiency-related drawback of permitting the exchange rate to float.

Under a system of fixed exchange rates, in contrast, the possibility of unanticipated governmental actions to alter exchange rate targets can pose risks of unhedged foreign exchange losses. Hence, we reach the following conclusion on the efficiency merits of fixed versus floating exchange rates:

> **There is a trade-off between the social costs incurred in hedging against foreign exchange risks in a system of floating exchange rates and the risk of experiencing unhedged losses as a result of unexpected devaluations in a system of fixed exchange rates.**

This means that a key criterion for evaluating the potential efficiency gain that a country might experience by switching from a floating exchange rate to a fixed exchange rate is the risk that the nation's government may face pressures to vary its exchange-rate targets. As we shall discuss in Chapter 13, a fundamental implication is that the credibility of the government's commitment to a fixed exchange rate is likely to be crucial in determining whether a system of fixed exchange rates is more efficient than a floating-exchange-rate system.

Fundamental ISSUES

#4 What is the basic economic efficiency trade-off faced in choosing between fixed and floating exchange rates?

On the one hand, members of society must incur large resource costs to hedge against foreign exchange market risks in a system of floating exchange rates. On the other hand, with fixed exchange rates there can be significant risks of unhedged losses stemming from unanticipated currency devaluations. Because these latter risks depend on the behavior of governments, a fixed-exchange-rate system is not necessarily preferable, on efficiency grounds, to a system of floating exchange rates.

Stability Arguments for Fixed versus Floating Exchange Rates

What should a country do if the fixed- and floating-exchange-rate systems happen to produce the same level of economic efficiency? Can other factors tip the balance in favor of one system? Or, alternatively, if one exchange-rate system is more efficient than the other, can other factors nevertheless induce a nation to adopt the alternative system of exchange rates?

One potentially important consideration in choosing between fixed and floating exchange rates is *economic stability.* There are a number of notions of economic stability, because there are several variables that a nations' citizens may desire for their government to try to stabilize. These include real income, the inflation rate, and the unemployment rate. For now we shall focus on real income stability under fixed versus floating exchange rates. It turns out that the implications for real income stability under the two exchange-rate systems are fundamentally the same, even if inflation and unemployment stability also are key policy goals, as we shall explain in Chapter 13. Hence, we can identify the key aspects of the *stability trade-off* entailed in the choice of a fixed or floating exchange rate by concentrating on the single policy goal of stable real income.

Autonomous Expenditure Volatility and Fixed versus Floating Exchange Rates One possible source of real income instability that any nation faces is variability in aggregate autonomous expenditures. Recall from Chapter 10 that variations in autonomous saving, import spending, investment, government spending, net taxes, or export spending cause changes in the equilibrium real income level, thereby resulting in changes in the position of the *IS* schedule. For example, consider the effect of a significant decline in real income in the rest of the world, denoted by y^* in Figure 12–11, from an initial level of y_1^* to a lower level of y_2^*. With less real income to allocate to purchases of domestic goods, foreign residents reduce their expenditures on domestic exports. This causes aggregate autonomous expenditures on domestic goods and services to decline, so the *IS* schedule shifts leftward, from

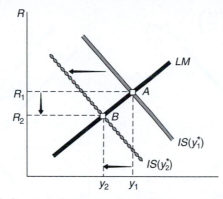

Figure 12–11   The Effects of a Decline in Aggregate Autonomous Expenditures

A decline in real income in the rest of the world, from y_1^* to y_2^*, causes foreign residents to reduce their expenditures on domestic exports, resulting in a fall in domestic aggregate autonomous expenditures and a leftward shift in the *IS* schedule. Consequently, equilibrium domestic real income declines from y_1 at point *A* to y_2 at point *B*, which indicates that volatility in real income in the rest of the world results in domestic real income instability.

$IS(y_1^*)$ to $IS(y_2^*)$, causing a movement along the *LM* schedule from point *A* to point *B*. As a result, equilibrium *domestic* real income declines, from y_1 to y_2.

Volatility in real income in the rest of the world results in domestic income instability, holding all other factors unchanged.

Does the choice between fixed and floating exchange rates have any bearing on domestic real income stability in the face of a decline in real income abroad? The answer to this question is yes, as Figure 12–12 on the following page illustrates for the case of a small open economy with perfect capital mobility. We draw Figure 12–12 under the assumption that there is no expected exchange-rate depreciation, in which case uncovered interest parity yields equality between the domestic nominal interest rate, R_1, and the nominal interest rate in the rest of the world, R^*. Hence, the *BP* schedule is horizontal at this world interest rate.

Panel (a) of the figure displays the effect on equilibrium domestic real income of a fall in foreign real income with a fixed exchange rate. As in Figure 12–11, a decline in real income in the rest of the world causes the domestic *IS* schedule to shift leftward, from $IS(y_1^*)$ to $IS(y_2^*)$, along the *LM* schedule, from point *A* to point *B*. At point *B*, however, the equilibrium domestic interest rate, R_2, lies below the world interest rate, R^*. This stimulates capital outflows, thereby resulting in a domestic balance-of-payments deficit and downward pressure on the value of the nation's currency. As we discussed in Chapter 11, to keep the exchange rate fixed, the central bank must respond by reducing the quantity of money. This causes the *LM* schedule to shift to the left, from $LM(M_1)$ to $LM(M_2)$. The final equilibrium real income level is equal to y_3, at point *C* in panel (a). Under a fixed exchange rate, therefore, a contraction in the money stock required to maintain a fixed exchange rate reinforces a decline in domestic real income following a fall in foreign real income.

Panel (b) of Figure 12–12 contrasts this result with what happens under a floating exchange rate. As before, a decline in real income in the rest of the world causes the *IS* schedule to shift leftward. This takes place at the *initial equilibrium exchange rate*, denoted S_1, so we label the new *IS* schedule as $IS(y_2^*, S_1)$. At the new *IS–LM* equilibrium point *B* that results from this shift, there again is a balance-of-payments deficit. This causes the market value of the domestic currency to decline,

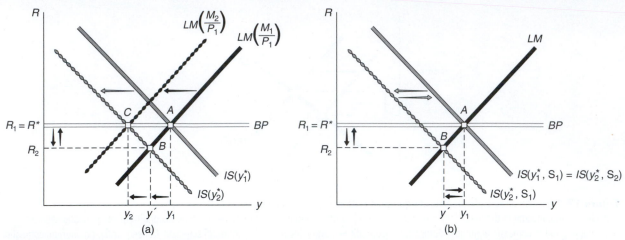

Figure 12–12   Real Income Stability in the Face of a Decline in Aggregate Autonomous Expenditures with Perfect Capital Mobility
Panel (a) shows that a fall in foreign real income with a fixed exchange rate causes the domestic *IS* schedule to shift leftward, inducing a movement from point *A* to point *B*. The resulting domestic balance-of-payments deficit places downward pressure on the value of the nation's currency. To keep the exchange rate fixed, the central bank must reduce the money stock and shift the *LM* schedule leftward. This monetary policy response yields a final equilibrium at point *C* in panel (a) and reinforces the real income effect of the fall in foreign real income. Panel (b) indicates that under a floating exchange rate, the fall in foreign real income that induces a movement to point *B* causes the equilibrium exchange rate to rise from S_1 to S_2, which induces a rise in net export spending and a rightward shift in the *IS* schedule. Hence, real income is more stable under a floating exchange rate as compared with a fixed exchange rate.

so the exchange rate rises to a higher value, S_2. The depreciation in the domestic currency spurs net export spending, which causes the *IS* schedule to shift back to its original position, now labeled $IS(y_2^*, S_2)$, at point *A*. At this point, the nation reattains balance-of-payments equilibrium, and the equilibrium level of domestic real income once again is equal to y_1, its initial value. By permitting the exchange rate to float, a nation's policymakers *automatically* ensure real income stability in the face of a decline in real income in the rest of the world. Real income is more stable, therefore, under a floating exchange rate, as compared with a fixed exchange rate.

Indeed, we would have obtained this same basic conclusion if we had considered *any* factor that causes a decline in aggregate autonomous expenditures and if we had evaluated a situation of imperfect capital mobility. Equilibrium real income is more stable in the face of variations in aggregate autonomous expenditures under a floating exchange rate.

Financial Volatility and Fixed versus Floating Exchange Rates This conclusion does not necessarily mean that a floating exchange rate always promotes real income stability, however. To see why, let's begin by considering another possible source of real income instability, which is volatility in the financial sector of the economy.

For example, suppose that people suddenly lose confidence in long-term prospects in the bond market. This induces them to shift much of their wealth from bonds to holdings of money. Thus, the demand for real money balances increases at any given level of real income. As shown in panel (a) of Figure 12–13 on the following page, an initial real income level of y_1 causes a rightward shift in the demand schedule for real money balances, from $m_1^d(y_1)$ to $m_2^d(y_1)$. The result is a rise in the equilibrium interest rate, from R_1 at point *A* to R' at point *B*, and, as shown in panel (b), an upward shift in the *LM* schedule at the initial income level y_1, from $LM_1(M_1/P_1)$

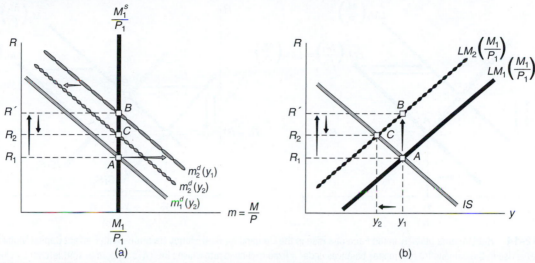

Figure 12-13   The Effects of a Rise in the Demand for Real Money Balances

A rise in the demand for money caused by any factor other than an increase in real income causes an increase in the equilibrium nominal interest rate, from R_1 at point A in panel (a) to R' at point B. At the initial level of real income, the new real income–interest rate combination that maintains money market equilibrium, given by point B in panel (b), lies above the initial real income–interest rate combination given by point A. Thus, an increase in the demand for real money balances not stemming from a rise in real income generates an upward and leftward shift in the LM schedule. This causes equilibrium real income to decline to y_2 in panel (b), which induces a leftward shift in the money demand schedule in panel (a). The net effect is a rise in the equilibrium interest rate and a decline in equilibrium real income.

at point A to $LM_2(M_1/P_1)$ at point B. Thus, the rise in the demand for money causes the LM schedule to shift, even though the quantity of real money balances does not change. The rise in the interest rate causes a decline in desired investment, as reflected by an upward movement along the IS schedule in panel (b), so equilibrium real income declines from y_1 to y_2. At the final IS–LM equilibrium point C, therefore, real income is lower than before. The decline in real income causes the demand for real money balances to fall somewhat, so the equilibrium interest rate falls back to R_2 at point C in panel (a).

Figure 12–13 indicates that variations in the demand for real money balances can lead to real income instability. Now let's consider how the extent of such instability can depend on the choice between fixed versus floating exchange rates. Figure 12–14 on the next page provides a comparison between the real income effects of money demand variations for the two exchange-rate systems, again under the assumption of a small open economy with perfect capital mobility. Panel (a) shows the effect of a rise in the demand for real money balances under a fixed exchange rate. This causes the LM schedule to shift to the left, from $LM_1(M_1/P_1)$ to $LM_2(M_1/P_1)$, which tends to push up the equilibrium domestic interest rate, from R_1 at point A toward R_2 at point B.

Because R_2 exceeds the world interest rate, R^*, at point B, the domestic economy experiences a capital inflow that contributes to a balance-of-payments surplus. As a result, there is upward pressure on the value of the domestic currency in foreign exchange markets. To keep the exchange rate fixed, the domestic central bank must purchase foreign-currency-denominated assets. If the domestic central bank conducts nonsterilized interventions, this action generates a rise in the domestic money stock, which shifts the LM schedule back to the right in panel (a), to $LM_2(M_2/P_2)$ at point A. By maintaining a fixed exchange rate, therefore, the central

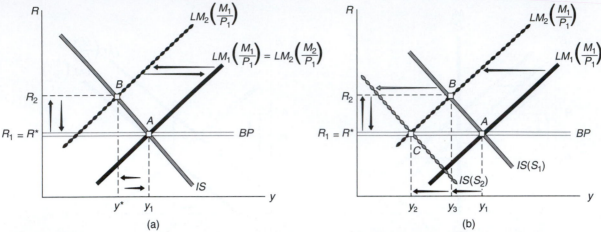

Figure 12–14   Real Income Stability in the Face of a Rise in the Demand for Real Money Balances with Perfect Capital Mobility

In panel (a), a rise in the demand for real money balances under a fixed exchange rate causes the *LM* schedule to shift leftward, inducing a movement from point *A* to point *B*. The resulting rise in the domestic interest rate causes a capital inflow. To keep the exchange rate fixed, the domestic central bank must purchase foreign assets, which leads to a rise in the domestic money stock and causes the *LM* schedule to shift back to the right. In panel (b), the movement to point *B* caused by a rise in the demand for real money balances with a floating exchange rate leads to a decline in the equilibrium exchange rate from S_1 to S_2. As a result, there is decline in net export expenditures in the domestic economy that causes the *IS* schedule to shift leftward to the final equilibrium point *C*. At this point, real income is below the initial equilibrium income level, so real income is less stable in the face of money demand variations under a floating exchange rate.

bank *automatically* offsets the real income effect of a rise in money demand. Equilibrium real income is more stable in the face of variations in the demand for real money balances under a fixed exchange rate.

Panel (b) of Figure 12–14 shows how equilibrium real income responds to a rise in the demand for real money balances in a system of floating exchange rates. The increase in money demand shifts the *LM* schedule leftward, from $LM_1(M_1/P_1)$ to $LM_2(M_1/P_1)$. This places upward pressure on the domestic interest rate, which tends to rise from R_1 at point *A* toward R_2 at point *B*. The result is an inflow of capital and a balance-of-payments surplus. In a floating-exchange-rate system, this causes the domestic currency to appreciate, so the equilibrium exchange rate declines from an initial value, S_1, to a lower level, S_2.

Consequently, the domestic price of goods imported from abroad falls, and the foreign price of domestic exports rises, thereby inducing a decline in net export expenditures in the domestic economy. This reduces aggregate desired expenditures on domestic goods and services, which causes the *IS* schedule to shift leftward in panel (b), from $IS(S_1)$ to $IS(S_2)$. At the final equilibrium point *C*, real income is equal to y_3, which unambiguously is less than the initial equilibrium income level y_1. By adopting a system of floating exchange rates, a nation's policymakers thereby expose real income to greater instability as a result of money demand variations.

The Stability Trade-Off These examples illustrate a fundamental *stability trade-off* that nations face when they choose between adopting fixed or floating exchange rates:

1. **Variations in aggregate desired expenditures lead to real income instability under a fixed-exchange-rate system. Permitting the exchange**

rate to float automatically reduces the real income effects of volatility in desired expenditures.

2. **Variations in the demand for real money balances contribute to real income instability under a floating-exchange-rate system. Fixing the exchange rate automatically reduces the real income effects of volatility in money demand.**

This stability trade-off indicates that, holding economic efficiency criteria constant, a nation should opt for a fixed exchange rate if the main source of real income instability arises from financial volatility that causes variations in the demand for real money balances. In contrast, in a nation in which there is considerable volatility in desired expenditures, a system of floating exchange rates is preferable.

Clearly, it is possible that a system of floating exchange rates might be preferable on the grounds of stability, yet be less desirable than a system of fixed exchange rates from the perspective of economic efficiency. Alternatively, maintaining a fixed exchange rate could, under some circumstances, be the better policy choice from the standpoint of achieving greater real income stability, but adopting a system of floating exchange rates might lead to a higher level of overall economic efficiency. In either of these situations, a nation would have to make a difficult choice between minimizing real income instability and maximizing economic efficiency.

Monetary Policy Autonomy and Fixed versus Floating Exchange Rates

Our analyses of economic policymaking in Chapter 11 and in this chapter indicate that there is at least one other factor that can influence a nation's choice to fix its exchange rates or to allow them to float in foreign exchange markets. This is the nation's desire for *monetary policy autonomy*, or the extent to which monetary policies can exert independent effects on overall economic performance.

As you learned in Chapter 11, when nations' economies are interdependent, the choice between a system of fixed or floating exchange rates affects the ability of each nation's central bank to conduct independent policy actions to influence its own nation's economic performance. Under a fixed exchange rate, a central bank's actions to keep the value of its nation's currency unchanged preclude the potential for any efforts to vary the quantity of money for purposes of domestic real income stabilization. In a sense, adopting a fixed exchange rate in a world of interdependent economies makes a nation's monetary policy a "slave" to events in other nations.

In contrast, earlier in this chapter we noted in our two-economy analysis of a floating-exchange-rate system that a central bank's policy actions can influence its nation's equilibrium real income level. Hence, adopting a system of floating exchange rates gives a nation's central bank policy autonomy that it does not possess under a system of fixed exchange rates.

As you can see, nations must truly consider many factors when they determine the exchange-rate policies that are best for their own interests. Economic efficiency trade-offs, economic stability trade-offs, and the issue of monetary policy autonomy all can influence a country's final decision. In the next chapter we will show how one more factor can play a role in affecting this decision. This is the extent to which the price level is flexible. Policymakers must also consider variations in the price level and inflation when they choose the exchange-rate systems for their nations.

monetary policy autonomy
The capability of a central bank to engage in monetary policy actions independent of the actions of other central banks.

Fundamental ISSUES

#5 How does the choice between fixed and floating exchange rates depend in part on the implications for economic stability and monetary policy autonomy?

With fixed exchange rates, the effects of variability in aggregate autonomous expenditures on a nation's output of goods and services causes real-income instability, whereas flexibility of exchange rates automatically mutes such instability in a system of floating exchange rates. With floating exchange rates, money demand volatility can make a nation's real-income level more unstable, whereas maintaining fixed exchange rates automatically offsets the extent to which changes in the demand for real-money balances influence equilibrium real income. Hence, a floating-exchange-rate system is preferable to a system of fixed exchange rates if the variability of aggregate autonomous expenditures is significantly larger than the volatility of money demand. Another consideration favoring a system of floating exchange rates is that central banks can engage in independent policy actions when exchange rates float. Under a system of fixed exchange rates, central banks must sacrifice their policy autonomy.

Chapter SUMMARY

1. **How Monetary and Fiscal Policy Actions Affect a Nation's Real Income under Floating Exchange Rates:** An increase in the amount of money in circulation induces a balance-of-payments deficit. This causes a depreciation of a nation's currency that stimulates net export expenditures and raises equilibrium real income. The effects of fiscal policy actions on a nation's balance of payments and the value of its currency depend on the extent to which a nation's borders are open to flows of financial resources. Under most circumstances, an expansionary fiscal policy action induces a short-run increase in a nation's real income level. The amount of the resulting increase in real income tends to fall as the degree of capital mobility increases.

2. **Perfect Capital Mobility and the Relative Effectiveness of Monetary and Fiscal Policy Actions in a Small Open Economy That Permits Its Exchange Rates to Float:** With perfect capital mobility and floating exchange rates, monetary policy actions exert their greatest possible effects on equilibrium real income in a small open economy. In contrast, fiscal policy actions have no short-run real income effects under floating exchange rates and perfect capital mobility.

3. **The Effects of Policy Actions in One Nation on Economic Activity in the Other Nation with a Floating Exchange Rate:** With a floating exchange rate and interdependent economies, a monetary policy expansion in one nation tends to raise equilibrium real income in that nation while reducing equilibrium real income in the other country. In contrast, an expansionary fiscal policy expansion in one nation tends to stimulate equilibrium real income levels in both countries.

4. **The Basic Economic Efficiency Trade-Off Faced in Choosing between Fixed and Floating Exchange Rates:** To shield themselves against risks of loss caused by exchange-rate volatility that can arise with floating exchange rates, individuals and businesses must allocate significant resources to hedging activities. By reducing the variability of exchange rates, a system of fixed exchange rates largely eliminates the incentive to engage in such activities, thereby yielding a potential resource saving.

Nevertheless, adopting fixed exchange rates exposes individuals and firms to the possibility of incurring sizable unhedged losses as a result of unexpected devaluations.

5. **Economic Stability, Monetary Policy Autonomy, and the Choice between Fixed and Floating Exchange Rates:** Changes in aggregate autonomous expenditures lead to real income instability in a system of fixed exchange rates but do not affect the level of real income under floating exchange rates. Variations in the demand for real money balances cause instability in the real income level in a system of floating exchange rates but do not affect the level of real income under fixed exchange rates. Therefore, a system of floating exchange rates promotes greater real income stability if the variability of aggregate autonomous expenditures is sizable relative to the volatility of money demand. A floating exchange rate also allows central banks to conduct independent monetary policies, whereas central banks lose policy autonomy under fixed exchange rates.

QUESTIONS and PROBLEMS

1. Explain, in your own words, why a currency depreciation shifts the *BP* schedule rightward.

2. Suppose that a national government adopts, and is able to enforce, a system of capital controls that permits absolutely no flows of financial resources across its borders, so that the *BP* schedule is vertical. Explain what effects an expansionary fiscal policy action would have on equilibrium real income in such an environment.

3. The government of a small open economy with relatively low capital mobility and a floating exchange rate decides that its top policy objective is to reduce its budget deficit via a reduction in government expenditures. Trace through the likely effects of this policy action within the *IS–LM–BP* framework.

4. The central bank of a small open economy with relatively high capital mobility and a floating exchange rate implements a contractionary monetary policy. Trace through the likely effects of this policy action within the *IS–LM–BP* framework.

5. Consider a two-country model in which both the domestic central bank and the foreign central bank permit the exchange rate to float. Begin with an initial equilibrium like the one illustrated in Figure 11–11 on page 338, and work out the effects of a foreign fiscal contraction.

6. Redo Question 5, but this time examine the effects of a domestic fiscal contraction.

7. In the early 1990s, as the United States struggled to emerge from a short but sharp real income contraction, its government prevailed upon the Japanese government to increase government spending and cut taxes. Assuming that capital mobility between the United States and Japan is nearly perfect and that the dollar–yen exchange rate floats in the foreign exchange market, would this request appear to have been consistent with U.S. interests? Justify your answer.

8. Referring back to the situation described in Question 7, what *monetary policy* actions would the U.S. government have preferred the Japanese government to pursue in the early 1990s? Explain your reasoning.

9. Following the late 1950s, most nations of Western Europe sought to maintain a system of nearly fixed exchange rates, on the grounds that such a system would promote greater efficiency by limiting the need to hedge against foreign exchange risks that would arise under floating exchange rates. These nations realigned their exchange rates over a dozen

times between 1979 and 1999. Did this fact strengthen or weaken the case for fixed exchange rates in Western Europe? Explain.

10. Consider a nation in which the demand for money is relatively stable. Export and import expenditures have fluctuated considerably in recent years, however, and political instability has led to considerable variation in government spending. If the country's primary goal is real income stability, should it adopt a system of fixed or floating exchange rates? Justify your answer.

Online APPLICATIONS

Internet URL: *http://www.bankofengland.co.uk*

Title: Bank of England

Navigation: The above address connects you with the home page for the Bank of England.

Application: Click on *Statistics* at the left of the page, and then click on *Interactive Database.* Then select *Tables,* and then *Money and Lending.*. Answer the following questions:

1. Click on *Monthly Growth rates of M4 and M4 lending* to download this table. Select *M4, Seasonally adjusted.* Examine the recent three- and six-month growth rates in M4, Britain's main measure of the quantity of money.

2. Go back to the *Tables Page* and click on *Interest and exchange rates* (right column) to download these data. Use the data for the U.S. dollar exchange rate of the British currency, the pound sterling, to calculate rates of British currency appreciation or depreciation during recent months. Does there appear to be a relationship between the M4 money growth rate and the rate of appreciation or depreciation of the pound sterling? Does this square with theory?

SELECTED REFERENCES and FURTHER READINGS

Belke, Ansgar, and Daniel Gros. "Asymmetries in Transatlantic Monetary Policymaking: Does the ECB Follow the Fed?" *Journal of Common Market Studies 43* (2005): 921–946.

Bergin, Paul, and Oscar Jorda. "Measuring Monetary Policy Interdependence." *Journal of International Money and Finance 23* (2004): 761–793.

Corden, Max. *Too Sensational: On the Choice of Exchange Rate Regimes.* Cambridge, MA: MIT Press, 2002.

Daniels, Joseph P., Peter Toumanoff, and Marc van der Ruhr. "Optimal Basket-Peg Arrangements for Developing Nations." *Journal of Economic Integration 16* (March 2001): 128–145.

Duttagupta, Rupa, and Inci Otker-Robe. "Exits from Pegged Regimes: An Empirical Analysis." International Monetary Fund, IMF Working Paper WP/03/147 (July 2003).

Edwards, Sebastian, and Eduardo Levy Yeyati. "Flexible Exchange Rates as Shock Absorbers." *European Economic Review 49* (2005): 2079–2105.

Ehrmann, Michael, and Marcel Fratzscher. "Exchange Rates and Fundamentals: New Evidence from Real Time Data." *Journal of International Money and Finance 24* (2005): 317–341.

Engel, Charles, and Kenneth West. "Exchange Rates and Fundamentals." *Journal of Political Economy 113* (2005): 487–517.

Forssback, Jens, and Lars Oxelheim. "On the Link between Exchange-Rate Regimes, Capital Controls, and Monetary Policy." *The World Economy 29* (2006): 341–368.

Frankel, Jeffrey, Seerio Schmakler, and Luis Serven. "Global Transmission of Interest Rates: Monetary Independence and Currency Regime." *Journal of International Money and Finance 24* (2005): 387–412.

Ghosh, Atish, Ann-Marie Gulde, and Holger Wolf. *Exchange Rate Regimes: Choices and Consequences.* Cambridge, MA: MIT Press, 2002.

Glick, Reuven, and Michael Hutchison. "Capital Controls and Exchange Rate Instability in Developing Economies." *Journal of International Money and Finance 24* (2005): 387–412.

Klein, Michael, and Jay Shambaugh. "Fixed Exchange Rates and Trade." *Journal of International Economics 70* (2006): 359–383.

Neely, Christopher, and Lucio Sarno. "How Well Do Monetary Fundamentals Forecast Exchange Rates?" Federal Reserve Bank of St. Louis, Working Paper 2002-007A (May 2002).

Reinhart, Carmen, and Kenneth Rogoff. "The Modern History of Exchange Rate Regimes: A Reinterpretation." *Quarterly Journal of Economics 119* (2004): 1–48.

13

The Price Level, Real Output, and Economic Policymaking

Fundamental ISSUES

1. What is the aggregate demand schedule?

2. What factors determine the extent to which changes in the quantity of money can influence aggregate demand in an open economy?

3. What factors determine the extent to which fiscal policy actions can influence aggregate demand in an open economy?

4. What is the aggregate supply schedule?

5. How are a nation's price level and volume of real output determined, and how might economic policymakers influence inflation and real output?

6. Why does the rational expectations hypothesis indicate that economic policies may have limited real output effects and that the credibility of policymakers is important?

From the late 1990s through the mid-2000s, central bank officials worldwide were singing to the same tune: inflation targeting. Following the lead of Canada, New Zealand, and the United Kingdom, central banks of more than two dozen developing nations opted to establish target rates of inflation. In fact, instead of aiming to achieve their target inflation rates on average, most of these nations began regarding their targets as upper limits. Even in the United States, where the Employment Act of 1946 requires the Federal Reserve to take into account explicit objectives for unemployment as well as inflation, top policymakers began debating the advantages and disadvantages of pursuing an explicit inflation target.

By the end of the 2000s, however, most of the world's central banks utilizing explicit inflation targets were experiencing actual rates of inflation well above formal target levels. In the developing world, inflation rates exceeded target levels in every single nation in which a central bank claimed to be utilizing inflation targets. And in the United States, in which the average inflation rate in recent years has more than doubled from its early-2000s low, during the early 2010s all Federal Reserve discussion of the merits of inflation targeting had come to an abrupt halt.

In recent years, households and businesses around the globe have been adjusting to the greatest inflation variability in more than twenty-five years. It remains to be seen whether they will have to learn to live with higher inflation variability—or in some nations perhaps even accelerating rates of inflation—during the years to come.

In previous chapters, we have focused on how equilibrium real income and the equilibrium nominal interest rate are determined in open economies. To concentrate on how varying degrees of capital mobility affect the transmission of policy actions, we also have abstracted from the important roles that the price level plays in this process. Consequently, at this point we have not developed a complete framework for understanding the factors that affect *real* economic variables, such as aggregate labor employment. Nor have we explored theories of how nominal gross domestic product (GDP) is split between its price level and real GDP components.

Our objectives in this chapter are to address these issues. To do so, we shall need to explain the determination of the price level in an open economy, how variations in the price level influence the transmission of monetary and fiscal policies, and ways in which the actions of policymakers themselves can affect a nation's price level and its rate of change, the rate of inflation (or deflation). Furthermore, we shall seek to explain the relationships between the price level and real output and between the inflation rate and unemployment rate.

AGGREGATE DEMAND

Any theory of price-level determination must begin with a theory of the total demand for all goods and services produced within a nation. Economists refer to this as the *aggregate demand for real output*. As you will now learn, in the preceding three chapters we have laid all the groundwork for understanding the factors that determine aggregate demand.

The Aggregate Demand Schedule

You first learned in Chapter 10 that the point of intersection of the *IS* schedule and the *LM* schedule is a single real income–nominal interest rate combination at which aggregate desired expenditures equal real income *and* at which the market for real money balances is in equilibrium. Subsequently, you learned how variations in aggregate autonomous expenditures can affect the equilibrium real income level and nominal interest rate. In addition, you saw how changes in the nominal money stock and the demand for real money balances can influence these variables.

These factors, it turns out, are also the fundamental determinants of the aggregate demand for a nation's output of goods and services. The reason is that the *IS–LM* framework provides the underpinning for the theory of aggregate demand.

To see why this is so, consider Figure 13–1 on the following page. Panel (a) displays the *IS–LM* diagram. The initial point at which the *IS* and *LM* schedules cross is point *A*. The position of the *LM* schedule, as we discussed in Chapter 10, depends on the quantity of *real money balances*. At point *A*, the nominal money stock is M_1 and the value of the GDP deflator is P_1. Thus, the quantity of real money balances is equal to M_1/P_1, and the *LM* schedule is $LM (M_1/P_1)$.

Now consider what happens following a rise in the price level from P_1 to a higher level, P_2. This causes real money balances to decline, from M_1/P_1 to M_1/P_2. The effect of such a decline in real money balances on the position of the *LM* schedule is the same as if the nominal money stock had declined with an unchanged price level, which causes the *LM* schedule to shift upward and to the left. Thus, as

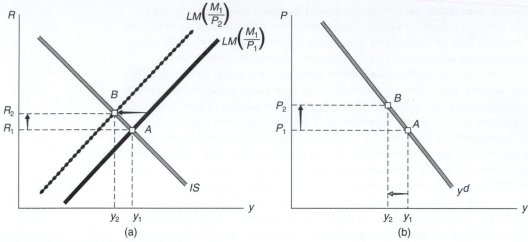

Figure 13–1   Deriving the Aggregate Demand Schedule

Panel (a) shows that a rise in the price level induces an increase in the equilibrium nominal interest rate through the real balance effect, as the *LM* schedule shifts back along the *IS* schedule from point *A* to point *B*. Because equilibrium real income falls as the price level increases, the aggregate demand schedule containing real income–price level combinations *A* and *B* slopes downward in panel (b).

aggregate demand schedule

Combinations of real income and the price level that maintain *IS–LM* equilibrium and thereby ensure that real income is equal to aggregate desired expenditures and that the market for real money balances is in equilibrium.

shown in panel (a) of Figure 13–1, a rise in the price level causes a shift in the *LM* schedule *LM* (M_1/P_2), yielding a new *IS–LM* equilibrium point *B*. The decline in the supply of real money balances resulting from the price level increase causes the equilibrium nominal interest rate to rise. This increase in the interest rate causes desired investment spending to decline. Hence, there is a fall in aggregate desired expenditures, which generates a fall in equilibrium real income. Consequently, at point *B* the equilibrium nominal interest rate is higher, as compared with the initial point *A*, at R_1, and the equilibrium real income level is lower, at y_2.

Panel (b) of the figure shows the relationship between equilibrium real income and the price level implied by panel (a). Both real income–price level combinations in panel (a), y_1 and P_1 at point *A* and y_2 and P_2 at point *B*, are consistent with *IS–LM* equilibrium. Therefore, *both* of these real income–price level combinations maintain equilibrium real income *and* equilibrium in the market for real money balances. The complete set of real income–price level combinations consistent with *IS–LM* equilibrium, which includes points *A* and *B*, is the ***aggregate demand schedule***, denoted y^d. This schedule, by definition, is the set of combinations of real income and the price level that is consistent with *IS–LM* equilibrium, which means that these combinations simultaneously maintain an equality of aggregate desired expenditures *and* real income and money market equilibrium.

#1 What is the aggregate demand schedule?

The aggregate demand schedule consists of real income–price level combinations that achieve equality of real income and aggregate desired expenditures while at the same time maintaining equilibrium in the market for real money balances. Consequently, every point along an aggregate demand schedule corresponds to a point of *IS–LM* equilibrium.

Factors That Determine the Position of the Aggregate Demand Schedule in an Open Economy

In Figure 13–1, we derived the aggregate demand schedule by considering the effect on equilibrium real income following an increase in the price level, *holding all other factors unchanged*. This means that variations in other factors that influence the positions of the *IS* or *LM* schedules can alter the position of the aggregate demand schedule. Thus, changes in aggregate autonomous expenditures, which affect the position of the *IS* schedule, and variations in the nominal money stock, which influence the position of the *LM* schedule, can cause the aggregate demand schedule to shift. Via these channels, therefore, fiscal and monetary policy actions can influence the aggregate demand schedule's position.

As you learned in Chapters 11 and 12, however, the degree of capital mobility conditions the extent to which monetary and fiscal policy actions can affect equilibrium real income. In addition, the real income effects of monetary and fiscal policies vary, depending on whether a nation adopts fixed or floating exchange rates. It follows that the extent to which aggregate demand responds to monetary or fiscal policy actions in an open economy depends on the degree of capital mobility and the system of exchange rates that is in place.

Monetary Policy and Aggregate Demand Before we explore ways in which capital mobility and exchange-rate flexibility condition the effects of monetary policy actions on aggregate demand, let's first focus on the basic linkage between changes in the quantity of money and the aggregate demand schedule. To do this, let's initially consider a *closed economy* in which the issues of capital mobility and exchange rate-flexibility are irrelevant.

In a closed economy, if a nation's central bank increases the nominal quantity of money supplied from M_1 to a larger amount M_2, then, as shown in panel (a) of Figure 13–2, at a given price level such as P_1, the result is a downward and

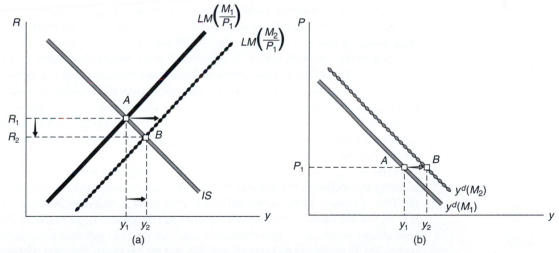

Figure 13–2   **The Effect of an Increase in the Money Stock on Aggregate Demand in a Closed Economy**
With an unchanged price level, an increase in the nominal quantity of money in circulation causes an increase in the amount of real money balances and shifts the *LM* schedule downward and to the right along the *IS* schedule from point *A* to point *B* in panel (a). Because the resulting real income level at point *B* in panel (b) corresponds to the same price level, this new equilibrium real income–price level combination lies on a new aggregate demand schedule to the right of the real income–price level combination at point *A* on the original aggregate demand schedule. Thus, an increase in the nominal money stock causes an increase in aggregate demand.

rightward shift in the *LM* schedule from $LM(M_1/P_1)$ to $LM(M_2/P_1)$. Thus, there is a movement from an initial *IS–LM* equilibrium at point *A* to a new equilibrium at point *B*. The increase in the nominal money stock reduces the equilibrium nominal interest rate, from R_1 to R_2, and induces a rise in equilibrium real income, from y_1 to y_2.

As you can see in panel (b), the real income–price level combination y_2 and P_1 lies to the right of the original aggregate demand schedule, denoted as $y^d(M_1)$. Nevertheless, this new point *B* in panel (b) is consistent with the *IS–LM* equilibrium at point *B* in panel (a). By definition, the aggregate demand schedule is a set of real income–price level combinations that maintain *IS–LM* equilibrium, so point *B* in panel (b) is on a *new* aggregate demand schedule. Consequently, a rise in the nominal quantity of money shifts the aggregate demand schedule to the right. That is:

> **In a closed economy, a rise in the nominal money stock always causes an increase in aggregate demand.**

Now that you see how monetary policy actions affect aggregate demand in a closed economy, let's turn our attention to the effects of central bank policies in open economies.

Monetary Policy and Aggregate Demand in an Open Economy with a Fixed Exchange Rate In Chapters 11 and 12, you learned that the effects of monetary policy actions on equilibrium real income in an open economy depend on whether exchange rates are fixed or flexible and on the degree of capital mobility. Thus, you might expect that the effects of monetary policy actions on aggregate demand should depend on these same factors.

Figure 13–3 illustrates how monetary policy actions might—or might not—affect the position of the aggregate demand schedule in a system of fixed exchange rates. The figure displays three pairs of diagrams in panels (a), (b), and (c). Each pair consists of *IS–LM–BP* diagrams above corresponding aggregate demand schedules. Panel (a) displays a situation of low capital mobility and a relatively steep *BP* schedule, whereas panel (b) shows a situation of high capital mobility and a more shallow *BP* schedule. Finally, panel (c) illustrates an environment in which there is perfect capital mobility, so that the *BP* schedule is horizontal.

In panel (a), as in Figure 13–2, an increase in the money stock from M_1 to M_2 causes the *LM* schedule to shift downward and to the right, so there is a movement from point *A* to point *B* in diagram (a1). The equilibrium nominal interest rate declines from R_1 toward R_2, and equilibrium real income rises from y_1 toward y_2. Thus, holding other factors constant, at a given price level P_1 there is a rightward shift in the aggregate demand schedule, in diagram (a1), from $y^d(M_1)$ toward the dashed schedule denoted $y^d(M_2)$.

The increase in real income spurs import spending, and with low capital mobility the decline in the nominal interest rate induces a meager outflow of capital. Thus, a balance-of-payments deficit arises at point *B*, and there is downward pressure on the value of the nation's currency in foreign exchange markets. If the central bank sterilizes its interventions to maintain a fixed exchange rate, then the money stock remains at its higher level, M_2, and the aggregate demand schedule shifts fully to the position $y^d(M_2)$ in diagram (a2).With nonsterilized interventions, however, the money stock falls back toward its original level of M_1 as the central bank's foreign exchange reserves decline. Thus, the aggregate demand ultimately returns to its original position, $y^d(M_1)$, in diagram (a2), as the *LM* schedule shifts back to its initial position in diagram (a1).

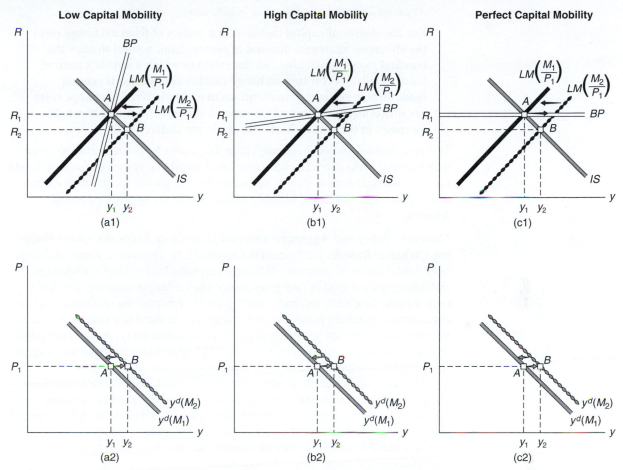

Figure 13–3   The Effect of an Increase in the Money Stock on Aggregate Demand in an Open Economy with a Fixed Exchange Rate
In all three pairs of panels, an increase in the money stock causes the *LM* schedule to shift downward and to the right, resulting in a movement from point *A* to point *B*. The induced increase in real income causes import spending to rise, and the induced decline in the nominal interest rate results in capital outflows, and these effects together lead to a balance-of-payments deficit. If the central bank sterilizes its interventions to maintain a fixed exchange rate, then the money stock remains at its higher level, M_2, and the aggregate demand schedule shifts fully to the position $y^d(M_2)$. With unsterilized interventions, however, the money stock falls back toward its original level of M_1 as the central bank's foreign exchange reserves decline. Consequently, the aggregate demand ultimately returns to its original position, $y^d(M_1)$, regardless of the degree of capital mobility, as the *LM* schedule shifts back to its initial position.

As shown in panels (b) and (c), these same basic conclusions follow in environments of high and perfect capital mobility. In diagram (b1), a balance-of-payments deficit again follows an expansion of the money stock, with more significant capital outflows accounting for much of the deficit. In diagram (b2), therefore, aggregate demand again rises only if the central bank were to sterilize its foreign exchange interventions. In diagram (c1), the decline in the nominal interest rate generates capital outflows that account fully for the balance-of-payments deficit, and in diagram (c2) we again see that the aggregate demand schedule shifts rightward only with sterilized interventions. Otherwise, an increase in the quantity of money in circulation ultimately has no effect on aggregate demand.

Thus, we can reach the following conclusion:

For any degree of capital mobility, in a system of fixed exchange rates the effects on aggregate demand of central bank actions to alter the nominal money stock hinge on the extent to which a nation's central bank sterilizes its foreign exchange market operations. If central bank foreign exchange interventions to maintain fixed exchange rates are unsterilized, then efforts to expand aggregate demand through increases in the money stock ultimately are ineffective.

This conclusion does not necessarily mean that there are no circumstances under which central banks can influence aggregate demand in a system of fixed exchange rates. As we shall discuss shortly, central banks may choose to vary their exchange-rate objectives as a means of bringing about shifts in the aggregate demand schedule.

Monetary Policy and Aggregate Demand in an Open Economy with a Floating Exchange Rate As you learned in Chapter 12, in a system in which exchange rates float, balance-of-payments deficits or surpluses lead to market exchange-rate adjustments instead of foreign exchange market interventions by a nation's central bank. Panels (a), (b), and (c) of Figure 13–4 display the implications of an expansionary monetary policy action for aggregate demand in a system of floating exchange rates with low, high, and perfect capital mobility. Again, each panel displays pairs of diagrams depicting IS–LM–BP equilibrium positions and diagrams showing the corresponding aggregate demand schedules.

First consider panel (a), in which the steep slope of the BP schedule reflects the assumption of low capital mobility. An increase in the quantity of money in circulation from M_1 to a larger quantity M_2 causes the LM schedule to shift downward and to the right in diagram (a1), leading to a movement from point A to point B and a decline in the equilibrium nominal interest rate from R_1 toward R_2 and a rise in equilibrium real income from y_1 toward y_2.

Because capital mobility is low in diagram (a1), the fall in the equilibrium interest rate causes a relatively small capital outflow. Nevertheless, the increase in real income stimulates increased import spending, which leads to a balance-of-payments deficit at point B. As a result, there is downward pressure on the value of the nation's currency, leading to a domestic currency depreciation. Thus, the exchange rises from an initial value, denoted as S_1, to a higher value, S_2.

This currency depreciation reduces the effective price of the nation's exports while increasing the effective price of imports. Consequently, net export spending rises, causing an increase in aggregate autonomous expenditures and a rightward shift in the IS schedule in diagram (a1), from $IS(S_1)$ to $IS(S_2)$. Likewise, the domestic currency depreciation causes the BP schedule to shift downward and to the right, from $BP(S_1)$ to $BP(S_2)$, to maintain balance-of-payments equilibrium as the interest rate rises and real income increases. At point C, there is a balance-of-payments equilibrium, and there is no further upward pressure on the exchange rate. At this final equilibrium point, the equilibrium interest rate is equal to R_2, and the equilibrium real income level is equal to y_2.

Thus, at the current price level P_1, there is a higher corresponding level of real income, y_2, that is consistent with IS–LM equilibrium. It follows that in diagram (a2), there is a rightward shift in the aggregate demand schedule, from $y^d(M_1)$ to $y^d(M_2)$. In contrast to the case of a fixed exchange rate, an expansionary monetary policy action raises aggregate demand under a floating exchange rate.

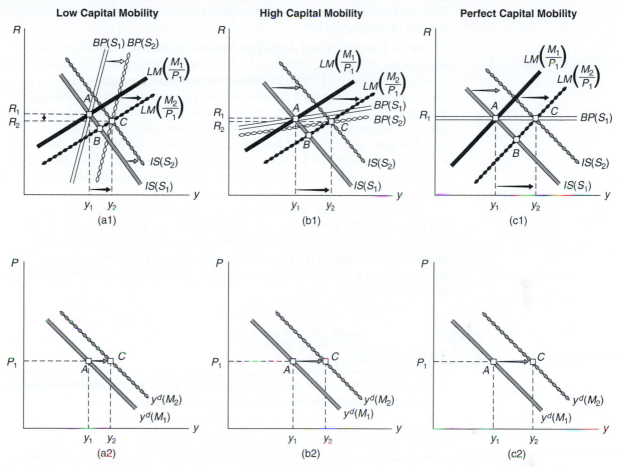

Figure 13–4   The Effect of an Increase in the Money Stock on Aggregate Demand in an Open Economy with a Floating Exchange Rate
In all three pairs of panels, an increase in the money stock causes the *LM* schedule to shift rightward, resulting in a balance-of-payments deficit, which, in turn, causes a domestic currency depreciation. The rise in the exchange rate stimulates greater net export expenditures and raises equilibrium real income. With higher capital mobility, the extent of capital outflow and, consequently, the size of the resulting depreciation and real income effect, will rise. Hence, higher capital mobility enhances the amount of the expansion in aggregate demand induced by a rise in the money stock.

Panels (b) and (c) of Figure 13–4 illustrate that this same conclusion follows with high and perfect capital mobility. Note in diagram (b1), however, that with high capital mobility, a given monetary expansion causes a larger capital outflow and, hence, greater currency depreciation, as compared with the case of low capital mobility in diagram (a1). This generates a larger rise in net export spending, and so the *IS* schedule shifts farther to the right. Consequently, equilibrium real income rises by a larger amount under high capital mobility, so that the aggregate demand schedule shifts farther to the right in diagram (b2).

In panel (c) you can see that the rise in aggregate demand resulting from a monetary expansion is even more pronounced under perfect capital mobility. We may conclude the following:

In a system of floating exchange rates, an expansionary monetary policy action unambiguously raises aggregate demand. The size of the effect on aggregate demand becomes greater as the degree of capital mobility increases.

Thus, under floating exchange rates, greater capital mobility enhances the potential strength of monetary policy.

Exchange-Rate Policy and Aggregate Demand in an Open Economy If we interpret the shifts displayed in Figure 13–4 somewhat differently, we can also explain how an exchange-rate devaluation can influence aggregate demand. Suppose that the central bank had held the exchange rate fixed at S_1 but then decided to devalue its nation's currency. This requires an increase in the exchange-rate target to a new, higher level, denoted S_2. To bring about this change in the exchange rate, the central bank would need to expand the money stock for a time until the exchange rate settled at the central bank's higher target value. This would shift the *LM* schedule rightward. At the same time, the increase in the exchange rate would cause the *IS* and *BP* schedules to shift to the right.

These effects are the same as those illustrated in panels (a), (b), and (c) of Figure 13–4. Therefore, this figure also illustrates the essential effects of an exchange-rate devaluation in a system of fixed exchange rates. Such a devaluation would, as illustrated in Figure 13–4, cause aggregate demand to increase. The amount of the expansion in aggregate demand would be greater with higher degrees of capital mobility.

$\$¥£€$Fundamental ISSUES

#2 What factors determine the extent to which changes in the quantity of money can influence aggregate demand in an open economy?

The effects of an increase in the money stock on aggregate demand depend on the exchange-rate system that is in place and on the degree of capital mobility. Under fixed exchange rates, an unsterilized increase in the quantity of money does not influence aggregate demand. Exchange-rate devaluations, in contrast, induce an increase in aggregate demand, and the same effect arises from an increase in the amount of money in circulation under a floating exchange rate. In these latter situations, greater capital mobility enhances the amount of the increase in aggregate demand.

Fiscal Policy and Aggregate Demand To understand the basic linkage between fiscal policy actions and the aggregate demand schedule, let's again start by considering the case of a closed economy. Panel (a) of Figure 13–5 displays the *IS–LM* effects of a rise in real government expenditures, from g_1 to a higher level g_2, for a given price level, P_1. As discussed in Chapter 12, the direct result is a rightward shift in the *IS* schedule by the amount of the government spending increase times the autonomous spending multiplier, $1/(1 - MPC)$. The rise in real income causes the demand for real money balances to rise, thereby generating an increase in the equilibrium nominal interest rate. As a result, real investment spending declines, but not sufficiently to prevent a net rise in equilibrium real income, from y_1 at point *A* to y_2 at point *B*.

Point *B* in panel (a) is a new *IS–LM* equilibrium, so the real income–price level combination y_2 and P_1 must lie on a new aggregate demand schedule, $y^d(g_2)$, at point *B* in panel (b). Thus, in a closed economy the increase in government spending causes an increase in aggregate demand.

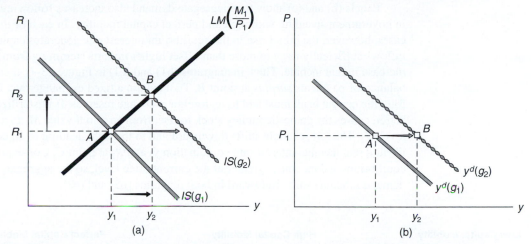

(a)   (b)

Figure 13–5   The Effect of an Increase in Government Spending on Aggregate Demand in a Closed Economy
With an unchanged price level, an increase in government spending shifts the *IS* schedule rightward along the *LM* schedule from point *A* to point *B* in panel (a). The resulting real income level at point *B* in panel (b) corresponds to the same price level, and this new equilibrium real income–price level combination is located on a new aggregate demand schedule to the right of the real income–price level combination at point *A* on the original aggregate demand schedule. Consequently, an increase in government spending causes an increase in aggregate demand.

Fiscal Policy and Aggregate Demand in an Open Economy with a Fixed Exchange Rate Now consider the implications of an expansionary fiscal policy action in an open economy with a fixed exchange rate. Panels (a), (b), and (c) of Figure 13–6 on the following page display the effects of an increase in government spending under low, high, and perfect capital mobility. In the upper diagram in each panel, the rise in government spending causes the *IS* schedule to shift from $IS(g_1)$ to $IS(g_2)$, generating an initial movement from point *A* to point *B*. Thus, the equilibrium nominal interest rate initially rises from R_1 to R', and equilibrium real income increases from y_1 to y'.

As we discussed in Chapter 11, the effects of a fiscal expansion on a nation's balance of payments depend on the openness of its borders to flows of financial resources. In the case of low capital mobility, illustrated in diagram (a1), the rise in the equilibrium nominal interest rate resulting from the increase in government expenditures induces a capital inflow that is too small to compensate for an increase in import spending caused by the rise in real income. As a result, there is a balance-of-payments deficit at point *B*. This places downward pressure on the value of the domestic currency. To keep the exchange rate fixed, the central bank must sell foreign exchange reserves. If the central bank's interventions are unsterilized, this causes a reduction in the nominal money stock, from M_1 to a smaller amount M_2, thereby shifting the *LM* schedule upward and to the left, from $LM(M_1)$ to $LM(M_2)$. The resulting *IS–LM–BP* equilibrium is at point *C*, at which there is still a net rise in the equilibrium interest rate, to R_2, and a net increase in equilibrium real income, to y_2.

Because equilibrium real income rises from its initial level of y_1 to the higher level of y_2 at the current price level, P_1, this new real income–price level combination at point *C* lies on a new aggregate demand schedule in diagram (a2). Thus, on net the increase in government spending shifts the aggregate demand schedule to the right, from $y^d(g_1, M_2)$ to $y^d(g_2, M_2)$.

Panels (b) and (c) show that aggregate demand also increases following a rise in government spending with high and perfect capital mobility. In each of these cases, however, the initial rise in the equilibrium interest rate generates capital inflows sufficiently large to more than offset higher imports stemming from an increase in real income. Thus, in diagrams (b1) and (c1) in Figure 13–6, there is a balance-of-payments *surplus* at point B. To maintain a fixed exchange rate, therefore, the central bank must add to its foreign exchange reserves. If unsterilized, this action causes the domestic money stock to rise, from an initial value M_1 to a higher level M_2. The LM schedule shifts downward and to the right, leading to an equilibrium real income–interest rate combination y_2 and R_2 at point C. Consequently, equilibrium real income is greater at the current price level, so the aggregate demand schedule shifts rightward in both diagrams (b2) and (c2).

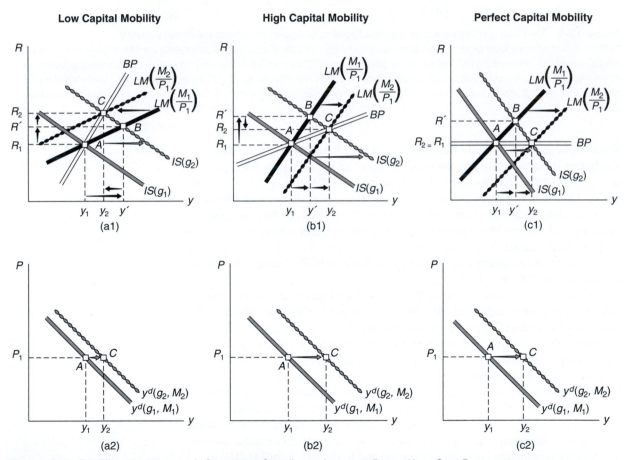

Figure 13–6 The Effect of an Increase in Government Spending on Aggregate Demand in an Open Economy with a Fixed Exchange Rate

In all three pairs of panels, an increase in government expenditures causes the *IS* schedule to shift rightward, inducing initial increases in the equilibrium nominal interest rate from R_1 to R′ and in the level of equilibrium real income from y_1 to y'. Panel (a1) shows that with low capital mobility, there is a balance-of-payments deficit at point B, which requires the central bank to sell foreign exchange reserves to keep the exchange rate fixed, thereby resulting in a final equilibrium at point C and a slight rise in aggregate demand, shown in panel (a2). Panels (b) and (c) show that with higher or perfect capital mobility, a rise in government spending causes a balance-of-payments surplus at point B. To keep the exchange rate from declining in both cases, the central bank must purchase foreign exchange reserves, which leads to a final equilibrium at point C and larger increases in aggregate demand.

Note that panels (a), (b), and (c) indicate that as the degree of capital mobility increases, the extent to which central bank interventions generate money stock changes that reinforce the expansionary effects of fiscal policy actions rises. We may conclude the following:

> **In a system of fixed exchange rates, an expansionary fiscal policy action unambiguously raises aggregate demand. The size of the effect on aggregate demand becomes greater as the degree of capital mobility increases.**

Thus, under fixed exchange rates, greater capital mobility enhances the potential strength of fiscal policy.

Fiscal Policy and Aggregate Demand in an Open Economy with a Floating Exchange Rate If a nation's central bank permits exchange rates to float, then fiscal policy actions do not lead to changes in the quantity of money in circulation. Instead, they result in changes in the equilibrium value of the nation's currency.

Panels (a), (b), and (c) of Figure 13–7 on the next page show how the relationship between fiscal policy actions and aggregate demand varies with the degree of capital mobility in a system of floating exchange rates. Panel (a) depicts a situation of low capital mobility. At the current market exchange rate S_1, an increase in the amount of government spending, from g_1 to g_2, causes the IS schedule to shift to the right in diagram (a1), from $IS(g_1, S_1)$ to $IS(g_2, S_1)$. With low capital mobility, the increase in the equilibrium nominal interest rate stemming from the rise in government spending generates insufficient capital account improvements to counter an increase in import spending caused by the rise in equilibrium real income. Hence, there is a balance-of-payments deficit at point B.

This causes the domestic currency to depreciate, so the equilibrium exchange rate rises to S_2. This depreciation spurs net exports, so the IS schedule shifts farther to the right, to $IS(g_2, S_2)$. In addition, the rise in the exchange rate causes the BP schedule to shift downward and to the right, to $BP(S_2)$. At the final equilibrium point C, there is balance-of-payments equilibrium at the higher exchange rate S_2, the higher nominal interest rate R_2, and the higher real income level y_2. As shown in diagram (a2), this produces a new real income–price level combination, y_2 and P_1, that is consistent with an IS–LM equilibrium. Thus, the rise in government spending causes the aggregate demand schedule to shift rightward, from $y^d(g_1)$ to $y^d(g_2)$.

In a situation in which there is high capital mobility, the effect of a government spending increase on aggregate demand is much more muted, however, as shown in panel (b) of Figure 13–7. In diagram (b1), the initial increase in the equilibrium nominal interest rate, from R_1 at point A to R' at point B, causes a capital account improvement that more than offsets the decline in the current account. Hence, there is a balance-of-payments *surplus* at point B in diagram (b1). This causes the exchange rate to *fall* from an initial value S_1 to a *lower* value S_2, which reduces net export spending and causes the IS schedule to shift back to the left, to $IS(g_2, S_2)$. Although real income on net is higher, at y_2, at the final equilibrium point C, as compared with the case of low capital mobility in panel (b), there is a smaller increase in equilibrium real income following the rise in government spending. The aggregate demand schedule, therefore, shifts by a smaller amount in diagram (b2) as compared with diagram (a2).

Panel (c) depicts a situation of perfect capital mobility. In this case, there is a significant balance-of-payments surplus at point B in diagram (c1), as the increase in the nominal interest rate generates sizable capital inflows. As a result, there is a

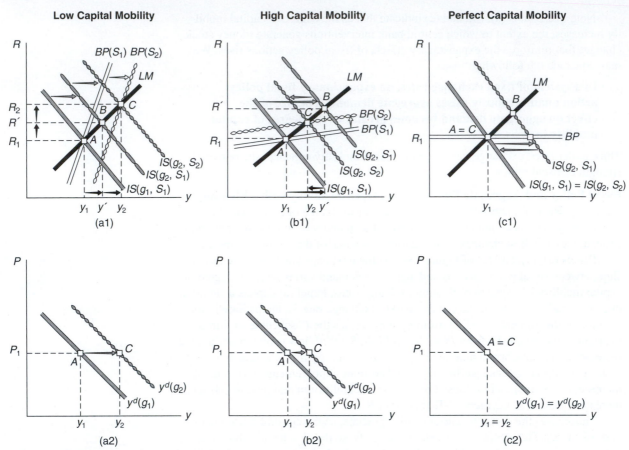

Figure 13–7 The Effect of an Increase in Government Spending on Aggregate Demand in an Open Economy with a Floating Exchange Rate

In all three pairs of panels, an increase in government expenditures causes the *IS* schedule to shift rightward, inducing initial increases in the equilibrium nominal interest rate from R_1 to R' and in the level of equilibrium real income from y_1 to y'. Panel (a1) depicts a situation of low capital mobility, in which the rise in government spending causes a balance-of-payments deficit at point B, which induces a currency depreciation and an additional rightward shift in the *IS* schedule. At the final equilibrium point C there is a potentially sizable expansion in aggregate demand in panel (a2). With high or perfect capital mobility, in contrast, an increase in government spending causes a balance-of-payments surplus, a currency appreciation, and a partially [panel (b1)] or fully [panel (c)] offsetting leftward shift in the *IS* schedule. Thus, the aggregate demand effect of a rise in government expenditures is mitigated by higher capital mobility.

sizable domestic currency appreciation, which ultimately causes the *IS* schedule to shift back to its original position. The final equilibrium point C corresponds to the initial equilibrium point A, and equilibrium real income remains at its initial level, y_1. Thus, there is no movement from point A in diagram (c2). Aggregate demand is unaffected by the rise in government expenditures with perfect capital mobility and a floating exchange rate.

This reasoning leads to the following conclusion:

> **Under floating exchange rates, the size of the effect of a given fiscal policy action on aggregate demand declines as the degree of capital mobility increases. Under perfect capital mobility, fiscal policy cannot influence the position of the aggregate demand schedule.**

Consequently, adopting a system of floating exchange rates tends to mute the effects that fiscal policy actions can exert on aggregate demand.

Fundamental ISSUES

#3 What factors determine the extent to which fiscal policy actions can influence aggregate demand in an open economy?

The key factors influencing the aggregate demand effects of fiscal policy actions are capital mobility and the exchange-rate system that a government adopts. In a system of fixed exchange rates, an increase in government spending causes aggregate demand to increase, and greater capital mobility enhances this effect. In a system of floating exchange rates, the aggregate demand effects of increased government expenditures are more muted, and they dissipate further as the degree of capital mobility increases.

AGGREGATE SUPPLY

As we shall discuss, the equilibrium price level is the price level at which firms and workers are willing and able to produce the aggregate output of goods and services that is consistent with the aggregate demand for those goods and services. Hence, to contemplate how the price level is determined, we must first consider the behavior of firms and workers.

Output and Employment Determination

Changes in the price of an *individual* good or service typically induce firms to alter the amount of inputs, such as labor, that they use in production and to vary the quantity of the good or service that they produce and offer for sale in the marketplace. A long-standing issue, however, is the extent to which changes in the *overall* price level affect the *aggregate* levels of employment and output. As you will learn, resolving this issue is crucial to determining whether monetary or fiscal policies can influence aggregate employment and output levels in an open economy.

The Production Function The aggregate *production function* is the relationship between the quantities of productive factors—labor, capital, land, and entrepreneurship—employed by all firms in the economy and their total output of goods and services, given the technology currently available. We shall focus on short-run production decisions, which firms must make over a time horizon sufficiently brief that firms cannot adjust fixed factors of production, such as capital, land, and entrepreneurship. Hence, in the short run the factor of production that firms can vary is the quantity of labor that they employ, denoted N.

Economists have three approaches to measuring of the quantity of labor employed by firms. One approach is to measure the number of people employed during a given period. Another approach is to measure the total time worked by all individuals employed by firms, which is just the total hours that workers were employed during a given interval. Finally, economists can combine these approaches by measuring the number of *person-hours*.

Firms use labor in conjunction with other productive factors to produce goods and services. The aggregate production function determines the economy-wide level of real output, y, resulting from firms' employment of the total quantity of labor, N:

$$y = F(N).$$

production function
The relationship between the quantities of factors of production employed by firms and their output of goods and services using the current technology.

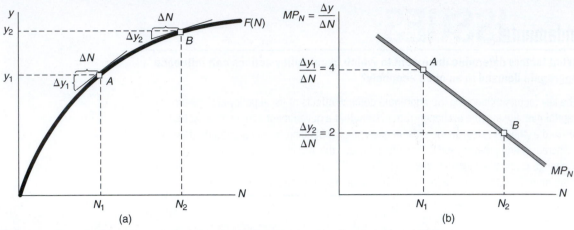

Figure 13–8 The Aggregate Production Function and the Marginal-Product-of-Labor (MP_N) Schedule
Given a fixed stock of capital and a current state of technology, higher levels of labor employment are necessary to achieve increased production of real output. The bowed, or concave, shape of the production function in panel (a) reflects the law of diminishing returns, which states that total output increases at a decreasing rate for each additional one-unit rise in employment of labor. Consequently, as shown in panel (b), the marginal product of labor declines as employment rises.

This equation indicates that the aggregate amount of firms' real output is a *function* of the amount of labor that they employ.

Panel (a) of Figure 13–8 displays a diagram of the aggregate production function, $F(N)$. At any point along this function, we can see how much real output firms can produce given a particular level of employment. For example, if firms employ N_1 units of labor at point A, then aggregate real output would equal y_1. Increasing employment to N_2, at point B, leads to production of a higher real output level, y_2.

The Marginal Product of Labor The *slope* of the production function is a change in output resulting from a change in employment, or *rise*, divided by a corresponding change in employment, or *run*. By definition, the slope of the production function, $\Delta y/\Delta N$, is the additional amount of output that firms can produce by employing an additional unit of labor, which economists call the ***marginal product of labor***, or MP_N. That is, $MP_N \equiv \Delta y/\Delta N$, or the slope of the production function at a given quantity of labor.

marginal product of labor

The additional quantity of output that firms can produce by employing another unit of labor.

Because the aggregate production function in panel (a) of Figure 13–8 is *concave*, or bowed downward, its slope declines as employment increases. For instance, the slope of the function at point A is equal to the slope of the line tangent to the function at this point, or $\Delta y_1/\Delta N$, where the symbol Δ denotes a change in a quantity. At the higher employment level N_2 at point B, however, an identical change in employment, ΔN, leads to a smaller change in output, Δy_2. As a result, the slope of the production function at point B, which is equal to $\Delta y_2/\Delta N$, must be smaller than the slope of the production function at point A. Thus, the marginal product of labor declines as labor employment at firms increases. This is consistent with the ***law of diminishing marginal returns***, which states that eventually the additional output produced by an additional unit of labor declines as firms employ more units of labor given at least one fixed input.

law of diminishing marginal returns

The fact that the additional output produced by an additional unit of labor ultimately falls as firms employ more units of labor.

Panel (b) of Figure 13–8 depicts the marginal-product-of-labor schedule, or MP_N *schedule*. The MP_N schedule shows the marginal product of labor, or slope of the production function, at any given quantity of labor. The schedule's downward slope reflects the law of diminishing marginal returns. At the employment level N_1, the marginal product of labor is equal to $\Delta y_1/\Delta N$, which is the slope of the production function at point A, which we assume is equal to a value of four units of output per unit of labor. If total employment were to increase to N_2 at point B, then the slope of the production function would fall to $\Delta y_2/\Delta N$, which we assume is equal to two units of output per unit of labor.

The Demand for Labor To determine how many units of labor to employ, any firm must weigh the revenue gain from the sale of the additional production generated by another unit of labor against the cost of hiring that labor unit. To maximize its profits over a given period, a firm must produce output to the point at which its marginal revenue (MR), or additional revenue stemming from production and sale of an additional unit of output, is just equal to its marginal cost (MC), or additional production cost that it incurs in this endeavor. On the one hand, if MR is greater than MC at a given production level, then the firm earns a positive net profit from the last unit of production, which gives the firm an incentive to increase production. On the other hand, if MC is greater than MR, then the firm's net profit on the last unit produced is negative, which gives the firm an incentive to reduce production. At the output level at which $MR = MC$, therefore, the firm earns positive net profits for every unit up to the last unit produced, which thereby maximizes profits on its total output production.

If firms are purely competitive, then no individual firm can influence the market price of a unit of output. Thus, each unit of output yields the same marginal revenue, which is the market price. It follows that purely competitive firms produce output up to the point at which

$$MR \equiv P = MC,$$

which indicates that under pure competition, price equals marginal cost.

A firm's marginal cost of producing output stems from the expense that it incurs by employing labor. This is the *nominal wage*, denoted W and measured in units of domestic currency per labor unit, that it pays for each unit of labor. For example, suppose that the current market wage rate is $W_1 =$ \$20 per unit of labor. If, as at point B in Figure 13–8, the marginal product of labor at the firm's current output level is $MP_N = \Delta y/\Delta N = 2$ units of output per unit of labor, then we can compute the firm's marginal cost of producing output by dividing W_1 by MP_N. This yields $MC = (\$20$ per unit of labor$)/(2$ units of output per unit of labor$) = \$10$ per unit of output. Hence, marginal cost by definition is equal to W/MP_N.

This implies that we can rewrite a purely competitive firm's profit-maximizing condition, $P = MC$, as

$$P = W/MP_N.$$

Multiplying both sides of this equation by MP_N yields

$$P \times MP_N = (W/MP_N) \times MP_N = W.$$

Therefore, an alternative way to express the firm's profit-maximizing condition is

$$W = P \times MP_N.$$

This equation tells us that a purely competitive, profit-maximizing firm will employ labor to the point at which the money wage that the firm pays each unit of labor is equal to the price it receives for each unit of output that labor produces times the marginal product of labor. Economists call this latter product the

**value of the marginal
product of labor**

The price of output times the
marginal product of labor.

value of the marginal product of labor, or $VMP_N = P \times MP_N$. For example, if the market price of a firm's output is $5 per unit of output and the marginal product of labor is two units of output per unit of labor, then the value of labor's marginal product is equal to the product of these two figures, or $10 per unit of labor.

Figure 13–9 illustrates the value-of-marginal-product-of-labor schedule, or VMP_N schedule, which we obtain by multiplying the firm's output price, P, times the MP_N schedule in panel (b) of Figure 13–8 on page 390. If the nominal wage that a firm pays each unit of labor is $W_1 = 20 per unit of labor, then the firm employs labor to the point at which the value of labor's marginal product is equal to $20 per unit of labor. This, the figure shows, implies employment of an amount of labor N_1. At a lower wage rate of $W_2 = 10 per unit of labor, however, the firm requires a smaller value of marginal product to maximize its profit, and so it *increases* the amount of labor it employs, to the quantity of labor N_2. A fall in the market wage rate causes the firm to increase the quantity of labor it demands.

Hence, a firm decides how many units of labor that it desires to employ by moving along its VMP_N schedule. This leads to the following important conclusion:

> **The VMP_N schedule for a purely competitive firm is that firm's labor
> demand schedule showing how many units of labor, N, that the firm
> demands at any given nominal wage, W.**

Wage Flexibility, Aggregate Supply, and the Price Level

The process by which nominal wages are determined can vary considerably across firms and industries within individual countries. In addition, there is significant variation in the extent to which certain institutional structures for wage determination may predominate. Every nation also has its own laws governing the interactions between firms and workers. As a result, no single theory of wage determination fits every nation. This means that the manner in which total employment and the aggregate output level are determined also differs across countries.

The Determination of Nominal Wages In a number of nations, for example, most workers and firms establish contracts that set the terms, such as wages and benefits,

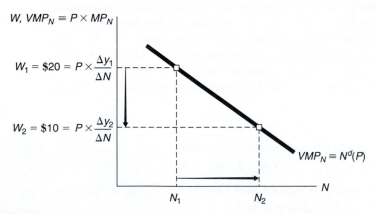

Figure 13–9   The Demand for Labor

A profit-maximizing firm employs labor to the point at which the value of labor's marginal product is equal to the nominal wage. Thus, a rise in the nominal wage reduces the quantity of labor demanded by a firm. This means that the quantity of labor actually employed by firms depends on three factors. One is the prices at which firms are able to sell their products. Another is the productivity of labor. The third, to which we now turn our attention, is the process by which nominal wages are determined.

that govern the employment of workers with the firms over a given time period, such as one to three years. In some nations, such as Belgium, Finland, Norway, and Sweden, more than half of all workers are members of unions that negotiate *explicit contracts*, or formal, written agreements between workers and firms. In a few countries, such as Austria and Italy, unions may coordinate wage bargaining, leading to a highly centralized process of determining nominal wages that strengthens the wage-setting powers of unions. In other countries, such as France and Japan, the legal environment extends many aspects of union agreements to nonunionized workers. In Japan, for example, the national government, rather than unions, coordinates the wage-determination process by establishing a synchronized, nationwide schedule for nominal wage adjustments.

In other countries, the process by which workers and firms establish nominal wages is much more decentralized. This is particularly true in countries such as the United Kingdom and the United States, in which the legal setting promotes more individualized labor contracting and the extent of unionization is lower. Of course, wage contracts need not exist only in unionized industries. For instance, most U.S. firms offering employment to new recipients of undergraduate degrees usually extend job offers stating initial salaries and policies on the amount of time that will pass before the next salary review. In addition, *implicit contracts*, or unwritten, tacit agreements, may exist, so even in the absence of explicit wage agreements, workers and firms may follow certain unstated patterns of behavior in establishing standards for wage determination. Nevertheless, most U.S. and British workers and firms establish wage bargains on an individual basis, rather than through a centralized procedure. Indeed, in many industries within these nations, labor markets may function very much like those for goods and services, with the nominal wage adjusting to equilibrate the quantity of labor supplied by workers with the quantity of labor demanded by firms. (The fact that labor productivity is a key determinant of the demand for labor has important implications for open economies with relatively high corporate income tax rates; see *Management Notebook: In a Globalized Economy, Higher Corporate Income Taxes Translate into Lower Wages for Workers*.)

MANAGEMENT Notebook

In a Globalized Economy, Higher Corporate Income Taxes Translate into Lower Wages for Workers

Figure 13–10 displays maximum corporate tax rates in selected nations, ranging from nearly 40 percent in Japan, the United States, and Germany to a maximum rate less than half as high in Slovakia, Poland, Hungary, and Ireland. Politicians around the world commonly suggest that higher corporate income taxes are aimed at wealthy individuals. Nevertheless, in countries with flexible wages, one impact of increasing corporate income tax rates is likely to be lower wages for their workers. Higher corporate income tax rates induce managers of firms to cut back on their gross investment expenditures. Of course, businesses engage in such spending to replace worn-out capital goods or to expand their capital stock beyond its existing level. If they cut back on capital expenditures, this reduces the amount of capital goods available to workers and thereby reduces workers' productivity. Thus, other things being equal, when a country elects to establish a relatively high corporate tax rate in a globalized economy in which funds can readily

Figure 13–10

Maximum Corporate Income Tax Rates in Selected Nations

The top corporate income tax rate varies considerably across nations, from as high as nearly 40 percent in Japan to just over 12 percent in Ireland.

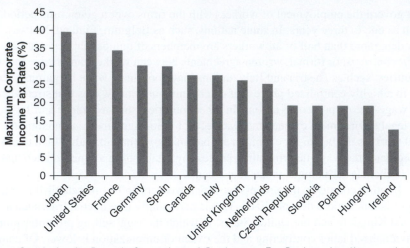

Source: Organization for Economic Cooperation and Development, *Tax Database, http://www.oecd.org/tax/taxpolicyanalysis/oecdtaxdatabase.htm.*

move from high-tax-rate countries to low-tax-rate nations, it risks an outflow of foreign capital investment and, ultimately, decreased labor productivity and hence lower wages.

In fact, Kevin Hassert and Aparna Mathur of the American Enterprise Institute estimate that for the average nation, a 1-percentage-point increase in the corporate income tax rate is associated with a 0.8-percentage-point drop in wages during the next five years. Furthermore, their study suggests that, on average, a 1-percentage-point cut in the corporate income tax rate in a neighboring country causes a nation's wages to decline by 0.5 percentage point within five years. Thus, even a nation that leaves its corporate income tax rate unchanged can, in the face of a corporate-tax-rate reduction by a neighboring country, undergo a wage reduction when capital resources flow away to the lower-tax country and domestic labor productivity falls in response.

For Critical Analysis

Why do you suppose that wages have risen considerably in Ireland since its government slashed corporate income tax rates?

Employment and Aggregate Supply with Fixed versus Flexible Nominal Wages To see why the process of wage determination is so important, consider Figure 13–11. In panel (a), the overall level of nominal wages is *fixed* at a level W^f. The general level of nominal wages could be inflexible in the short term because of long-term contracts negotiated in concert by national unions or via governmental coordination of a nationwide bargaining process. Another reason for wage stickiness might be minimum wage laws that fix the wages of the lowest-paid workers. Although fewer than 5 percent of workers in the United States, Austria, Belgium, and the Netherlands work for a minimum wage, in France, Greece, and Luxembourg, 10 to 20 percent of workers earn a legally mandated minimum wage.

Aggregate supply with inflexible nominal wages As shown in diagram (a1), if wages are inflexible, then the overall level of nominal wages W^f does not vary

Inflexible Wages with Price Level Change

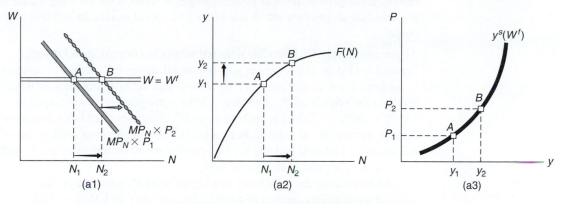

(a1)   (a2)   (a3)

Flexible Wages with Price Level Change

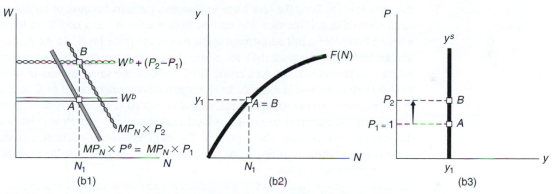

(b1)   (b2)   (b3)

Figure 13–11   Employment and Output Determination with Fixed versus Flexible Nominal Wages
The (a) panels show that if wages are inflexible, then the overall level of nominal wages W^f does not vary with a change in the position of the VMP_N schedule resulting from a rise in the price level. Consequently, employment rises from N_1 at point A to N_2 at point B, as the value of workers' marginal product increases, inducing firms to demand more labor. The resulting increase in employment causes a movement from point A to point B along the aggregate production function, so that aggregate real output increases from y_1 to y_2. Hence, the aggregate supply schedule slopes upward with fixed nominal wages. In contrast, the (b) panels show that if W^b is an initial, base level of wages, then automatic contractual adjustment of wages in response to an increase in the price level, to $W^b + (P_2 - P_1)$, results in no change in employment or output. Hence, with complete wage adjustment to price changes, the aggregate supply schedule is vertical.

with a change in the position of the VMP_N schedule resulting from a rise in the price level, from an initial price level P_1 to a higher price level P_2. As a result, employment increases from N_1 at point A to N_2 at point B, as the value of workers' marginal product rises, inducing firms to demand more labor so as to expand their output of goods and services in pursuit of greater profits. In diagram (a2), this increase in employment causes a movement from point A to point B along the aggregate production function, so that aggregate real output increases from y_1 to y_2. Therefore, in diagram (a3) there is a movement from the initial real output–price level combination y_1 and P_1, at point A, to a new combination y_2 and P_2, at point B. Points A and B in diagram (a3) lie along an upward-sloping *aggregate supply schedule*, which shows how real output that all workers and firms in the economy are willing and able to produce varies with changes in the price level. The aggregate supply schedule in diagram (a3) includes all real output–price

aggregate supply schedule

A schedule depicting volumes of real output produced by all workers and firms at each possible price level.

level combinations consistent with the fixed nominal wage W^f in diagram (a1). Hence, if the general level of nominal wages is fixed, a nation's aggregate supply schedule slopes upward: A rise in the price level causes an increase in real output.

Aggregate supply with flexible nominal wages In contrast, panel (b) of Figure 13–11 depicts a setting in which nominal wages fully adjust to changes in the price level. In diagram (b1), we assume that W^b is an initial, *base* wage level. At the price level P_1, the value of labor's marginal product is equal to $VMP_N^1 = MP_N \times P_1$, and at the base wage W^b, the quantity of labor demanded by firms is equal to N_1, at point A. In diagram (b2), the real output level produced by this amount of labor is equal to y_1. This yields the real output–price level combination y_1 and P_1 at point A in diagram (b3).

An increase in the price level, to a higher level P_2, again causes a rise in the value of the marginal product of labor in diagram (b1), to $VMP_N^2 = MP_N \times P_2$. Now, however, we suppose that nominal wages flexibly adjust to this change in the price level to keep the *real* wage unchanged, perhaps because of contractual arrangements that call for such adjustment, from a level W^b to a new level $W^b + \Delta P$, where ΔP denotes a full adjustment to the rise in the price level. At the new equilibrium point B in diagram (b1), the nominal wage thereby rises in proportion to the increase in the price level. As a result, firms demand the same amount of labor as they did before the rise in the price level. Employment remains equal to N_1 at point B in diagram (b1), so the amount of real output produced is equal to y_1 in diagram (b2). As a result, the new real output–price level combination y_1 and P_2 at point B in diagram (b3) lies directly above point A. The aggregate supply schedule containing these points is vertical. A rise in the price level does not induce an increase in the nation's real output level.

What types of labor market arrangements can cause nominal wages to adjust equiproportionately to changes in the price level? One possibility is if workers' contracts call for full *indexation* of wages, so that firms automatically ratchet workers' wages upward in response to inflation. Workers' contracts might be indexed directly to price-level variations, or they might be indexed less directly, via arrangements such as profit-sharing contracts. Another possibility would be situations in which markets for labor skills are highly competitive and unregulated, so that they essentially function as *auction markets*, with wages determined via a bidding process. In such markets, firms would bid wages upward in response to increases in the price level, so that nominal wages would vary in direct proportion to prices.

Many economists argue that in the long run, labor markets should function like auction markets. That is, given the passage of a sufficient span of time, labor contracts or other institutional wage arrangements should reflect such factors as the productivity of a nation's workers, the size of its labor force, and general willingness of workers to supply their skills to firms. In a long-run equilibrium, therefore, the nominal wage should adjust equiproportionately to changes in the price level. Thus, the long-run aggregate supply schedule for an economy is vertical, as in Figure 13–11.

The Aggregate Supply Schedule with Partial Wage Adjustment In most nations, the general level of nominal wages is neither completely fixed nor fully flexible in the face of changes in the price level. The overall wage level within a country typically adjusts *partially* to movements in prices, at least over short-run periods.

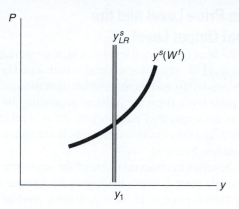

Figure 13–12

The Short-Run and Long-Run Aggregate Supply Schedules

Over the short run, when nominal wages are fixed and do not adjust to changes in the price level, the aggregate supply schedule, y^s (W^f), slopes upward. In the long run, which is a sufficiently lengthy interval during which the wage determination process can account for an increase in the price level, the aggregate supply schedule is vertical, as illustrated by the schedule denoted y^s_{LR}.

This means that for most nations, over a short-run interval the aggregate supply schedule, y^s, slopes upward, as in Figure 13–12. Consequently, as compared with the situation that arises if the general level of nominal wages were fixed, as illustrated by the much shallower aggregate supply schedule $y^s(W^f)$, inducing a given rise in real output production may require relatively significant increases in the price level. At the same time, because all wages in a nation generally are not fully indexed to inflation and because institutional arrangements usually prevent labor markets from functioning as auction markets in the short run, the aggregate supply schedule is not vertical. Only in the long run—which is a period sufficiently lengthy that the wage determination process takes into account all the elements influencing worker and firm preferences—does a rise in the price level fail to yield higher real output, as is the case along the vertical schedule denoted y^s_{LR}.

Fundamental ISSUES

#4 What is the aggregate supply schedule?

The aggregate supply schedule consists of combinations of real output and the price level that are consistent with firms' production capabilities and the total amount of labor employed, given the process by which workers' nominal wages are determined. If the overall wage level adjusts in proportion to changes in the price level, which is most likely to occur only if contracts fully index wages to changes in the price level or if sufficient time passes for wages otherwise to make such a complete adjustment, then the aggregate supply schedule is vertical. Any wage inflexibility, however, causes the aggregate supply schedule to slope upward, and the schedule is most shallow if contracts or legal restraints fix nominal wages.

REAL OUTPUT, THE PRICE LEVEL, AND ECONOMIC POLICYMAKING

The aggregate demand and aggregate supply schedules together provide a foundation for understanding the determination of a country's price level and its volume of real output. In addition, as you will learn in this section, they also provide a framework for examining how economic policies may influence a nation's real GDP and inflation rate.

The Equilibrium Price Level and the Equilibrium Real Output Level

The *equilibrium price level* is the price level at which all workers and firms are willing to produce a level of output that maintains both equality of real income and aggregate desired expenditures and money market equilibrium. Thus, at an economy's equilibrium price level, firms are satisfied producing the current output of goods and services at the wages they pay workers, there is no tendency for current real income to change, and the current interest rate is consistent with equilibrium in the market for real money balances.

Figure 13–13 illustrates the determination of the equilibrium price level, P_1, which arises at the single point E where the aggregate demand and aggregate supply schedules cross. At this price level, the equilibrium level of real output, y_1, by definition corresponds to a real income level consistent with an *IS–LM* equilibrium, because point E is on the aggregate demand schedule. Therefore, real income is equal to aggregate desired expenditures, and the market for real money balances is in equilibrium. At the same time, point E is on the aggregate supply schedule, so y_1 also constitutes a level of real output that firms are willing and able to produce, given the available technology and the nominal wages that they pay workers. It follows that y_1 is the *equilibrium real output level* for the economy.

To see why P_1 and y_1 constitute the equilibrium price level–real output combination, suppose that the actual price level happens to equal P_2. At this price level, the real value of money balances supplied by the central bank is driven upward, thereby pushing down the equilibrium nominal interest rate in the money market. This raises aggregate desired expenditures to an amount consistent with the real income level y_3 in Figure 13–13. At the same time, however, the lower price level P_2 reduces the value of labor's marginal product, inducing firms to demand less labor at any given nominal wage and, therefore, to produce less real output. Thus, the actual level of real output produced is equal to y_2. A rise

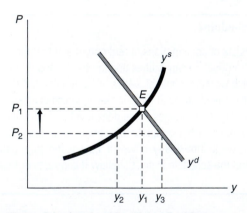

Figure 13–13   Determination of the Equilibrium Price Level and Equilibrium Real Output

The equilibrium price level and the equilibrium level of real output arise at the intersection of the aggregate demand and aggregate supply schedules. This point, denoted E, is on the aggregate demand schedule and corresponds to a point of *IS–LM* equilibrium, so the market for real money balances is in equilibrium and real income is equal to aggregate desired expenditures. At the same time, this point is on the aggregate supply schedule, and so at the price level corresponding to point E, workers and firms are willing and able to produce the equilibrium real output level. If the price level happened to equal P_2, then the level of aggregate desired expenditures is consistent with an output level equal to y_3, but the aggregate output level that firms produce is equal to y_2. Thus, the equilibrium price level must rise to P_1 at point E, which yields the equilibrium output level y_1.

in the price level thereby must occur to push the value of real money balances downward. This increases the equilibrium interest rate and depresses investment expenditures, thereby reducing aggregate spending and the quantity of real output demanded. In addition, an increase in the price level raises the value of the marginal product of labor, causing firms to increase employment of labor and output production. Hence, there must be upward pressure on the price level if the price level is equal to P_2, and the price level rises toward P_1 to reattain full equilibrium.

The Output and Price-Level Effects of Economic Policies with Floating versus Fixed Exchange Rates

Monetary and fiscal policies can affect the position of the aggregate demand schedule. In turn, aggregate demand, together with aggregate supply, determines the equilibrium price level and the equilibrium volume of real output. It follows that monetary and fiscal policies may play roles in influencing the level of GDP and the inflation rate in an open economy.

Aggregate Demand, Output, and Inflation   To see how monetary or fiscal policy actions might have short-run effects on real output and the price level, consider Figure 13–14. You learned in the opening section of this chapter that monetary and fiscal policies can, under certain circumstances, influence the position of the aggregate demand schedule. Figure 13–14 illustrates a situation in which a policy action induces a rise in aggregate demand, thereby causing the aggregate demand schedule to shift to the right along the short-run aggregate supply schedule.

As a result of the increase in aggregate demand, at the initial equilibrium price level P_1, the desired quantity of real output demanded increases. To induce a rise in the actual amount of production, however, the price level must rise to a new equilibrium level, P_2. This rise in the price level raises the value of the marginal product of labor, thereby inducing firms to employ more workers and produce a larger volume of goods and services. Consequently, the level of real output increases from its initial equilibrium level, y_1, to a new, higher level, y_2.

Thus, in principle, an expansionary policy action that yields an increase in aggregate demand has the following key effects. First, it produces inflation, because it pushes up the price level. Second, in the short run, the rise in the price level generates increased real output. Finally, total employment increases in conjunction with the rise in real output.

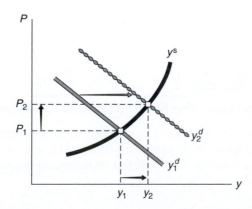

Figure 13–14

The Effects of a Policy-Induced Increase in Aggregate Demand

An expansionary monetary, exchange-rate, or fiscal policy action causes the aggregate demand schedule to shift to the right along the short-run aggregate supply schedule. This results in a rise in the equilibrium price level and an increase in equilibrium real output.

Economic Policies, Output, and Inflation with Floating versus Fixed Exchange Rates As we discussed earlier, how monetary and fiscal policies influence aggregate demand depends both on the degree of capital mobility and whether exchange rates float in the foreign exchange markets or are fixed through central bank interventions. It follows that these same factors condition the potential effects that policy actions may exert on a nation's price level and volume of aggregate real output.

Policy effects on real output and the price level under floating exchange rates In the first part of this chapter, we determined that monetary policy actions always influence aggregate demand in a system of floating exchange rates. In contrast, fiscal policy actions have more limited effects on aggregate demand, and the effects of fiscal policy actions dissipate with increased capital mobility.

For this reason, adopting a system of floating exchange rates enhances the potential for monetary policy actions to have significant short-run effects on real output. Expansions in the money stock also tend to have more inflationary consequences under floating exchange rates, as compared with expansionary fiscal policy actions.

Policy effects on real output and the price level under fixed exchange rates In a system of fixed exchange rates, a nation's central bank must intervene in foreign exchange markets as needed to maintain the value of the nation's currency. Barring sustained sterilization of such interventions, the result is that any efforts to expand aggregate demand via an expansion of the quantity of money in circulation typically place downward pressure on the value of the nation's currency that must be offset by a contraction in the money stock. Therefore, changes in the quantity of money generally have muted effects on aggregate demand and, thus, on real output and the price level, under fixed exchange rates. By way of contrast, maintaining fixed exchange rates enhances the potential influence of fiscal policy actions on aggregate demand and, consequently, on equilibrium real output and prices.

Another manner in which policymakers might bring about an expansion in aggregate demand, a short-run rise in equilibrium real output, and an associated increase in the price level is through a currency *devaluation*. A devaluation induces a rise in net export spending and, thus, causes an increase in aggregate demand. (Within a two-country or even multi-country perspective, economic spillover effects from one nation to other trading partners suggests that real output levels in clusters of nations could move together over time; see *Policy Notebook: Are Nations' Business Cycles More Nearly Synchronized Than in Years Past?*)

POLICY Notebook

Are Nations' Business Cycles More Nearly Synchronized Than in Years Past?

You learned in Chapter 12 about various economic factors, such as sudden changes in autonomous aggregate expenditures in the demand for real money balances, can affect an individual country's equilibrium real income. In addition, you learned from the two-country models discussed in

Chapters 11 and 12 that changes in a domestic nation's equilibrium real income can, by altering its residents' desired expenditures on exports in a second country, affect the latter country's equilibrium real income as well. Taken together, these facts suggest that real outputs in countries that are trading partners might be related. A domestic real output decline during a domestic business-cycle contraction might contribute to a change in real output in a country that is a trading partner, and vice versa. Thus, the possibility that the economies of many of the world's nations may have become more closely linked in recent years might seem to suggest that changes in their levels of real output potentially may have become more synchronized—that is, move more nearly in tandem—over time.

Nevertheless, you also learned in Chapters 11 and 12 that feedback effects from one nation's economy to another depend on whether the nations have a floating or fixed exchange rate. For instance, a decline in domestic autonomous aggregate expenditures tends to induce a corresponding decline in a foreign trading partner's equilibrium income and, hence, aggregate demand and equilibrium output if the exchange rate floats or if the domestic central bank maintains a fixed exchange rate. If the foreign trading partner's central bank acts to keep the exchange rate fixed, however, foreign aggregate demand and equilibrium real output tend to rise in response to a fall in domestic autonomous aggregate expenditures. Likewise, the effects of a sudden fall in the domestic demand for real money balances also depend on whether the exchange rate floats or is fixed. Under a floating exchange rate, an unexpected drop in domestic money demand generates an increase in aggregate demand and real output for a foreign trading partner. In contrast, if the foreign central bank maintains a fixed exchange rate, the effects of the domestic drop in money demand would be decreases in foreign aggregate demand and real output. This reasoning suggests, therefore, that under either floating or fixed exchange rates, the overall net real output effects of simultaneous decreases in aggregate autonomous expenditures and in the demand for real money balances in one nation likely would be ambiguous across a number of trading partners.

Perhaps it is not surprising, therefore, that recent research has reached mixed conclusions about whether business cycles have become more nearly synchronized across clusters of nations. Michael Bordo of Rutgers University and Thomas Helbling of the International Monetary Fund find evidence of some business-cycle synchronization over the past thirty years for sixteen major industrialized nations. Lourdes Montoya of the College of Europe and Jakob de Haan of the University of Groningen reach an analogous conclusion for the advanced nations that currently utilize the euro. In a study of 125 years of data for twenty-five industrialized and emerging economies, Michael Artis of the Centre for Economic Policy Research and George Chouliarakis and P.K.G. Harischandra of the University of Manchester also find evidence of greater business-cycle synchronization for industrialized nations. For emerging countries, however, they conclude that real-output spillover effects in other nations are dwarfed by events that occur within those countries themselves. Thus, there is some evidence that levels of real output tend to move together for groups of developing nations but not for less advanced countries.

For Critical Analysis

Why do you suppose that some economists suggest that nations with more nearly synchronized business cycles might stand to gain if their monetary and fiscal policymakers worked together to coordinate policy actions?

Fundamental ISSUES

#5 How are a nation's price level and volume of real output determined, and how might economic policymakers influence inflation and real output?

The intersection of the aggregate demand and aggregate supply schedules determines the equilibrium level of real output and the equilibrium price level. At equilibrium, all workers and firms are willing and able to produce the amount of real output that yields a real income level equal to aggregate desired expenditures and money market equilibrium at the current price level. Under floating exchange rates, changes in the money stock are the key means by which economic policymaking might influence aggregate demand, the price level, and real output. Under fixed exchange rates, fiscal policy actions and devaluations are economic policy actions that are most likely to affect aggregate demand, the price level, and real output.

RULES VERSUS DISCRETION IN ECONOMIC POLICYMAKING

The preceding analysis indicates that there are a number of circumstances under which it appears that monetary, fiscal, and exchange-rate policies *potentially* can influence the economy's volume of real output and, by implication, employment level. An important issue, however, is whether such policies *actually* can play a role in affecting a nation's real economic performance.

Expectations and the Flexibility of Nominal Wages

Many economists are skeptical about the likelihood that most monetary, fiscal, or exchange-rate policy actions can have significant, long-lived effects on a nation's real output and employment levels. The basis for their skepticism is their doubts that economic policymakers can initiate policy actions without altering the behavior of private individuals and businesses. If workers and firms can *anticipate* the effects of particular policy actions, these economists argue, then it is less likely that such actions can influence real output and employment.

rational expectations hypothesis

The hypothesis that people form expectations using all available past and current information, plus their understanding of how the economy operates.

The Rational Expectations Hypothesis The linchpin of this view is called the *rational expectations hypothesis*. According to this hypothesis, a person attempts to make the best possible forecast of an economic variable using all available past *and current* information *and* drawing on an understanding of what factors affect the determination of the economic variable.

For instance, as workers bargain with firms over their nominal wages, they must try to forecast the level of prices so that they can try to maintain a desired purchasing power of their wages. If workers' expectations are *rational*, then they will use all information available to them at the time they negotiate their wages. In addition, they will take into account all the factors that play a role in determining the price level during the period that their wage bargain will be in force.

Wages, Employment, and Output When Policy Actions Are Anticipated
Figure 13–15 depicts the implication that the rational expectations hypothesis has for wage and employment determination. At the initial points labeled *A* in the

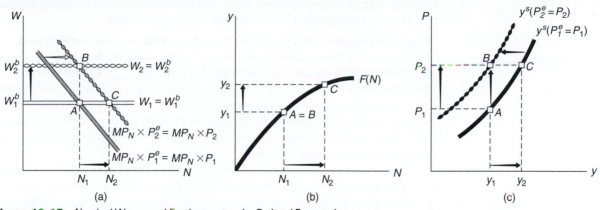

Figure 13–15   Nominal Wages and Employment under Rational Expectations

At the initial points labeled A, workers and firms have established an initial base wage, W_1^b, given their expectation of the price level, $P_1^e = P_1$ and their anticipation of the value of the marginal product of labor, $VMP_N^1 = MP_N \times P_1^e = MP_N \times P_1$ in panel (a). If workers and firms form expectations rationally and recognize that a policy action is likely to raise the price level, then they will raise their price expectation to $P_2^e = P_2$ and negotiate a higher base nominal wage W_2^b. As a result, equilibrium real output will remain unchanged in panel (b), so that the aggregate supply schedule will shift upward by the amount of the anticipated increase in the price level, from point A to point B in panel (c). Only if workers and firms fail to anticipate policy actions that cause rise in the price level would movements from point A to point C, and corresponding short-run increases in employment and output, take place.

figure, we assume that workers and firms have established an initial base wage, denoted W_1^b. We assume in panel (a) that they have set this base wage in light of their *expectation* of the price level, $P_1^e = P_1$ (where the superscript e denotes an expectation) and, consequently, their *anticipation* of the value of the marginal product of labor, $VMP_N^1 = MP_N \times P_1^e = MP_N \times P_1$, during the period in which firms pay workers the base wage W_1^b. If the actual price level in fact turns out to equal P_1, then the employment level equals N_1 at point A. As a result, in panel (b) the level of real output is equal to y_1. Hence, in panel (c) the resulting real output–price level combination y_1 and P_1 is at point A on the aggregate supply schedule $y^s(W_1^b)$.

Suppose, however, that just before workers agree to the base wage W_1^b, they learn that an economic policymaker intends to embark on a new policy strategy that is likely to increase the price level. Such a price increase would erode the purchasing power of their wages. Thus, as shown in panel (a), workers have an incentive to renegotiate a higher base wage, W_2^b, in light of their forecast of the higher price level that they would expect to arise following the policy action, denoted $P_2^e = P_2$. To keep the purchasing power of their wages the same, workers thereby insist on an increase in the base wage in proportion to the expected rise in the price level. For instance, if P_2^e were 5 percent higher than P_1^e, workers would negotiate a base nominal wage W_2^b that would be 5 percent above W_1^b.

As you can see in panel (b), if the actual price level rises to P_2—by the amount workers anticipate when they renegotiate their wages—the result is no change in employment at point B. Thus, in panel (b), we can see that real output remains unchanged following the correctly anticipated rise in the price level from P_1 to P_2. As shown in panel (c), this means that the aggregate supply schedule shifts *upward* by the amount of the anticipated increase in the price level, to $y^s(W_1^b)$. We may conclude that if workers are able to correctly anticipate an increase in the price level resulting from an economic policy action, the result would be no change in real output. Thus, the policy action also would not affect employment.

Wages, Employment, and Output When Policy Actions Are Unanticipated
This is not to say that economic policies could never affect output and employment. For example, consider the points labeled C in Figure 13–15. These points denote the outcomes of an *unanticipated* rise in the price level from P_1 to P_2. In this situation workers expected the price level to equal P_1 when they negotiated their contract, but it actually turns out to be equal to P_2. Unless contracts indexed wages fully to such a price increase, the result in panel (a) would be an increase in employment at the base wage W_1^b from N_1 to N_2 at point C.

The increase in employment of labor causes real output to rise from y_1 to y_2 at point C in panel (b), which implies a movement from point A to point C in panel (c). Thus, under the rational expectations hypothesis, an *unexpected* rise in the price level induced by an expansion in aggregate demand can induce an increase in equilibrium real output.

Our reasoning on the effects of anticipated versus unanticipated policies leads to the following conclusion:

> **If workers form price-level expectations rationally and can adjust their wage bargains with their employers in light of those expectations, then correctly anticipated policy actions have no effect on real output and employment. Only unanticipated policy changes can influence the levels of output and employment.**

This conclusion has important policy implications. One is that even if monetary, fiscal, or exchange-rate policies affect aggregate demand, from a theoretical standpoint they will not necessarily influence a nation's real GDP. Note that this implication hinges on the hypothesis of rational expectations and on the extent to which workers can adjust their wage bargains. Although most economists conclude that the rational expectations hypothesis is reasonable, in many nations the process by which wages are determined may not, as we noted earlier, permit speedy wage adjustments. Nevertheless, to the extent that workers can bargain for higher wages in anticipation of higher prices stemming from expansionary policy actions, the real effects of those policies are likely to be limited.

Another key implication, it turns out, is that one result of well-intentioned policymaking can be persistent inflation, such as the consistently positive rates of inflation many nations of the world have experienced since the middle of the twentieth century. Let's look at why this is so.

Discretion, Credibility, and Inflation
Figure 13–16 displays consumer price inflation rates for selected nations in various regions of the world since the mid-1980s. We could have selected a number of other nations to include in the figure, but in all countries that we otherwise might have chosen, we also would have depicted positive consumer price inflation rates in nearly every single year. Why is this true, given that governments and central banks commonly express a desire to eliminate inflation?

The Inflation Bias of Discretionary Economic Policymaking A possible answer, it turns out, follows from our analysis of the determination of wages, employment, and output under rational expectations. To understand why, consider Figure 13–17. In the figure, we suppose that, given an initial base wage level W_1^b,

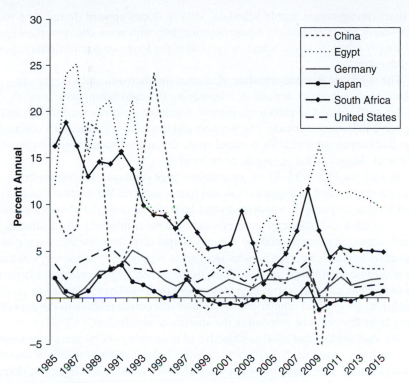

Source: International Monetary Fund, *World Economic Outlook Database.*

Figure 13–16

Inflation in Selected Nations

Since the mid-1980s, consumer price inflation rates in the United States, Germany, and Japan have been well below those in most other nations. Nevertheless, all nations typically have experienced positive inflation in nearly every year.

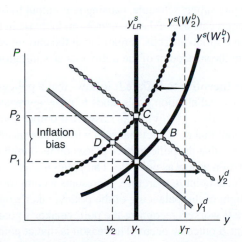

Figure 13–17   The Inflation Bias of Discretionary Policymaking

If the current equilibrium for the economy is point *A*, and if the policymaker's goals are to raise output toward the capacity output level y_T but to keep inflation low, then the policymaker's temptation is to split the difference between these conflicting objectives by inducing a rise in aggregate demand, to point *B*. But if workers realize that the policymaker has an incentive to permit prices to rise, then they will bargain for higher contract wages, thereby raising labor costs for businesses and shifting the aggregate supply schedule leftward. This means that if the policymaker ignores the temptation to induce a rise in aggregate demand, the result will be higher prices and lower real output at point *D*. To avoid this, the policymaker must raise aggregate demand as workers expect. The final equilibrium in the absence of policymaker credibility not to increase inflation, therefore, is at point *C*, with unchanged real output but a higher price level. The increase in the price level caused by a movement from point *A* to point *C* is an *inflation bias* resulting from discretionary policymaking.

the short-run aggregate supply schedule, $y^s(W_1^b)$, slopes upward. In the long run, when wages are able to adjust equiproportionately with price changes, the aggregate supply schedule is y_{LR}^s, which is vertical at the long-run equilibrium output level denoted y_1.

The aggregate demand schedule y_1^d crosses the short-run and long-run aggregate supply schedules at point A, determining the equilibrium price level P_1. Consequently, point A depicts a situation in which the short-run equilibrium and the long-run equilibrium coincide. The workers and firms have negotiated a contract wage that happens to match the nominal wage that arises if wages are completely flexible to changes in the aggregate price level.

In addition, Figure 13–17 on the previous page displays a *target* output level, denoted y_T, that policymakers would like to achieve. We assume that this target level of output is the **capacity output level**, or the real GDP that firms could produce if labor and other factors of production were employed to their utmost. Actual output can never exceed the capacity output level, because the assessment of taxes on workers' incomes induces workers to supply fewer labor services than they otherwise would have desired. Thus, in the presence of income taxes firms are able to produce less real output than they otherwise would have planned to produce. In addition, government regulations can reduce real output relative to the capacity output level that could be attained in the absence of regulations.

We shall assume that another objective of economic policymakers is to keep inflation as low as possible. Nevertheless, a policymaker's primary means of increasing output in the short run is through policy actions that move the aggregate demand schedule upward along the short-run aggregate supply schedule. This means that policymakers face a short-run trade-off between the goals of higher equilibrium output and minimum inflation. To see this, note that an increase in aggregate demand from point A in Figure 13–17 causes a rightward movement along the short-run aggregate supply schedule, causing real output to rise toward the target y_T. But a rise in aggregate demand also induces an increase in the price level, thereby generating higher inflation. Thus, remaining at the current equilibrium point A is more desirable from the standpoint of the policymaker's inflation objective.

The Incentive to Inflate It follows that a policymaker who cares about both the output and inflation goals tends to raise aggregate demand somewhat from point A, such as from y_1^d to y_2^d. This raises real output at the cost of additional inflation. The amount that the policymaker is willing to expand aggregate demand depends on the weight that the policymaker places on its output objective relative to its aim to keep inflation as low as possible. The policymaker's intended short-run equilibrium outcome at point B, therefore, represents a compromise outcome for the policymaker in light of this balancing of the policymaker's output and inflation goals.

If workers recognize the policymaker's goals, however, they will not let the point B outcome occur. The reason is that at point B, the price level is higher than workers and firms anticipated when determining the base wage W_1^b. Hence, the purchasing power of wages, or real wages, that workers had intended to earn is lower at point B than they would desire. Point B, therefore, is inconsistent with the wage strategy of workers.

Workers' Response Instead, workers recognize at the time that they negotiate their wages that the policymaker has an incentive to increase aggregate demand from y_1^d to y_2^d. They react by increasing their price expectation and negotiating a higher base wage, W_2^b, thereby inducing a leftward shift in the aggregate supply schedule,

capacity output level
The level of real GDP that could be produced if all factors of production were fully employed.

from $y^s(W_1^b)$ to $y^s(W_2^b)$. This yields point C in Figure 13–17. At point C, workers maintain the desired purchasing power of their wages, and the policymaker follows through on the aim to raise aggregate demand in an effort to increase output while holding down inflation. Thus, in contrast to point B, point C is a possible equilibrium point. At point C, however, the policymaker ultimately fails to increase real output, which remains equal to y_1.

Why doesn't the policymaker recognize that point B is unattainable when workers can respond by adjusting their wages and leave aggregate demand at the position y_1^d? The reason is that if workers fail to believe that the policymaker can follow through on such a commitment, then they will still raise their price expectation and negotiate an increase in their base wage. This wage increase causes the aggregate supply schedule to shift from $y^s(W_1^b)$ to $y^s(W_2^b)$. Consequently, if the policymaker does follow through with a commitment to leave aggregate demand at y_1^d, point D results. Point D, however, is entirely inconsistent with the policymaker's aims. At this point, after all, inflation occurs and real output falls even *further* below the capacity output target y_T, to the level y_2. Therefore, point D is not a feasible equilibrium point.

Note, however, that *if* workers *can* believe a policymaker's commitment to keep the aggregate demand schedule at y_1^d, then point A is maintained as the final equilibrium point. In this special circumstance of a *credible* commitment to a zero-inflation policy, the policymaker accepts its inability to raise real output toward the capacity level. There is no inflation.

The Problem of Policy Credibility We conclude that points A and C in Figure 13–17 are the two possible equilibrium points arising from the interaction between the policymaker's setting of aggregate demand and the determination of nominal wages by workers and firms. Point A results from commitment to a monetary policy rule, and so it denotes a *commitment equilibrium*. In contrast, point C follows from the inability or unwillingness by workers to believe that a policymaker renounces its ability to act in a discretionary manner by honoring such a commitment. Point C, in other words, is a point of *discretionary equilibrium*. Hence, these two points constitute the alternative outcomes that result from ollowing a policy rule or pursuing discretionary policymaking.

Clearly, *policy credibility*, or the believability of the policymaker's willingness and ability to stick to a policy commitment, is the key determinant of which equilibrium point arises. Such credibility is difficult to achieve in the example illustrated in Figure 13–17 because of the *time inconsistency problem* that exists in the example. This problem is that although honoring a policy commitment yields zero inflation at point A in Figure 13–17, such an action is inconsistent with the aims of the policymaker, which has the ability to alter its policies at any time. In our example, after workers have committed to a base wage, the policymaker can expand aggregate demand, which benefits the policymaker but not workers (point B). This induces workers to bargain for an increase in their base wage, thereby forcing even a policymaker who might otherwise prefer to honor a commitment to zero inflation to raise aggregate demand in an effort to prevent a fall in real output (point D).

The result of the time inconsistency problem and the lack of policy credibility in our example is a higher price level at point C as compared with point A. Economists refer to the difference between the resulting price level P_2 at point C and the initial price level P_1 at point A as the *inflation bias* of discretionary economic policymaking. This is a bias toward inflation that stems from the ability of a policymaker to determine its policies in a discretionary manner in the presence of a

policy credibility
The believability of a policymaker's commitment to a stated intention.

time inconsistency problem
A situation in which a policymaker can better attain its objectives by violating a prior policy stance.

inflation bias
The tendency for an economy to experience persistent inflation as a result of the time inconsistency problem and the lack of policy credibility.

time inconsistency problem and in the absence of policy credibility. (To think about what the theory of discretionary policymaking suggests that we can infer from recent increases in actual and expected rates of inflation, see *Policy Notebook: When Measured Inflation Expectations Creep Upward, So Does the Apparent Inflation Bias of Discretionary Policymaking.*)

POLICY Notebook

When Measured Inflation Expectations Creep Upward, So Does the Apparent Inflation Bias of Discretionary Policymaking

There are two basic ways to try to measure inflation expectations. One is through surveys—that is, asking individuals or even economists and other professional forecasters for their predictions of inflation. Another approach is to infer expected inflation rates from the difference between the nominal interest rate on a security, such as a U.S. Treasury security, that includes no special adjustments for inflation, and the nominal interest rate on a security that does adjust for inflation, such as an inflation-indexed U.S. Treasury security.

In 2003 and 2004, both measures of inflation expectations indicated that the anticipated annual rate of inflation was just over 2 percent in the European Monetary Union, about 1 percent in the United Kingdom, and about 2.5 percent in the United States. Between 2004 and the 2008 financial crisis, measures of inflation expectations exhibited a general upswing, indicating expected inflation as high as just over 4 percent in the European Monetary Union, nearly 5.5 percent in the United Kingdom, and above 5 percent in the United States. Actual inflation rates in these regions also increased throughout the 2000s. Finally, during the years since 2009, measures of anticipated inflation rates in these regions have been back to a range between 2 and 3 percent, and actual inflation rates also have tended to end up within this range.

The theory of discretionary policymaking indicates that these associated swings in expected and actual inflation are consistent with increased inflation biases. One likely culprit, the theory suggests, has been some loss of anti-inflation credibility on the part of central banks.

For Critical Analysis

During the remainder of the 2010s, how might the European Central Bank, the Bank of England, and the Federal Reserve go about regaining some credibility and further reducing actual and expected rates of inflation?

Making Economic Policies Credible Three types of economic policymaking can stimulate aggregate demand and are thereby subject to the time inconsistency problem illustrated in Figure 13–17 on page 405: monetary policy, fiscal policy, and exchange-rate policy. The same basic time inconsistency problem arises in all three areas of policymaking. This is that a policymaker may gain from short-run expansions of aggregate demand after workers negotiate their nominal wages.

How can economic policymakers gain sufficient credibility to honor commitments to noninflationary policies? It turns out that there are several possible mechanisms for reducing or even eliminating the inflation bias that can arise from discretionary policymaking.

Constitutional limitations on monetary policy One approach, which has been advocated by a number of observers, such as Milton Friedman of the Hoover Institution at Stanford University, would be for nations to adopt firm legal prohibitions against discretionary policymaking. In Germany, for instance, the nation's constitution required the Bundesbank, Germany's central bank, to pursue a policy of price stability. The German constitution also limited the ability of the German government to interfere with the Bundesbank's policies. This made a Bundesbank commitment to low inflation policies much more credible than it would be otherwise.

Learn more about the Bundesbank's structure at *http://www.bundesbank.de/index.en.php.*

Establishing a reputation In the absence of constitutional limitations, a policymaker might gain credibility by establishing and maintaining a reputation as an "inflation hawk." To see how a policymaker might do this, reconsider Figure 13–17. Recall that if a policymaker honors a commitment not to raise aggregate demand in pursuit of short-term output gains but is not believed by workers and firms, then the result is higher inflation and reduced output, as depicted in Figure 13–17 by a movement from point *A* to point *D*. If the policymaker cares only about the current real output level and inflation rate, it never desires for point *D* to occur. If the central bank wishes to establish a future reputation as an inflation hawk, however, then it might be willing to let output fall to point *D* in the figure. From that time onward, the policymaker's promises not to raise aggregate demand in pursuit of short-term output gains might then be credible.

Appointing a "conservative," independent policymaker The theory of the discretionary inflation bias implies that a key factor influencing the size of the inflation bias is how much a policymaker dislikes inflation relative to how much the policymaker desires to try to raise real output toward its capacity level. Thus, appointing a *conservative policymaker*, or an individual who dislikes inflation more than the average citizen, may be one means of reducing the size of the inflation bias.

Most proposals for the appointment of conservative policymakers as a possible way to limit the discretionary inflation bias have focused on central banks. One reason is that in most nations the officials who head such institutions are, indeed, appointed by elected leaders. Another reason is that central banks can be powerful policymaking institutions under either floating or fixed exchange rates. On the one hand, in a system of flexible exchange rates, expansionary monetary policies have the potential to be highly inflationary. On the other hand, even in a system of fixed exchange rates, central banks may have considerable input into decisions to devalue a nation's currency. Thus, the credibility of a commitment to an exchange-rate target intended to be consistent with low inflation may depend in large part on the credibility of a nation's central bank.

Recently a number of economists, and notably Carl Walsh of the University of California at Santa Cruz, have proposed the use of *central banker contracts*, or legally binding agreements between governments and appointed central bank officials. Under such contracts, central bank officials would be punished, or perhaps rewarded, depending on the nation's inflation performance. One real-world example

conservative policymaker

A central bank official who dislikes inflation more than an average citizen in society and who thereby is less willing to induce discretionary increases in the quantity of money in an effort to achieve short-run increases in real output.

central banker contact

A legally binding agreement between a government and a central banking official that holds the official responsible for a nation's inflation performance.

of a central banker contract has been in effect in New Zealand since 1989. Under the New Zealand central banking arrangement, consistent departures from price stability that clearly stem from aggregate demand expansions may lead to dismissal of the head of the central bank.

The point of central banker contracts is to make central bank officials more *accountable*. Nevertheless, adopting central banker contracts does not preclude granting central bank officials considerable *independence* to conduct the monetary or exchange-rate policies that they feel would be needed to keep inflation low. In fact, a number of economists contend that central bank independence may be a key element in a successful low-inflation policy. They argue that establishing a reputation as an inflation hawk is difficult for a central bank official who is constrained by political pressures to achieve other objectives as well, such as a low unemployment rate or a high growth rate for real output. Thus, these economists argue that governments should make central banks *politically independent* by insulating them from such political pressures. Furthermore, they argue, accountability for a country's inflation performance is an unfair burden to place on central bank officials if governments fail to grant these officials *economic independence,* or the power to determine their own budget or to provide direct financial support for government policy initiatives. From this perspective, a fully independent central bank would be both politically and economically independent.

Visit the Reserve Bank of New Zealand at *http://www.rbnz.govt.nz.*

Support for Central Bank Independence To support their contention about the potential desirability of central bank independence, advocates of this approach point to evidence such as that depicted in panels (a) and (b) of Figure 13–18. Each panel plots an index measure of central bank overall political and economic independence along the horizontal axis. Panel (a) plots average annual inflation rates along the vertical axis and illustrates that there has been an *inverse relationship* between central bank independence and average inflation. Hence, nations with more independent central banks, such as Germany, Switzerland, and the United States, typically have experienced lower average inflation.

Panel (b) of Figure 13–18 plots the variance of inflation along the vertical axis and indicates that there also has been an inverse relationship between central bank independence and inflation variability. That is, nations with more independent central banks tend to experience less inflation volatility. Together, panels (a) and (b) therefore indicate that greater central bank independence tends to yield more stable inflation rates, as well as reduced average inflation.

This evidence supporting the theoretical arguments favoring more independent central banks has induced a number of countries, such as France, Japan, Mexico, Pakistan, and the United Kingdom, to grant significantly greater political and economic independence to their central banks. In addition, the evidence, plus the low-inflation experience of Germany under its highly independent Bundesbank, led European nations to agree that when a European central bank ultimately was established, the central bank had considerable independence from national governments.

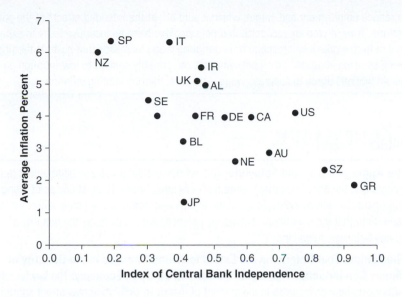

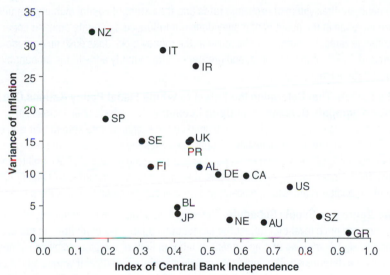

Source: From Alex Cukierman, *Central Bank Strategy, Credibility, and Independence,* Cambridge, MA: MIT Press, 1992; and the International Monetary Fund, *International Financial Statistics.*

Figure 13–18

Central Bank Independence, Average Inflation, and Inflation Variability

As panel (a) shows, nations with more independent central banks, such as Germany, Switzerland, and the United States, have lower inflation rates as compared with countries with less independent central banks. Panel (b) indicates that nations with more independent central banks also have experienced less inflation variability.

Fundamental ISSUES

#6 Why does the rational expectations hypothesis indicate that economic policies may have limited real output effects and that the credibility of policymakers is important?

The rational expectations hypothesis is that people use all available information and their understanding of how the economy functions to predict the price level. Hence, if workers make rational price-level forecasts when negotiating their nominal wages, they will bargain for higher nominal wages when they correctly anticipate that policymakers plan to enact policies to expand real output. Such wage increases would induce firms to reduce employment and output, which would offset the intended effects of the policy actions. Thus, if workers recognize that policymakers have an incentive to try to expand real output, workers will respond by negotiating wage increases that push up the price level, spurring inflation. Only if policymakers can credibly commit to low-inflation policies would workers agree to suppress wage increases, thereby limiting inflation.

Chapter SUMMARY

1. **The Aggregate Demand Schedule:** This schedule displays all combinations of real income and the price level that maintain *IS–LM* equilibrium. Thus, at any point along an aggregate demand schedule, real income equals aggregate desired expenditures at the same time that the quantity of real money balances supplied equals the quantity of real money balances demanded.

2. **The Factors That Determine the Extent to which Changes in the Quantity of Money Can Influence Aggregate Demand in an Open Economy:** The key factors influencing how an increase in the amount of money in circulation may affect aggregate demand are the system of exchange rates and the extent of capital mobility. An unsterilized increase in the quantity of money does not influence aggregate demand under fixed exchange rates. In contrast, an increase in the money stock does push up aggregate demand if exchange rates float, and greater capital mobility adds to the amount by which aggregate demand rises.

3. **The Factors That Determine the Extent to which Fiscal Policy Actions Can Influence Aggregate Demand in an Open Economy:** The effects of an increase in government spending on aggregate demand depend on the exchange-rate system that is in place and on the degree of capital mobility. Under fixed exchange rates, an increase in government spending causes aggregate demand to increase, and greater capital mobility enlarges this effect. Under floating exchange rates, the aggregate demand effects of higher government expenditures are less significant, and greater capital mobility mutes them even further.

4. **The Aggregate Supply Schedule:** This schedule depicts all combinations of real output and the price level that reflect the production capabilities of all firms in the economy and the aggregate level of employment of labor in light of the process by which nominal wages are determined. The aggregate supply schedule is vertical if wages adjust equiproportionately to changes in the price level, which can occur only if contracts specify full wage indexation or if sufficient time passes to permit such a complete wage adjustment. To the extent that nominal wages are less flexible, however, the aggregate supply schedule exhibits a more shallow, upward slope.

5. **A Nation's Price Level and Volume of Real Output and the Effect of Economic Policies on Inflation and Real Output:** The intersection of the aggregate demand and aggregate supply schedules determines the equilibrium price level and real output level. At the point where these schedules cross, all workers and firms are willing and able to produce the amount of real output that yields a real income level equal to aggregate desired expenditures and money market equilibrium at the prevailing price level. If exchange rates float, then monetary policy actions are the primary means by which aggregate demand, the price level, and real output might be influenced by economic policymaking. Under fixed exchange rates, fiscal policy actions or currency devaluations are economic policy actions that have the greatest effects on aggregate demand, the price level, and real output.

6. **Why the Rational Expectations Hypothesis Indicates That Economic Policies May Have Limited Real Output Effects and That the Credibility of Policymakers Is Important:** According to the rational expectations hypothesis, individuals use all the information they have, plus their knowledge of how the economy functions, when they forecast the price level. Hence, workers who make rational price-level forecasts when negotiating their nominal wages will bargain for wage increases if they correctly anticipate expansionary monetary, fiscal, or exchange-rate policies intended to raise real output. The resulting rise in the overall wage level would induce firms to reduce employment and output, thereby offsetting the policy actions. Hence, if workers recognize that policymakers desire to raise real output, workers will bargain for inflationary wage increases. The key means by which policymakers might limit inflation would be by credibly committing to low-inflation policies.

QUESTIONSandPROBLEMS

1. True or false? "In today's world with floating exchange rates and nearly perfect capital mobility among industrialized nations, the individual monetary policy actions of central banks are becoming irrelevant to their nations' inflation performances." Explain.

2. When European Monetary Union nations moved toward a system of irrevocably fixed exchange rates in 1999, they qualified for entry by restraining their fiscal policies in clearly defined ways. Explain why such fiscal policy restraints might have made sense if one key goal of European countries was to limit inflation.

3. Use an aggregate demand–aggregate supply diagram to explain why, in a system of fixed exchange rates, a currency devaluation typically results in domestic inflation. If workers' expectations are rational and if workers are able to renegotiate wage adjustments rapidly, under what circumstances would a devaluation induce an increase in real output? Under what circumstances would a devaluation fail to generate a rise in real output? Explain your reasoning.

4. Suppose that workers in a country gain clout in the wage bargaining process and are able to raise their base wages. If no other events occur, what would happen to the nation's price level and to its real GDP? Use an aggregate demand–aggregate supply diagram to explain your answer.

5. Suppose that workers in a small open economy with a fixed exchange rate realize that their nation's central bank and government wish to increase real GDP by 7 percent during the year leading up to an election, in the hope that higher employment would garner more votes for current leaders. Workers realize that 10 percent inflation would be required to yield this desired increase in real GDP. The nation has no constraints on the ability of its central bank and government to change its current exchange-rate targets, and there is no central bank or governmental concern about high inflation. According to the basic theory of discretionary policymaking discussed in this chapter, would you predict that the central bank and government will devalue the nation's currency? If so, and if workers can bargain for wage changes, would you predict a rise in inflation and in real GDP for this nation? Justify your answers.

6. Suppose that the wages of all workers in a nation are fully indexed to inflation, so that wages always adjust in lockstep to changes in the price level. Under the theory of discretionary monetary policy, is there an incentive for this nation's central bank to produce an inflation bias? (*Hint*: Recall that the slope of the aggregate supply schedule varies with the degree of wage flexibility and that short-run output gains are feasible only when the aggregate supply schedule slopes upward.)

7. Consider the situation described in Question 6. Would full indexation be desirable if aggregate demand is stable but aggregate supply is subject to shifts caused by changes in the prices of important resources such as oil?

8. Evaluate the following statement: "A real strength of performance contracts for central bankers is that they give central bankers policy discretion while subjecting them to a societal rule."

9. Between the mid-1990s and the early 2010s, average nominal wages in China more than tripled, a fact that many observers credited in large part to an increase in Chinese workers' productivity.
    a. Simplify by assuming that the amount of labor supplied in China remained nearly unchanged between the mid-1990s and the early 2010s, and suppose that Chinese workers' productivity did indeed increase considerably. In principle, could such a rise in productivity by itself explain the significant increase in the nominal wages earned by Chinese workers?
    b. Between the mid-1990s and the early 2010s, the average rate of inflation in China exceeded 4 percent per year. As a consequence, the nation's price level at the beginning of the 2010s was nearly 90 percent larger than it was in 1995. Discuss how this fact could help to account for the significant increase in Chinese workers' wages during this period.
    c. Based on the information provided in part b, how could the theory of discretionary policymaking help to explain the simultaneous increases in the levels of prices and wages in China between the mid-1990s and the early 2010s?

10. Evaluate the following statement: "According to the basic theory of discretionary monetary policy and inflation, central bank independence alone will not necessarily restrain a central bank from pursuing inflationary policies. Thus, it should be no surprise to economists that there is no apparent relationship between the degree of central bank independence and inflation outside of the world's developed nations."

Online APPLICATIONS

If the aggregate supply schedule slopes upward, then a rise in the price level should induce an increase in a nation's real output. It follows that higher inflation should be associated with higher employment, or equivalently, with lower unemployment rates. This application allows you to take a direct look at unemployment and inflation data to judge for yourself whether or not the two variables appear to be related in the United States.

Internet URL: *http://www.bls.gov/eag/eag.us.htm*

Title: U.S. Bureau of Labor Statistics: Economy at a Glance

Navigation: Begin at the home page of the U.S. Bureau of Labor Statistics (http://www.bls.gov). Click on the *Home* dropdown window and under *At a Glance Tables*, select *U.S. Economy.*

Application: Perform the indicated operations, and answer the following questions:

1. In the *Economy At a Glance Tables,* click on *Consumer Price Index,* then *CPI Tables,* and then *Consumer Price Index History Table.* How much has the inflation varied in recent years? Compare this with previous years, especially the mid-1970s to the mid-1980s.

2. Back up to *Economy at a Glance,* and now click on *Unemployment Rate,* then *CPS Tables,* and then *Employment status of the population, 1940's to date.* During what recent years was the unemployment rate approaching its peak value? Do you note any appearance of an inverse relationship between the unemployment rate and the inflation rate (part 1)?

SELECTED REFERENCES and FURTHER READINGS

Artis, Michael, George Chouliarakis, and P. K. G. Harischandra. "Business Cycle Synchronization since 1880." *Manchester School 79* (2011): 173–207.

Bleaney, Michael, and Manuela Francisco. "Exchange Rate Regimes and Inflation: Only Hard Pegs Make a Difference." *Canadian Journal of Economics 38* (2005): 1453–1476.

Bordo, Michael, and Thomas Helbling. "International Business Cycle Synchronization in Historical Perspective." *Manchester School 79* (2011): 208–238.

Brumm, Harold. "Inflation and Central Bank Independence: Conventional Wisdom Redux." *Journal of Money, Credit, and Banking 32* (2000): 807–819.

Bryson, Jay, Chih-huan Chen, and David VanHoose. "Implications of Economic Interdependence for Endogenous Wage Indexation Decisions." *Scandinavian Journal of Economics 100* (1998): 693–710.

Calmfors, Lars, and John Driffill. "Bargaining Structure, Corporatism, and Macroeconomic Performance." *Economic Policy 3* (1988): 14–61.

Cukierman, Alex. *Central Bank Strategy, Credibility, and Independence.* Cambridge, MA: MIT Press, 1992.

Daniels, Joseph, Farrokh Nourzad, and David VanHoose. "Openness, Centralized Wage Bargaining, and Inflation." *European Journal of Political Economy 22* (2006): 969–988.

Gonçalves, Carlos, and Alexandre Carvalho. "Inflation Targeting Matters: Evidence from OECD Countries' Sacrifice Ratios." *Journal of Money, Credit, and Banking 41* (2009): 233–243.

James, Jonathan, and Phillip Lawler. "Productivity, Indexation, and Macroeconomic Outcomes: The Implications of Goods Market Competition and Wage Bargaining Structure." *Journal of Economics and Business 58* (2006): 465–479.

Ling, Shu, and Haichua Ye. "Does Inflation Targeting Really Make a Difference? Evaluating the Treatment Effect of Inflation Targeting in Seven Industrial Countries." *Journal of Monetary Economics 54* (2007): 2521–2533.

Mafi-Kreft, Elham, and Steven Krett. "Importing Credible Monetary Policy: A Way for Transition Economies to Fight Inflation." *Economics Letters 92* (2006): 1–6.

Montoya, Lourdes Acedo, and Jakob de Haan. "Regional Business Cycle Synchronization in Europe?" *International Economics and Economic Policy 5* (2008): 123–137.

Ratti, Ronald. "On Optimal Contracts for Central Bankers and Inflation- and Exchange-Rate-Targeting Regimes." *Journal of Money, Credit, and Banking 34* (2002): 678–685.

Stella, Peter. "Central Bank Financial Strength, Policy Constraints, and Inflation." International Monetary Fund, Working Paper WP/08/49 (February 2008).

Surico, Paulo. "Measuring the Time Inconsistency of U.S. Monetary Policy." *Economica 75* (2008): 22–38.

Walsh, Carl. "Optimal Contracts for Central Bankers. *American Economic Review 85* (1) (March 1995): 150–167.

PART 5

■

DOMESTIC AND MULTINATIONAL POLICYMAKING IN A GLOBAL ECONOMY

14 Domestic Economic Policymaking in a Global Economy

15 Policy Coordination, Monetary Union, and Target Zones

14

Domestic Economic Policymaking in a Global Economy

Fundamental ISSUES

1. What is the policy assignment problem?
2. What is exchange rate overshooting, and why might it occur?
3. Why does increased openness of a nation's economy have an uncertain net effect on the responsiveness of output to changes in the price level?
4. Is there an inverse relationship between openness and inflation?
5. What is the new open economy macroeconomics?

Recently, a report issued by the International Monetary Fund discussed factors contributing to generally lower, as compared with earlier periods, worldwide rates of inflation. According to the report, "Some analysts have argued that low and stable inflation reflects more intense global competition, which prevents firms from raising prices and puts downward pressures on wages in many sectors. If so, and given that lower-cost producers in emerging markets and developing countries will continue to integrate into the global trading system, these forces are likely to ensure low inflation in the foreseeable future, reminiscent of the secular deflation associated with broad productivity increases during the classical gold standard in the late nineteenth century." Thus, the report suggested, increased "globalization"—a shorthand term for an increased extent of openness of the world's economies to international trade in goods and services and a greater degree of mobility of financial capital—could result in a long-lasting reduction in inflation around the world.

Does globalization reduce inflation? If so, through what channels do increased trade openness and greater capital mobility bring about a disinflationary trend? This chapter will address these and other questions regarding the impacts of globalization.

THE POLICY ASSIGNMENT PROBLEM

Whether because they recognize that international factors influence domestic goals or because of political pressures that they face from mercantilist advocates, monetary and fiscal policymakers commonly espouse their interest in attaining international objectives. Once they commit themselves to achieving international goals, however, policymakers must confront a fundamental problem: Domestic and international objectives sometimes clash. For instance, increasing government expenditures might be regarded as an appropriate fiscal policy action to spur growth in a nation's real income, yet the rise in real income tends to spur import spending and raise the merchandise trade deficit. Reducing money growth may be the best policy for a central bank to pursue to restrain inflation, but the interest rate reduction that results may cause capital to flow out of the country, thereby inducing a balance-of-payments deficit.

In principle, the solution to this potential conflict might seem straightforward. After all, there are two policymakers: a central bank and a governmental fiscal authority. And there are two basic types of goals that they might pursue: international objectives and domestic objectives. Why not just assign one set of goals to the central bank and the other set to the fiscal authority?

Indeed, this is a possible solution to conflicts that can emerge between international and domestic goals. Nevertheless, a problem remains. Which policymakers should take responsibility for achieving the alternative objectives? Should the central bank seek to attain a nation's real output goals while the government aims for balance-of-payments equilibrium, or should the assignment of policymakers between the two goals be reversed? This question is known as the ***assignment problem*** in policymaking. Let's consider how the problem might be addressed in various circumstances that a nation with an open economy might face.

Finding the Best Policy Mix for Internal and External Balance

Suppose, for instance, that both a nation's central bank and its finance ministry (or, in some nations, such as the United States, its treasury department) agree that the nation has two key economic goals, which each will actively pursue on a week-to-week basis. One is an *internal-balance objective,* which is to achieve a desired level of real GDP. The other is an *external-balance objective,* which is to maintain balanced-of-payments equilibrium. Hence, the central bank could seek to conduct monetary policy with an intent to achieve the internal GDP objective or the external balance-of-payments objective. At the same time, the finance ministry could vary its spending and taxation policies in an effort to attain one objective or the other. It would be redundant for both authorities to aim at the same objective. Consequently, it makes sense for one authority to seek to achieve the internal-balance objective of a desired real GDP level while the other authority aims to achieve the external-balance objective of a balance-of-payments equilibrium.

For a nation with a floating exchange rate, would it be in the nation's best interest for the central bank to adjust the money stock to achieve the desired real GDP level while the finance ministry varies the composition of its budget in an effort to attain balanced-of-payments equilibrium? Or should the central bank seek to maintain the quantity of money in circulation at a level consistent with the external-balance objective, leaving the finance ministry with the responsibility for influencing real GDP through its budgetary policies?

assignment problem
The problem of determining whether the central bank or the finance ministry should assume responsibility for achieving a nation's domestic or international policy objectives.

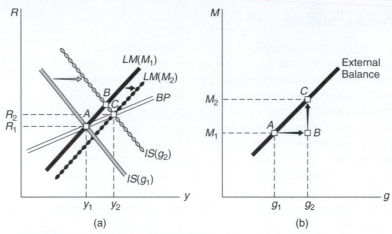

Figure 14–1   Monetary and Fiscal Policy Combinations for External Balance with High Capital Mobility and a Floating Exchange Rate
In panel (a), an increase in government spending causes the *IS* schedule to shift rightward from point *A*, resulting in a higher equilibrium interest rate at point *B* that generates a capital inflow and a balance-of-payments surplus. To reestablish a balance-of-payments equilibrium, the central bank can increase the quantity of money in circulation, thereby causing the *LM* schedule to shift rightward and generating a fall in the domestic interest rate that reverses the flow of financial resources and thereby reattains external balance at point *C*. Consequently, maintaining external balance in the face of increased government spending requires an increase in the money stock, which implies that the external-balance schedule slopes upward in panel (b).

Achieving External Balance To think about the fundamental nature of the assignment problem, let's begin by considering Figure 14–1. Point *A* in panel (a) displays an initial *IS–LM–BP* equilibrium position at point *A* for an economy with high, but imperfect, capital mobility that is initially in balance-of-payments equilibrium at a level of government spending equal to g_1. Let's suppose that the central bank concentrates on achieving the nation's external-balance objective by setting the money stock appropriately. Now consider what happens if the government increases spending from g_1 to g_2. As shown in panel (a), the *IS* schedule shifts rightward. The resulting rise in the equilibrium domestic interest rate generates a capital inflow, which, because capital is highly mobile, more than offsets the increase in imports caused by a rise in equilibrium real income. Thus, the nation begins to run a balance-of-payments surplus at point *B*.

Under a floating exchange rate, a domestic currency appreciation would eventually bring about adjustments in the positions of the *IS* and *BP* schedules consistent with a new balance-of-payments equilibrium (see Figure 12–4 on page 352) in the absence of any central bank action. To work toward immediate attainment of balance-of-payments equilibrium, however, the central bank must boost the money stock from the initial level of M_1 to a higher value of M_2, which shifts the *LM* schedule rightward. This results in a reduction in the domestic interest rate that generates capital outflows and a further increase in equilibrium real income. This, in turn, stimulates greater import spending, both of which result in speedier movement toward balance-of-payments equilibrium at point *C* in panel (a).

Thus, both points *A* and *C* in panel (b) of Figure 14–1 are part of a set of combinations of government spending and the quantity of money in circulation that maintains external balance. These combinations make up the upward-sloping *external-balance schedule* in panel (b). This schedule indicates that to maintain the nation's external-balance objective, the central bank must increase the money stock whenever the government increases its spending.

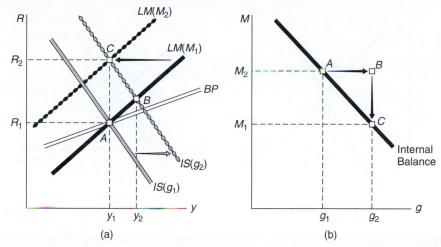

Figure 14–2 Monetary and Fiscal Policy Combinations for Internal Balance with High Capital Mobility and a Floating Exchange Rate
In panel (a), an increase in government spending causes the *IS* schedule to shift rightward from point *A*, resulting in a higher equilibrium level of real income. To return real income to its initial level, the central bank can reduce the quantity of money in circulation, thereby causing the *LM* schedule to shift leftward to reestablish internal balance at point *C*. Consequently, maintaining external balance in the face of increased government spending requires a decrease in the money stock, which implies that the external-balance schedule slopes downward in panel (b).

Achieving Internal Balance Figure 14–2 considers what it takes for policymakers to achieve *internal* balance in the face of increased government spending. At point *A* in panel (a), equilibrium real income is equal to y_1, which happens to correspond to the real-income objective for government policymakers. If the government raises its spending, then equilibrium real income rises to y_2 at point *B*, above the target income level, at which point there is once again a balance-of-payments surplus.

To push the nation's economy back to a position of internal balance, the central bank must reduce the money stock, thereby inducing a leftward shift of the *LM* schedule in panel (a), so that real income returns to its original level consistent with internal balance at point *C*. Both points *A* and *C* in panel (b) of Figure 14–2 lie along a schedule of points giving combinations of government spending and a quantity of money in circulation that maintain external balance. These policy combinations comprise the downward-sloping *internal-balance schedule* in panel (b). This schedule indicates that to maintain the nation's internal-balance goal level of real income, the central bank must reduce the money stock whenever the government increases its spending.

Assigning Internal and External Objectives

Panel (a) in Figure 14–3 on the next page shows both the external-balance schedule and the internal-balance schedule. The point where these schedules cross, denoted as *E*, is the only point that lies on both schedules. Thus, this point gives the single combination of the government's expenditures and the central bank's money stock, denoted g^* and M^*, that can simultaneously achieve external and internal balance.

Suppose that the central bank aims to achieve internal balance, while the government's finance ministry seeks to achieve external balance. Panel (a) shows what happens if the money stock is above the level consistent with internal balance, M_1 at point *A*, and government spending is below the value consistent with the external balance objective, g_1. Given the quantity of money M_1, the finance ministry raises spending to g_2 in order to achieve its balance-of-payments objective at point *B* on

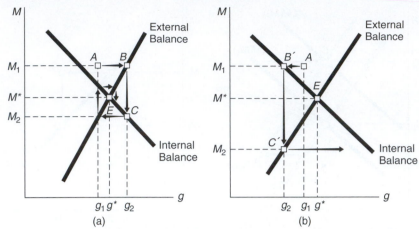

Figure 14–3 Policy Assignment and Internal and External Balance with High Capital Mobility and a Floating Exchange Rate
At point *A* in both panels, the quantity of money M_1 is above the level consistent with internal balance, and the level of government spending g_1 is below the value consistent with external balance. In panel (a), the finance ministry's assignment is to aim for external balance. It thus increases government spending, which results in point *B*. The central bank, then, is assigned the task of aiming for internal balance and therefore reduces the money stock, which yields point *C*. Successive actions by the two policymakers ultimately will generate point *E*, which is consistent with both external balance and internal balance. In panel (b), in which the assignments are reserved, then at point *A* the government reduces its spending to move to point *B'*, which induces the central bank to reduce the money stock to move to point *C'*, and so on, in movements progressively farther from point *E*. Thus, the correct policy assignment is for the finance ministry to strive for external balance and the central bank to aim for internal balance, as in panel (a).

the external-balance schedule. To attain the goal level of real income at this higher level of government expenditures, the central bank decreases the quantity of money to M_2 at point *C* on the internal-balance schedule. Ultimately, as shown in panel (b), such back-and-forth responses by the two policymakers attain the government spending–exchange rate combination g^* and M^* at point *E*.

An Incorrect Assignment Now suppose that the assignment of goals is reversed: The central bank seeks to attain external balance, while the finance ministry aims to achieve internal balance. The initial point in panel (b) again is point *A* with the policy combination g_1 and M_1. Given the quantity of money M_1, the government decreases its spending to g_2 in order to achieve its real-income objective at point *B'* on the internal-balance schedule. To attain a balance-of-payments equilibrium at this lower level of government expenditures, the central bank decreases the money stock to M_2 at point *C'* on the external-balance schedule. Clearly, with this assignment of objectives, interactions between the two policymakers pushes government spending and the quantity of money in circulation *farther* from g^* and M^* at point *E*.

In this example, the appropriate policy assignment entails having the government aim to achieve external balance and the central bank adjust the money stock in an effort to attain internal balance. Thus, Figure 14–3 depicts a situation in which a nation's central bank can better attain international goals while a finance ministry can do a more creditable job of achieving domestic objectives.

In some cases, however, it could be better for the central bank to work toward attaining domestic objectives while the finance ministry focuses on purely international goals. For instance, Question 1 at the end of the chapter examines the situation of low capital mobility and a floating exchange rate, in which it turns out that the assignment definitely should be reversed: In this situation, the central bank should aim for the external balance objective while the finance ministry should seek to achieve internal balance.

Difficulties in Solving the Assignment Problem Clearly, the degree of capital mobility makes a difference in solving the assignment problem. So does the flexibility of the exchange rate. In our example, the exchange rate was flexible, but under a fixed exchange rate in which the central bank varies the exchange rate peg and the finance ministry adjusts its budgetary policies, alternative solutions to the assignment problem also emerge, depending on the relative mobility of capital.

These considerations suggest that the appropriate assignment of policy objectives varies from nation to nation, depending on the specific circumstances that they face. The assignment problem can become a contentious issue. Officials of a nation's central bank may feel confident that it would be more efficient for the government to restrict its policy interests to domestic issues, leaving the international sphere to the central bank. Government officials, however, may be reluctant to accept this assignment. It is not unusual, therefore, for central banks and government officials to squabble about these issues. Sometimes disagreements about the appropriate solution to a nation's policy assignment problem can become public spats and escalate into serious political disputes.

Fundamental ISSUES

#1 What is the policy assignment problem?

The policy assignment problem is the issue of determining whether monetary or fiscal policymakers should aim their policies at internal or external policy goals. Under some circumstances, policies can be mismatched with ultimate goals. As a result, efforts by foreign ministers to conduct fiscal policy and by central banks to vary the quantity of money in circulation or an exchange-rate peg can conflict, causing both policymakers to fail to achieve their ultimate economic goals.

EXCHANGE-RATE RESPONSES TO POLICY ACTIONS WITH STICKY WAGES AND PRICES—EXCHANGE-RATE OVERSHOOTING

In Chapter 13, you learned that in a short-run situation in which nominal wages are fully indexed to changes in the price level, the aggregate supply schedule is vertical. Consequently, the short-run effects of a rise in aggregate demand induced, say, by an increase in the quantity of money in circulation, are the fullest possible increase in the price level and no change in equilibrium output. These outcomes contrast with those that arise when nominal wages are fixed in the short run. In this environment, stickiness in nominal wages makes a nation's aggregate supply curve upward sloping, so that an equal-sized rise in aggregate demand generates a short-run increase in equilibrium real output. In addition, the increase in aggregate demand causes the price level to rise somewhat less than if wages were fully indexed.

Thus, short-run wage stickiness causes the aggregate price level to adjust less completely to changes in aggregate demand than it would otherwise. That is, wage stickiness leads to short-run sluggishness in price-level adjustments to factors such as monetary policy actions that can affect the position of the aggregate demand

exchange-rate overshooting

A situation in which the short-run effect of an increase in aggregate demand is a rise in the nominal exchange rate above its long-run equilibrium value.

schedule. This fact, it turns out, potentially has an important consequence for the response of the exchange rate to policy actions that induce a change in aggregate demand. ***Exchange-rate overshooting*** can occur, meaning that in the short run, a rise in aggregate demand can cause the nominal exchange rate to rise above its long-run equilibrium value. Short-run stickiness in the price level, therefore, can generate additional short-term variability in the exchange rate.

The Long-Run Adjustment of the Exchange Rate to a Monetary Expansion

To understand the concept of exchange-rate overshooting, let's begin by considering the long-run adjustment of a floating exchange rate to an increase in aggregate demand. Furthermore, let's suppose that the rise in aggregate demand is brought about by an increase in the quantity of money.

Long-Run Equilibrium In the long run, as shown in panel (a) of Figure 14–4, the aggregate supply schedule, y_{LR}^s, is vertical, because given enough adjustment time, nominal wages vary in equal measure to changes in the price level. The long-run equilibrium price level is determined by the intersection of aggregate demand with this long-run aggregate supply schedule.

Suppose that in the long run, the domestic price level adjusts to satisfy the condition $P = k \times P^* \times S$, where k is a constant factor of proportionality. Because k is constant, $\%\Delta k = 0$, so that this condition implies $\%\Delta P = \%\Delta P^* + \%\Delta S$, which is the relative-purchasing-power-parity condition. Hence, this condition ensures that relative purchasing power holds in the long run. Panel (b) of Figure 14–4 displays the condition $P = k \times P^* \times S$ as a straight-line relationship between the domestic price level P and the nominal exchange rate S, in which the factor $k \times P^*$ is the slope.

Exchange-Rate Adjustment in the Long Run Figure 14–4 also shows the long-run effects of a rise in aggregate demand generated by an increase in the money stock. The increase in aggregate demand has the long-run effect of raising the

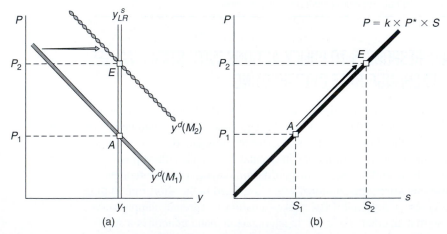

(a)   (b)

Figure 14–4   Long-Run Adjustment of the Exchange Rate to an Increase in the Money Stock

Points A in panels (a) and (b) display initial long-run determination of real output, the price level, and the exchange rate. An increase in the quantity of money, from M_1 to M_2, causes aggregate demand to increase in panel (a). In the market for output, therefore, the long-run effects are a rise in the equilibrium price level, from P_1 to P_2, but no change in equilibrium real output. Panel (b) shows the relative-purchasing-power-parity condition, $P = k \times P^* \times S$, which indicates that the rise in the price level induces a proportionate long-run increase in the exchange rate, from S_1 to S_2.

equilibrium price level from P_1 at point A to P_2 at point E. It leaves the level of real output unaffected, at y_1.

As shown in panel (b), the increase in the price level resulting from the rise in the quantity of money shifts brings about a long-run rise in the exchange rate, from S_1 at point A to S_2 at point E. Thus, consistent with the various theories you learned about in previous chapters, the long-run effect of an expansionary monetary policy action must be a domestic currency depreciation.

Exchange-Rate Overshooting

The basic idea of the exchange-rate-overshooting concept is that the exchange rate is unlikely to rise smoothly to its long-run equilibrium value following a monetary expansion. During the adjustment process in which the price level initially fails to reach its long-run value, there will first be a significant depreciation of the domestic currency. That is, the exchange rate will first rise above the long-run equilibrium value of S_2 in Figure 14–4. In this sense, the exchange rate will overshoot its long-run equilibrium value. Then a domestic currency *appreciation* must occur as the price level increases the rest of the way to its long-run equilibrium value.

Moving from the Short Run to the Long Run To understand the exchange-rate-overshooting idea, consider Figure 14–5 on the following page, in which we assume that a small, open economy has perfect capital mobility. In contrast to Figure 14–4, this figure considers the full process by which adjustment to long-run equilibrium occurs when there is incomplete short-run adjustment in the price level.

As in Figure 14–4, panel (a) of Figure 14–5 shows an increase in aggregate demand. As displayed in panel (c), this rise in aggregate demand is generated by an increase in the quantity of money, which shifts the LM schedule rightward. At the new IS–LM equilibrium point B, there is now a balance-of-payments deficit, so the domestic currency begins to depreciate. The value of S, therefore, must rise in the short run. Because the price level does not immediately rise completely to its long-run equilibrium value, the result is a *real* domestic currency depreciation, which results in an increase in spending on domestic exports. The IS schedule shifts rightward from IS_1 to IS_2, and in the short run the economy tends toward point C in panel (c). This point corresponds to point C in panel (a), at which equilibrium real income at the initial price level begins to rise, so that the aggregate demand schedule shifts rightward.

In a short-run equilibrium, equilibrium real income rises toward y', and the equilibrium price level increases toward P'. A rise in the price level, however, causes real money balances to decline, so the LM schedule begins to shift back to the left once more in panel (c). This generates a movement along the *new IS* curve, IS_2, to an equilibrium point such as point D. At point D, there is a balance-of-payments surplus, so the domestic currency must *appreciate*. The value of the exchange rate must begin to fall somewhat, and a *real* domestic currency appreciation results that causes export spending to decline toward its original level. The IS curve thereby returns to its original position, and the final equilibrium is point E in panel (c), which arises at the long-run equilibrium real income level y_1 consistent with point E in panel (a).

Tracing the Adjustment of the Exchange Rate Now let's review what happens to the exchange rate during the adjustment process just described. Initially, it *rises* from S_1 to a value of S' as the domestic currency depreciates immediately in

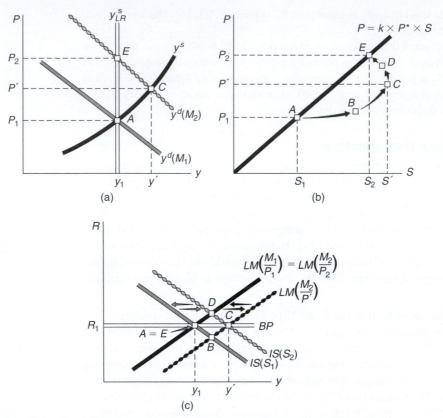

Figure 14–5 Short- and Long-Run Adjustments of the Exchange Rate to an Increase in the Money Stock
Points A in panels (a), (b), and (c) display initial long-run determination of real output, the price level, the exchange rate, and the nominal interest rate. An increase in the quantity of money, from M_1 to M_2, causes the LM schedule to shift rightward, which generates a balance-of-payments deficit at point B in panel (c). Because of short-term nominal rigidities, the price level does not immediately adjust to long-run equilibrium when aggregate demand rises in panel (a), so in panel (b) the exchange rate rises relatively more than the price level, thereby overshooting its long-run value. As the exchange rate continues to rise, to point C in panel (b), domestic exports increase, which causes the IS schedule to shift rightward. The short-run equilibrium positions for IS and LM and the market for real output are at points C in panels (a) and (c). As the price level completes its long-run adjustment to P_2, the LM schedule shifts back to point D in panel (c), resulting in a balance-of-payments surplus that induces a decline in the exchange rate to point D in panel (b). This appreciation causes the IS schedule to shift back to its original position as well. The final long-run equilibrium is attained at points E in all three panels.

response to the monetary expansion. At some point it must then *decline* to its long-run value of S_2. But in the long run, the final equilibrium value of the exchange rate, S_2, must exceed the starting value, S_1.

This implies that the exchange rate must follow the path including the points A, B, C, D, and E in panel (b). During the initial adjustments between points A and C in panels (a) and (c), the exchange rate jumps above the long-run value S_2, thereby rising from S_1 at point A in panel (b) toward the value S' at point C. Then as the price level eventually increases to its long-run equilibrium value between points C and E in panels (a) and (c), the exchange rate must decline somewhat in panel (b) before reaching its long-run equilibrium level, S_2.

Hence, because of the failure of the price level to adjust immediately to its long-run value following the monetary expansion, the exchange rate must initially bypass *its* long-run value. This is *exchange-rate overshooting*.

Implications of Exchange-Rate Overshooting This example shows how exchange-rate overshooting naturally arises when nominal wages and prices are sticky in the short run. There are two reasons that the exchange-rate overshooting concept is important. One is that for a number of nations with open economies, overshooting is likely to be a key aspect of the process of adjustment from the initial impact of a policy action that boosts aggregate demand to the ultimate, long-run effects. Even if the near-term inflationary consequences are muted, the exchange rate will tend to respond more markedly, which potentially can result in significant domestic currency depreciation almost immediately following the policy action.

More broadly, the overshooting analysis helps to explain why nominal exchange rates in most nations are typically much more variable than the prices of goods and services. It also indicates that short-term jumps in the exchange rate in response to variations in aggregate demand are likely to be especially pronounced in countries with greater nominal wage and price stickiness. In these countries, therefore, the overshooting analysis helps to explain why the volatility of exchange rates is several orders of magnitude greater than the variability of the price level.

 Fundamental ISSUES

#2 What is exchange-rate overshooting, and why might it occur?

Exchange-rate overshooting occurs when a policy action or other event that changes aggregate demand causes a short-run overadjustment in the exchange rate relative to the long-run adjustment that will take place. A key factor that can explain exchange-rate overshooting is sluggish adjustment of a nation's price level as a result of short-run stickiness in nominal wages and prices. For instance, the direct effect of a rise in domestic aggregate demand is a home currency depreciation. But if the price level rises only part of the way to its long-run value following the increase in aggregate demand, then a continuing upward adjustment of the price level following an initial currency depreciation must ultimately result in an appreciation of the home currency. This means that the short-run depreciation has to be greater than the long-run depreciation.

OPENNESS AND THE OUTPUT–INFLATION RELATIONSHIP—HOW GLOBALIZATION ALTERS THE EFFECTS OF POLICIES

Analysis of exchange-rate overshooting indicates that the responsiveness of real output to the price level is the fundamental determinant of whether a demand-induced increase in the price level has the potential to boost a nation's output in the short run. If real output is relatively insensitive to changes in the price level, then a short-run increase in national output can be generated via an expansion of aggregate demand only at the cost of a relatively significant increase in the price level—a relatively large inflationary boost. If the real output responds relatively strongly to changes in the price level, then an identical increase in output can be achieved at the cost of a more modest overall economy-wide increase in the prices of goods and services.

In the basic aggregate demand–aggregate supply model, the responsiveness of output to the price level is governed by the shape of the aggregate supply schedule. This shape depends largely on the extent of economy-wide nominal wage rigidity, which is determined by the willingness of workers and firms to enter in contracts that fix nominal wages for lengthy intervals. Economists have determined that a number of important factors likely influence this decision. Table 14–1 summarizes several of these factors and explains how they influence the willingness of workers to enter into nominal wage contracts with firms. As indicated in the table, higher and more variable inflation, more stable firm and industry output, and a lower degree of central bank independence all tend to reduce the incentive to enter into contracts that fix nominal wages. In the basic aggregate demand–aggregate supply framework, therefore, the result is that nominal wages are more market-responsive. This steepens the aggregate supply schedule and reduces the sensitivity of aggregate real output to changes in the price level.

The *openness* of a nation's economy is another potentially important factor that affects the responsiveness of a nation's real output to changes in the price level. As economies become more globalized, this factor assumes greater importance. From a theoretical standpoint, however, it turns out that openness can have conflicting effects on the output–inflation relationship.

How Increased Openness Can Make Output Less Responsive to Inflation

When economists first began to think about how greater openness might affect the sensitivity of real output to changes in the price level, they focused on the basic aggregate demand–aggregate supply framework. Within this approach, two alternative perspectives lead to the conclusion that nations with more open economies could have steeper aggregate supply schedules and, consequently, a reduced responsiveness of real output to inflation. (Determining how openness affects the output–inflation relationship in the real world requires a measure of openness; a way to measure openness is discussed in *Policy Notebook: Measuring Openness*.)

Table 14–1

Key Factors Affecting the Willingness of Workers to Establish Nominal Wage Contracts

Four fundamental determinants of the desirability of utilizing nominal wage contracts are the level of inflation, the volatility of aggregate demand and aggregate supply, the variability of firm- or industry-specific demand and supply, and the degree of central bank independence.

Level of inflation	A higher inflation rate reduces the incentive to set fixed nominal wages, because the real value of wages will decline during the contract interval.
Variability of aggregate demand and aggregate supply	Greater volatility of either aggregate demand or aggregate supply increases inflation variability, creating volatility in real value of wages, thereby reducing the incentive to set fixed contract wages.
Variability of firm- or industry-specific demand and supply	If demand for a firm's or industry's output or the firm's or industry's supply of output is relatively stable, then letting firm- or industry-level market conditions determine wages is preferable to establishing fixed contract wages.
The degree of central bank independence	Less central bank independence raises average inflation and thereby reduces the incentive to fix nominal wages.

POLICY Notebook

Measuring Openness

How do economists decide just how "open" a nation's economy is to international flows of goods and services? The most commonly used measures in most studies are the ratio of a nation's imports to its GDP and the ratio of the sum of its imports and exports to its GDP.

For some nations, measures of openness can vary considerably from year to year. Thus, Figure 14–6 displays an *average* value of the latter measure of openness for selected nations between the mid-1980s and the late 2000s. Using this measure of openness, among this set of nations, Singapore, Malta, Malaysia, and Belgium have the open economies. The United States, India, Sudan, and Bangladesh have economies that are least open.

For Critical Analysis

Can you think of another way of trying to measure the openness of a nation's economy?

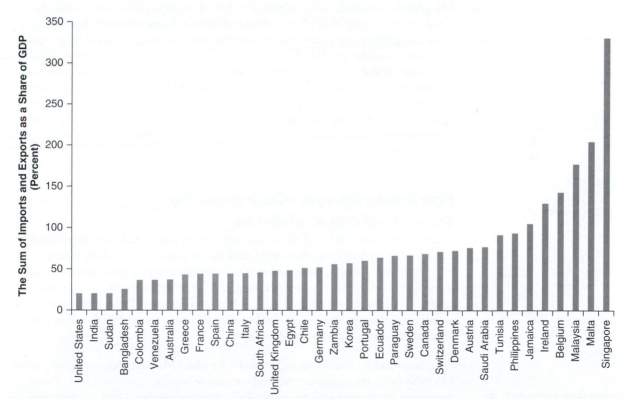

Figure 14–6   The Sum of Imports and Exports as a Share of Total Expenditures in Selected Nations

Among this set of industrialized nations, using imports as a share of total expenditures as a measure of openness indicates that Singapore is most open and that the United States is least open.

Source: World Bank, *World Development Indicators.*

Partially Indexed Wage Contracts To understand one way that greater openness can make real output less sensitive to changes in the price level, let's consider an example. In Japan, imports account for only a little over 15 percent of total national expenditures, but imports make up more than 75 percent of Luxembourg's aggregate expenditures. It seems likely that a larger portion of workers in Luxembourg than in Japan will desire for their nominal wages to be more responsive to a domestic depreciation that raises the prices of imported goods and services and thereby boosts the consumer price index.

One way to ensure that nominal wages are more likely to rise in tandem with a depreciation of the domestic currency is to increase the degree to which wages are indexed to changes in the CPI. As you learned in Chapter 13, increased indexation of nominal wages makes equilibrium employment less sensitive to changes in the price level, which steepens the aggregate supply schedule. Thus, one possible effect of increased openness is to raise the degree of wage indexation, which reduces the responsiveness of a nation's real output to changes in the price level.

Greater Openness and Imported Inputs Firms in some nations import a large portion of the inputs, such as raw materials, that they require to produce final goods and services. In some countries, such as parts of Europe where domestic population growth rates recently have been very low, or even negative, many firms rely considerably on imported labor. For such industries, home currency depreciations cause domestic output prices and input costs—raw materials prices or wages paid to foreign workers—to rise in tandem.

Suppose that in such countries, greater openness results in an enlargement in the number of firms and industries utilizing imported inputs. As a consequence, proportionate changes in the price level and in input prices will tend to be more nearly equalized in the short run. The result will be a steepening of the aggregate supply curve. Hence, greater openness may cause real output to be less sensitive to inflation.

How Greater Openness Can Increase the Sensitivity of Output to Inflation

Each of the world's national economies has its own unique features. Some have considerable competition across most markets for goods and services, whereas others have very limited competition in any product markets. Several nations have monetary policymakers that are independent of other branches of government; in other nations, monetary policymaking is highly politicized. These significant cross-country differences, it turns out, can have considerable bearing on the short-run relationships between output and inflation.

imperfect competition
A market environment in which there are only a few firms, each of which individually can influence the market price by varying its production.

Openness and Competition in Domestic Product Markets An important problem with using the aggregate demand–aggregate supply framework to evaluate the effects of openness on the output–inflation relationship is that the theory of aggregate supply presumes that firms sell their products in perfectly competitive markets. Many nations restrain competition through elaborate systems of domestic regulations and protect firms from foreign competition using trade barriers. In a number of these countries, therefore, *imperfect competition* exists in a significant portion of the markets for goods and services. This means that there are only a few producers, each of which can, by varying its output, individually influence—or, in the case in which a single firm is a monopoly producer, determine—the market price. (A common factor contributing to restraints on competition in a nation's industries is extensive governmental regulation of product markets; see *Management Notebook: Which Nations' Industries Face the Most Extensive Regulations?*)

MANAGEMENT Notebook

Which Nations' Industries Face the Most Extensive Regulations?

Economists commonly argue that governments imposing extensive regulations boost costs faced by firms contemplating entering industries. Raising entry costs via regulations, they suggest, reduces the degree of domestic competition.

Figure 14–7 displays an index measure of the extensiveness of product-market regulations for a number of countries. This measure indicates that among this set of nations, product-market regulations are most extensive in Poland, Turkey, and Mexico. They are least widespread in Austria, the United Kingdom, and Iceland.

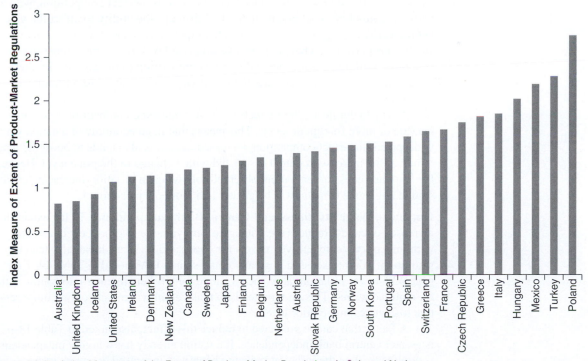

Figure 14–7   Index Measures of the Extent of Product-Market Regulations in Selected Nations

This figure displays an index measure of the extensiveness of governmental regulations in domestic markets for goods and services in various nations. Among this set of countries, the measure indicates that products are least widespread in Austria and most extensive in Poland.

Source: Organization for Economic Cooperation and Development.

For Critical Analysis

What are some possible ways that various forms of regulation of product markets—health and safety regulations, environmental regulations, advertising regulations, product quality regulations, and the like—might raise the costs of entering an industry?

In a country with widespread imperfect competition, there are few close substitutes for each firm's product. Each firm has considerable ability to vary the price of its product in response to a change in consumer demand. Thus, a rise in total consumption, brought about perhaps by an expansionary monetary policy action that raises demand in each market throughout the economy, generates a significant increase in price at each imperfectly competitive firm. Associated increases in firm production, however, tend to be more muted. A relatively small rise in aggregate output is thereby associated with a relatively large proportionate increase in the price level in a nation with widespread imperfect competition.

Suppose that the nation's government were to adopt policies promoting the entry of new firms into these imperfectly competitive markets. The range of substitute products available to consumers would increase. Consequently, the quantity of each firm's output demanded would be more sensitive to a change in price, so an increase in desired consumption at each firm would be associated with a smaller price increase. That is, with more firms competing in the marketplace, each firm's *pricing power* is reduced. (In the limit of perfect competition, with a very large number of sellers, no individual firm has the ability to affect the market price.) Thus, a given rise in aggregate output is associated with a relatively smaller proportionate change in the overall price level in a more competitive economy. With more widespread domestic competition in the nation's markets for goods and services, therefore, the sensitivity of real output to inflation will be greater.

A way to duplicate these effects of greater domestic competition is to allow the sale of more foreign products. This means that in an economy of a nation with widespread imperfect competition, increased openness also tends to boost the magnitude of the increase in output associated with a change in the price level. Hence, the responsiveness in real output observed following an inflation-increasing expansion in aggregate demand will be greater in a more open economy.

Openness, Wage Stickiness, and Central Bank Independence To the extent that increased openness reduces the pricing power available to producers in a country with imperfectly competitive markets for goods and services, it can also tend to restrain inflation (discussed in greater detail shortly). As noted in Table 14–1 on page 428, lower inflation raises the incentive for workers to enter into contracts that fix nominal wages. This, in turn, tends to make employment and output more sensitive to changes in the price level.

A factor that can be predicted to reduce this effect, also noted in Table 14–1, is greater central bank independence. If a nation already has a highly independent central bank, then the inflation-reducing benefit of increased openness is more subdued. So the effect of openness on the output–inflation relationship operating through the incentive to establish fixed-wage contracts is most likely to apply to nations with less independent central banks.

Evidence on Openness and the Output–Inflation Relationship

The basic aggregate demand–aggregate supply framework indicates that greater openness should, if a nation's product markets are highly competitive, lead to greater wage indexation and more close alignment of changes in the costs of imported inputs with changes in the overall level of prices of produced goods and services. Both of these effects of greater openness would tend to make aggregate real output *less* responsive to inflation. At the same time, however, in nations with imperfectly competitive product markets, increased openness could reduce the extent to which firms can boost their prices. In addition, to the extent that greater openness reduces inflation, the incentive to establish nominal wage contracts would rise (although greater central bank independence would tend to diminish this effect). These two effects of increased openness would tend to make aggregate real output *more* responsive to inflation.

This leads to two conclusions. First, the net effect of increased openness on the short-run output–inflation relationship is likely to vary from country to country. In a nation with highly competitive markets for goods and services and in which firms utilize a number of imported inputs, it is more likely that greater openness will make real output less sensitive to variations in the price level, so that a policy-induced expansion in aggregate demand will boost output by a smaller amount in the short run. In a different country in which product markets are more imperfectly competitive and in which inflation is significantly reduced by greater openness, a rise in the degree of openness will make real output more responsive to price-level changes. Then an expansionary policy action will generate a larger short-run output increase.

Responsiveness of Output to Inflation: International Evidence Figure 14–8 plots an index measure of output responsiveness to inflation in relation to the sum of imports and exports as a percentage of GDP for more than 90 nations over a period stretching from the mid-1980s through the mid-2000s. As indicated, the trend relationship among these points slopes upward, suggesting a potentially positive association between openness and the responsiveness of output to inflation.

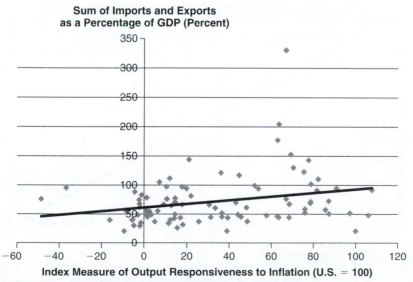

Sum of Imports and Exports as a Percentage of GDP (Percent)

Index Measure of Output Responsiveness to Inflation (U.S. = 100)

Figure 14–8

Openness and an Index Measure of Output Responsiveness to Inflation

This figure plots the 1985–2004 average value of CPI inflation against the average value of the same period of an index measure of the responsiveness of output to inflation for more than 90 nations. The result is an apparently slightly upward-sloping relationship.

Source: Harald Badinger, "Globalization, the Output-Inflation Tradeoff, and Inflation," *European Economic Review* 53(8) (November 2009): 888–907.

Whether or not there is *actually* a positive relationship between openness and the sensitivity of output to changes in inflation remains an unsettled question, however. Jonathan Temple of the University of Bristol first explored the relationship between openness and the output–inflation relationship by studying data for a set of developed nations early in the 2000s. He concluded that the relationship did not appear to be very robust from a statistical standpoint. As our earlier discussion indicated, the problem that economists face in evaluating how openness affects the responsiveness of output to inflation is that national economic structures can differ considerably. This makes it hard to assess the true nature of the relationship between openness and the responsiveness of output to inflation without taking into account factors specific to each individual nation.

Central Bank Independence, Openness, and the Output–Inflation Relationship
To see the important effects that country-specific factors can have on the relationship between openness and the output–inflation relationship, recall that one of these factors is the independence of a nation's central bank. In countries that already have independent central banks, inflation is relatively low, which results in workers and firms establishing more fixed-wage contracts, thereby increasing the responsiveness of output to changes in the inflation rate. Hence, a greater level of central bank independence detracts from the extent to which greater openness can boost the sensitivity of output to inflation.

Figure 14–9 depicts how estimates of the net effect of openness on the sensitivity of output to inflation tend to be positive or negative, depending on the level of central bank independence. In nations that in past years have had the least independent central banks, such as New Zealand, Sweden, and Finland, there has been more latitude for greater openness to restrain inflation, induce establishment of more nominal wage contracts, and thereby make output more sensitive to price changes. Hence, there is a net positive effect of openness on the responsiveness of

Figure 14–9

Central Bank Independence and the Net Effect of Openness on the Output–Inflation Relationship

In nations that have had relatively independent central banks, greater openness has tended to reduce the sensitivity of output to inflation. Increased openness has been associated with a greater responsiveness of output to inflation in countries with less central bank independence.

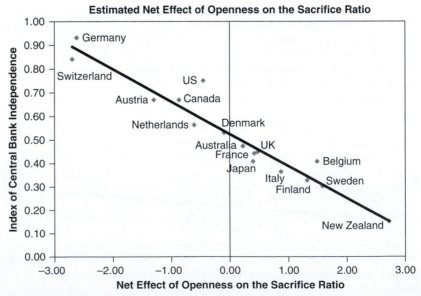

Source: Estimates developed by the authors and Farrokh Nourzad of Marquette University.

output to inflation. Greater central bank independence in nations such as Germany, Switzerland, and the United States has constrained the extent to which increased openness can have a positive effect on a measure of the responsiveness of output to inflation called the "sacrifice ratio," so in these nations the estimated net effect of openness is negative.

Thus, for a nation with a very independent central bank, highly competitive markets for goods and services, and indexed wages or speedily adjusting prices of raw materials imported in relatively large volumes, greater openness generated by globalization will tend to *reduce* the inflation responsiveness of output. In contrast, increased openness is more likely to *increase* the sensitivity of output to inflation in a country with relatively less independent central banks, more imperfectly competitive product markets, and sticky nominal wages.

Additional Evidence Regarding the Interaction between Openness and the Output–Inflation Relationship In addition to the degree of central bank independence, another factor that appears to influence the association between openness and the sensitivity of output to inflation is exchange-rate flexibility. For instance, Christopher Bowdler of the University of Oxford suggests that there is more likely to be a positive effect of openness on the responsiveness of output to inflation when exchange rates are less flexible. Bowdler has provided support for this hypothesis by comparing the measured impact of greater openness on the sensitivity of output to inflation before 1980, when there was considerable worldwide exchange-rate inflexibility, and since 1980, when exchange rates have been much more flexible.

Nevertheless, other recent evidence appears to support a generally positive relationship between openness to trade and the output-inflation relationship. For instance, Harald Badinger of the Vienna University of Economics has examined data on openness, output, and inflation for the nations displayed in Figure 14–8. After controlling for a number of factors, his conclusion is that the upward-sloping relationship depicted in the figure holds true on net.

To sum up, the short-run sensitivity of real output to price-level changes determines the effectiveness of domestic policies aimed at achieving national policy objectives. The greater degree of openness that has been accompanying the trend toward increased globalization likely is influencing the inflation responsiveness of output in many of the world's nations. Increased openness can exert several different, and potentially conflicting, effects on the output–inflation relationship. At present, most evidence from study of data from a variety of nations suggests that a greater degree of openness makes output more sensitive to inflation, but research on this issue is continuing.

Fundamental ISSUES

#3 Why does increased openness of a nation's economy have an uncertain net effect on the responsiveness of output to changes in the price level?

The immediate effects of policy actions that alter aggregate demand for a nation's total output of goods and services depend on the sensitivity of output to a change in the price level, which, in turn, can be influenced by increased openness of the nation's economy to international trade. Greater openness tends to reduce the sensitivity of output to a change in the price level in countries with central banks that are very independent, that have highly competitive product markets, and that have indexed wages or rapidly adjusting prices of imported raw materials. Increased openness tends to raise the inflation responsiveness of output in nations with relatively less independent central banks, imperfectly competitive markets for goods and services, and sticky nominal wages. These characteristics often vary across nations, so the net effect of openness on the inflation sensitivity of an individual country's output can be either positive or negative.

OPENNESS AND INFLATION

In the preceding evaluation of how openness affects the responsiveness of output to changes in the price level, we noted that increased openness may have a tendency to reduce inflation. Is there an inverse relationship between openness and inflation? If so, why might greater openness restrain inflation?

The Global Openness–Inflation Relationship

The net effect of openness on the output–inflation relationship appears to be positive in some countries but negative in others. This is why the evidence concerning the output–inflation relationship is so mixed when viewed across the world's nations.

In contrast, examination of openness and inflation across the world's nations indicates an unambiguous inverse relationship, as you can see in Figure 14–10, which plots average sums of exports and imports as shares of national expenditures in relation to average annual inflation rates since 1985 for more than 100 nations. This apparent relationship was first verified in a more detailed statistical analysis conducted by David Romer of the University of California at Berkeley. From a global perspective, increased openness appears to be associated with lower inflation. (The degree of openness to international trade may also influence a nation's potential exposures to abrupt drops in capital inflows; see *Policy Notebook: Is a More Open Economy More or Less Prone to "Sudden Stops"?*)

Figure 14–10

The Relationship between Openness and Inflation for a Large Set of Nations

This figure shows that there is an apparent inverse relationship between openness and inflation for more than 100 developed and less developed nations.

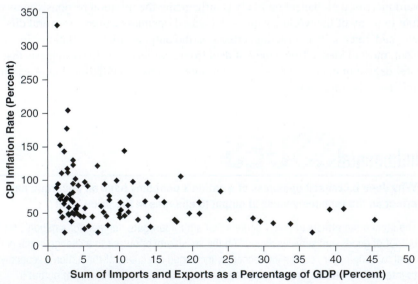

Source: World Bank, *World Development Indicators.*

POLICY Notebook

Is a More Open Economy More or Less Prone to "Sudden Stops"?

International economists refer to a situation in which a nation experiences an abrupt halt to capital inflows as a *sudden stop*. These sorts of sudden-stop episodes are infrequent, but when sudden stops do occur, they typically accompany financial or currency crises and sharp declines in real output.

Some observers have suggested that countries with economies more open to international trade are particularly vulnerable to sudden stops, perhaps because a weakening in the volume of exports in more open countries may be more likely trigger a falloff in capital inflows. Other observers make the contrary argument that a greater degree of openness to international trade makes nations less susceptible to sudden stops, because creditors believe that the ability of open economies to earn income from their trade with other nations makes them more likely to repay their debts.

Eduardo Cavallo of the Inter-American Bank and Jeffrey Frankel of Harvard University study the experiences of 141 nations between the 1970s and the 2000s and identify 85 sudden-stop episodes. They find that increasing the ratio of international trade to GDP by 10 percentage points—which they point out would be like shifting from Argentina's currently low trade-to-GDP ratio to Australia's much higher ratio—generates a nearly 40 percent *reduction* in the probability of experiencing a sudden stop. Thus, Cavallo and Frankel conclude that greater openness to trade makes nations *less* vulnerable to sudden stops.

For Critical Analysis

Why do you suppose that declines in real GDP so often accompany sudden stops?

sudden stop
An immediate end to capital inflows to a nation.

There are two key reasons greater openness might reduce inflation. One, suggested by Romer, is that in countries in which greater openness makes output less sensitive to changes in the price level, there is a lower potential output gain from any given boost in inflation. As you learned in Chapter 13, this would tend to restrain the inflationary tendencies of central banks that would like to raise output toward the capacity level. The second reason, which is more applicable to nations with imperfectly competitive product markets, is that increased openness exposes domestic firms to more competition, thereby reducing their ability to set prices above perfectly competitive levels. Thus, the overall price level is less responsive to central bank policies in a more open economy, which can tend to reduce the temptation for central banks to engage in expansionary policy actions intended to induce output increases via higher prices.

Just How Strong Is the Openness–Inflation Relationship?

It is sometimes misleading to assume that an apparent cross-country relationship actually reflects structural factors arising within each and every nation. This is also true of the relationship between openness and inflation displayed in Figure 14–10, which masks important differences across countries.

Differences in How Openness and Inflation Relate in Developed versus Less Developed Nations Romer's study of the openness–inflation relationship was completed in the early 1990s. Since then, the global relationship has weakened

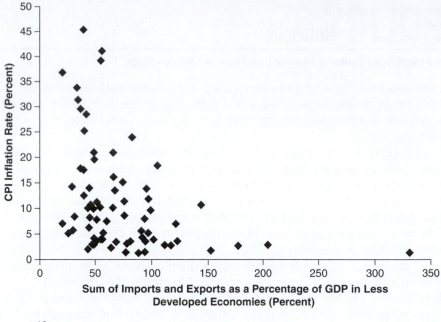

Figure 14–11

Openness and Inflation in Developed and Less Developed Economies, 1985–Present

Panel (a) shows that for years since 1985, there is barely a hint of a negative relationship between openness and inflation in the world's most developed economies. Panel (b) shows that there still generally appears to be an inverse relationship for less developed economies, however.

Source: International Monetary Fund, *International Financial Statistics.*

somewhat. The reason for this can be seen in Figure 14–11. Panel (a) shows that the relationship between openness and inflation in developed nations is very weak. As you can see in panel (b), however, the negative relationship between openness and inflation for less developed nations is as strong as the overall relationship between countries that is shown in Figure 14–10.

One possible reason openness might affect developed and less developed countries differently is that in developed nations, central banks tend to be much more insulated from political pressures. Hence, central banks in developed nations already have considerable capability to rein in inflation, which leaves less scope for increased openness to further reduce the inflation rate. In contrast, in less developed nations with weaker policymaking institutions, the competition-enhancing effects of increased openness can have more significant effects on inflation.

Accounting for Cross-Country Differences in the Impacts of Globalization
Looking within individual developed and developing nations, the relationship between openness and inflation has exhibited varying patterns. As the extent of globalization has risen over time, average inflation has risen in some nations and fallen in others. In the case of the United States, a recent study by Laurence Ball of Johns Hopkins University concludes that increased openness has had no effect on inflation.

Indeed, there are a number of factors that likely determine the impact that an increased degree of openness has on a given nation's inflation rate, such as the extent to which workers' wages are fixed for intervals of time and the degree of competition involving domestic firms within home industries. If wages are already highly flexible and adjust quickly to price changes, there is less likelihood that output will respond to inflation in any event, and if a nation's markets for goods and services are already highly competitive, increased openness to trade with foreign firms is less likely to help hold down price increases.

Another factor that influences the impact of globalization on inflation across countries is the structure of nations' income-tax systems. In a more *progressive* income-tax system in which the share of income transmitted to the government rises as income increases, it turns out that output is less sensitive to price-level changes, which reduces the incentive for policymakers to try to boost output via inflationary policies. Thus, increased income-tax progressivity reduces inflationary tendencies within an economy and thereby leaves less scope for increased openness to further reduce inflation.

Alongside central bank independence, these factors help to explain why increased openness has less of an impact on inflation in developed nations, in which these factors tend to be observed more often than in less developed nations. Variations in these factors across all nations also help to explain why we witness differing responses of inflation to globalization among the world's nations.

 Fundamental ISSUES

#4 Is there an inverse relationship between openness and inflation?

Cross-country comparisons indicate an inverse relationship between openness and inflation. This relationship could stem from a tendency for greater openness to make output less sensitive to inflation, thereby giving central banks less incentive to engage in discretionary policies that boost the inflation rate. Alternatively, in countries with imperfectly competitive product markets, increased openness could reduce the ability of domestic firms to raise prices, thereby dampening increases in the economy-wide price level. A negative relationship between openness and inflation is not as clear-cut in developed nations, however. Furthermore, the openness–inflation relationship can vary considerably from country to country.

NEW OPEN ECONOMY MACROECONOMICS AND ITS POLICY IMPLICATIONS

The responsiveness of output to inflation has long been a concern within the field of *macroeconomics*, which refers broadly to the study of a nation's total economic activity. Economists who seek to apply concepts from macroeconomics to better

open economy macroeconomics

The study of factors affecting the overall economic performance of a country that permits cross-border exchanges of goods, services, and financial assets.

understand open economies engage in *open economy macroeconomics,* or the study of factors that influence the aggregate economic performance of a nation that is open to international trade in goods, services, and financial assets. Naturally, as the trend toward increased globalization has continued, the distinction between macroeconomics and open economy macroeconomics has narrowed.

The differing economic effects of globalization across countries has posed problems for economists, because past theories of open economy macroeconomics have often failed to account for factors such as differing degrees of wage rigidity, price-adjustment speed, and product-market competition. In recent years some economists have responded by seeking to develop a new approach to analyzing policymaking in open economies, called the *new open economy macroeconomics.* This approach explicitly considers the interplay among nominal wage stickiness, sluggish price adjustment, and imperfect competition, typically within theories that seek to explain choices nations' residents make over time.

new open economy macroeconomics

An approach to open economy macroeconomics that focuses on how nominal wage stickiness, sluggish price adjustment, and imperfect competition affect the transmission of policy actions, often in the context of theories aimed at predicting decisions that nations' residents make over time.

Features of the New Open Economy Macroeconomics

There are three key elements of the new open economy macroeconomics approach to analyzing national policymaking. First, this approach spotlights the role of sticky product prices. Second, it takes into account imperfect competition in markets for goods and services. Third, it evaluates how a country's residents make choices affecting employment, output, and international trade and capital flows from month to month and from year to year.

price inertia

Slow short-term adjustment of a nation's price level to variations in factors affecting aggregate demand and overall business production costs.

Sources of Price Stickiness Within the new open economy macroeconomics perspective, economic policies can have short-run effects on a nation's output of goods and services, in part because product prices adjust slowly. To explain overall *price inertia*, or short-term sluggishness in adjustment of a nation's price level, proponents of the new open economy macroeconomics have developed theories in which price stickiness arises from the profit-maximizing decisions of firms.

menu costs

Small but nontrivial costs that firms incur when they alter product prices.

In these theories, short-term price stickiness typically arises from *menu costs,* which are small but measurable costs that firms must incur when they change the prices that they charge their customers. These costs could take the form of expenses entailed in printing new price tags, menus, and catalogs. They also could include costs incurred in bringing together firm managers for meetings on price changes or in renegotiating business deals with customers. (In recent years, economists have sought to investigate whether, as commonly assumed in theories associated with the new open economy macroeconomics, prices are indeed sticky; see *Management Notebook: Are Product Prices Really Sticky?*)

MANAGEMENT Notebook

Are Product Prices Really Sticky?

To consider the question of whether prices are sticky, many economists have tried to *infer* how slowly prices adjust within nations based on observed changes in the nations' overall price levels. They usually do so using a theory suggesting that the key determinants of price changes are the inflation-adjusted marginal costs incurred by firms and the public's expectation of future prices. Applying methods suggested by this theory to the rate of change in the GDP deflator or consumer price index has indicated that, on average, prices change only about every eighteen months in the United Sates and even less often in European nations.

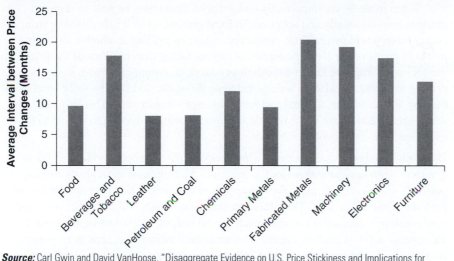

Figure 14–12

Estimated Intervals between Price Changes in Selected Industries

Examination of producer price indexes indicates that in some industries, inferred periods between price changes are 18 months or longer. In other industries, however, prices appear to adjust more than twice as quickly.

Source: Carl Gwin and David VanHoose, "Disaggregate Evidence on U.S. Price Stickiness and Implications for Sticky-Price Macro Models," *Economic Inquiry 46* (October 2008): 561–575.

When a similar approach is applied to a measure of the level of prices that firms actually charge—presumably the prices that sticky-price theories suggest are slow to adjust—called the All-Commodities Producer Price Index, the estimated average period between U.S. price changes drops to not much more than nine months. Additionally, adjusting for structural changes in inflation-adjusted marginal costs that have occurred over time reduces this estimate to six months or even less.

Applying this commonly used technique for measuring price stickiness to *industry*-level producer price indexes reveals that price adjustment times turn out to vary considerably across selected U.S. industries, as shown in Figure 14–12. The prices charged by some industries do appear to take at least eighteen months to change, but other prices adjust much more rapidly. Thus, although there is evidence of considerable price stickiness in some industries, prices of many goods appear to be relatively flexible.

For Critical Analysis

Why might the relative shares of real GDP produced by industries with differing degrees of price stickiness help in determining whether the idea of sticky prices is relevant to a nation's entire economy?

Imperfect Competition To understand why profit-maximizing firms might fail to adjust their prices to long-run equilibrium levels in the short run, the new open economy macroeconomics presumes that firms are imperfectly competitive. Thus, this approach departs from the aggregate supply analysis in Chapter 13 that implicitly assumed perfectly competitive markets for goods and services with many buyers and sellers, free entry into and exit from markets, and indistinguishable products.

Instead, the new open economy macroeconomics applies to situations in which economies are dominated by markets with limited numbers of buyers or sellers, in which there may be barriers to market entry or exit, or in which firm products or factors of services may be differentiated. Such market environments, proponents of this approach contend, are commonplace throughout much of the world.

pricing to market
A situation in which imperfectly competitive firms selling products abroad set prices in terms of the local currencies of purchasers located in the countries where the items are sold.

dynamic open economy theories
Economic models intended to explain how variables such as real output, employment, the price level, the current account, and the capital account interact and vary over time.

When markets are imperfectly competitive, firms may be able to segment markets internationally and set prices in local currencies at levels differing from a competitive world price. Thus, producers engage in ***pricing to market,*** or setting prices in terms of the local currencies of buyers rather than in terms of the prices in the locations where firms produce their products. In conjunction with sticky prices, pricing to market breaks the linkage between domestic and foreign price levels and thereby allows for the nominal and real exchange rates to vary. This helps explain why exchange rates are more volatile than prices without having to appeal to the exchange-rate-overshooting rationale.

Dynamic Analysis Much of the new open economy macroeconomics considers ***dynamic open economy theories*** that take into account how individuals and imperfectly competitive firms make consumption and production decisions from one period of time to the next. Thus, this approach commonly offers predictions about how a nation's economic variables such as real output, employment, the price level, the current account, and the capital account should adjust over time in response to policy actions and other factors that influence aggregate demand or firms' production costs.

There are three fundamental advantages of this emphasis on dynamic decision making by individuals and firms. First, this type of analysis rules out consideration of situations in which consumers, workers, or firms make decisions at any point that turn out to be inconsistent with their long-term consumption and production capabilities. Second, although short-term nominal wage and price stickiness explain how policies exert short-run effects on real output and employment, a typical property of these frameworks is that output and employment equal the values predicted by the basic long-run theory of aggregate supply discussed in Chapter 13. Third, the dynamic theories suggest likely time paths of responses of variables—the current account, the exchange rate, employment, real output, domestic output prices and consumer prices, and the like—to changes in policy parameters or to economic shocks. In principle, this offers numerous predictions that can be evaluated using actual data from countries around the world.

Policy Implications of the New Open Economy Macroeconomics

The reason that price stickiness is important in many theories employed by proponents of the new open economy macroeconomics is that failure of the price level to reach its long-run equilibrium value in the near term causes the real exchange rate to diverge as well from its long-run equilibrium value. This means that economic policies that influence aggregate demand can affect the terms of trade faced by individuals and firms, which respond by making short-term changes in their consumption and production plans. Thus, in an environment of sluggish prices, policymakers can exert output and employment effects in the short run.

Welfare Evaluations This provides a motivation for policies that actively "manage" aggregate demand, because a change in aggregate demand at a national level can move domestic output toward its efficient level. In a global economy with international trade, this implies that the active pursuit of such policies by national policymakers might be able to improve both domestic *and* global welfare. Indeed, because the new open economy macroeconomics approach seeks to develop theories based on the choices made by individuals and firms, it allows for direct predictions about whether policy actions really *do* raise social welfare.

Still a Long Way to Go The new open economy macroeconomics shows promise of allowing economists to resolve issues relating to the effects of globalization on domestic policymaking, including the effects of globalization on the output–inflation relationship and national inflation rates. In addition, economists have used this approach to develop a number of interesting theories aimed at predicting how equilibrium exchange rates may be influenced by incomplete exchange-rate pass-through effects resulting from pricing to market.

At present, however, the new open economy macroeconomics has some hurdles to overcome. For example, so far most theories using this approach assume that people in all nations are *representative agents*. Thus, these theories assume that all individuals at home and abroad have the same tastes concerning which goods and services to consume, the same risk preferences, and the same views about the types of market structures and policy institutions to establish. Proponents of the new theories point out that their lack of consideration of such factors in spite of considerable cultural and legal diversity is also a common failing in more traditional open economy theories. Critics argue that this is a more glaring problem in the new theories because a key rationale for the new open economy macroeconomics has been to explain how individual responses to policy actions influence the policies' effects.

A second hurdle for the new open economy macroeconomics lies in the difficulties caused by competing interests. Proponents of the new open economy macroeconomics have developed intricate theories of how representative agents maximize their own welfare when confronted with policy changes, but so far they have not taken discretionary policymaking (see Chapter 13) into account in their theories. As a consequence, the approach is currently inconsistent: Individuals and firms act in their own best interest, but policymakers do not. Indeed, many of the theories assume that policy actions are essentially random events.

Finally, there are many more theories than there is evidence regarding the relevance of the new open economy macroeconomics. Paul Bergin of the University of California at Davis has found some evidence that the basic new open economy macroeconomics approach may better explain movements in output and prices than previous theories of open economies. At the same time, however, he finds the approach is less successful in explaining variations in exchange rates. It remains to be seen, therefore, whether the new open economy macroeconomics ultimately will be useful as a guide to policymaking in increasingly globalized economies.

Fundamental ISSUES

#5 What is the new open economy macroeconomics?

The new open economy macroeconomics is an approach to understanding the transmission of policy actions in open economies that emphasizes the roles of nominal wage stickiness, sluggish price adjustment, and imperfect competition, typically within theories aimed at predicting decisions that nations' residents make over time. A suggested advantage of the new open economy macroeconomics is its potential ability to explain how policy actions may improve the welfare of the residents of a nation with an open economy. Another is that theories in this vein may be able to provide ways to gauge welfare improvements from policy actions. Possible pitfalls may result from the inability of representative-agent theories to take into account preference differences between residents of different nations, the failure of the new theories to recognize incentives that policymakers face, and current uncertainties about the real-world relevance of these theories.

Chapter SUMMARY

1. **The Policy Assignment Problem:** This is the issue of deciding whether monetary or fiscal policymakers should seek to achieve internal or external policy goals. Failure to match each policymaker with an appropriate ultimate objective can cause the efforts of governments and central banks to work at cross-purposes, and both policymakers will fail to attain their ultimate economic objectives.

2. **Exchange Rate Overshooting and Why It Might Occur:** Exchange rate overshooting refers to a short-run overadjustment in the exchange rate, relative to its long-run value, following a policy action or other event that alters aggregate demand. Sluggish adjustment of a nation's price level as a result of short-run stickiness in nominal wages and prices can explain why exchange-rate overshooting might occur. In the case of an increase in aggregate demand, the immediate effect is a domestic currency depreciation. If the price level moves only partway to its higher long-run value in the short run, then the ongoing rise in the price level following the initial currency depreciation will eventually result in a domestic currency appreciation. In order for these long-run adjustments in the price level and the exchange rate to occur, the amount of the initial depreciation must be larger than will take place in the long run.

3. **Why Increased Openness of a Nation's Economy Has Uncertain Effects on the Responsiveness of Output to Changes in the Price Level:** The output effects of policy actions that influence aggregate demand depend on how responsive a nation's output is to a change in the price level. Increased openness to international trade tends to lower the sensitivity of output to a change in the price level in nations with very independent central banks, highly competitive markets for goods and services, and indexed wages or rapidly adjusting prices of imported raw materials. Greater openness tends to increase the responsiveness of output to changes in the price level in countries with relatively less independent central banks, imperfectly competitive product markets, and sticky nominal wages. Because these features typically differ from country to country, the net effect of openness on the inflation sensitivity of any given nation's output can be either positive or negative.

4. **The Relationship between Openness and Inflation:** Examination of openness and inflation in numerous countries appears to indicate an inverse relationship between the two variables. One possible explanation offered for this relationship is that if greater openness makes output less sensitive to inflation, there are lessened incentives for central banks to engage in discretionary policies that bring about higher inflation. Another proposed explanation is that in nations with imperfectly competitive markets for goods and services, increased openness could reduce the pricing power of domestic firms, which reduces the extent to which increases in the overall price level can occur. Nevertheless, the openness–inflation relationship in the most developed nations has been very weak in recent years, and the relationship between openness and inflation can vary dramatically across individual nations.

5. **New Open Economy Macroeconomics:** The new open economy macroeconomics is an approach to evaluating policymaking in open economies that stresses the implications of sticky nominal wages, incomplete short-run price adjustment, and imperfect competitive goods markets, often using theories that predict the decisions of nations' residents across time. One possible advantage of the new open economy macroeconomics is that it may illustrate the ways in which welfare benefits can arise from policymaking in open economies. Another potential benefit of the approach is that it could suggest ways to measure such welfare benefits. Potential drawbacks of the approach might include an overreliance on representative-agent theories that do not account for possible preference differences among residents of the world's nations, failure to fully consider the incentives of policymakers, and incomplete evidence regarding whether the theories are relevant to the real world.

QUESTIONSandPROBLEMS

1. Suppose that a small, open economy has a floating exchange rate and capital mobility sufficiently *low* that the *BP* schedule is *steeper* than the *LM* schedule. The central bank, by changing the money stock, and the fiscal authority, by changing the amount of government spending, desire to bring about both internal and external balance as speedily as possible.
   a. Consider an increase in government spending, and explain how to derive the internal-balance schedule.
   b. Consider an increase in government spending, and explain how to derive the external-balance schedule.
   c. Determine the appropriate assignment of objectives.

2. Suppose that a small open economy has a fixed exchange rate and capital mobility sufficiently *high* that the *BP* schedule is *shallower* than the *LM* schedule. The central bank, by changing the target exchange rate, and the fiscal authority, by changing the amount of government spending, desire to bring about both internal and external balance as speedily as possible. (*Hint:* Recall that changes in the exchange rate shift both the *BP* schedule and the *IS* schedule; also keep in mind that changes in the money stock, which shift the *LM* schedule, must occur to adjust to the central exchange-rate target.)
   a. Consider an increase in government spending, and explain how to derive the internal-balance schedule, with the exchange rate *S* measured along the vertical axis and government spending *g* measured along the horizontal axis.
   b. Consider an increase in government spending, and explain how to derive the external-balance schedule, with the exchange rate *S* measured along the vertical axis and government spending *g* measured along the horizontal axis.
   c. Determine the appropriate assignment of objectives.

3. A small open economy has a fixed exchange rate and capital mobility sufficiently *low* that the *BP* schedule is *steeper* than the *LM* schedule. The central bank, by changing the target exchange rate, and the fiscal authority, by changing the amount of government spending, desire to bring about both internal and external balance as speedily as possible. (*Hint:* Recall that changes in the exchange rate shift both the *BP* schedule and the *IS* schedule; also keep in mind that changes in the money stock, which shift the *LM* schedule, must occur to adjust to the central exchange-rate target.)
   a. Consider an increase in government spending, and explain how to derive the internal-balance schedule, with the exchange rate *S* measured along the vertical axis and government spending *g* measured along the horizontal axis.

b. Consider an increase in government spending, and explain how to derive the external-balance schedule, with the exchange rate S measured along the vertical axis and government spending g measured along the horizontal axis.

c. Determine the appropriate assignment of objectives.

4. The central bank in a small open economy with perfect capital mobility and a floating exchange rate reduces the nation's money stock. Use appropriate diagrams to explain how the exchange rate must adjust in the long run when relative purchasing power is assumed to hold.

5. Suppose that nominal rigidities make the short-run aggregate supply schedule for the economy in Question 4 slope upward. Based on the long-run reasoning provided in your answer to Question 4, use appropriate diagrams to explain how exchange-rate overshooting can occur in the short run if there is a contraction in the quantity of money in circulation.

6. A nation's economy becomes more open, and as a consequence, aggregate real output becomes less responsive to short-run changes in the price level. Discuss factors that might help explain why this has occurred.

7. In a different country than in Question 6, the short-run sensitivity of output to price-level variations has increased following an increase in the degree of openness of the country's economy. Discuss factors that might help explain why this has occurred.

8. Discuss two possible reasons why greater openness of a nation's economy might be associated with lower inflation.

9. Explain why a relatively high level of central bank independence might limit the inflation-reducing effect that otherwise tends to result from a rise in the degree of openness of a particular nation's economy.

10. Briefly discuss the three key features of the new open economy macroeconomics. In addition, briefly evaluate the key ways that these features are different from the basic characteristics of the approaches to analyzing policy effects used in Chapters 10 through 13.

Online APPLICATIONS

Internet URL: *http://www.imf.org/external/pubs/ft/weo/2006/01/index.htm*

Title: IMF World Economic Outlook: Globalization and Inflation

Navigation: Go to the above URL. Click on *Summary* under *Chapter III: How Has Globalization Affected Inflation?*

Application: Read the summary, and answer the following questions:

1. According to the summary, what are key factors influencing how globalization affects inflation?

2. As explained in the summary, why are some industries likely to be affected more by globalization than others?

For Group Study and Analysis: Have the class read all of *Chapter III: How Has Globalization Affected Inflation?* What factors, aside from openness, appear to reduce inflation in the world's nations? Propose and evaluate various reasons for why each factor might have an effect on inflation.

SELECTED REFERENCES and FURTHER READINGS

Badinger, Harald. "Globalization, the Output-Inflation Tradeoff, and Inflation," *European Economic Review 53*(8), November 2009): 888–907.

Ball, Laurence. "Has Globalization Changed Inflation?" National Bureau of Economic Research, Working Paper No. 12687 (November 2006).

Bergin, Paul. "Putting the 'New Open Economy Macroeconomics' to a Test." *Journal of International Economics 60* (May 2003): 3–34.

Bowdler, Christopher. "Openness, Exchange Rate Regimes, and the Phillips Curve." *Journal of International Money and Finance 28*(1), February 2009): 148–160.

Cavallo, Eduardo, and Jeffrey Frankel. "Does Openness to Trade Make Countries More Vulnerable to Sudden Stops, or Less?" *Journal of International Money and Finance 27* (December 2008): 1430–1452.

Cavelaars, Paul. "Does Globalization Discipline Monetary Policymakers?" Journal of International Money and Finance 28 (April 2009): 392–405.

Daniels, Joseph, and David VanHoose. "Trade Openness, Capital Mobility, and the Sacrifice Ratio." *Open Economies Review 20*(3), September 2009): 473–487.

Daniels, Joseph, and David VanHoose. "Openness, the Sacrifice Ratio, and Inflation: Is There a Puzzle?" *Journal of International Money and Finance 25* (December 2006): 1336–1347.

Daniels, Joseph, Farrokh Nourzad, and David VanHoose. "Openness, Central Bank Independence, and the Sacrifice Ratio." *Journal of Money, Credit, and Banking 37* (April 2005): 371–379.

Duarte, Margarida. "International Pricing in New Open-Economy Models." Federal Reserve Bank of Richmond, *Economic Quarterly 87* (2001): 53–70.

Gwin, Carl, and David VanHoose. "Disaggregate Evidence on Price Stickiness and Implications for Macro Models," *Economic Inquiry 46*(4), October 2008): 561–575.

Karras, George. "Openness and the Effects of Monetary Policy." *Journal of International Money and Finance 18* (February 1999): 13–26.

Lane, Philip. "The New Open Economy Macroeconomics: A Survey." *Journal of International Economics 54* (2001): 518–538.

Obstfeld, Maurice. "International Macroeconomics: Beyond the Mundell–Fleming Model." *IMF Staff Papers 47* (2001): 1–39.

Rogoff, Kenneth. "Dornbusch's Overshooting Model after Twenty-Five Years." *IMF Staff Papers 49* (2002): 1–34.

Romer, David. "Openness and Inflation: Theory and Evidence." *Quarterly Journal of Economics 108* (November 1993): 869–903.

Razin, Assaf, and Prakash Loungani. "Globalization and Equilibrium Output-Inflation Tradeoffs." In Jeffrey Frankel and Christopher Pissarides, eds., *NBER International Seminar on Macroeconomics, 2005*. Cambridge, MA: MIT Press.

Sarno, Lucio. "Towards a New Paradigm in Open Economy Modeling: Where Do We Stand?" Federal Reserve Bank of St. Louis, *Review 83* (May/June 2001): 21–36.

Temple, Jonathan. "Openness, Inflation, and the Phillips Curve: A Puzzle." *Journal of Money, Credit, and Banking 34* (May 2002): 450–468.

VanHoose, David. "The New Open Economy Macroeconomics: A Critical Appraisal." *Open Economic Review 15* (April 2004): 193–215.

15

Policy Coordination, Monetary Union, and Target Zones

Fundamental ISSUES

1. What is structural interdependence, and how can it lead nations to cooperate or to coordinate their policies?
2. What are the potential benefits of international policy coordination?
3. What are the potential drawbacks of international policy coordination?
4. Could nations gain from adopting a common currency?
5. What are vehicle currencies?
6. What is an exchange-rate target zone?

On October 7, 2008, six central banks engaged in an unprecedented act of coordinated policymaking. The European Central Bank, the Federal Reserve, the Bank of Canada, the Bank of England, Sweden's Riksbank, and the Swiss National Bank simultaneously engaged in expansionary monetary policy actions aimed at pushing down market interest rates. They also engaged in coordinated reductions in the rates of interest at which they were willing to lend to private banks. In a joint statement, the central banks indicated that in light of declines in commodity prices, inflationary pressures had "started to moderate." The statement continued, "The recent intensification of the financial crisis has augmented the downside risks to growth and thus diminished further the upside risks to price stability. Some easing of global monetary conditions is therefore warranted."

Why is the widespread coordination of monetary policy actions, such as the coordinated interventions of October 7, 2008, a rare event? What factors can motivate central banks to coordinate their monetary policies? In this chapter, we shall address these and other questions relating to the coordination of policymaking. Consequently, we begin by trying to understand why nations might choose to work together in implementing economic policies.

INTERNATIONAL INTERDEPENDENCE

Why might nations contemplate the joint determination of their economic policy actions or even consider sharing the same currency? In most cases, the answer is that international transactions in goods, services, and financial assets connect them so that they share common interests.

Structural Interdependence and International Policy Externalities

Economists are known to disagree about some issues. One general area of agreement, however, concerns the increasing openness of the world's economies. Economists widely concur that national economies are increasingly interconnected, as demonstrated in Chapter 1.

Structural Interdependence and Its Consequences In today's world, in which countries' citizens trade significant amounts of goods and services and exchange sizable volumes of financial instruments across national boundaries, national economies are *structurally interdependent*. This means nations' economic systems—their markets for goods and services, financial markets, and payment systems—are interlinked.

An important consequence of structural interdependence is that events that benefit or harm the interests of one country may also have a bearing on the interests of citizens of another nation. This means that collective actions that citizens of a nation undertake in their own interest may spill over to influence the welfare of other countries' residents. Economists refer to such spillover effects as *externalities*. These are benefits or costs experienced by one individual or group as a result of actions by another individual or group in a separate location or market.

Externalities may be either *negative* or *positive*. A negative externality arises when market transactions among one set of individuals harm others. A commonly cited negative externality is pollution, in which the act of producing a good that benefits one group of firms and consumers fouls the air or water, thereby reducing the well-being of others. Likewise, a negative *international externality* may arise if the actions of a body of individuals in one nation adversely affect the economic performance of another nation. It is also possible that the collective actions of one nation's residents may improve the economic performance in another country. This constitutes a positive international externality.

International Policy Externalities A nation's political system typically charges individual leaders, groups of representatives or delegates, or government agencies with conducting economic policies on behalf of the nation's citizens. As we have discussed in the preceding chapters, such policies can alter the choices of private residents and businesses, thereby influencing a country's overall economic performance.

If national economies are structurally interdependent, then *international policy externalities*, or benefits or costs of policy effects that spill over onto other nations, may result. For instance, as the two-country models in prior chapters illustrated, *locomotive effects* or *beggar-thy-neighbor effects* can occur when a policy action in one nation affects the economic performance of other nations. If a locomotive effect arises, then a policy-induced increase in real income in one country also engenders a rise in real income in another country. Hence, the locomotive effect is an example of a positive international policy externality. In contrast, the

structural interdependence
The interconnectedness of countries' markets for goods and services, financial markets, and payment systems, which causes events in one nation to have effects on the economy of another nation.

externality
A benefit or cost felt by one individual or group stemming from actions by another individual or group in another location or market.

international policy externality
A benefit or cost for one nation's economy owing to a policy action undertaken in another nation.

beggar-thy-neighbor effect, which arises if a policy action raises real income at home at the expense of reduced real income abroad, constitutes a negative international policy externality.

National policymakers recognize that their policy actions may affect other countries. They also realize that decisions by foreign policymakers may influence economic performance at home. This gives policymakers an incentive to engage in *strategic policymaking*, meaning that they develop a plan for achieving objectives for their own nation, taking into account the extent to which their nation is structurally linked to others and courses of action that other nations' policymakers may pursue. Recognition that positive and negative externalities may result from policies that policymakers undertake also may induce them to band together to minimize the negative consequences of their individual policy choices and to enhance the positive spillovers that might result.

Accounting for Interdependence: International Policy Cooperation and Coordination

There are two ways that nations might try to work together to achieve their economic performance objectives.

International Policy Cooperation The first of these is through *international policy cooperation*. This refers to the formal establishment of institutions and processes through which national policymakers can collaborate on their national goals, provide information about specific approaches they intend to follow in implementing policies, and share information and data about their countries' economic performances.

An example of an institutional arrangement that facilitates international policy cooperation is the *Group of Seven (G7)*. As we discussed in Chapter 3, this is a collection of seven nations—Canada, France, Germany, Italy, Japan, the United Kingdom, and the United States—whose chief economic policy officials meet on a regular basis. At these meetings, G7 officials discuss their broad policy objectives and plans, as well as more specific economic issues of concern to the member nations.

International Policy Coordination As noted at the beginning of this chapter, in October 2008, several of the world's central banks—the European Central Bank, the Federal Reserve, the Bank of Canada, the Bank of England, Sweden's Riksbank, and the Swiss National Bank—worked together to push down global interest rates. This action represented a striking example of *international policy coordination*, which refers to the joint determination of national economic policies for the mutual benefit of a group of countries.

By coordinating their monetary policies, these central banks sought to prevent international policy externalities that might otherwise have arisen if they alternatively had implemented disjoint policy actions that would have yielded substantial interest rate spreads across countries. In so doing, the central banks sought to ensure that exchange rates did not exhibit wide swings that could have led to unintended beggar-thy-neighbor effects for some nations as others sought to contain a growing financial crisis.

Proponents of international policy coordination argue that nations around the world could gain considerably from broad-based policy coordination. Rather than just coordinating their policies from time to time, as in the case of the joint monetary policy action initiated in October 2008, these observers contend that nations

strategic policymaking
The formulation of planned policy actions in light of the structural linkages among nations and the manner in which other countries' policymakers may conduct their own policies.

international policy cooperation
The adoption of institutions and procedures by which national policymakers can inform each other about their objectives, policy strategies, and national economic data.

international policy coordination
The joint determination of economic policies within a group of nations for the intended benefit of the group as a whole.

should make policy coordination a day-to-day process. Indeed, many argue that countries could reap considerable gains from coordinating *all* their economic policies, including those aimed at broad output and inflation objectives.

Fundamental ISSUES

#1 What is structural interdependence, and how can it lead nations to cooperate or to coordinate their policies?

When national economies are linked together, then they are structurally interdependent. As a result, policy actions in one country can have spillover effects, or international policy externalities, that influence economic performance in other nations. International policy externalities are said to be positive if they improve other countries' economic performances. They are negative if they worsen those nations' prospects. To enhance the potential for positive policy externalities, or to reduce the likelihood of negative externalities, nations may choose to cooperate by sharing information about economic data and policy objectives. They also may choose to coordinate their policymaking by determining policy actions that are in their joint interest.

PERFECT CAPITAL MOBILITY REVISITED: CAN INTERNATIONAL POLICY COORDINATION PAY?

In Chapters 11 and 12, we contemplated the implications of policy actions for the economic performances of two nations that were completely open to cross-border capital flows, under the assumption that the nations' price levels were unaffected by policy actions. To consider how international policy coordination might be beneficial for two nations, let's again assume that capital is completely mobile across the nations' borders. In addition, suppose that the rate of exchange of the two nations' currencies floats freely in the foreign exchange market. Now, however, let's be more realistic by contemplating a flexible price level in both countries.

The Aggregate Demand Effects of National Monetary Policies

As we discussed in Chapter 13, if the domestic central bank increases the nominal quantity of domestic money in circulation, then, as shown in panel (a) of Figure 15–1 (p. 452), at the current price level P_1 there is a rise in the quantity of real money balances, from an initial level M_1/P_1 to a higher level M_2/P_1. The result is a rightward shift in the domestic LM schedule, from $LM(M_1/P_1)$ to $LM(M_2/P_1)$. This causes the domestic interest rate to fall from its initial equilibrium value of R_1 at point A toward a lower value of R' at point B, below the BP schedule, denoted BP_1, that corresponds to the initial equilibrium exchange rate. Under our maintained assumption of perfect capital mobility, this decrease in the domestic interest rate induces a movement of financial resources from the domestic country to the foreign country. Thus, there is an increase in the domestic demand for foreign currency and a reduction in the foreign demand for domestic currency. Consequently, the value of the domestic currency depreciates relative to the foreign currency, so the equilibrium exchange rate rises from its initial value of S_1 to a higher level, S_2.

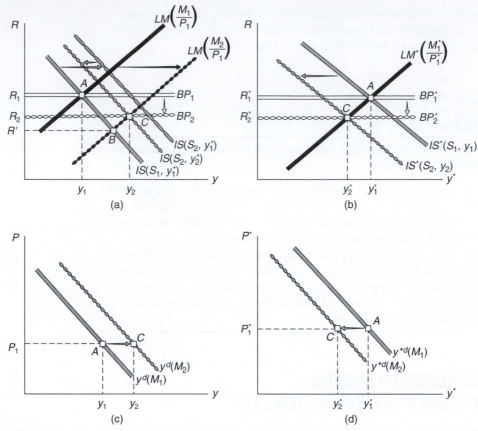

Figure 15–1   Aggregate Demand Effects of a Domestic Monetary Expansion in a Two-Country Model with Perfect Capital Mobility and a Floating Exchange Rate

A rise in the domestic money stock shifts the domestic *LM* schedule rightward from point *A* to point *B* in panel (a). The resulting fall in the domestic interest rate induces capital to flow from the domestic country to the foreign country, causing the equilibrium exchange rate to rise from S_1 to S_2. This domestic currency depreciation causes the domestic *IS* schedule to shift rightward in panel (a) and, assuming that the net effect on the domestic trade balance of the domestic currency depreciation and rise in foreign real income is negative, it causes the foreign *IS* schedule to shift leftward in panel (b). The rise in foreign real income then causes the domestic *IS* schedule to shift leftward somewhat. In panels (a) and (b), points *C* are the final equilibrium points, which indicates that aggregate demand rises in the domestic country, as shown in panel (c), while aggregate demand falls in the foreign country, as shown in panel (d).

Because the domestic currency depreciation reduces domestic imports and increases domestic exports, at the initial level of foreign real income, y_1^* the domestic *IS* schedule shifts to the right in panel (a) of Figure 15–1, from $IS(S_1, y_1^*)$ to $IS(S_2, y_1^*)$. In the foreign country, by way of contrast, the appreciation of the foreign currency increases foreign imports and reduces foreign exports. We assume that this direct negative effect on the foreign trade balance is greater than the positive effect stemming from the offsetting rise in foreign exports generated by the rise in domestic real income, so that the foreign *IS* schedule shifts to the left on net in panel (b), from $IS^*(S_1, y_1)$ to $IS^*(S_2, y_2)$. The net decline in foreign real income causes foreign import spending to decline somewhat, so that domestic exports decline, inducing the domestic *IS* schedule to shift back to the left somewhat, from $IS(S_1, y_1^*)$ to $IS(S_2, y_2^*)$. At the final equilibrium points *C* in both panels, the equilibrium domestic nominal interest rate converges to an equality with the equilibrium foreign interest rate, with $R_2 = R_2^*$, as the *BP* schedules for both nations shift downward.

On the one hand, at the equilibrium point C in panel (a), the equilibrium level of domestic real income, y_2, is greater than its initial equilibrium value, y_1. As panel (c) indicates, this implies a rightward shift in the domestic aggregate demand schedule, from $y^d(M_1)$ to $y^d(M_2)$. Hence, as we saw in Chapter 12 for the case of a small, open economy, an increase in the domestic money stock raises domestic aggregate demand.

On the other hand, at point C in panel (b), equilibrium foreign real income, y_2^*, is less than its initial level, y_1^*. As shown in panel (d), this is true at the current foreign price level, denoted P_1^*. Hence, as you learned in Chapter 13, under a floating exchange rate and perfect capital mobility, a domestic monetary expansion typically has a beggar-thy-neighbor effect on the foreign country. As panel (d) indicates, the rise in the quantity of domestic money in circulation, because of the response of the exchange rate, shifts the foreign aggregate demand schedule leftward, from $y^{*d}(M_1)$ to $y^{*d}(M_2)$. Thus, an increase in the domestic money stock *reduces* foreign aggregate demand and thereby constitutes a negative international policy externality for the foreign country.

A foreign monetary expansion also constitutes a negative international policy externality from the perspective of the domestic country. It causes the foreign LM^* schedule to shift to the right and then induces a rightward shift of the foreign IS^* schedule as the foreign currency's value depreciates and a leftward shift of the domestic IS schedule as the domestic currency's value appreciates. This generates declines in equilibrium nominal interest rates in both nations, a rise in equilibrium foreign real income, and a decline in equilibrium domestic real income.

Conflicting Monetary Policies and the Potential Role of Policy Coordination

The preceding discussion indicates that in a two-country setting with a floating exchange rate and perfect capital mobility, there is a natural *conflict* in monetary policymaking. Figure 15–2 illustrates such a policy conflict. In panel (a), we suppose that the domestic central bank desires to bring about a short-run increase in equilibrium domestic output, from y_1 to a target output level denoted y_T. To accomplish this

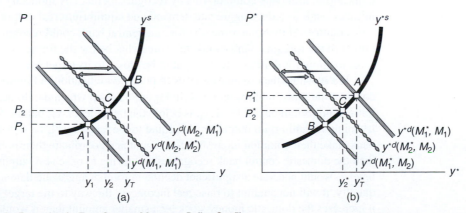

Figure 15–2   An Example of a Two-Country Monetary Policy Conflict

In panel (a), the domestic central bank increases the domestic money stock to try to raise real output to a target level, y_T, at point B. The resulting foreign currency appreciation causes the foreign aggregate demand schedule to shift leftward, pushing foreign output below the foreign central bank's target output level, y_T^* at point B in panel (b). This induces the foreign central bank to increase the foreign money stock, yielding a final equilibrium at point C in panel (b), and causing the domestic aggregate demand schedule to shift back to the left in panel (a) to a final equilibrium at point C. Thus, on net, the final equilibrium output levels in the two countries can end up well below desired levels.

objective, the domestic central bank must increase the quantity of domestic money in circulation from an initial value, M_1, to a higher level, M_2. Given the current level of the foreign money stock, M_1^*, this action causes the domestic aggregate demand schedule to shift rightward, from $y^*(M_1, M_1^*)$ to $y^*(M_2, M_1^*)$. Holding all else constant, equilibrium domestic real output then rises from y_1 at point A to y_T at point B.

As we discussed earlier, however, this domestic monetary policy action causes the foreign aggregate demand schedule to shift leftward, from $y^{*d}(M_1^*, M_1)$ to $y^{d*}(M_1^*, M_2)$. In an effort to offset this resulting decline in foreign real output from the foreign central bank's initial target real output level y_T^*, which we assume it initially had achieved, the foreign central bank must raise the foreign money stock toward a level such as M_2^*. As shown in panel (b) of Figure 15–2, this foreign action shifts the foreign aggregate demand schedule to right from $y^{*d}(M_1^*, M_2)$ to a position such as that shown by $y^{*d}(M_1^*, M_2)$ Thus, we suppose that the foreign central bank's response is insufficient to completely offset the negative effect of the domestic monetary expansion. In this instance, equilibrium foreign output declines somewhat in the short run, to y_2^* at point C.

In the domestic country, the rise in the foreign money stock causes the domestic aggregate demand schedule to shift back to the left in panel (a), from $y^d(M_1, M_1^*)$ to $y^d(M_2, M_2^*)$. As a result, the net short-run effect is a net increase of domestic real income only to the level denoted y_2 at point C.

Thus, if the two central banks pursue their real income goals *independently*, pursuing the monetary policies that are only in the best interest of their own countries, they tend to work at cross-purposes. An expansionary policy action by one central bank tends to be offset by an expansionary policy action by the other central bank. As a result, it is possible, as shown in panels (a) and (b) of Figure 15–2, that both countries could end up in situations in which their real output levels are well below desired levels.

A Potential Gain from Policy Coordination

In principle, it might be possible for the two central banks to reduce the negative consequences of the policy conflict that they face in our previous example. The domestic central bank could do this by recognizing that any monetary expansion it initiates tends to reduce aggregate demand and equilibrium real output in the foreign country. At the same time, the foreign central bank could recognize that real output in the foreign country must fall somewhat below the foreign output target level to allow for domestic real output to be closer to its target level.

We illustrate the possible benefits of policy coordination in Figure 15–3. We consider the same initial situation as in Figure 15–2, in which the domestic country's initial equilibrium output level, y_1, is below the target level, y_T, but the foreign country's initial equilibrium output level is equal to the target level, y_T^*. If both central banks take their common interests into account and coordinate their policy efforts, then the domestic central bank recognizes that trying to raise real output to the target level y_T would generate a significant decline in foreign aggregate demand. Consequently, it will not attempt to raise real income all the way to the target level. Instead, it increases the domestic money stock by a smaller amount than it would if it were to act independently, from the initial quantity M_1 to a somewhat higher amount denoted M_2'. This action initially shifts the domestic aggregate demand schedule from $y^d(M_1, M_1^*)$ to $y^d(M_2', M_1^*)$, causing a movement from point A to point B in panel (a).

With coordinated monetary policies, the foreign central bank likewise takes into account the effects of its policies on the domestic country. Therefore, when the

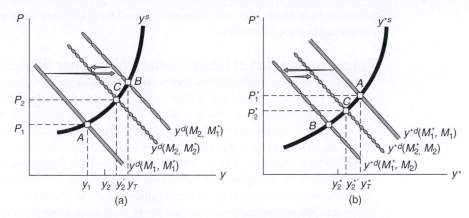

Figure 15–3   An Illustration of the Potential Benefits of International Monetary Policy Coordination
If two nations' central banks coordinate their policies, then the domestic central bank increases the domestic money stock by a smaller amount than it would have if it had acted independently, thereby inducing movement from point A to point B in panel (a). In response to the smaller decline in foreign real output shown by the movement from point A to point B in panel (b), the foreign central bank responds by increasing in the foreign money stock by a smaller amount than it would have under independent policymaking. Hence, foreign real output falls only slightly below the foreign output target, to $y_2^{*\prime}$ at point C in panel (b), which is above the level y_2^* that would have arisen without coordination (see Figure 15–2 on page 453). The moderate increase in the foreign money stock causes a slight reduction in domestic aggregate demand. Hence, domestic output falls somewhat below the target level, to $y_2^\prime$ at point C in panel (a), which is closer to the domestic output target, as compared with the output level y_2 that would have arisen in the absence of coordination.

mild domestic monetary policy expansion results in a reduction in foreign aggregate demand in panel (b) of Figure 15–3, from $y^{*d}(M_1^*, M_1)$ to $y^{*d}(M_1^*, M_2^\prime)$, the foreign central bank responds with a more moderate increase in the foreign money stock, as compared with the case of independent policymaking that we considered in Figure 15–2. This causes a moderate rise in foreign aggregate demand, from $y^{*d}(M_1^*, M_2^\prime)$ to $y^{*d}(M_2^{*\prime}, M_2^\prime)$. As a result, equilibrium foreign real output falls only slightly below the foreign output target, to $y_2^{*\prime}$, at point C. Although the foreign country's output thereby is somewhat less than the target level, this equilibrium foreign output level under coordinated policymaking nonetheless is greater than y_2^*, which is the output level that Figure 15–2 indicated would otherwise arise in the absence of coordination.

In the domestic country, the moderate increase in the foreign money stock causes a slight reduction in domestic aggregate demand in panel (a) of Figure 15–3, from $y^d(M_2^\prime, M_1^*)$ to $y^d(M_2^\prime, M_2^{*\prime})$. Consequently, on net, equilibrium domestic output still falls somewhat below the target level, to $y_2^\prime$ at point C. Nevertheless, it is closer to the domestic output target under coordinated policymaking than it would have been in the absence of coordination. With independent policymaking, as determined in Figure 15–2, domestic output would have been at the lower level, y_2.

Essentially, under coordinated policymaking the two nations' central banks partially sacrifice their own nations' individual interests for the common good of both nations. As a result, both nations are, in our example, better off than they would have been if their central banks were unwilling to make this sacrifice.

THE PROS AND CONS OF INTERNATIONAL POLICY COORDINATION

The previous example is a concrete illustration of the fact that nations potentially can benefit from working together to aim toward their national economic goals. There are several general arguments in favor of international policy coordination, however. In addition, there are some strong reasons to question whether policy coordination is always beneficial.

Potential Benefits of International Policy Coordination

Proponents of international policy coordination typically propose three broad rationales. The example depicted in Figures 15–2 and 15–3 on pages 453 and 455 illustrates the first of these, which is that coordination of policies can take into account and potentially minimize policy externalities. The second justification for coordination is that if national policymakers work together, they may be able to achieve a larger number of goals with their available policy instruments than they would achieve by acting alone. Finally, proponents of coordinated policymaking argue that coordination permits national policymakers to present a "united front" in the face of home political pressures that could push them toward pursuing mutually inconsistent and, therefore, ultimately harmful policies.

Internalizing International Policy Externalities The act of coordinating policies for the mutual benefit of a group of countries effectively requires the nations' policymakers to behave as if their countries were a single entity. Thus, international policy coordination *internalizes* the externalities that individually formulated national policies would tend to produce. This essentially is why policy coordination can pay in the example depicted in Figures 15–2 and 15–3. Internalizing the spillovers resulting from monetary policy actions permitted the nations' central banks to keep equilibrium output levels as close to target levels as possible. Likewise, in the real-world example of the Basel Agreement on bank capital regulation, recognizing the potential for negative competitive consequences for national banking systems may have permitted G10 nations to avoid those adverse outcomes.

Getting the Most Out of Limited Sets of Policy Instruments It also is possible that international coordination can permit national policymakers to achieve a larger number of goals with the limited policy instruments they possess. As a simple example, suppose that two nations' central banks each have the same two goals: to achieve an increase in equilibrium domestic output and to minimize exchange-rate variability. Each, therefore, has an incentive to increase its money stock. But if the central banks increase their money stocks at different rates, then the rate of exchange between their currencies must vary. To prevent volatility of the exchange rate while achieving their common goal of raising national output levels, the central banks can coordinate their actions.

This is an intentionally simplified example, but it illustrates the basic point. If national policymakers have few policy instruments but related goals, then by working together to determine the appropriate settings of their policy instruments, they potentially could come closer to achieving their multiple objectives. Coordination thereby might be mutually beneficial.

Gaining Support from Abroad The third rationale for international policy coordination is that policymakers in various countries might gain additional strength to withstand domestic political pressures by banding together with other policymakers. When faced with internal pressures to enact policies that might provide short-term gains at the expense of long-term social costs, policymakers could use their commitment to international coordination agreements as a justification for holding the line against such actions.

#2 What are the potential benefits of international policy coordination?

The most significant gain that might arise from policy coordination is the internalization of international policy externalities, meaning that working together toward joint goals could permit national policymakers to minimize the ill effects of negative externalities or improve the prospect for benefits of positive externalities. It also is possible that policy coordination might increase the number of policy instruments that could be aimed at policymakers' objectives. In addition, establishing formal policy coordination agreements or institutions could assist a policymaker's efforts to resist domestic political pressures to enact shortsighted policies with potentially harmful long-term effects.

Some Potential Drawbacks of International Policy Coordination

In our example depicted in Figures 15–2 and 15–3, both nations unambiguously gained from policy coordination. Our example, however, was designed to illustrate a circumstance in which coordination might pay. International policy coordination *might* make two nations better off in certain circumstances, but it need not always be the best course for nations to follow.

There are several possible drawbacks associated with international policy coordination. For one thing, for coordination to work, countries must be willing and able to sacrifice at least a portion of their own interests. In addition, national policymakers must trust in the willingness and ability of their counterparts in other nations to make such sacrifices. Finally, well-intentioned efforts to coordinate policies might have negative consequences, such as higher average inflation rates.

How Much Autonomy Should a Nation Sacrifice? Ultimately, what defines any nation is its *sovereignty*, or the supremacy of its citizens' own control of the resources within their country's geographic borders. If international policy coordination is to achieve benefits for a nation, its citizens and leaders must be amenable to giving up some degree of sovereignty. They must be willing to pursue *international* objectives along with purely domestic goals.

For instance, suppose that on January 1, 2010, a group of nations were to agree that their relative currency values must be fixed beginning March 1, 2018. At the end of February of that year, however, one of the nations determines that it could gain by devaluing its currency relative to the currencies of the other countries in the group. Nevertheless, to abide by the policy coordination agreement, the nation's leaders would have to sacrifice the nation's discretion to pursue its own self-interest by devaluing its currency.

Can Other Countries Be Trusted? This last example illustrates a fundamental problem with international policy coordination, which is that there typically are incentives for countries that enter into coordination agreements to cheat. To see why, consider Figure 15–4 on the following page. Each cell in the figure gives hypothetical values, in "welfare units," of the citizens of two countries, denoted A and B, when their countries do or do not coordinate their policies. In the upper-left-hand cell of Figure 15–4, we see that if country A and country B conduct independent, noncoordinated policies, each derives a welfare level of 50 units. In contrast, if both

	Country B Does Not Coordinate	Country B Coordinates
Country A Does Not Coordinate	Country A welfare = 50 Country B welfare = 50 Total welfare = 100	Country A welfare = 100 Country B welfare = 25 Total welfare = 125
Country A Coordinates	Country A welfare = 25 Country B welfare = 100 Total welfare = 125	Country A welfare = 75 Country B welfare = 75 Total welfare = 150

Figure 15–4 Hypothetical Welfare Levels for Two Nations
If policymakers in two nations fail to coordinate their policies, then their combined welfare is 100 units. If both work together to coordinate policy actions, however, their total welfare is 150 units. The difficulty is that if either nation "cheats" and does not coordinate as promised, it can raise its own welfare to 100 units while generating a 25-unit decline in the other nation's welfare.

nations coordinate their policymaking, then the lower-right-hand cell indicates that they both attain welfare levels of 75 units. Thus, policy coordination is beneficial for both countries.

Nevertheless, the potential for each country to gain from cheating could still result in a failure to coordinate policies. Country A's policymakers know that country A's welfare can be raised to 100 units if country A fails to follow through on a coordination agreement with country B while country B's policymakers continue to honor the agreement. Consequently, there is an incentive for the policymakers in country A to renege on the deal to achieve higher national welfare. As a result, as indicated in the upper-right-hand cell of Figure 15–4, country B's welfare declines to 25 units. Hence, country A gains, but only at country B's expense. At the same time, country B's policymakers face the same temptation to cheat and pursue a beggar-thy-neighbor policy, as the lower-left-hand cell of the figure shows.

Clearly, in this example the combined welfare of both nations' citizens is highest, at 150 units, if policymakers in the two nations follow through and coordinate their policies. Yet each nation has an incentive to renege in favor of a beggar-thy-neighbor policy that yields a lower welfare level of 125 units. If *both* countries cheat simultaneously, however, then total welfare is at its lowest, at 100 units. Nevertheless, each individual country might think that it is better off than it would be if it were to stick with the agreement only to be cheated by the other nation's policymakers.

This example illustrates a key problem of international policy coordination. Agreements to coordinate national policies can work only if all participants trust each other. Hence, each nation's commitment to an international policy coordination arrangement must be *credible* to other participating nations. In the absence of such credibility, each nation would recognize that it is worse off by agreeing to coordinate and exposing its citizens to the adverse effects caused by other nations' cheating.

Putting Faith in Other Nations' Policymakers The potential for deception and cheating is not the only factor that can cause individual nations to lose from agreeing to coordinate their policies with those of other countries. Another problem that a nation encounters when it sacrifices some sovereignty in hopes of reaping gains from coordination is the possibility that other nations' policymakers may lack competence to pursue the best common policy. That is, to be willing to cede some of its policymaking sovereignty to another country, a nation must be confident in two things. The nation must have confidence that policymakers in the other country will honor the coordination agreement. The nation also must believe that the other nation's policymakers have the ability to do their jobs effectively.

There is also the possibility that policymakers of coordinating nations may have conflicting outlooks on the appropriate policies for all nations to pursue jointly, even if the policymakers otherwise trust themselves to honor their agreements and to competently implement policy actions. Such conflicts may arise because of different policymaker preferences concerning, say, how much relative weight to place on real output versus inflation objectives. Alternatively, policymakers might not agree about the best way to implement a coordination agreement.

Could "Successful" Coordination Actually Be Counterproductive? Finally, even if nations agree to coordinate, stick to their agreement, and determine their policies taking joint welfare into account, there is still the possibility that in the end their citizens could be worse off. Economists have identified a key circumstance under which this could happen.

Discretionary monetary policies and inflation without coordination This circumstance in which successful policy coordination actually may reduce welfare was first pointed out by Kenneth Rogoff of Princeton University. Figure 15–5 illustrates Rogoff's basic argument. Panel (a) depicts an initial aggregate demand–aggregate supply equilibrium at point A for the domestic economy in the two-country, floating-exchange-rate, perfect-capital-mobility setting that we considered earlier in this chapter. At point A, the initial domestic price level is P_1, and the initial real output level, which we assume is equal to the long-run equilibrium output level, is y_1. As in Chapter 13, we assume that this output level is lower than it otherwise would be if there were no income taxes or government regulations that act to push real output below a socially desired output level equal to y_T. Panel (b) shows an analogous situation faced in the foreign

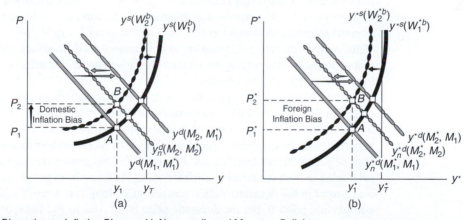

Figure 15–5 Discretionary Inflation Biases with Noncoordinated Monetary Policies

If policymakers in two countries seek to push their nations' output levels toward target levels given y_T and y_T^* but also dislike inflation, then they have an incentive to increase their stocks of money and raise aggregate demand somewhat at the cost of some inflation. An increase in the money stock in either nation, however, tends to depress aggregate demand in the other nation. In the end, noncoordinated monetary policies thereby result in aggregate demand schedules located at the positions given by $y_n^d(M_2, M_2^*)$ in panel (a) and $y_n^{*d}(M_2^*, M_2)$ in panel (b). Consequently, noncoordinated policymaking leads to policy externalities that reduce the extent to which the two policymakers are able to expand aggregate demand in their nations, which reduces the inflation biases that result from negotiation of higher base wages, W_2^b and W_2^{*b}, by workers and firms in the two countries.

economy, in which the initial equilibrium price level is equal to P_1^*, and the initial equilibrium output level is equal to y_1^*, which is below a desired output level that is equal to y_T^*.

In both panels, the positions of the nations' short-run aggregate supply schedules depend on the overall base level of nominal wages, initially given by W_1^b and W_1^{*b}. As we discussed in Chapter 13, workers and firms within the two countries establish these base wages in light of their price-level expectations. The positions of the aggregate demand schedules depend on both nation's money stocks, which initially equal M_1 and M_1^*. As noted earlier in this chapter, with a floating exchange rate and perfect capital mobility, a rise in the domestic money stock typically increases domestic aggregate demand while depressing foreign aggregate demand. Likewise, an increase in the foreign money stock typically raises foreign aggregate demand while reducing domestic aggregate demand.

If policymakers desire to try to push real output toward the target levels y_T and y_T^* but simultaneously dislike inflation, then typically they have an incentive to raise aggregate demand in the hope of a short-run output expansion but at the cost of some inflation. Thus, the domestic central bank has an incentive to increase the domestic money stock to try to place the domestic aggregate demand schedule in a position such as the dashed schedule labeled $y^d(M_2, M_1^*)$ in panel (a). At the same time, the foreign central bank has an incentive to increase the foreign money stock to shift the foreign aggregate demand schedule rightward to a location such as that given by the dashed schedule denoted $y^{*d}(M_2^*, M_1)$ in panel (b).

As we discussed earlier, however, an increase in the domestic money stock results in a domestic currency depreciation that causes aggregate demand to decline in the foreign country. Thus, the domestic monetary expansion depresses somewhat the extent to which foreign aggregate demand increases. Consequently, on net the final position of the foreign aggregate demand schedule is at the somewhat lower level, denoted as $y_n^{*d}(M_2^*, M_2)$ in panel (b), where the subscript n indicates that monetary policies are *noncoordinated*. Likewise, an expansionary monetary policy action by the foreign central bank generates foreign currency depreciation that reduces domestic exports, causing the final position of the domestic aggregate demand schedule to be in a location such as that given by $y_n^d(M_2, M_2^*)$ in panel (a). Thus, noncoordinated policymaking in both nations leads to policy externalities that generate smaller aggregate demand changes than the countries' central banks have incentives to try to achieve.

As in Chapter 13, suppose that workers in both nations negotiate their base wages in light of their rational expectations of the price levels determined in part by the monetary policy actions of their nations' central banks. If workers recognize that their central banks have an incentive to increase their money stocks, then they negotiate higher base wages, W_2^b and W_2^{*b}. This causes the aggregate supply schedules in both countries to shift leftward. As a result, in panel (a), equilibrium real output in the domestic nation remains at its long-run level of y_1 at the final equilibrium point B, but the domestic price level rises to P_2. Thus, discretionary monetary policy by the domestic central bank generates a domestic inflation bias. In like manner, in panel (b), equilibrium foreign real output remains at y_1^*, but there is a foreign inflation bias owing to the higher foreign price level P_2^*.

Discretionary monetary policies and inflation with coordination Now let's consider what happens if both central banks coordinate their discretionary policy choices, by *working together* to maintain a fixed exchange rate between their nations' currencies. To see how coordination can alter the inflation biases that the countries experience as a result of discretionary policymaking, consider Figure 15–6. Again, both central banks have an incentive to expand aggregate demand in their countries by raising their money stocks. Thus, the domestic central bank seeks to shift the domestic aggregate demand schedule rightward to the position given by $y_n^d(M_2, M_1^*)$ in panel (a). At the same time, the foreign central bank has an incentive to increase the foreign money stock to shift the foreign aggregate demand schedule to shift rightward to $y_n^{*d}(M_2^*, M_1)$ in panel (b).

As you saw in Figure 15–5 on page 459, in the *absence* of coordinated monetary policies, exchange-rate adjustments cause the aggregate demand schedules in both nations to shift back to the left somewhat, to positions labeled $y_n^d(M_2, M_2^*)$ and $y_n^{*d}(M_2^*, M_2)$. But if both countries coordinate their policies to keep the exchange rate from changing, then they eliminate spillover effects that exchange rate adjustments have on their imports and exports. This keeps the domestic monetary expansion from causing a contraction in foreign aggregate demand. It also prevents the foreign monetary expansion from inducing a decline in domestic aggregate demand. Hence, with coordinated policymaking, the final positions of the nation's aggregate demand schedules, denoted $y_c^d(M_2', M_2^{*'})$ and $y_c^{*d}(M_2^{*'}, M_2')$, correspond to the locations that each central bank desires to achieve.

Again, however, if workers in the two countries negotiate their base wages in light of their understanding that the central banks have the incentive to increase their money stocks, then they negotiate higher base wages W_2^b and W_2^{b*}. As a result, the aggregate supply schedules in both nations again shift leftward, and the final equilibrium points are points B' in panels (a) and (b) of Figure 15–6. Thus, in panel (a) the equilibrium domestic price level rises to P_2' with monetary policy coordination, and in panel (b) the equilibrium foreign price level increases to $P_2^{*'}$. If the central banks had not coordinated their policies, however, the ultimate equilibrium points would have been those from Figure 15–5, which are points B at the

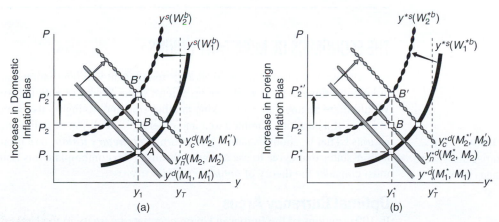

Figure 15–6   Discretionary Inflation Biases with Coordinated Monetary Policies

If two central banks with an incentive to expand their money stocks to raise output toward target levels work together to keep the exchange rate from changing, then they can push out their nations' aggregate demand by greater amounts, to $y_c^d(M_2', M_2^{*'})$ and $y_c^{*d}(M_2^{*'}, M_2')$, as compared with the aggregate demand levels that they could achieve without policy coordination, $y_n^d(M_2, M_2^*)$ and $y_n^{*d}(M_2^*, M_2)$. As a result, with coordinated policymaking both nations experience larger inflation biases resulting from adoption of discretionary policies by their central banks.

price levels given by P_2 and P_2^*. Therefore, Rogoff's conclusion is that coordination of discretionary monetary policies tends to lead to a larger inflation bias in each country.

The reason that the discretionary inflation bias is greater for both countries is that policy coordination that pegs the exchange rate eliminates the policy externalities that otherwise would restrain the increases in aggregate demand caused by discretionary monetary expansions. As a result, aggregate demand in each nation rises by a greater amount following a central bank increase in the money stock. The result is higher average inflation than each country would have experienced if its central banks had not coordinated their policies.

This does not mean that policy coordination is *necessarily* harmful. As we noted earlier, limiting international policy externalities can reduce policy conflicts and thereby help to stabilize equilibrium real output levels in interdependent nations. Nevertheless, Rogoff's argument illustrates a potential cost of the coordination of discretionary monetary policies: Such policies can lead to higher average inflation in the countries whose central banks coordinate their policies.

Fundamental ISSUES

#3 What are the potential drawbacks of international policy coordination?

One difficulty with entering into policy coordination agreements is that nations must give up at least some measure of national sovereignty to implement such agreements. In addition, they must trust each other both to pursue promised policy actions and to do so in a competent manner. Yet there typically will be an incentive for one nation to cheat on a policy coordination agreement, in the pursuit of gains at another country's expense, and there is always the possibility that one nation's policymakers will fail to pursue policies that another nation believes to be appropriate. Finally, international policy coordination can, if policymakers' credibility levels are low within their own countries, lead to higher average inflation rates.

THE ECONOMICS OF MONETARY UNIONS

As we have discussed, if a nation chooses to enter into an international policy coordination arrangement, it must give up at least some degree of national sovereignty. Would there be any gain from taking another step and giving up its own currency in favor of a currency common to it and others in a coalition of policy-coordinating nations? That is, should a nation join a formal ***monetary union,*** or a grouping of nation-states that agree to use a single currency? To contemplate this issue, we must consider the theory of *optimal currency areas*.

monetary union
A set of countries that choose to use a common currency.

Optimal Currency Areas

In 1991, nations of the European Union negotiated a treaty in the Netherlands city of Maastricht. Among other things, the Maastrict Treaty established a European Central Bank that began issuing a single European currency, the *euro,* in 2002.

Although many European government officials and citizens hailed the treaty as a triumph of coordination and unity in the region, a number of economists questioned whether European countries truly would benefit from these monetary provisions of the agreement. These naysayers base their arguments on an economic theory developed more than thirty years ago by Robert Mundell of Columbia University. This is the ***theory of optimal currency areas,*** which is an analytical approach to determining the extent of a geographic area whose residents would be better off by fixing their exchange rates or even by using a common currency.

Each day, financial newspapers such as the *Wall Street Journal* or the *Financial Times* publish listings of exchange rates for more than fifty national currencies. These are not complete exchange-rate listings, however, because these newspapers list only the currencies with large trading volumes in the foreign exchange markets.

Why are there so many different national currencies? Why is it that residents of all fifty states of the United States use the same currency, even though states such as California and New York have higher volumes of GDP than most nations of the world? Would all nations in Europe actually benefit from following the example of the fifty U.S. states? The theory of optimal currency areas seeks to address these issues.

How Separate Currencies and a Floating Exchange Rate Can Be Beneficial

To understand the essential features of the theory of optimal currency areas, let's consider two hypothetical regions. People in one region, which we shall call region A, specialize in producing low-cholesterol foods. Residents of the other region, denoted region B, manufacture textiles. In both regions, wages and prices are sticky in the short run. Initially, both regions experience balanced trade.

Suppose that residents of one region are unable to move to the other region in pursuit of employment in the other region's industry. One possible reason for this state of affairs could be that there are language or cultural barriers that effectively prohibit employment in the other regions' firms. Another reason could be that one or both of the regions might have established restrictions that prevent region A residents who are employed in low-cholesterol food production from moving to region B to make clothing, and vice versa.

Nevertheless, let's suppose that residents of both regions face no restrictions on their ability to purchase the goods produced in both regions. Finally, let's suppose that each region has its own currency. The exchange rate for these currencies could either float in the foreign exchange market, or regional policymakers could fix the exchange rate.

A Shift in Relative Demands Consider now what happens if residents of both regions were to lose their interest in keeping up with the most recent fads in clothing styles, thereby reducing the demand for the textiles produced in region B. At the same time, suppose that both regions' residents also become more health conscious, so that the demand for region A's low-cholesterol foods increases. As a result, region A begins to run a trade surplus, and its output and employment increase. In contrast, region B begins to experience a trade deficit, and its output and employment decline.

If the rate of exchange between the regions' currencies is fixed, then the assumed short-run stickiness of wage and prices causes unemployment to persist for some time in region B following the changes in consumers' tastes. In the long run, of course, the price of the low-cholesterol foods manufactured in region A increases, and the price of the textiles made in region B declines, leading to an ultimate rebalancing of trade between the two regions. Until this long-run adjustment occurs, however, region B can experience a significant unemployment problem.

theory of optimal currency areas
A means of determining the size of a geographic area within which residents' welfare is greater if their governments fix exchange rates or adopt a common currency.

A Flexible Exchange Rate If the exchange rate is flexible, however, then the trade surplus in region A and trade deficit in region B induce a rapid depreciation in the value of region B's currency relative to the currency of region A. This causes an immediate fall in the effective price of region B's textile goods as perceived by residents of region A and a speedy rise in the effective price of region A's low-cholesterol foods faced by residents of region B. As a result, trade between the two nations is balanced much more rapidly with a floating exchange rate, and region B's unemployment problem is much more short-lived.

This example illustrates a situation in which two regions benefit from using separate currencies whose relative values adjust freely in the foreign exchange market. Fixing the rate of exchange between the currencies, or taking the further step of adopting a single currency, eliminates the exchange rate's role as a mechanism for short-run adjustment to changes in relative demands for the regions' goods. This exposes the regions to the potential for chronic payments imbalances and unemployment problems.

Certainly, with separate currencies and a market-determined exchange rate, residents of both nations face foreign exchange risks arising from exchange-rate movements and costs of converting one currency to another when they wish to purchase another region's goods. Nonetheless, adopting individual currencies and a floating exchange rate protects the regions from unemployment dangers that arise from language, cultural, or legal barriers to worker migration.

When Could Using a Single Currency Pay Off? Now suppose that the conditions that have led to past constraints on worker migration break down. As a result, residents of region A can move freely to region B to work, and vice versa. Let's further suppose that shortly following this development, there once again is a rise in the demand for region A's low-cholesterol foods and a decline in the demand for region B's textile products.

The immediate results, again, are a trade surplus, higher output, and higher employment in region A and a trade deficit, lower output, and lower employment in region B. As a result, some residents of region B find themselves without work. Now, however, these unemployed region B residents can migrate—or perhaps even commute—to newly available jobs in region A. Thus, region B unemployment is at worst a temporary phenomenon. Indeed, unemployment for both regions together is minimized in the face of such changes in the relative demands for their products.

In this example, there is no reason that the rates of exchange between the two regions cannot be fixed, thereby permitting residents of both regions to avoid foreign exchange risks. Indeed, economists would conclude that the two regions together constitute an *optimal currency area,* or a geographical area within which fixed exchange rates may be maintained without slowing regional adjustments to changing regional circumstances. Furthermore, within such an optimal currency area, separate regions find it beneficial to adopt a *common currency* if the cost of converting currencies for regional trade exceeds any perceived gain from having separate currencies. If, for example, the residents of regions A and B continue to perceive sizable benefits from using separate currencies even though no barriers otherwise separate their regions, then they might wish to continue to incur currency conversion costs that arise when they trade goods. But if currency conversion costs are sufficiently large relative to the potential benefits of maintaining separate regional currencies, then the residents of the two regions that constitute an optimal currency area may gain, on net, from adopting a single, common currency. (Proposals have been advanced for the nations of North America to utilize the same

optimal currency area
A geographic area within which labor is sufficiently mobile to permit speedy adjustments to payment imbalances and regional unemployment, so that exchange rates can be fixed and a common currency can be adopted.

currency; see *Policy Notebook: Will North Americans Eventually Use the "Amero" as a Medium of Exchange?*)

POLICY Notebook

Will North Americans Eventually Use the "Amero" as a Medium of Exchange?

A few years ago, the president of Mexico suggested that the three nations participating in the North American Free Trade Agreement—Canada, Mexico, and the United States—should eventually adopt a single currency. Private Canadian groups, such as the C.D. Howe Institute, have even drawn up proposals aimed at serving as guidelines for a "North American Monetary Union." Some have even proposed a name for an imagined North American currency: the "amero."

A common argument offered by proponents of a common North American currency is the significant upswing in international trade among Canada, Mexico, and the United States. U.S. trade with Canada and Mexico now accounts for more than 30 percent of total U.S. international trade. Since 1990, Mexico's share of total Canadian trade has more than tripled, and Canada's share of Mexican trade has increased by more than 500 percent.

So far, however, these increases in cross-border flows of goods and services have not yet translated into considerably freer mobility of factors of production across national borders of the three North American nations. Furthermore, there is very little evidence that the United States would gain from the proposed monetary union. Most studies find that gains that might arise—mainly in the form of reduced costs of converting currencies and additional trade benefits—would accrue to Canada and Mexico. Thus, at present there is little incentive for the United States to participate in a North American currency union.

For Critical Analysis

Based on the theory of optimal currency areas, what is the main argument against a North American monetary union?

Rationales for Separate Currencies

What benefits might residents of two regions with few or no barriers to worker mobility perceive as sufficiently large to justify maintaining separate currencies? One possible answer might be that residents of either region might regard the loss of their own region's currency as a sacrifice of sovereignty. If a region were a nation-state with its own cultural history that its residents associated in part with the region's currency—for instance, Britain with its pound sterling that evokes memories of a former empire or Germany with its deutsche mark that symbolized the nation's commitment to low inflation—then convincing residents to give up their currency could prove difficult.

Removal of Currency Competition Nationalism is not the only factor that might dissuade a country from joining others in using a single currency. Another potential justification for retaining separate currencies is the potential for welfare gains stemming from *currency competition*. This idea was first put forward by the economist Frederick Hayek. He argued that a central bank may be hesitant to place too much currency in circulation if it recognizes that so doing reduces the exchange value of its nation's currency relative to those of other nations, thereby inducing people to prefer to hold less of its currency. Thus, fear of lost business to competing currencies issued by other central banks could lead a country's central bank to hold back on inflationary money growth.

Hayek argued that having many national currencies effectively in competition with each other could be advantageous to the residents of all nations. As a result, they could lose out if governments were to band together and adopt a common currency. Such a move reduces the extent of currency competition and can thereby remove an important check on inflation in regions that might adopt a common currency.

Lack of Fiscal Integration Nations' governments maintain their own budgets with their own sources of revenues and distributions of expenditures. Conflicts related to differences in national budgetary policies can complicate successfully maintaining a monetary union.

Absence of a system of fiscal transfers Most nations are collections of regions, and a number of countries subdivide their political governance structures regionally, typically in the form of states or provinces. These fiscal governance subdivisions can sometimes create frictions that hinder the mobility of factors of production and consequently slow adjustments to economic shocks that affect regions asymmetrically.

For this reason, most relatively large nations that utilize single currencies establish mechanisms for providing transfer payments to people located in areas subjected to adverse economic shocks. Because there is no exchange rate to help rebalance regional economic activity, the mobility frictions that political subdivisions create cause temporary unemployment problems. A system of fiscal transfers directs funds to people in regions hardest hit by asymmetric shocks to assist them in withstanding their economic effects until they are able to adjust to them over a longer period of time, perhaps by moving to another locale where jobs are more plentiful.

seigniorage

Central bank profits resulting from the value of a flow increase in a country's money stock over and above the cost of money production.

Seigniorage issues The key source of any government's revenues is taxes. One type of taxation is *seigniorage,* or central bank profits earned from producing money whose market value exceeds its cost of production. Modern central banks earn seigniorage by receiving interest on securities but not passing it on to holders of currencies they issue or to banks that must hold reserves with the central banks. Seigniorage is a relatively small portion of any nation's tax revenues. Nevertheless, in some nations it is a more important share of tax revenues than it is for others, meaning that such nations might have to undertake the politically painful task of increasing other taxes if they were to lose seigniorage following adoption of a common currency. Thus, these nations might value having a separate currency more than others.

For instance, in our hypothetical example of regions A and B, suppose that the two regions together were to constitute an optimal currency area. In principle, therefore, the two regions could maintain a fixed exchange rate without experiencing long-term trade imbalances or unemployment. Nonetheless, if the government of region A were to depend to a much larger extent upon seigniorage as a revenue source, then region A might be unwilling to agree to adopt a common currency. As a result, the two regions might keep their exchange rate fixed yet continue to use separate currencies.

Fiscal deficit and debt divergences Another obstacle to successful operation of a single currency can arise if there are substantial divergences in participating governments' budget deficits—flows of government expenditures in excess of revenues funded by government borrowing—and resulting stocks of public indebtedness at different points in time. Such divergences potentially can create a number of financial pressures that can complicate the task of maintaining the single currency.

Consider, for instance, a situation in which two nations adopt a single currency, yet one country's government persistently runs significant deficits and begins accumulating a much higher public debt—a debt so large that investors begin to question whether it can be repaid. Eventually, investors may substitute away from holding debt instruments issued by the high-deficit government in favor of the other nation's government's debt instruments they regard as having less risky returns. The result will be a sudden and potentially considerably capital outflow from the high-government-deficit nation and a consequent balance-of-payments deficit in that nation. Because the nations share the same currency, however, no exchange-rate adjustment can take place to rebalance their international accounts. If there are any frictions that constrain mobility of productive factors across the nation's borders, then a sizeable asymmetric shock may be experienced across economies of the two nations, resulting in reduced production and higher unemployment in the high-deficit country. Hence, in the face of these divergences in fiscal deficit and debt conditions, the nations likely would have been better off with separate currencies, which would enable the exchange rate to help to act as a shock absorber.

Trials and Tribulations of the European Monetary Union

Under the terms of the Maastricht Treaty on European Union (EU), eleven members of the then-fifteen-nation EU adopted a common currency in 1999. This group of countries, which became the European Monetary Union (EMU), began using the new currency, the euro, in hand-to-hand transactions in 2002. During the following decade, six more EU member nations elected to utilize the euro as well, and had their central banks join the European System of Central Banks and a centralized institution, the European Central Bank (ECB), in managing circulation of the euro.

By the early 2010s, however, the longer-term future of the euro was in some doubt. Although some observers believed that the EMU might remain intact and eventually even expand once more, others suggested that ultimately only a subset of euro-utilizing nations would continue as EMU members. The most pessimistic observers suggested, however, that in the end the EMU might cease to exist altogether, with member countries likely to readopt their original currencies—albeit at exchange rates perhaps radically altered from their early-2000s levels.

Take a look at the most recent data on European Union nations at
http://epp.eurostat.ec.europa.eu.

Why did a currency union that initially seemed to function well find itself suddenly subject to so much uncertainty after only ten years in operation? The answer to this question has two parts. First, there has always been doubt about whether the degree of mobility of factors of production—in particular, labor—across the full set of EMU member nations was ever sufficient for the EMU to constitute an optimal currency area. Second, fiscal policy failures have caused divergences in economic performances among EMU countries that have contributed to worsening unemployment problems in several member nations.

Does the Eurozone Constitute an Optimal Currency Area? Ever since discussion of the possibility of establishing a single European currency began in earnest during the 1980s, there has been considerable uncertainty about whether all the EU nations actually constitute an optimal currency area. For instance, research by Barry Eichengreen of the University of California at Berkeley compared measures of labor mobility in Western Europe with those of other countries with single currencies, such as the United States and Canada. His evidence indicated that labor is much less mobile in Western Europe, implying that this portion of the world really has never been an especially strong candidate for an optimal currency area.

Most subsequent studies reached conclusions similar to Eichengreen's. Indeed, some researchers contemplated existing monetary arrangements in other nations and found that some geographic regions already using common currencies conceivably might be better off with their own separate currencies. Some studies, for example, suggested that from the standpoint of mobility of factors of production, the entire United States may not constitute an optimal currency area. (Some observers have suggested that the nations of East Asia should contemplate adopting a common currency, even though the argument for these nations may be even weaker than for European countries; see *Policy Notebook: Pros and Cons of an East Asian Monetary Union*.)

POLICY Notebook

Pros and Cons of an East Asian Monetary Union

In recent years, some observers have proposed currency unions involving nations of East Asia. Country groupings that might wish to contemplate a common currency, these observers suggest, include the Association of Southeast Asian Nations—Indonesia, Malaysia, Philippines, Thailand, and several smaller countries—or the Newly Industrialized Economies—Korea, Hong Kong, Taiwan, and Singapore. Others have proposed a wider currency union including China and Japan.

A common argument offered by proponents of a common East Asian currency is the significant upswing in international trade among nations in this part of the world. In 1980, intraregional trade accounted for about 35 percent of all international trade of East Asian nations. Today, more than 50 percent of East Asian trade is intraregional, which is almost as large as the intraregional trade share within the European Union.

So far, however, these increases in cross-border flows of goods and services have not yet translated into considerably freer mobility of factors of production across national borders of East Asian nations. Furthermore, there is very little evidence that either China or Japan would gain from a monetary union encompassing all of East Asia. Most studies find that gains that might arise—mainly in the form of reduced costs of converting currencies and additional trade benefits—would accrue to smaller countries. Thus, at present there is little incentive for either China or Japan to participate in an East Asian currency union.

For Critical Analysis

Based on the theory of optimal currency areas, what is the main argument against an East Asian monetary union?

Fiscal Crisis and the Euro The founders of the euro recognized that in the presence of frictions on mobility of factors of production, significant cross-country divergences of fiscal deficits and debts could eventually cause problems for the EMU. For this reason, the Maastricht Treaty governing the management of the euro requires a country wishing to join the EMU to have a government budget deficit no larger than 3 percent of its GDP and total government debt no greater than 60 percent of its GDP.

The Maastricht Treaty was silent, however, about whether nations that joined the EMU had to *maintain* government deficits and public debts within these limits during subsequent years. Within a few years' time, several EMU governments, including those of France and Germany, decided to operate with deficits or debts exceeding the Maastricht Treaty limits. Then, when a global recession following on the heels of the 2008 U.S. financial panic caused national incomes to level off or even drop and tax revenues to stagnate even as public expenditures continued to grow, most EMU nations' governments began running significant deficits and accumulating much larger levels of public indebtedness.

This fiscal response was particularly pronounced among the so-called PIIGS nations of the EMU—Portugal, Ireland, Italy, Greece, and Spain, whose annual government deficit–GDP ratios rose to more than double the 3 percent Maastricht limit and whose public debt–GDP ratios increased to well above the Maastricht Treaty's 60 percent threshold. Indeed, by the early 2010s, public debt–GDP ratios exceeded 100 percent in all of the PIIGS nations except Spain, and in Greece this ratio grew to above 150 percent.

Public debt ratios in France and Germany also increased to above 80 percent, but economic activity in these and other non-PIIGS nations remained at a level sufficient to convince investors that this set of EMU nations' governments likely could successfully continue to pay interest and repay principal. Investors developed doubts about the capabilities of PIIGS nations' governments to be able to honor their debts. Thus, they began substituting away from holdings of those nations' governments' debt instruments to those of non-PIIGS countries' governments. Indeed, in early 2012, many European investors were buying German government bonds offering *negative* interest yields, meaning that they were sufficiently anxious to avoid the risks of holding assets in many other EMU nations that they were willing to get back a smaller amount of principal than they initially paid when purchasing German government bonds.

The substantial shifts of financial capital from PIIGS nations to other EMU countries contributed to rising balance-of-payments deficits among the former group. Weak north-south mobility of labor and other productive factors caused unemployment problems to fester in the EMU's southern tier, whereas in Ireland many people responded by moving to other EMU countries to seek employment. Thus, in Portugal, Italy, Greece, and Spain, unemployment problems escalated. In the absence of an EMU fiscal transfer system, incomes in these southern-tier nations decreased, and their governments experienced further reductions in tax revenues. This revenue decrease contributed to a further worsening of their fiscal deficit and debt positions.

Many economists, such as Carmen Reinhart of the Peterson Institute for International Economics and Kenneth Rogoff of Harvard University, project that the debt problems plaguing the majority of EMU member nations will persist for at least another decade. It remains to be seen how many EMU nations will still be using the euro as their currency by the early 2020s, given the pressures in place for PIIGS nations to abandon the currency in favor of flexible exchange rates that can allow imbalances to adjust—or perhaps for non-PIIGS countries either to ask some of the former nations to leave the EMU or to give up on the monetary union themselves. (Since 1948, more than half of the efforts by two or more nations to use a common currency have broken down; see the *Policy Notebook: When Have Past Currency Unions Collapsed?*)

POLICY Notebook

When Have Past Currency Unions Collapsed?

In a study of 245 efforts by two or more countries to utilize a common currency since 1948, Volker Nitsch of Free University Berlin seeks to identify the reasons for the dissolutions of 128 of the attempted currency unions. Nitsch finds two key economic factors that cause such efforts to collapse. One is an increase in the difference between national inflation rates. Another is a low level of international trade among the nations. An attempt by at least two nations to use a common currency when one or more of the nations do not engage in very much trade typically leads to failure of the common currency. Alternatively, a significant drop-off in trade in one or more of the nations typically generates a currency breakup, even if nations experienced relatively large trade flows at the outset.

For Critical Analysis

Why do you suppose that maintaining a significant level of international trade among nations can help to perpetuate use of a common currency?

Fundamental ISSUES

#4 Could nations gain from adopting a common currency?

Countries qualify as an optimal currency area, or a geographic area in which movements of workers among regions alleviate unemployment and payments imbalances without the need for exchange-rate adjustment, if labor is highly mobile across national boundaries. In such an environment, nations could save their residents from incurring foreign exchange risks and currency conversion costs by joining a monetary union with a common currency. Nevertheless, even countries within an optimal currency area may resist joining a monetary union (1) if countries fear that the loss of currency competition could remove restraints on inflationary policymaking, (2) if their national governments would lose seigniorage revenues that they could not recoup via other sources of taxation, or (3) if nations allow substantial divergences in fiscal policies by failing to provide for fiscal transfer mechanisms or permitting significant deficits and debts to create intra-union payments imbalances.

VEHICLE CURRENCIES

vehicle currency

A currency that individuals and businesses most often use to conduct international transactions.

As shown in the previous sections, issues of securities and money market instruments can be denominated in any number of currencies. *Vehicle currencies* are used worldwide to denominate international transactions and international financial instruments. Specifically, a ***vehicle currency*** is a currency that individuals and businesses most often use to conduct international transactions. For example, a firm in Japan may issue a bond denominated in U.S. dollars that is purchased by a European household. In this situation, the U.S. dollar serves as a vehicle currency. The transaction is denominated in the U.S. dollar, but a U.S. household is not party to the transaction at all. (To consider recent evidence regarding a key factor contributing to the decision by firms to use a vehicle currency in international trade, see *Policy Notebook: Determination of Invoicing Currencies in International Trade.*)

POLICY Notebook

Determination of Invoicing Currencies in International Trade

Vehicle currencies are commonly used to denominate, or *invoice*, payments for traded goods and services. Linda Goldberg and Cédric Tille of the Federal Reserve Bank of New York have developed a three-country theory of the choice of which country's currency will most often be utilized in invoicing trade among nations. Their theory indicates that firms in industries offering products for which demands are very price-sensitive are more likely than firms in other industries to opt to utilize a particular country's currency for invoicing international transactions. The reason is that firms selling goods that have many close substitutes have an incentive to limit movements of their product prices relative to those of competitors. One way to do this is to invoice in the same currency as the one utilized by their competitors.

Goldberg and Tille study export and import data for twenty-four countries and show that the dollar is the invoice currency for most U.S. transactions and also is extensively used in trade not involving the United States. Consistent with their theory, they find evidence that most dollar-invoicing of non-U.S. trade involves goods sold by firms operating in highly competitive industries. Thus, many of the non-U.S. firms engaging in international trade not involving the United States apparently "herd" toward use of the dollar simply because most other firms use the dollar to denominate their export and import payments.

For Critical Analysis

What does Goldberg and Tille's theory suggest might happen if a large share of companies around the world that operate in highly competitive markets were to begin invoicing their trade in euros instead of dollars?

The Dollar's Predominance

Since the end of World War II, the U.S. dollar has been the dominant vehicle currency. The world's major banks denominate most assets and liabilities used in cross-border transactions in dollars. Traditionally most financial instruments issued in international money and capital markets also have been denominated in dollars.

Since the early 1980s, however, there has been a gradual shift toward the use of multiple currencies in international transactions. As a result, there have been periods when it appeared that the dollar might lose its dominant position. For example, during the 1960s dollar crises that preceded the break-up of the Bretton Woods system and the dollar depreciation of the early 1990s, there was speculation as to whether the dollar would remain the leading vehicle currency. Even today, following the full introduction of the euro, some experts question whether the U.S. dollar can maintain its position as the world's leading currency. They wonder if the dollar will eventually be replaced by another predominant currency, as Table 15–1 shows has occurred throughout world history.

Evidence Regarding Today's Vehicle Currencies

Table 15–2 presents evidence on the use of four leading vehicle currencies, the U.S. dollar, the euro, the Japanese yen, and the British pound. As shown by the data, in international financial markets, the U.S. dollar remains the dominant vehicle currency, used to denominate over 57 percent of banks' cross-border positions, more

Table 15–1

A Timeline of Vehicle Currencies

The U.S. dollar is the latest in a long line of vehicle currencies.

Period	Nation	Currencies
Pre–7th century B.C.	Babylonia	Shekel
6th–7th centuries B.C.	Persia	Daric
5th–3rd centuries B.C.	Greece, Macedonia	Drachma, Stater
3rd century B.C.–4th century A.D.	Rome	Solidus, Denarius, Seterce, Aureus
4th–13th centuries	Byzantium	Solidus, Besant
7th–13th centuries	Mecca	Dirham, Dinar
9th–13th centuries	China	Tael, Chuen
13th–16th centuries	Italy	Florin, Grosso, Sequin, Ducat
16th–17th centuries	Spain	Real, Escudo
17th–18th centuries	France	Denier, Sol, Louis d'or
18th century	India	Rupee, Mohur
19th century	France	Franc
19th–20th centuries	Britain	Shilling, Pound
20th–early 21st centuries	United States	Dollar

Source: Robert Mundell, "The International Impact of the Euro and Its Implications for Transition Economies," in Mario Blejer and Marko Skreb, eds., *Central Banking, Monetary Policies, and the Implications for Transition Economies,* Boston: Kluwer Academic Publishers, 1999, pp. 403–428.

than one-third of international money market instruments, and almost 39 percent of international notes and bonds.

The evidence from foreign exchange markets suggests that the dollar is even more heavily utilized in international trade. On any given day, the U.S. dollar is involved in more than 80 percent of trades of one currency for another in the world's foreign exchange markets. Consequently, the dollar is utilized more than twice as

Table 15–2 Leading Vehicle Currencies

Shares of Market %	Banks' Cross-Border Positions in Foreign Currencies (Assets)	Banks' Cross-Border Positions in Foreign Currencies (Liabilities)	International Money Market Instruments	International Bonds and Notes
U.S. dollar	58.0	59.1	30.1	41.1
Euro	21.7	20.1	45.4	43.2
British pound	4.4	4.5	16.5	7.6
Japanese yen	3.1	3.7	1.6	2.5
All other	13.2	12.6	6.4	5.6

Source: Data from Bank for International Settlements, 2012.

often in overall exchange for other currencies as the second most commonly traded currency, the European euro. The dollar is involved in currency exchanges more than four times as often as either the third and fourth most commonly exchanged currencies, the British pound and the Japanese yen.

A few years ago, there was widespread speculation that the euro might eventually replace the dollar as the leading vehicle currency. Currently, however, the bulk of the evidence supports the conclusion that the dollar's position as the world's primary vehicle currency remains unchallenged.

Fundamental ISSUES

#5 What are vehicle currencies?

Vehicle currencies are currencies that individuals and businesses most often use to conduct international transactions. Since the end of the World War II, the U.S. dollar has been the world's primary vehicle currency. The euro and the Japanese yen are the next two predominant vehicle currencies.

SPLITTING THE DIFFERENCE: EXCHANGE-RATE TARGET ZONES

In previous chapters, you learned that open economies face advantages and disadvantages when contemplating either a system of floating exchange rates or a system of fixed exchange rates. In this chapter, you have seen that failure to coordinate monetary policies can, with floating exchange rates, expose interdependent economies to negative policy externalities that might be at least partially offset via international policy coordination. Yet, coordinating their policies to fix the exchange rate can push up their average inflation rates.

In recent years some economists, such as Paul Krugman of Stanford University, have questioned whether nations of the world must really make a stark choice between fixed or floating exchange rates. They have proposed an approach that seeks a middle ground between these extremes. In a sense, this approach "splits the difference" by limiting exchange-rate volatility while still permitting some variation in countries' currency values.

Target Zones

How can central banks limit exchange-rate movements but allow the exchange rate to vary, nonetheless? Figure 15–7 illustrates one possible answer, which is the establishment of an exchange-rate *target zone,* or a range within which central banks permit exchange rates to vary.

Establishing a Target Zone In Figure 15–7 on the next page, there are upper and lower *bands*, or limits, for permissible values of the exchange rate, S. The upper band is denoted S_U and the lower band is denoted S_L. In a target zone system, a nation's central bank (or perhaps a group of central banks, such as those agreeing to participate in the European Monetary System) establishes specific values for these exchange-rate bands. The central bank commits itself to intervening in the foreign exchange markets to ensure that its nation's currency value will not rise above the upper band or fall below the lower band. For instance, if the exchange

target zone
A range of permitted exchange-rate variation between upper and lower exchange-rate bands that a central bank defends by selling or purchasing foreign exchange reserves.

Figure 15–7

An Exchange-Rate Target Zone

A target zone is a range within which a central bank permits the exchange rates to vary. If the exchange rate approaches the upper band S_U, then the central bank sells foreign exchange reserves in sufficient quantities to prevent additional depreciation of its nation's currency. In contrast, if the exchange rate approaches the lower band S_L, then the central bank purchases sufficient amounts of foreign exchange reserves to stem any further currency appreciation. Between the upper and lower bands, however, the central bank does not intervene in the foreign exchange market.

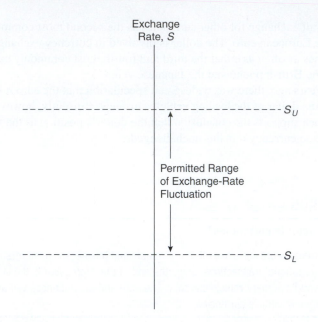

rate approaches the upper band S_U, then the central bank must sell foreign exchange reserves in sufficient quantities to prevent additional depreciation of its nation's currency. In contrast, if the exchange rate approaches the lower band S_L, then the central bank must purchase sufficient amounts of foreign exchange reserves to halt any further currency appreciation.

Between the upper and lower bands, the central bank does not intervene in the foreign exchange markets. Thus, the exchange rate floats freely within the target zone. Because it does not move outside the zone, however, the scope for exchange-rate variability is limited by the size of the upper and lower bands. On the one hand, if the values of S_U and S_L are very small, then the target zone essentially amounts to a fixed-exchange-rate system. On the other hand, if the central bank establishes a very large range between S_U and S_L, then the target zone looks much like a floating-exchange-rate arrangement.

The Behavior of the Exchange Rate Inside the Target Zone How will the exchange rate vary inside the target zone? To address this question, consider Figure 15–8. The upward-sloping dashed line shows how the exchange rate might vary in response to changes in factors that determine its value in a system of floating exchange rates, assuming for simplicity that there is a linear relationship between the exchange rate and these factors. As you learned in Chapter 12, with a floating exchange rate, variations in the quantity of money at home and abroad are important factors influencing a country's currency value.

It is tempting to envision that the exchange rate should vary along the dashed line in a target zone system, with the central bank intervening as soon as the exchange rate reaches either the upper or lower band of the target zone, at points *A* or *B*. Under this view, a target zone system truly amounts to a floating exchange rate within the zone, with a fixed exchange-rate "limit" at the top and bottom of the zone.

In fact, it is unlikely that the exchange rate will vary along the dashed line. The reason is that speculators in the foreign exchange market alter their demand for the nation's currency if they anticipate a central bank intervention near either band of the zone. For example, if the exchange rate rises toward the upper band S_U in

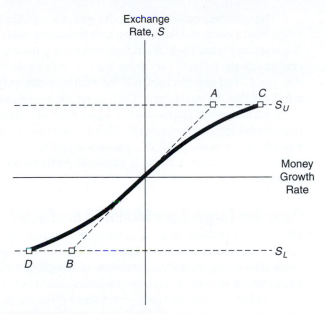

Figure 15–8 The Behavior of the Exchange Rate within a Target Zone

The upward-sloping dashed line between points *A* and *B* shows how the exchange rate varies in response to changes in the domestic money growth. An oversimplified view of how the exchange rate might vary inside a target zone is that it floats along this dashed line within the target zone, with fixed exchange rate limits at the top and bottom of the zone. In fact, however, speculators in the foreign exchange market alter their demands for the nation's currency if they anticipate a central bank intervention near either band of the zone. Hence, the equilibrium exchange rate in a target zone actually should lie below the dashed line as the exchange rate approaches the upper band of the zone, with the central bank obliged to intervene by selling foreign exchange reserves only at an extreme limiting point beyond point *A*, such as point *C*. Likewise, the exchange rate should lie above the dashed line as the exchange rate approaches the lower band of the zone, inducing actual central bank interventions only at a point such as *D*, farther to the left from point *B*. As a result, the equilibrium exchange rate should lie along a smooth, S-shaped curve.

Figure 15–8, then foreign exchange market speculators anticipate that central bank foreign exchange reserve sales will take place to prevent the exchange rate from rising above S_U. Consequently, in this situation speculators expect that it is more likely that the exchange rate will decline in the future. They respond to this anticipation by increasing their current demand for the nation's currency, in the hope of earning future profits by selling the currency when the exchange rate declines and its value appreciates. The resulting current rise in the demand for the nation's currency, however, results in a current appreciation. Hence, foreign exchange market speculation depresses the exchange rate somewhat relative to its value under a true float.

This reasoning implies that the dashed line in Figure 15–8 cannot depict the actual values of the exchange rate in a target zone system. The exchange rate does not truly "float" freely within the target zone. Instead, the equilibrium exchange rate in a target zone should lie below the dashed line as the exchange rate approaches the upper band of the zone. Only at an extreme limiting point beyond point *A*, such as point *C*, is the central bank ultimately obliged to intervene by selling foreign exchange reserves. In contrast, if the exchange rate declines toward the lower band, S_L, speculators demand less of the nation's currency, which tends to push the equilibrium exchange rate upward. Hence, the equilibrium exchange rate should lie above the dashed line as the exchange rate approaches the lower band of the zone, inducing actual central bank interventions only at a point such as *D*, farther to the left from point *B*.

Thus, holding other factors unchanged, the equilibrium exchange rate in a target zone system should lie along a smooth curve such as the S-shaped curve displayed in Figure 15–8. As factors determining the exchange rate change, the exchange rate then should vary along this curve. Because this curve is more shallow than the dashed line that applies if the exchange rate truly floats between the bands, it follows that the establishment of a target zone does more than place absolute limits on exchange-rate fluctuations. A target zone also should lead to less exchange-rate variability *between* the bands. This is one of the potential benefits of adopting a target zone system, if one of a nation's objectives is to reduce foreign exchange risks and to prevent variations in economic performance arising from exchange-rate volatility.

Does the Target Zone Model Fit the Facts?

The reasoning behind the S-curve model of the exchange rate under a target zone seems inescapable. This led a number of economists to spend much of the early 1990s developing theoretical extensions of Krugman's initial reasoning. They determined how a number of economic variables should behave in a target zone environment, including short- and long-term interest rates, the price level, and the balance of payments—all under the assumption that the S-curve reasoning should fit the facts.

Real-World Evidence Nevertheless, a number of economists also began searching for evidence supporting this reasoning. In what Lars Svensson of Stockholm University has called "an excellent example of 'the great tragedy of Science—the slaying of a beautiful hypothesis by an ugly fact' (T. H. Huxley)"—these economists almost uniformly found little evidence of an S-curve relationship between exchange rates in real-world examples of target-zone-type arrangements, such as the Bretton Woods system and the European Monetary System.

The basic S-curve model failed the test of empirical relevance along a number of dimensions. For instance, one essential prediction of the model is the S-curve shape. In fact, economists have been able to find few historical cases in which movements in any nation's exchange rate traced out such a relationship. Indeed, there is little evidence of any long-lasting deterministic relationship between the exchange rate and factors that theory otherwise predicts should affect it. Furthermore, additional predictions about how variables such as interest rates and the price level should behave also receive very little support from real-world data.

Salvaging the Target Zone Theory Today, most economists agree that the basic S-curve model of target zones cannot be salvaged without taking into account two key factors. One is *imperfect policy credibility*. Any system that entails policy commitments to fix or otherwise limit movements in exchange rates generally is not fully credible. There always tends to be some doubt in the minds of foreign exchange market traders about whether a central bank will stand by an announced intention to defend an exchange-rate target—or a zone limiting the range of movement of the exchange rate. As Krugman himself pointed out when he proposed the basic S-curve model, if there is a probability that central banks may fail to intervene as the exchange rate approaches an announced band, then the S-curve model has to be modified to account for that. The result is a lower likelihood of an S-shaped relationship between the exchange rate and factors that determine its value, such as money growth rates.

In addition, central banks may not intervene in foreign exchange markets only at the bands of a target zone. They also may conduct *intra-marginal interventions*,

intra-marginal interventions
Central bank purchases or sales of foreign exchange reserves at exchange-rate levels within a target zone.

or foreign exchange market interventions designed to move exchange rates to desired levels *within* a target zone. It turns out that if central banks conduct intra-marginal interventions, as many of them have done and continue to do, then the basic reasoning of the target zone model is still correct, but it is less likely that there is a fixed S-shaped relationship between the equilibrium exchange rate and its essential determinants.

This has led economists to modify the basic target zone framework to account for these two factors. For example, Michael Klein of Tufts University and Karen Lewis of the University of Pennsylvania developed a target zone model that allows for the possibility that people alter their beliefs about the true target zone bands that central banks are willing and able to defend based on their observations of actual central bank interventions. Klein and Lewis applied their amended target zone model to actual experience during a period of coordinated interventions by the German Bundesbank, Bank of Japan, and Federal Reserve between February and October of 1987. They found evidence that even though these central banks made strong efforts to make their policies credible by coordinating their foreign exchange market interventions and signaling their intentions, traders' perceptions of the intended target zone varied greatly during that eight-month interval.

This and other studies appear to indicate that the target zone model maybe a useful explanation of exchange-rate behavior within the bands of a target zone as long as the model accounts for imperfect credibility and intra-marginal interventions. Economists continue to explore how target zones have functioned in the past and may yet function in the future.

 Fundamental ISSUES

#6 What is an exchange-rate target zone?

An exchange-rate target zone is a region between upper and lower exchange-rate bands, announced by central banks, within which exchange-rate movements must remain. In the case of a credible target zone, a country's central bank pre-commits itself to selling foreign exchange reserves to keep the nation's exchange rate at or below the upper band of the zone and to buying foreign exchange reserves to keep the nation's exchange rate at or above the lower band of the zone. The basic theory of exchange-rate determination in a target zone indicates that the exchange rate should lie on an S-shaped curve. Real-world experience, however, indicates that imperfect policy credibility and intra-marginal interventions require modification of this basic target zone model.

Chapter SUMMARY

1. **Structural Interdependence and International Policy Cooperation or Coordination:** National economies are said to be structurally interdependent if one country's economy responds to events affecting the performance of another. In such situations, international policy externalities can exist, meaning that policy actions in one country can have spillover effects on the economies of other nations. Positive international policy externalities exert beneficial spillover effects on other nations' economic performances, whereas negative international policy externalities contribute to a worsening of those nations' economic performances. To enhance positive externalities or mitigate negative externalities, nations

may decide to establish institutional structures for sharing data or for collaborating on national goals. They also may decide to coordinate their policies by determining policy actions that are best for their common good.

2. **The Potential Benefits of International Policy Coordination:** The most important potential gain that policy coordination might achieve is the internalization of international policy externalities. That is, joint determination of policy actions could allow policymakers to minimize negative externalities or to enhance positive externalities. Policy coordination might also enlarge the number of policy instruments that policymakers could aim at their collective goals. Finally, by joining a formal international policy coordination arrangement, a national policymaker may have more success in resisting domestic political pressures to engage in policy actions that have near-term benefits but potentially negative long-term effects.

3. **The Potential Drawbacks of International Policy Coordination:** One way in which a nation loses by entering into a policy coordination arrangement is that its policymakers sacrifice at least part of their national sovereignty. Furthermore, there must be mutual faith that nations will not cheat on a policy coordination agreement at the expense of other countries and that otherwise well-meaning policymakers in other nations will not pursue counterproductive policies. Another potential pitfall of international policy coordination is that it can, if policymakers' credibility levels are low among residents of their own nations, lead to the adoption of more inflationary policies.

4. **The Possibility That Nations Could Gain from Adopting a Common Currency:** Nations lie inside an optimal currency area if there is sufficient mobility of workers across national boundaries to alleviate unemployment and payments imbalances without the need for exchange-rate adjustment. Countries in an optimal currency area could, in principle, eliminate foreign exchange risks and currency conversion costs faced by their residents if they were to form a monetary union with a common currency. Nonetheless, nations within an optimal currency area may choose to forgo using a common currency (1) if nations worry that reduced currency competition could remove restraints on inflationary biases inherent in monetary policymaking, (2) if countries' governments would experience seigniorage losses that could not be replaced by other revenue sources, or (3) if nations allow significant divergences in fiscal policies via a lack of fiscal transfer mechanisms or allowance of substantial government deficits and debts that generate destabilizing payments imbalances.

5. **Vehicle Currencies:** Vehicle currencies are currencies that individuals and businesses most often use to conduct international transactions. Traditionally, the U.S. dollar has been the world's primary vehicle currency. Others are the British pound, the Japanese yen, and, more recently, the European Monetary Union's euro. Although the euro has made inroads into the dollar's preeminent position in international money and capital markets, banks continue to use the dollar to denominate most cross-border transactions, and evidence from foreign exchange market trading suggests that the dollar remains the primary vehicle currency in international trade.

6. **Exchange-Rate Target Zones:** An exchange-rate target zone is a region between upper and lower exchange-rate bands, or upper and lower limits, within which central banks seek to restrain exchange-rate variations. If a target zone policy is credible, then a nation's central bank can pre-commit to a policy of selling foreign exchange reserves to keep the nation's exchange rate at or below the upper band of the zone and purchasing foreign exchange reserves to keep the nation's exchange rate at or above the lower band of the zone. According to the basic target zone theory of exchange-rate determination,

the exchange rate should lie on an S-shaped curve. Actual evidence from periods in which target zone policies have been pursued, however, implies that imperfect policy credibility and intra-marginal interventions must be taken into account for the target zone model to fit the facts.

QUESTIONSandPROBLEMS

1. Suppose that two nations were to establish a central clearing house for interbank payments that cross their borders. In addition, the staffs of their central banks work together to develop rules and regulations for this clearing house, and they jointly fund and operate an agency charged with regulating this institution. Would this best be termed an example of policy cooperation or of policy coordination? Explain your reasoning.

2. A domestic government enacts a significant cut in taxes intended to spur its domestic industries. In addition, however, the tax cut gives foreign-owned firms an incentive to relocate their offices and production facilities within domestic borders. The tax cut also has been carefully crafted to avoid spurring increased imports by domestic citizens. Would these effects of this domestic policy action be an example of a positive or negative international policy externality? Explain.

3. Workers who speak a common language and share a common culture are completely mobile within a region that encompasses three small economies that engage in large volumes of international trade and have floating exchange rates. Residents in each country must incur sizable costs each time they convert their home currency into a foreign currency, and they face significant foreign exchange risks. Is this region a potential candidate for monetary union? Justify your answer.

4. As noted in this chapter, there is not strong evidence that all nations of Western Europe constitute an optimal currency area in the conventional sense. Yet several countries outside the European Monetary Union continue to express interest in adopting the euro. Can you think of any other arguments that leaders of these nations might give to support the goal of joining the European Monetary Union? Explain.

5. Suppose that a country's residents speak a language that most others around the world do not know. There also are legal and natural impediments to movements of factors of production across the nation's borders. The nation's central bank maintains a fixed exchange rate. Recently, there has been a worldwide fall in the demand for the nation's primary products. Could this nation gain from letting its exchange rate float? Explain your reasoning.

6. Why might Europe benefit more fully from its adoption of a single currency if all of its residents shared knowledge of at least one common language? Explain.

7. Discuss the potential advantages of coordinating national monetary policies. Of these, which do you think is most important? Explain.

8. Discuss the likely disadvantages of international monetary policy coordination. Which do you believe to be the greatest disadvantage? Take a stand, and justify your position.

9. In light of the trade-offs entailed in coordinating national monetary policies, why might central banks agree only to coordinate their policies intermittently, such as when unexpected negative events like world energy-price jumps take place? Explain your reasoning.

10. There have recently been proposals for a currency union involving several nations located in southern and central Africa. These nations tend to experience common reactions to world shocks, and they engage in considerable trade with one another. There is very little

movement of labor or capital across their borders. Several of the countries' governments rely on seigniorage to fund large shares of their public spending, while others do not. In your view, is a currency union a good idea at this time? Explain your reasoning.

11. Suppose that a nation's central bank announces that it intends to intervene in foreign exchange markets to defend upper and lower limits on its nation's exchange rate. Yet foreign exchange market traders learn that the central bank has no foreign exchange reserves to use in such interventions. Would you expect the exchange rate to lie on the S-curve predicted by the basic target zone model? If so, why? If not, how do you think the schedule for the exchange rate on the target zone diagram would be shaped? Explain.

Online**APPLICATIONS**

Member nations of the European Union continue to try to work out a framework for adopting a single currency. This application acquaints you with issues concerning monetary policy in the European Monetary Union.

Internet URL: *http://www.ecb.int*

Title: About the European Central Bank

Navigation: Begin at http://www.ecb.int, the address for the home page of the European Central Bank. Click on the tab titled *The Europen Central Bank*. On the left-hand side of the page click on *Educational*. Scroll down to *Our videos*.

Application: The European Central Bank and member nations of the European Monetary Union continue to adjust to a single currency. Read the videos listed below to learn about the various issues concerning the ECB and monetary policy in the EMU, and then answer the following questions:

1. Click on and watch the short video titled *Role and tasks* What is the main difference between the ECB and other central banks around the world? What is the main objective of the ECB? What are the six activities the ECB is involved in to ensure the functioning of the euro?

2. Now select and watch the video titled *Monetary policy strategy*. What is the inflation target of the ECB? What are the nine key economic indicators watched by the ECB when formulating monetary policy?

SELECTED REFERENCES**and**FURTHER READINGS

Bauer, Christian, Paul DeGrauwe, and Stefan Reitz. "Exchange Rate Dynamics in a Target Zone: A Heterogeneous Expectations Approach." Deutsche Bundesbank, Discussion Paper No. 11 (2007).

Bottazzi, Laura, and Paulo Manasse. "Credibility and Seigniorage in a Common Currency Area," *Journal of Money, Credit, and Banking 34* (2002): 1034–1046.

Chinn, Menzie, and Jeffrey Frankel. "The Euro May over the Next 15 Years Surpass the Dollar as Leading International Currency." National Bureau of Economic Research, Working Paper No. 13909 (April 2008).

Chriszt, Michael. "Perspectives on a Potential North American Monetary Union." Federal Reserve Bank of Atlanta, *Economic Review*, 4th Quarter (2000): 29–39.

Daniels, Joseph, and David VanHoose. "Currency Substitution, Seigniorage, and Currency Crises in Interdependent Economies." *Journal of Economics and Business 55* (May/June 2003): 221–232.

Glick, Reuven. "Does Europe's Path to Monetary Union Provide Lessons for East Asia?" Federal Reserve Bank of San Francisco, *Economic Letter* No. 2005-19 (August 12, 2005).

Goldberger, Linda, and Cédric Tille. "Vehicle Currency Use in International Trade." Federal Reserve Bank of New York, Staff Report No. 200 (January 2005).

Kenen, Peter, and Ellen Meade. *Regional Monetary Integration*. Cambridge, UK: Cambridge University Press, 2008.

Kirton, John J., and Joseph P. Daniels, eds. *The G8 Role in the New Millennium*. Aldershot, UK: Ashgate Publishing Ltd. (1999).

Kokotsis, Ella, and Joseph P. Daniels. "G8 Summits and Compliance." In Michael R. Hodges, John J. Kirton, and Joseph P. Daniels, eds. *The G8's Role in the New Millennium*. Aldershot, UK: Ashgate Publishing, 1999.

Krugman, Paul, and Marcus Miller, eds. *Exchange Rate Targets and Currency Bands*. Cambridge, UK: Cambridge University Press, 1992.

Melvin, Michael, Lukas Menishoff, and Maik Schmeling. "Automating Exchange Rate Target Zones: Intervential via an Electronic Limit Order Book." CESifo, Working Paper No. 2221 (February 2008).

Mundell, Robert. "A Theory of Optimal Currency Areas." *American Economic Review 51* (1961): 657–665.

Murdaca, B. Gabriela. "Central Bank Interventions and Exchange Rate Board Regimes." *Journal of International Money and Finance 20* (2001): 677–700.

Nitsch, Volker. "Have a Break, Have a…National Currency: When Do Monetary Unions Fall Apart?" CESifo, Working Paper No. 1113 (January 2004).

Portes, Richard. "The Euro and the International Financial System." In Marco Buti and Andre Sapir, eds. *EMU and Economy Policy in Europe: The Challenge of the Early Years*. London: Edward Elgar, 2003.

Reinhart, Carmen, and Kenneth Rogoff. *A Decade of Debt*. Washington, D.C.: Peterson Institute for International Economics, September 2011.

Rose, Andrew, and Charles Engel. "Currency Unions and International Integration." *Journal of Money, Credit, and Banking 39* (2002): 1067–1089.

Van Overtveldt, Johan. *The End of the Euro: The Uneasy Future of the European Union*. Jackson, TN: Agate Publishing, 2011.

GLOSSARY

A

absorption approach A theory of balance-of-payments and exchange-rate determination that emphasizes the role of a nation's expenditures, or absorption, and income. According to the absorption approach, if a nation's real income exceeds the amount of goods and services that it absorbs, then the nation will run a current account surplus.

absorption instrument A government's ability to increase or decrease a nation's absorption by changing its own purchases of domestic output or by influencing consumption and investment expenditures.

absorption A nation's total expenditures on final goods and services net of exports.

adverse selection The potential for those who borrow funds to undertake unworthy, high-risk investment projects.

aggregate demand schedule Combinations of real income and the price level that maintain *IS–LM* equilibrium and thereby ensure that real income is equal to aggregate desired expenditures and that the market for real money balances is in equilibrium.

aggregate expenditures schedule A schedule depicting total desired expenditures on domestic goods and services by households, firms, the government, and foreign residents at each and every level of real national income.

aggregate net autonomous expenditures The total amount of autonomous consumption, autonomous investment, autonomous government spending, and autonomous export spending, which is assumed to be independent of the level of national income.

aggregate supply schedule A schedule depicting volumes of real output produced by all workers and firms at each possible price level.

American option An option in which the holder may buy or sell a security any time before or including the date at which the contract expires.

announcement effect A change in private market interest rates or exchange rates that results from an anticipation of near-term changes in market conditions signaled by a central bank policy action.

assignment problem The problem of determining whether the central bank or the finance ministry should assume responsibility for achieving a nation's domestic or international policy objectives.

asymmetric information Possession of information by one party in a financial transaction that is not available to the other party.

autonomous expenditures multiplier A measure of the size of the multiplier effect on equilibrium real income caused by a change in aggregate autonomous expenditures, which is equal to $1/(MPS + MPIM) = 1/(1 - MPC)$.

autonomous consumption The amount of household consumption spending on domestically produced goods and services that is independent of the level of real income.

autonomous investment spending Desired investment expenditures that are independent of the level of real income.

B

balance-of-payments system A system of accounts that measures transactions of goods, services, income, and financial assets between domestic residents, businesses, and governments and the rest of the world during specific time period.

Bank for International Settlements (BIS) An institution based in Basel, Switzerland, that serves as an agent for central banks and a center of economic cooperation among the largest industrialized nations.

base year A reference year for price-level comparisons, which is a year in which nominal GDP is equal to real GDP, so that the GDP deflator's value is equal to one.

beggar-thy-neighbor effect A policy action of one nation that benefits that nation's economy but worsens economic performance in another nation.

bid–ask margin The difference between the ask price, or price at which a currency is offered for sale, and the bid price, or price offered for the purchase of the currency, expressed as a percent of the ask price.

bid–ask spread The difference between the bid price, or price offered for the purchase of a currency, and the ask price, or price at which the currency is offered for sale.

bonds Long-term promissory notes.

book-entry security systems Computer systems that the Federal Reserve uses to maintain records of sales of U.S. Treasury securities and interest and principal payments.

***BP* schedule** A set of real income–nominal interest rate combinations that is consistent with a balance-of-payments equilibrium in which the current account balance and capital account balance sum to zero.

business cycles Periods of fluctuation in real GDP around its natural level.

C

call option An option contract giving the owner the right to purchase a financial instrument at a specific price.

Cambridge equation A theory of the demand for money developed by economists at Cambridge University. The Cambridge equation postulates that the quantity of money demanded is a fraction of nominal income.

capacity output level The level of real GDP that could be produced if all factors of production were fully employed.

capital account   A tabulation of the flows of financial assets among domestic private residents, foreign private residents, and domestic and foreign governments; sometimes referred to as the *financial account*.

capital controls   Legal restrictions on the ability of a nation's residents to hold and exchange assets denominated in foreign currencies.

capital gain   A rise in the value of a financial instrument at the time it is sold, as compared with its market value at the time it was purchased.

capital loss   A decline in the market value of a financial instrument at the time it is sold, as compared with its market value at the time it was purchased.

capital market liberalization   Policy actions designed to allow relatively open issuance and competition in a nation's stock and bond markets.

capital mobility   The extent to which financial resources can flow across a nation's borders.

capital requirements   Minimum equity capital standards that national regulatory agencies impose on banks.

central banker contact   A legally binding agreement between a government and a central banking official that holds the official responsible for a nation's inflation performance.

Clearing House Interbank Payments System (CHIPS)   A privately owned and operated large-value wire transfer system linking about 50 U.S. banks, which allows them to transmit large payments relating primarily to foreign exchange and Eurocurrency transactions.

Cologne Debt Initiative   A follow-up program to the HIPC Initiative that expanded the list of nations that could potentially qualify for debt relief, expanded the amount of proposed debt relief, and accelerated the time table.

composite currency   A currency unit in which the value is expressed as a weighted average of a selected basket of currencies.

conditionality   The set of limitations on the range of allowable actions of a government of a country that is a recipient of IMF loans.

conservative policymaker   A central bank official who dislikes inflation more than an average citizen in society and who thereby is less willing to induce discretionary increases in the quantity of money in an effort to achieve short-run increases in real output.

consumer price index (CPI)   A weighted sum of the prices of goods and services that the government determines a typical consumer purchases each year.

convertibility   The ability to freely exchange a currency for a reserve commodity or reserve currency.

core capital   Defined by the Basel capital standards as shareholders' equity plus retained earnings.

corners hypothesis   The view that policymakers should choose fully flexible or hard-peg-exchange-rate regimes over intermediate regimes such as adjustable-peg, crawling-peg, or basket-peg arrangements.

country risk   The possibility of losses on holdings of financial instruments issued in another nation because of political uncertainty within that nation.

covered exposure   A foreign exchange risk that has been completely eliminated with a hedging instrument.

covered interest parity   A condition relating interest differentials to the forward premium or discount.

crawling peg   An exchange-rate arrangement in which a country pegs its currency to the currency of another nation, but allows the parity value to change at regular time intervals.

credit entry   A positive entry in the balance of payments that records a transaction resulting in a payment from abroad to a domestic resident.

credit risk   The risk of loss that could take place if one party to an exchange were to fail to abide by terms under which both parties originally had agreed to make the exchange.

cross rate   A bilateral exchange rate calculated from two other bilateral exchange rates.

cross-border mergers and acquisitions   The combining of firms located in different nations in which one firm absorbs the assets and liabilities of another firm (merger) or purchases the assets and liabilities of another firm (acquisition).

crowding-out effect   A decline in real private investment spending induced by a rise in the demand for money and the equilibrium nominal interest rate caused by a rise in equilibrium real income that follows an expansionary fiscal policy action.

currency board or independent currency authority   An independent monetary agency that substitutes for a central bank. The currency board pegs the value of the domestic currency, and changes in the foreign reserve holdings of the currency board determine the level of the domestic money stock.

currency future   An agreement to deliver to another a standardized quantity of a specific nation's currency at a designated future date.

currency option   A contract granting the right to buy or sell a given amount of a nation's currency at a certain price within a specific period of time.

currency swap   An exchange of payment flows denominated in different currencies.

currency-basket peg   An exchange-rate arrangement in which a country pegs its currency to the weighted average value of a basket, or selected number, of currencies.

current account   Measures the flow of goods, services, income, and transfers or gifts between domestic residents, businesses, and governments and the rest of the world.

cyclical unemployment   The fraction of a nation's labor force composed of individuals who have lost employment owing to business-cycle fluctuations.

D

debit entry   A negative entry in the balance of payments that records a transaction resulting in a payment abroad by a domestic resident.

default risk   The possibility that an individual or business that issues a financial instrument may be unable to meet its obligations to repay the principal or to make interest payments.

derivative credit risks   Risks stemming from the potential default by a party in a derivative contract or from unexpected changes in credit exposure because of changes in the market yields of instruments on which derivative yields depend.

derivative market risks   Risks arising from unanticipated changes in derivatives market liquidity or payments-system failures.

derivative operating risks   Risks owing to a lack of adequate management controls or from managerial inexperience with derivative securities.

derivative security   A financial instrument in which the return depends on the returns of other financial instruments.

devalue   A situation in which a nation with a pegged-exchange-rate arrangement changes the pegged, or parity, value of its currency so that it takes a greater number of domestic currency units to purchase one unit of the foreign currency to which the nation's currency value is pegged.

discounted present value   The value today of a payment to be received at a future date.

dollar-standard exchange-rate system   An exchange-rate system in which a country pegs its currency to the U.S. dollar and freely exchanges the domestic currency for the dollar at the pegged rate.

domestic credit   Total domestic securities and loans held as assets by a central bank.

dynamic open economy theories   Economic models intended to explain how variables such as real output, employment, the price level, the current account, and the capital account interact and vary over time.

E

early-warning system   A mechanism that multinational institutions might use to track financial crisis indicators to determine that a crisis is on the horizon, thereby permitting a rapid response to head off the crisis.

economic efficiency   The allocation of scarce resources at minimum cost.

economic exposure   The risk that changes in exchange values might alter a firm's present value of the future income streams.

economic fundamentals   Basic factors determining a nation's current exchange rate, such as the country's present and likely future economic policies and performance.

economies of scale   Cost savings from pooling funds for centralized management.

effective exchange rate   A measure of the weighted-average value of a currency relative to a selected group of currencies.

elasticities approach   An approach that emphasizes changes in the prices of goods and services as the main determinant of a nation's balance of payments and the exchange value of its currency.

equities   Ownership shares that might or might not pay the holder a dividend; their values rise and fall with savers' perceived value of the issuing enterprise.

Eurobonds   Long-term debt instruments denominated in a currency other than that of the country in which instrument is issued.

Eurocommercial paper   Unsecured short-term debt instrument issued in a currency other than that of the country in which the instrument is issued.

Eurocurrency market   A market for the borrowing and lending of Eurocurrency deposits.

Eurocurrency   A bank deposit denominated in a currency other than that of the nation in which the bank deposit is located.

Euronotes   Short- and medium-term debt instruments issued in a currency other than that of the country in which the instrument is issued.

European option   An option in which the holder may buy or sell a financial instrument only on the day that the contract expires.

***ex ante* conditionality**   The imposition of IMF lending conditions before the IMF grants the loan.

***ex post* conditionality**   The imposition of IMF lending conditions after a loan has already been granted.

exchange-rate instability   A situation in which a currency depreciation increases the difference between the quantity of foreign exchange supplied and the quantity of foreign exchange demanded instead of reducing the difference.

exchange-rate overshooting   A situation in which the short-run a effect of an increase in aggregate demand is a rise in the nominal exchange rate above its long-run equilibrium value.

exchange-rate parity bands   A range of exchange values, with an upper and lower limit within which the exchange value of the domestic currency can fluctuate.

exchange-rate system   A set of rules that determines the international value of a currency.

exercise price   The price at which the holder of an option has the right to buy or sell a financial instrument; also known as the strike price.

expectations theory   A theory of the term structure of interest rates that views bonds with differing maturities as perfect substitutes, causing their yields to differ solely because traders anticipated that short-term interest rates will rise or fall.

expenditure-switching instrument   A government's ability to alter, or switch, expenditures among imports and exports by enacting policies that change their relative prices.

externality   A benefit or cost felt by one individual or group stemming from actions by another individual or group in another location or market.

externality   A spillover from the actions of one set of individuals to others who otherwise are not involved in the transactions among that group.

F

Fedwire   A large-value wire transfer system operated by the Federal Reserve that is open to all banking institutions that legally must maintain required cash reserves with the Fed.

financial crisis indicator   An economic variable that normally moves in a specific direction and by a certain relative amount in advance of a financial crisis, thereby helping to predict a coming crisis.

financial crisis   A situation that arises when financial instability becomes so severe that the nation's financial system is unable to function. A financial crisis typically involves a banking crisis, a currency crisis, and a foreign debt crisis.

financial instability   When a nation's financial sector is no longer able to allocate funds to the most productive projects.

financial intermediation   Indirect finance through the services of financial institutions that channel funds from savers to those who ultimately make capital investments.

financial sector   A designation for the sector of the economy where people trade in financial assets.

financial-sector development   The strengthening and growth of a nation's financial sector institutions, payments systems, and regulatory agencies.

fiscal agent   A term describing a central bank's role as an agent of its government's finance ministry or treasury department, in which the central bank issues, services, and redeems debts on the government's behalf.

Fisher equation   A condition that defines the real interest rate as the nominal interest rate less the expected rate of inflation.

flexible-exchange-rate system   An exchange-rate system whereby a nation allows market forces to determine the international value of its currency.

foreign direct investment   The acquisition of foreign financial assets that results in an ownership share in the foreign entity of 10 percent or greater.

foreign exchange market efficiency   A situation in which the equilibrium spot and forward exchange rates adjust to reflect all available information, in which case the forward premium is, on average, equal to the expected rate of currency depreciation plus any risk premium. This, in turn, implies that the forward exchange rate predicts, on average, the expected future spot exchange rate.

foreign exchange risk   The risk that the value of a future receipt or obligation will change due to a change in foreign exchange rates.

45-degree line   A line that cuts in half the 90-degree angle of the coordinate axes on a diagram relating real income to aggregate desired expenditures and that provides a potential set of equilibrium points at which real income equals aggregate desired expenditures.

forward exchange market   A market for contracts that ensure the future delivery of a foreign currency at a specified exchange rate.

forward premium or discount   The difference between the forward exchange rate and the spot exchange rate, expressed as a percentage of the spot exchange rate.

frictional unemployment   The fraction of a nation's labor force composed of people who are temporarily out of work.

futures contract   An agreement to deliver to another a given amount of a standardized commodity or financial instrument at a designated future date.

futures options   Options to buy or sell futures contracts.

G

GDP price deflator   A measure of the overall price level; equal to nominal gross domestic product divided by real gross domestic product.

gross domestic product (GDP)   The market value of all final goods and services produced within a nation's borders during a given period.

Group of Five (G5)   The nations of France, Germany, Japan, the United Kingdom, and the United States.

Group of Seven (G7)   The G5 plus Canada and Italy.

Group of Ten (G10)   Belgium, Canada, France, Germany, Italy, Japan, the Netherlands, Sweden, the United Kingdom, and the United States.

H

hedging   The act of offsetting or eliminating risk exposure.

Herstatt risk   Liquidity, credit, and systemic risks across international borders.

HIPC Initiative   A program of debt relief for the heavily indebted poor countries developed by the leaders of the seven major industrialized nations. The initiative established a set of conditions and time table required for debt relief.

I

imperfect competition   A market environment in which there are only a few firms, each of which individually can influence the market price by varying its production.

income identity   A truism stating that real income is allocated among real household consumption, real household saving, real net taxes, and real imports.

inflation bias   The tendency for an economy to experience persistent inflation as a result of the time inconsistency problem and the lack of policy credibility.

insolvency   A situation in which the value of a bank's assets falls below the value of its liabilities.

interbank funds markets   Markets for large-denomination interbank loans and one-day to one-week maturities.

interest rate forward contract   Contracts committing the issuer to sell a financial instrument at a given interest rate as of a specific date.

interest rate futures   Contracts to buy or sell a standardized denomination of a specific financial instrument at a given price at a certain date in the future.

interest rate risk   The possibility that the market value of a financial instrument will change as interest rates vary.

interest rate swap   A contractual exchange of one set of interest payments for another.

international capital markets   Markets for cross-border exchange of financial instruments that have maturities of one year or more.

international financial architecture   The international institutions, governmental and nongovernmental organizations, and policies that govern activity in the international monetary and financial markets.

international financial diversification   Holding financial instruments issued in various countries to spread portfolio risks.

International Monetary Fund (IMF)   A multinational organization with more than 180 member nations that seeks to encourage global economic growth by promoting international monetary cooperation and effective exchange arrangements and by providing temporary and longer-term financial assistance to nations experiencing balance-of-payments difficulties.

international money markets   Markets for cross-border exchange of financial instruments with maturities of less than one year.

international policy cooperation   The adoption of institutions and procedures by which national policymakers can inform each other about their objectives, policy strategies, and national economic data.

international policy coordination   The joint determination of economic policies within a group of nations for the intended benefit of the group as a whole.

international policy externality   A benefit or cost for one nation's economy owing to a policy action undertaken in another nation.

intra-marginal interventions   Central bank purchases or sales of foreign exchange reserves at exchange-rate levels within a target zone.

IS–LM equilibrium   A single point shared in common by the *IS* and *LM* schedules, at which the economy simultaneously attains both an income–expenditure equilibrium and equilibrium in the money market.

IS schedule   A set of possible combinations of real income and the nominal interest rate that is necessary to maintain the income–expenditure equilibrium, $y = c + i + g + x$, for a given level of aggregate net autonomous expenditures.

J

J-curve effect   A phenomenon in which a depreciation of the domestic currency causes a nation's balance of payments to worsen before it improves.

Jamaica Accords   A meeting of the member nations of the IMF, occurring in January 1976, amending the constitution of the IMF to allow, among other things, each member nation to determine its own exchange-rate arrangement.

L

large-value wire transfer systems   Payments systems such as Fedwire and CHIPS that permit the electronic transmission of large volumes of funds.

law of diminishing marginal returns   The fact that the additional output produced by an additional unit of labor ultimately falls as firms employ more units of labor.

leaning against the wind   Central bank interventions to halt or reverse the current trend in the market exchange value of its nation's currency.

leaning with the wind   Central bank interventions to support or speed along the current trend in the market exchange value of its nation's currency.

lender of last resort   A central banking function in which the central bank stands willing to lend to any temporarily illiquid but otherwise solvent banking institution to prevent its illiquid position

from leading to a general loss of confidence in that institution.

liquidity effect   A reduction in the equilibrium nominal interest rate stemming from an increase in the nominal quantity of money in circulation.

liquidity risk   The risk of loss that may occur if a payment is not received when due.

LM schedule   A set of combinations of real income and the nominal interest rate that maintains money market equilibrium.

locomotive effect   A stimulus to real income growth in one nation due to an increase in real income in another country.

Lombard rate   The specific name given to the interest rate on central bank advances that the European Central Bank and Swiss National Bank set above current market interest rates.

London Club   A forum for debtor nations to initiate negotiations with private-sector lenders to reschedule payments on commercial bank debt.

long position   An obligation to purchase a financial instrument at a given price and at a specific time.

Louvre Accord   A meeting of the central bankers and finance ministers of the G7 nations, less Italy, that took place in February 1987. The participants announced that the exchange value of the dollar had fallen to a level consistent with "economic fundamentals" and that central banks would intervene in the foreign exchange market only to ensure the stability of exchange rates.

M

managed or dirty float   An exchange-rate arrangement in which a nation allows the international value of its currency to be primarily determined by market forces, but intervenes from time to time to stabilize its currency.

marginal product of labor   The additional quantity of output that firms can produce by employing another unit of labor.

marginal propensity to consume (MPC) The additional consumption resulting from an increase in disposable income; a change in consumption spending divided by a corresponding change in disposable income; the slope of the consumption function.

marginal propensity to import (MPIM) The additional import expenditures stemming from an increase in disposable income; a change in import spending divided by a corresponding change in disposable income; the slope of the import function.

marginal propensity to save (MPS) The additional saving caused by an increase in disposable income; a change in saving divided by a corresponding change in disposable income; the slope of the saving function.

market-based regulation Using information gleaned from financial markets to determine appropriate bank regulatory standards.

Marshall–Lerner condition A necessary condition for exchange-rate stability, in which the sum of the elasticity of import demand and the elasticity of export supply must exceed unity.

menu costs Small but nontrivial costs that firms incur when they alter product prices.

mercantilism A view that a primary determinant of a nation's wealth is its inflows of payments resulting from international trade and commerce, so that a nation can gain by enacting policies that spur exports while limiting imports.

monetary approach Relates changes in a nation's balance of payments and the exchange value of its currency to differences between the quantity of money demanded and the quantity of money supplied.

monetary base Central bank holdings of domestic securities and loans plus foreign exchange reserves, or the sum of currency and bank reserves.

monetary order A set of laws and regulations that establishes the framework within which individuals conduct and settle transactions.

monetary policy autonomy The capability of a central bank to engage in monetary policy actions independent of the actions of other central banks.

monetary union A set of countries that choose to use a common currency.

money multiplier The number by which a reserve measure is multiplied to obtain the total money stock of an economy.

moral hazard The possibility that a borrower might engage in more risky behavior after receiving the funds from a lender.

multiplier effect The ratio of a change in the equilibrium real income to an increase in autonomous net aggregate expenditures. When the aggregate expenditure schedule shifts vertically, the equilibrium level of national income changes by a multiple of the amount of the shift, and the *IS* schedule shifts by this magnitude.

N

natural rate of unemployment The sum of the rates of frictional and structural unemployment, or the unemployment rate that would arise if a nation's economy were always on its long-run growth path.

natural real gross domestic product A level of real GDP that lies on a nation's long-run growth path.

net creditor A nation whose total claims on foreigners exceed the total claims of foreigners on the nation.

net debtor A nation whose total claims on foreigners are less than the total claims of foreigners on the nation.

netting The process of combining separate risk exposures that a firm faces in its foreign-currency-denominated payments and receipts into a single net risk exposure.

new open economy macroeconomics An approach to open economy macroeconomics that focuses on how nominal wage stickiness, sluggish price adjustment, and imperfect competition affect the transmission of policy actions, often in the context of theories aimed at predicting decisions that nations' residents make over time.

nominal exchange rate A bilateral exchange rate that is unadjusted for changes in the two nations' price levels.

nominal gross domestic product The current market value of all final goods and services produced by a nation during a given period with no adjustment for prices.

normal profit A profit level just sufficient to compensate bank owners for holding equity shares in banks rather than other enterprises.

O

off-balance-sheet banking Bank activities that earn income without expanding the assets and liabilities that they report on their balance sheets.

official settlements balance A balance-of-payments account that tabulates transactions of reserve assets by official government agencies.

open economy macroeconomics The study of factors affecting the overall economic performance of a country that permits cross-border exchanges of goods, services, and financial assets.

open-market operations Central bank purchases or sales of government or private securities.

optimal currency area A geographic area within which labor is sufficiently mobile to permit speedy adjustments to payment imbalances and regional unemployment, so that exchange rates can be fixed and a common currency can be adopted.

option A financial contract giving the owner the right to buy or sell an underlying financial instrument at a certain price within a specific period of time.

overvalued currency A currency in which the current market-determined value is higher than the value predicted by an economic theory or model.

P

Paris Club A forum that allows debtor nations to initiate negotiations with creditor nations to reschedule payments on official debt.

pass-through effect   The effect of a currency depreciation that results in higher domestic prices of imported goods and services.

payment system   A term that broadly refers to the set of mechanisms by which consumers, businesses, governments, and financial institutions make payments.

pegged-exchange-rate system   An exchange-rate system in which a country pegs the international value of the domestic currency to the currency of another nation.

penalty rate   The general term for any interest rate on central bank advances that is set above prevailing market interest rates.

per capita gross domestic product   The total value of final goods and services produced within a country during a given year divided by the number of people residing in the country.

perpetuity   A bond with an infinite term to maturity.

peso problem   An upward bias in depreciation expectations resulting from a perceived small probability of a large currency realignment.

Plaza Agreement   A meeting of the central bankers and finance ministers of the G5 nations that took place at the Plaza Hotel in New York in September 1985. The participants announced that the exchange value of the dollar was too strong and that the nations would coordinate their intervention actions in order to drive down the value of the dollar.

policy credibility   The believability of a policymaker's commitment to a stated intention.

policy instruments   A financial variable that central banks can control in an effort to attain their policy objectives.

policy-created distortion   When a government policy results in a market producing a level of output that is different from the economically efficient level of output. The policy, therefore, causes a less-than-optimal allocation of an economy's scarce resources.

portfolio approach   Relates changes in a nation's balance of payments and the exchange value of its currency to the quantities demanded and supplied of domestic money, domestic securities, and foreign securities.

portfolio balance effect   An exchange-rate adjustment resulting from changes in government or central bank holdings of foreign-currency-denominated financial instruments that influences the equilibrium prices of the instruments.

portfolio diversification   Holding financial instruments with different characteristics so as to spread risks across the entire set of instruments.

portfolio investment   The acquisition of foreign financial assets that results in less than a 10 percent ownership share in the entity.

portfolio motive   Modern term for Keynes's essential argument for a speculative motive for holding money, in which people hold both money and bonds and adjust their holdings of both components of financial wealth based on their anticipations concerning interest rate movements.

precautionary motive   The motive to hold money for use in unplanned exchanges.

preferred habitat theory   A theory of the term structure of interest rates that views bonds as imperfectly substitutable, so that yields on longer-term bonds must be greater than those on shorter-term bonds even if short-term interest rates are not expected to rise or fall.

price elasticity of demand   A measure of the proportional change of the quantity demanded to a proportional change in price.

price elasticity of supply   A measure of the proportional change of the quantity supplied to a proportional change in its price.

price inertia   Slow short-term adjustment of a nation's price level to variations in factors affecting aggregate demand and overall business production costs.

pricing to market   A situation in which imperfectly competitive firms selling products abroad set prices in terms of the local currencies of purchasers located in the countries where the items are sold.

principal   The amount of credit extended when one makes a loan or purchases a bond.

private capital account   A tabulation of the flows of financial assets between domestic private residents and foreign private residents.

producer price index (PPI)   A weighted average of the prices of goods and services that the government determines a typical business receives from selling its products during a given period.

product identity   A truism stating that real national product is the sum of real household consumption, real realized investment, real government spending, and real export spending.

production function   The relationship between the quantities of factors of production employed by firms and their output of goods and services using the current technology.

purchasing power parity (PPP)   A condition that states that if international arbitrage is unhindered, the price of a good or service in one nation should be the same as the exchange-rate-adjusted price of the same good or service in another nation.

put option   An option contract giving the owner the right to sell a financial instrument at a specific price.

Q

quota subscription   The funds deposited by IMF member nations that together form the pool of funds that IMF managers can use for loans to member nations experiencing financial difficulties.

R

rational expectations hypothesis   The hypothesis that people form expectations using all available past and current information, plus their understanding of how the economy operates.

real consumption spending   The real amount of expenditures by households on domestically produced goods and services.

real disposable income   A household's real after-tax income.

real exchange rate   A bilateral exchange rate that has been adjusted for price changes that occurred in the two nations.

real export spending   Real value of goods and services produced by domestic firms and exported to other countries.

real gross domestic product   A price-adjusted measure of aggregate output, or nominal GDP divided by the GDP price deflator.

real import spending   The real flow of expenditures by households for the purchase of goods and services from firms in other countries.

real interest parity   A condition that postulates that in equilibrium the real rates of interest on similar financial instruments of two nations are equal.

real interest rate   The nominal interest rate less the rate of price inflation expected to prevail over the maturity period of the financial instrument.

real money balances   The price-level-adjusted value of the nominal quantity of money, defined as the nominal money stock divided by the price level.

real net taxes   The amount of real taxes paid to the government by households, net of transfer payments.

real realized investment spending   Actual real firm expenditures in the product markets.

real saving   The amount of income that households save through financial markets.

real sector   A designation for the sector of the economy engaged in the production and sale of goods and services.

realignment   A change in an official-exchange-rate target.

reinvestment risk   The possibility that available yields on short-term financial instruments may decline, so that holdings of longer-term instruments might be preferable.

reserve currency   The currency commonly used to settle international debts and to express the exchange value of other nations' currencies.

reserve requirements   Central bank regulations requiring private banks to hold specified fractions of transactions and term deposits either as vault cash or as funds on deposit at the central bank.

revalue   A situation in which a nation with a pegged-exchange-rate arrangement changes the pegged, or parity, value of its currency so that it takes a smaller number of domestic currency units to purchase one unit of the foreign currency to which the nation's currency value is pegged.

risk premium   An increase in the return offered on a higher-risk financial instrument to compensate individuals for the additional risk they undertake.

risk structure of interest rates   The relationship among yields on financial instruments that have the same maturity but differ because of variations in default risk, liquidity, and tax rates.

risk-adjusted assets   A weighted average of bank assets that regulators compute to account for risk differences across assets.

S

segmented markets theory   A theory of the term structure of interest rates that views bonds with differing maturities as nonsubstitutable, so that their yields differ because they are determined in separate markets.

seigniorage   Central bank profits resulting from the value of a flow increase in a country's money stock over and above the cost of money production.

short position   An obligation to sell a financial instrument at a given price and at a specific time.

spatial arbitrage   The act of profiting from exchange-rate differences that prevail in different markets.

Special Drawing Right (SDR)   A composite currency of the International Monetary Fund in which the value is based on a weighted-average value of the currencies of five member nations.

speculative attack   A concerted effort by financial market speculators to induce abandonment of an exchange-rate target that will yield them profits in derivative markets.

spot market   A market for contracts requiring the immediate sale or purchase of an asset.

sterilization   A central bank policy of altering domestic credit in an equal and opposite direction relative to any variation in foreign exchange reserves so as to prevent the monetary base from changing.

stock options   Options to buy or sell firm equity shares.

stock-index futures   Promises of future delivery of a portfolio of stocks represented by a stock price index.

strategic policymaking   The formulation of planned policy actions in light of the structural linkages among nations and the manner in which other countries' policymakers may conduct their own policies.

structural interdependence   The interconnectedness of countries' markets for goods and services, financial markets, and payment systems, which causes events in one nation to have effects on the economy of another nation.

structural unemployment   The fraction of a nation's labor force composed of people who would like to be employed but who do not possess skills and other characteristics required to obtain jobs.

sudden stop   An immediate end to capital inflows to a nation.

supplementary capital   A measure that many national banking regulators use to calculate required capital, which includes certain preferred stock and most subordinated debt.

swap   A contract entailing an exchange of payment flows between two parties.

systemic risk   The risk that some payment intermediaries may not be able to meet the terms of payment agreements because of failures by other institutions to settle transactions that otherwise are not related.

T

target zone   A range of permitted exchange-rate variation between upper and lower exchange-rate bands that a central bank defends by selling or purchasing foreign exchange reserves.

term premium   An amount by which the yield on a long-term bond must exceed the yield on a short-term bond to make individuals willing to hold either bond if they expect short-term bond yields to remain unchanged.

term structure of interest rates   The relationship among yields on financial instruments with identical risk, liquidity, and tax characteristics but differing terms to maturity.

theory of optimal currency areas   A means of determining the size of a geographic area within which residents' welfare is greater if their governments fix exchange rates or adopt a common currency.

time inconsistency problem   A situation in which a policymaker can better attain its objectives by violating a prior policy stance.

total capital   Under the Basel bank capital standards, this is the sum of core capital and supplementary capital.

transaction exposure   The risk that the cost of a transaction, or the proceeds from a transaction, in terms of the domestic currency, may change due to changes in exchange rates.

transactions motive   The motive to hold money for use in planned exchanges.

transfer payments   Governmentally managed income redistributions.

translation exposure   Foreign exchange risk that results from the conversion of the value of a firm's foreign-currency-denominated assets and liabilities into a common currency value.

triangular arbitrage   Three transactions undertaken in three different markets and/or in three different currencies in order to profit from differences in prices.

Trilemma   The idea that policymakers may choose a combination of two, but not all three of the following policy options: fixed exchange rates, discretionary monetary policy, and liberalized capital markets.

U

uncovered interest parity   A condition relating interest differentials to an expected change in the spot exchange rate of the domestic currency.

undervalued currency   A currency in which the current market-determined value is lower than that predicted by an economic theory or model.

unemployment rate   The percentage of a nation's labor force that is unemployed.

V

value of the marginal product of labor   The price of output times the marginal product of labor.

vehicle currency   A currency that individuals and businesses most often use to conduct international transactions.

W

World Bank   A sister institution to the International Monetary Fund that is more narrowly specialized in making loans to about 100 developing nations in an effort to promote their long-term development and growth.

world index fund   A portfolio of globally issued financial instruments with yields that historically have moved in offsetting directions.

Y

yield curve   A chart giving the relationship among yields on bonds that differ only in their terms to maturity.

Z

zero-coupon bonds   Bonds that pay lump-sum amounts at maturity.

INDEX

A

Absolute purchasing power parity, 49–52
Absorption, 234
Absorption approach to the balance of
   payments, 233–237
   See also Balance of payments
Absorption instrument, 236
Accion International, 208
   Web site, 208
Adverse selection, 153, 193
Aggregate autonomous expenditures,
Aggregate demand, 377–389
   aggregate demand schedule
      defined, 378
      derivation in a closed economy,
         377–378
   effects of national monetary policies,
   exchange rate policy in an open
      economy, 384
   fiscal policy in a closed economy,
      384–385
   fiscal policy in an open economy with a
      fixed exchange rate, 385–387
   fiscal policy in an open economy with a
      floating exchange rate, 387–388
   monetary policy in a closed economy,
      379–380
   monetary policy in an open economy with
      a fixed exchange rate, 380–382
   monetary policy in an open economy with
      a floating exchange rate, 382–384
   output and inflation and,
Aggregate desired expenditures, 292
Aggregate expenditures schedule, 292
Aggregate net autonomous expenditures, 292
Aggregate supply, 389–397
   aggregate supply schedule with partial
      wage adjustment, 396–397
   demand for labor, 391–392
   employment and aggregate supply, fixed
      vs. flexible nominal wages,
      394–396
   marginal product of labor, 390–391
   nominal wages, 392–393
   output and employment determination,
      389–392
   production function, 389–390
   wage flexibility and the price level, 392–397
Aizenman, Joshua, 204, 254
Alexander, Sidney, 236
Altunbas, Yener, 156
American option, 139
Announcement effect, 175, 267
Appreciation, currency, 32

Arbitrage
   covered interest, 96–97
   covered interest and saving flows, 96
   deviations from real interest parity as a
      measure of international market
      arbitrage, 129–130
   foreign exchange, 42–43
   purchasing power parity and, 50–51
   spatial, 42
   triangular, 42–43
   See also international financial arbitrage
Argentina, 3, 197, 200
Artificial currency unit. *See* Composite
   currencies
Ask price, 34
Assignment problem, 419
Asymmetric information, 153, 193
Automobile import example, 18–19
Autonomous consumption, 287
Autonomous dissaving, 286
Autonomous expenditures multiplier, 297
Autonomous import spending, 287
Autonomous investment spending, 293

B

Badinger, Harald, 435
Bahmani-Oskooee, Mohsen, 231
Balance of payments, 10–24
   as a double-entry bookkeeping system,
      10–12
   absorption approach, 233–237
      defined, 233
      determination of the current account
         balance, 234–235
      economic expansion and contraction,
         235–236
      modeling, 233–235
      policy instruments, 236–237
   capital account, 14–15
   characteristics of traditional approaches,
   current account, 12–14
      goods, 12
      income, 13
      services, 12–13
      unilateral transers, 14
   deficits and surpluses, 16–18
   defined, 10
   derivation of the demand for foreign
      exchange, 221–222
   derivation of the supply of foreign
      exchange, 223–224
   determining a nation's, 307–309
   elasticities approach, 226–233
      defined, 226

   exchange rate and, 226–228
   J-curve effect, 229–231
   Marshall-Lerner condition, 228–229
   measures of import and export price
      elasticities, 228
   pass-through effects, 232–233
   short- and long-run measures, 228
   elasticity and the demand for foreign
      exchange, 222–223
   elasticity and the supply of foreign
      exchange, 224–225
   equilibrium, 16
   international examples, 18–20
   monetary approach to, 255–263
      Cambridge approach to money
         demand, 255–256
      fixed-exchange-rate arrangement,
         257–259
      flexible-exchange-rate arrangement,
         259–260
      two-country setting, 260–262
   official settlements balance, 15–16
   overall, 16
   portfolio approach to, 263–268
      defined, 263
      households' allocation of wealth,
         263–265
      intervention, 265–266
      sterilization,266–268
   recording a U.S. firm's export, 12
   summary statement of U.S., 10–12
   See also BP schedule; Exchange-rate
      systems
Balance on merchandise trade, 17
Balance sheet,
   central bank's, 244
   of the Bank of Canada, 171
Ball, Laurence, 439
banco, 157
Bank for International Settlements,
   26, 63, 166
   Web site, 26, 83, 184
Bank market efficiency, 164
Bank of Canada, 171
Bank of England, 62, 172–175
   effective exchange rates, 40
   Web site, 40, 374
Bank of Estonia, Web site,
Bank of Japan,
   as central bank, 174–175
   BOJNET system, 157–158
   Web site, 250
Bank of Mexico, Web site, 365
Bank of Russia, Web site, 270

Bank (origin of word), 157
Bank regulation, 163–169
    See also Central banks; International
        banking; Monetary policy
Bankhaus I.D. Herstatt, 160
    See also Herstatt risk
Banks
    Equity as a percentage of assets in the
        U.S., 167
    See also Central banks; International
        banking
Banque de France, 172
Barings Bank, 133
Base year, 37
Basel III, 166
Basel capital requirements, 166–169
Basel pillars, 167
Basel regulatory system, 167–168
    Pillar 1 (Basel capital
        requirements), 167
    Pillar 2 (supervisory-review-process
        guideline guidelines), 168
    Pillar 3 (information disclosure guidelines),
        168
Beggar-thy-neighbor effect, 342
Beige Book, Web site, 311–312
Bekaert, Geert, 127
Berg, Andrew, 201–202
Bergin, Paul, 443]
Bid-ask margin, 34
Bid-ask spread, 34
Bid price, 34
Bilateral exchange rates, 32
Bilateral weights, 37–38
Blair, Tony, 69
BOJNET system (Japan), 157–158
Bolhasani, Marzieh, 231
Bond performance requirement, 138
Bonds, 113–126
    capital losses on bonds with differing
        maturities, 118–119
    defined, 105
    estimates of excess returns on
        international bond trading,
        125–126
    market price and discounted present
        value, 113–117
    zero coupon bonds, 118
    See also Interest rates
Book-entry security systems, 172
Borensztein, Eduardo, 201–202
Bowdler, Christopher, 435
BP schedule, 305–306
Brazil, 3, 201, 335
Break-even point, options, 141
Bretton Woods system, 64–68
    See also Exchange-rate systems
Britain, CHAPS system, 157–158
British consols (2.5 Consolidated Stock
    of 1921), 116

British Financial Services Authority,
    Web site, 165
Brookings Institution, Web site, 232
Bullet swap (plain vanilla swap), 144
Bundesbank, 67
    Web site, 49
Bureau of Economic Analysis, Web site, 10
Bureau of Labor Statistics, Web site, 281
Business cycles, 317
    synchronization of, 400–401
Bussière, Matthieu, 228
Buying price, 34

C

Call options
    defined, 139
    limited losses and potential profits from
        using currency call options,
        139–141
Cambridge equation, 255–256
Canada, 7, 8, 70
    and arbitrage across the U.S. border, 52
    inflation targeting in, 376
Capacity output level, 406
Capital
    core, 166
    supplementary, 166
    total, 166
Capital accounts, 11, 14–16, 21–24
    defined, 14
    example, 21
    surplus, 21–22
Capital controls, 199–200, 315, 320
Capital flows, 6–8, 23–24
    cross-border mergers and acquisitions,
        189–190
    current account balance and, 23–24
    economic growth and, 191–193
        long-term development and, 191–192
        smoothing the domestic economy, 192
    emerging economies, 190–191
    foreign direct investment (FDI), 196–199
    foreign direct investment (FDI) and
        developed nations, 188–189
    maximizing benefits and minimizing risks,
        195–196
    misallocations
        financial instability and crises,
            161–163, 194
        market imperfections, 193
        policy-created distortions, 193–194
    portfolio capital flows, 196–197
    recent crisis episodes and,
        capital controls, 199–200
        foreign direct investment as a stabiliz-
            ing element, 198–199
Capital gains, 113
Capital inflows (credit), 18
Capital losses, 118–119

Capital market liberalization, 194
Capital markets, defined, 105
Capital misallocations, 161–163, 193–194
Capital mobility
    defined, 320
    high, 320, 322
    low, 321–322
    perfect, 322–323
    shape of *BP* schedule, 321–323
    See also Fixed exchange rates
Capital outflows (debit), 18
Capital requirements, banks, 166–169
Carry trade, 102–103
Carter, Jimmy, 70
Cavallo, Eduardo, 437
CBOT. *See* Chicago Board of Trade
CDI. *See* Cologne Debt Initiative
Central Bank of Brazil, Web site, 335
Central Bank of Venezuela, Web site, 325
Central banker contract, 409
Central banks, 170–177,
    assets,170–171
    balance sheet, 170–171, 244–248
        monetary base and money stock
            relationship, 247–248
        a nation's monetary base, 244–245
        a nation's money stock, 246–247
    as bankers' banks, 173–174
    as government banks, 172–173
    as fiscal agents, 172
    externalities as rationale for, 173
    independence and, 410
    inflation and, 404–407
    liabilities and net worth, 171
    as monetary policymakers, 174–178
        interest-rate regulations and direct
            credit controls, 177
        interest rates on advances, 174–175
        open-market operations, 176–177
        reserve requirements, 177
    number of (1670–present), 170
    policy instruments, 174
    support for independence for, 410–411
    See also Bank of Japan; European
        System of Central Banks;
        Federal Reserve System,
        Monetary policy
*Centre d'Etudes Prospectives et
    d'Informations Internationales*,
    Web site, 15
CHAPS system (Britain), 157–158
Charitable organizations, humanitarian aid
    and, 20
Chicago Mercantile Exchange
    (CME), 136–137
    executing derivatives
        transactions, 137
    Web site, 136, 149
Chile, 79
    capital controls and, 199

China, 3
    foreign exchange reserves, 245
    link from Chinese wages to U.S. consumer
        prices, 280–281
    private investment flows to, 197
    Q coins, 59
    saving as a share of national income, 274
Chinn, Menzi, 204
CHIPS. *See* Clearing House Interbank
        Payments System
CIA World Factbook, Web site, 346
Circular flow of income and expenditures, 283
Civil War, U.S., 60
Clearing House Interbank Payments System
        (CHIPS), 158
Closed economy, aggregate demand in,
        377–378
College students,
    balance of payments example, 19
    study abroad programs and, 44
Cologne Debt Initiative (CDI), 209
Colombia, 79
Commitment equilibrium, 407
Commodity-backed money, 59
Commodity money, 59
Composite currencies, 40–42
        See also Special Drawing Right (SDR)
Conservative policymaker, 409
Consumer price indexes (CPIs), 35–36, 280
Consumption function, 287
Contagion effects, 162, 193
Convertibility, 60
Core capital, 166
Corners hypothesis, 201
Country risk, 102
Coupon payments, 116
Covered exposure, defined, 88
Covered interest parity
    adjustment to an equilibrium, 97–99
    covered interest arbitrage, 96
    covered interest arbitrage and saving
        flows, 97–99
    covered-interest-parity grid, 96–97
    defined, 96
    exchange uncertainty and, 95–99
CPI. *See* Consumer Price Index
Crawling band, 79
Crawling pegs, 78–79
        See also Exchange-rate systems
Credit, change in domestic, 245
Credit controls, 177
Credit entry, 10
Credit position, U.S. (1980-present), 22
Credit risks, 159–160, 363
Cross-border mergers and acquisitions,
        189–190
Cross-border transactions, 6–7
Cross-currency swap, 144
Cross rates, 33–34
Crowding-out effect, 331, 357

Currencies
    currency competition, 465–466
    devaluing, 65
    optimal currency areas, 462–475
    overvalued, 49
    reserve, 65
    revaluing, 65
    undervalued, 49
Currency appreciation and
        depreciation, 32
Currency-basket peg, 76–78
Currency board (independent currency
        authority), 75–76
Currency futures, 136–139
    defined, 136
    hedging with, 137–139
Currency notes, 171
Currency options, 139
Currency swaps, 143
Currency trading, online, 31
Current account, 12–14
    capital flows and, 23–24
Cyclical unemployment, 318

D

Daly, Deirdre, 233
Debit entry, 10
Debt stock, 22
Default risk, 123
Deficits, balance of payments and, 16–18
Demand
    Cambridge approach to money demand,
        255–256
    change in, 47–48
    change in quantity of money demanded,
        258, 260
    for currencies, 45
    derivation of the demand for foreign
        exchange, 221–222
    loanable funds and, 93
    measures of import and export price
        elasticities, 228
    for money, 298–301
    real money balances, 301–302
        See also Aggregate demand
Demand curves, 43–45
Denmark, peg with bands, 75–76
Depreciation, 275
    currency, 32
Derived demand, 43
Derivative credit risk, 145
Derivative market risk, 145
Derivative operating risks, 145
Derivative securities, 131–145
    defined, 131
    forward contracts, 135
    futures
        currency, 136–139
        daily settlement, 138–139

        interest rate, 136
        stock-index, 136
    hedging with forward contracts, 132
    major losses since 1990, 134
    options
        American options, 139
        call options, 139
        currency options, 139
        European options, 139
        exercise price, 139
        futures options, 139
        limited losses and potential profits
            from using currency call options,
            139–141
        limited losses and potential profits
            from using currency put options,
            141–142
        netting, 142–142
        stock options, 139
        types of, 139
    risks and regulation, 145
        measuring, 145
        types of derivatives risks, 145
    speculation with, 132–134
    speculative gains and losses, 133
    swaps, 143–144
        currency, 143
        defined, 143
        interest rate, 143
        types of, 144
d'Estaing, Valery Giscard, 69
Devaluing, 65
Direct finance, 152
Dirty float (managed float), 71
Discount rate, 175
Discounted present value, 113
Discretionary equilibrium, 408
Diversification, international financial, 154
Dollar-standard exchange-rate system, 64
Dollarization, 74–75
    benefits of, 201–202
    costs of, 202
    dollarized economies, 202
    East Timor, 202
    Ecuador, 202
    El Salvador, 202
Dollar's prominence, 471
Domestic consumption spending, 244
    change in, 257–258, 259–260
Domestic industries, government regulations
        by selected countries, 431
Domestic investment, 23–24
Domestic saving, 23–24
Dominguez, Kathryn, 267
Double-entry bookkeeping system, 10–12
Dynamic open economy theories, 442

E

Early warning systems, 211
East Timor, 202

ECB. *See* European Central Bank
Economic efficiency, 363
Economic exposure, 88
Economic fundamentals, 161
Economic trade-offs, 363
Economies of scale, 154
    in information processing, 156
Economist
    Web site, 52, 56
Economic stability, 363, 366
Ecuador, 74, 202
Edwards, Sebastian, 74, 199–200
Effective exchange rates, 36–40
    See also Foreign exchange market
Efficiency
    bank, 164–165
    economic, 363
    fixed versus floating exchange rates,
        363–366
    See also market efficiency
Eichengreen, Barry, 468
El Salvador, 74–75, 202
Elasticities approach to balance of payments,
        226–233
    See also Balance of payments
Elasticity, and the demand for foreign
        exchange, 222–223
Elasticity, and the supply of foreign exchange,
        224–225
Emerging economies
    capital flows and, 190–191
    See also Less developed economies
Employment
    wages and output when policy actions are
        anticipated, 402–404
    wages and output when policy actions are
        unanticipated, 404
    See also Nominal wages
EMU. *See* European Monetary Union
Equilibrium
    adjustment to, 97–99
    balance-of-payments, 16, 306
    BP schedule, 305–306
    commitment, 407
    discretionary, 407
    IS schedule and income-expenditure,
        294–296
    IS-LM, 307
    LM schedule and money market,
        302–303
    price level and real output level, 398
Equilibrium exchange rate, 47–49
Equilibrium income, expenditures and,
        291–293
Equities, 105
ESCB. *See* European System of Central Banks
ESF. *See* Exchange Stability Fund
Euro, 72–73
    demand for and supply of, 43–49
    problems with, 72–73

Eurobonds, 105
Eurocommercial paper, 106
Eurocurrencies, 105–106
    defined, 106
    interest rates, 107–108
    origins of, 106
    relationship to the forward market,
        107–108
Euronotes, 106
European Borrowing Unit (Ebu), 78
European Central Bank (ECB), 72, 467
    Web site, 228, 480
European Economic Community, 68
European Monetary Union (EMU),
        467–470
    TARGET system, 157–158
European option, 139
European Payments Union, 65
European Union (EU), 75
    Web site, 467
Ex ante conditionality, 204–205
Ex post conditionality, 204–205
Excess returns, 124–127
    defined, 125
    estimates of international bond trading,
        125–126
Exchange-rate band, 473
Exchange-rate instability, 229
Exchange-rate overshooting, 423–427
    defined, 424
    long-run adjustment of the exchange rate,
        424–425
    moving from the short run to the
        long run, 425
    tracing the adjustment of the exchange
        rate, 425–427
Exchange-rate systems, 58–84
    Bretton Woods system, 64–68
        Performance of, 66–68
        Smithsonian Agreement and the snake
            in the tunnel, 68–69
    crawling pegs, 78–79
        Nicaragua's, 79
        parity band, 79
    currency baskets, 76–78
    definitions, 59
    dollarization, 201–202
    financial crisis and,
        corners hypothesis, 201
        dollarization and, 201–202
        ex ante versus ex post conditionality at
            the IMF, 204–205
        World Bank and, 206–207
    fixed versus floating rates, 80
    flexible-exchange-rate system, 69–73
        defined, 69
        economic summits and a new
            order, 69
        the euro, 72–73
        performance of, 69–70

Plaza Agreement and the Louvre
            Accord, 70–72
    gold standard, 60–63
        collapse of, 63
        performance of, 62–63
    independent currency authorities or
            currency boards, 75–76
    portfolio approach, 263–268
        defined, 263
        households' allocation of wealth,
            263–265
        intervention effectiveness, 265–266
        sterilization, 266–268
    summary pie chart of, 73
    trilemma, 203–204
    See also Balance of Payments, Fixed
            Exchange Rates; Floating
            exchange rates; Foreign exchange
            market
Exchange-rate parity bands, 76
Exchange-rate target zones, 473–477
Exchange rates
    defined, 35
    See also Exchange-rate systems, Foreign
            exchange market
Exchange Stabilization Fund (ESF), 249
Exchange-traded derivative instruments,
Exercise price, 139
Expectations theory, 120–121
Expected return, 95
Expenditure-switching instrument, 237
Expenditures, 284–291
    See also Open economy framework
Explicit contracts, 393
Exports, 11
    pass-through effects, 232–233
    recording a U.S. firm's, 12
External balance, 319
Externalities
    defined, 449
    internalizing international policy
            externalities, 456
    international policy, 449
structural interdependence and, 449

F
FASB. *See* Financial Accounting Standards
        Board
FDI. *See* Foreign direct investment
Federal Deposit Insurance Corporation, 165
Federal funds rate, 175
Federal Open Market Committee (FOMC), 176
    FOMC Directive, 176
Federal Reserve Bank of New York, Web site,
        164, 236
Federal Reserve System (Fed)
    as central bank, 172
    Interest rates Web site, 115
    See also Central banks

Fedwire, 158
Fiat money, 59
Financial crises
    Argentina, 200
    capital controls and, 199–200
    capital flows and, 198–200
    capital misallocations and, 193–199
    ex ante versus ex post conditionality at the
        IMF, 204–205
    exchange-rate systems and, 200–210
        See also Exchange-rate systems
    foreign direct investment and,
        196–197
    Mexico, 198, 200–201, 203
    Russia, 200
    Southeast Asia, 200
    trilemma, 203–204
    Turkey, 200
        See also International banking
Financial crisis
    defined, 161
    indicator, 201–211
Financial engineers, 144
Financial instability, 161
    capital misallocations and, 193–195
Financial intermediation, 152–156
    defined, 153
Financial markets, 104–108
    eurobonds, 105
    eurocommercial paper, 106
    eurocurrencies, 106
    Eurocurrency market, 106
    euronotes, 106
    international capital markets, 105
    international money markets, 105
        See also Derivative securities
Financial sector, 4
Financial-sector development,
    192–193
Financial Service Authority, Web site, 165
Financial Times,
    Web site, 35
Financial volatility, 197
Fiscal agents, central banks as, 172
Fiscal policy
    aggregate demand in a closed
        economy, 384
    aggregate demand in an open economy
        with a fixed exchange rate,
        385–387
    aggregate demand in an open economy
        with a floating exchange rate,
        387–389
    fixed exchange rates and, 330–334
    perfect capital mobility and, 387–388
        See also Fixed exchange rates; Floating
        exchange rates
Fisher equation, 128
Fixed-exchange-rate arrangement, 48
    and monetary approach, 257–259

capital controls, 320
capital mobility, 320–323
    defined, 320
    high, 320, 322
    low, 321–322
    perfect, 322–323
    shape of *BP* schedule, 321–323
external balance objectives,
    319–320
    international and domestic
        goals, 319
    mercantilism, 320
imperfect capital mobility
    fiscal policy with and without steriliza-
        tion, 332–334
    fiscal policy and the balance of pay-
        ments, 331–332
    fiscal policy, the nominal interest rate,
        and real income, 330–331
    monetary approach to balance of pay-
        ments revisited, 329
    monetary policy and the balance of
        payments, 327–329
    monetary policy, the nominal interest
        rate, and real income, 325–329
    nonsterilized monetary policy, 328–329
    sterilized monetary policy,
        327–328
internal balance objectives, 315–318
    employment goals, 317–318
    inflation goals, 318
    per capita GDP, 315
    real-income goals, 315–317
monetary policy and aggregate demand in
    an open economy, 380–382
perfect capital mobility
    fiscal policy with, 337
    fixed versus floating exchange rates,
        357–358
    monetary policy with, 336
    two-country example, 338–344
policy effects on real output and the price
    level under, 400
versus floating exchange rates, 363–371
    See also Floating exchange rates
Fixed-weight price indexes, 279–281
Flexible-exchange-rate system, 69–73
    See also Exchange-rate systems
Flexible-weight price index, 280
Floating exchange rates
    exchange-rate volatility, British pound, 364
    fiscal policy and aggregate demand in an
        open economy, 385–389
    imperfect capital mobility,
        exchange-rate variations and the *BP*
            schedule, 350
        exchange-rate variations and the *IS*
            schedule, 349–350
        fiscal policy, 353–354
        monetary policy, 350–353

monetary policy and aggregate demand in
    an open economy, 380–384
perfect capital mobility, 355–358
    fiscal policy with, 356–357
    fixed versus floating exchange rates,
        357–358
    monetary policy with, 355–356
    two-country example, 358–362
policy effects on real output and the price
    level under, 399–400
relationship between changes in effective
    exchange rates and current
    account balances, selected
    nations, 352
versus fixed exchange rates, 363–371
    efficiency arguments for fixed versus
        floating exchange rates,
        363–366
    monetary policy autonomy and, 371
    stability arguments for fixed versus
        floating exchange rates,
        366–371
        See also Exchange-rate systems
FOMC. *See* Federal Open Market
    Committee
Ford, Gerald, 69
Foreign assets, ten largest MNEs, 9
Foreign direct investment (FDI), 15
    average annual growth of world FDI and
        world exports, 189
    capital flows and, 188–189
    capital liberalization and, 196–197
    defined, 15
    developed nations and, 188–189
    geographical distribution of FDI inflows, of
        total inflows, 190
Foreign exchange interventions, 248–254
    financing interventions, 249–250
    intervention transactions, 248–249
    leaning with or against the wind, 249
    and the money stock, 250–252
        example, 251–252
    sterilization of interventions, 252–254
Foreign exchange market, 28–57
    arbitrage, 50–51
    bid-ask spreads and trading margins, 34
    composite currencies, 40–42
        defined, 40
        Special Drawing Right (SDR),
    cross-border transactions, 6–7
    defined, 29
    demand for a currency, 45
    effect of price changes, 35–36
    effective exchange rates, 36–40
        constructing, 36–37
        defined, 36
        two-country example, 37–38
    efficiency and, 103–104
        evidence on, 104
    equilibrium exchange rate, 47–49

Foreign exchange market (*continued*)
exchange rates as relative prices, 32
cross rates, 33–34
currency appreciation and
depreciation, 32
market intervention, 48–49
nominal exchange rates, 35
online trading, 31
purchasing power parity (PPP), 49–53
absolute, 49–52
relative, 52–53
real exchange rates, 35
role of, 29–30
spot market, 30–31
supply of a currency, 45–46
turnover and world exports, 6
See also Balance of payments; Fixed
exchange rates; Floating exchange
rates
Foreign exchange reserves, countries with
largest holdings, 245
Foreign exchange risk, 87–89
defined, 87
economic exposure, 88
hedging, 88
transaction exposure, 87
translation exposure, 87
Foreign investment, versus trade, 15
Fort Knox, 67
45-degree line, 293
Forward contracts
hedging with, 132
interest rate forward contracts, 132
See also Derivative securities
Forward discount, 91
Forward exchange market, 89–92
covering a transaction with a forward
contract, 89–90
defined, 89
determination of forward exchange
rates, 90
eurocurrency and, 105–106
forward exchange rate as a predictor of
the future spot exchange rate,
90–92, 103–104
Forward premium, 91
Forward swap, 144
Frankel, Jeffrey, 210, 267, 437
France, 7, 70
Free trade, 4
Frictional unemployment, 318
Friedman, Milton, 69
Future spot exchange rate, forward exchange
rate as, 90–92
Futures contracts, 135–139
defined, 135
currency futures, 136
hedging with currency futures, 137–139
interest rate futures, 136
stock-index futures, 136

See also Derivative securities
Futures Industry Association, Web site, 136
Futures options, 139
FX Solutions, 31

G
G5. *See* Group of Five
G7. *See* Group of Seven
G10. *See* Group of Ten
Gain Capital, 31
GATT. *See* General Agreement on Tariffs
and Trade
GDP. *See* Gross domestic product
General Agreement on Tariffs and Trade
(GATT), 64
Germany, 6, 7
GDP,
Giro systems, 157–158
Glick, Reuven, 254
Global trade
in goods and services, 3–5
selected nations' trade in goods and
services, 5
See also Trade
Globalization, 3
ten largest multinational enterprises
(MNEs), 9
top twenty globalized nations, 8
See also Integration
Gold pool, 66–67
Gold standard, 60–63
See also Exchange-rate systems
Gold window, Nixon and, 68
Goldberg, Linda, 471
Goldstein, Morris, 210
Goods
defined, 12
world trade in, 3–5
Goodwill, 13
Government banks, central banks
as, 172–173
Government depositories, central banks
as, 172
Government spending, net taxes
and, 290–290
Great Depression, 63
Great Society, 66
Greece, 72
Gross domestic product (GDP)
defined, 275
natural real GDP, 317
per capita, 315
price deflator, 277
real versus nominal, 276–277
for selected countries, 276
Group of Five (G5), 70
Group of Seven (G7), 71
Group of Ten (G10), 68
Guatemala, 74

H
Hale, Galina, 281
Harvard University's Center for International
Development, Web site, 198
Hassert, Kevin, 394
Hayek, Friedrich, 465–466
Hedging
with currency futures, 137–139
defined, 88
foreign exchange risk, 87–89
with forward contracts, 132
Hellerstein, Rebecca, 233
Herding behavior, 193
Herstatt risk, 160–161
See also Bankhaus I.D. Herstatt
Higgins, Matthew, 24
High capital mobility, 320, 322
HIPC initiative, 209
Hobijn, Bart, 281
Hot-money flows, 196
Humanitarian aid, 13
Hume, David, 255
Hungary, 100
Huxley, T.H., 476

I
IBM-Toshiba currency swap example,
143–144
Iceland, 163
Illiquidity, 164
IMF. *See* International Monetary Fund
IMF World Economic Outlook, Web site, 446
Imperfect capital mobility, 321–322
See also Fixed exchange rates; Floating
exchange rates
Imperfect competition, 430
Imperfect policy credibility, 476
Implicit contracts, 393
Import function, 287
Imports, 11
as a share of total expenditures in
selected nations, 429
balance of payments example, 18–19
measures of the price elasticity of import
demand, 228
openness and, 429
Income
defined, 13
See also Equilibrium income
Income-expenditure equilibrium, 291–293
Income identity, 283
Independent currency authority (currency
board), 75–76
Indirect finance, 152
Indonesia
exchange market pressures and, 201
private investment flows to, 197
Induced import spending, 287
Induced saving, 286

Infinite sum, 116
Inflation
    aggregate demand and output, 402–404
    costs of, 318
    discretionary monetary policies and
        inflation with coordination,
        459–460
    discretionary monetary policies and
        inflation without coordination,
        460–462
    incentive for, 406
    inflation bias of discretionary
        policymaking, 404–411
    openness and, 436–439
    in selected nations, 411
Insolvencies, 164
Integration, 3–10
    world trade in goods and services, 3–5
    See also Globalization
Interbank funds market, 171
Interbank FX, 31
Interdependence. *See* International
        interdependence
Interest, defined, 113
Interest parity, 94
    See also Covered interest parity;
        Uncovered interest parity
Interest rate forward contract, 132
Interest rate futures, 136
Interest rate risk
    defined, 118
    hedging, 131
    possible responses, 130–131
    strategies for limiting, 119
    term to maturity and, 118–119
    See also Risk
Interest rate swap, 143
Interest rates
    defined, 113
    determining, 93–94
    and discounted present value, 113
    discounted present value and the market
        price of bonds, 113–115
    excess returns and uncovered interest
        parity, 124–127
    financing and investing terminology Web
        site, 115
    interest parity, 94–95
    nominal, 127
    perpetuities and relationship between
        interest yields and bond prices,
        116–117
    present values of a future dollar, 114
    real
        defined, 128
        Fisher equation, 128
    real interest parity, 127–130
        combining relative purchasing power
            parity and uncovered interest
            parity, 128–129

deviations from as a measure of inter-
        national market arbitrage,
        129–130
    regulations and direct credit controls, 177
    risk, 118
        default risk, 122
        liquidity, 123–124
        tax differences, 124
    risk premium and the failure of interest
        rate convergence, 101
    term structure of, 119–122
        expectations theory, 120–121
        preferred habitat theory, 122
        segmented markets theory, 120
        yield curves, 119–120
    term to maturity and interest-rate risk,
        118–119
    See also Covered Interest Parity;
        Uncovered interest parity
Intermediation. *See* Financial intermediation
Internal balance objectives, 315–318
    employment goals, 317–318
    inflation goals, 318
    per capita GDP, 315
    real-income goals, 315–317
International Bank for Reconstruction and
        Development, 64
    See also World Bank; General Agreement
        on Tariffs and Trade
International banking
    bank (origin of word), 157
    bank versus market finance, 152
    capital requirements, 166–169
        computing, 166
        core capital, 166
        off-balance-sheet banking, 166
        risk-adjusted assets, 166
        supplementary capital, 166
        total capital, 166
        toughening the Basel capital stand-
            ards, 166–168
    economies of scale, 154
    financial instability and financial crisis,
        161–163
        contagion effects, 162, 193
        moral hazard problems, 162–163, 193
        self-fulfilling expectations, 162
        speculative attack, 162
    financial intermediation, 152–156
        across national boundaries, 154–156
    payment-system risks, 158–161
        credit risk, 159–160
        Herstatt risk, 160–161
        liquidity risk, 159
        systemic risk, 160
    payment systems, 157
        electronic, 158
        nonelectronic, 157–158
    regulation, 164–165
        limiting the scope for bank insolvencies

and failures, 164
        maintaining bank liquidity, 164
        market-based, 168
        promoting an efficient system,
            164–165
        world's largest banks, 155
        See also Central banks
International capital flows, 188–191
International financial arbitrage, 92–99
    exchange uncertainty and covered
        interest parity, 95–99
    interest parity, 95–96
    interest rate determination (loanable
        funds), 93–94
    See also Arbitrage
International financial architecture
    alternative institutional structures for
        limiting financial crises,
        212–213
    crises prediction and early warning
        systems, 211
    defined, 188
    rethinking long-term development lending,
        211–212
    See also Capital flows; Exchange-rate
        systems
International financial diversification, 154
International interdependence, 449–451
    accounting for interdependence,
        450–451
        international policy cooperation, 450
        international policy coordination,
            450–451
    policy externalities, 449–450
    strategic policymaking, 450
    structural interdependence, 449
    See Bretton Woods system; Exchange-
        rate systems
International Monetary Fund (IMF), 64,
        178–182
    conditionality, 179
    ex ante versus ex post conditionality at,
        204–205
    financing facilities, 180
    founding under Bretton Woods, 64
    growth in membership (since 1945), 179
    quota subscriptions, 179
International policy cooperation, 450
International policy coordination, 451–462
    benefits
        gaining support from abroad, 456
        getting the most out of limited sets of
            policy instruments, 456
        internalizing international policy exter-
            nalities, 456
    drawbacks
        autonomy and, 457
        discretionary monetary policy and
            inflation with coordination,
            460–462

International policy coordination (*continued*)
  discretionary monetary policy and infla-
    tion without coordination, 459–460
  putting faith in other nations' policy-
    makers, 458–459
  trust, 457–458
  perfect capital mobility
    aggregate demand effects of national
      monetary policies, 451–453
    conflicting monetary policies, 453–454
    gains from coordination, 454–455
International policy externality, 449
Interventions. *See* Foreign exchange
  inteventions
Intra-marginal interventions, 476
Inventory investment, 275
Investment spending, desired, 288–290
Iraq, 354
Italy, 7, 70
Ito, Hiro, 204
IS-LM-BP model, 305–309
IS schedule
  exchange-rate variations, 349–350
See also Open economy framework

J
J-curve effect, 229–231
  defined, 230
Jamaica Accords, 69
Japan, 5, 7
  See also Bank of Japan
J.P. Morgan nominal index, 30, 39

K
Kaminsky, Graciele, 201
Kenen, Peter, 68
Keynes, John Maynard, 62, 64
Klein, Michael, 477
Klitgaard, Thomas, 24
KOF Economic Institute, Web site, 7
Korea, exchange market pressures and, 201
Krugman, Paul, 473
Kuwait, 258

L
Labor
  demand for, 391–392
  law of diminishing marginal returns, 390
  marginal product of labor, 390
  value of the marginal product of labor,
    391–392
Lamfalussy standards, 159
Large-value wire transfer systems, 158
Law of diminishing marginal returns, 390
Leading indicators, 210
Leaning against the wind, 249
Leaning with the wind, 249
Lender of last resort, 173–174

Less-developed economies
  Openness and inflation in, 437–439
  See also Emerging economies
Lewis, Karen, 477
Libor
  See London interbank offered rate
Liquidity effect, of monetary policy, 326
Liquidity premium, 124
Liquidity risk, 159
LM schedule, 302–305
  See also Open economy framework
Loanable funds
  market for, 93–94, 97–99
Locomotive effect, 340
Lombard rate, 174
London Club, 209
London interbank offered rate (Libor), 117–118
Long position, 90, 135
Long run
  adjustment of the exchange rate to a
    monetary expansion, 424–425
  moving from short run to, 425–427
Long-Term Capital Management, 133
Louvre Accord (G7), 70–72
Low capital mobility, 320–321

M
Macroeconomics, new open economy,
  439–444
Mahar, Molly, 194
Maintenance margin, 138
Mama Mike, 299
Managed float, 71
Margin account, 139
Marginal product of labor, 390
  value of, 392
Marginal propensity to consume (MPC), 285
Marginal propensity to import (MPIM), 285
Marginal propensity to save (MPS), 285
Market-to-market procedure, 138
Market-based regulation, 168
Market efficiency, foreign exchange
  defined, 104
  evidence on, 104
  foreign exchange, 103–104
Market for real money balances, 298–303
Market imperfections, 193
Market intervention. *See* Foreign exchange
  interventions
Market risks, 363
Marsh, Christina, 233
Marshall-Lerner condition, 228–229
Marshall Plan, 65
Marston, Richard, 129
Mathur, Aparna, 394
Mauritius, 75
Maximum corporate income tax rates,
  selected nations, 394
Megabanks, 155–156

Meissner, Christopher, 329–330
Menu costs, 440
Mercantilism, 320
Mexico
  Banco de Mexico Web site, 315
  financial crisis, 198–200–201, 203
  realignment, 364–365
Microlending, 207–208
Middle East, 58
  deserting sinking dollar, 259–260
  War, 70
Monetary approach to balance of payments,
  255–263
  two-country setting, 260–262
  See also Balance of payments
Monetary base, 244–245
  money stock and, 246–248
Monetary order, 59
Monetary policy
  aggregate demand in a closed economy,
    379–380
  aggregate demand in an open economy
    with a fixed exchange rate,
    380–382
  aggregate demand in an open economy
    with a floating exchange rate,
    382–384
  central banks and, 174–178
  fixed exchange rate and, 325–329, 336
  flexible exchange rate and,
    330–335, 337
  inflation and, 404–411
  See also Central banks; Fixed exchange
    rates, Floating exchange rates;
    Monetary approach to the balance
    of payments
Monetary policy autonomy, 457
Monetary union, 462–470
  defined, 462
  European Monetary Union (EMU), 467–470
    as optimal currency area, 467–468
    fiscal crisis, 468–470
    rationales for separate currencies,
      465–467
    currency competition, 465–466
    fiscal deficit and debt divergences,
      468–469
    lack of fiscal integration, 466
    seigniorage issues, 467
  theory of optimal currency areas, 462–465
    defined, 463
    optimal currency area, 464
    separate currencies and a floating
      exchange rate, 464
    separate currencies rationales, 464
    shift in relative demands, 463–464
Money, demand for, 298–302
Money markets, defined, 105
Money multiplier, 246–247
  defined, 247

Money stock
    interventions and, 250–252
    monetary base and, 247–248
Moral hazard, 153–154
Molyneux, Philip, 156
MPC. *See* Marginal propensity to consume
MPIM. *See* Marginal propensity to import
MPS. *See* Marginal propensity to save
Multinational enterprises (MNEs), 8–9
    ten largest ranked by foreign assets, 9
    ten largest ranked by transnationality, 9
Multiplier effect, 295–397
    defined, 295
    explanation of, 297
Mundell, Robert, 463

N
Natural real gross domestic product, 317
Natural rate of unemployment, 318
Net creditor, 22
Net debtors
    defined, 22
    United States as, 22–23
Netting, 142–143
New open economy macroeconomics, 439–444
    features, 440–442
        dynamic analysis, 442
        imperfect competition, 441–442
        price stickiness, 440–441
    policy implications, 442–443
        hurdles for policy analysis, 443
        welfare evaluations, 442
New Zealand
    inflation targeting in, 376
    Reserve Bank of, Web site, 262
Nicaragua,
    crawling-peg arrangement, 79
    dollarization contemplation, 74
Nitsch, Voker, 470
Nixon, Richard, gold window and, 68
Nominal effective exchange rate since 1980
    (Bank of England), 39
Nominal exchange rates, 35
Nominal gross domestic product, 277
Nominal wages
    aggregate supply schedule with
        partial wage adjustment,
        396–397
    employment and aggregate supply
        with fixed versus flexible,
        394–396
    expectations and the flexibility of,
        402–404
    factors affecting willingness of workers to
        establish wage contracts, 428
    indexed contracts, 396
Normal profits, 164
Notional value of derivatives, 145

O
Oanda
    Web site, 31
Off-balance-sheet banking, 166
Official settlements balance, 15–16
Online foreign exchange trading, 31
Oomes, Nienke, 329–330
OPEC. *See* Organization of Oil and Petroleum
        Exporting Countries
Open economy. *See* Aggregate demand
Open economy framework
    balance of payments
        BP schedule, 305–306,
        deficit, 306
        equilibrium, 305
        IS-LM-BP model, 305–309
        surplus, 309
    BP schedule
        capital mobility and, 321–323
        defined, 306
        derivation of, 305–306
        exchange-rate variations and, 350
        slope of, 320–321
    demand for money, 298–302
    expenditures
        aggregate desired, 292
        desired investment spending,
            288–290
        equilibrium national income and,
            292–293
        export spending, 291
        saving, import spending, and con-
            sumption spending, 284–288
    fixed- and flexible-weight price measures,
        279–281
    gross domestic product (GDP)
        base year, 277–278
        defined, 275
        GDP price deflator, 277
        real versus nominal, 276–277
        of selected nations, 276
    IS schedule, 293–297
        defined, 295
        derivation of, 294–295
        determining the position of, 295
        multiplier effect, 295–297
    IS-LM equilibrium, 307
    LM schedule, 302–305
        defined, 304
        determining the position of, 304–305
        money market equilibrium and,
            303–304
Open economy macroeconomics, 440
Open-market operations, 176–177
    alternative procedures for, 176–177
Open-market transactions, 176, 246
Openness and globalization, 427–439
    inflation and, 436–439
        cross-country differences in impacts
            of globalization, 439

differences in developed versus less
    developed nations, 437–438
global openness-inflation relationship,
    436–437
output-inflation relationship, 427–435
    competition in domestic product
        markets, 430–432
    evidence, 433–435
    imported inputs and, 430
    measuring openness, 428–429
    product-market regulation, selected
        nations, 431
    wage stickiness and central bank
        independence, 432
    willingness of workers to establish
        nominal wage contracts, 428–429
    See also New open economy
        macroeconomics; Open economy
        macroeconomics
Operating risks, 145
Optimal currency areas, 462
Options, 139–143
    See also Derivative securities
Organization for Economic Cooperation and
        Development, Web site, 190
Organization of Oil and Petroleum Exporting
        Countries (OPEC), 70
Orange County, California, 133
Output
    aggregate demand and inflation and, 399
    capacity, 406
    equilibrium, 398–399
    policy effects on output and price level
        under fixed exchange rates, 400
    policy effects on output and price level
        under floating exchange rates,
        399–400
    wages and employment when policy
        actions are anticipated, 402–404
    wages and employment when policy
        actions are unanticipated, 404
    See also Real output
Outright transaction, 176
Over-the-counter contracts, 139
Overall balance of payments, 16
Overshooting, 424
    See also Exchange-rate overshooting
Overvalued currency, 49

P
Pakistan, 197
Paris Club, 209
Parity band, 79
Pass-through effects, 232–233
Paul, Ron, 62
Payment intermediaries, 157
Payment systems,
    electronic, 158
    nonelectronic, 157–158

Payment systems (*continued*)
  risks and, 158–161
  See also International banking
PCE index. *See* Personal consumption
    expenditure price index
Pegged-exchange-rate system, 64
Penalty rate, 174
Penn World Tables, Web site, 279
Per capita gross domestic product,
    315–316
  annual rates of growth in real, G7
    nations, 316
  defined, 315
  per capita GDP growth, 315–316
Perfect capital mobility
  international policy coordination and,
    451–453
  See also Fixed exchange rates; Floating
    exchange rates
Perfect hedge, 131
Perfect substitutes, 120
Perpetuities
  defined, 116
  and the relationship between interest
    yields and bond prices, 116–117
Peso problem, 126
PIIGS nations (Portugal, Ireland, Italy, Greece
    Spain), 469
Plain vanilla swap (bullet swap), 144
Plaza Agreement (G5), 70–72, 267
Policy assignment problem, 419–423
  assigning internal and external objectives,
    421–423
  defined, 419
  external balance, 420
  internal balance, 421
Policy coordination. *See* International policy
    coordination
Policy-created distortions, 193–194
Policy credibility, 407
  imperfect, 476
Policy instruments, central bank, 174
Policymaking
  rules versus discretion in, 402–411
    expectations and the flexibility of
      nominal wages, 402–404
    inflation bias, 404–406
    policy credibility, 407–409
    support for central bank
      independence, 410–411
  strategic, 450
  See also Fiscal policy; Fixed exchange
    rates; Floating exchange rates;
    Monetary policy
Portfolio approach to exchange-rate
    determination, 263–268
  See also Exchange-rate systems
Portfolio balance effect, 267
Portfolio motive for money demand,
    300–301

Portfolios, 14
  diversification of, 131
PPI. *See* Producer price index
PPP. *See* Purchasing power parity
Precautionary motive for money demand, 299
Preferred habitat theory, 122
Price changes, effect of, 35–36
Price deflator, 277
Price elasticity of demand, 222
  See also Elasticity
Price elasticity of supply, 222
  See also Elasticity
Price indexes, GDP deflator, 277–279
Price inertia, 440
Price level, equilibrium, 398–399
Price stickiness, 440–441
Pricing power, 432
Pricing to market, 442
Principal, 113
Private capital account, 14–15
Producer price index (PPI), 281
Product identity, 284
Production function, 389–390
Protectionist trade policies, 63
Purchasing power parity (PPP), 49–53
  absolute, 49–52
  defined, 49
  relative, 52–53
  See also Foreign exchange market
Put options,
  defined, 139
  limited losses and potential profits using
    currency put options, 141–142

Q

Q coins, 59
Qatar, 259

R

Rational expectations hypothesis, 402
Real consumption spending, 282
  declining impact of interest rate variations
    on, 288
Real disposable income, 284
Real effective exchange rates, 39–40
Real exchange rates, 35
Real export spending, 283
Real gross domestic product, 277
Real import spending, 282
Real income and expenditures, 282–284
  circular flow of, 283
  See also IS schedule
Real interest parity, 127–130
Real interest rates, 128, 288–289
Real money balances
  defined, 301
  demand for, 301–302
Real net taxes, 282
Real output, 389

  equilibrium, 398
  See also Output
Real realized investment spending, 283
Real saving, 282
Real sector, 4
Realignments, 364
Realized return, 95
Regulatory arbitrage, 194
Regulatory tripwires, 168
Reinhart, Carmen, 210, 469
Reinvestment risk, 131
Relative prices
  defined, 32
  exchange rates as, 32–34
Relative purchasing power parity, 52–53
Replacement-cost credit exposure, 145
Representative agents, 443
Repurchase agreements, 176
  reverse, 176
Required capital, 166
Reserve Bank of Australia, Web site, 262
Reserve Bank of New Zealand, Web site, 262
Reserve currency, 65
Reserve requirements, 177
Revaluing, 65
Reverse repurchase agreements, 176
Ricardian equivalence, 334
Ricardo, David, 334
Risk
  country risk, 102
  credit, 159–160
  default, 122
  derivatives risks and regulations, 145
  foreign exchange, 97–99
  Herstatt, 160–161
  Interest rate risk, 118
  liquidity, 159
  market, 363
  operating, 145
  payment-system, 158–161
  reinvestment, 131
  risk premium, 101, 124
  risk structure of interest rates, 122–124
  social cost from foreign exchange risks,
    systemic, 160
  uncovered interest parity and, 101–102
  See also Interest rate risk
Risk-adjusted capital, 166
Risk-based capital requirements, 166–169
  See also International banking
Risk premium, 101, 124
Risk structure of interest rates, 122–124
Rogoff, Kenneth, 459, 469
Romer, David, 436
Rose, Andrew, 210
Rugman, Alan, 8
Russia, 3
  financial crisis, 200–201
  foreign exchange reserves, 245
  ruble, 41–42

S

Sarno, Lucio, 267
Saving function, 286
SDR. *See* Special Drawing Right
Securities. *See* Derivative securities
Segmented markets theory, 120
Seigniorage, 466
Sekioua, Sofiane, 130
Self-fulfilling expectations, 162
Selling price, 34
Services
    defined, 12–13
    world trade in, 4–5
Short position, 89, 135
Short run
    moving to long run, 425–427
    versus long run, 423–424
Signaling effect, 267
Singapore
    foreign exchange reserves, 245
    spared an economic crisis, 194
Smithsonian Agreement, 68
Smoot-Hawley Act, 63
Snake in the tunnel, 68–69
Social costs, from foreign exchange risks, 363–364
Société Générale, 113–114, 133 é
South Africa, 197
South Korea, 3, 204
    GDP, 278
    Web site, 277
Southeast Asia, 200
Sovereign funds, 243, 335
Sovereignty, 457
Spatial arbitrage, 42
Special Drawing Right (SDR), 40–42
    calculation of, 41–42
    See also Composite currencies
Speculation
    with derivatives, 130–134
    gains and losses, 133
Speculative attack, 162
Spot exchange market, 30–36
    defined, 30
Stability, exchange rates and, 366–371
Standard forward premium, 91
Statistical discrepancy, 16
Statistics Canada, Web site, 240
Sterilization
    defined, 252
    fiscal policy and, 332–334
    and interventions, 252–254
    monetary policy and, 337–338
Sticky prices, 440–441
Stock-index futures, 136
Stock options, 139
Strategic policymaking, 450
Structural interdependence, 449
Structural unemployment, 318

Substitutes
    imperfect, 122
    perfect, 120
Sudden stop, 437
Supplementary capital, 166
Supply
    of currencies, 45–46
    derivation of the supply of foreign exchange, 223–224
    elasticity and the supply of foreign exchange, 224–225
    loanable funds and, 93
    See also Aggregate supply
Supply curves, 46
Supranational financial policymaking institutions, 178–182
    International Monetary Fund (IMF), 178–181
    Word Bank, 181–182
Surpluses
    balance of payments and, 16–18
    capital account and, 21–23
Svensson, Lars, 476
Sveriges Riksbank (Sweden), 169
Swap options (swaption), 144
Swaps, 143–144
    See also Derivative securities
Swaption (swap option), 144
Swedish Riksbank, Web site, 169
Swiss National Bank, 174
Switzerland, 8
Syria, 258
Synchronization of business cycles, 400–401
Systemic risk, 160, 363

T

TARGET system (European Monetary Union), 157–158
Target zones, 473–477
    defined, 473
    establishing, 473–474
    exchange-rate behavior inside, 474–476
    imperfect policy credibility, 476
    intra-marginal interventions, 476
    real-world evidence, 476
Taxation
    government spending and, 290–291
    interest rates and, 124
    maximum corporate income tax rates, selected nations, 394
    real net taxes, 282
Taylor, Mark, 267
Temple, Jonathan, 434
Term premium, 122
Term structure of interest rates, 119–122
    See also Interest rates
Term to maturity, 118–119
Thailand, 5

Tille, Cédric, 471
Time inconsistency problem, 407–408
Toshiba-IBM currency swap example, 143–144
Total capital, 166
Trade
    balance on merchandise, 17
    See also Global trade; Integration
Trade deficit, 2, 17
Trading margin, 34
Transaction exposure, 87
Transactions motive for money demand, 298–299
Transfer payments, 282
Translation exposure, 87
Transnationality index, 8–9
    ten largest MNEs, 9
Triangular arbitrage, 42–43
Trilemma, 203–204
Turkey, 200
Two-country monetary model, 260–262
Tzu, Sun, 165

U

Unbiased predictor, 104
Uncertainty, and covered interest parity, 93–99
Uncovered interest parity, 99–103
    arbitrage, 99–100
    combining relative purchasing power parity and, 128–129
    defined, 100
    risk and, 101–102
    risks other than foreign exchange risk, 101–102
    tests of, 102
    uncovered interest arbitrage, 99–100
UNCTAD. *See* United Nations Conference on Trade and Development
Undervalued currency, 49
Unemployment
    cyclical, 318
    frictional, 318
    natural rate of, 318
    rate, 317
    rates in selected nations, 317
    structural, 318
Unilateral transfers, 13
United Kingdom, 6, 7, 63, 70, 194, 376
United Nations Committee on Trade and development (UNCTAD), 188
    Web site, 188
United States
    and arbitrage across the Canadian border, 52
    GDP, 281–282
    as net debtor, 22
University of Toronto G8 Research Group, Web site, 70

V

Value of the marginal product of labor, 391–392
Vehicle currency, 470–473
   defined, 470
   dollar's predominance, 471
   evidence, 471–473
   timeline, 472
Venezuela, 197, 325
Vietnam conflict, 66
Volcker, Paul, 70

W

Wage stickiness, 392–393, 428
Wages. *See* Nominal wage
Wall Street Journal, 22
Walsh, Carl, 410
Wealth identity, 263
Web sites
   Accion International, 208
   Bank for International Settlements, 26, 83, 184
   Bank of England, 40, 374
   Bank of Japan, 250
   Bank of Mexico, 365
   Bank of Russia, 270
   Beige Book, 311–312
   British Financial Services Authority, 165
   Brookings Institution, 232
   Bundesbank, 409
   Bureau of Economic Analysis, 10
   Central Bank of Brazil, 335
   Central Bank of Venezuela, 325

Centre d'Etudes Prospectives et d'Informations Internationales, 15
Chicago Mercantile Exchange, 137, 149
CHIPS, 158
CIA World Factbook, 346
Economist, The, 52, 56
European Central Bank, 228, 480
European Union, 467
Federal Reserve System, interest rates, 116
Federal Reserve Bank of New York, 164, 236
Finance and investing terminology, 115
Financial Service Authority, 165
Financial Times, 35
KOF Economic Institute, 7
Futures Industry Association, 136
Harvard University's Center for International Development, 198
IMF World Economic Outlook, 446
Oanda, 31
Organization for Economic Cooperation and Development, 190
Penn World Tables, 279
Reserve Bank of Australia, 262
Reserve Bank of New Zealand, 262
South Korean economy, 277
Statistics Canada, 240
Swedish Riksbank, 169
United Nations Conference on Trade and Development (UNCTAD), 188
University of Toronto G8 Research Group, 70

U.S. Bureau of Labor Statistics, 281
World Bank, 110, 316
   World Investment Report, 216
Wei, Min, 127
Weights, 37
   bilateral, 37–38
Welfare evaluations, 442
Welfare levels, hypothetical for two nations, 457–458
Williamson, John, 194
World Bank
   defined, 181
   establishment, 64
   financial crises and, 206–207
   institutions of, 181
   Web site, 110, 316
World Index fund, 155
World Investment Report,
   Web site, 216
World War I, trade and, 4

X

Xing, Yuhang, 127

Y

Yeltsin, Boris, 69
Yield curves, 119–120
   for selected nations, 119–120
Yunus, Muhammad, 207–208

Z

Zero-coupon bonds, 118